INTRODUCTION TO THE LITERATURE OF EUROPE IN THE 15th, 16th, AND 17th CENTURIES

Engraved by William Holl.

Henry Hallam

From a Painting by Thomas Phillips, R.A. in the possession of Mr Murray.

INTRODUCTION TO THE LITERATURE OF EUROPE IN THE 15th, 16th, AND 17th CENTURIES

HENRY HALLAM

Volume I

FREDERICK UNGAR PUBLISHING CO.
NEW YORK

Republished 1970
from the edition of 1873
Reprinted from a copy in the collections of
The New York Public Library
Astor, Lenox and Tilden Foundations

Printed in the United States of America

Library of Congress Catalog Card No. 74-118869

ISBN (3-volume set) 0-8044-2331-8
Volume I 0-8044-2332-6
Volume II 0-8044-2333-4
Volume III 0-8044-2334-2

PREFACE

TO

THE FIRST EDITION.

THE ADVANTAGES of such a synoptical view of literature as displays its various departments in their simultaneous condition through an extensive period, and in their mutual dependency, seem too manifest to be disputed. And, as we possess little of this kind in our own language, I have been induced to undertake that to which I am, in some respects at least, very unequal, but which no more capable person, as far as I could judge, was likely to perform. In offering to the public this introduction to the literary history of three centuries—for I cannot venture to give it a title of more pretension— it is convenient to state my general secondary sources of information, exclusive of the acquaintance I possess with original writers; and, at the same time, by showing what has already been done, and what is left undone, to furnish a justification of my own undertaking.

The history of literature belongs to modern, and chiefly to almost recent times. The nearest approach to it that the ancients have left us is contained in a single chapter of Quintilian, the first of the tenth book, wherein he passes rapidly over the names and characters of the poets, orators, and historians of Greece and Rome. This, however, is but a sketch; and the valuable work of Diogenes Laertius preserves too little of chronological order to pass for a history of ancient philosophy, though it has supplied much of the materials for all that has been written on that subject.

In the sixteenth century, the great increase of publications, and the devotion to learning which distinguished that period, might suggest the scheme of a universal literary history. Conrad Gesner, than whom no one, by extent and variety of erudition, was more fitted for the labour, appears to have framed a plan of this kind. What he has published, the Bibliotheca Universalis, and the Pandectæ Universales, are, taken together, the materials that might have been thrown into an historical form; the one being an alphabetical catalogue of authors and their writings; the other a digested and minute index to all departments of knowledge, in twenty-one books, each divided into titles, with short references to the texts of works on every head in his comprehensive classification. The order of time is therefore altogether disregarded. Possevin, an Italian Jesuit, made somewhat a nearer approach to this in his Bibliotheca Selecta, published at Rome in 1593. Though his partitions are rather encyclopædic than historical, and his method, especially in the first volume, is chiefly argumentative, he gives under each chapter a nearly chronological catalogue of authors, and sometimes a short account of their works.

Lord Bacon, in the second book De Augmentis Scientiarum, might justly deny, notwithstanding these defective works of the preceding century, that any real history of letters had been written; and he compares that of the world, wanting this, to a statue of Polypheme deprived of his single eye. He traces the method of supplying this deficiency in one of those luminous and comprehensive passages which bear the stamp of his vast mind: the origin and antiquities of every science, the methods by which it has been taught, the sects and controversies it has occasioned, the colleges and academies in which it has been cultivated, its relation to civil government and common society, the physical or temporary causes which have influenced its condition, form, in his plan, as essential a part of such a history, as the lives of famous authors, and the books they have produced.

No one has presumed to fill up the outline which Bacon

himself could but sketch; and most part of the seventeenth century passed away with few efforts on the part of the learned to do justice to their own occupation; for we can hardly make an exception for the Prodromus Historiæ Literariæ (Hamburg, 1659) of Lambecius, a very learned German, who, having framed a magnificent scheme of a universal history of letters, was able to carry it no farther than the times of Moses and Cadmus. But, in 1688, Daniel Morhof, professor at Kiel in Holstein, published his well-known Polyhistor, which received considerable additions in the next age at the hands of Fabricius, and is still found in every considerable library.

Morhof appears to have had the method of Possevin in some measure before his eyes; but the lapse of a century, so rich in erudition as the seventeenth, had prodigiously enlarged the sphere of literary history. The precise object, however, of the Polyhistor, as the word imports, is to direct, on the most ample plan, the studies of a single scholar. Several chapters, that seem digressive in an historical light, are to be defended by this consideration. In his review of books in every province of literature, Morhof adopts a sufficiently chronological order; his judgments are short, but usually judicious; his erudition so copious, that later writers have freely borrowed from the Polyhistor, and, in many parts, added little to its enumeration. But he is far more conversant with writers in Latin than the modern languages; and, in particular, shows a scanty acquaintance with English literature.

Another century had elapsed, when the honour of first accomplishing a comprehensive synopsis of literary history in a more regular form than Morhof, was the reward of Andrès, a Spanish Jesuit, who, after the dissolution of his order, passed the remainder of his life in Italy. He published at Parma, in different years, from 1782 to 1799, his Origine, Progresso, e Stato attuale d' ogni Litteratura. The first edition is in five volumes quarto; but I have made use of that printed at Prato, 1806, in twenty octavo volumes. Andrès, though a Jesuit, or perhaps because a Jesuit, accommodated himself in some measure to the tone of the age wherein his book appeared, and is always temperate, and often candid. His learning is very extensive in surface, and sometimes minute and curious, but not, generally speaking, profound; his style is flowing, but diffuse and indefinite; his characters of books have a vagueness unpleasant to those who seek for precise notions; his taste is correct, but frigid; his general views are not injudicious, but display a moderate degree of luminousness or philosophy. This work is, however, an extraordinary performance, embracing both ancient and modern literature in its full extent, and, in many parts, with little assistance from any former publication of the kind. It is far better known on the Continent than in England, where I have not frequently seen it quoted; nor do I believe it is common in our private libraries.

A few years after the appearance of the first volumes of Andrès, some of the most eminent among the learned of Germany projected a universal history of modern arts and sciences on a much larger scale. Each single province, out of eleven, was deemed sufficient for the labours of one man, if they were to be minute and exhaustive of the subject: among others, Bouterwek undertook poetry and polite letters; Buhle speculative philosophy; Kästner the mathematical sciences; Sprengel anatomy and medicine; Heeren classical philology. The general survey of the whole seems to have been assigned to Eichhorn. So vast a scheme was not fully executed; but we owe to it some standard works, to which I have been considerably indebted. Eichhorn published, in 1796 and 1799, two volumes, intended as the beginning of a General History of the Cultivation and Literature of modern Europe, from the twelfth to the eighteenth century. But he did not confine himself within the remoter limit; and his second volume, especially, expatiates on the dark ages that succeeded the fall of the Roman Empire. In consequence, perhaps, of this diffuseness, and also of the abandonment, for some reason with which I am unacquainted, of a large portion of the original undertaking, Eichhorn prosecuted this work no farther in its original form. But,

altering slightly its title, he published, some years afterwards, an independent universal 'History of Literature'
from the earliest ages to his own. This is comprised in six
volumes, the first having appeared in 1805, the last in 1811.

The execution of these volumes is very unequal. Eichhorn
was conversant with oriental, with theological literature,
especially of his own country, and in general with that contained in the Latin language. But he seems to have been
slightly acquainted with that of the modern languages, and
with most branches of science. He is more specific, more
chronological, more methodical in his distribution than
Andrès: his reach of knowledge, on the other hand, is less
comprehensive; and though I could praise neither highly
for eloquence, for taste, or for philosophy, I should incline
to give the preference in all these to the Spanish Jesuit.
But the qualities above mentioned render Eichhorn, on the
whole, more satisfactory to the student.

These are the only works, as far as I know, which deserve
the name of general histories of literature, embracing all
subjects, all ages, and all nations. If there are others, they
must, I conceive, be too superficial to demand attention.
But in one country of Europe, and only in one, we find a
national history so comprehensive as to leave uncom-
memorated no part of its literary labour. This was first
executed by Tiraboschi, a Jesuit born at Bergamo, and in his
later years librarian of the Duke of Modena, in twelve
volumes quarto: I have used the edition published at Rome
in 1785. It descends to the close of the seventeenth century. In full and clear exposition, in minute and exact
investigation of facts, Tiraboschi has few superiors; and
such is his good sense in criticism, that we must regret the
sparing use he has made of it. But the principal object of
Tiraboschi was biography. A writer of inferior reputation,
Corniani, in his Secoli della Litteratura Italiana dopo il suo
Risorgimento (Brescia, 9 vols., 1804—1813), has gone more
closely to an appreciation of the numerous writers whom he
passes in review before our eyes. Though his method is
biographical, he pursues sufficiently the order of chronology

to come into the class of literary historians. Corniani is not
much esteemed by his countrymen, and does not rise to a
very elevated point of philosophy; but his erudition appears
to me considerable, his judgments generally reasonable, and
his frequent analyses of books give him one superiority over
Tiraboschi.

The Histoire Littéraire de l'Italie, by Ginguéné, is well
known: he had the advantage of following Tiraboschi; and
could not so well, without his aid, have gone over a portion
of the ground, including in his scheme, as he did, the Latin
learning of Italy; but he was very conversant with the
native literature of the language, and has, not a little
prolixly, doubtless, but very usefully, rendered much of easy
access to Europe, which must have been sought in scarce
volumes, and was in fact known by name to a small part of
the world. The Italians are ungrateful, if they deny their
obligations to Ginguéné.

France has, I believe, no work of any sort, even an indifferent one, on the universal history of her own literature;
nor can we claim for ourselves a single attempt of the most
superficial kind. Warton's History of Poetry contains much
that bears on our general learning; but it leaves us about
the accession of Elizabeth.

Far more has been accomplished in the history of particular departments of literature. In the general history of
philosophy, omitting a few older writers, Brucker deserves
to lead the way. There has been of late years some disposition to depreciate his laborious performance, as not sufficiently imbued with a metaphysical spirit, and as not
rendering with clearness and truth the tenets of the philosophers whom he exhibits. But the Germany of 1744 was
not the Germany of Kant and Fichte; and possibly Brucker
may not have proved the worse historian for having known
little of recent theories. The latter objection is more material; in some instances he seems to me not quite equal
to his subject. But upon the whole he is of eminent usefulness; copious in his extracts, impartial and candid in his
judgments.

In the next age after Brucker, the great fondness of the
German learned both for historical and philosophical investigation produced more works of this class than I know
by name, and many more than I have read. The most
celebrated, perhaps, is that of Tennemann; but of which I
only know the abridgment, translated into French by M.
Victor Cousin, with the title Manuel de l'Histoire de Philosophie. Buhle, one of the society above mentioned, whose
focus was at Göttingen, contributed his share to their scheme
in a History of Philosophy from the revival of letters. This
I have employed through the French translation in six
volumes. Buhle, like Tennemann, has very evident obligations to Brucker; but his own erudition was extensive, and
his philosophical acuteness not inconsiderable.

The history of poetry and eloquence, or fine writing, was
published by Bouterwek, in twelve volumes octavo. Those
parts which relate to his own country, and to Spain and
Portugal, have been of more use to me than the rest. Many
of my readers must be acquainted with the Littérature du
Midi, by M. Sismondi; a work written in that flowing and
graceful style which distinguishes the author, and succeeding
in all that it seeks to give,—a pleasing and popular, yet not
superficial or unsatisfactory, account of the best authors in
the southern languages. We have nothing historical as to
our own poetry but the prolix volumes of Warton. They
have obtained, in my opinion, full as much credit as they
deserve: without depreciating a book in which so much may
be found, and which has been so great a favourite with the
literary part of the public, it may be observed that its errors
as to fact, especially in names and dates, are extraordinarily
frequent, and that the criticism, in points of taste, is not of
a very superior kind.

Heeren undertook the history of classical literature,—a
great desideratum, which no one had attempted to supply.
But unfortunately he has only given an introduction, carrying us down to the close of the fourteenth century, and a
history of the fifteenth. These are so good, that we must
much lament the want of the rest; especially as I am aware

of nothing to fill up the vacuity. Eichhorn, however, is
here of considerable use.

In the history of mathematical science, 1 have had recourse
chiefly to Montucla, and, as far as he conducts us, to Kästner,
whose catalogue and analysis of mathematical works is far
from complete, but his own observations less perspicuous and
philosophical. Portal's History of Anatomy, and some other
books, to which I have always referred, and which it might
be tedious to enumerate, have enabled me to fill a few pages
with what I could not be expected to give from any original
research. But several branches of literature, using the word,
as I generally do, in the most general sense for the knowledge imparted through books, are as yet deficient in any
thing that approaches to a real history of their progress.

The materials of literary history must always be derived
in great measure from biographical collections, those, especially, which intermix a certain portion of criticism with
mere facts. There are some, indeed, which are almost entirely of this description. Adrian Baillet, in his Jugemens
des Sçavans, published in 1685, endeavoured to collect the
suffrages of former critics on the merits of all past authors.
His design was only executed in a small part, and hardly
extends beyond grammarians, translators, and poets; the
latter but imperfectly. Baillet gives his quotations in
French, and sometimes mingles enough of his own to raise
him above a mere compiler, and to have drawn down the
animosity of some contemporaries. Sir Thomas Pope Blount
is a perfectly unambitious writer of the same class. His
Censura celebriorum autorum, published in 1690, contains
nothing of his own, except a few short dates of each author's
life, but diligently brings together the testimonies of preceding critics. Blount omits no class, nor any age; his
arrangement is nearly chronological, and leads the reader
from the earliest records of literature to his own time. The
polite writers of modern Europe, and the men of science, do
not receive their full share of attention; but this volume,
though not, I think, much in request at present, is a very
convenient accession to any scholar's library.

Bayle's Dictionary, published in 1697, seems at first sight an inexhaustible magazine of literary history. Those who are conversant with it know that it frequently disappoints their curiosity; names of great eminence are sought in vain, or are very slightly treated; the reader is lost in episodical notes perpetually frivolous, and disgusted with an author who turns away at every moment from what is truly interesting to some idle dispute of his own time, or some contemptible indecency. Yet the numerous quotations contained in Bayle, the miscellaneous copiousness of his erudition, as well as the good sense and acuteness he can always display when it is his inclination to do so, render his dictionary of great value, though I think chiefly to those who have made a tolerable progress in general literature.

The title of a later work by Père Niceron, Mémoires pour servir à l'histoire des hommes illustres de la république des lettres, avec un catalogue raisonné de leurs ouvrages, in forty-three volumes 12mo, published at Paris from 1727 to 1745, announces something rather different from what it contains. The number of 'illustrious men' recorded by Niceron is about 1600, chiefly of the sixteenth and seventeenth centuries. The names, as may be anticipated, are frequently very insignificant; and, in return, not a few of real eminence, especially when Protestant, and above all English, are overlooked, or erroneously mentioned. No kind of arrangement is observed; it is utterly impossible to conjecture in what volume of Niceron any article will be discovered. A succinct biography, though fuller than the mere dates of Blount, is followed by short judgments on the author's works, and by a catalogue of them, far more copious, at least, than had been given by any preceding bibliographer. It is a work of much utility; but the more valuable parts have been transfused into later publications.

The English Biographical Dictionary was first published in 1761. I speak of this edition with some regard, from its having been the companion of many youthful hours; but it is rather careless in its general execution. It is sometimes ascribed to Birch; but I suspect that Heathcote had more to do with it. After several successive enlargements an edition of this dictionary was published in thirty-two volumes, from 1812 to 1817, by Alexander Chalmers, whose name it now commonly bears. Chalmers was a man of very slender powers, relatively to the magnitude of such a work; but his life had been passed in collecting small matters of fact, and he has added much of this kind to British biography. He inserts, beyond any one else, the most insignificant names, and quotes the most wretched authorities. But as the faults of excess, in such collections, are more pardonable than those of omission, we cannot deny the value of his Biographical Dictionary, especially as to our own country, which has not fared well at the hands of foreigners.

Coincident nearly in order of time with Chalmers, but more distinguished in merit, is the Biographie universelle. The eminent names appended to a large proportion of the articles contained in its fifty-two volumes are vouchers for the ability and erudition it displays. There is doubtless much inequality in the performance; and we are sometimes disappointed by a superficial notice, where we had a right to expect most. English literature, though more amply treated than had been usual on the Continent, and with the benefit of Chalmers's contemporaneous volumes, is still not fully appreciated : our chief theological writers, especially, are passed over almost in silence. There seems, on the other hand, a redundancy of modern French names; those, above all, who have, even obscurely and insignificantly, been connected with the history of the Revolution; a fault, if it be one, which is evidently gaining ground in the supplementary volumes. But I must speak respectfully of a work to which I owe so much, and without which, probably, I should never have undertaken the present.

I will not here characterise several works of more limited biography; among which are the Bibliotheca Hispana Nova of Antonio, the Biographia Britannica, the Bibliothèque française of Goujet; still less is there time to enumerate particular lives, or those histories which relate to short periods, among the sources of literary knowledge. It will

be presumed, and will appear by my references, that I have
employed such of them as came within my reach. But I am
sensible that, in the great multiplicity of books of this kind,
and especially in their prodigious increase on the Continent
of late years, many have been overlooked from which I might
have improved these volumes. The press is indeed so active,
that no year passes without accessions to our knowledge,
even historically considered, upon some of the multifarious
subjects which the present volumes embrace. An author
who waits till all requisite materials are accumulated to his
hands, is but watching the stream that will run on for ever;
and though I am fully sensible that I could have much improved what is now offered to the public by keeping it back
for a longer time, I should but then have had to lament
the impossibility of exhausting my subject. ΕΠΟΙΕΙ, the
modest phrase of the Grecian sculptors, well expresses the
imperfection that attaches to every work of literary industry
or of philosophical investigation. But I have other warnings
to bind up my sheaves while I may,—my own advancing
years, and the gathering in the heavens.

I have quoted, to my recollection, no passage which I have
not seen in its own place; though I may possibly have transcribed in some instances, for the sake of convenience, from
a secondary authority. Without censuring those who suppress the immediate source of their quotations, I may justly
say that in nothing I have given to the public has it been
practised by myself. But I have now and then inserted in
the text characters of books that I have not read on the
faith of my guides; and it may be the case that intimation
of this has not been always given to the reader.

It is very likely that omissions, not, I trust, of great consequence, will be detected; I might in fact say, that I am
already aware of them; but perhaps these will be candidly
ascribed to the numerous ramifications of the subject, and
the necessity of writing in a different order from that in
which the pages are printed. And I must add that some
omissions have been intentional: an accumulation of petty
facts, and especially of names to which little is attached,

fatigues unprofitably the attention; and as this is very frequent in works that necessarily demand condensation, and
cannot altogether be avoided, it was desirable to make some
sacrifice in order to palliate the inconvenience. This will be
found, among many other instances, in the account of the
Italian learned of the fifteenth century, where I might easily
have doubled the enumeration, but with little satisfaction to
the reader.

But, independently of such slighter omissions, it will appear that a good deal is wanting in these volumes, which
some might expect in a history of literature. Such a history
has often contained so large a proportion of biography, that
a work in which it appears very scantily, or hardly at all,
may seem deficient in necessary information. It might be
replied, that the limits to which I have confined myself, and
beyond which it is not easy perhaps, in the present age, to
obtain readers, would not admit of this extension; but I may
add that any biography of the authors of these centuries,
which is not servilely compiled from a few known books of
that class, must be far too immense an undertaking for one
man, and, besides its extent and difficulty, would have been
particularly irksome to myself, from the waste of time, as I
deem it, which an inquiry into trifling facts entails. I have
more scruple about the omission of extracts from some of the
poets and best writers in prose, without which they can be
judged very unsatisfactorily; but in this also I have been
influenced by an unwillingness to multiply my pages beyond
a reasonable limit. But I have, in some instances, gone
more largely into analyses of considerable works than has
hitherto been usual. These are not designed to serve as
complete abstracts, or to supersede, instead of exciting, the
reader's industry; but I have felt that some books of traditional reputation are less fully known than they deserve.

Some departments of literature are passed over, or partially touched. Among the former are books relating to
particular arts, as agriculture or painting; or to subjects of
merely local interest, as those of English law. Among the
latter is the great and extensive portion of every library, the

historical. Unless where history has been written with peculiar beauty of language, or philosophical spirit, I have generally omitted all mention of it; in our researches after truth of fact, the number of books that possess some value is exceedingly great, and would occupy a disproportionate space in such a general view of literature as the present. For a similar reason, I have not given its numerical share to theology.

It were an impertinence to anticipate, for the sake of obviating, the possible criticism of a public which has a right to judge, and for whose judgments I have had so much cause to be grateful, nor less so to dictate how it should read what it is not bound to read at all; but perhaps I may be allowed to say, that I do not wish this to be considered as a book of reference on particular topics, in which point of view it must often appear to disadvantage; and that, if it proves of any value, it will be as an entire and synoptical work.

ADVERTISEMENT

TO

THE FOURTH EDITION.

THE text of this work has been revised, and such errors as the Author detected have been removed. The few additional notes are distinguished by the dates of the publication of the different editions in the years 1842, 1847, and 1853.

CONTENTS

OF

THE FIRST VOLUME.

———◆◇◆———

PART I.

ON THE LITERATURE OF THE FIFTEENTH AND FIRST HALF OF
THE SIXTEENTH CENTURY.

CHAPTER I.

ON THE GENERAL STATE OF LITERATURE IN THE MIDDLE AGES
TO THE END OF THE FOURTEENTH CENTURY.

a 2

CHAPTER II.

ON THE LITERATURE OF EUROPE FROM 1400 TO 1440.

CHAPTER III.

ON THE LITERATURE OF EUROPE FROM 1440 TO THE CLOSE OF THE FIFTEENTH CENTURY.

CHAPTER IV.

ON THE LITERATURE OF EUROPE FROM 1500 TO 1520.

CHAPTER V.

HISTORY OF ANCIENT LITERATURE IN EUROPE FROM 1520 TO 1550.

CHAPTER VI.

HISTORY OF THEOLOGICAL LITERATURE IN EUROPE FROM 1520 TO 1550.

CHAPTER VII.

HISTORY OF SPECULATIVE, MORAL, AND POLITICAL PHILOSOPHY, AND OF JURISPRUDENCE, IN EUROPE, FROM 1520 TO 1550.

CHAPTER VIII.

HISTORY OF THE LITERATURE OF TASTE IN EUROPE FROM 1520 TO 1550.

CHAPTER IX.

ON THE SCIENTIFIC AND MISCELLANEOUS LITERATURE OF EUROPE FROM 1520 TO 1550.

PART II.

ON THE LITERATURE OF THE LATTER HALF OF THE SIXTEENTH CENTURY.

CHAPTER I.

HISTORY OF ANCIENT LITERATURE IN EUROPE FROM 1550 TO 1600.

CHAPTER II.

HISTORY OF THEOLOGICAL LITERATURE IN EUROPE FROM 1550 TO 1600.

INTRODUCTION

TO THE

LITERATURE OF EUROPE

IN THE FIFTEENTH, SIXTEENTH, AND
SEVENTEENTH CENTURIES.

PART I.

ON THE LITERATURE OF THE FIFTEENTH AND FIRST HALF
OF THE SIXTEENTH CENTURY.

CHAPTER I.

ON THE GENERAL STATE OF LITERATURE IN THE MIDDLE AGES TO THE END OF THE FOURTEENTH CENTURY.

Loss of ancient Learning in the Fall of the Roman Empire—First Symptoms of its Revival—Improvement in the Twelfth Century—Universities and Scholastic Philosophy—Origin of Modern Languages—Early Poetry—Provençal, French, German, and Spanish—English Language and Literature — Increase of Elementary Knowledge—Invention of Paper — Roman Jurisprudence—Cultivation of Classical Literature—Its Decline after the Twelfth Century—Less visible in Italy—Petrarch.

1. ALTHOUGH the subject of these volumes does not comprehend the literary history of Europe anterior to the commencement of the fifteenth century, a period as nearly coinciding as can be expected in any arbitrary division of time with what is usually denominated the revival of letters, it appears necessary to prefix such a general retrospect of the state of knowledge for some preceding ages as will illustrate its subsequent progress. In this, however, the reader is not to expect a regular history of mediæval literature, which would be nothing less than the extension of

Retrospect of learning in middle ages necessary.

a scheme already perhaps too much beyond my powers of execution.[a]

2. Every one is well aware that the establishment of the
Loss of learning in fall of Roman empire. barbarian nations on the ruins of the Roman empire in the West was accompanied or followed by an almost universal loss of that learning which had been accumulated in the Latin and Greek languages, and which we call ancient or classical—a revolution long prepared by the decline of taste and knowledge for several preceding ages, but accelerated by public calamities in the fifth century with overwhelming rapidity. The last of the ancients, and one who forms a link between the classical period of literature and that of the
Boethius— his Consolation of Philosophy. middle ages, in which he was a favourite author, is Boethius, a man of fine genius, and interesting both from his character and his death. It is well known that, after filling the dignities of consul and senator in the court of Theodoric, he fell a victim to the jealousy of a sovereign, from whose memory, in many respects glorious, the stain of that blood has never been effaced. The Consolation of Philosophy, the chief work of Boethius, was written in his prison. Few books are more striking from the circumstances of their production. Last of the classic writers, in style not impure, though displaying too lavishly that poetic exuberance which had distinguished the two or three preceding centuries, in elevation of sentiment equal to any of the philosophers, and mingling a Christian sanctity with their lessons, he speaks from his prison in the swan-like tones of dying eloquence. The philosophy that consoled him in bonds was soon required in the sufferings of a cruel death. Quenched in his blood, the lamp he had trimmed with a skilful hand gave no more light; the language of Tully and Virgil soon ceased to be spoken; and many ages were to pass away before learned diligence restored its purity, and the union of genius with imitation taught a few modern writers to surpass in eloquence the Latinity of Boethius.

---

[a] The subject of the following chapter has been already treated by me in another work, the History of Europe during the Middle Ages. I have not thought it necessary to repeat all that is there said: the reader, if he is acquainted with those volumes, may consider the ensuing pages partly as supplemental, and partly as correcting the former where they contain anything inconsistent.

3. The downfall of learning and eloquence, after the death of Boethius in 524, was inconceivably rapid. His contemporary Cassiodorus, Isidore of Seville, and Martianus Capella, the earliest but worst of the three, by very indifferent compilations, and that encyclopedic method which Heeren observes to be an usual concomitant of declining literature, superseded the use of the great ancient writers, with whom, indeed, in the opinion of Meiners, they were themselves acquainted only through similar productions of the fourth and fifth centuries. Isidore speaks of the rhetorical works of Cicero and Quintilian as too diffuse to be read.[b] The authorities upon which they founded their scanty course of grammar, logic, and rhetoric, were chiefly obscure writers, no longer extant; but themselves became the oracles of the succeeding period, wherein the trivium and quadrivium, a course of seven sciences, introduced in the sixth century, were taught from their jejune treatises.[c]

Rapid decline of learning in sixth century.

4. This state of general ignorance lasted, with no very sensible difference, on a superficial view, for about five centuries, during which every sort of knowledge was almost wholly confined to the ecclesiastical order; but among them, though instances of gross ignorance were exceedingly frequent, the necessity of preserving the Latin

A portion remains in the church

---

[b] Meiners, Vergleichung der Sitten, &c., des Mittelalters mit denen unsers Jahrhunderts, 3 vols. Hanover, 1793. Vol. ii. p. 333. Eichhorn, Allgemeine Geschichte der Cultur und Litteratur, vol. ii. p. 29. Heeren, Geschichte des Studiums der classischen, Litteratur. Göttingen, 1797. These three books, with the Histoire littéraire de la France, Brucker's history of Philosophy, Turner's and Henry's Histories of England, Muratori's 43rd Dissertation, Tiraboschi, and some few others, who will appear in the notes, are my chief authorities for the dark ages. But none, in a very short compass, is equal to the third discourse of Fleury, in the 13th volume of the 12mo. edition of his Ecclesiastical History.

[c] The trivium contained grammar, logic, and rhetoric; the quadrivium, arithmetic, geometry, music, and astronomy, as in these two lines, framed to assist the memory:—

'Gramm. loquitur; Dia. vera docet; Rhet. verba colorat; Mus. canit; Ar. numerat: Geo. ponderat; Ast. colit astra.'

But most of these sciences, as such, were hardly taught at all. The arithmetic, for instance, of Cassiodorus or Capella, is nothing but a few definitions mingled with superstitious absurdities about the virtues of certain numbers and figures. Meiners, ii. 339. Kästner, Geschichte der Mathematik, p. 8. The arithmetic of Cassiodorus occupies little more than two folio pages, and does not contain one word of the common rules. The geometry is much the same; in two pages we have some definitions and axioms, but nothing farther. His logic is longer and better, extending to sixteen folio pages. The grammar is very short and trifling, the rhetoric the same.

language, in which the Scriptures, the canons, and other
authorities of the church, and the regular liturgies were
written, and in which alone the correspondence of their well-
organised hierarchy could be conducted, kept flowing, in the
worst seasons, a slender but living stream; and though, as has
been observed, no great difference may appear, on a superficial
view, between the seventh and eleventh centuries, it would
easily be shown that, after the first prostration of learning, it
was not long in giving signs of germinating afresh, and that
a very slow and gradual improvement might be dated farther
back than is generally believed.[d]

5. Literature was assailed in its downfall by enemies from
within as well as from without. A prepossession
Prejudices of the clergy against profane learning. against secular learning had taken hold of those
ecclesiastics who gave the tone to the rest. It was
inculcated in the most extravagant degree by Gregory I., the
founder, in a great measure, of the papal supremacy, and the
chief authority in the dark ages.[e] It is even found in Alcuin,
to whom so much is due, and it gave way very gradually in
the revival of literature. In some of the monastic foundations,
especially in that of Isidore, though himself a man of considerable learning, the perusal of heathen authors was prohibited. Fortunately Benedict, whose order became the most
widely diffused, while he enjoined his brethren to read, copy,
and collect books, was silent as to their nature, concluding,
probably, that they would be wholly religious. This, in course
of time, became the means of preserving and multiplying
classical manuscripts.[f]

---

[d] M. Guizot confirms me in a conclusion to which I had previously come,
that the seventh century is the *nadir* of
the human mind in Europe, and that its
movement in advance began before the
end of the next, or, in other words,
with Charlemagne. Hist. de la Civilisation en France, ii. 345. A notion
probably is current in England, on the
authority of the older writers, such as
Cave or Robertson, that the greatest
darkness was later; which is true as to
England itself. It was in the seventh
century that the barbarians were first
tempted to enter the church, and obtain
bishoprics, which had, in the first age

after their invasion, been reserved to
Romans. Fleury, p. 18.

[e] Gregory has been often charged, on
the authority of a passage in John of
Salisbury, with having burned a library
of heathen authors. He has been warmly
defended by Tiraboschi, iii. 102. Even
if the assertion of our countryman were
more positive, he is of too late an age to
demand much credit. Eichhorn, however, produces vehement expressions of
Gregory's disregard for learning, and
even for the observance of grammatical
rules. ii. 443.

[f] Heeren, p. 59. Eichhorn, ii. 11, 12,
40, 49, 50.

6. If, however, the prejudices of the clergy stood in the way of what we more esteem than they did, the study of philological literature, it is never to be forgotten Their usefulness in preserving it. that but for them the records of that very literature would have perished. If they had been less tenacious of their Latin liturgy, of the vulgate translation of Scripture, and of the authority of the fathers, it is very doubtful whether less superstition would have grown up, but we cannot hesitate to pronounce that all grammatical learning would have been laid aside. The influence of the church upon learning, partly favourable, partly the reverse, forms the subject of Eichhorn's second volume, whose comprehensive views and well-directed erudition, as well as his position in a great protestant university, give much weight to his testimony; but we should remember also that it is, as it were, by striking a balance that we come to this result; and that in many respects the clergy counteracted that progress of improvement which in others may be ascribed to their exertions.

7. It is not unjust to claim for these islands the honour of having first withstood the dominant ignorance, and even led the way in the restoration of knowledge. First appearances of reviving learning in Ireland and England. As early as the sixth century, a little glimmer of light was perceptible in the Irish monasteries; and in the next, when France and Italy had sunk in deeper ignorance, they stood, not quite where national prejudice has sometimes placed them, but certainly in a very respectable position.[g] That island both drew students from the continent, and sent forth men of comparative eminence into its schools and churches. I do not find, however, that they contributed much to the advance of secular, and especially of grammatical learning. This is rather due to England, and to the happy influence of Theodore, Archbishop of Canterbury, an Asiatic Greek by birth, sent hither by the Pope in 668, through whom, and his companion Adrian, some knowledge of the Latin and even Greek languages was propagated in the Anglo-Saxon church. The Venerable Bede, as he was afterwards styled, early in the eighth century, surpasses

[g] Eichhorn, ii. 176, 188. See also the first volume of Moore's History of Ireland, where the claims of his country are stated favourably, and with much learning and industry, but not with extravagant partiality.

every other name of our ancient literary annals ; and though little more than a diligent compiler from older writers, may perhaps be reckoned superior to any man whom the world (so low had the East sunk like the West) then possessed. A desire of knowledge grew up ; the school of York, some-what later, became respectable, before any liberal education had been established in France ; and from this came Alcuin, a man fully equal to Bede in ability, though not in eru-dition.[h] By his assistance, and that of one or two Italians, Charlemagne laid in his vast dominions the foundations of learning, according to the standard of that age, which dispelled, at least for a time, some part of the gross igno-ance wherein his empire had been enveloped.[i]

8. The praise of having originally established schools belongs to some bishops and abbots of the sixth century. They came in place of the imperial schools overthrown by the barbarians.[k]   In the downfall of that temporal dominion, a spiritual aristocracy was providentially raised up, to save from extinction the remains of learning, and religion itself.   Some of those schools seem to have been preserved in the south of Italy, though merely, perhaps, for elementary instruction ; but in France the barbarism of the latter Merovingian period was so complete that, before the reign of Charlemagne, all liberal studies had come to an end.   Nor was Italy in a much better state at his accession, though he called two or

Few schools before the age of Charle-magne.

---

[h] Eichhorn, ii. 188, 207, 263. Hist. litt. de la France, vols. iii. and iv. Henry's History of England, vol. iv. Turner's History of Anglo-Saxons. No one, however, has spoken so highly or so fully of Alcuin's merits as M. Guizot, in his Histoire de la Civilisation en France, vol. ii. pp. 344-385.

[The writings of Alcuin are not highly appreciated by the learned and judicious author of Biographia Britannica Lite-raria, especially in relation to their in-fluence upon English literature. The truth is, that Alcuin was a polite scho-lar for the age in which he lived, but no real poet. 'He has, on the whole,' says Mr. Wright, ' more simplicity and less pretension in his poetry than his prede-cessor Aldhelm, and so far he is more pleasing ; but, unfortunately, when the

latter was turgid and bombastic, the former too often went into the opposite extreme of being flat and spiritless.' p. 46. This criticism seems not unjust. Alcuin, however, is an easy versifier, and has caught the tone of Ovid, some-times of Virgil, with some success.—1847.]

[i] Besides the above authors, see, for the merits of Charlemagne, as a restorer of letters, his Life by Gaillard and An-drès, Origine, &c., della Litteratura, i. 165.

[k] Eichhorn, ii. 5, 45. Guizot (vol. ii. p. 116) gives a list of the episcopal schools in France before Charlemagne.

[m] Ante ipsum Carolum regem in Gal-lia nullum fuerat studium liberalium artium. Monachus Engolimensis, apud Launoy de Scholis celebrioribus.

three scholars from thence to his literary councils. The libraries were destroyed, the schools chiefly closed; wherever the Lombard dominion extended, illiteracy was its companion.[n]

9. The cathedral and conventual schools, created or restored by Charlemagne, became the means of preserving that small portion of learning which continued to exist. They flourished most, having had time to produce their fruits, under his successors, Louis the Debonair, Lothaire, and Charles the Bald.[o] It was, doubtless, a fortunate circumstance that the revolution of language had now gone far enough to render Latin unintelligible without grammatical instruction. Alcuin, and others who, like him, endeavoured to keep ignorance out of the church, were anxious, we are told, to restore orthography; or, in other words, to prevent the written Latin from following the corruptions of speech. They brought back also some knowledge of better classical authors than had been in use. Alcuin's own poems could at least not have been written by one unacquainted with Virgil:[p] the faults are numerous, but the style is not always inelegant; and from this time, though quotations from the Latin poets, especially Ovid and Virgil, and sometimes from Cicero, are not very frequent, they occur sufficiently to show that manuscripts had been brought to this side of the Alps. They were, however, very rare: Italy was still, as might be expected, the chief depository of ancient writings; and Gerbert speaks of the facility of obtaining them in that country.[q]

10. The tenth century used to be reckoned by mediæval historians the darkest part of this intellectual night. It was the iron age, which they vie with one another in describing as lost in the most consummate ignorance. This, however, is much rather applicable to

Beneficial effects of those established by him.

The tenth century more progressive than usually supposed.

---

[n] Tiraboschi. Eichhorn. Heeren.

[o] The reader may find more of the history of these schools in a little treatise by Launoy, De Scholis celebrioribus a Car. Mag. et post Car. Mag. instauratis; also in Hist. litt. de la France, vols. iii. and iv.; Crevier, Hist. de l'Université de Paris, vol. i.; Brucker's Hist. Phil. iii.; Muratori, Dissert. xliii.;

Tiraboschi, iii. 158; Eichhorn, 261, 295; Heeren and Fleury.

[p] A poem by Alcuin, De Pontificibus Ecclesiæ Eboracensis, is published in Gale's XV. Scriptores, vol. iii.

[q] Nosti quot scriptores in urbibus aut in agris Italiæ passim habeantur. Gerbert. Epist. 130, apud Heeren, p. 166.

Italy and England than to France and Germany. The former were both in a deplorable state of barbarism;[r] and there are, doubtless, abundant proofs of ignorance in every part of Europe. But, compared with the seventh and eighth centuries, the tenth was an age of illumination in France; and Meiners, who judged the middle ages somewhat, perhaps, too severely, but with a penetrating and comprehensive observation, of which there had been few instances, has gone so far as to say, that 'in no age, perhaps, did Germany possess more learned and virtuous churchmen of the episcopal order than in the latter half of the tenth, and beginning of the eleventh century.'[s] Eichhorn points out indications of a more extensive acquaintance with ancient writers in several French and German ecclesiastics of this period.[t] In the eleventh century this continued to increase; and towards its close we find more vigorous and extensive attempts at throwing off the yoke of barbarous ignorance, and either retrieving what had been lost of ancient learning, or supplying its place by the original powers of the mind.

11. It is the most striking circumstance in the literary annals of the dark ages, that they seem to us still more deficient in native, than in acquired ability. The mere ignorance of letters has sometimes been a little exaggerated, and admits of certain qualifications; but a tameness and mediocrity, a servile habit of merely compiling from others, runs through the writers of these centuries. It is not only that much was lost, but that there was nothing to compensate for it; nothing of original genius in the province of imagination; and but two extraordinary men, Scotus Erigena and Gerbert, may be said to stand out from the crowd in literature and philosophy. It must be added, as to the former, that his writings contain, at least in such extracts as I have seen, unintelligible rhapsodies of mysticism, in which, perhaps, he should not even have the credit of originality. Eichhorn, however, bestows great praise on

Want of genius in the dark ages.

---

[r] [See Tiraboschi for the one, and Turner's History of Anglo-Saxons for the other. But I do not know that England was *more* dark in the tenth century than in the ninth.—1842.]

[s] Vergleichung der Sitten. ii. 384.

The eleventh century he holds far more advanced in learning than the sixth. Books were read in the latter, which no one looked at in the earlier. P. 399.

[t] Allg. Gesch. ii. 335, 398.

Scotus; and the modern historians of philosophy treat him with respect.[u]

12. It would be a strange hypothesis, that no man endowed with superior gifts of nature lived in so many ages. Though the pauses of her fertility in these high endowments are more considerable, I am disposed to think, than any previous calculation of probabilities would lead us to anticipate, we could not embrace so extreme a paradox. Of military skill, indeed, and civil prudence, we are not now speaking. But, though no man appeared of genius sufficient to burst the fetters imposed by ignorance and bad taste, some there must have been who, in a happier condition of literature, would have been its legitimate pride. We perceive, therefore, in the deficiencies of these writers, the effect which an oblivion of good models and the prevalence of a false standard of merit may produce in repressing the natural vigour of the mind. Their style, where they aim at eloquence, is inflated and redundant, formed upon the model of the later fathers, whom they chiefly read; a feeble imitation of that vicious rhetoric which had long overspread the Latinity of the empire.[x]

Prevalence of bad taste.

---

[u] Extracts from John Scotus Erigena will be found in Brucker, Hist. Philosophiæ, vol. iii. p. 619; in Meiners, ii. 373; or more fully, in Turner's History of England, vol. i. 447, and Guizot, Hist. de la Civilisation en France, iii. 137, 178. The reader may consult also Buhle, Tennemann, and the article on Thomas Aquinas in the Encyclopædia Metropolitana, ascribed to Dr. Hampden. But, perhaps, Mr. Turner is the only one of them who has seen, or at least read, the metaphysical treatise of John Scotus, entitled De Divisione Naturæ, in which alone we find his philosophy. It is very rare out of England, nor common in it.

[x] Fleury, l. xlv. § 19, and Troisième Discours (in vol. xiii.), p. 6. Turner's History of England, iv. 137, and History of Anglo-Saxons, iii. 403. It is sufficient to look at any extracts from these writers of the dark ages to see the justice of this censure. Fleury, at the conclusion of his excellent third discourse, justly and candidly apologises for these five ages, as not wholly destitute of learning, and far less of virtue. They have been, he says, outrageously depreciated by the humanists of the sixteenth century, who thought good Latin superior to everything else; and by protestant writers, who laid the corruptions of the church on its ignorance. Yet there is an opposite extreme into which those who are disgusted with the common-places of superficial writers sometimes run; an estimation of men by their relative superiority above their own times, so as to forget their position in comparison with a fixed standard.

An eminent living writer who has carried the philosophy of history, perhaps, as far as any other, has lately endeavoured, at considerable length, to vindicate in some measure the intellectual character of this period. (Guizot, vol. ii. pp. 123–224.) It is with reluctance that I ever differ from M. Guizot; but the passages adduced by him (especially if we exclude those of the fifth century, the poems of Avitus, and the homilies of Cæsarius) do not appear adequate to redeem the age by any signs of genius they display. It must always be a question of degree; for no one is absurd enough to deny the existence of a relative superiority of talent

13. It might naturally be asked, whether fancy and feeling
Deficiency of poetical talent. were extinct among the people, though a false taste
might reign in the cloister. Yet it is here that we
find the most remarkable deficiency, and could appeal scarce
to the vaguest tradition, or the most doubtful fragment,
in witness of any poetical talent worthy of notice, except a
little in the Teutonic languages. The Anglo-Saxon poetry
has occasionally a wild spirit, rather impressive, though it is
often turgid, and always rude. The Scandinavian, such as the
well-known song of Regner Lodbrog, if that be as old as the
period before us, which is now denied, displays a still more
poetical character. Some of the earliest German poetry, the
song on the victory of Louis III. over the Normans in 883,
and, still more, the poem in praise of Hanno, archbishop of
Cologne, who died in 1075, are warmly extolled by Herder and
Bouterwek.[y] In the Latin verse of these centuries we find,
at best, a few lines among many which show the author to
have caught something of a classical style; the far greater
portion is very bad.[z]

---

or the power of expressing moral emotions, as well as relative facts, with
some warmth and energy. The legends
of saints, an extensive though quite neglected portion of the literature of the
dark ages, to which M. Guizot has had
the merit of directing our attention,
may probably contain many passages,
like those he had quoted, which will be
read with interest; and it is no more
than justice that he has given them in
French, rather than in that half-barbarous Latin, which, though not essential to the author's mind, never fails,
like an unbecoming dress, to show the
gifts of nature at a disadvantage. But
the questions still recur: Is this in itself excellent? Would it indicate,
wherever we should meet with it, powers
of a high order? Do we not make a
tacit allowance in reading it, and that
very largely, for the mean condition in
which we know the human mind to have
been placed at the period? Does it
instruct us, or give us pleasure?
In what M. Guizot has said of the
moral influence of these legends, in humanising a lawless barbarian race (p.
157), I should be sorry not to concur: it
is a striking instance of that candid and

catholic spirit with which he has always
treated the mediæval church.
[y] Herder, Zerstreute Blätter, vol. v.
pp. 169, 184. Heinsius, Lehrbuch der
Deutschen Sprachwissenschaft, iv. 29.
Bouterwek, Geschichte der Poesie und
Beredsamkeit, vol. ix. pp. 78, 82. The
author is unknown; aber dem unbekann-
ten sichert sein Werk die Unsterblich-
keit, says the latter critic. One might
raise a question as to the capacity of an
anonymous author to possess immortal
fame. Nothing equal to this poem, he
says, occurs in the earlier German poetry: it is an outpouring of genius, not
without faults, but full of power and
feeling: the dialect is still Frankish,
but approaches to Swabian. Herder
calls it 'a truly Pindaric song.' He
has given large extracts from it in the
volume above quoted, which glows with
his own fine sense of beauty.
[z] Tiraboschi supposes Latin versifiers
to have been common in Italy. Le Città
al pari che le campagne risuonavan di
versi. iii. 207.
The specimens he afterwards produces,
p. 219, are miserable. Hroswitha, abbess of Gandersheim, has, perhaps, the
greatest reputation among these Latin

14. The very imperfect state of language, as an instrument of refined thought, in the transition of Latin to the Imperfect state of language may account for this. French, Castillian, and Italian tongues, seems the best means of accounting in any satisfactory manner for this stagnation of the poetical faculties. The delicacy that distinguishes in words the shades of sentiment, the grace that brings them to the soul of the reader with the charm of novelty united to clearness could not be attainable in a colloquial jargon, the offspring of ignorance, and indeterminate possibly in its forms, which those who possessed any superiority of education would endeavour to avoid. We shall soon have occasion to advert again to this subject.

15. At the beginning of the twelfth century we enter upon a new division in the literary history of Europe. Improvement at beginning of twelfth century. From this time we may deduce a line of men conspicuous, according to the standard of their times, in different walks of intellectual pursuit, and the commencement of an interesting period, the later middle ages, in which, though ignorance was very far from being cleared away, the natural powers of the mind were developed in considerable activity. We shall point out separately the most Leading circumstances in progress of learning. important circumstances of this progress, not all of them concurrent in efficacy with each other, for they were sometimes opposed, but all tending to rouse Europe from indolence, and to fix its attention on literature. These are, 1st. The institution of universities, and the methods pursued in them; 2nd. The cultivation of the modern languages, followed by the multiplication of books and the extension of the art of writing ; 3rd. The investigation of the Roman law; and, lastly, the return to the study of the Latin language in its ancient models of purity. We shall thus come down to the fifteenth century, and judge better of what is meant by the revival of letters when we apprehend with more exactness their previous condition.

16. Among the Carlovingian schools it is doubtful whether we can reckon one at Paris ; and though there are Origin of the university of Paris. some traces of public instruction in that city about

---

poets. She wrote, in the tenth century, sacred comedies in imitation of Terence, which I have not seen, and other poetry which I saw many years since, and thought very indifferent.

the end of the ninth century, it is not certain that we can assume it to be more ancient. For two hundred years more, indeed, it can only be said that some persons appear to have come to Paris for the purposes of study.[a] The commencement of this famous university, like that of Oxford, has no record. But it owes its first reputation to the sudden spread of what is usually called the scholastic philosophy.

17. There had been hitherto two methods of treating theo-

Modes of treating the science of theology.

logical doctrines : one, that of the fathers, who built them on Scripture, illustrated and interpreted by their own ingenuity, and in some measure also on the traditions and decisions of the church; the other, which is said by the Benedictines of St. Maur to have grown up about the eighth century (though Mosheim seems to refer it to the sixth), using the fathers themselves, that is, the chief writers of the first six hundred years, who appear now to have acquired that distinctive title of honour as authority, conjointly with Scripture and ecclesiastical determinations, by means of extracts or compends of their writings. Hence about this time we find more frequent instances of a practice which had begun before—that of publishing *Loci communes* or *Catenæ patrum,* being only digested extracts from the authorities under systematic heads.[b] Both these methods were usually called positive theology.

18. The scholastic theology was a third method; it was in

Scholastic philosophy; its origin.

its general principle an alliance between faith and reason; an endeavour to arrange the orthodox system of the church, such as authority had made it, according to the rules and methods of the Aristotelian dialectics

---

[a] Crevier, i. 137–5.

[b] Fleury, 3me discours, p. 48. (Hist. ecclés. vol. xiii. 12mo.' ed.) Hist. litt. de la France, vii. 147. Mosheim, in Cent. vi. et post. Muratori, Antichità Italiane, dissert. xliii. p. 610. In this dissertation, it may be observed by the way, Muratori gives the important fragment of Caius, a Roman presbyter before the end of the second century (as some place him), on the canon of the New Testament, which has not been quoted, as far as I know, by any English writer, nor, which is more remarkable, by Michaelis. It will be found in Eichhorn, Einleitung in das Neue Testament,

iv. 35; [and I have learned, since the publication of my first edition, that it is printed in Routh's Reliquiæ Sacræ.— 1842.]

Upon this great change in the theology of the church, which consisted principally in establishing the authority of the fathers, the reader may see M. Guizot, Hist. de la Civilisation, iii. 121. There seem to be but two causes for this : the one, a consciousness of ignorance and inferiority to men of so much talent as Augustin and a few others ; the other, a constantly growing jealousy of the free exercise of reason, and a determination to keep up unity of doctrine.

and sometimes upon premises supplied by metaphysical reasoning. Lanfranc and Anselm made much use of this method in the controversy with Berenger as to transubstantiation, though they did not carry it so far as their successors in the next century.[c] The scholastic philosophy seems chiefly to be distinguished from this theology by a larger infusion of metaphysical reasoning, or by its occasional inquiries into subjects not immediately related to revealed articles of faith.[d] The origin of this philosophy, fixed by Buhle and Tennemann in the ninth century, or the age of Scotus Erigena, has been brought down by Tiedemann, Meiners, and Hampden [e] so low as the thirteenth. But Roscelin of Compiègne, a little before 1100, may be accounted so far the founder of the schoolmen, that the great celebrity of their disputations and the rapid increase of students are to be traced to the influence of his theories, though we have no proof that he ever taught at Paris. Roscelin also, having been the first to

Roscelin.

---

[c] Hist. litt. de la France, ubi suprà. Tennemann, Manuel de l'Hist. de la Philosophie, i. 332. Crevier, i. 100. Andrès, ii. 15.

[d] A jesuit of the sixteenth century thus shortly and clearly distinguishes the positive from the scholastic, and both from natural or metaphysical theology. At nos theologiam scholasticam dicimus, quæ certiori methodo et rationibus imprimis ex divina Scriptura, ac traditionibus seu decretis patrum in conciliis definitis veritatem eruit, ac discutiendo comprobat. Quod cum in scholis præcipue argumentando comparetur, id nomen sortita est. Quamobrem differt a positiva theologia, non re sed modo, quemadmodum item alia ratione non est eadem cum naturali theologia, quo nomine philosophi metaphysicen nominarunt. Positiva igitur non ita res disputandas proponit, sed pæne sententiam ratam et firmam ponit, præcipue in pietatem incumbens. Versatur autem et ipsa in explicatione Scripturæ sacræ, traditionum conciliorum et sanctorum patrum. Naturalis porro theologia Dei naturam per naturæ argumenta et rationes inquirit, cum supernaturalis, quam scholasticam dicimus, Dei ejusdem naturam, vim, proprietates, cæterasque res divinas per ea principia vestigat, quæ sunt hominibus revelata divinitus. Possevin, Bibliotheca Selecta, l. 3, c. i.

Both positive and scholastic theology were much indebted to Peter Lombard, whose Liber Sententiarum is a digest of propositions extracted from the fathers, with no attempt to reconcile them. It was therefore a prodigious magazine of arms for disputation.

[e] The first of these, according to Tennemann, begins the list of schoolmen with Hales; the two latter agree in conferring that honour on Albertus Magnus. Brucker inclines to Roscelin, and has been followed by others. It may be added, that Tennemann divides the scholastic philosophy into four periods, which Roscelin, Hales, Ockham, and the sixteenth century terminate; and Buhle into three, ending with Roscelin, Albertus Magnus, and the sixteenth century. It is evident that, by beginning the scholastic series with Roscelin, we exclude Lanfranc and even Anselm; the latter of whom was certainly a deep metaphysician; since to him we owe the subtle argument for the existence of a Deity, which Des Cartes afterwards revived. Buhle, 679. This argument was answered at the time by one Gaunelo; so that metaphysical reasonings were not unknown in the eleventh century. Tennemann, 344.

revive the famous question as to the reality of universal ideas, marks, on every hypothesis, a new era in the history of philosophy. The principle of the schoolmen in their investigations was the expanding, developing, and, if possible, illustrating and clearing from objection, the doctrines of natural and revealed religion, in a dialectical method, and by dint of the subtlest reason. The questions which we deem altogether metaphysical, such as that concerning universal ideas, became theological in their hands.[f]

19. Next in order of time to Roscelin came William of Champeaux, who opened a school of logic at Paris in 1109 : and the university can only deduce the regular succession of its teachers from that time.[g] But his reputation was soon eclipsed, and his hearers drawn away by a more potent magician, Peter Abelard, who taught in the schools of Paris in the second decad of the twelfth century. Wherever Abelard retired, his fame and his disciples followed him ; in the solitary walls of the Paraclete, as in the thronged streets of the capital.[h] And the impulse given was so powerful, the fascination of a science which now appears arid and unproductive was so intense, that from this time for many generations it continued to engage the most intelligent and active minds. Paris, about the middle of the twelfth century, in the words of the Benedictines of St. Maur, to whom we owe the ' Histoire littéraire de la France,' was another Athens ; the number of students

Progress of scholasticism ; increase of university of Paris.

---

[f] Brucker, though he contains some useful extracts, and tolerable general views, was not well versed in the scholastic writers. Meiners (in his Comparison of the Middle Ages) is rather superficial as to their philosophy, but presents a lively picture of the schoolmen in relation to literature and manners. He has also, in the Transactions of the Göttingen Academy, vol. xii. pp. 26–47, given a succinct, but valuable, sketch of the Nominalist and Realist Controversy. Tennemann, with whose Manuel de la Philosophie alone I am conversant, is said to have gone very deeply into the subject in his larger history of Philosophy. Buhle appears superficial. Dr. Hampden, in his Life of Thomas Aquinas, and view of the scholastic philosophy, published in the Encyclopædia

Metropolitana, has the merit of having been the only Englishman, past or present, so far as I know, since the revival of letters, who has penetrated far into the wilderness of scholasticism. Mr. Sharon Turner has given some extracts in the fourth volume of his History of England.

[M. Cousin, in the fourth volume of his Fragmens philosophiques, has gone more fully than any one into the philosophy of Roscelin, and especially of Abelard. This is reprinted from the Introduction to the unpublished works of Abelard, edited by M. Cousin in the great series of Documens inédits.— 1847.]

[g] Crevier, i. 3.

[h] Hist. litt. de la France, vol. xii. Brucker, iii. 750.

(hyperbolically speaking, as we must presume) exceeding that of the citizens. This influx of scholars induced Philip Augustus some time afterwards to enlarge the boundaries of the city ; and this again brought a fresh harvest of students, for whom in the former limits it had been difficult to find lodgings. Paris was called, as Rome had been, the country of all the inhabitants of the world ; and we may add, as, for very different reasons, it still claims to be.[i]

20. Colleges, with endowments for poor scholars, were founded in the beginning of the thirteenth century, or even before, at Paris and Bologna, as they were afterwards at Oxford and Cambridge, by munificent patrons of letters ; charters incorporating the graduates and students collectively under the name of universities were granted by sovereigns, with privileges perhaps too extensive, but such as indicated the dignity of learning and the countenance it received.[k]   It ought, however, to be remembered that these foundations were not the cause, but the effect, of that increasing thirst for knowledge, or the semblance of knowledge, which had anticipated the encouragement of the great.   The schools of Charlemagne were designed to lay

Universities founded. Oxford.

---

[i] Hist. litt. de la France, ix. 78. Crevier. i. 274.

[k] Fleury, xvii. 13, 17.   Crevier, Tiraboschi, &c. A University, universitas doctorum et scholarium, was so called either from its incorporation, or from its professing to teach all subjects, as some have thought. Meiners, ii. 405. Fleury, xvii. 15. This excellent discourse of Fleury, the fifth, relates to the ecclesiastical literature of the later middle ages. [The first privilege granted to Bologna was by Frederic Barbarossa in 1158. But it gives an appeal to the bishops, not to the rector of the university, in case any scholar had cause of complaint against his teacher. In fact there was no rector, nor, properly speaking, any university till near the end of the twelfth century. Savigny, Gesch. des Römischen Rechts, 111, 152. And as at Bologna nothing was taught but jurisprudence for some time afterwards, it is doubted by some whether that school could be called an university, which ought to be a place of general instruction. Tiraboschi, v. 253. Upon the whole, the precedence must be allowed,

I think, to Paris ; but even there we cannot trace the university, as strictly such, so high as 1200. En ces temps-là, l'ensemble des écoles Parisiennes était appelé *studium generale* bien plutôt qu' *universitas* ; ce dernier nòm leur fut appliqué, peut-être pour la première fois, dans l'affaire d'Amaury de Chartres et de ses disciples en 1209. Il n'est point employé dans le diplôme de Philippe-Auguste, donné en 1201, à l'occasion d'une rixe violente entre les écoliers et les bourgeois de Paris.—Discours sur l'état des lettres au treizième siècle, in Hist. litt. de la France, vol. xvi. p. 46, par Daunou.

The university of Toulouse was incorporated with the same privileges as that of Paris by a bull of Gregory IX. in 1238 ; which seems to have been acknowledged as sufficient in France on several other occasions. Montpelier, which had for some time been a flourishing school of medicine, acquired the rights of an university before the end of the thirteenth century ; but no other is of equal antiquity. Id. pp. 57, 59.— 1842.]

the basis of a learned education, for which there was at that time no sufficient desire.[m] But in the twelfth century, the impetuosity with which men rushed to that source of what they deemed wisdom, the great university of Paris, did not depend upon academical privileges or eleemosynary stipends, which came afterwards, though these were undoubtedly very effectual in keeping it up. The university created patrons, and was not created by them. And this may be said also of Oxford and Cambridge in their incorporate character, whatever the former may have owed, if in fact it owed anything, to the prophetic munificence of Alfred. Oxford was a school of great resort in the reign of Henry II., though its first charter was only granted by Henry III. Its earlier history is but obscure, and depends chiefly on a suspicious passage in Ingulphus, against which we must set the absolute silence of other writers.[n] It became in the thirteenth century second only to Paris in the multitude of its students and the celebrity of its scholastic disputations. England indeed, and especially through Oxford, could show more names of the first class in this line than any other country.[o]

---

[m] These schools, established by the Carlovingian princes in convents and cathedrals, declined, as it was natural to expect, with the rise of the universities. Meiners, ii. 406. Those of Paris, Oxford, and Bologna, contained many thousand students.

[n] Giraldus Cambrensis, about 1180, seems the first unequivocal witness to the resort of students to Oxford, as an established seat of instruction. But it is certain that Vacarius read there on the civil law in 1149, which affords a presumption that it was already assuming the character of a university. John of Salisbury, I think, does not mention it. In a former work, I gave more credence to its foundation by Alfred than I am now inclined to do. Bologna, as well as Paris, was full of English students about 1200. Meiners, ii. 428.

[o] Wood expatiates on what he thought the glorious age of the university :—
'What university, I pray, can produce an invincible Hales, an admirable Bacon, an excellent well-grounded Middleton, a subtle Scotus, an approved Burley, a resolute Baconthorpe, a singular Ockham, a solid and industrious Holcot,

and a profound Bradwardin? all which persons flourished within the compass of one century. I doubt that neither Paris, Bologna, or Rome, that grand mistress of the Christian world, or any place else, can do what the renowned Bellosite (Oxford) hath done. And without doubt all impartial men may receive it for an undeniable truth, that the most subtle arguing in school divinity did take its beginning in England and from Englishmen ; and that also from thence it went to Paris, and other parts of France, and at length into Italy, Spain, and other nations, as is by one observed. So that though Italy boasted that Britain takes her Christianity first from Rome, England may truly maintain that from her (immediately by France) Italy first received her school divinity.' Vol. i. p. 159, A. D. 1168.
[If the authenticity of the History of Croyland Abbey, under the name of Ingulfus, cannot be maintained, as both Sir Francis Palgrave and Mr. Wright contend, the antiquity of the University of Oxford must, I fear, fall to the ground. See Biographia Britannica Litteraria, vol. ii. p. 28. Whether

21. Andrès is inclined to derive the institution of collegiate foundations in universities from the Saracens. Collegiate foundations derived from the Saracens. He finds no trace of these among the ancients; while in several cities of Spain, as Cordova, Granada, Malaga, colleges for learned education both existed and obtained great renown. These were sometimes unconnected with each other, though in the same city; nor had they, of course, those privileges which were conferred in Christendom. They were therefore more like ordinary schools or gymnasia than universities; and it is difficult to perceive that they suggested anything peculiarly characteristic of the latter institutions, which are much more reasonably considered as the development of a native germ, planted by a few generous men, above all by Charlemagne, in that inclement season which was passing away.[p]

22. The institution of the Mendicant orders of friars, soon after the beginning of the thirteenth century, Scholastic philosophy promoted by Mendicant Friars. caused a fresh accession, in enormous numbers, to the ecclesiastical state, and gave encouragement to the scholastic philosophy. Less acquainted, generally, with grammatical literature than the Benedictine monks, less accustomed to collect and transcribe books, the disciples of Francis and Dominic betook themselves to disputation, and found a substitute for learning in their own ingenuity and expertness.[q] The greatest of the schoolmen were the Dominican Thomas Aquinas, and the Franciscan Duns Scotus. They were founders of rival sects, which wrangled with each other for two or three centuries. But the authority of their writings, which were incredibly voluminous, especially those of the former,[r] impeded in some measure the growth of new men; and we find, after the middle of the fourteenth century, a diminution of eminent names in the series of the schoolmen, the last of whom that is much remembered in modern times was William Ockham.[s] He

---

Vacarius were the first lecturer, or chose that town because a school had already been established therein, seems not determinable, though the latter is more likely.—1847.]

[p] Andrès, ii. 129.

[q] Meiners, ii. 615, 629.

[r] The works of Thomas Aquinas are published in seventeen volumes folio; Rome, 1570: those of Duns Scotus in twelve; Lyons, 1639. It is presumed that much was taken down from their oral lectures; some part of these volumes is of doubtful authenticity. Meiners, ii. 718. Biogr. Univ.

[s] 'In them (Scotus and Ockham), and

revived the sect of the Nominalists, formerly instituted by
Roscelin, and, with some important variations of opinion,
brought into credit by Abelard, but afterwards overpowered
by the great weight of leading schoolmen on the opposite
side—that of the Realists. The disciples of Ockham, as well
as himself, being politically connected with the party in
Germany unfavourable to the high pretensions of the court
of Rome, though they became very numerous in the universities, passed for innovators in ecclesiastical as well as philosophical principles. Nominalism itself indeed was reckoned by the adverse sect cognate to heresy. No decline,
however, seems to have been as yet perceptible in the spirit
of disputation, which probably, at the end of the fourteenth
century, went on as eagerly at Paris, Oxford, and Salamanca,
the great scenes of that warfare, as before, and which in
that age gained much ground in Germany through the
establishment of several universities.

23. Tennemann has fairly stated the good and bad of the
Character scholastic philosophy. It gave rise to a great
of this
philosophy. display of address, subtlety, and sagacity, in the
explanation and distinction of abstract ideas, but at the
same time to many trifling and minute speculations, to a
contempt of positive and particular knowledge, and to much
unnecessary refinement.[t] Fleury well observes that the dry
technical style of the schoolmen, affecting a geometrical
method and closeness, is in fact more prolix and tedious

in the later schoolmen generally, down
to the period of the Reformation, there
is more of the parade of logic, a more
formal examination of arguments, a more
burthensome importunity of syllogizing,
with less of the philosophical power of
arrangement and distribution of the subject discussed. The dryness again in-
separable from the scholastic method is
carried to excess in the later writers,
and perspicuity of style is altogether neglected.' Encyclopædia Metropol. part
xxxvii. p. 805.

The introduction of this excess of
logical subtlety, carried to the most
trifling sophistry, is ascribed by Meiners
to Petrus Hispanus, afterwards Pope
John XXI. who died in 1271. ii. 705.
Several curious specimens of scholastic

folly are given by him in this place
They brought a discredit upon the name,
which has adhered to it, and involved
men of fine genius, such as Aquinas
himself, in the common reproach.

The barbarism of style, which
amounted almost to a new language, became more intolerable in Scotus and his
followers than it had been in the older
schoolmen. Meiners, 722. It may be
alleged, in excuse of this, that words are
meant to express precise ideas ; and that
it was as impossible to write metaphysics
in good Latin, as the modern naturalists
have found it to describe plants and
animals.

[t] Manuel de la Philosophie, i. 337.
Eichhorn, ii. 396.

than one more natural, from its formality in multiplying objections and answers.[u]   And as their reasonings commonly rest on disputable postulates, the accuracy they affect is of no sort of value.   But their chief offences were the interposing obstacles to the revival of polite literature, and to the free expansion of the mind.   Italy was the land where the schoolmen had least influence, though many of the Italians who had a turn for those discussions repaired to Paris.[x]   Public schools of theology were not opened in Italy till after 1360.[y]   Yet we find the disciples of Averroes numerous in the university of Padua about that time. *It prevails least in Italy.*

24. II. The universities were chiefly employed upon this scholastic theology and metaphysics, with the exception of Bologna, which dedicated its attention to the civil law, and of Montpellier, already famous as a school of medicine.   The laity in general might have remained in as gross barbarity as before, while topics so removed from common utility were treated in an unknown tongue.   We must therefore look to the rise of a truly native literature in the several languages of western Europe, as a more essential cause of its intellectual improvement; and this will render it necessary to give a sketch of the origin and early progress of those languages and that new literature. *Literature in modern languages.*

25. No one can require to be informed that the Italian, Spanish, and French languages are the principal of many dialects deviating from each other in the gradual corruption of the Latin, once universally spoken by the subjects of Rome in her western provinces. They have undergone this process of change in various degrees, but always from similar causes; partly from the retention of barbarous words belonging to their original languages, or the introduction of others through the settlement of the northern nations in the empire; but in a far greater proportion from ignorance of grammatical rules, or from vicious pronunciation and orthography.   It has been the labour of many distinguished writers to trace the source *Origin of the French, Spanish, and Italian languages.*

---

u See 5me discours, xvii. 30–50.   y Id. 137, 160.   De Sade, Vie de Pé-
x Tiraboschi, v. 115.   trarque. iii. 757.

and channels of these streams, which have supplied both the literature and the common speech of the south of Europe; and perhaps not much will be hereafter added to researches which, in the scarcity of extant documents, can never be minutely successful. Du Cange, who led the way in the admirable preface to his Glossary; Le Bœuf, and Bonamy, in several memoirs among the transactions of the Academy of Inscriptions about the middle of the last century; Muratori, in his ,32nd, 33rd, and 40th dissertations on Italian antiquities; and, with more copious evidence and successful industry than any other, M. Raynouard, in the first and sixth volumes of his Choix des Poésies des Troubadours, have collected as full a history of the formation of these languages as we could justly require.

26. The pure Latin language, as we read it in the best Corruption of colloquial Latin in the Lower Empire. ancient authors, possesses a complicated syntax and many elliptical modes of expression, which give vigour and elegance to style, but are not likely to be readily caught by the people. If, however, the citizens of Rome had spoken it with entire purity, it is to be remembered that Latin, in the later times of the republic, or under the empire, was not, like the Greek of Athens or the Tuscan of Florence, the idiom of a single city, but a language spread over countries in which it was not originally vernacular, and imposed by conquest upon many parts of Italy, as it was afterwards upon Spain and Gaul. Thus we find even early proofs that solecisms of grammar, as well as barbarous phrases and words unauthorised by use of polite writers, were very common in Rome itself; and in every succeeding generation, for the first centuries after the Christian era, these became more frequent and inevitable.[z] A vulgar Roman dialect, called *quotidianus* by Quintilian, *pedestris* by Vegetius, *usualis* by Sidonius, is recognised as distinguishable from the pure Latinity to which we give the name of classical. But

---

[z] [As the word 'barbarous' is applied at present with less strictness, it may be worth while to mention, that, in Latin, it meant only words borrowed from the languages of barbarians. This of course did not include Greek; for though the adoption of Greek words in Latin writers was sometimes reckoned an affectation, it could not pass for a barbarism. But perhaps the Provincial dialects of Italy were included; for it is said by Quintilian, that sometimes barbarous phrases had been uttered by the audience in the theatres; theatra exclamâsse barbarè.—1847.]

the more ordinary appellation of this inferior Latin was *rusticus*; it was the country language or *patois*, corrupted in every manner, and, from the popular want of education, incapable of being restored, because it was not perceived to be erroneous.[a] Whatever may have been the case before the fall of the Western Empire, we have reason to believe that in the sixth century the colloquial Latin had undergone, at least in France, a considerable change even with the superior class of ecclesiastics. Gregory of Tours confesses that he was habitually falling into that sort of error, the misplacing inflexions and prepositions, which constituted the chief original difference of the rustic tongue from pure Latinity. In the opinion indeed of Raynouard, if we take his expressions in their natural meaning, the Romance language, or that which afterwards was generally called Provençal, is as old as the establishment of the Franks in Gaul. But this is perhaps not reconcilable with the proofs we have of a longer continuance of Latin. In Italy it seems probable that the change advanced more slowly. Gregory the Great, however, who has been reckoned as inveterate an enemy of learning as ever lived, speaks with superlative contempt of a regard to grammatical purity in writing. It was a crime in his eyes for a clergyman to teach grammar; yet the number of laymen who were competent or willing to do so had become very small.

27. It may render this more clear if we mention a few of

---

[a] Du Cange, preface, pp. 13, 29; Rusticum igitur sermonem non humiliorem paulo duntaxat, et qui sublimi opponitur, appellabant; sed eum etiam, qui magis reperet, barbarismis soloecismisque scateret, quam apposite Sidonius squamam sermonis Celtici, &c. vocat.— Rusticum, qui nullis vel grammaticæ vel orthographiæ legibus astringitur. This is nearly a definition of the early Romance language; it was Latin without grammar or orthography.

The squama sermonis Celtici, mentioned by Sidonius, has led Gray, in his valuable remarks on rhyme, vol. ii. p. 53, as it has some others, into the erroneous notion that a real Celtic dialect, such as Cæsar found in Gaul, was still spoken. But this is incompatible with the known history of the French language; and Sidonius is one of those loose declamatory writers whose words are never to be construed in their proper meaning; the common fault of Latin authors from the third century. Celticus sermo was the patois of Gaul, which, having once been Gallia Celtica, he still called such. That a few proper names, or similar words, and probably some others, in French are Celtic, is well known.

Quintilian has said, that a vicious orthography must bring on a vicious pronunciation. Quod male scribitur, male etiam dici necesse est. But the converse of this is still more true, and was in fact the great cause of giving the new Romance language its *visible* form.

the growing corruptions which have in fact transformed the
Latin into French and the sister tongues.   The prepositions
were used with no regard to the proper inflexions of nouns
and verbs.   These were known so inaccurately, and so constantly put one for another, that it was necessary to have
recourse to prepositions instead of them.   Thus *de* and *ad*
were made to express the genitive and dative cases, which is
common in charters from the sixth to the tenth century.
Again, it is a real fault in the Latin language, that it wants
both the definite and indefinite article : *ille* and *unus*,
especially the former, were called in to help this deficiency.
In the forms of Marculfus, published towards the end of the
seventh century, *ille* continually occurs as an article; and it
appears to have been sometimes used in the sixth.   This, of
course, by an easy abbreviation, furnished the articles in
French and Italian.   The people came soon to establish
more uniformity of case in the noun, either by rejecting
inflexions or by diminishing their number.   Raynouard
gives a long list of old French nouns formed from the Latin
accusative by suppressing *em* or *am*.[b]   The active auxiliary
verb, than which nothing is more distinctive of the modern
languages from the Latin, came in from the same cause, the
disuse, through ignorance, of several inflexions of the tenses ;
to which we must add, that here also the Latin language is
singularly deficient, possessing no means of distinguishing
the second perfect from the first, or ‘ I have seen,’ from ‘ I
saw.’   The auxiliary verb was early applied in France and
Italy to supply this defect; and some have produced what

---

[b] See a passage of Quintilian, l. 9, c.
4, quoted in Hallam's Middle Ages,
chap. ix.
  In the grammar of Cassiodorus, a
mere compilation from old writers, and
in this instance from one Cornutus, we
find another remarkable passage, which
I do not remember to have seen quoted,
though doubtless it has been so, on the
pronunciation of the letter *M*.   To utter
this final consonant, he says, before a
word beginning with a vowel, is wrong,
durum ac barbarum sonat; but it is an
equal fault to omit it before one beginning with a consonant ; par enim atque
idem est vitium, ita cum vocali sicut
cum consonante *M* literam, exprimere.
Cassiodorus, De Orthographia, cap. 1.
Thus we perceive that there was a nicety
as to the pronunciation of this letter,
which uneducated persons would naturally not regard.   Hence in the inscriptions of a low age we frequently find
this letter omitted ; as in one quoted by
Muratori, Ego L. Contius me bibo [vivo]
archa [archam] feci, and it is very easy
to multiply instances.   Thus the neuter
and the accusative terminations were
lost.

they think occasional instances of its employment even in
the best classical authors.

28. It seems impossible to determine the progress of these
changes, the degrees of variation between the polite and
popular, the written and spoken Latin, in the best ages of
Rome, in the decline of the empire, and in the Continuance
kingdoms founded upon its ruins; or, finally, the of Latin in seventh
exact epoch when the grammatical language ceased century.
to be generally intelligible. There remains, therefore, some
room still for hypothesis and difference of opinion. The
clergy preached in Latin early in the seventh century, and
we have a popular song of the same age on the victory
obtained by Clotaire II. in 622 over the Saxons.[c] This has
been surmised by some to be a translation, merely because
the Latin is better than they suppose to have been spoken.
But, though the words are probably not given quite correctly,
they seem reducible, with a little emendation, to short verses
of an usual rhythmical cadence.[d]

29. But in the middle of the eighth century we find the
rustic language mentioned as distinct from Latin ;[e] It is changed
and in the council of Tours held in 813 it is ordered to a new language in
that homilies shall be explained to the people in eighth and ninth.
their own tongue, whether rustic Roman or Frankish. In
842 we find the earliest written evidence of its existence, in

---

[c] Le Bœuf, in Mém de l'Acad. des
Inscript. vol. xvii,—[Liron, in a dissertation on the origin of the French language, published in his Singularités
historiques, i. 103, contends, from a
passage in the life of St. Eligius, that
Latin was the vulgar tongue as late as
670. But the passage quoted is perhaps
not conclusive. He supposes that Latin
became unintelligible in the reign of
Pepin, or the first years of Charlemagne,
p. 116. But this is running too close ;
and even if he could be so exact as to
any one part of France, we have no
reason whatever to suppose that the
corruptions of language went on with
equal steps in every province.—1842.]

[d] Turner, in Archæologia, vol. xiv. 173.
Hallam's Middle Ages, chap. ix. Bouterwek, Gesch. der Französischen Poesie,
p. 18, observes, that there are many
fragments of popular Latin songs pre-

served. I have not found any quoted,
except one, which he gives from La
Ravillère, which is simple and rather
pretty; but I know not whence it is
taken. It seems the song of a female
slave, and is perhaps nearly as old as
the destruction of the empire.

At quid jubes, pusiole,
Quare mandas, filiole,
Carmen dulce me cantare
Cum sim longe exul valde
Intra mare,
O cur jubes canere ?

Intra seems put for trans. The metre is
rhymed trochaic; but that is consistent
with antiquity. It is, however, more
pleasing than most of the Latin verse of
this period, and is more in the tone of
the modern languages. As it is not at
all a hackneyed passage, I have thought
it worthy of quotation.

[e] Acad. des Inscript. xvii. 713.

the celebrated oaths taken by Louis of Germany and his brother Charles the Bald, as well as by their vassals, the former in Frankish or early German, the latter in their own current dialect. This, though with somewhat of a closer resemblance to Latin, is accounted by the best judges a specimen of the language spoken south of the Loire; afterwards variously called the Langue d'Oc, Provençal, or Limousin, and essentially the same with the dialects of Catalonia and Valencia.[f] It is decidedly the opinion of M. Raynouard, as it was of earlier inquirers, that the general language of France in the ninth century was the southern dialect, rather than that of the north, to which we now give the exclusive name of French, and which they conceive to have deviated from it afterwards.[g] And he has employed great labour to prove that, both in Spain and Italy, this language was generally spoken with hardly so much difference from that of France as constitutes even a variation of dialect; the articles, pronouns, and auxiliaries being nearly identical; most probably not with so much difference as would render the native of one country by any means unintelligible in another.[h]

---

[f] Du Cange, p. 35. Raynouard, passim. M. de la Rue has called it 'un Latin expirant.' Recherches sur les Bardes d'Armorique. Between this and 'un Français naissant' there may be only a verbal distinction; but, in accuracy of definition, I should think M. Raynouard much more correct. The language of this oath cannot be called Latin without a violent stretch of words, no Latin scholar, as such, would understand it, except by conjecture. On the other hand, most of the words, as we learn from M. R., are Provençal of the twelfth century. The passage has been often printed, and sometimes incorrectly. M. Roquefort, in the preface to his Glossaire de la Langue romane, has given a tracing from an ancient manuscript of Nitard, the historian of the ninth century, to whom we owe this important record of language.

[g] The chief difference was in orthography; the Northerns wrote Latin words with an *e* where the South retained *a*; as charitet, caritat; veritet, veritat; appelet, apelat. 'Si l'on rétablissait dans les plus anciens textes français les

a primitifs en place des *e*, on aurait identiquement la langue des troubadours.' Raynouard, Observations sur le Roman du Rou, 1829, p. 5.

[h] The proofs of this similarity occupy most part of the first and sixth volumes in M. Raynouard's excellent work. [The theory of M. Raynouard, especially so far as it involves the existence of a primitive Romance tongue, akin to the Provençal, itself derived from Latin, but spoken simultaneously, or nearly so, in Spain and Italy as well as France, and the mother of the Neo-Latin languages, has been opposed in the very learned Histoire de la Formation de la Langue française, by M. Ampère.— 1847.]

It is a common error to suppose that French and Italian had a double source, barbaric as well as Latin; and that the northern nations, in conquering those regions, brought in a large share of their own language. This is like the old erroneous opinion, that the Norman Conquest infused the French which we now find in our own tongue. There are certainly Teutonic words, both in French

30. Thus, in the eighth and ninth centuries, if not before, France had acquired a language, unquestionably Early specimens of French. nothing else than a corruption of Latin (for the Celtic or Teutonic words that entered into it were by no means numerous, and did not influence its structure), but become so distinct from its parent, through modes of pronunciation as well as grammatical changes, that it requires some degree of practice to trace the derivation of words in many instances. It might be expected that we should be able to adduce, or at least prove to have existed, a series of monuments in this new form of speech. It might naturally appear that poetry, the voice of the heart, would have been heard whenever the joys and sufferings, the hopes and cares of humanity, wherever the countenance of nature, or the manners of social life, supplied their boundless treasures to its choice; and among untutored nations it has been rarely silent. Of the existence of verse, however, in this early period of the new languages, we find scarce any testimony, a doubtful passage in a Latin poem of the ninth century excepted,[1] till we come to a production on the captivity of Boethius, versified chiefly from passages in his Consolation, which M. Raynouard, though Poem on Boethius. somewhat wishing to assign a higher date, places about the year 1000. This is printed by him from a manuscript formerly in the famous abbey of Fleury, · or St.

---

and Italian, but not sufficient to affect the proposition that these languages are merely Latin in their origin. These words in many instances express what Latin could not; thus *guerra* was by no means synonymous with *bellum*. Yet even Roquefort talks of ' un jargon composé de mots tudesques et romains,' Discours préliminaire, p. 19; forgetting which, he more justly remarks afterwards, on the oath of Charles the Bald, that it shows ' la langue romane est entièrement composée de Latin.' A long list could no doubt be made of French and Italian words that cannot easily be traced to any Latin with which we are acquainted; but we may be surprised that it is not still longer.

[1] In a Latin eclogue quoted by Paschasius Radbert (ob. 865) in the life of St. Adalhard, abbot of Corbie (ob. 826) the Romance-poets are called upon to join the Latins in the following lines:—

Rustica concelebret Romana Latinaque lingua,
Saxo, qui, pariter plangens, pro carmine dicat;
Vertite huc cuncti, cecinit quam maximus ille,
Et tumulum facite, et tumulo superaddite carmen.

Raynouard, Choix des Poésies, vol. ii. p. cxxxv. These lines are scarcely intelligible; but the quotation from Virgil, in the ninth century, perhaps deserves remark, though, in one of Charlemagne's monasteries, it is not by any means astonishing. Nennius, a Welsh monk, as some think, of the same age, who can hardly write Latin at all, has quoted another line :—

Purpurea intexti tollant aulæa Britanni.

Gale, XV. Scriptores, iii. 102.

Benoît-sur-Loire, and now in the public library of Orleans. It is a fragment of 250 lines, written in stanzas of six, seven, or a greater number of verses of ten syllables, sometimes deviating to eleven or twelve; and all the lines in each stanza rhyming masculinely with each other. It is certainly by much the earliest specimen of French verse;[k] even if it should only belong, as Le Bœuf thought, to the eleventh century.

31. M. Raynouard has asserted what will hardly bear dispute, that 'there has never been composed any considerable work in any language, till it has acquired determinate forms of expressing the modifications of ideas according to time, number, and person,' or, in other words, the elements of grammar.[m] But whether the Provençal or Romance language were in its infancy so defective, he does not say; nor does the grammar he has given lead us to that inference. This grammar, indeed, is necessarily framed, in great measure, out of more recent materials. It may be suspected, perhaps, that a language formed by mutilating the words of another, could not for many ages be rich or flexible enough for the variety of poetic expression. And the more ancient forms would long retain their prerogative in writing: or, perhaps, we can only say, that the absence of poetry was the effect, as well as the evidence, of that intellectual barrenness, more characteristic of the dark ages than their ignorance.

Provençal grammar.

32. In Italy, where we may conceive the corruption of lan-

---

[k] Raynouard, vol. ii. pp. 5, 6, and preface, p. cxxvii.

[m] Observations philologiques et grammaticales sur le Roman du Rou (1829), p. 26. Two ancient Provençal grammars, one by Raymond Vidal in the twelfth century, are in existence. The language therefore must have had its determinate rules before that time.

M. Raynouard has shown with a prodigality of evidence, the regularity of the French or Romance language in the twelfth century, and its retention of Latin forms, in cases when it had not been suspected. Thus it is a fundamental rule, that in nouns masculine, the nominative ends in s in the singular, but wants it in the plural; while the oblique cases lose it in the singular, but

retain it in the plural. This is evidently derived from the second declension in Latin. As for example—

Sing. Li princes est venus, et a este sacrez rois.
Plu. Li evesque et li plus noble baron se sont assemble.

Thus also the possessive pronoun is always *mes, tes, ses,* (meus, tuus, suus,) in the nominative singular; *mon, ton, son,* (meum, &c.) in the oblique regimen. It has been through ignorance of such rules that the old French poetry has seemed capricious, and destitute of strict grammar; and, in a philosophical sense, the simplicity and extensiveness of M. Raynouard's discovery entitle it to the appellation of beautiful. [It has, however, been since shown to require some limitation.]

guage to have been less extensive, and where the spoken patois had never acquired a distinctive name, like *lingua* Latin re-*Romana* in France, we find two remarkable proofs, tained in use as they seem, that Latin was not wholly unintel- Italy. ligible in the ninth and tenth centuries, and which therefore modify M. Raynouard's hypothesis as to the simultaneous origin of the Romance tongue. The one is a popular song of the soldiers, on their march to rescue the emperor Louis II. in 881, from the violent detention in which he had been placed by the duke of Benevento ; the other, a similar exhortation to the defenders of Modena in 924, when that city was in danger of siege from the Hungarians. Both of these were published by Muratori, in his fortieth dissertation on Italian Antiquities ; and both have been borrowed from him by M. Sismondi, in his Littérature du Midi.[n] The former of these poems is in a loose trochaic measure, totally destitute of regard to grammatical inflexions. Yet some of the leading peculiarities of Italian, the article and the auxiliary verb, do not appear. The latter is in accentual iambics, with a sort of monotonous termination in the nature of rhyme ; and in very much superior Latinity, probably the work of an ecclesiastic.[o] It is difficult to account for either of these, especially the former, which is merely a military song, except on the supposition that the Latin language was not grown wholly out of popular use.

33. In the eleventh century, France still affords us but few extant writings. Several, indeed, can be shown to French of have once existed. The Romance language, compre- century. hending the two divisions of Provençal and Northern French, by this time distinctly separate from each other, was now,

---

[n] Vol. i. pp. 23, 27.

[o] I am at a loss to know what Muratori means by saying, ' Son versi di dodici sillabe, ma computata la ragione de' tempi, vengono ad essere uguali a gli endecasillabi,' p. 551. He could not have understood the metre, which is perfectly regular, and even harmonious, on the condition only, that no ' ragione de' tempi,' except such as accentual pronunciation observes, shall be demanded. The first two lines will serve as a specimen :—

O tu, qui servas armis ista mænia,
Noli dormire, moneo, sed vigila.'

This is like another strange observation of Muratori in the same dissertation, that, in the well-known lines of the emperor Adrian to his soul, ' Animula vagula, blandula,' which could perplex no schoolboy, he cannot discover ' un' esatta norma di metro ;' and therefore takes them to be merely rhythmical.

say the authors of the Histoire littéraire de la France, employed in poetry, romances, translations, and original works in different kinds of literature; sermons were preached in it; and the code, called the Assises de Jerusalem, was drawn up under Godfrey of Bouillon in 1100.[p] Some part of this is doubtful, and especially the age of these laws. They do not mention those of William the Conqueror, recorded in French by Ingulfus. Doubts have been cast by a distinguished living critic on the age of this French code, and upon the authenticity of the History of Ingulfus itself; which he conceives, upon very plausible grounds, to be a forgery of Richard II.'s time : the language of the laws indeed appears to be very ancient, but not probably distinguishable at this day from the French of the twelfth century.[q] It may be said, in general, that, except one or two translations from books of Scripture, very little now extant has been clearly referred to an earlier period.[r] Yet we may suspect that the language was already

---

[p] Vol. vii. p. 107.

[q] [The French laws in Ingulfus are ascertained to be a translation from the Latin, made in the thirteenth century.]

[r] Roquefort, Glossaire de la Langue romane, p. 25, and État de la Poésie française, p. 42 and 206, mentions several religious works in the Royal Library, and also a metrical romance in the British Museum, lately published in Paris, on the fabulous voyage of Charlemagne to Constantinople. [But this romance is now referred by its editor, M. Michel, to the beginning of the twelfth century. And the translations of the books of Kings, mentioned in the text, are so far from being clearly referrible to an earlier period, that their editor, M. le Roux de Lincy, in Documens inédits, 1841, though wavering a little, evidently inclines to place them about the same time. In fact, we are not able to prove satisfactorily that any Norman French, except the version of Boethius above mentioned, belongs to the eleventh century. Roquefort and De la Rue assumed too much as to this. It may be mentioned here, that M. Michel distinguishes six dialects of Northern French in use during the twelfth century; spoken and written in Picardy, in Normandy, in the Isle of France, in Burgundy and some central provinces, in Lorraine, and, finally, in Poitou and

Anjou; the last of which had a tinge of the Langue d'Oc. Id. Introduction, p. 59.—1847.] Raynouard has collected a few fragments in Provençal. But I must dissent from this excellent writer in referring the famous poem of the Vaudois, La Nobla Leyczon, to the year 1100. Choix des Poésies des Troubadours, vol. ii. p. cxxxvii. I have already observed, that the two lines which contain what he calls ' la date de l'an 1100,' are so loosely expressed, as to include the whole ensuing century. (Hallam's Middle Ages, chap. ix.) And I am now convinced that the poem is not much older than 1200. It seems probable that they reckoned 1100 years, on a loose computation, not from the Christian era but from the time when the passage of Scripture to which these lines allude was written. The allusion may be to 1 Pet. i. 20. But it is clear that, at the time of the composition of this poem, not only the name of *Vaudois* had been imposed on those sectaries, but they had become subject to persecution. We know nothing of this till near the end of the century. This poem was probably written in the south of France, and carried afterwards to the Alpine valleys of Piedmont, from which it was brought to Geneva and England in the seventeenth century. La Nobla Leyczon is published at length by Ray-

employed in poetry, and had been gradually ramifying itself by the shoots of invention and sentiment; since, at the close of this age, and in the next, we find a constellation of gay and brilliant versifiers, the Troubadours of Southern France, and a corresponding class to the north of the Loire.

34. These early poets in the modern languages chiefly borrowed their forms of versification from the Latin. Metres of It is unnecessary to say, that metrical composition modern languages. in that language, as in Greek, was an arrangement of verses corresponding by equal or equivalent feet; all syllables being presumed to fall under a known division of long and short, the former passing for strictly the double of the latter in quantity of time. By this law of pronunciation all verse was measured; and to this not only actors, who were assisted by an accompaniment, but the orators also endeavoured to conform. But the accented, or, if we choose rather to call them so, emphatic syllables, being regulated by a very different though uniform law, the uninstructed people, especially in the decline of Latinity, pronounced, as we now do, with little or no regard to the metrical quantity of syllables, but according to their accentual differences. And this gave rise to the popular or rhythmical poetry of the Lower Empire; traces of which may be found in the second century, and even much earlier, but of which we have abundant proofs after the age of Constantine.[s] All metre, as Augustin says, was rhythm,

---

nouard. It consists of 479 lines, which seem to be rhythmical or aberrant Alexandrines; the rhymes uncertain in number, chiefly masculine. The poem censures the corruptions of the church, but contains little that would be considered heretical; which agrees with what contemporary historians relate of the original Waldenses. Any doubts as to the authenticity of this poem are totally unreasonable. M. Raynouard, an indisputably competent judge, observes, 'Les personnes qui l'examineront avec attention jugeront que le manuscrit n'a pas été interpolé,' p. cxliii.

I will here reprint, more accurately than before, the two lines supposed to give the poem the date of 1100:—

Ben ha mil et cent anez compli entièrement,
Que fo scripta l'ora car sen al derier temps.

Can M. Raynouard, or any one else, be warranted by this in saying, ' La date de l'an 1100, qu'on lit dans ce poème, mérite toute confiance'?

[The writings ascribed to the ancient Waldenses have lately been investigated with considerable acuteness and erudition in the British Magazine, and the spuriousness of the greater part seems demonstrated. But those who consider Leger as a forger, do not appear to doubt the authenticity of this poem, La Nobla Leyczon, though they entirely agree with me as to its probable date near the end of the twelfth century.—1842.]

[s] The well-known lines of Adrian to Florus, and his reply, ' Ego nolo Florus esse,' &c. are accentual trochaics, but not wholly so; for the last line, Scythicas pati pruinas, requires the word pati to be sounded as an iambic. They

but all rhythm was not metre: in rhythmical verse, neither
the quantity of syllables, that is, the time allotted to each by
metrical rule, nor even, in some degree, their number, was
regarded, so long as a cadence was retained in which the ear
could recognise a certain approach to uniformity.   Much popular poetry, both religious and profane, and the public hymns
of the church, were written in this manner; the distinction
of long and short syllables, even while Latin remained a
living tongue, was lost in speech, and required study to attain
it.   The accent or emphasis, both of which are probably, to a
certain extent, connected with quantity and with each other,
supplied its place ; the accented syllable being, perhaps, generally lengthened in ordinary speech ; though this is not the
sole cause of length, for no want of emphasis or lowness of
tone can render a syllable of many letters short.   Thus we
find two species of Latin verse : one metrical, which Pruden-
tius, Fortunatus, and others aspired to write; the other
rhythmical, somewhat licentious in number of syllables, and
wholly accentual in its pronunciation.   But this kind was
founded on the former, and imitated the ancient syllabic
arrangements.   Thus the trochaic, or line in which the stress
falls on the uneven syllables, commonly alternating by eight
and seven, a very popular metre from its spirited flow, was
adopted in military songs, such as that already mentioned of
the Italian soldiers in the ninth century.   It was also common
in religious chants.   The line of eight syllables, or dimeter
iambic, in which the cadence falls on the even places, was
still more frequent in ecclesiastical verse.   But these are the
most ordinary forms of versification in the early French or Provençal, Spanish, and Italian languages.   The line of eleven
syllables, which became in time still more usual than the
former, is nothing else than the ancient hendecasyllable, from
which the French, in what they call masculine rhymes, and
ourselves more generally, from a still greater deficiency of final
vowels, have been forced to retrench the last syllable.   The
Alexandrine of twelve syllables might seem to be the trimeter
iambic of the ancients.   But Sanchez has very plausibly re-

---

are not the earliest instance extant of   quotes some satirical lines on Julius
disregard to quantity ; for Suetonius   Cæsar.

ferred its origin to a form more usual in the dark ages, the pentameter; and shown it in some early Spanish poetry.[t] The Alexandrine, in the southern languages, had generally a feminine termination, that is, in a short vowel; thus becoming of thirteen syllables, the stress falling on the penultimate, as is the usual case in a Latin pentameter verse, accentually read in our present mode. The variation of syllables in these Alexandrines, which run from twelve to fourteen, is accounted for by the similar numerical variety in the pentameter.[u]

35. I have dwelt, perhaps tediously, on this subject, because vague notions of a derivation of modern metrical arrangements, even in the languages of Latin origin, from the Arabs or Scandinavians, have sometimes gained credit. It has been imagined also, that the peculiar characteristic of the new poetry, rhyme, was borrowed from the Saracens of Spain.[x] But the Latin language abounds so much in consonances, that those who have been accustomed to write verses in it well know the difficulty of avoiding them, as much as an ear formed on classical models demands; and as this gingle is certainly pleasing in itself, it is not wonderful that the less fastidious vulgar should adopt it in their rhythmical songs. It has been proved by Muratori, Gray, and Turner, beyond the possibility of doubt, that rhymed Latin verse was in use from the end of the fourth century.[y]

Origin of rhyme in Latin.

---

[t] The break in the middle of the Alexandrine, it will occur to every competent judge, has nothing analogous to it in the trimeter iambic, but exactly corresponds to the invariable law of the pentameter.

[u] Roquefort, Essai sur la Poésie française dans le 12me et 13me siècles, p. 66. Galvani, Osservazioni sulla Poesia de' Trovatori. (Modena, 1829.) Sanchez, Poesias Castellanas anteriores al 15mo siglo, vol. i. p. 122.

Tyrwhitt had already observed, 'The metres which the Normans used, and which we seem to have borrowed from them, were plainly copied from the Latin rhythmical verses, which, in the declension of that language, were current in various forms among those who either did not understand, or did not regard, the true quantity of syllables;

and the practice of rhyming is probably to be deduced from the same original.' Essay on the Language and Versification of Chaucer, p. 51.

[x] Andrès, with a partiality to the Saracens of Spain, whom, by a singular assumption, he takes for his countrymen, manifested in almost every page, does not fail to urge this. It had been said long before by Huet, and others who lived before these subjects had been thoroughly investigated. Origine e Progresso, &c., ii. 194. He has been copied by Ginguéné and Sismondi.

[y] Muratori, Antichità Italiane, Dissert. 40. Turner, in Archæologia, vol. xiv., and Hist. of England, vol. iv. pp. 328, 653. Gray has gone as deeply as any one into this subject; and though, writing at what may be called an early period of metrical criticism, he has

36. Thus, about the time of the first crusade, we find two Provençal dialects of the same language, differing by that time not inconsiderably from each other, the Provençal and French, possessing a regular grammar, established forms of versification (and the early troubadours added several to those borrowed from the Latin[z]), and a flexibility which gave free scope to the graceful turns of poetry. William, duke of Guienne, has the glory of leading the van of surviving Provençal songsters. He was born in 1070, and may probably have composed some of his little poems before he joined the crusaders in 1096. If these are genuine, and no doubt of them seems to be entertained, they denote a considerable degree of previous refinement in the language.[a] We do not, I believe, meet with any other troubadour till after the middle of the twelfth century. From that time till about the close of the thirteenth, and especially before the fall of the house of Toulouse in 1228, they were numerous almost as the gay insects of spring; names of illustrious birth are mingled in the list with those whom genius has saved from obscurity; they were the delight of a luxurious nobility, the pride of southern France, while the great fiefs of Toulouse and Guienne were in their splendour. Their style soon extended itself to the northern dialect. Abelard was the first of recorded name, who taught the banks of the Seine to resound a tale of love; and it was of Eloise that he sung.[b] 'You composed,' says that gifted and noble-spirited woman, in one of her letters to him, 'many verses in amorous measure, so sweet both in their language and their melody, that your name was incessantly in the mouths of all, and even the most illiterate could not be forgetful of you. This it was chiefly that made women admire you. And as most of these songs were on me and my love, they made me known in many countries, and

(margin note) Provençal and French poetry.

fallen into a few errors, and been too easy of credence, unanswerably proves the Latin origin of rhyme. Gray's Works by Mathias, vol. ii. p. 30–54.

[z] See Raynouard, Roquefort, and Galvani, for the Provençal and French metres, which are very complicated.

[a] Raynouard, Choix des Poésies des Troubadours, vol. ii. Auguis, Recueil des anciens Poëtes français, vol. i.

[b] Bouterwek, on the authority of La Ravaillère, seems to doubt whether these poems of Abelard were in French or Latin. (Gesch. der Französischen Poesie, p. 18.) I believe this would be thought quite paradoxical by any critic at present.

caused many women to envy me. Every tongue spoke of your Eloise; every street, every house resounded with my name.'° These poems of Abelard are lost; but in the Norman, or Northern French language, we have an immense number of poets belonging to the twelfth and the two following centuries. One hundred and twenty-seven are known by name in the twelfth alone, and above two hundred in the thirteenth.ᵈ Thibault, king of Navarre and count of Champagne, about the middle of the next, is accounted by some the best, as well as noblest, of French poets; but the spirited and satirical Rutebouf might contest the preference.

37. In this French and Provençal poetry, if we come to the consideration of it historically, descending from an earlier period, we are at once struck by the vast preponderance of amorous ditties. The Greek and Roman muses, especially

---

° Duo autem, fateor tibi specialiter inerant, quibus feminarum quarumlibet animos statim allicere poteras, dictandi videlicet et cantandi gratia; quæ cæteros minimè philosophos assecutos esse novimus. Quibus quidem quasi ludo quodam laborem exercitii recreans philosophici pleraque amatorio metro vel rithmo composita reliquisti carmina, quæ præ nimiâ suavitate tam dictaminis quam cantûs sæpius frequentata tuum in ore omnium nomen incessanter tenebant, ut etiam illiteratos melodiæ dulcedo tui non sineret immemores esse. Atque hinc maxime in amorem tui feminæ suspirabant. Et cum horum pars maxima carminum nostros decantaret amores, multis me regionibus brevi tempore nunciavit, et multarum in me feminarum accendit invidiam. And in another place: Frequenti carmine tuam in ore omnium Heloissam ponebas; me platæ omnes, me domus singulæ resouabant. Epist. Abælardi et Heloissæ. These epistles of Abelard and Eloisa, especially those of the latter, are, as far as I know, the first book that gives any pleasure in reading which had been produced in Europe for 600 years, since the consolation of Boethius. But I do not press my negative judgment. We may at least say that the writers of the dark ages, if they have left anything intrinsically very good, have been ill-treated by the learned, who have failed to extract it. Pope, it may be here observed, has done great injustice to Eloisa in

his unrivalled epistle, by putting the sentiments of a coarse and abandoned woman into her mouth. Her refusal to marry Abelard arose not from an abstract predilection for the name of mistress above that of wife, but from her disinterested affection, which would not deprive him of the prospect of ecclesiastical dignities, to which his genius and renown might lead him. She judged very unwisely, as it turned out, but from an unbounded generosity of character. He was, in fact, unworthy of her affection, which she expresses in the tenderest language. Deum testem invoco, si me Augustus universo præsidens mundo matrimonii honore dignaretur, totumque mihi orbem confirmaret in perpetuum præsidendum, charius mihi et dignius videretur tua dici meretrix quam illius imperatrix.

ᵈ Augis, Discours préliminaire, p. 2. Roquefort, État de la Poésie française aux 12me et 13me siècles. Hist. litt. de la France, xvi. 239.

[It ought to have been observed, that comparatively few of the poets of the twelfth century are extant; most of them are Anglo-Norman. At least ten times as much French verse of the thirteenth has been preserved. Hist. litt. de la France, p. 239. Notre prose et notre poésie française existaient avant 1200, mais c'est au treizième siècle qu'elles commencèrent à prendre un caractère national. Id. p. 254.—1847.]

the latter, seem frigid as their own fountain in comparison. Satires on the great, and especially on the clergy, exhortations to the crusade, and religious odes, are intermingled in the productions of the Troubadours ; but love is the prevailing theme. This tone they could hardly have borrowed from the rhythmical Latin verses, of which all that remain are without passion or energy. They could as little have been indebted to their predecessors for a peculiar gracefulness, an indescribable charm of gaiety and ease, which many of their lighter poems display. This can only be ascribed to the polish of chivalrous manners, and to the influence of feminine delicacy on public taste. The well-known dialogue, for example, of Horace and Lydia, is justly praised ; nothing extant of this amœbean character, from Greece or Rome, is nearly so good. But such alternate stanzas, between speakers of different sexes, are very common in the early French poets ; and it would be easy to find some quite equal to Horace in grace and spirit. They had even a generic name, *tensons*, contentions ; that is, dialogues of lively repartee, such as we are surprised to find in the twelfth century, an age accounted by many almost barbarous. None of these are prettier than what are called *pastourelles*, in which the poet is feigned to meet a shepherdess whose love he solicits, and by whom he is repelled (not always finally) in alternate stanzas.[e] Some of these may be read in Roquefort, État de la Poésie française dans le 12me et 13me siècles ; others in Raynouard, Choix des Poésies des Troubadours ; in Auguis, Recueil des Anciens Poètes français ; or in Galvani, Osservazioni sulla Poesia de' Trovatori.

---

[e] These have, as Galvani has observed, an ancient prototype in the twenty-seventh pastoral of Theocritus, which Dryden has translated with no diminution of its freedom. Some of the Pastourelles are also rather licentious ; but that is not the case with the greater part. M. Raynouard, in an article of the Journal des Savans for 1824, p. 613, remarks the superior decency of the southern poets, scarcely four or five transgressing in that respect ; while many of the fabliaux in the collections of Barbazan and Méon are of the most coarse and stupid ribaldry ; and such that even the object of exhibiting ancient manners and language scarcely warranted their publication in so large a number.

[A good many pastourelles, but all variations of the same subject, are published by M. Michel, in his Théâtre français au Moyen Âge, p. 31. These are in northern dialects, and may be referred to the twelfth and thirteenth centuries. Robin and Marion are always the shepherd or peasant and his rustic love ; and a knight always interferes, with or without success, to seduce or outrage Marion. We have nothing corresponding to these in England.—1847.]

38. In all these light compositions which gallantry or gaiety inspired, we perceive the characteristic excellences of French poetry, as distinctly as in the best vaudeville of the age of Louis XV. We can really sometimes find little difference, except an obsoleteness of language, which gives them a kind of poignancy. And this style, as I have observed, seems to have been quite original in France, though it was imitated by other nations.[f] The French poetry, on the other hand, was deficient in strength and ardour. It was also too much filled with monotonous common-places; among which the tedious descriptions of spring, and the everlasting nightingale, are eminently to be reckoned. These, perhaps, are less frequent in the early poems, most of which are short, than they became in the prolix expansion adopted by the allegorical school in the fourteenth century. They prevail, as is well known, in Chaucer, Dunbar, and several other of our own poets.

39. The metrical romances, far from common in Provençal,[g] but forming a large portion of what was written in the northern dialect, though occasionally picturesque, graceful, or animated, are seldom free from tedious or prosaic details. The earliest of these extant seems to be that of Havelok the Dane, of which an abridgment was made by Geoffrey Gaimar, before the middle of the twelfth century. The story is certainly a popular legend from the Danish part of England, which the French versifier has called, according to the fashion of romances, 'a Breton lay.' If this word meant any thing more than relating to Britain,

Metrical romances. Havelok the Dane.

---

[f] Andrès, as usual with him, whose prejudices are all that way, derives the Provençal style of poetry from the Arabians; and this has been countenanced, in some measure, by Ginguéné and Sismondi. Some of the peculiarities of the Troubadours, their tensons, or contentions, and the envoi, or termination of a poem, by an address to the poem itself or the reader, are said to be of Arabian origin. In assuming that rhyme was introduced by the same channel, these writers are probably mistaken. But I have seen too little of oriental, and, especially, of Hispano-Saracenic poetry, to form any opinion how far the more essential characteristics of Provençal verse may have been derived from it. One seems to find more of oriental hyperbole in the Castilian poetry.

[g] It has been denied that there are any metrical romances in Provençal. But one called the Philomena, on the fabulous history of Charlemagne, is written after 1173, though not much later than 1200. Journal des Savans, 1824. [The Philomena is in prose; but it has been pointed out to me, that four metrical romances in Provençal have been brought to light by Raynouard and others.—1842.]

it is a plain falsehood; and, upon either hypothesis, it may lead us to doubt, as many other reasons may also, what has been so much asserted of late years, as to the Armorican origin of romantic fictions; since the word Breton, which some critics refer to Armorica, is here applied to a story of mere English birth.[h] It cannot, however, be doubted, from the absurd introduction of Arthur's name in this romance of Havelok, that it was written after the publication of the splendid fables of Geoffrey.[i]

---

[h] The Recherches sur les Bardes d'Armorique, by that respectable veteran M. de la Rue, are very unsatisfactory. It does not appear that the Bretons have so much as a national tradition of any romantic poetry, nor any writings in their language older than 1450. The authority of Warton, Leyden, Ellis, Turner, and Price, has rendered this hypothesis of early Armorican romance popular; but I cannot believe that so baseless a fabric will endure much longer. Is it credible that tales of aristocratic splendour and courtesy sprung up in so poor and uncivilised a country as Bretagne? Traditional stories they might, no doubt, possess, and some of these may be found in the Lais de Marie, and other early poems; but not romances of chivalry. I do not recollect, though speaking without confidence, that any proof has been given of Armorican traditions about Arthur earlier than the history of Geoffrey; it seems too much to interpret the word *Britones* of them rather than of the Welsh. Mr. Turner, I observe, without absolutely recanting, has much receded from his opinion of an Armorican original for Geoffrey of Monmouth. [It is not easy to perceive how the story of Arthur, as a Welsh prince and conqueror, should have originated in Britany, which may have preserved some connexion with Cornwall, but none, as far as we know, with Wales. The Armoricans, at least, had no motive for inventing magnificent fables in order to swell the glory of a different, though cognate, people. Mr. Wright conceives that Arthur was a mythic personage in Britany, whose legend was confounded by Geoffrey with real history. But this wholly annihilates the historical basis, and requires us not only to reject Nen-

nius as a spurious or interpolated writer, which is Mr. Wright's hypothesis, but to consider all the Welsh poems which contain allusions to Arthur as posterior to the time of Geoffrey. 'The legends of the British kings,' he says, ' appear to have been brought over from Bretagne, and not to have had their origin among the Welsh; although we begin to observe traces of the legends relating to Arthur and Merlin before Geoffrey of Monmouth wrote, yet even the Welsh of that time appear to have rejected his narrative as fabulous.' Biogr. britann. littéraire, vol. ii. p. 145. If we can depend at all on the stories of the Mabinogion, which a lady has so honourably brought before the English public, the traditional legends concerning Arthur prevailed in Wales in an earlier age than that of Geoffrey; and perhaps William of Malmesbury alluded to them rather than to the recent forgery, in the words, Hic est Arthurus de quo Britonum nugæ hodieque delirant; dignus plane, quem non fallaces somniarent fabulæ, sed veraces prædicarent historiæ, quippe qui labantem patriam diu sustinuerit, infractosque civium mentes ad bellum acuerit. De Gestis Reg. Angl. l. 1. Arthur's victory at Mount Badon in 516, and his death in 537, are mentioned in the Annales Cambriæ, prepared by the late Mr. Petrie for publication; a brief chronicle, which seems, in part, at least, considerably older than the twelfth century, if not almost contemporary.— 1847.]

[i] The romance of Havelok was printed by Sir Frederick Madden in 1829; but not for sale. His Introduction is of considerable value. The story of Havelok is that of Curan and Argentile, in Warner's Albion's England, upon which Mason founded a drama. Sir F. Madden

40. Two more celebrated poems are by Wace, a native of Jersey; one, a free version of the history lately published by Geoffrey of Monmouth; the other, a narrative of the Battle of Hastings and Conquest of England. Many other romances followed. Much has been disputed for some years concerning these, as well as the lays and fabliaux of the northern trouveurs; it is sufficient here to observe, that they afforded a copious source of amusement and interest to those who read or listened, as far as the French language was diffused; and this was far beyond the boundaries of France. Not only was it the common spoken tongue of what is called the court, or generally of the superior ranks, in England, but in Italy and in Germany, at least throughout the thirteenth century. Brunetto Latini wrote his philosophical compilation, called Le Trésor, in French, ' because,' as he says, ' the language was more agreeable and usual than any other.' Italian, in fact, was hardly employed in prose at that time. But for those whose education had not gone so far, the romances and tales of France began to be rendered into German, as early as the latter part of the twelfth century, as they were long afterwards into English, becoming the basis of those popular songs, which illustrate the period of the Swabian emperors, the great house of Hohenstauffen, Frederic Barbarossa, Henry VI., and Frederic II.

Diffusion of French language.

41. The poets of Germany, during this period of extraordinary fertility in versification, were not less numerous than those of France and Provence.[k] From Henry of Veldek to the last of the lyric poets,

German poetry of Swabian period.

---

refers the English translation to some time between 1270 and 1290. The manuscript is in the Bodleian Library. The French original has since been reprinted in France, as I learn from Brunet's Supplément au Manuel du Libraire. Both this and its abridgment, by Geoffrey Gaimar, are in the British Museum.

k Bouterwek, p. 95. [Gervinus, in his Poetische Literatur der Deutschen, has gone more fully than his predecessor Bouterwek into the history of German mediæval poetry, which was more abundant, perhaps, than in any other

country. Ottfried, about 883, turned the Gospels into German verse; we here find rhyme instead of the ancient alliteration. But in the next two centuries we have chiefly Latin poetry, though some of it apparently derived from old lays of the Hunnish or Burgundian age. In the beginning of the twelfth century the vernacular poetry revived in a number of chivalric stories, of which Alexander and Charlemagne were generally the heroes. The Franconian emperors did not encourage letters. But under the Swabian line poetry eminently flourished. Several epics besides the Nibel-

soon after the beginning of the fourteenth century, not less than two hundred are known by name. A collection made in that age by Rudiger von Manasse of Zurich contains the productions of one hundred and forty; and modern editors have much enlarged the list.[m] Henry of Veldek is placed by Eichhorn about 1170, and by Bouterwek twenty years later; so that at the utmost we cannot reckon the period of their duration more than a century and a half. But the great difference perceptible between the poetry of Henry and that of the old German songs proves him not to have been the earliest of the Swabian school; he is as polished in language and versification as any of his successors; and though a northern, he wrote in the dialect of the house of Hohenstauffen. Wolfram von Eschenbach, in the first years of the next century, is, perhaps, the most eminent name of the Minne-singers, as the lyric poets were denominated, and is also the translator of several romances. The golden age of German poetry was before the fall of the Swabian dynasty, at the death of Conrad IV. in 1254. Love, as the word denotes, was the peculiar theme of the Minne-singers; but it was chiefly from the northern or southern dialects of France, especially the latter, that they borrowed their amorous strains.[n] In the latter part of the thirteenth century, we

---

ungen Lied belong to the latter part of the twelfth century or beginning of the next, and are much superior in spirit and character to anything that followed. —1853.]

[m] Bouterwek, p. 98. This collection was published in 1758 by Bodmer.

[n] Herder, Zerstreute Blätter, vol. v. p. 206. Eichhorn, Allg. Geschichte der Cultur, vol. i. p. 226. Heinsius, Teut, oder Lehrbuch der Deutschen Sprachwissenschaft, vol. iv. pp. 32–80. Weber's Illustrations of Northern Antiquities, 1814. This work contains the earliest analysis, I believe, of the Nibelungen Lied. But, above all, I have been indebted to the excellent account of German poetry by Bouterwek, in the ninth volume of his great work, the History of Poetry and Eloquence since the thirteenth century. In this volume the mediæval poetry of Germany occupies nearly four hundred closely-printed pages. I have since met with a pleasing little volume, on the Lays of the Minne-

singers, by Mr. Edgar Taylor. It contains an account of the chief of those poets, with translations, perhaps in too modern a style, though it may be true that no other would suit our modern taste.

A species of love-song, peculiar, according to Weber (p. 9), to the Minne-singers, are called Watchmen's Songs. These consist in a dialogue between a lover and the sentinel who guards his mistress. The latter is persuaded to imitate 'Sir Pandarus of Troy;' but, when morning breaks, summons the lover to quit his lady; who, in her turn, maintains that 'it is the nightingale, and not the lark,' with almost the pertinacity of Juliet.

Mr. Taylor remarks, that the German poets do not go so far in their idolatry of the fair as the Provençals, p. 127. I do not concur altogether in his reasons; but as the Minne-singers imitated the Provençals, this deviation is remarkable. I should rather ascribe it to the hyper-

find less of feeling and invention, but a more didactic and moral tone, sometimes veiled in Æsopic fables, sometimes openly satirical. Conrad of Würtzburg is the chief of the later school; but he had to lament the decline of taste and manners in his own age.

42. No poetry, however, of the Swabian period is so national as the epic romances, which drew their subjects from the highest antiquity, if they did not even adopt the language of primæval bards, which, perhaps, though it has been surmised, is not compatible with their style. In the two most celebrated productions of this kind, the Helden Buch, or Book of Heroes, and the Nibelungen Lied, the Lay of the Nibelungen, a fabulous people, we find the recollections of an heroic age, wherein the names of Attila and Theodoric stand out as witnesses of traditional history, clouded by error and coloured by fancy. The Nibelungen Lied, in its present form, is by an uncertain author, perhaps about the year 1200;° but it comes, and as far as we can judge with

---

bolical tone which the Troubadours had borrowed from the Arabians, or to the susceptibility of their temperament.

° Weber says,—'I have no doubt whatever that the romance itself is of very high antiquity, at least of the eleventh century, though, certainly, the present copy has been considerably modernised.' Illustrations of Northern Romances, p. 26. But Bouterwek does not seem to think it of so ancient a date; and I believe it is commonly referred to about the year 1200. Schlegel ascribes it to Henry von Offerdingen. Heinsius, iv. 52.

It is highly probable, that the 'barbara et antiquissima carmina,' which, according to Eginhard, Charlemagne caused to be reduced to writing, were no other than the legends of the Nibelungen Lied, and similar traditions of the Gothic and Burgundian time. Weber, p. 6. I will here mention a curious Latin epic poem on the wars of Attila, published by Fischer in 1780. He conceives it to be of the sixth century; but others have referred it to the eighth. [Raynouard (Journal des Savans, Aug. (1833) places it in the tenth. And my friend the Hon. and Rev. W. Herbert, in the notes to his poem on Attila (1837), a production displaying an union of

acuteness and erudition with great poetical talents, has, probably with no knowledge of Raynouard's judgment, come to the same determination, from the mention of Iceland, under the name of Thile, which was not discovered till 861. 'The poem resembles in style and substance the later Scandinavian sagas, and it is probably a Latin version of some such prose narrative; and the spelling of Thule, Thile, seems to have been derived from the Scandinavian orthography Thyle. At the end of the tenth century the Scandinavians, who were previously illiterate, began to study in Italy, and the discovery of Iceland would have transpired through them. It is probable that this may be the earliest work in which the name Thule has been applied to Iceland, and it is most likely a production of the tenth century. The MS. is said to be of the thirteenth.' It appears, however, by M. Raynouard's article that the MS. in the Royal Library at Paris contains a dedication to an archbishop of Rome near the close of the tenth century, which, in the absence of any presumption to the contrary, may pass for the date of the poem.—1842.] The heroes are Franks; but the whole is fabulous, except the name of Attila and his Huns.

little or no interpolation of circumstances, from an age anterior to Christianity, to civilisation, and to the more refined
forms of chivalry. We cannot well think the stories later
than the sixth or seventh centuries. The German critics
admire the rude grandeur of this old epic; and its fables,
marked with a character of barbarous simplicity wholly
unlike that of later romance, are become, in some degree,
familiar to ourselves.

43. The loss of some accomplished princes, and of a near
Decline of German poetry. intercourse with the south of France and with Italy,
as well as the augmented independence of the
German nobility, only to be maintained by unceasing warfare, rendered their manners, from the latter part of the
thirteenth century, more rude than before. They ceased to
cultivate poetry, or to think it honourable in their rank.
Meantime a new race of poets, chiefly burghers of towns,
sprang up about the reign of Rodolph of Hapsburg, before
the lays of the Minne-singers had yet ceased to resound.
These prudent, though not inspired votaries of the muse,
chose the didactic and moral style as more salutary than the
love-songs, and more reasonable than the romances. They
became known in the fourteenth century, by the name of

I do not know whether this has any connexion with a history of Attila by a
writer named Casola, existing in manuscript at Modena, and being probably a
translation in prose from Latin into
Provençal. A translation of this last
into Italian was published by Rossi at
Ferrara in 1568: it is a very scarce book,
but I have seen two copies of it. Weber's
Illustrations, p. 23. Eichhorn, Allg.
Gesch. ii. 178. Galvani, Osservazioni
sulla Poesia de' Trovatori, p. 16.

The Nibelungen Lied seems to have
been less popular in the middle ages
than other romances; evidently because
it relates to a different state of manners.
Bouterwek, p. 141. Heinsius observes
that we must consider this poem as the
most valuable record of German antiquity, but that to over-rate its merit,
as some have been inclined to do, can
be of no advantage. [The Nibelungen
Lied is placed by Gervinus about 1210.
It was not liked by the clergy, doubtless
on account of its heathenish character;

nor by the courtly poets, who thought
it too rude; and in fact the style is
much behind that of the age. The
sources of this poem are unknown: that
the author had traditional legends, and
probably lays, to guide him, will of
course hardly be doubted; little more
than a few great names, Attila, Theodoric, Gunther, belong to real history;
but the whole complexion of the poem
is so different from that of the twelfth
century, that we must believe the poet
to have imbued himself by some such
means with the spirit of times long past.
No disparagement, but the reverse, to
the genius of him who, in these respects,
as well as in his animated and picturesque language, so powerfully reminds
us of the father of poetry. The Nibelungen Lied has been lately modernised
in German, and is read perhaps with
more pleasure in that form, though it
displays less of its original raciness.
—1853.]

Meister-singers, but are traced to the institutions of the twelfth century, called singing-schools, for the promotion of popular music, the favourite recreation of Germany. What they may have done for music I am unable to say; it was in an evil hour for the art of poetry that they extended their jurisdiction over her. They regulated verse by the most pedantic and minute laws, such as a society with no idea of excellence but conformity to rule would be sure to adopt; though nobler institutions have often done the same, and the Master-burghers were but prototypes of the Italian academicians. The poetry was always moral and serious, but flat. These Meister-singers are said to have originated at Mentz, from which they spread to Augsburg, Strasburg, and other cities, and in none were more renowned than Nuremburg. Charles IV., in 1378, incorporated them by the name of Meistergenoss-schaft, with armorial bearings and peculiar privileges. They became, however, more conspicuous in the sixteenth century; scarce any names of Meister-singers before that age are recorded; nor does it seem that much of their earlier poetry is extant.[p]

44. The French versifiers had by this time, perhaps, become less numerous, though several names in the same style of amatory song do some credit to their age. But the romances of chivalry began now to be written in prose; while a very celebrated poem, the Roman de la Rose, had introduced an unfortunate taste for allegory into verse, from which France did not extricate herself for several generations. Meanwhile the Provençal poets, who, down to the close of the thirteenth century, had flourished in the south, and whose language many Lombards adopted, came to an end : after the re-union of the fief of Toulouse to the Crown, and the possession of Provence by a northern line of princes, their ancient and renowned tongue passed for a dialect, a patois of the people. It had never been much employed in prose, save in the kingdom of Aragon, where, under the name of Valencian, it continued for two

Poetry of France and Spain.

---

[p] Bouterwek, ix. 271-291. Heinsius, iv. 85-98. See also the Biographie universelle, art. Folcz; and a good article in the Retrospective Review, vol. x. p. 113. [See also Gervinus, Poetische Literatur der Deutschen, p. 112 and post.]

centuries to be a legitimate language, till political circumstances of the same kind reduced it, as in southern France, to a provincial dialect. The Castilian language, which, though it has been traced higher in written fragments, may be considered to have begun, in a literary sense, with the poem of the Cid, not later, as some have thought, than the middle of the twelfth century, was employed by a few extant poets in the next age, and in the fourteenth was as much the established vehicle of many kinds of literature in Spain as the French was on the other side of the mountains.[q] The names of Portuguese poets not less early than any in Castile are recorded; fragments are mentioned by Bouterwek as old as the twelfth century, and there exists a collection of lyric poetry in the style of the Troubadours, which is referred to no late part of the next age.[r] Nothing has been published

---

[q] Sanchez, Coleccion de Poesias Castellanas anteriores al siglo 15mo. Velasquez, Historia della Poesia Español; which I only know by the German translation of Dieze (Göttingen, 1769), who has added many notes. Andrès, Origine d' ogni Litteratura, ii. 158. Bouterwek's History of Spanish and Portuguese Literature. I shall quote the English translation of this work.

[r] This very curious fact in literary history has been brought to light by Lord Stuart of Rothesay, who printed at Paris, in 1823, twenty-five copies of a collection of ancient Portuguese songs, from a manuscript in the library of the College of Nobles at Lisbon. An account of this book, by M. Raynouard, will be found in the Journal des Savans for August, 1825; and I have been favoured by my noble friend the editor with the loan of a copy; though my ignorance of the language prevented me from forming an exact judgment of its contents. In the preface the following circumstances are stated. It consists of seventy-five folios, the first part having been torn off, and the manuscript attached to a work of a wholly different nature. The writing appears to be of the fourteenth century, and in some places older. The idiom seems older than the writing: it may be called, if I understand the meaning of the preface, as old as the beginning of the thirteenth century, and certainly older than the reign of

Denis, pode appellidarse coevo do seculo xiii, e de certo he anterior ao reynado de D. Deniz. Denis king of Portugal reigned from 1279 to 1325. It is regular in grammar, and for the most part in orthography; but contains some Gallicisms, which show either a connexion between France and Portugal in that age, or a common origin in the southern tongues of Europe; since certain idioms found in this manuscript are preserved in Spanish, Italian, and Provençal, yet are omitted in Portuguese dictionaries. A few poems are translated from Provençal, but the greater part are strictly Portuguese, as the mention of places, names, and manners shows. M. Raynouard, however, observes, that the thoughts and forms of versification are similar to those of the Troubadours. The metres employed are usually of seven, eight, and ten syllables, the accent falling on the last; but some lines occur of seven, eight, or eleven syllables, accented on the penultimate, and these are sometimes interwoven, at regular intervals, with the others.

The songs, as far as I was able to judge, are chiefly, if not wholly, amatory: they generally consist of stanzas, the first of which is written (and printed) with intervals for musical notes, and in the form of prose, though really in metre. Each stanza has frequently a burden of two lines. The plan appeared to be something like that of the Castilian

in the Castilian language of this amatory style older than
1400.

45. Italy came last of those countries where Latin had
been spoken to the possession of an independent Early Italian
language and literature.   No industry has hitherto language.
retrieved so much as a few lines of real Italian till near the
end of the twelfth century;[s] and there is not much before
the middle of the next.   Several poets, however, whose versification is not wholly rude, appeared soon afterwards.   The
Divine Comedy of Dante seems to have been commenced
before his exile from Florence in 1304.   The Italian language
was much used in prose during the times of Dante and
Petrarch, though very little before.

46. Dante and Petrarch are, as it were, the morning stars
of our modern literature.   I shall say nothing more of Dante and
the former in this place : he does not stand in such Petrarch.
close connexion as Petrarch with the fifteenth century, nor
had he such influence over the taste of his age.   In this
respect Petrarch has as much the advantage over Dante, as
he was his inferior in depth of thought and creative power.
He formed a school of poetry, which, though no disciple
comparable to himself came out of it, gave a character to the
taste of his country.   He did not invent the sonnet, but he,
perhaps, was the cause that it has continued in fashion for
so many ages.[t]   He gave purity, elegance, and even stability

---

glosas of the fifteenth century, the subject of the first stanza being repeated,
and sometimes expanded, in the rest.   I
do not know that this is found in any
Provençal poetry.   The language, according to Raynouard, resembles Provençal more than the modern Portuguese does.   It is a very remarkable
circumstance, that we have no evidence,
at least from the letter of the Marquis
of Santillana early in the fifteenth century, that the Castilians had any of
these love-songs till long after the date
of this Cancioneiro ; and that we may
rather collect from it, that the Spanish
amatory poets chose the Gallician or
Portuguese dialect in preference to their
own.   Though the very ancient collection to which this note refers seems to
have been unknown, I find mention of
one by Don Pedro, count of Barcelos,

natural son of King Denis, in Dieze's
notes on Velasquez. Gesch. der Span.
Dichtkunst, p. 70.   This must have
been in the first part of the fourteenth
century.
  [s] Tiraboschi, iii. 323, doubts the authenticity of some inscriptions referred
to the twelfth century.   The earliest
genuine Italian seems to be a few lines
by Ciullo d'Alcamo, a Sicilian, between
1187 and 1193, vol. iv. p. 340. [Mura-
tori thinks it probable that Italian
might be written sometimes in the
twelfth century.   Quando ciò precisa-
mente avvenisse, noi nol sappiamo,
perchè l' ignoranza e barbarie di que'
tempi non ne lasciò memoria, o non
compose tale opere, che meritassero di
vivere infino ai tempi nostri.   Della
perfetta Poesia, v. i. p. 6.—1842.]
  [t] Crescimbeni (Storia della vulgar

to the Italian language, which has been incomparably less
changed during near five centuries since his time, than it was
in one between the age of Guido Guinizzelli and his own;
and none have denied him the honour of having restored a
true feeling of classical antiquity in Italy, and consequently
in Europe.

47. Nothing can be more difficult than to determine, ex-
Change of cept by an arbitrary line, the commencement of the
Anglo-Saxon
to English. English language; not so much, as in those of the
Continent, because we are in want of materials, but rather
from an opposite reason, the possibility of tracing a very
gradual succession of verbal changes that ended in a change
of denomination. We should probably experience a similar
difficulty if we knew equally well the current idiom of France
or Italy in the seventh and eighth centuries. For when we
compare the earliest English of the thirteenth century with
the Anglo-Saxon of the twelfth, it seems hard to pronounce
why it should pass for a separate language, rather than a
modification or simplification of the former. We must conform, however, to usage, and say that the Anglo-Saxon was
converted into English : 1. by contracting or otherwise modi-
fying the pronunciation and orthography of words; 2. by
omitting many inflections, especially of the noun, and consequently making more use of articles and auxiliaries; 3. by
the introduction of French derivatives; 4. by using less
inversion and ellipsis, especially in poetry. Of these the
second alone, I think, can be considered as sufficient to
describe a new form of language; and this was brought
about so gradually that we are not relieved from much of
our difficulty whether some compositions shall pass for the
latest offspring of the mother or the earliest fruits of the
daughter's fertility.[u]

48. The Anglo-Norman language is a phrase not quite so
unobjectionable as the Anglo-Norman constitution; and, as
it is sure to deceive, we might better lay it aside altogether.[x]

Poesia, vol. ii. p. 269) asserts the claim
of Guiton d'Arezzo to the invention of
the regular sonnet, or at least the perfection of that in use among the Provençals.

  [u] It is a proof of this difficulty, that
he best masters of our ancient language
have lately introduced the word Semi-
Saxon, which is to cover every thing
from 1150 to 1250. See Thorpe's preface to Analecta Anglo-Saxonica, and
many other recent books.

  [x] A popular and pleasing writer has
drawn a little upon his imagination in

In the one instance there was a real fusion of laws and government, to which we can find but a remote analogy, or rather none at all, in the other. It is probable, indeed, that the converse of foreigners might have something to do with those simplifications of the Anglo-Saxon grammar which appear about the reign of Henry II., more than a century after the Conquest; though it is also true that languages of a very artificial structure, like that of England before that revolution, often became less complex in their forms, without any such violent process as an amalgamation of two different races.[y] What is commonly called the Saxon Chronicle is continued to the death of Stephen in 1154, and in the same language, though with some loss of its purity. Besides the neglect of several grammatical rules, French words now and then obtrude themselves, but not very frequently, in the latter pages of this Chronicle. Peterborough, however, was quite an English monastery; its endowments, its abbots, were Saxon; and the political spirit the Chronicle breathes, in some passages, is that of the indignant subjects, *servi ancor frementi*, of the Norman usurpers. If its last compilers, therefore, gave way to some innovations of language, we may presume that these prevailed more extensively in places less secluded, and especially in London.

49. We find evidence of a greater change in Layamon, a translator of Wace's romance of Brut from the French. Layamon's age is uncertain; it must have been after 1155, when the original poem was completed, and can hardly be placed below 1200. His language is accounted rather

---

the following account of the language of our forefathers after the Conquest: —'The language of the Church was Latin; that of the king and nobles, Norman; that of the people, Anglo-Saxon; *the Anglo-Norman jargon was only employed in the commercial intercourse between the conquerors and the conquered.*' Ellis's Specimens of Early English Poets, vol. i. p. 17. What was this jargon? and where do we find a proof of its existence? and what was the commercial intercourse hinted at? I suspect Ellis only meant, what has often been remarked, that the animals which bear a Saxon name in the field acquire a French one in the shambles. But even this is more ingenious than just; for muttons, beeves, and porkers are good old words for the living quadrupeds. [It has of late years been more usual to call the French poetry written in English, Anglo-Norman.—1842.]

[y] 'Every branch of the low German stock from whence the Anglo-Saxon sprung, displays the same simplification of its grammar.' Price's preface to Warton, p. 110. He therefore ascribes little influence to the Norman conquest or to French connexions. [It ought, however, to be observed, that the simplifications of the Anglo-Saxon grammar had begun before the reign of Henry II.; the latter part of the Saxon Chronicle affords full proof of this.—1847.]

Anglo-Saxon than English; it retains most of the distinguishing inflections of the mother-tongue, yet evidently differs considerably from that older than the Conquest by the introduction, or at least more frequent employment, of some new auxiliary forms, and displays very little of the characteristics of the ancient poetry, its periphrases, its ellipses, or its inversions. But though translation was the means by which words of French origin were afterwards most copiously introduced, very few occur in the extracts from Layamon hitherto published; for we have not yet the expected edition of the entire work. He is not a mere translator, but improves much on Wace. The adoption of the plain and almost creeping style of the metrical French romance, instead of the impetuous dithyrambics of Saxon song, gives Layamon at first sight a greater affinity to the new English language than in mere grammatical structure he appears to bear.[z]

50. Layamon wrote in a village on the Severn;[a] and it is agreeable to experience that an obsolete structure of language should be retained in a distant province, while it has undergone some change among the less rugged inhabitants of a capital. The disuse of Saxon forms crept on by degrees; some metrical lives of saints, apparently written not far from the year 1250,[b] may be deemed

Progress of English language.

---

[a] See a long extract from Layamon in Ellis's Specimens. This writer observes, that 'it contains no word which we are under the necessity of referring to a French root.' *Duke* and *Castle* seem exceptions; but the latter word occurs in the Saxon Chronicle before the Conquest, A.D. 1052.

[a] [I believe that Ernley, of which Layamon is said to have been priest, is Over Arley, near Bewdley.—1842.]

[Sir F. Madden says Lower Arley, another village a few miles distant.— 1847.]

[b] Ritson's Dissertat. on Romance. Madden's Introduction to Havelok. Notes of Price, in his edition of Warton. Warton himself is of no authority in this matter. Price inclines to put most of the poems quoted by Warton near the close of the thirteenth century. It should here be observed, that the language underwent its metamorphosis

into English by much less rapid gradations in some parts of the kingdom than in others. Not only the popular dialect of many counties, especially in the north, retained long, and still retains, a larger proportion of the Anglo-Saxon peculiarities, but we have evidence that they were not everywhere disused in writing. A manuscript in the Kentish dialect, if that phrase is correct, bearing the date of 1340, is more Anglo-Saxon than any of the poems ascribed to the thirteenth century, such as we read in Warton, such as the legends of saints, or the Ormulum. This very curious fact was first made known to the public by Mr. Thorpe, in his translation of Cædmon, preface, p. xii.; and an account of the manuscript itself, rather fuller than that of Mr. T., has since been given in the catalogue of the Arundel MSS. in the British Museum.

[The edition of Layamon alluded to

English; but the first specimen of it that bears a precise date is a proclamation of Henry III., addressed to the people of Huntingdonshire in 1258, but doubtless circular throughout England.[c] A triumphant song, composed probably in London, on the victory obtained at Lewes by the confederate barons in 1264, and the capture of Richard Earl of Cornwall, is rather less obsolete in its style than this proclama-

---

in the text has now been published by Sir Frederick Madden, at the expense of the Society of Antiquaries, and will prove an important accession to the history of our language, being by much the most extensive remains of that period denominated Semi-Saxon. The date of this long poem is now referred by the editor to the reign of John at the beginning of the thirteenth century. A passage, formerly quoted by Mr. Sharon Turner, but which had escaped my recollection, manifestly was written after the death of Henry II. in 1189, and probably after that of his queen Eleanor in 1203. Mr. Turner has, therefore, inclined to the same period as Sir Frederick Madden; and others had acceded to his opinion. The chief objection, and, indeed, the only one, may be the antiquity of Layamon's language, compared with the Ormulum, a well-known, but hitherto unpublished, poem of a certain Orm, and with another poem, which has been printed, entitled the Owl and the Nightingale. Nothing can exhibit a transitional state of language better than the great work of Layamon, consisting of near 30,000 lines. These are all short, and though very irregular, coming far nearer to the old Anglo-Saxon than to the octo-syllabic French rhythm. Some of them are rhymed, but in a much larger proportion the alliterative euphony of the northern nations is preferred. The publication of the entire poem enables us to correct some of the judgments founded on mere extracts; thus I should qualify what is said in the text, that Layamon 'adopted the plain and almost creeping style of the metrical French romance.' His poem has more spirit and fire, in the Scandinavian and Anglo-Saxon style, than had been supposed. Upon the whole, Layamon must be reckoned far more of the older than the newer formation; he is an *eocene*, or at most a *miocene*; while his contemporaries, as

they seem to be, belong philologically to a later period.

The poem of the Owl and the Nightingale is supposed by its editor, Mr. Stevenson, to have been written soon after the death of Henry II., who is mentioned in it. But I do not see why the passage leads us to more than that no other king of that name had reigned. We need not, therefore, go higher than the age of John. The Ormulum contains, I believe, no evidence of its date; but the language is very decidedly more English, the versification more borrowed from Norman models, than that of Layamon. Since it is natural to presume that the change of language would not be alike in all parts of England, and even that individuals might continue to preserve forms which were going into comparative disuse, we cannot rely on these varieties as indicating difference of age. The editor of Layamon informs us that the French words in the older copy of that writer do not amount to fifty. The hypothesis, if we are to use such a word, that the transition of our language from Saxon to English took place more rapidly in some districts than in others, acquires strong confirmation from a few lines preserved in Roger de Hoveden and Benedict Abbas about the year 1190. They seem to be printed inaccurately, and I shall consequently omit them here; but the language is English of Henry III.'s reign. It is possible that it has been a little modernised in the manuscripts of these historians.—1847.]

[c] Henry's Hist. of Britain, vol. viii. appendix. 'Between 1244 and 1258,' says Sir F. Madden, 'we know, was written the versification of part of a meditation of St. Augustine, as proved by the age of the prior, who gave the manuscript to the Durham library,' p. 49. This, therefore, will be strictly the oldest piece of English, to the date of which we can approach by more than conjecture.

tion, as might naturally be expected. It could not have been written later than that year, because in the next the tables were turned on those who now exulted by the complete discomfiture of their party in the battle of Evesham. Several pieces of poetry, uncertain as to their precise date, must be referred to the latter part of this century. Robert of Gloucester, after the year 1297, since he alludes to the canonisation of St. Louis,[d] turned the chronicle of Geoffrey of Monmouth into English verse; and, on comparing him with Layamon, a native of nearly the same part of England, and a writer on the same subject, it will appear that a great quantity of French had flowed into the language since the loss of Normandy. The Anglo-Saxon inflections, terminations, and orthography had also undergone a very considerable change. That the intermixture of French words was very slightly owing to the Norman conquest will appear probable by observing at least as frequent an use of them in the earliest specimens of the Scottish dialect, especially a song on the death of Alexander III. in 1285. There is a good deal of French in this, not borrowed, probably, from England, but directly from the original sources of imitation.

51. The fourteenth century was not unproductive of men,
English of the 14th century. Chaucer. Gower. both English and Scotch, gifted with the powers of poetry. Laurence Minot, an author unknown to Warton, but whose poems on the wars of Edward III. are referred by their publisher Ritson to 1352, is perhaps the first original poet in our language that has survived, since such of his predecessors as are now known appear to have been merely translators, or, at best, amplifiers, of a French or Latin original. The earliest historical or epic narrative is due to John Barbour, archdeacon of Aberdeen, whose long poem in the Scots dialect, The Bruce, commemorating the deliverance of his country, seems to have been completed in 1373. But our greatest poet of the middle ages, beyond comparison, was Geoffrey Chaucer; and I do not know that any other country, except Italy, produced his equal in variety of invention, acuteness of observation, or felicity of expression. A vast interval must be made between

---

[d] Madden's Havelok, p. 52.

Chaucer and any other English poet; yet Gower, his contemporary, though not, like him, a poet of nature's growth, had some effect in rendering the language less rude, and exciting a taste for verse; if he never rises, he never sinks low; he is always sensible, polished, perspicuous, and not prosaic in the worst sense of the word. Longlands, the supposed author of Piers Plowman's Vision, with far more imaginative vigour, has a more obsolete and unrefined diction.

52. The French language was spoken by the superior classes of society in England from the Conquest to the reign of Edward III., though it seems probable that they were generally acquainted with English, at least in the latter part of that period. But all letters, even of a private nature, were written in Latin till the beginning of the reign of Edward I., soon after 1270, when a sudden change brought in the use of French.[e] In grammar school boys were made to construe their Latin into French; and in the statutes of Oriel College, Oxford, we find a regulation so late as 1328, that the students shall converse together, if not in Latin, at least in French.[f] The minutes of the corporation of London, recorded in the Town Clerk's office, were in French, as well as the proceedings in Parliament, and in the courts of justice; and oral discussions were perhaps carried on in the same language, though this is not a necessary consequence. Hence the English was seldom written, and hardly employed in prose, till after the middle of the fourteenth century. Sir John Mandeville's travels were written in 1356. This is our earliest English book.[g] Wicliffe's translation of the Bible, a great work that

General disuse of French in England.

---

[e] I am indebted for this fact, which I have ventured to generalise, to the communication of Mr. Stevenson, late subcommissioner of public records. [I find, however, that letters, even in France, are said to have been written only in Latin to the end of the century. On n'écrivait encore que très-peu de lettres en langue française. Discours sur l'état des Lettres au 13me siècle, in Hist. littéraire de la France, vol. xvi. p. 168. It is probable, therefore, that I have used too strong words as to the general usage.—1842.]

[f] Si qua inter se proferant, colloquio Latino vel saltem Gallico perfruantur.

Warton, i. 6. In Merton College statutes, given in 1271, Latin alone is prescribed.

[g] [This is only true as to printed books. For there are several copies of a translation of the Psalter and Church Hymns, by Rolle, commonly called the hermit of Hampole, who has subjoined a comment on each verse. Rolle is said by Mr. Sharon Turner to have died in 1349; we must therefore place him a little before Mandeville. Even in him we find a good deal of French and Latin, which indeed he seems to have rather studiously sought, in order 'that they

enriched the language, is referred to 1383. Trevisa's version
of the Polychronicon of Higden was in 1385, and the Astro-
labe of Chaucer in 1392. A few public instruments were
drawn up in English under Richard II.; and about the
same time, probably, it began to be employed in epistolary
correspondence of a private nature. Trevisa informs us
that when he wrote (1385) even gentlemen had much left
off to have their children taught French, and names the
schoolmaster (John Cornwall) who soon after 1350 brought
in so great an innovation as the making his boys read Latin
into English.[h] This change from the common use of
French in the upper ranks seems to have taken place as
rapidly as a similar revolution has lately done in Germany.
By a statute of 1362 (36 E. III. c. 15), all pleas in courts
of justice are directed to be pleaded and judged in English,
on account of French being so much unknown. But the
laws, and, generally speaking, the records of Parliament,
continued to be in the latter language for many years;
and we learn from Sir John Fortescue, a hundred years
afterwards, that this statute itself was not fully enforced.[i]
The French language, if we take his words literally, even in
the reign of Edward IV., was spoken in affairs of mercantile
account, and in many games, the vocabulary of both being
chiefly derived from it.[k]

53. Thus by the year 1400 we find a national literature sub-
State of sisting in seven European languages, three spoken
European in the Spanish Peninsula, the French, the Italian,
languages the German, and the English, from which last the
about 1400.
Scots dialect need not be distinguished. Of these the Italian
was the most polished, and had to boast of the greatest
writers; the French excelled in their number and variety.
Our own tongue, though it had latterly acquired much
copiousness in the hands of Chaucer and Wicliffe, both of
whom lavishly supplied it with words of French and Latin

---

that knowes noght the Latyne be the
Ynglys may come to many Latyne
wordis.'—Baber's preface to Wicliffe's
translation of New Testament.—1847.]

[h] The passage may be found quoted
in Warton, ubi supra, or in many other
books.

[i] 'In the courts of justice they for-

merly used to plead in French, till, in
pursuance of a law to that purpose, that
custom was *somewhat restrained*, but not
hitherto quite disused.' De Laudibus
Legum Angliæ, c. xlviii. I quote from
Waterhouse's translation; but the Latin
runs *quam plurimum* restrictus est.

[k] Ibid.

derivation, was but just growing into a literary existence.
The German, as well as that of Valencia, seemed to decline.
The former became more precise, more abstract, more intellectual (*geistig*), and less sensible (*sinnlich*) (to use the words
of Eichhorn), that is, less full of ideas derived from sense, and
of consequence less fit for poetry; it fell into the hands of
lawyers and mystical theologians. The earliest German
prose, a few very ancient fragments excepted, is the collection of Saxon laws (Sachsenspiegel), about the middle of the
thirteenth century; the next the Swabian collection (Schwa-
benspiegel), about 1282.[m] But these forming hardly a part
of literature, though Bouterwek praises passages of the latter
for religious eloquence, we may deem John Tauler, a Dominican friar of Strasburg, whose influence in propagating what
was called the mystical theology gave a new tone to his
country, to be the first German writer in prose. 'Tauler,'
says a modern historian of literature, 'in his German
sermons mingled many expressions invented by himself,
which were the first attempt at a philosophical language, and
displayed surprising eloquence for the age wherein he lived.
It may be justly said of him that he first gave to prose that
direction in which Luther afterwards advanced so far.'[n]
Tauler died in 1361. Meantime, as has been said before, the
nobility abandoned their love of verse, which the burghers
took up diligently, but with little spirit or genius; the
common language became barbarous and neglected, of which
the strange fashion of writing half Latin, half German verses
is a proof.[o] This had been common in the darker ages: we
have several instances of it in Anglo-Saxon, and also after
the Conquest, nor was it rare in France; but it was late to
adopt it in the fourteenth century.

54. The Latin writers of the middle ages were chiefly
ecclesiastics. But of these in the living tongues a
large proportion were laymen. They knew, therefore, how to commit their thoughts to writing; and
hence the ignorance characteristic of the darker ages must
seem to be passing away. This, however, is a very difficult

Ignorance of reading and writing in darker ages.

---

[m] Bouterwek, p. 163. There are some
novels at the end of the thirteenth, or beginning of the fourteenth, century. Ib.

[n] Heinsius, iv. 76.
[o] Eichhorn, Allg. Gesch. i. 240.

though interesting question, when we come to look nearly at
the gradual progress of rudimental knowledge. I can offer
but an outline, which those who turn more of their attention
towards the subject will be enabled to correct and complete.
Before the end of the eleventh century, and especially after
the ninth, it was rare to find laymen in France who could
read and write.[p] The case was probably not better anywhere
else, except in Italy. I should incline to except Italy on the
authority of a passage in Wippo, a German writer soon
after the year 1000, who exhorts the Emperor, Henry II., to
cause the sons of the nobility to be instructed in letters,
using the example of the Italians, with whom, according
to him, it was a universal practice.[q] The word clerks or
clergymen became in this and other countries synonymous
with one who could write or even read ; we all know the
original meaning of benefit of clergy, and the test by which
it was claimed. Yet from about the end of the eleventh, or
at least of the twelfth century, many circumstances may lead
us to believe that it was less and less a conclusive test, and
that the laity came more and more into possession of the
simple elements of literature.

55. I. It will of course be admitted that all who adminis-
Reasons for tered or belonged to the Roman law were masters of
supposing
this to have reading and writing, though we do not find that they
diminished
after 1100. were generally ecclesiastics, even in the lowest sense
of the word, by receiving the tonsure. Some, indeed, were
such. In countries where the feudal law had passed from
unwritten custom to record and precedent, and had grown
into as much subtlety by diffuseness as the Roman, which
was the case of England from the time of Henry II., the
lawyers, though laymen, were unquestionably clerks or

---

[p] Hist. litt. de la France, vii. 2. Some
nobles sent their children to be educated
in the schools of Charlemagne, especially
those of Germany, under Raban, Notker,
Bruno, and other distinguished abbots.
But they were generally destined for
the church. Meiners, ii. 377. The
signatures of laymen are often found to
deeds of the eighth century, and sometimes of the ninth. Nouv. Traité de la
diplomatique, ii. 422. The ignorance of
the laity, according to this authority, was
not strictly parallel to that of
church.

[q] Tunc fac edictum per terram Teutonicorum
Quilibet ut dives sibi natos instruat omnes
Litterulis, legemque suam persuadeat illis,
Ut cum principibus placitandi venerit usus,
Quisque suis libris exemplum proferat illis.
Moribus his dudum vivebat Roma decenter,
His studiis tantos potuit vincere tyrannos.
Hoc servant Itali post prima crepundia cuncti.

I am indebted for this quotation to
Meiners, ii. 344.

learned. II. The convenience of such elementary knowledge to merchants, who, both in the Mediterranean and in
these parts of Europe, carried on a good deal of foreign commerce, and indeed to all traders, may induce us to believe
that they were not destitute of it; though it must be confessed that the word clerk rather seems to denote that
their deficiency was supplied by those employed under them.
I do not, however, conceive that the clerks of citizens were
ecclesiastics.[r] III. If we could rely on a passage in Ingulfus,
the practice in grammar schools of construing Latin into
French was as old as the reign of the Conqueror;[s] and it
seems unlikely that this should have been confined to children
educated for the English church. IV. The poets of the
north and south of France were often men of princely or
noble birth, sometimes ladies; their versification is far too
artificial to be deemed the rude product of an illiterate mind ;
and to these, whose capacity of holding the pen few will
dispute, we must surely add a numerous class of readers, for
whom their poetry was designed. It may be surmised that
the itinerant minstrels answered this end, and supplied the
ignorance of the nobility. But many ditties of the troubadours were not so well adapted to the minstrels, who seem to
have dealt more with metrical romances. Nor do I doubt
that these also were read in many a castle of France and
Germany. I will not dwell on the story of Francesca of
Rimini, because no one perhaps is likely to dispute that a
Romagnol lady in the age of Dante would be able to read the
tale of Lancelot. But that romance had long been written ;
and other ladies doubtless had read it, and possibly had left
off reading it in similar circumstances, and as little to their
advantage. The fourteenth century abounded with books in
French prose, nor were they by any means wanting in the
thirteenth, when several translations from Latin were made;[t]

---

[r] The earliest recorded bills of ex-
change, according to Beckmann, Hist.
of Inventions, iii. 430, are in a passage
of the jurist Baldus, and bear date in
1328. But they were by no means in
common use till the next century. I
do not mention this as bearing much on
the subject of the text.

[s] Et pueris etiam in scholis principia literarum Gallicè et non Anglicè
traderentur.

[t] Hist. litt. de la France, xvi. 144.
Notre prose et notre poésie française
existaient avant 1200; mais c'est au
treizième siècle qu'elles commencèrent
à prendre un caractère national. Id,
254.

the extant copies of some are not very few; but no argument against their circulation could have been urged from their scarcity in the present day. It is not of course pretended that they were diffused as extensively as printed books have been. V. The fashion of writing private letters in French, instead of Latin, which, as has been mentioned, came in among us soon after 1270, affords perhaps a presumption that they were written in a language intelligible to the correspondent, because he had no longer occasion for assistance in reading them, though they were still generally from the hand of a secretary. But at what time this disuse of Latin began on the Continent of Europe I cannot exactly determine.

56. The art of reading does not imply that of writing; it seems likely that the one prevailed before the other. Increased knowledge of writing in fourteenth century. The latter was difficult to acquire, in consequence of the regularity of characters preserved by the clerks and their complex system of abbreviations, which rendered the cursive handwriting introduced about the end of the eleventh century almost as operose to those who had not much experience of it as the more stiff characters of older manuscripts. It certainly appears that even autograph signatures are not found till a late period. Philip the Bold, who ascended the French throne in 1272, could not write, though this is not the case with any of his successors. I do not know that equal ignorance is recorded of any English sovereign, though we have, I think, only a series of autographs beginning with Richard II. It is said by the authors of Nouveau Traité de la Diplomatique, Benedictines of laborious and exact erudition, that the art of writing had become rather common among the laity of France before the end of the thirteenth century: out of eight witnesses to a testament in 1277 five could write their names; at the beginning of that age it is probable, they think, that not one could have done so.[u] Signatures to deeds of private persons, however, do not begin to appear till the fourteenth, and were not in established use in France till about the middle of the

---

[u] Vol. ii. p. 423. Charters in French are rare at the beginning of the thirteenth century, but become common under Philip III. Hist. litt. de la France, xvi. 155.

fifteenth, century.[x]   Indorsements upon English deeds, as well as mere signatures, by laymen of rank, bearing date in the reign of Edward II., are in existence; and there is an English letter from the lady of Sir John Pelham to her husband in 1399, which is probably one of the earliest instances of female penmanship. By the badness of the grammar we may presume it to be her own.[y]

57. Laymen, among whom Chaucer and Gower are illustrious examples, received occasionally a learned education; and indeed the great number of gentlemen who studied in the inns of court is a conclusive proof that they were not generally illiterate. The common law required some knowledge of two languages. Upon

Average state of knowledge in England.

---

[x] Vol. ii. p. 434 et post.

[y] I am indebted for a knowledge of this letter to the Rev. Joseph Hunter, who recollected to have seen it in an old edition of Collins' Peerage. Later editions have omitted it as an unimportant redundancy, though interesting even for its contents, independently of the value it acquires from the language. On account of its scarcity, being only found in old editions now not in request, I shall insert it here; and till any other shall prefer a claim, it may pass for the oldest private letter in the English language. I have not kept the orthography, but have left several incoherent and ungrammatical phrases as they stand. It was copied by Collins from the archives of the Newcastle family.

My dear Lord,—I recommend me to your high lordship with heart and body and all my poor might, and with all this I thank you as my dear lord dearest and best beloved of all earthly lords I say for me, and thank you my dear lord with all this that I say before of your comfortable letter that ye sent me from Pontefract that come to me on Mary Magdalene day; for by my troth I was never so glad as when I heard by your letter that ye were strong enough with the grace of God for to keep you from the malice of your enemies. And dear Lord if it like to your high lordship that as soon as ye might that I might hear of your gracious speed; which as God Almighty continue and increase. And my dear lord if it like

you for to know of my fare, I am here by laid in manner of a siege with the county of Sussex, Surrey, and a great parcel of Kent, so that I may nought out no none victuals get me but with much hard. Wherefore my dear if it like you by the advice of your wise counsel for to get remedy of the salvation of your castle and withstand the malice of the shires aforesaid. And also that ye be fully informed of their great malice workers in these shires which that haves so despitefully wrought to you, and to your castle, to your men, and to your tenants for this country have they wasted for a great while. Farewell my dear lord, the Holy Trinity you keep from your enemies, and ever send me good tidings of you. Written at Pevensey in the castle on St. Jacob day last past,

By your own poor
J. PELHAM.
To my true Lord.

[Sir Henry Ellis says: 'We have nothing earlier than the fifteenth century which can be called a familiar letter.'— Original Letters, first series, vol. i. This of Lady Pelham, however, is an exception, and perhaps others will be found; at least it cannot now be doubtful that some were written, since a lady is not likely to have set the example. Sir H. E., nevertheless, is well warranted in saying that letters previous to the reign of Henry V. were usually written in French or Latin.— 1847.]

the whole we may be inclined to think that in the year 1400, or at the accession of Henry IV., the average instruction of an English gentleman of the first class would comprehend common reading and writing, a considerable familiarity with French, and a slight tincture of Latin; the latter retained or not, according to his circumstances and character, as school learning is at present. This may be rather a favourable statement; but after another generation it might be assumed, as we shall see, with more confidence as a fair one.[z]

58. A demand for instruction in the art of writing would increase with the frequency of epistolary correspondence, which, where of a private or secret nature, no one would gladly conduct by the intervention of a secretary. Better education, more refined manners, a closer intercourse of social life, were the primary causes of this increase in private correspondence. But it was greatly facilitated by the invention, or rather, extended use of paper as the vehicle of writing instead of parchment; a revolution, as it may be called, of high importance, without which both the art of writing would have been much less practised, and the invention of printing less serviceable to mankind. After the subjugation of Egypt by the Saracens, the importation of the papyrus, previously in general use, came in no long time to an end; so that, though down to the end of the seventh century all instruments in France were written upon it, we find its place afterwards supplied by parchment; and, under the house of Charlemagne, there is hardly an instrument upon any other material.[a] Parchment, however, a much more durable and useful vehicle than papyrus,[b] was expensive, and its cost not only excluded the necessary waste which a free

Marginal note: Invention of paper.

---

[z] It might be inferred from a passage in Richard of Bury, about 1343, that none but ecclesiastics could read at all. He deprecates the putting of books into the hands of *laici*, who do not know one side from another. And in several places it seems that he thought they were meant for 'the tonsured' alone. But a great change took place in the ensuing half century; and I do not believe he can be construed strictly even as to his own time.

[a] Montfaucon, in Acad. des Inscript. vol. vi. But Muratori says that the papyrus was little used in the seventh century, though writings on it may be found as late as the tenth Dissert. xliii. This dissertation relates to the condition of letters in Italy as far as the year 1100; as the xlivth does to their subsequent history.

[b] Heeren justly remarks (I do not know that others have done the same), of how great importance the general use of parchment, to which, and afterwards to paper, the old perishable papyraceous manuscripts were transferred, has been to the preservation of literature. P. 74.

use of writing requires, but gave rise to the unfortunate practice of erasing manuscripts in order to replace them with some new matter. This was carried to a great extent, and has occasioned the loss of precious monuments of antiquity, as is now demonstrated by instances of their restoration.

59. The date of the invention of our present paper, manufactured from linen rags, or of its introduction into Europe, has long been the subject of controversy. That paper made from cotton was in use sooner, is admitted on all sides. Some charters written upon that material not later than the tenth century were seen by Montfaucon; and it is even said to be found in papal bulls of the ninth.[c] The Greeks, however, from whom the west of Europe is conceived to have borrowed this sort of paper, did not much employ it in manuscript books, according to Montfaucon, till the twelfth century, from which time it came into frequent use among them. Muratori had seen no writing upon this material older than 1100, though, in deference to Montfaucon, he admits its occasional employment earlier.[d] It certainly was not greatly used in Italy before the thirteenth century. Among the Saracens of Spain, on the other hand, as well as those of the East, it was of much greater antiquity. The Greeks called it *charta Damascena*, having been manufactured or sold in the city of Damascus. And Casiri, in his catalogue of the Arabic manuscripts in the Escurial, desires us to understand that they are written on paper of cotton or linen, but generally the latter, unless the contrary be expressed.[e] Many in this catalogue were written before the thirteenth, or even the twelfth century.

60. This will lead us to the more disputed question as to the antiquity of linen paper. The earliest distinct instance I have found, and which I believe has hitherto been overlooked, is an Arabic version of the Aphorisms of Hippocrates, the manuscript bearing the date of 1100. This Casiri observes to be on linen paper, not as in itself remarkable, but as accounting for its injury by wet.

Linen paper, when first used.

Cotton paper.

Linen paper as old as 1100.

[c] Mém. de l'Acad. des Inscriptions, vi. 604. Nouveau Traité de Diplomatique, i. 517. Savigny, Gesch. des Römischen Rechts, iii. 534.
[d] Dissert. xliii.

[e] Materiæ, nisi membraneus sit codex, nulla mentio: cæteros bombycinos, ac. maximam partem, chartaceos esse colligas. Præfatio, p. 7.

It does not appear whether it were written in Spain, or, like many in that catalogue, brought from Egypt or the East.[f]

61. The authority of Casiri must confirm beyond doubt
Known to a passage in Peter, abbot of Clugni, which has
Peter of
Clugni. perplexed those who place the invention of linen paper very low. In a treatise against the Jews, he speaks of books, ex pellibus arietum, hircorum, vel vitulorum, sive ex biblis vel juncis Orientalium paludum, aut ex *rasuris veterum pannorum,* seu ex aliâ quâlibet forte viliore materia compactos. A late English writer contends that nothing can be meant by the last words, ' unless that all sorts of inferior substances capable of being so applied, among them, perhaps, hemp and the remains of cordage, were used at this period in the manufacture of paper.'[g] It certainly at least seems reasonable to interpret the words ' ex rasuris veterum pannorum,' of linen rags; and when I add that Peter Cluniacensis passed a considerable time in Spain about 1141, there can remain, it seems, no rational doubt that the Saracens of the peninsula were acquainted with that species of paper, though perhaps it was as yet unknown in every other country.

62. Andrès asserts, on the authority of the Memoirs of
and in 12th the Academy of Barcelona, that a treaty between
and 13th
centuries. the kings of Aragon and Castile, bearing the date of 1178, and written upon linen paper, is extant in the archives of that city.[h] He alleges several other instances in the next age; when Mabillon, who denies that paper of linen was then used in charters, which, indeed, no one is likely to maintain, mentions, as the earliest specimen he had seen in France, a letter of Joinville to St. Louis, which must be older than 1270. Andrès refers the invention to the Saracens of Spain, using the fine flax of Valencia and Murcia; and conjectures that it was brought

---

[f] Casiri, N. 787. Codex anno Christi 1100, chartaceus, &c.

[g] See a memoir on an ancient manuscript of Aratus, by Mr. Ottley, in Archæologia, vol. xxvi.

[h] Vol. ii. p. 73. Andrès has gone much at length into this subject, and has collected several important passages which do not appear in my text. The letter of Joinville has been supposed to be addressed to Louis Hutin in 1314, but this seems inconsistent with the writer's age.

into use among the Spaniards themselves by Alfonso X. of Castile.[i]

63. In the opinion of the English writer to whom we have above referred, paper, from a very early period, was manufactured of mixed materials, which have sometimes been erroneously taken for pure cotton. We have in the Tower of London a letter addressed to Henry III. by Raymond, son of Raymond VI., Count of Toulouse, and consequently between 1216 and 1222, when the latter died, upon very strong paper, and certainly made, in Mr. Ottley's judgment, of mixed materials; while in several of the time of Edward I., written upon genuine cotton paper of no great thickness, the fibres of cotton present themselves everywhere at the backs of the letters so distinctly that they seem as if they might even now be spun into thread.[k] *Paper of mixed materials.*

64. Notwithstanding this last statement, which I must confirm by my own observation, and of which no one can doubt who has looked at the letters themselves, several writers of high authority, such as Tiraboschi and Savigny, persist not only in fixing the invention of linen paper very low, even after the middle of the fourteenth century, but in maintaining that it is undistinguishable from that made of cotton, except by the eye of a manufacturer.[m] Were this indeed true, it would be sufficient for the purpose we have here in view, which is not to trace the origin of a particular discovery, but the employment of a useful vehicle of writing. If it be true that cotton paper was fabricated in Italy of so good a texture *Invention of paper placed by some too low.*

---

[i] Vol. ii. p. 84. He cannot mean that it was never employed before Alfonso's time, of which he has already given instances.

[k] Archæologia, ibid. I may however observe, that a gentleman as experienced as Mr. Ottley himself inclines to think the letter of Raymond written on paper wholly made of cotton, though of better manufacture than usual.

[m] Tiraboschi, v. 85. Savigny, Gesch. des Römischen Rechts, iii. 534. He relies on a book I have not seen, Wehrs vom Papier, Hall, 1789. This writer, it is said, contends that the words of

Peter of Clugny, ex rasuris veterum pannorum, mean cotton paper. Heeren, p. 208. Lambinet, on the other hand, translates them, without hesitation, 'chiffons de linge.' Hist. de l'Origine de l'Imprimerie, i. 93.

Andrès has pointed out, p. 70, that Maffei merely says he has seen no paper of linen earlier than 1300, and no instrument on that material older than one of 1367, which he found among his own family deeds. Tiraboschi, overlooking this distinction, quotes Maffei for his own opinion as to the lateness of the invention.

that it cannot be discerned from linen, it must be considered as of equal utility. It is not the case with the letters on cotton paper in our English repositories; most, if not all, of which were written in France or Spain. But I have seen in the Chapter House at Westminster a letter written from Gascony about 1315, to Hugh Despencer, upon thin paper, to all appearance made like that now in use, and with a water mark. Several others of a similar appearance, in the same repository, are of rather later time. There is also one in the King's Remembrancer's Office of the 11th of Edward III. (1337 or 1338), containing the accounts of the King's ambassadors to the count of Holland, and probably written in that country. This paper has a water mark, and if it is not of linen, is at least not easily distinguishable. Bullet declares that he saw at Besançon a deed of 1302 on linen paper: several are alleged to exist in Germany before the middle of the century; and Lambinet mentions, though but on the authority of a periodical publication, a register of expenses from 1323 to 1354, found in a church at Caen, written on two hundred and eight sheets of that substance.[n] One of the Cottonian manuscripts (Galba, B. I.) is called Codex Chartaceus in the catalogue. It contains a long series of public letters, chiefly written in the Netherlands, from an early part of the reign of Edward III. to that of Henry IV. But upon examination I find the title not quite accurate; several letters, and especially the earliest, are written on parchment, and paper does not appear at soonest till near the end of Edward's reign.[o] Sir Henry Ellis has said that ' very few instances indeed occur before the fifteenth century of letters written upon paper.'[p] The use of cotton paper was by no means general, or even, I believe, frequent, except in Spain and Italy, perhaps also in the south of France. Nor was it much employed, even in Italy, for books. Savigny tells us there are few manuscripts of law

---

[n] Lambinet, ubi supra. [Linen paper, it is said, in Hist. littéraire de la France, xvi. 38, is used in some proceedings against the Templars in 1309 ; but the author knows of none earlier. He does not mention cotton paper at all ; writing was on vellum or parchment.—1842.]

[o] Andrès, p. 68, mentions a note written in 1342, in the Cotton Library, as the earliest English specimen of linen paper. I do not know to what this refers ; in the above-mentioned Codex Chartaceus is a letter of 1341, but it is on parchment.

[p] Ellis's Original Letters, i. 1.

books among the multitude that exist which are not written
on parchment.

65. It will be manifest from what has been said how
greatly Robertson has been mistaken in his position, Not at first
that 'in the eleventh century the art of making very important.
paper, in the manner now become universal, was invented, by
means of which not only the number of manuscripts increased, but the study of the sciences was wonderfully facilitated.'[q]　Even Ginguéné, better informed on such subjects
than Robertson, has intimated something of the same kind.
But paper, whenever or wherever invented, was very sparingly
used, and especially in manuscript books, among the French,
Germans, or English, or linen paper, even among the
Italians, till near the close of the period which this chapter
comprehends.　Upon the 'study of the sciences' it could
as yet have had very little effect.　The vast importance of
the invention was just beginning to be discovered.　It is to
be added, as a remarkable circumstance, that the earliest
linen paper was of very good manufacture, strong and
handsome, though perhaps too much like card for general
convenience ; and every one is aware that the first printed
books are frequently beautiful in the quality of their paper.

66. III. The application of general principles of justice
to the infinitely various circumstances which may Importance
of legal
arise in the disputes of men with each other is in studies.
itself an admirable discipline of the moral and intellectual
faculties.　Even where the primary rules of right and policy
have been obscured in some measure by a technical and
arbitrary system, which is apt to grow up, perhaps inevitably,
in the course of civilisation, the mind gains in precision and
acuteness, though at the expense of some important qualities ; and a people wherein an artificial jurisprudence is
cultivated, requiring both a regard to written authority, and
the constant exercise of a discriminating judgment upon
words, must be deemed to be emerging from ignorance.
Such was the condition of Europe in the twelfth century.
The feudal customs, long unwritten, though latterly become
more steady by tradition, were in some countries reduced

---

[q] Hist. of Charles V. vol. i. note 10.　Heeren inclines to the same opinion,
p. 200.

into treatises; we have our own Glanvil, in the reign of
Henry II., and in the next century much was written upon
the national laws in various parts of Europe. Upon these it
is not my intention to dwell; but the importance of the
civil law in its connexion with ancient learning, as well as
with moral and political science, renders it deserving of a
place in any general account either of mediæval or modern
literature.

67. That the Roman laws, such as they subsisted in the
Roman laws never wholly unknown. western empire at the time of its dismemberment
in the fifth century, were received in the new
kingdoms of the Gothic, Lombard, and Carlovingian dynas-
ties, as the rule of those who by birth and choice submitted
to them, was shown by Muratori and other writers of the
last century. This subject has received additional illustration from the acute and laborious Savigny, who has
succeeded in tracing sufficient evidence of what had been,
in fact, stated by Muratori, that not only an abridgment of
the Theodosian code, but that of Justinian, and even the
Pandects, were known in different parts of Europe long
before the epoch formerly assigned for the restoration of
that jurisprudence.[r] The popular story, already much discredited, that the famous copy of the Pandects, now in the
Laurentian library at Florence, was brought to Pisa from
Amalfi, after the capture of that city by Roger king of Sicily
with the aid of a Pisan fleet in 1135, and became the means
of diffusing an acquaintance with that portion of the law
through Italy, is shown by him not only to rest on very
slight evidence, but to be unquestionably, in the latter and
more important circumstance, destitute of all foundation.[s]
It is still indeed an undetermined question whether other

[r] It can be no disparagement to Savigny, who does not claim perfect originality, to say that Muratori, in his
44th dissertation, gives several instances
of quotations from the Pandects in
writers older than the capture of
Amalfi.
[The most decisive proof that Savigny
has adduced for the use of the Pandects
before the twelfth century is from a
work bearing the name of Petrus, called
Exceptiones Legum Romanorum, which
he supposes to have been written at
Valence before the time of Gregory VII.
The Pandects are herein cited so copiously, as to leave no doubt that Peter
was acquainted with the entire collection. In other instances, it might be
doubted whether the quotation implies
more than a partial knowledge. Savigny,
Gesch. Römisch. Rechts, vol. ii. Appendix.—1847.]
[s] Savigny, Geschichte des Römischen
Rechts im Mittelalter, iii. 83.

existing manuscripts of the Pandects are not derived from
this illustrious copy, which alone contains the entire fifty
books, and which has been preserved with a traditional
veneration indicating some superiority; but Savigny has
shown, that Peter of Valence, a jurist of the eleventh century, made use of an independent manuscript; and it is
certain that the Pandects were the subject of legal studies
before the siege of Amalfi.

68. Irnerius, by universal testimony, was the founder of
all learned investigation into the laws of Justinian. Irnerius,—
He gave lectures upon them at Bologna, his native his first successors.
city, not long, in Savigny's opinion, after the commencement
of the century.[t]   And besides this oral instruction, he began
the practice of making glosses, or short marginal explanations, on the law books, with the whole of which he was
acquainted.   We owe also to him, according to ancient
opinion, though much controverted in later times, an
epitome, called the Authentica, of what Gravina calls the
prolix and difficult (salebrosis atque garrulis) Novels of
Justinian, arranged according to the titles of the Code.   The
most eminent sucessors of this restorer of the Roman law
during the same century were Martinus Gosias, Bulgarus,
and Placentinus.   They were, however, but a few among
many interpreters, whose glosses have been partly though
very imperfectly preserved.   The love of equal liberty and
just laws in the Italian cities rendered the profession of
jurisprudence exceedingly honourable; the doctors of Bologna
and other universities were frequently called to the office of
podestà, or criminal judge, in these small republics; in
Bologna itself they were officially members of the smaller
or secret council; and their opinions, which they did not
render gratuitously, were sought with the respect that had
been shown at Rome to their ancient masters of the age of
Severus.

69. A gloss, γλῶσσα, properly meant a word from a
foreign language, or an obsolete or poetical word, Their
or whatever requires interpretation.   It was after- glosses.
wards used for the interpretation itself; and this sense,

---

[t] Vol. iv. p. 16.   Some have erroneously thought Irnerius a German.

which is not strictly classical, may be found in Isidore, though some have imagined Irnerius himself to have first employed it.[u] In the twelfth century it was extended from a single word to an entire expository sentence. The first glosses were interlinear; they were afterwards placed in the margin, and extended finally in some instances to a sort of running commentary on an entire book. These were called an Apparatus.[x]

70. Besides these glosses on obscure passages, some law-yers attempted to abridge the body of the law. Placentinus wrote a summary of the Code and Institutes. But this was held inferior to that of Azo, which appeared before 1220. Hugolinus gave a similar abridgment of the Pandects. About the same time, or a little after, a scholar of Azo, Accursius of Florence, undertook his celebrated work, a collection of the glosses, which, in the century that had elapsed since the time of Irnerius, had grown to an enormous extent, and were of course not always consistent. He has inserted little, probably, of his own, but exercised a judgment, not perhaps a very enlightened one, in the selection of his authorities. Thus was compiled his Corpus Juris Glossatum, commonly called Glossa, or Glossa Ordinaria: a work, says Eichhorn, as remarkable for its barbarous style and gross mistakes in history as for the solidity of its judgments and practical distinctions. Gravina, after extolling the conciseness, acuteness, skill, and diligence in comparing remote passages, and in reconciling apparent inconsistencies, which distinguished Accursius, or rather those from whom he compiled, remarks the injustice of some moderns, who reproach his work with the ignorance inevitable in his age, and seem to think the chance of birth which has thrown them into more enlightened times, a part of their personal merit.[y]

Abridgments of law.

Accursius's Corpus Glossatum.

71. Savigny has taken still higher ground in his admiration, as we may call it, of the early jurists, those from the appearance of Irnerius to the publication of the Accursian body of glosses. For the execution of this

Character of early jurists.

---

[u] Alcuin defines glossa, ' unius verbi vel nominis interpretatio.' Ducange, præfat. in Glossar. p. 38.

[x] Savigny, iii. 519.
[y] Origines Juris, p. 184.

work indeed he testifies no very high respect; Accursius did
not sufficient justice to his predecessors; and many of the
most valuable glosses are still buried in the dust of unpublished manuscripts.[z] But the men themselves deserve our
highest praise. The school of Irnerius rose suddenly; for
in earlier writers we find no intelligent use, or critical interpretation, of the passages which they cite. To reflect upon
every text, to compare it with every clause or word that
might illustrate its meaning in the somewhat chaotic mass
of the Pandects and Code, was reserved for these acute and
diligent investigators. 'Interpretation,' says Savigny, 'was
considered the first and most important object of glossers, as
it was of oral instructors. By an unintermitting use of the
original law-books, they obtained that full and lively acquaintance with their contents, which enabled them to
compare different passages with the utmost acuteness, and
with much success. It may be reckoned a characteristic
merit of many glossers, that they keep the attention always
fixed on the immediate subject of explanation, and, in the
richest display of comparisons with other passages of the
law, never deviate from their point into anything too indefinite and general; superior often in this to the most
learned interpreters of the French and Dutch schools, and
capable of giving a lesson even to ourselves. Nor did the
glossers by any means slight the importance of laying a
sound critical basis for interpretation, but on the contrary laboured earnestly in the recension and correction of
the text.'[a]

72. These warm eulogies afford us an instance, to which
there are many parallels, of such vicissitudes in literary
reputation, that the wheel of fame, like that of fortune,
seems never to be at rest. For a long time, it had been the
fashion to speak in slighting terms of these early jurists;
and the passage above quoted from Gravina is in a much
more candid tone than was usual in his age. Their trifling
verbal explanations of *etsi* by *quamvis*, or *admodum* by *valde;*
their strange ignorance in deriving the name of the Tiber
from the Emperor Tiberius, in supposing that Ulpian and

---

[z] Vol. v. pp. 258–267.   [a] Vol. v. pp. 199–211.

Justinian lived before Christ, in asserting that Papinian was put to death by Mark Antony, and even in interpreting *pontifex* by *papa* or *episcopus*, were the topics of ridicule to those whom Gravina has so well reproved.[b] Savigny, who makes a similar remark, that we learn, without perceiving it and without any personal merit, a multitude of things which it was impossible to know in the twelfth century, defends his favourite glossers in the best manner he can, by laying part of the blame on the bad selection of Accursius, and by extolling the mental vigour which struggled through so many difficulties.[c] Yet he has the candour to own, that this rather enhances the respect due to the men, than the value of their writings; and without much acquaintance with the ancient glossers, one may presume to think, that in explaining the Pandects, a book requiring, beyond any other that has descended to us, an extensive knowledge of the language and antiquities of Rome, their deficiencies, if to be measured by the instances we have given, or by the general character of their age, must require a perpetual exercise of our lenity and patience.

73. This great compilation of Accursius made an epoch Decline of jurists after Accursius. in the annals of jurisprudence. It put an end in great measure to the oral explanations of lecturers which had prevailed before. It restrained at the same time the ingenuity of interpretation. The glossers became the sole authorities, so that it grew into a maxim,—No one can go wrong who follows a gloss; and some said, a gloss was worth a hundred texts.[d] In fact, the original was continually unintelligible to a student. But this was accompanied, according to the distinguished historian of mediæval jurisprudence, by a decline of the science. The jurists in the latter part of the thirteenth century are far inferior to the school of Irnerius. It might be possible to seek a general cause, as men are now always prone to do, in the loss of self-government in many of the Italian republics. But Savigny, superior

[b] Gennari, author of Respublica Jurisconsultorum, a work of the last century, who, under colour of a fiction, gives rather an entertaining account of the principal jurists, exhibits some curious specimens of the ignorance of the Accursian interpreters, such as those in the text. See too the article Accursius in Bayle.

[c] v. 213.

[d] Bayle, ubi supra. Eichhorn, Gesch. der Litteratur, ii. 461. Savigny, v. 268.

great sch

In the fo

decline; t

graduates

jurispruden

alone produ

in France a

great reputa

77. IV. 1

derived from

bian interpr

with the com

perverted him

m In this sligh
lawyers, I have be
the reader will hav
vina and Savigny,
neat and succinct
Gesch. der Litte
The Origines Juris
enjoyed a considerab
Savigny observes
Gravina has thoug
his style than his s
says of the old jurists
less through its emp
criticism. iii. 72. (
toire de la Jurisprud
speaks in still lower t
n It has been a subj
whether the physical
writings of Aristotle
to Europe at the begin
teenth century, throug
or through Arabic tra
former supposition res
what seems good aut
Rigord, a contemporary
the latter is now mor
ceived, and is said to
dissertation which I ha
M. Jourdain. Tennema
l'Hist. de la Philos. i
Arabic translations were
made directly from the G
the Syriac. It is thought
the logic of Aristotle w
Europe sooner.
[The prize essay of Jour
entitled Recherches critiqu
et l'Origine des Traduc
d'Aristote, was republishe
his son. The three poin

---

to this affectation of philosophy, admits that this is neither a cause adequate in itself, nor chronologically parallel to the decline of jurisprudence. We must therefore look upon it as one of those revolutions, so ordinary and so unaccountable, in the history of literature, where, after a period fertile in men of great talents, there ensues, perhaps with no unfavourable change in the diffusion of knowledge, a pause in that natural fecundity, without which all our endeavours to check a retrograde movement of the human mind will be of no avail. The successors of Accursius in the thirteenth century contented themselves with an implicit deference to the glosses; but this is rather a proof of their inferiority than its cause.[e]

74. It has been the peculiar fortune of Accursius, that his name has always stood in a representative capacity to engross the praise or sustain the blame of the great body of glossers from whom he compiled. One of those proofs of national gratitude and veneration was paid to his memory which it is the more pleasing to recount, that, from the fickleness and insensibility of mankind, they do not very frequently occur. The city of Bologna was divided into the factions of Lambertazzi and Gieremei. The former, who were Ghibelins, having been wholly overthrown and excluded, according to the practice of Italian republics, from all civil power, a law was made in 1306, that the family of Accursius, who had been on the vanquished side, should enjoy all the privileges of the victorious Guelf party, in regard to the memory of one 'by whose means the city had been frequented by students, and its fame had been spread through the whole world.'[f] *Respect paid to him at Bologna.*

75. In the next century a new race of lawyers arose, who, by a different species of talent, almost eclipsed the greatest of their predecessors. These have been called the scholastic jurists, the glory of the schoolmen having excited an emulous desire to apply their dialectic methods in jurisprudence.[g] Of these the most conspicuous were Bartolus and Baldus, especially the former, whose authority became *Scholastic jurists. Bartolus.*

e Savigny, v. 320.
f Ib. v. 268.
g The employment of logical forms

in law is not new; instances of it may be found in the earlier jurists. Savigny, v. 330; vi. 6.

still
tolu
did
nora
unles
disti
subje
it wer
do to
code,
numbe
many
subtlet
who c
tolus
origina
tical e
chiefly
with for
between
have no
which ar
prudence

76. Th

with phil
cessors, ar
by which a
of subsidia
with hardl

ʰ Geschichte
Bartolus even sa
jurisconsultus.
thority for thi
whom perhaps I
nenus, Historia
Vergleichung de
seems, however, i
ᶦ Origines Juri
ᵏ Savigny, vi.

their native poetry, much more the glosses of the civil lawyers, are not what is commonly meant by the revival of learning. In this we principally consider the increased study of the Latin and Greek languages, and in general of what we call classical antiquity. In the earliest of the dark ages, as far back as the sixth century, the course of liberal instruction, as has been said above, was divided into the trivium and the quadrivium; the former comprising grammar, logic, and rhetoric; the latter music, arithmetic, geometry, and astronomy. But these sciences, which seem tolerably comprehensive, were in reality taught most superficially or not at all. The Latin grammar, in its merest rudiments, from a little treatise ascribed to Donatus, and extracts of Priscian,° formed the only necessary part of the trivium in ecclesiastical schools. Even this seems to have been introduced afresh by Bede and the writers of the eighth century, who much excel their immediate predecessors in avoiding gross solecisms of grammar.ᵖ It was natural that in England, where Latin had never been a living tongue, it should be taught better than in countries which still affected to speak it. From the time of Charlemagne it was lost on the Continent in common use, and preserved only through glossaries, of which there were many. The style of Latin in the dark period, independently of its want of verbal purity, is in very bad taste; but no writers seem to have been more inflated and empty than the English.�q

the Arabic, the orthography of Greek words is never correct; sometimes an Arabic word is left.

Writers of the thirteenth century mention translations of the philosophical works by Boethius. But as this could not be the great Boethius, Jourdain finds some traces of another bearing the name; or it may have been an error in referring a work to a known author.

The quotations from Aristotle in Albertus Magnus show that some were derived from Greek, some from Arabic. He says in one place, 'Quod autem hæc vera sint quæ dicta sunt, testatur Aristotelis translatio Arabica quæ sic dicit. . . . Græca autem translatio discordat ab hoc, et, ut puto, est mendosa.'—Jourdain, p. 38. By 'Arabica translatio,' he means, of course, a translation from the Arabic.

The translation of Aristotle's Metaphysics, published in 1483, is from the Greek.—1853.]

° Fleury, xvii. 18.   Andrès, ix. 284.

ᵖ Eichhorn, Allg. Gesch. ii. 73. The reader is requested to distinguish, at least if he cares about references, Eichhorn's Allgemeine Geschichte der Cultur, from his Geschichte der Litteratur, with which, in future, we shall have more concern.

q Fleury, xvii. 23. Ducange, preface to Glossary, p. 10. The Anglo-Saxon charters are distinguished for their pompous absurdity; and it is the general character of our early historians. One Ethelwerd is the worst; but William of Malmesbury himself, perhaps in some measure by transcribing passages from others, sins greatly in this respect.

The distinction between the ornaments adapted to poetry and to prose had long been lost, and still more the just sense of moderation in their use. It cannot be wondered at that a vicious rhetoric should have overspread the writings of the ninth and tenth centuries, when there is so much of it in the third and fourth.

78. Eichhorn fixes upon the latter part of the tenth century as an epoch from which we are to deduce, in its beginnings, the restoration of classical taste; it was then that the scholars left the meagre introductions to rhetoric formerly used for the works of Cicero and Quintilian.[r] In the school of Paderborn, not long after 1000, Sallust and Statius, as well as Virgil and Horace, appear to have been read.[s] Several writers, chiefly historical, about this period, such as Lambert of Aschaffenburg, Ditmar, Wittikind, are tolerably exempt from the false taste of preceding times; and if they want a truly classical tone, express themselves with some spirit.[t] Gerbert, who by an uncommon quickness of parts shone in very different provinces of learning, and was beyond question the most accomplished man of the dark ages, displays in his epistles a thorough acquaintance with the best Latin authors and a taste for their excellences.[u] He writes with the feelings of Petrarch, but in a less auspicious period. Even in England, if we may quote again the famous passage of Ingulfus, the rhetorical works of Cicero, as well as some book which he calls Aristotle, were read at Oxford under Edward the Confessor. But we have no indisputable name in the eleventh century, not even that of John de Garlandiâ, whose Floretus long continued to be a text-book in schools. This is a poor collection of extracts from Latin authors. It is uncertain whether or not the compiler were an Englishman.[x]

Improvement in tenth and eleventh centuries.

[r] Allg. Gesch. ii. 79.

[s] Viguit Horatius magnus atque Virgilius, Crispus et Sallustius, et Urbanus Statius, ludusque fuit omnibus insudare versibus et dictaminibus jucundisque cantibus. Vita Meinwerci in Leibnitz Script. Brunsvic. apud Eichhorn, ii. 399.

[t] Eichhorn, Gesch. der Litteratur, i. 807. Heeren, p. 157.

[u] Heeren, p. 165. It appears that Cicero de Republicâ was extant in his time.

[x] Hist. litt. de la France, viii. 84. The authors give very inconclusive reasons for robbing England of this writer, who certainly taught here under William the Conqueror, if not before, but it is possible enough that he came over from France. They say there is no such surname in England as Garland, which

79. It is admitted on all hands that a remarkable im-
Lanfranc and provement both in style and in the knowledge of
his schools. Latin antiquity, was perceptible towards the close
of the eleventh century. The testimony of contemporaries
attributes an extensively beneficial influence to Lanfranc.
This distinguished person, born at Pavia in 1005, and early
known as a scholar in Italy, passed into France about 1042,
to preside over a school at Bec, in Normandy. It became
conspicuous under his care for the studies of the age, dialectics and theology. It is hardly necessary to add that
Lanfranc was raised by the Conqueror to the primacy of
England, and thus belongs to our own history. Anselm, his
successor both in the monastery of Bec and the see of Canterbury, far more renowned than Lanfranc for metaphysical
acuteness, has shared with him the honour of having diffused
a better taste for philological literature over the schools of
France. It has, however, been denied by a writer of high
authority that either any knowledge or any love of classical
literature can be traced in the works of the two archbishops.
They are in this respect, he says, much inferior to those of
Lupus, Gerbert, and others of the preceding ages.[y] His
contemporaries, who extol the learning of Lanfranc in hyperbolical terms, do so in very indifferent Latin of their own;
but it appears indeed more than doubtful whether the
earliest of them meant to praise him for this peculiar species
of literature.[z] The Benedictines of St. Maur cannot find
much to say for him in this respect. They allege that he

---

happens to be a mistake; but the native
English did not often bear surnames in
that age.

[In this note I have been misled by
the Histoire littéraire de la France.
John de Garlandiâ, the grammarian,
author of the Floretus, lived in the
thirteenth century. But there was a
writer on arithmetic, named Garland,
in the reign of William the Conqueror.
See Wright's Biographia Britannica Literaria, vol. ii. p. 16.—1847.]

The Anglo-Saxon clergy were inconceivably ignorant, ut cæteris esset stu-
pori qui grammaticam didicisset. Will.
Malmesbury, p. 101. This leads us
to doubt the Aristotle and Cicero of
Ingulfus.

[y] Heeren, p. 185. There seems certainly nothing above the common in
Lanfranc's epistles.

[z] Milo Crispinus, Abbot of Westminster, in his life of Lanfranc, says of
him, 'Fuit quidam vir magnus Italia
oriundus, quem Latinitas in antiquum
scientiæ statum ab eo restituta tota
supremum debito cum amore et honore
agnoscit magistrum, nomine Lanfrancus.'
This passage, which is frequently
quoted, surely refers to his eminence in
dialectics. The words of William of
Malmesbury go farther. 'Is literatura
perinsignis liberales artes quæ jamdu-
dum sorduerant, a Latio in Gallias
vocans acumine suo expolivit.'

and Anselm wrote better than was then usual—a very moderate compliment; yet they ascribe a great influence to their public lectures, and to the schools which were formed on the model of Bec;[a] and perhaps we could not without injustice deprive Lanfranc of the credit he has obtained for the promotion of polite letters. There is at least sufficient evidence that they had begun to revive in France not long after his time.

80. The signs of gradual improvement in Italy during the eleventh century are very perceptible; several schools, among which those of Milan and the convent of Monte Casino are most eminent, were established; and some writers, such as Peter Damiani and Humbert, have obtained praise for rather more elegance and polish of style than had belonged to their predecessors.[b] The Latin vocabulary of Papias was finished in 1053. This is a compilation from the grammars and glossaries of the sixth and seventh centuries; but though many of his words are of very low Latinity, and his etymologies, which are those of his masters, absurd, he shows both a competent degree of learning and a regard to profane literature, unusual in the darker ages, and symptomatic of a more liberal taste.[c] *Italy— Vocabulary of Papias.*

81. It may be said with some truth, that Italy supplied the fire from which other nations in this first, as afterwards in the second era of the revival of letters, lighted their own torches. Lanfranc, Anselm, Peter Lombard, the founder of systematic theology in the twelfth *Influence of Italy upon Europe.*

---

[a] Hist. litt. de la France, vii. 17, 107; viii. 304. The seventh volume of this long and laborious work begins with an excellent account of the literary condition of France in the eleventh century. At the beginning of the ninth volume we have a similar view of the twelfth.

[b] Bettinelli, Risorgimento d' Italia dopo il mille. Tiraboschi, iii. 248.

[c] The date of the vocabulary of Papias had been placed by Scaliger, who says he has as many errors as words, in the thirteenth century. But Gaspar Barthius, in his Adversaria, c. i., after calling him ' veterum Glossographorum compactor non semper futilis,' observes, that Papias mentions an emperor, Henry II., as then living, and thence fixes the era of his book in the early part of the eleventh century, in which he is followed by Bayle, art. Balbi. It is rather singular that neither of those writers recollected the usage of the Italians to reckon as Henry II., the Prince whom the Germans call Henry III., Henry the Fowler not being included by them in the imperial list; and Bayle himself quotes a writer, unpublished in the age of Barthius, who places Papias in the year 1053. This date, I believe, is given by Papias himself. Tiraboschi, iii. 300. A pretty full account of the Latin glossaries, before and after Papias, will be found in the preface to Ducange, p. 38.

century, Irnerius, the restorer of jurisprudence, Gratian, the
author of the first compilation of canon law, the school of
Salerno, that guided medical art in all countries, the first
dictionaries of the Latin tongue, the first treatise of algebra,
the first great work that makes an epoch in anatomy, are
as truly and exclusively the boast of Italy as the restoration
of Greek literature and of classical taste in the fifteenth
century; [d] but if she were the first to propagate an impulse towards intellectual excellence in the rest of Europe,
it must be owned that France and England, in this dawn
of literature and science, went in many points of view far
beyond her.

82. Three religious orders, all scions from the great
Increased Benedictine stock, that of Clugni, which dates from
copying of
manuscripts. the first part of the tenth century, the Carthusians,
founded in 1084, and the Cistercians in 1098, contributed
to propagate classical learning. [e] The monks of these foundations exercised themselves in copying manuscripts; the
arts of calligraphy, and, not long afterwards, of illumination, became their pride; a more cursive handwriting and
a more convenient system of abbreviations were introduced;
and thus from the twelfth century we find a great increase
of manuscripts, though transcribed mechanically as a monastic duty, and often with much incorrectness. The abbey
of Clugni had a rich library of Greek and Latin authors;
but few monasteries of the Benedictine rule were destitute
of one; it was their pride to collect and their business to
transcribe books. [f] These were, in a vast proportion, such
as we do not highly value at the present day; yet almost
all we do possess of Latin classical literature, with the exception of a small number of more ancient manuscripts, is
owing to the industry of these monks. In that age there
was perhaps less zeal for literature in Italy, and less practice in copying, than in France. [g] This shifting of intellectual exertion from one country to another is not peculiar
to the middle ages; but, in regard to them, it has not

---

[d] Bettinelli, Risorgimento d' Italia,
p. 71.
[e] Fleury. Hist. litt. de la France,
ix. 113.

[f] Fleury. Hist. litt. de la France,
ix. 139.
[g] Heeren, p. 197.

always been heeded by those who, using the trivial metaphor of light and darkness, which it is not easy to avoid, have too much considered Europe as a single point under a receding or advancing illumination.

83. France and England were the countries where the revival of classical taste was chiefly perceived. In Germany no sensible improvement in philological literature can be traced, according to Eichhorn and Heeren, before the invention of printing, though I think this must be understood with exceptions, and that Otho of Frisingen, Saxo Grammaticus, and Gunthor, author of the poem entitled Ligurinus (who belongs to the first years of the thirteenth century), might stand on an equal footing with any of their contemporaries. But in the schools which are supposed to have borrowed light from Lanfranc and Anselm a more keen perception of the beauties of the Latin language, as well as an exacter knowledge of its idiom, was imparted. John of Salisbury, himself one of their most conspicuous ornaments, praises the method of instruction pursued by Bernard of Chartres about the end of the eleventh century, who seems indeed to have exercised his pupils vigorously in the rules of grammar and rhetoric. After the first grammatical instruction out of Donatus and Priscian, they were led forward to the poets, orators, and historians of Rome; the precepts of Cicero and Quintilian were studied, and sometimes observed with affectation.[h] An admiration of the great classical writers, an excessive love of philology, and disdain of the studies that drew men from it, shine out in the two curious treatises of John of Salisbury. He is perpetually citing the poets, especially Horace, and had read most of Cicero. Such, at least, is the opinion of Heeren, who bestows also a good deal of praise upon his Latinity.[i] Eichhorn places him at the head of all his contemporaries. But no one has admired his style so much as Meiners, who declares that he has no equal in the writers of the third, fourth, or fifth centuries,

John of Salisbury.

---

[h] Hist. litt. de la France, vii. 16.
[i] P. 203. Hist. litt. de la France, ix. 47. Peter of Blois also possessed a very respectable stock of classical literature.

except Lactantius and Jerome.[k] In this I cannot but think there is some exaggeration; the style of John of Salisbury, far from being equal to that of Augustin, Eutropius, and a few more of those early ages, does not appear to me by any means elegant; sometimes he falls upon a good expression, but the general tone is not very classical. The reader may judge from the passage in the note.[m]

84. It is generally acknowledged that in the twelfth century we find several writers, Abelard, Eloisa Bernard of Clairvaux, Saxo Grammaticus, William of Malmesbury, Peter of Blois, whose style, though never correct (which, in the absence of all better dictionaries than that of Papias, was impossible), and sometimes affected, sometimes too florid and diffuse, is not wholly destitute of spirit, and even of elegance;[n] the Latin poetry, instead of Leonine rhymes, or attempts at regular hexameters almost equally bad, becomes, in the hands of Gunther, Gualterus de Insulis, Gulielmus Brito, and Joseph Iscanus,

Improvement of classical taste in 12th century.

---

[k] Vergleichung der Sitten, ii. 586. He says nearly as much of Saxo Grammaticus and William of Malmesbury. If my recollection of the former does not deceive me, he is a better writer than our monk of Malmesbury.

[m] One of the most interesting passages in John of Salisbury is that above cited, in which he gives an account of the method of instruction pursued by Bernard of Chartres, whom he calls exundantissimus modernis temporibus fons literarum in Gallia. John himself was taught by some who trod in the steps of this eminent preceptor. Ad hujus magistri formam præceptores mei in grammatica, Gulielmus de Conchis, et Richardus cognomento Episcopus, officio nunc archidiaconus Constantiensis, vita et conversatione vir bonus, suos discipulos aliquando informaverunt. Sed postmodum ex quo opinio veritati præjudicium fecit, et homines videri quam esse philosophi maluerunt, professoresque artium se totam philosophiam brevius quam triennio aut quadriennio transfusuros auditoribus pollicebantur, impetu multitudinis imperitæ victi cesserunt. Exinde autem minus temporis et diligentiæ in grammaticæ studio impensum est. Ex quo contigit ut qui

omnes artes, tam liberales quam mechanicas profitentur, nec primam noverint, sine qua frustra quis progredietur ad reliquas. Licet autem et aliæ disciplinæ ad literaturam proficiant, hæc tamen privilegio singulari facere dicitur literatum. Metalog. lib. i. c. 24.

[n] Hist. litt. de la France, ix. 146. The Benedictines are scarcely fair towards Abelard (xii. 147), whose style, as far as I have seen, which is not much, seems equal to that of his contemporaries.

[The best writers of Latin in England, prose as well as verse, flourished under Henry II. and his sons. William of Malmesbury, who belongs to the reign of Stephen, though not destitute of some skill as well as variety, displays too much of the Anglo-Saxon Latinity, tumid and redundant. But Giraldus Cambrensis and William of Newbury were truly good writers : very few indeed even of the fourth century can be deemed to excel the latter. In verse, John de Hauteville, author of the Architrenius, Nigellus Wireker, and Alexander Neckam, are deserving of praise. Short extracts will be found in Wright. —1847.]

to whom a considerable number of names might be added, always tolerable, sometimes truly spirited;[o] and amidst all that still demands the most liberal indulgence we cannot but perceive the real progress of classical knowledge, and the development of a finer taste in Europe.[p]

85. The vast increase of religious houses in the twelfth century rendered necessary more attention to the rudiments of literature.[q] Every monk, as well as every secular priest, required a certain portion of Latin. In the ruder and darker ages many illiterate persons had been ordained: there were even kingdoms, as, for example, England, where this is said to have been almost general. But the canons of the church demanded of course such a degree of instruction as the continual use of a dead language made indispensable; and in this first dawn of learning there can be, I presume, no doubt that none received the higher orders, or became professed in a monastery for which the order of priesthood was necessary, without some degree of grammatical knowledge. Hence this kind of education in the rudiments of Latin was imparted to a greater number of individuals than at present.

Influence of increased number of clergy.

86. The German writers to whom we principally refer have expatiated upon the decline of literature after the middle of the twelfth century, unexpectedly disappointing the bright promise of that age, so that for almost two hundred years we find Europe fallen back in learning where we might have expected her progress.[r] This, however, is by no means true, in the most limited sense, as to the latter part of the twelfth century, when that purity of classical taste, which Eichhorn and others seem chiefly to have had in their minds, was dis-

Decline of classical literature in 13th century.

---

[o] Warton has done some justice to the Anglo-Latin poets of this century. The Trojan War and Antiocheis of Joseph Iscanus, he calls 'a miracle in this age of classical composition.' The style, he says, is a mixture of Ovid, Statius, and Claudian. Vol. i. p. 163. The extracts Warton gives seem to me a close imitation of the second. The Philippis of William Brito must be of the thirteenth century, and Warton refers the Ligurinus of Gunther to 1206.

[p] Hist. litt. de la France, vol. ix. Eichhorn, All. Gesch. der Cultur, ii. 30, 62. Heeren. Meiners.

[q] Hist. litt. de la France, ix. 11.

[r] Meiners, ii. 605. Heeren, p. 228. Eichhorn, Allg. Gesch. der Litteratur, ii. 63–118.

The running title of Eichhorn's section, Die Wissenschaften verfallen in Barbarey, seems much too generally expressed.

played in better Latin than had been written before. In a general view the thirteenth century was an age of activity and ardour, though not in every respect the best directed. The fertility of the modern languages in versification, the creation, we may almost say, of Italian and English in this period, the great concourse of students to the universities, the acute, and sometimes profound, reasonings of the scholastic philosophy, which was now in its most palmy state, the accumulation of knowledge, whether derived from original research or from Arabian sources of information, which we find in the geometers, the physicians, the natural philosophers of Europe, are sufficient to repel the charge of having fallen back, or even remained altogether stationary, in comparison with the preceding century. But in politeness of Latin style it is admitted that we find an astonishing and permanent decline both in France and England. Such complaints are usual in the most progressive times; and we might not rely on John of Salisbury when he laments the decline of taste in his own age.[s] But, in fact, it would have been rather singular if a classical purity had kept its ground. A stronger party, and one hostile to polite letters, as well as ignorant of them—that of the theologians and dialecticians—carried with it the popular voice in the church and the universities. The time allotted by these to philological literature was curtailed, that the professors of logic and philosophy might detain their pupils longer. Grammar continued to be taught in the university of Paris, but rhetoric, another part of the trivium, was given up; by which it is to be understood, as I conceive, that no classical authors were read, or, if at all, for the sole purpose of verbal explanation.[t] The thirteenth century, says Heeren, was one of the most unfruitful for the study of ancient literature.[u] He does not seem to except Italy, though there, as we shall soon see, the remark is hardly just. But in Germany the tenth century, Leibnitz declares, was a golden age of learning, compared with the thirteenth;[x] and France itself is

---

[s] Metalogicus, l. i. c. 24. This passage has been frequently quoted. He was very inimical to the dialecticians, as philologers generally are.

[t] Crevier, ii. 376.
[u] P. 237.
[x] Introductio in Script. Brunswic. § lxiii., apud Heeren, et Meiners, ii. 631.

but a barren waste in this period.[y] The relaxation of manners among the monastic orders, which, generally speaking, is the increasing theme of complaint from the eleventh century, and the swarms of worse vermin, the mendicant friars, who filled Europe with stupid superstition, are assigned by Meiners and Heeren as the leading causes of the return of ignorance.[z]

87. The writers of the thirteenth century display an incredible ignorance, not only of pure idiom, but of the common grammatical rules. Those who attempted to write verse have lost all prosody, and relapse into Leonine rhymes and barbarous acrostics. The historians use a hybrid jargon intermixed with modern words. The scholastic philosophers wholly neglected their style, and thought it no wrong to enrich the Latin, as in some degree a living language, with terms that seemed to express their meaning. In the writings of Albertus Magnus, of whom Fleury says that he can see nothing great in him but his volumes, the grossest errors of syntax frequently occur, and vie with his ignorance of history and science. Through the sinister example of this man, according to Meiners, the notion that Latin should be written with regard to ancient models was lost in the universities for three hundred years; an evil, however, slight in comparison with what he inflicted on Europe by the credit he gave to astrology, alchemy, and magic.[a] Duns Scotus and his

Relapse into barbarism.

No one has dwelt more fully than this last writer on the decline of literature in the thirteenth century, out of his cordial antipathy to the schoolmen. P. 589 et post.

Wood, who has no prejudices against popery, ascribes the low state of learning in England under Edward III. and Richard II. to the misconduct of the mendicant friars, and to the papal provisions that impoverished the church.

[y] [Abelard, Peter of Blois, and others, might pass for models in comparison with Albertus, Aquinas, and the rest of the writers of the thirteenth century. La décadence est partout sensible; elle est progressive dans les cours des règnes de St. Louis, de Philippe III, et de Philippe IV; et quoique le Français

restât dans l'enfance, la Latinité déjà si vieille avant l'année 1200 vieillissait et dépérissait encore. Hist. litt. de la France, xvi. 145.—1842.]

[z] Meiners, ii. 615. Heeren, 235.

[a] Meiners, ii. 692. Fleury, 5me discours, in Hist. eccles. xvii. 44. Buhle, i. 702. [A far better character of Albertus Magnus is given by Jourdain: 'Albert, considéré comme théologien ou philosophe, est sans doute l'un des hommes les plus extraordinaires de son siècle; je pourrais même dire l'un des génies les plus étonnants des âges passés.' P. 302. His History of Animals 'est un monument précieux, qui, présentant l'état des opinions et des connaissances du moyen âge, remplit une longue lacune, et lie l'ancienne

disciples, in the next century, carried this much farther, and introduced a most barbarous and unintelligible terminology, by which the school metaphysics were rendered ridiculous in the revival of literature.[b] Even the jurists, who more required an accurate knowledge of the language, were hardly less barbarous. Roger Bacon, who is not a good writer, stands at the head in this century.[c] Fortunately, as has been said, the transcribing ancient authors had become a mechanical habit in some monasteries. But it was done in an ignorant and slovenly manner. The manuscripts of these latter ages, before the invention of printing, are by far the most numerous, but they are also the most incorrect, and generally of little value in the eyes of critics.[d]

88. The fourteenth century was not in the slightest No improvement in 14th century. degree superior to the preceding age. France, England, and Germany were wholly destitute of good Latin scholars in this period. The age of Petrarch and Boccaccio, the age before the close of which classical learning truly revived in Italy, gave no sign whatever of animation throughout the rest of Europe; the genius it produced, and in this it was not wholly deficient, displayed itself in other walks of literature.[e] We may justly praise Richard of Bury. Richard of Bury for his zeal in collecting books, and still more for his munificence in giving his library to the university of Oxford, with special injunctions that they should be lent to scholars. But his erudition appears crude and uncritical, his style indifferent, and his thoughts superficial.[f] Yet I am not aware that he had any equal in England during this century.

---

histoire de la science à celle des temps modernes.' P. 325. His original source in this work was Aristotle's History of Animals, in Michael Scot's translation from the Arabic. The knowledge of Greek possessed by Albertus seems to have been rather feeble.—1853.]

  [b] Meiners, ii. 721.

  [c] Heeren, p. 245.

  [d] Id. p. 304.

  [e] Id. p. 300. Andrès, iii. 10.

[f] The Philobiblon of Richard Aungerville, often called Richard of Bury, Chancellor of Edward III., is worthy of being read, as containing some curious illustrations of the state of literature. He quotes a wretched poem de Vetulâ as Ovid's, and shows little learning, though he had a great esteem for it. See a note of Warton, History of English Poetry, i. 146, on Aungerville.

89. The patronage of letters, or collection of books, are not reckoned among the glories of Edward III.; _{Library} though, if any respect had been attached to learn- _{formed by Charles V.} ing in his age and country, they might well have _{at Paris.} suited his magnificent disposition. His adversaries, John, and especially Charles V. of France, have more claims upon the remembrance of a literary historian. Several Latin authors were translated into French by their directions;[g] and Charles, who himself was not ignorant of Latin, began to form the Royal Library of the Louvre. We may judge from this of the condition of literature in his time. The number of volumes was about 900. Many of these, especially the missals and psalters, were richly bound and illuminated. Books of devotion formed the larger portion of the library. The profane authors, except some relating to French history, were in general of little value in our sight. Very few classical works are in the list, and no poets except Ovid and Lucan.[h] This library came, during the subsequent English wars, into the possession of the Duke of Bedford; and Charles VII. laid the foundations of that which still exists.[i]

90. This retrograde condition, however, of classical literature was only perceptible in Cisalpine Europe. _{Some improvement in Italy during 13th century.} By one of those shiftings of literary illumination to which we have alluded, Italy, far lower in classical taste than France in the twelfth century, deserved a higher place in the next. Tiraboschi says that the progress in polite letters was slow, but still some was made; more good books were transcribed, there were more readers, and of these some took on them to imitate what they read; so that gradually the darkness which overspread the land began to be dispersed. Thus we find that those who wrote at the end of the thirteenth century were less rude in style

---

[g] Crevier, ii. 424. Warton has amassed a great deal of information, not always very accurate, upon the subject of early French translations. These form a considerable portion of the literature of that country in the fourteenth and fifteenth centuries. Hist. of English Poetry, ii. 414–430. See also de Sade, Vie de Pétrarque, iii. 548; and Crevier,

Hist. de l'Univ. de Paris, ii. 424.
[h] Warton adds Cicero to the classical list; and I am sorry to say that, in my History of the Middle Ages, I have been led wrong by him. Bouvin, his only authority, expressly says, pas un seul manuscrit de Cicéron. Mém. de l'Acad. des Inscript. ii. 693.
[i] Id. 701.

than their predecessors at its commencement.[k]   A more
elaborate account of the state of learning in the thirteenth
century will be found in the life of Ambrogio Traversari,
by Mehus; and several names are there mentioned, among
whom that of Brunetto Latini is the most celebrated.
Latini translated some of the rhetorical treatises of Cicero.[m]
And we may perhaps consider as a witness to some degree
of progressive learning in Italy at this time the Catholicon
Catholicon   of John Balbi, a Genoese monk, more frequently
of Balbi.   styled Januensis.   This book is chiefly now heard
of because the first edition, printed by Gutenberg in 1460,
is a book of uncommon rarity and price.   It is, however,
deserving of some notice in the annals of literature.   It
consists of a Latin grammar, followed by a dictionary,
both perhaps superior to what we should expect from the
general character of the times.   They are at least copious;
the Catholicon is a volume of great bulk.   Balbi quotes
abundantly from the Latin classics, and appears not wholly
unacquainted with Greek; though I must own that Tiraboschi and Eichhorn have thought otherwise.   The Catholicon, as far as I can judge from a slight inspection of it,
deserves rather more credit than it has in modern times
obtained.   In the grammar, besides a familiarity with the
terminology of the old grammarians, he will be found to
have stated some questions as to the proper use of words,
with *dubitari solet, multum quæritur*; which, though they
are superficial enough, indicate that a certain attention was
beginning to be paid to correctness in writing.   From the
great size of the Catholicon its circulation must have been
very limited.[n]

---

[k] Tiraboschi, iv. 420.   The Latin
versifiers of the thirteenth century
were numerous, but generally very indifferent.   Id. 378.

[m] Mehus, p. 157.   Tiraboschi, p.
418.

[n] Libellum hunc (says Balbi at the
conclusion) ad honorem Dei et gloriosæ
Virginis Mariæ, et beati Domini patris
nostri et omnium sanctorum electorum,
necnon ad utilitatem meam et ecclesiæ
sanctæ Dei, ex diversis majorum meorum
dictis multo labore et diligenti studio
compilavi.   Operis quippe ac studii mei

est et fuit multos libros legere et ex
plurimis diversos carpere flores.

Eichhorn speaks severely, and, I am
disposed to think, unjustly, of the Catholicon, as without order and plan, or
any knowledge of Greek, as the author
himself confesses (Gesch. der Litteratur,
ii. 238).   The order and plan are alphabetical, as usual in a dictionary ; and
though Balbi does not lay claim to much
Greek, I do not think he professes entire
ignorance of it.   Hoc difficile est scire
et minimè mihi non bene scienti linguam
Græcam :—apud Gradenigo, Litteratura

91. In the dictionary, however, of John of Genoa, as in those of Papias and the other glossarists, we find little distinction made between the different grada- tions of Latinity. The Latin tongue was to them, except so far as the ancient grammarians whom they copied might indicate some to be obsolete, a single body of words; and, ecclesiastics as they were, they could not understand that Ambrose and Hilary were to be proscribed in the vocabulary of a language which was chiefly learned for the sake of reading their works. Nor had they the means of pronoun- cing, what it has cost the labour of succeeding centuries to do, that there is no adequate classical authority for innume- rable words and idioms in common use. Their knowledge of syntax also was very limited. The prejudice of the church against profane authors had by no means wholly worn away; much less had they an exclusive possession of the grammar schools, most of the books taught in which were modern. Papias, Uguccio, and other indifferent lexicographers, were of much authority.[o] The general ignorance in Italy was still very great. In the middle of the fourteenth century we read of a man, supposed to be learned, who took Plato and Cicero for poets, and thought Ennius a contemporary of Statius.[p]

Imperfection of early dic- tionaries.

92. The first real restorer of polite letters was Petrarch. His fine taste taught him to relish the beauties of Virgil and Cicero, and his ardent praises of them inspired his compatriots with a desire for classical knowledge. A generous disposition to encourage letters began to show itself among the Italian princes. Robert, king of Naples, in the early part of this century, one of the first patrons of Petrarch, and several of the great families of Lombardy, gave this proof of the humanising effects of peace and prosperity.[q] It has been thought by some, that but for the appearance and influence of Petrarch at that period, the

Restoration of letters due to Petrarch.

Greco-Italiana, p. 104. I have observed that Balbi calls himself *philocalus*, which indeed is no evidence of much Greek erudition.

[o] Mehus. Muratori, Dissert. 44.

[p] Mehus, p. 211. Tiraboschi, v. 82.

[q] Tiraboschi, v. 20, et post. Ten universities were founded in Italy

during the fourteenth century, some of which did not last long. Rome and Fermo in 1303; Perugia in 1307; Tre- viso about 1320; Pisa in 1339; Pavia not long after; Florence in 1348; Siena in 1357; Lucca in 1369; and Ferrara in 1391.

manuscripts themselves would have perished, as several had
done in no long time before; so forgotten and abandoned to
dust and vermin were those precious records in the dungeons
of monasteries.[r] He was the first who brought in that almost
deification of the great ancient writers, which, though carried
in following ages to an absurd extent, was the animating
sentiment of solitary study; that through which its fatigues
were patiently endured, and its obstacles surmounted. Petrarch tells us himself, that while his comrades at school
were reading Æsop's Fables, or a book of one Prosper, a
writer of the fifth century, his time was given to the study
of Cicero, which delighted his ear long before he could understand the sense.[s] It was much at his heart to
acquire a good style in Latin. And, relatively to his
predecessors of the mediæval period, we may say that he was
successful. Passages full of elegance and feeling, in which
we are at least not much offended by incorrectness of style,
are frequent in his writings. But the fastidious scholars of
later times contemned these imperfect endeavours at purity.
'He wants,' says Erasmus, 'full acquaintance with the language, and his whole diction shows the rudeness of the preceding age.'[t] An Italian writer, somewhat earlier, speaks
still more unfavourably. 'His style is harsh, and scarcely
bears the character of Latinity. His writings are indeed
full of thought, but defective in expression, and display the
marks of labour without the polish of elegance.'[u]

Character of his style.

I incline to agree with Meiners in rating the style of
Petrarch rather more highly.[x] Of Boccace the writer above
quoted gives even a worse character. 'Licentious and inaccurate in his diction, he has no idea of selection. All his
Latin writings are hasty, crude, and unformed. He labours
with thought, and struggles to give it utterance; but his

---

[r] Heeren, 270.

[s] Et illa quidem ætate nihil intelligere poteram, sola me verborum dulcedo
quædam et sonoritas detinebat ut quicquid aliud vel legerem vel audirem,
raucum mihi dissonumque videretur.
Epist. Seniles, lib. xv., apud de Sade,
i. 36.

[t] Ciceronianus.

[u] Paulus Cortesius de hominibus doc-

tis. I take the translations from Roscoe's Lorenzo de' Medici, c. vii.

[x] Vergleichung der Sitten, iii. 126.
Meiners has expatiated for fifty pages,
pp. 94–147, on the merits of Petrarch
in the restoration of classical literature;
he seems unable to leave the subject.
Heeren, though less diffuse, is not less
panegyrical. De Sade's three quartos
are certainly a little tedious.

sentiments find no adequate vehicle, and the lustre of his native talents is obscured by the depraved taste of the times.' Yet his own mother-tongue owes its earliest model of grace and refinement to his pen.

93. Petrarch was more proud of his Latin poem called Africa, the subject of which is the termination of the second Punic war, than of the sonnets and odes His Latin poetry. which have made his name immortal, though they were not the chief sources of his immediate renown. It is indeed written with elaborate elegance, and perhaps superior to any preceding specimen of Latin versification in tho middle ages, unless we should think Joseph Iscanus his equal. But it is more to be praised for taste than correctness; and though in the Basle edition of 1554, which I have used, the printer has been excessively negligent, there can be no doubt that the Latin poetry of Petrarch abounds with faults of metre. His eclogues, many of which are covert satires on the court of Avignon, appear to me more poetical than the Africa, and are sometimes very beautifully expressed. The eclogues of Boccaccio, though by no means indifferent, do not equal those of Petrarch.

94. Mehus, whom Tiraboschi avowedly copies, has diligently collected the names, though little more than the names, of Latin teachers at Florence in the fourteenth century.[y] John of Ravenna. But among the earlier of these there was no good method of instruction, no elegance of language. The first who revealed the mysteries of a pure and graceful style was John Malpaghino, commonly called John of Ravenna, one whom in his youth Petrarch had loved as a son, and who not very long before the end of the century taught Latin at Padua and Florence.[z] The best scholars of the ensuing age were his disciples, and among them was Gasparin of Barziza, or, as generally called, of Bergamo, justly Gasparin of Barziza. characterised by Eichhorn as the father of a pure and elegant Latinity.[a] The distinction between the genuine Latin lan-

---

[y] Vita Traversari, p. 348.
[z] A life of John Malpaghino of Ravenna is the first in Meiners' Lebensbeschreibungen berühmter Männer, 3 vols. Zurich, 1795; but it is wholly taken from Petrarch's Letters, and from Mehus's Life of Traversari, p. 348. See also Tiraboschi, v. 554.
[a] Geschichte der Litteratur, ii. 241.

guage and that of the Lower Empire was from this generally
recognised; and the writers who had been regarded as
standards were thrown away with contempt. This is the
proper era of the revival of letters, and nearly coincides with
the beginning of the fifteenth century.

95. A few subjects, affording less extensive observation,
we have postponed to the next chapter, which will contain
the literature of Europe in the first part of the fifteenth
century. Notwithstanding our wish to preserve in general
a strict regard to chronology, it has been impossible to avoid
some interruptions of it without introducing a multiplicity
of transitions incompatible with any comprehensive views;
and which, even as it must inevitably exist in a work of this
nature, is likely to diminish the pleasure, and perhaps the
advantage, that the reader might derive from it.

CHAPTER II.

ON THE LITERATURE OF EUROPE FROM 1400 TO 1440.

Cultivation of Latin in Italy—Revival of Greek Literature—Vestiges of it
during the Middle Ages—It is taught by Chrysoloras—his Disciples—
and by learned Greeks—State of Classical Learning in other Parts of
Europe—Physical Sciences—Mathematics—Medicine and Anatomy—
Poetry in Spain, France, and England—Formation of new Laws of
Taste in Middle Ages — Their Principles — Romances — Religious
Opinions.

1. Ginguéné has well observed, that the fourteenth century
left Italy in the possession of the writings of three
great masters, of a language formed and polished by
them, and of a strong relish for classical learning.
But this soon became the absorbing passion; fortunately,
no doubt, in the result, as the same author has elsewhere
said, since all the exertions of an age were required to explore the rich mine of antiquity, and fix the standard of
taste and purity for succeeding generations. The ardour
for classical studies grew stronger every day. To write
Latin correctly, to understand the allusions of the best
authors, to learn the rudiments at least of Greek, were the
objects of every cultivated mind.

2. The first half of the fifteenth century has been sometimes called the age of Poggio Bracciolini, which
it expresses not very inaccurately as to his literary
life, since he was born in 1381, and died in 1459; but it
seems to involve too high a compliment. The chief merit
of Poggio was his diligence, aided by good fortune, in re-
covering lost works of Roman literature, that lay mouldering
in the repositories of convents. Hence we owe to this one
man eight orations of Cicero, a complete Quintilian, Co-
lumella, part of Lucretius, three books of Valerius Flaccus,
Silius Italicus, Ammianus Marcellinus, Tertullian, and
several less important writers : twelve comedies of Plautus

were also recovered in Germany through his directions.[a]
Poggio, besides this, was undoubtedly a man of considerable learning for his time, and still greater sense and spirit
as a writer, though he never reached a very correct or
elegant style.[b] And this applies to all those who wrote
before the year 1440, with the single exception of Gasparin; to Coluccio Salutato, Guarino of Verona, and even
Leonard Aretin.[c] Nor is this any disparagement to their
abilities and industry. They had neither grammars nor

---

[a] Shepherd's Life of Poggio. Tiraboschi. Corniani. Roscoe's Lorenzo,
ch. 1. Fabricius, in his Bibliotheca
Latina mediæ et infimæ ætatis, gives a
list not quite the same; but Poggio's
own authority must be the best. The
work first above quoted is for the literary history of Italy in the earlier half
of the fifteenth century, what Roscoe's
Lorenzo is for the latter. Ginguéné has
not added much to what these English
authors and Tiraboschi had furnished.

[b] Mr. Shepherd has judged Poggio a
little favourably, as became a biographer, but with sense and discrimination. His Italian translator, Tonelli
(Firenze, 1825), goes much beyond the
mark in extolling Poggio above all his
contemporaries, and praising his ' vastis-
sima erudizione' in the strain of hyperbole too familiar to Italians. This vast
learning, even for that time, Poggio
did not possess: we have no reason to
believe him equal to Guarino, Filelfo, or
Traversari, much less to Valla. Erasmus
however was led by his partiality to
Valla into some injustice towards Poggio, whom he calls rabula adeo indoctus,
ut etiamsi vacaret obscœnitate, tamen
indignus esset qui legeretur, adeo autem
obscœnus, ut etiamsi doctissimus esset,
tamen esset a viris bonis rejiciendus.
Epist. ciii. This is said too hastily;
but in his Ciceronianus, where we have
his deliberate judgment, he appreciates
Poggio more exactly. After one of the
interlocutors has called him vividæ cujusdam eloquentiæ virum, the other
replies:—Naturæ satis erat, artis et
eruditionis non multum ; interim im-
puro sermonis fluxu, si Laurentio Vallæ
credimus. Bebel, a German of some
learning, rather older than Erasmus, in
a letter quoted by Blount (Censura
Auctorum, in Poggio), praises Poggio
very highly for his style, and prefers

him to Valla. Paulus Cortesius seems
not much to differ from Erasmus about
Poggio, though he is more severe on
Valla.

It should be added, that Tonelli's
notes on the life of Poggio are useful;
among other things he points out that
Poggio did not learn Greek of Emanuel
Chrysoloras, as all writers on this part of
literary history had hitherto supposed,
but about 1423, when he was turned of
forty.

[c] Coluccio Salutato belongs to the
fourteenth century, and was deemed
one of its greatest ornaments in learning.
Ma a dir vero, says Tiraboschi, who
admits his extensive erudition, relatively to his age, benchè lo stil di Coluccio abbia non rare volte energia e
forza maggiore che quello della maggior
parte degli altri scrittori di questi tempi,
è certo però, che tanto è diverso da
quello di Cicerone nella prosa, e ne'
versi da quel di Virgilio, quanto appunto
è diversa una scimia da un uomo. v. 537.

Cortesius, in the dialogue quoted
above, says of Leonard Aretin:—Hic
primus inconditam scribendi consuetudinem ad numerosum quendam sonum
inflexit, et attulit hominibus nostris
aliquid certe splendidius. . . . Et ego
video hunc nondum satis esse limatum,
nec delicatiori fastidio tolerabilem.
Atqui dialogi Joannis Ravennatis vix
semel leguntur, et Coluccii Epistolæ,
quæ tum in honore erant, non apparent;
sed Boccaccii Genealogiam legimus, uti-
lem illam quidem, sed non tamen cum
Petrarchæ ingenio conferendam. At
non videtis quantum his omnibus desit ?
p. 82. Of Guarino he says afterwards:
—Genus tamen dicendi inconcinnum
admodum est et salebrosum ; utitur
plerumque imprudens verbis poeticis,
quod est maxime vitiosum ; sed magis
est in eo succus, quam color laudandus.

dictionaries, in which the purest Latinity was distinguishable from the worst; they had to unlearn a bar- Latin style
barous jargon, made up with scraps of the Vulgate indifferent.
and of ecclesiastical writers, which pervades the Latin of
the middle ages; they had great difficulty in resorting
to purer models, from the scarcity and high price of manuscripts, as well as from their general incorrectness, which it
required much attention to set right.   Gasparin of Barziza
took the right course, by incessantly turning over the pages
of Cicero; and thus by long habit gained an instinctive
sense of propriety in the use of language, which no secondary
means at that time could have given him.

3. This writer, often called Gasparin of Bergamo, his own
birthplace being in the neighbourhood of that city, Gasparin of
was born about 1370, and began to teach before Barziza.
the close of the century. He was transferred to Padua by
the senate of Venice in 1407; and in 1410 accepted the
invitation of Filippo Maria Visconti to Milan, where he remained till his death in 1431. Gasparin had here the good
fortune to find Cicero de Oratore, and to restore the text of
Quintilian by the help of the manuscript brought from St.
Gall by Poggio, and another found in Italy by Leonard
Aretin. His fame as a writer was acquired at Padua, and
founded on his diligent study of Cicero.

4. It is impossible to read a page of Gasparin without
perceiving that he is quite of another order of Merits of his
scholars from his predecessors. He is truly style.
Ciceronian in his turn of phrases and structure of sentences,
which never end awkwardly, or with a wrong arrangement
of words, as is habitual with his contemporaries. Inexact
expressions may of course be found, but they do not seem
gross or numerous. Among his works are several orations
which probably were actually delivered : they are the earliest
models of that classical declamation which became so usual
afterwards, and are elegant, if not very forcible. His Epistolæ ad Exercitationem accommodatæ was the first book
printed at Paris. It contains a series of exercises for his

Memoria tenco, quendam familiarem famæ suæ consuluisse, si nihil unquam
meum solitum dicere, melius Guarinum scripsisset. p. 14.

pupils, probably for the sake of double translation, and merely designed to exemplify Latin idioms.[d]

5. If Gasparin was the best writer of this generation, the most accomplished instructor was Victorin of Feltre, to whom the Marquis of Mantua entrusted the education of his own children.

Victorin of Feltre.

Many of the Italian nobility, and some distinguished scholars, were brought up under the care of Victorin in that city; and, in a very corrupt age, he was still more zealous for their moral than their literary improvement. A pleasing account of his method of discipline will be found in Tiraboschi, or more fully in Corniani, from a life written by one of Victorin's pupils named Prendilacqua.[e] 'It could hardly be believed,' says Tiraboschi, 'that in an age of such rude manners a model of such perfect education could be found: if all to whom the care of youth is entrusted would make it theirs, what ample and rich fruits they would derive from their labours!' The learning of Victorin was extensive; he possessed a moderate library, and, rigidly demanding a minute exactness from his pupils in their interpretation of ancient authors, as well as in their own compositions, laid the foundations of a propriety in style which the next age was to display. Traversari visited the school of Victorin, for whom he entertained a great regard, in 1433: it had then been for some years established.[f] No writings of Victorin have been preserved.

6. Among the writers of these forty years, after Gasparin of Bergamo, we may probably assign the highest place in politeness of style to Leonardo Bruni, more commonly called Aretino, from his birthplace, Arezzo. ' He

Leonard Aretin.

---

[d] Morhof, who says, primus in Italia aliquid balbutire cœpit Gasparinus, had probably never seen his writings, which are a great deal better in point of language than his own. Cortesius however blames Gasparin for too elaborate a style; nimia cura attenuabat orationem.

He once uses a Greek word in his letters; what he knew of the language does not otherwise appear; but he might have heard Guarino at Venice. He had not seen Pliny's Natural History,

nor did he possess a Livy, but was in treaty for one. Epist. p. 200, A.D. 1415 .

[e] Tiraboschi, vii. 306. Corniani, ii. 53. Heeren, p. 235. He is also mentioned with much praise for his mode of education, by his friend Ambrogio Traversari, a passage from whose Hodœporicon will be found in Heeren, p. 237. Victorin died in 1447, and was buried at the public expense, his liberality in giving gratuitous instruction to the poor having left him so.

[f] Mehus, p. 421.

was the first,' says Paulus Cortesius, 'who replaced the rude structure of periods by some degree of rhythm, and introduced our countrymen to something more brilliant than they had known before, though even he is not quite as polished as a fastidious delicacy would require.' Aretin's History of the Goths, which, though he is silent on the obligation, is chiefly translated from Procopius, passes for his best work. In the constellation of scholars who enjoyed the sunshine of favour in the palace of Cosmo de' Medici, Leonard Aretin was one of the oldest and most prominent. He died at an advanced age in 1444, and is one of the six illustrious dead who repose in the church of Santa Croce.[g]

7. We come now to a very important event in literary history—the resuscitation of the study of the Greek language in Italy. During the whole course of the middle ages we find scattered instances of scholars in the west of Europe, who had acquired some knowledge of Greek; to what extent it is often a difficult question to determine. In the earlier and darker period we begin with a remarkable circumstance, already mentioned, of our own ecclesiastical history. The infant Anglo-Saxon churches, desirous to give a national form to their hierarchy, solicited the pope Vitalian to place a primate at their head. He made choice of Theodore, who not only brought to England a store of Greek manuscripts, but, through the means of his followers, imparted a knowledge of it to some of our countrymen. Bede, half a century afterwards, tells us, of course very hyperbolically, that there were still surviving disciples of Theodore and Adrian who understood the Greek and Latin languages as well as their own.[h] From these he

Revival of Greek language in Italy.

Early Greek scholars of Europe.

---

[g] Madame de Staël unfortunately confounded this respectable scholar, in her Corinne, with Pietro Aretino. I remember well that Ugo Foscolo could never contain his wrath against her for this mistake.

[h] Hist. Eccles. l. v. c. 2. Usque hodie supersunt ex eorum discipulis, qui Latinam Græcamque linguam æque ac propriam in qua nati sunt, norunt. Bede's own knowledge of Greek is attested by his biographer Cuthbert;

præter Latinam etiam Græcam comparaverat.

[Bede's acquaintance with Greek is attested still better by many proofs which his own works contain. Aldhelm was also a Greek scholar. See Wright's Biograph. Literaria, vol. i. p. 40, 51, 275. But when Mr. W. adds: 'We might bring many passages together which seem *almost* to prove that Homer continued to be read in the schools till the end of the thirteenth century,'

derived, no doubt, his own knowledge, which may not
have been extensive; but we cannot expect more, in such
very unfavourable circumstances, than a superficial progress
in so difficult a study. It is probable that the lessons of
Theodore's disciples were not forgotten in the British and
Irish monasteries. Alcuin has had credit, with no small
likelihood, if not on positive authority, for an acquaintance
with Greek;[1] and as he, and perhaps others from these
islands, were active in aiding the efforts of Charlemagne for
the restoration of letters, the slight tincture of Greek which
we find in the schools founded by that emperor may have
been derived from their instruction. It is, however,
an equally probable hypothesis that it was communicated by Greek teachers, whom it was easy to procure. Charlemagne himself, according to Eginhard, could
read, though he could not speak, the Greek language. Thegan
reports the very same, in nearly the same words, of Louis the
Debonair.[k] The former certainly intended that it should be
taught in some of his schools;[m] and the Benedictines of St.
Maur, in their long and laborious Histoire littéraire de la

Under Charlemagne and his successors.

I must withhold my assent till the passages have been both produced and well
sifted.—1847.]

A manuscript in the British Museum
(Cotton, Galba, i. 18) is of some importance in relation to this, if it be truly
referred to the eighth century. It contains the Lord's Prayer in Greek, written
in Anglo-Saxon characters, and appears
to have belonged to some one of the
name of Athelstan. Mr. Turner (Hist.
of Anglo-Saxons, vol. iii. p. 396) has
taken notice of this manuscript, but
without mentioning its antiquity. The
manner in which the words are divided
shows a perfect ignorance of Greek in
the writer; but the Saxon is curious in
another respect, as it proves the pronunciation of Greek in the eighth century to have been modern or Romaic,
and not what we hold to be ancient.

[1] C'était un homme habile dans le
Grec comme dans le Latin. Hist. litt.
de la France, iv. 8.

[M. Jourdain observes that Thomas
Aquinas understood Greek, and that he
criticises the translations of Aristotle.
Recherches critiques, p. 393. But we

ought not to acquiesce in this general
position without examining the proofs.
I doubt much whether Thomas Aquinas
could read Aristotle in the original.—
1853.]

[k] The passages will be found in Eichhorn, Allg. Gesch. ii. 265 and 290.
That concerning Charlemagne is quoted
in many other books. Eginhard says in
the same place, that Charles prayed in
Latin as readily as in his own language;
and Thegan, that Louis could speak
Latin perfectly.

[m] Osnabrug has generally been named
as the place where Charlemagne peculiarly designed that Greek should be
cultivated. It seems, however, on considering the passage in the Capitularies
usually quoted (Baluze, ii. 419), to have
been only one out of many. Eichhorn
thinks that the existence of a Greek
school at Osnabrug is doubtful, but that
there is more evidence in favour of
Saltzburg and Ratisbon. Allg. Gesch.
der Cultur, ii. 383. The words of the
Capitulary are, Græcas et Latinas Scholas in perpetuum manere ordinavimus.

France, have enumerated as many as seventeen persons within
France, or at least the dominions of the Carlovingian house,
to whom they ascribe, on the authority of contemporaries, a
portion of this learning.[n] These were all educated in the
schools of Charlemagne, except the most eminent in the list,
John Scotus Erigena. It is not necessary by any means to
suppose that he had acquired by travel the Greek tongue,
which he possessed sufficiently to translate, though very indifferently, the works attributed in that age to Dionysius the
Areopagite.[o] Most writers of the ninth century, according
to the Benedictines, make use of some Greek words. It
appears by a letter of the famous Hincmar, archbishop of
Rheims, who censures his nephew Hincmar of Laon for doing
this affectedly, that glossaries, from which they picked those
exotic flowers, were already in use. Such a glossary in Greek
and Latin, compiled under Charles the Bald for the use of
the church of Laon, was, at the date of the publication of
the Histoire littéraire de la France, near the middle of the
last century, in the library of St. Germain des Prés.[p] We
may thus perceive the means of giving the air of more learning than was actually possessed ; and are not to infer from
these sprinklings of Greek in mediæval writings, whether in
their proper characters, or Latinised, which is much more
frequent, that the poets and profane, or even ecclesiastical,
writers were accessible in a French or English monastery.
Neither of the Hincmars seem to have understood the Greek
language ; and Tiraboschi admits that he cannot assert any
Italian writer of the ninth century to be acquainted with it.[q]

8. The tenth century furnishes not quite so many proofs
of Greek scholarship. It was, however, studied _{In the}
by some brethren in the abbey of St. Gall, a cele- _{tenth and eleventh}
brated seat of learning for those times, and the _{centuries.}
library of which, it is said, still bears witness, in its copious

---

[n] Hist. litt. de la France, vol. v.
Launoy had commenced this enumeration in his excellent treatise on the
schools of Charlemagne; but he has not
carried it quite so far. See, too, Eichhorn, Allg. Gesch. ii. 420; and Gesch.
der Litt. i. 824. Meiners thinks that
Greek was better known in the ninth

century, through Charlemagne's exertions, than for five hundred years afterwards, ii. 367.
[o] Eichhorn, ii. 227. Brucker. Guizot.
[p] Hist. litt. de la France, vol. iv.
Ducange, præf. in Glossar. p. 40.
[q] iii. 206.

collection of manuscripts, to the early intercourse between
the scholars of Ireland and those of the Continent. Baldric,
bishop of Utrecht,[r] Bruno of Cologne, and Gerbert, besides
a few more whom the historians of St. Maur record, possessed a tolerable acquaintance with the Greek language.
They mention a fact that throws light on the means by which
it might occasionally be learned. Some natives of that
country, doubtless expatriated Catholics, took refuge in the
diocese of Toul, under the protection of the bishop, not long
before 1000. They formed separate societies, performing
divine service in their own language, and with their own
rites.[s] It is probable, the Benedictines observe, that Humbert, afterwards a cardinal, acquired from them that knowledge of the language by which he distinguished himself in
controversy with their countrymen.[t] This great schism of
the church, which the Latins deeply felt, might induce some
to study a language from which alone they could derive
authorities in disputation with these antagonists. But it
had also the more unequivocal effect of drawing to the west
some of those Greeks who maintained their communion with
the church of Rome. The emigration of these into the
diocese of Toul is not a single fact of the kind, and it is probably recorded from the remarkable circumstance of their
living in community. We find from a passage in Heric, a
prelate in the reign of Charles the Bald, that this had already
begun—at the commencement, in fact, of the great schism.[u]
Greek bishops and Greek monks are mentioned as settlers
in France during the early part of the eleventh century.
This was especially in Normandy, under the protection of
Richard II., who died in 1028. Even monks from Mount
Sinai came to Rouen to share in his liberality.[x] The Benedictines ascribe the preservation of some taste for the Greek
and oriental tongues to these strangers. The list, however,

---

[r] Baldric lived under Henry the
Fowler; his biographer says:—Nullum
fuit studiorum liberalium genus in omni
Græca et Latina eloquentia quod ingenii sui vivacitatem aufugeret. Launoy,
p. 117. Hist. litt. vi. 50.
[s] Hist. litt. vi. p. 57.
[t] Ib. vii. p. 528.
[u] Ducange, præfat. in Glossar. p. 41.

[x] Hist. litt. de la France, vii. 69,
124 et alibi. A Greek manuscript in
the Royal Library at Paris, containing
the Liturgy according to the Greek
ritual, was written in 1022, by a monk
named *Helie* (they do not give the Latin
name), who seems to have lived in Normandy. If this stands for Elias, he
was probably a Greek by birth.

of the learned in them is very short, considering the erudition
of these fathers, and their disposition to make the most of
all they met with. Greek books are mentioned in the few
libraries of which we read in the eleventh century.[y]

9. The number of Greek scholars seems not much more
considerable in the twelfth century, notwithstand- In the
ing the general improvement of that age. The twelfth.
Benedictines reckon about ten names, among which we do
not find that of Bernard.[z] They are inclined also to deny
the pretensions of Abelard;[a] but, as that great man finds a
very hostile tribunal in these fathers, we may pause about
this, especially as they acknowledge Eloise to have understood both the Greek and Hebrew languages. She established a Greek mass for Whitsunday in the Paraclete
convent, which was sung as late as the fifteenth century;
and a Greek missal in Latin characters was still preserved
there.[b] Heeren speaks more favourably of Abelard's learning, who translated passages from Plato.[c] The pretensions
of John of Salisbury are slighter; he seems proud of his
Greek, but betrays gross ignorance in etymology.[d]

10. The thirteenth century was a more inauspicious period
for learning; yet here we can boast, not only of John In the
Basing, archdeacon of St. Alban's, who returned thirteenth.
from Athens about 1240, laden, if we are bound to believe
this literally, with Greek books, but of Roger Bacon and
Robert Grostête, bishop of Lincoln. It is admitted that
Bacon had some acquaintance with Greek; and it appears
by a passage in Matthew Paris that a Greek priest who had

---

[y] Id. p. 48.

[z] Hist. litt. de la France, pp. 94, 151.
Macarius, abbot of St. Fleury, is said to
have compiled a Greek lexicon, which
has been several times printed under
the name of Beatus Benedictus. [It is
one of the glossaries which follow the
Thesaurus of Henry Stephens. Journal
des Savans, May 1829–1842.]

[a] Hist. litt. de la France, xii. 147.
[Mr. Cousin, who has paid more atten-
tion than anyone to the writings of
Abelard, thinks that he was ignorant of
Greek beyond a few words; probably
Eloise had not much surpassed her pre-
ceptor. Fragmens philosophiques, vol.

iv. p. 687, or Introduction aux Œuvres
d'Abélard, in Documens inédits, p. 44.
Abelard only says of her, that she was
Græcæ non expers literaturæ; afterwards, indeed, he uses the words, peri-
tiam adepta.—1847.]

[b] Id. xii. 642.

[c] P. 204. His Greek was no doubt
rather scanty, and not sufficient to give
him an insight into ancient philosophy;
in fact, if his learning had been greater,
he could only read such manuscripts as
fell into his hands; and there were very
few then in France. Vide supra.

[d] Ibid. John derives analytica from
ἀνὰ and λέξις.

obtained a benefice at St. Alban's gave such assistance to
Grostête as enabled him to translate the Testament of the
Twelve Patriarchs into Latin.[e] This is a confirmation of
what has been suggested above as the probable means by
which a knowledge of that language, in the total deficiency
of scholastic education, was occasionally imparted to persons
of unusual zeal for learning. And it leads us to another reflection, that by a knowledge of Greek, when we find it
asserted of a mediæval theologian like Grostête, we are not
to understand an acquaintance with the great classical
authors, who were latent in eastern monasteries, but the power
of reading some petty treatise of the fathers, or, as in this
instance, an apocryphal legend, or at best, perhaps, some of
the later commentators on Aristotle. Grostête was a man of
considerable merit, but has had his share of applause.

11. The titles of mediæval works are not unfrequently
Little ap-
pearance of
it in the 14th
century. taken from the Greek language, as the Polycraticus
and Metalogicus of John of Salisbury, or the Philo-
biblon of Richard Aungerville of Bury. In this
little volume, written about 1343, I have counted five instances of single Greek words. And, what is more important,
Aungerville declares that he had caused Greek and Hebrew
grammars to be drawn up for students.[f] But we have no
other record of such grammars. It would be natural to infer
from this passage that some persons, either in France or
England, were occupied in the study of the Greek language.
And yet we find nothing to corroborate this presumption;
all ancient learning was neglected in the fourteenth century;
nor do I know that one man on this side of the Alps, except
Aungerville himself, is reputed to have been versed in
Greek during that period. I cannot speak positively as to

---

[e] Matt. Par. p. 520. See also Turner's History of England, iv. 180. It is
said in some books that Grostête made
a translation of Suidas. But this is to
be understood merely of a legendary
story found in that writer's lexicon.
Pegge's Life of Grostête, p. 291. The
entire work he certainly could not have
translated, nor is it at all credible that
he had a copy of it. With respect to
the doubt I have hinted in the text as
to the great number of manuscripts said

to be brought to England by John
Basing, it is founded on their subsequent non appearance. We find very
few, if any, Greek manuscripts in England at the end of the fifteenth century.
Michael Scott, 'the wizard of dreaded
fame,' pretended to translate Aristotle;
but is charged with having appropriated
the labours of one Andrew, a Jew, as his
own. Meiners, ii. 664.
[f] C. x.

Berchœur, the most learned man in France. The council of
Vienne, indeed, in 1311 had ordered the establishment of
professors in the Greek, Hebrew, Chaldaic, and Arabic
languages, at Avignon, and in the universities of Paris,
Oxford, Bologna, and Salamanca. But this decree remained
a dead letter.

12. If we now turn to Italy, we shall find, as is not wonderful, rather more frequent instances of acquaint- Some traces
ance with a living language in common use with of Greek in Italy.
a great neighbouring people. Gradenigo, in an essay on
this subject,[g] has endeavoured to refute what he supposes to be the universal opinion, that the Greek tongue
was first taught in Italy by Chrysoloras and Guarino at
the end of the fourteenth century; contending that, from
the eleventh inclusive, there are numerous instances of
persons conversant with it; besides the evidence afforded
by inscriptions in Greek characters found in some churches,
by the use of Greek psalters and other liturgical offices,
by the employment of Greek painters in churches, and by
the frequent intercourse between the two countries. The
latter presumptions have in fact considerable weight; and
those who should contend for an absolute ignorance of
the Greek language, oral as well as written, in Italy, would
go too far. The particular instances brought forward by
Gradenigo are about thirty. Of these the first is Papias,
who has quoted five lines of Hesiod.[h] Lanfranc had also a
considerable acquaintance with the language.[i] Peter Lombard, in his Liber Sententiarum, the systematic basis of scholastic theology, introduces many Greek words, and explains
them rightly.[k] But this list is not very long; and when we
find the surname Bifarius given to one Ambrose of Bergamo
in the eleventh century, on account of his capacity of speaking both languages, it may be conceived that the accomplish-
ment was somewhat rare. Mehus, in his very learned life of
Traversari, has mentioned two or three names, among whom

---

[g] Ragionamento istorico-critico sopra
la Litteratura Greco-Italiana. Brescia,
1759.

[h] P. 37. These are very corruptly
given, through the fault of a transcriber;

for Papias has translated them into
tolerable Latin verse.

[i] Hist. litt. de la France, vii. 144.

[k] Meiners, iii. 11.

is the emperor Frederic II. (not indeed strictly an Italian),
that do not appear in Gradenigo.[m] But Tiraboschi conceives,
on the other hand, that the latter has inserted some on insufficient grounds. Christine of Pisa is mentioned, I think,
by neither; she was the daughter of an Italian astronomer,
but lived at the court of Charles V. of France, and was the
most accomplished literary lady of that age.[n]

13. The intercourse between Greece and the west of

Corruption of Greek language itself.

Europe, occasioned by commerce and by the crusades, had little or no influence upon literature.
For, besides the general indifference to it in those
classes of society which were thus brought into some degree
of contact with the Eastern Empire, we must remember that,
although Greek, even to the capture of Constantinople by
Mahomet II., was a living language in that city, spoken by
the superior ranks of both sexes with tolerable purity, it
had degenerated among the common people, and almost
universally among the inhabitants of the provinces and
islands, into that corrupt form, or rather new language,
which we call Romaic.[o] The progress of this innovation
went on by steps very similar to those by which the Latin
was transformed in the West, though it was not so rapid or
complete. A manuscript of the twelfth century, quoted by
Du Cange from the Royal Library at Paris, appears to be the
oldest written specimen of the modern Greek that has been
produced; but the oral change had been gradually going
forward for several preceding centuries.[p]

---

[m] Pp. 155, 217, &c. Add to these
authorities, Muratori, dissert. 44; Brucker, iii. 644, 647; Tiraboschi, v. 393.

[n] Tiraboschi, v. 388, vouches for
Christine's knowledge of Greek. She
was a good poetess in French, and altogether a very remarkable person.

[o] Filelfo says, in one of his epistles,
dated 1441, that the language spoken in
Peloponnesus 'adeo est depravata, ut
nihil omnino sapiat priscæ illius et elo-
quentissimæ Græciæ.' At Constantinople the case was better; 'viri eruditi
sunt nonnulli, et culti mores, et sermo
etiam nitidus.' In a letter of Coluccio
Salutato, near the end of the fourteenth
century, he says that Plutarch had been
translated de Græco in Græcum vulgare.

Mehus, p. 294. This seems to have
been done at Rhodes. I quote this to
remove any difficulty that others may
feel, for I believe the Romaic Greek is
much older. The progress of corruption
in Greek is sketched in the Quarterly
Review, vol. xxii., probably by the pen
of the Bishop of London. Its symptoms
were very similar to those of Latin in
the West; abbreviation of words, and
indifference to right inflections. See
also Col. Leake's Researches in the
Morea. Eustathius has many Romaic
words; yet no one in the twelfth century
had more learning.

[p] Du Cange, præfatio in Glossarium
mediæ et infimæ Græcitatis.

14. The Byzantine literature was chiefly valuable by illustrating, or preserving in fragments, the his- Character of torians, philosophers, and, in some measure, the literature. poets of antiquity. Constantinople and her empire produced abundantly men of erudition, but few of genius or of taste. But this erudition was now rapidly on the decline. No one was left in Greece, according to Petrarch, after the death of Leontius Pilatus, who understood Homer; words not, perhaps, to be literally taken, but expressive of what he conceived to be their general indifference to the poet: and it seems very probable that some ancient authors, whom we should most desire to recover, especially the lyric poets of the Doric and Æolic dialects, have perished, because they had become unintelligible to the transcribers of the Lower Empire; though this has also been ascribed to the scrupulousness of the clergy. An absorbing fondness for theological subtilties, far more trifling among the Greeks than in the schools of the West, conspired to produce a neglect of studies so remote as heathen poetry. Aurispa tells Ambrogio Traversari that he found they cared little about profane literature. Nor had the Greek learning ever recovered the blow that the capture of Constantinople by the crusaders in 1204, and the establishment for sixty years of a Latin and illiterate dynasty, inflicted upon it.[q] We trace many classical authors to that period, of whom we know nothing later, and the compilations of ancient history by industrious Byzantines came to an end. Meantime the language, where best preserved, had long lost the delicacy and precision of its syntax; the true meaning of the tenses, moods, and voices of the verb was overlooked or guessed at; a kind of Latinism, or something at least not ancient in structure and rhythm, shows itself in their poetry; and this imperfect knowledge of their once beautiful language is unfortunately too manifest in the grammars of the Greek exiles of the fifteenth century, which have so long been the groundwork of classical education in Europe.

---

[q] An enumeration, and it is a long one, of the Greek books not wholly lost till this time will be found in Heeren, p. 125; and also in his Essai sur les Croisades.

15. We now come to the proper period of the restoration
of Greek learning. In the year 1339, Barlaam, a
Calabrian by birth, but long resident in Greece, and
deemed one of the most learned men of that age, was entrusted by the emperor Cantacuzenus with a mission to
Italy.[r] Petrarch, in 1342, as Tiraboschi fixes the time, endeavoured to learn Greek from him, but found the task too
arduous, or rather had not sufficient opportunity to go on
with it.[s] Boccaccio, some years afterwards, succeeded better
with the help of Leontius Pilatus, a Calabrian also by birth,[t]
who made a prose translation of Homer for his use, and for
whom he is said to have procured a public appointment as
teacher of the Greek language at Florence in 1361. He
remained here about three years ; but we read nothing of
any other disciples ; and the man himself was of too unsocial
and forbidding a temper to conciliate them.[u]

Petrarch and Boccace learn Greek.

16. According to a passage in one of Petrarch's letters,
fancifully addressed to Homer, there were at that
time not above ten persons in Italy who knew how
to value the old father of the poets; five at the
most in Florence, one in Bologna, two in Verona, one in
Mantua, one in Perugia, but none at Rome.[x] Some pains
have been thrown away in attempting to retrieve the names
of those to whom he alludes : the letter shows, at least, that
there was very little pretension to Greek learning in his age;
for I am not convinced that he meant all these ten persons,
among whom he seems to reckon himself, to be considered
as skilled in that tongue. And we must not be led away by

Few acquainted with the language in their time.

---

[r] Mehus. Tiraboschi, v. 398. De Sade, i. 406. Biog. univ. : Barlaam.

[s] Incubueram alacri spe magnoque desiderio, sed peregrinæ linguæ novitas et festina præceptoris absentia præcide-runt propositum meum. It has been said, and probably with some truth, that Greek, or at least a sort of Greek, was preserved as a living language in Calabria ; not because Greek colonies had once been settled in some cities, but because that part of Italy was not lost to the Byzantine empire till about three centuries before the time of Barlaam and Pilatus. They, however, had gone to a better source ; and I should have great doubts as to the goodness of Ca-

labrian Greek in the fourteenth century, which of course are not removed by the circumstance that in some places the church service was performed in that language. Heeren, I find, is of the same opinion. p. 287.

[t] Many have taken Pilatus for a native of Thessalonica : even Hody has fallen into this mistake, but Petrarch's letters show the contrary.

[u] Hody de Græcis illustribus, p. 2. Mehus, p. 273. De Sade, iii. 625. Gibbon has erroneously supposed this translation to have been made by Boccace himself.

[x] De Sade, iii. 627. Tiraboschi, v. 371, 400. Heeren, 294.

the instances partially collected by Gradenigo out of the whole mass of extant records, to lose sight of the great general fact that Greek literature was lost in Italy for seven hundred years, in the words of Leonard Aretin, before the arrival of Chrysoloras. The language is one thing, and the learning contained in it is another. For all the purposes of taste and erudition there was no Greek in western Europe during the middle ages; if we look only at the knowledge of bare words, we have seen there was a very slender portion.

17. The true epoch of the revival of Greek literature in Italy, these attempts of Petrarch and Boccace having produced no immediate effect, though they evidently must have excited a desire for learning, cannot be placed before the year 1395,[y] when Emanuel Chrysoloras, previously known as an ambassador from Constantinople to the western powers, in order to solicit assistance against the Turks, was induced to return to Florence as public teacher of Greek. He passed from thence to various Italian universities, and became the preceptor of several early Hellenists.[z] The first, and perhaps the most eminent and useful of these, was Guarino Guarini of Verona, born in 1370. He acquired his knowledge of Greek under Chrysoloras at Constantinople, before the arrival of the latter in Italy. Guarino, upon his return, became

It is taught by Chryso- loras about 1395.

His disciples.

---

[y] This is the date fixed by Tiraboschi; others refer it to 1391, 1396, 1397, or 1399.

[z] Literæ per hujus belli intercapedines mirabile quantum per Italiam increvere; accedente tunc primum cognitione litera- rum Græcarum, quæ septingentis jam annis apud nostros homines desierant esse in usu. Retulit autem Græcam disciplinam ad nos Chrysoloras, Byzan- tinus, vir domi nobilis ac literarum Græ- carum peritissimus. Leonard Aretin apud Hody, p. 28. See also an extract from Manetti's Life of Boccace, in Hody, p. 61.

Satis constat Chrysoloram Byzantinum transmarinam illam disciplinam in Ita- liam advexisse; quo doctore adhibito primum nostri homines totius exercita- tiones atque artis ignari, cognitis Græcis literis, vehementer sese ad eloquentiæ studia excitaverunt. P. Cortesius de hominibus doctis, p. 6.

The first visit of Chrysoloras had pro- duced an inclination towards the study of Greek. Coluccio Salutato, in a letter to Demetrius Cydonius, who had accom- panied Chrysoloras, says, Multorum ani- mos ad linguam Helladum accendisti, ut jam videre videar multos fore Græcarum literarum post paucorum annorum cur- ricula non tepide studiosos. Mehus, p. 356.

The Erotemata of Chrysoloras, an in- troduction to Greek grammar, was the first, and long the only, channel to a knowledge of that language, save oral instruction. It was several times printed, even after the grammars of Gaza and Lascaris had come more into use. An abridgment by Guarino of Verona, with some additions of his own, was printed at Ferrara in 1509. Gin- guéné, iii. 283.

professor of rhetoric, first at Venice and other cities of
Lombardy, then at Florence, and ultimately at Ferrara,
where he closed a long life of unremitting and useful labour
in 1460. John Aurispa of Sicily came to the field rather
later, but his labours were not less profitable. He brought
back to Italy 238 manuscripts from Greece about 1423, and
thus put his country in possession of authors hardly known
to her by name. Among these were Plato, Plotinus, Diodorus,
Arrian, Dio Cassius, Strabo, Pindar, Callimachus, Appian.
After teaching Greek at Bologna and Florence, Aurispa also
ended a length of days under the patronage of the house of
Este, at Ferrara. To these may be added, in the list of
public instructors in Greek before 1440, Filelfo, a man still
more known by his virulent disputes with his contemporaries
than by his learning; who, returning from Greece in 1427,
laden with manuscripts, was not long afterwards appointed
to the chair of rhetoric, that is, of Latin and Greek philology,
at Florence; and, according to his own account, excited the
admiration of the whole city.[a] But his vanity was excessive, and his contempt of others not less so. Poggio was one
of his enemies; and their language towards each other is a
noble specimen of the decency with which literary and
personal quarrels were carried on.[b] It has been observed
that Gianozzo Manetti, a contemporary scholar, is less
known than others, chiefly because the mildness of his
character spared him the altercations to which they owe a
part of their celebrity.[c]

---

[a] Universa in me civitas conversa est;
omnes me diligunt, honorant omnes, ac
summis laudibus in cœlum efferunt.
Meum nomen in ore est omnibus. Nec
primarii cives modo, cum per urbem in-
cedo, sed nobilissimæ fœminæ honorandi
mei gratiâ loco cedunt, tantumque mihi
deferunt, ut me pudeat tanti cultûs.
Auditores sunt quotidie ad quadringen-
tos, vel fortassis et amplius; et hi quidem magna in parte viri grandiores et
ex ordine senatorio.   Phileph. Epist.
ad ann. 1428.

[b] Shepherd's Life of Poggio, ch. vi.
and viii.

[c] Hody was perhaps the first who
threw much light on the early studies
of Greek in Italy; and his book, De

Græcis illustribus, linguæ Græcæ in-
stauratoribus, will be read with pleasure and advantage by every lover of
literature; though Mehus, who came
with more exuberant erudition to the
subject, has pointed out a few errors.
But more is to be found as to its native
cultivators, Hody being chiefly concerned with the Greek refugees, in
Bayle, Fabricius, Niceron, Mehus, Zeno,
Tiraboschi, Meiners, Roscoe, Heeren,
Shepherd, Corniani, Ginguéné, and the
Biographie universelle, whom I name
in chronological order.

As it is impossible to dwell on the
subject within the limits of these pages,
I will refer the reader to the most useful of the above writings, some of

18. Many of these cultivators of the Greek language devoted their leisure to translating the manuscripts Translations from Greek into Latin. brought into Italy. The earliest of these was Peter Paul Vergerio (commonly called the elder, to distinguish him from a more celebrated man of the same names in the sixteenth century), a scholar of Chrysoloras, but not till he was rather advanced in years. He made, by order of the emperor Sigismund, and therefore not earlier than 1410, a translation of Arrian, which is said to exist in the Vatican library; but we know little of its merits.[d]　A more renowned person was Ambrogio Traversari, a Florentine monk of the order of Camaldoli, who employed many years in this useful labour. No one of that age has left a more respectable name for private worth : his epistles breathe a spirit of virtue, of kindness to his friends, and of zeal for learning. In the opinion of his contemporaries he was placed, not quite justly, on a level with Leonard Aretin for his knowledge of Latin, and he surpassed him in Greek.[e]　Yet neither his translations, nor those of his contemporaries, Guarino of Verona, Poggio, Leonardo Aretino, Filelfo, who, with several others, rather before 1440, or not long afterwards, rendered the historians and philosophers of Greece familiar to Italy, can be extolled as correct, or as displaying what is truly to be called a knowledge of either language. Vossius, Casaubon, and Huet speak with much dispraise of most of these early translations from Greek into Latin. The Italians knew not

which, being merely biographical collections, do not give the connected information he would require. The lives of Poggio and of Lorenzo de' Medici will make him familiar with the literary history of Italy for the whole fifteenth century, in combination with public events, as it is best learned. I need not say that Tiraboschi is a source of vast knowledge to those who can encounter two quarto volumes. Ginguéné's third volume is chiefly borrowed from these, and may be read with great advantage. Finally, a clear, full, and accurate account of those times will be found in Heeren. It will be understood that all these works relate to the revival of Latin as well as Greek.

[d] Biogr. univ. : Vergerio. He seems to have written very good Latin, if we

may judge by the extracts in Corniani, ii. 61.

[e] The Hodœporicon of Traversari, though not of importance as a literary work, serves to prove, according to Bayle (Camaldoli, note D), that the author was an honest man, and that he lived in a very corrupt age. It is an account of the visitation of some convents belonging to his order. The life of Ambrogio Traversari has been written by Mehus very copiously, and with abundant knowledge of the times : it is a great source of the literary history of Italy. There is a pretty good account of him in Niceron, vol. xix., and a short one in Roscoe ; but the fullest biography of the man himself will be found in Meiners, Lebensbeschreibungen berühmter Männer, vol. ii. pp. 222–307.

enough of the original, and the Greeks were not masters
enough of Latin. Gaza, upon the whole, ' than whom no
one is more successful,' says Erasmus, ' whether he renders
Greek into Latin, or Latin into Greek,' is reckoned the most
elegant, and Argyropulus the most exact. But George of
Trebizond, Filelfo, Leonard Aretin, Poggio, Valla, Perotti,
are rather severely dealt with by the sharp critics of later
times.[f] For this reproach does not fall only on the scholars
of the first generation, but on their successors, except
Politian, down nearly to the close of the fifteenth century.
Yet, though it is necessary to point out the deficiencies of
classical erudition at this time, lest the reader should hastily
conclude that the praises bestowed upon it are less relative
to the previous state of ignorance, and the difficulties with
which that generation had to labour, than they really are,
this cannot affect our admiration and gratitude towards men
who, by their diligence and ardour in acquiring and communicating knowledge, excited that thirst for improvement,
and laid those foundations of it, which rendered the ensuing
age so glorious in the annals of literature.

19. They did not uniformly find any great public en-
Public en-   couragement in the early stages of their teaching.
couragement
delayed.   On the contrary, Aurispa met with some opposition
to philological literature at Bologna.[g] The civilians and
philosophers were pleased to treat the innovators as men who
wanted to set showy against solid learning. Nor was the
state of Italy and of the papacy during the long schism very
favourable to their object. Ginguéné remarks that patronage
was more indispensable in the fifteenth century than it had
been in the last. Dante and Petrarch shone out by a

---

[f] Baillet, Jugemens des Savans, ii.
376, &c. Blount, Censura Auctorum, in
nominibus nuncupatis. Hody, sæpies.
Niceron, vol. ix. in Perotti. See also a
letter of Erasmus in Jortin's Life, ii. 425.
Filelfo tells us of a perplexity into
which Ambrogio Traversari and Carlo
Marsupini, perhaps the two principal
Greek scholars in Italy after himself and
Guarino, were thrown by this line or
Homer :—

Βούλομ' ἐγὼ λαὸν σόον ἔμμεναι, ἢ ἀπόλεσθαι·

The first thought it meant populum

aut salvum esse aut perire; which
Filelfo justly calls, inepta interpretatio
et prava. Marsupini said ἢ ἀπόλεσθαι
was, aut ipsum perire. Filelfo, after ex-
ulting over them, gives the true meaning. Phileph. Epist. ad ann. 1440.
Traversari complains much, in one of
his letters, of the difficulty he found
in translating Diogenes Laertius, lib.
vii. epist. ii. ; but Meiners, though admitting many errors, thinks this one of
the best among the early translations,
ii. 290.

[g] Tiraboschi, vii. 301.

paramount force of genius; but the men of learning required the encouragement of power in order to excite and sustain their industry.

20. That encouragement, however it may have been delayed, had been accorded before the year 1440. But fully accorded before Eugenius IV. was the first pope who displayed an 1440. inclination to favour the learned. They found a still more liberal patron in Alfonso, king of Naples, who, first of all European princes, established the interchange of praise and pension, both, however, well deserved, with Filelfo, Poggio, Valla, Beccatelli, and other eminent men. This seems to have begun before 1440, though it was more conspicuous afterwards until his death in 1458. The earliest literary academy was established at Naples by Alfonso, of which Antonio Beccatelli, more often called Panormita from his birthplace, was the first president, as Pontano was the second. Nicolas of Este, marquis of Ferrara, received literary men in his hospitable court. But none were so celebrated or useful in this patronage of letters as Cosmo de' Medici, the Pericles of Florence, who, at the period with which we are now concerned, was surrounded by Traversari, Niccolo Niccoli, Leonardo Aretino, Poggio ; all ardent to retrieve the treasures of Greek and Roman learning. Filelfo alone, malignant and irascible, stood aloof from the Medicean party, and poured his venom in libels on Cosmo and the chief of his learned associates. Niccoli, a wealthy citizen of Florence, deserves to be remembered among these; not for his writings, since he left none ; but on account of his care for the good instruction of youth, which has made Meiners call him the Florentine Socrates, and for his liberality as well as diligence in collecting books and monuments of antiquity. The public library of St. Mark was founded on a bequest by Niccoli, in 1437, of his own collection of eight hundred manuscripts. It was, too, at his instigation, and that of Traversari, that Cosmo himself, about this time, laid the foundation of that which, under his grandson, acquired the name of the Laurentian library.[h]

---

[h] I refer to the same authorities, but especially to the life of Traversari in Meiners, Lebensbeschreibungen, ii. 294. The suffrages of older authors are collected by Baillet and Blount.

21. As the dangers of the eastern empire grew more
Emigration of learned Greeks to Italy. imminent, a few that had still endeavoured to preserve in Greece the purity of their language, and the speculations of ancient philosophy, turned their eyes towards a haven that seemed to solicit the glory of protecting them. The first of these that is well known was Theodore Gaza, who fled from his birthplace, Thessalonica, when it fell under the Turkish yoke in 1430. He rapidly acquired the Latin language by the help of Victorin of Feltre.[1] Gaza became afterwards, but not, perhaps, within the period to which this chapter is limited, rector of the university of Ferrara. In this city Eugenius IV. held a council in 1438, removed next year, on account of sickness, to Florence, in order to reconcile the Greek and Latin churches. Though it is notorious that the appearances of success which attended this hard bargain of the strong with the weak were very fallacious, the presence of several Greeks, skilled in their own language, and even in their ancient philosophy, Pletho, Bessarion, Gaza, stimulated the noble love of truth and science that burned in the bosoms of enlightened Italians. Thus, in 1440, the spirit of ancient learning was already diffused on that side the Alps: the Greek language might be learned in at least four or five cities, and an acquaintance with it was a recommendation to the favour of the great; while the establishment of universities at Pavia, Turin, Ferrara, and Florence, since the beginning of the present century, or near the close of the last, bore witness to the generous emulation which they served to redouble and concentrate.

22. It is an interesting question, What were the causes
Causes of enthusiasm for antiquity in Italy. of this enthusiasm for antiquity which we find in the beginning of the fifteenth century?—a burst of public feeling that seems rather sudden, but prepared by several circumstances that lie farther back in Italian history. The Italians had for some generations learned more to identify themselves with the great people that had subdued the world. The fall of the house of

---

[1] Victorin perhaps exchanged instruction with his pupil; for we find by a letter of Traversari (p. 421, edit. Me- hus), that he was himself teaching Greek in 1433.

Swabia, releasing their necks from a foreign yoke, had
given them a prouder sense of nationality; while the name
of Roman emperor was systematically associated by one
party with ancient tradition; and the study of the civil law,
barbarously ignorant as its professors often were, had at
least the effect of keeping alive a mysterious veneration for
antiquity. The monuments of ancient Italy were perpetual
witnesses; their inscriptions were read; it was enough that
a few men like Petrarch should animate the rest; it was
enough that learning should become honourable, and that
there should be the means of acquiring it. The story of
Rienzi, familiar to every one, is a proof what enthusiasm
could be kindled by ancient recollections. Meantime the
laity became better instructed; a mixed race, ecclesiastics,
but not priests, and capable alike of enjoying the benefices,
of the church, or of returning from it to the world, were
more prone to literary than theological pursuits. The
religious scruples which had restrained churchmen, in the
darker ages, from perusing heathen writers, by degrees gave
way, as the spirit of religion itself grew more objective, and
directed itself more towards maintaining the outward church
in its orthodoxy of profession, and in its secular power, than
towards cultivating devout sentiments in the bosom.

23. The principal Italian cities became more wealthy
and more luxurious after the middle of the thir- Advanced
teenth century. Books, though still very dear, society.
comparatively with the present value of money, were much
less so than in other parts of Europe.[k] In Milan, about
1300, there were fifty persons who lived by copying them.
At Bologna, it was also a regular occupation at fixed prices.[m]

---

[k] Savigny thinks the price of books
in the middle ages has been much exaggerated; and that we are apt to judge
by a few instances of splendid volumes,
which give us no more notion of ordinary prices than similar proofs of luxury
in collectors do at present. Thousands
of manuscripts are extant, and the sight
of most of them may convince us that
they were written at no extraordinary
cost. He then gives a long list of law-
books, the prices of which he has found
recorded. Gesch. des Römischen Rechts,
iii. 549. But unless this were accompanied with a better standard of value

than a mere monetary one, which last
Savigny has given very minutely, it can
afford little information. The impression left on my mind, without comparing
these prices closely with those of other
commodities, was that books were
in real value very considerably dearer
(that is, in the ratio of several units to
one) than at present, which is confirmed
by many other evidences.

[m] Tiraboschi, iv. 72–80. The price
for copying a Bible was eighty Bolognese
livres; three of which were equal to two
gold florins.

In this state of social prosperity, the keen relish of Italy
for intellectual excellence had time to develop itself. A
style of painting appeared in the works of Giotto and his
followers, rude and imperfect, according to the skilfulness of
later times, but in itself pure, noble, and expressive, and
well adapted to reclaim the taste from the extravagance of
romance to classic simplicity. Those were ready for the
love of Virgil, who had formed their sense of beauty by the
figures of Giotto and the language of Dante. The subject
of Dante is truly mediæval; but his style, the clothing of
poetry, bears the strongest marks of his acquaintance with
antiquity. The influence of Petrarch was far more direct,
and has already been pointed out.

24. The love of Greek and Latin absorbed the minds of
Exclusive   Italian scholars, and effaced all regard to every
study of
antiquity.   other branch of literature. Their own language
was nearly silent; few condescended so much as to write
letters in it; as few gave a moment's attention to physical
science, though we find it mentioned, perhaps as remarkable,
in Victorin of Feltre, that he had some fondness for geometry, and had learned to understand Euclid.[n] But even in
Latin they wrote very little that can be deemed worthy of
remembrance, or even that can be mentioned at all. The
ethical dialogues of Francis Barbaro, a noble Venetian, on
the married life (de re uxoria),[o] and of Poggio on nobility,
are almost the only books that fall within this period
except declamatory invectives or panegyrics, and other productions of circumstance. Their knowledge was not yet
exact enough to let them venture upon critical philology;
though Niccoli and Traversari were silently occupied in the
useful task of correcting the texts of manuscripts, faulty
beyond description in the later centuries. Thus we must
consider Italy as still at school, active, acute, sanguine, full

---

[n] Meiners, Lebensbesch. ii. 293.

[o] Barbaro was a scholar of Gasparin
in Latin. He had probably learned
Greek of Guarino, for it is said that, on
the visit of the emperor John Paleologus
to Italy in 1423, he was addressed by
two noble Venetians, Leonardo Giustiniani and Francesco Barbaro, in as good
language as if they had been born in
Greece. Andrès, iii. 33. The treatise

de re uxoria, which was published about
1417, made a considerable impression in
Italy. Some account of it may be found
in Shepherd's Life of Poggio, ch. iii.,
and in Corniani, ii. 137; who thinks it
the only work of moral philosophy in the
fifteenth century which is not a servile
copy of some ancient system. He was
grandfather of the more celebrated Hermolaus Barbarus.

of promise, but not yet become really learned, or capable of doing more than excite the emulation of other nations.

25. But we find very little corresponding sympathy with this love of classical literature in other parts of Classical Europe; not so much owing to the want of inter- learning in France low. course, as to a difference of external circumstances, and still more, of national character and acquired habits. Clemangis, indeed, rather before the end of the fourteenth century, is said by Crevier to have restored the study of classical antiquity in France, after an intermission of two centuries;[p] and Eichhorn deems his style superior to that of most contemporary Italians.[q] Even the Latin verses of Clemangis are praised by the same author, as the first that had been tolerably written on this side the Alps for two hundred years. But we do not find much evidence that he produced any effect upon Latin literature in France. The general style was as bad as before. Their writers employed not only the barbarous vocabulary of the schools, but even French words with Latin terminations adapted to them.[r] We shall see that the renovation of polite letters in France must be dated long afterwards. Several universities were established in that kingdom; but even if universities had been always beneficial to literature, which was not the case during the prevalence of scholastic disputation, the civil wars of one unhappy reign, and the English invasions of another, could not but retard the progress of all useful studies. Some Greeks, about 1430, are said to have demanded a stipend, in pursuance of a decree of the council of Vienne in the preceding century, for teaching their language in the university of Paris. The nation of France, one of the four into which that university was divided, assented to this suggestion; but we find no other steps taken in relation to it. In 1455, it is said that the Hebrew language was publicly taught.[s]

[p] Hist. de l'Université de Paris, iii. 189. [q] Gesch. der Litteratur, ii. 242. Meiners (Vergleich. der Sitten, iii. 33) extols Clemangis in equally high terms. He is said to have read lectures on the rhetoric of Cicero and Aristotle. Id. ii. 647. Was there a translation of the latter so early?

[r] Bulæus. Hist. univ. Paris, apud Heeren, p. 118.

[s] Crevier, iv. 43. Heeren, p. 121.— [Daunou says (Journal des Savans, May 1829), that we might find names and books to show that the study of Greek was not totally interrupted in France from 1300 to 1453.—1842.]

26. Of classical learning in England we can tell no favour-
Much more able story. The Latin writers of the fifteenth
so in Eng-
land. century, few in number, are still more insignificant
in value; they possess scarce an ordinary knowledge of
grammar; to say that they are full of barbarisms and perfectly inelegant, is hardly necessary. The university of
Oxford was not less frequented at this time than in the
preceding century, though it was about to decline; but its
pursuits were as nugatory and pernicious to real literature
as before.[t] Poggio says, more than once, in writing from
England about 1420, that he could find no good books, and
is not very respectful to our scholars. 'Men given up to
sensuality we may find in abundance; but very few lovers
of learning; and those barbarous, skilled more in quibbles
and sophisms than in literature. I visited many convents;
they were all full of books of modern doctors, whom
we should not think worthy so much as to be heard.
They have few works of the ancients, and those are much
better with us. Nearly all the convents of this island
have been founded within four hundred years: but that
was not a period in which either learned men, or such
books as we seek, could be expected, for they had been lost
before.'[u]

27. Yet books began to be accumulated in our public
Library of libraries: Aungerville, in the preceding century,
Duke of
Gloucester. gave part of his collection to a college at Oxford;
and Humphrey, duke of Gloucester, bequeathed six hundred volumes, as some have said, or one hundred and
twenty-nine only, according to another account, to that
university.[x] But these books were not of much value in a

---

[t] No place was more discredited for
bad Latin. 'Oxoniensis loquendi mos'
became a proverb. This means that,
being disciples of Scotus and Ockham,
the Oxonians talked the jargon of their
masters.

[u] Pogg. Epist. p. 43 (edit. 1832).

[x] The former number is given by
Warton; the latter I find in a short
tract on English monastic libraries
(1831), by the Rev. Joseph Hunter. In
this there is also a catalogue of the library in the priory of Bretton in York-
shire, consisting of about 150 volumes;
but as late as the middle of the sixteenth
century. [The libraries of Aungerville,
Cobham, and others were united at
Oxford in 1480 to that of the duke of
Gloucester, and remained till the plunder under Edward VI. This may account for the discrepancy as to the
number of books (manuscript) in the
latter.—1842.]

literary sense, though some may have been historically useful. I am indebted to Heeren for a letter of thanks from the
duke of Gloucester to Decembrio, an Italian scholar of
considerable reputation, who had sent him a translation of
Plato de Republica. It must have been written before July,
1447, the date of Humphrey's death, and was probably as
favourable a specimen of our Latinity as the kingdom could
furnish.[y]

28. Among the Cisalpine nations, the German had the
greatest tendency to literary improvement, as we Gerard
Groot's
college at
Deventer.
may judge by subsequent events, rather than by
much that was apparent so early as 1440. Their
writers in Latin were still barbarous, nor had they partaken
in the love of antiquity which actuated the Italians. But
the German nation displayed its best characteristic — a
serious, honest, industrious disposition, loving truth and
goodness, and glad to pursue whatever part seemed to lead
to them. A proof of this character was given in an institution of considerable influence both upon learning and
religion, the college, or brotherhood, of Deventer, planned
by Gerard Groot, but not built and inhabited till 1400,
fifteen years after his death. The associates of this, called
by different names, but more usually Brethren of the Life
in Common (Gemeineslebens), or Good Brethren and Sisters, were dispersed in different parts of Germany and the
Low Countries, but with their head college at Deventer.
They bore an evident resemblance to the modern Moravians,
by their strict lives, their community, at least a partial one,
of goods, their industry in manual labour, their fervent
devotion, their tendency to mysticism. But they were as
strikingly distinguished from them by the cultivation of

---

[y] Hoc uno nos longe felicem judicamus, quod tu totque florentissimi viri
Græcis et Latinis literis peritissimi, quot
illic apud vos sunt nostris temporibus,
habeantur, quibus nesciamus quid lau-
dum digne satis possit excogitari. Mitto
quod facundiam priscam illam et priscis
viris dignam, quæ prorsus perierat, huic
sæculo renovatis; nec id vobis satis fuit,
et Græcas literas scrutati estis, ut et
philosophos Græcos et vivendi magistros,
qui nostris jam obliterati erant et oc-
culti, reseratis, et eos Latinos facientes
in propatulum adducitis. Heeren quotes
this, p. 135, from Sassi de studiis Me-
diolanensibus. Warton also mentions
the letter, ii. 388. The absurd solecism
exemplified in 'nos felicem judicamus'
was introduced affectedly by the writers
of the twelfth century. Hist. litt. de
la France, ix. 146.

knowledge, which was encouraged in brethren of sufficient capacity, and promoted by schools both for primary and for enlarged education. 'These schools were,' says Eichhorn, 'the first genuine nurseries of literature in Germany, so far as it depended on the knowledge of languages; and in them was first taught the Latin, and in the process of time the Greek and Eastern tongues.'[z] It will be readily understood, that Latin only could be taught in the period with which we are now concerned; and, according to Lambinet, the brethren did not begin to open public schools till near the middle of the century.[a] These schools continued to flourish, till the civil wars of the Low Countries and the progress of the Reformation broke them up. Groningen had also a school, St. Edward's, of considerable reputation. Thomas à Kempis, according to Meiners, whom Eichhorn and Heeren have followed, presided over a school at Zwoll, wherein Agricola, Hegius, Langius, and Dringeberg, the restorers of learning in Germany, were educated. But it seems difficult to reconcile this with known dates, or with other accounts of that celebrated person's history.[b] The brethren Gemeineslebens had forty-five houses in 1430, and in 1460 more than thrice the number. They are said by some to have taken regular vows, though I find a difference in my authorities as to this, and to have professed celibacy. They were bound to live by the labour of their hands, observing the ascetic discipline of monasteries, and not to beg; which made the mendicant orders their enemies. They were protected, however, against these malignant calumniators by the favour of the pope. The passages quoted by Revius, the historian of Deventer, do not quite bear out the reputation for love of literature which Eichhorn has given them; but they were much occupied in copying and binding books.[c] Their house at Bruxelles began to print books instead of copying them, in 1474.[d]

---

[z] Meiners, Lebensbeschreibungen berühmter Männer, ii. 311–324. Lambinet, Origines de l'Imprimerie, ii. 170. Eichhorn, Geschichte der Litteratur, ii. 134, iii. 882. Revius, Daventria Illustrata. Mosheim, cent. xv. c. 2, § 22. Biogr. univ. : Gerard, Kempis.

[a] Origines de l'Imprimerie, p. 180.
[b] Meiners, p. 323. Eichhorn, p. 137. Heeren, p. 145. Biog. univ. : Kempis. Revius, Davent. Illust.
[c] Daventria Illustrata, p. 35.
[d] Lambinet.

29. We have in the first chapter made no mention of the physical sciences, because little was to be said, and Physical it seemed expedient to avoid breaking the subject sciences in middle ages. into unnecessary divisions. It is well known that Europe had more obligations to the Saracens in this, than in any other province of research. They indeed had borrowed much from Greece, and much from India; but it was through their language that it came into use among the nations of the West. Gerbert, near the end of the tenth century, was the first who, by travelling into Spain, learned something of Arabian science. A common literary tradition ascribes to him the introduction of their numerals, and of the arithmetic founded on them, into Europe. This has been disputed, and again re-asserted, in modern times.[e] It is sufficient to say

---

[e] See Andrès, the Archæologia, vol. viii. and the Encyclopædias Britannic and Metropolitan, on one side against Gerbert; Montucla, i. 502, and Kästner, Geschichte der Mathematik, i. 35, and ii. 695, in his favour. The latter relies on a well-known passage in William of Malmesbury concerning Gerbert: Abacum certe primus a Saracenis rapiens, regulas dedit, quæ a sudantibus abacistis vix intelliguntur; upon several expressions in his writings, and upon a manuscript of his geometry, seen and mentioned by Pez, who refers it to the twelfth century, in which Arabic numerals are introduced. It is answered, that the language of Malmesbury is indefinite, that Gerbert's own expressions are equally so, and that the copyist of the manuscript may have inserted the ciphers.

It is evident that the use of the numeral signs does not of itself imply an acquaintance with the Arabic calculation, though it was a necessary step to it. Signs bearing some resemblance to these (too great for accident) are found in MSS. of Boethius, and are published by Montucla (vol. i. planch. xi.). In one MS. they appear with names written over each of them, not Greek, or Latin or Arabic, or in any known language. These singular names, and nearly the same forms, are found also in a manuscript well deserving of notice,—No. 343 of the Arundel MSS. in the British Museum, and which is said to have belonged to a convent at Mentz. This

has been referred by some competent judges to the twelfth, and by others to the very beginning of the thirteenth century. It purports to be an introduction to the art of multiplying and dividing numbers; quicquid ab abacistis excerpere potui, compendiose collegi. The author uses nine digits, but none for ten or zero, as is also the case in the MS. of Boethius. Sunt vero integri novem sufficientes ad infinitam multiplicationem, quorum nomina singulis sunt superjecta. A gentleman of the British Museum, who had the kindness, at my request, to give his attention to this hitherto unknown evidence in the controversy, is of opinion that the rudiments, at the very least, of our numeration are indicated in it, and that the author comes within one step of our present system, which is no other than supplying an additional character for zero. His ignorance of this character renders his process circuitous, as it does not contain the principle of juxtaposition for the purpose of summing; but it does contain the still more essential principle, a decuple increase of value for the same sign, in a progressive series of location from right to left. I shall be gratified if this slight notice should cause the treatise, which is very short, to be published, or more fully explained. [This manuscript, as well as that of Boethius, has drawn some attention lately, and is noticed in the publications of Mr. J. O. Halliwell, and of M. Charles at Paris.— 1842.]

here, that only a very unreasonable scepticism has questioned
the use of Arabic numerals in calculation during the thirteenth
Arabian nu- century; the positive evidence on this side cannot
merals and
method. be affected by the notorious fact, that they were not
employed in legal instruments, or in ordinary accounts : such
an argument indeed would be equally good in comparatively
modern times. These numerals are found, according to
Andrès, in Spanish manuscripts of the twefth century ; and,
according both to him and Cossali, who speak from actual
inspection, in the treatise of arithmetic and algebra by
Leonard Fibonacci of Pisa, written in 1220.[f] This has
never been printed.[g] It is by far our earliest testimony to
the knowledge of algebra in Europe : but Leonard owns that
he learned it among the Saracens. ' This author appears,'
says Hutton, or rather Cossali, from whom he borrows, ' to
be well skilled in the various ways of reducing equations to
their final simple state by all the usual methods.' His
algebra includes the solution of quadratics.

30. In the thirteenth century, we find Arabian numerals
Proofs of employed in the tables of Alfonso X., king of
them in
thirteenth Castile, published about 1252. They are said to
century. appear also in the Treatise of the Sphere, by John
de Sacro Bosco, probably about twenty years earlier; and a
treatise, De Algorismo, ascribed to him, treats expressly of
this subject.[h] Algorismus was the proper name for the
Arabic notation and method of reckoning. Matthew Paris,
after informing us that John Basing first made Greek numeral figures known in England, observes, that in these any
number may be represented by a single figure, which is not

---

[f] Montucla, whom several other writers
have followed, erroneously places this
work in the beginning of the fifteenth
century.

[g] [(1836). It has since been published by M. Libri, at Paris, in his Histoire des Sciences mathématiques en
Italie, vol. ii., from a MS. in the Maglio-
becchi Library. It occupies 170 pages
in M. Libri's volume. The editor
places Fibonacci at the head of the ma
thematicians of the middle ages.—1842.]

[h] Several copies of this treatise are in
the British Museum. Montucla has

erroneously said that this arithmetic of
Sacro Bosco is written in verse. Wallis,
his authority, informs us only that some
verses, two of which he quotes, are subjoined to the treatise. This is not the
case in the manuscripts I have seen. I
should add, that only one of them bears
the name of Sacro Bosco, and that in a
later handwriting. [I have called this
an unpublished treatise in my first edition, on the authority of the Biographie
universelle. But Professor De Morgan
has informed me that it was printed at
Venice in 1523.—1842.]

the case ' in Latin, nor in Algorism.' [1] It is obvious that in
some few numbers only this is true of the Greek; but the
passage certainly implies an acquaintance with that notation,
which had obtained the name of Algorism. It cannot, therefore, be questioned that Roger Bacon knew these figures;
yet he has, I apprehend, never mentioned them in his writings; for a calendar, bearing the date 1292, which has been
blunderingly ascribed to him, is expressly declared to have
been framed at Toledo. In the year 1282, we find a single
Arabic figure 3 inserted in a public record; not only the
first indisputable instance of their employment in England,
but the only one of their appearance in so solemn an instrument.[k] But I have been informed that they have been found
in some private documents before the end of the century. In
the following age, though they were still by no means in
common use among accountants, nor did they begin to be so
till much later, there can be no doubt that mathematicians
were thoroughly conversant with them, and instances of their
employment in other writings may be adduced.[m]

31. Adelard of Bath, in the twelfth century, translated the
elements of Euclid from the Arabic, and another version was
made by Campano in the next age. The first printed editions
are of the latter.[n] The writings of Ptolemy became known
through the same channel; and the once celebrated   Mathemati-
treatise on the Sphere by John de Sacro Bosco   cal treatises.
(Holywood, or, according to Leland, Halifax), about the beginning of the thirteenth century, is said to be but an

---

[1] Hic insuper magister Joannes figuras
Græcorum numerales, et earum notitiam
et significationes in Angliam portavit, et
familiaribus suis declaravit. Per quas
figuras etiam literæ repræsentantur. De
quibus figuris hoc maxime admirandum,
quod unica figura quilibet numerus re-
presentatur; quod non est in Latino, vel
in Algorismo. Mat. Paris, A.D. 1252,
p. 721.

[k] Parliamentary Writs, i. 232, edited
under the Record Commission, by Sir
Francis Palgrave. It was probably inserted for want of room, not enough
having been left for the word iii[um]. It
will not be detected with ease, even by
the help of this reference.

[m] Andrès, ii. 92, gives on the whole
the best account of the progress of

numerals. The article by Leslie in the
Encyclopædia Britannica is too dogmatical in denying their antiquity. That in
the Encyclopædia Metropolitana, by Mr.
Peacock, is more learned. Montucla is
but superficial, and Kästner has confined
himself to the claims of Gerbert; admitting which, he is too indifferent
about subsequent evidence. [Dr. Thomson, in his History of the Royal Society,
refers to several papers in their Transactions on the use of Arabic numerals in
England, and quotes one in 1741, which
asserts that an unquestionable instance
of their employment as early as 1011
occurs in the parish church of Romsey
(p. 241). But this, I conceive, must be
wholly rejected.—1853.]

[n] [M. Charles Jourdain, in his edition

abridgment of the Alexandrian geometer.[o] It has been
frequently printed, and was even thought worthy of a commentary by Clavius. Jordan of Namur (Nemorarius), near
the same time, shows a considerable insight into the properties of numbers.[p] Vitello, a native of Poland, not long afterwards, first made known the principles of optics in a treatise
in ten books, several times printed in the sixteenth century,
and indicating an extensive acquaintance with the Greek
and Arabian geometers. Montucla has charged Vitello with
having done no more than compress and arrange a work on
the same subject by Alhazen; which Andrès, always partial
to the Arabian writers, has not failed to repeat. But the
author of an article on Vitello in the Biographie universelle
repels this imputation, which could not, he says, have proceeded from any one who had compared the two writers. A
more definite judgment is pronounced by the laborious
German historian of mathematics, Kästner. ' Vitello,' he
says, ' has with diligence and judgment collected, as far as
lay in his power, what had been previously known; and,
avoiding the tediousness of Arabian verbosity, is far more
readable, perspicuous, and methodical than Alhazen; he has
also gone much farther in the science.'[q]

32. It seems hard to determine whe her or not Roger
Bacon be entitled to the honours of a discoverer in
science; that he has not described any instrument
analogous to the telescope, is now generally admitted; but
he paid much attention to optics, and has some new and important notions on that subject. That he was acquainted
with the explosive powers of gunpowder, it seems unreasonable to deny; the mere detonation of nitre in contact with
an inflammable substance, which of course might be casually
observed, is by no means adequate to his expressions in the
well-known passage on that subject. But there is no ground

Roger
Bacon.

---

of his father's Recherches critiques sur
les Traductions d'Aristote, p. 98, has
observed that I have reproduced an
error pointed out by Tiraboschi, iv.
151. Campano did not translate Euclid,
though he commented upon him The
only translation was by Adelard.—1853.]
    [o] Montucla, i. 506. Biogr. univ.
Kästner.

[p] Montucla. Kästner. Drinkwater's
Life of Galileo.
    [q] Gesch. der Mathem. ii. 263. The
true name is Vitello, as Playfair has remarked (Dissertat. in Encycl. Brit.),
but Vitellio is much more common.
Kästner is correct, always copying the
old editions.

for doubting, that the Saracens were already conversant with gunpowder.

33. The mind of Roger Bacon was strangely compounded of almost prophetic gleams of the future course His resemblance to of science, and the best principles of the inductive Lord Bacon. philosophy, with a more than usual credulity in the superstitions of his own time. Some have deemed him overrated by the nationality of the English.[r] But if we may have sometimes given him credit for discoveries to which he has only borne testimony, there can be no doubt of the originality of his genius. I have in another place remarked the singular resemblance he bears to Lord Bacon, not only in the character of his philosophy, but in several coincidences of expression. This has since been followed up by a later writer,[s] who plainly charges Lord Bacon with having borrowed much, and with having concealed his obligations. The Opus Majus of Roger Bacon was not published till 1733, but the manuscripts were not uncommon, and Selden had thoughts of printing the work. The quotations from the Franciscan and the Chancellor, printed in parallel columns by Mr. Forster, are sometimes very curiously similar; but he presses the resemblance too far; and certainly the celebrated distinction, in the Novum Organum, of four classes of *Idola* which mislead the judgment, does not correspond, as he supposes, with that of the causes of error assigned by Roger Bacon.

34. The English nation was not at all deficient in mathematicians during the fourteenth century; on English mathematicians of the contrary, no other in Europe produced nearly cians of fourteenth so many. But their works have rarely been pub- century. lished. The great progress of physical science, since the invention of printing, has rendered these imperfect treatises interesting only to the curiosity of a very limited class of readers. Thus Richard Suisset, or Swineshead, author of a book entitled, as is said, the Calculator, of whom Cardan

[r] Meiners, of all modern historians of literature, is the least favourable to Bacon, on account of his superstition, and credulity in the occult sciences. Vergleichung der Sitten, ii. 710, and iii. 232. Heeren, p. 244, speaks more candidly of him. It is impossible, I think, to deny that credulity is one of the points of resemblance between him and his namesake.
[s] Hist. of Middle Ages, iii. 539. Forster's Mahometanism Unveiled, ii. 312.

speaks in such language as might be applied to himself, is scarcely known, except by name, to literary historians; and though it has several times been printed, the book is of great rarity.[t] But the most conspicuous of our English geometers was Thomas Bradwardin, archbishop of Canterbury; yet more for his rank, and for his theological writings, than for the arithmetical and geometrical speculations which give him a place in science. Montucla, with a carelessness of which there are too many instances in his valuable work, has placed Bradwardin, who died in 1348, at the beginning of the sixteenth century, though his treatise was printed in 1495.[u]

35. It is certain that the phenomena of physical astronomy were never neglected; the calendar was

Astronomy.

known to be erroneous, and Roger Bacon has even been supposed by some to have divined the method of its restoration, which has long afterwards been adopted. The Arabians understood astronomy well, and their science was transfused more or less into Europe. Nor was astrology, the favourite superstition of both the eastern and western world, without its beneficial effect upon the observation and registering of the planetary motions.

Alchemy.

Thus, too, alchemy, which, though the word properly means but chemistry, was generally confined to the mystery that all sought to penetrate, the transmutation of metals into gold, led more or less to the processes by which

---

[t] The character of Suisset's book given by Brucker, iii. 852, who had seen it, does not seem to justify the wish of Leibnitz that it should be republished. It is a strange medley of arithmetical and geometrical reasoning with the scholastic philosophy. Kästner (Geschichte der Mathematik, i. 50) appears not to have looked at Brucker, and, like Montucla, has a very slight notion of the nature of Suisset's book. His suspicion that Cardan had never seen the book he so much extols, because he calls the author the Calculator, which is the title of the work itself, seems unwarrantable. Suisset probably had obtained the name from his book, which is not uncommon; and Cardan was not a man to praise what he had never read. [One of the later editions is in the British Museum, with

a manuscript date, 1520, but entered in the catalogue as Venice, 1505. It may be added, that the title in this edition is not the Calculator, though it appears by Brunet to have been so called in the first edition, that of Pavia, 1498; but Subtilissimi Ricardi Suisseti Anglici Calculationes noviter impressæ atque revisæ. I am informed that the work, in one edition or another, is less scarce than, on the authority of Brucker, I had conceived.—1842.]

[u] It may be considered a proof of the attention paid to geometry in England, that two books of Euclid were read at Oxford about the middle of the fifteenth century. Churton's Life of Smyth, p. 151, from the University Register. We should not have expected to find this.

a real knowledge of the component parts of substances has been attained.[x]

36. The art of medicine was cultivated with great diligence by the Saracens both of the East and of Spain, but with little of the philosophical science that had immortalised the Greek school. The writings, however, of these masters were translated into Arabic; whether correctly or not, has been disputed among oriental scholars; and Europe derived her acquaintance with the physic of the mind and body, with Hippocrates as well as Aristotle, through the same channel. But the Arabians had eminent medical authorities of their own, Rhases, Avicenna, Albucazi, who possessed greater influence. In modern times, that is, since the revival of Greek science, the Arabian theories have been in general treated with much scorn. It is admitted, however, that pharmacy owes a long list of its remedies to their experience, and to their intimacy with the products of the East. The school of Salerno, established as early as the eleventh century,[y] for the study of medicine, from whence the most considerable writers of the next ages issued, followed the Arabians in their medical theory. But these are deemed rude, and of little utility at present.

Medicine.

37. In the science of anatomy an epoch was made by the treatise of Mundinus, a professor at Bologna, who died in 1326. It is entitled Anatome omnium humani corporis interiorum membrorum. This book had one great advantage over those of Galen, that it was founded on the actual anatomy of the human body. For Galen is supposed to have only dissected apes, and judged of mankind by analogy; and though there may be reason to doubt whether this were altogether the case, it is certain that he had very little practice in human dissection. Mundinus seems to have been more fortunate in his opportunities of this kind than later anatomists, during the prevalence of a superstitious prejudice, have found them-

Anatomy.

---

[x] I refer to Dr. Thomson's history of Chemistry for much curious learning on the alchemy of the Middle Ages. In a work like the present, it is impossible to follow up every subject; and I think that a general reference to a book of re-putation and easy accessibility is better than an attempt to abridge it.

[y] Meiners refers it to the tenth, ii. 413; and Tiraboschi thinks it may be as ancient, iii. 347.

selves. His treatise was long the text-book of the Italian
universities, till, about the middle of the sixteenth century,
Mundinus was superseded by greater anatomists. The
statutes of the university of Padua prescribed, that anatomical lectures should adhere to the literal text of Mundinus. Though some have treated this writer as a mere
copier of Galen, he has much, according to Portal, of his
own. There were also some good anatomical writers in
France during the fourteenth century.[z]

38. Several books of the later middle ages, sometimes of
great size, served as collections of natural history,
Encyclopæ-
dic works of and, in fact, as encyclopædias of general know-
middle ages. ledge. The writings of Albertus Magnus belong,
in part, to this class. They have been collected, in
twenty-one volumes folio, by the Dominican Peter Jammi,
and published at Lyons in 1651. After setting aside
much that is spurious, Albert may pass for the most fertile
writer in the world. He is reckoned by some the founder
of the schoolmen; but we mention him here as a compiler,
from all accessible sources, of what physical knowledge had
been accumulated in his time. A still more comprehensive
Vincent of contemporary writer of this class was Vincent de
Beauvais. Beauvais, in the Speculum naturale, morale, doctrinale et historiale, written before the middle of the thirteenth century. The second part of this vast treatise in
ten volumes folio, usually bound in four, Speculum morale,
seems not to be written by Vincent de Beauvais, and is
chiefly a compilation from Thomas Aquinas, and other
theologians of the same age. The first, or Speculum
naturale, follows the order of creation as an arrangement;
and after pouring out all the author could collect on the
heavens and earth, proceeds to the natural kingdoms; and,
finally, to the corporeal and mental structure of man. In
the third part of this encyclopædia, under the title Speculum doctrinale, all arts and sciences are explained; and
the fourth contains an universal history.[a] The sources of

---

[z] Tiraboschi, v. 209–244, who is very
copious for a non-medical writer. Portal, Hist de l'Anatomie. Biogr. univ.:
Mondino, Chauliac. Eichhorn, Gesch.

der Lit. ii. 416–447.
   [a] Biogr. univ.: Vincentius Bellova-
censis.

this magazine of knowledge are of course very multifarious. In the Speculum naturale, at which alone I have looked, Aristotle's writings, especially the history of animals, those of other ancient authors, of the Arabian physicians, and of all who had treated the same subjects in the middle ages, are brought together in a comprehensive, encyclopædic manner, and with vast industry, but with almost a studious desire, as we might now fancy, to accumulate absurd falsehoods. Vincent, like many, it must be owned, in much later times, through his haste to compile, does not give himself the trouble to understand what he copies. But, in fact, he relied on others to make extracts for him, especially from the writings of Aristotle, permitting himself or them, as he tells us, to change the order, condense the meaning, and explain the difficulties.[b] It may be easily believed that neither Vincent of Beauvais, nor his amanuenses, were equal to this work of abridging and transposing their authors. Andrès, accordingly, has quoted a passage from the Speculum naturale, and another to the same effect from Albertus Magnus, relating, no doubt, in the Arabian writer from whom they borrowed, to the polarity of the magnet, but so strangely turned into nonsense, that it is evident they could not have understood in the least what they wrote. Probably, as their language is nearly the same, they copied a bad translation.[c]

Vincent of Beauvais.

39. In the same class of compilation with the Speculum of Vincent of Beauvais, we may place some later works, the Trésor of Brunetto Latini, written in French about 1280, the Reductorium, Repertorium, et Dictionarium morale of Berchorius, or Berchœur, a monk, who died at Paris in 1362,[d] and a treatise by Bartholomew Glanvil, De proprietatibus rerum, soon after that time. Reading all they could find, extracting from all they read, digesting their extracts under some natural, or, at worst,

Berchorius.

---

[b] A quibusdam fratribus excerpta susceperam ; non eodem penitus verborum schemate, quo in originalibus suis jacent, sed ordine plerumque transposito, nonnunquam etiam mutata perpaululum ipsorum verborum forma, manente tamen auctoris sententia ; prout ipsa vel prolixitatis abbreviandæ vel multitudinis in unam colligendæ, vel etiam obscuritatis explanandæ necessitas exigebat.

[c] Andrès, ii. 112. See also xiii. 141.

[d] This book, according to De Sade, Vie de Pétrarque, iii. 550, contains a few good things among many follies. I have never seen it.

alphabetical classification, these laborious men gave back
their studies to the world with no great improvement of the
materials, but sometimes with much convenience in their
disposition. This, however, depended chiefly on their ability
as well as diligence; and in the mediæval period, the want of
capacity to discern probable truth was a very great drawback
from the utility of their compilations.

40. It seems to be the better opinion, that few only of the
Spanish ballads. Spanish romances or ballads founded on history or
legend, so many of which remain, belong to a period
anterior to the fifteenth century. Most of them should be
placed still lower. Sanchez has included none in his collection of Spanish poetry, limited by its title to that period;
though he quotes one or two fragments which he would refer
to the fourteenth century.[e] Some, however, have conceived,
perhaps with little foundation, that several in the general
collections of romances, have been modernised in language
from more ancient lays. They have all a highly chivalrous
character; every sentiment congenial to that institution,
heroic courage, unsullied honour, generous pride, faithful
love, devoted loyalty, were displayed in Castilian verse, not
only in their real energy, but sometimes with an hyperbolical
extravagance to which the public taste accommodated itself,
and which long continued to deform the national literature.
The ballad of the Conde de Alarcos, which may be found
in Bouterwek, or in Sismondi, and seems to be ancient,
though not before the fifteenth century, will serve as a sufficient specimen.[f]

41. The very early poetry of Spain (that published by
Metres of Spanish poetry. Sanchez) is marked by a rude simplicity, a rhythmical, and not very harmonious versification, and,
especially in the ancient poem of the Cid, written, according
to some, before the middle of the twelfth century, by occa-

---

[e] The Marquis of Santillana, early in
the fifteenth century, wrote a short letter
on the state of poetry in Spain to his own
time. Sanchez has published this with
long and valuable notes.

[f] Bouterwek's History of Spanish and
Portuguese Poetry, i. 55. See also Sismondi, Littérature du Midi, iii. 228, for
the romance of the Conde de Alarcos.
Sismondi refers it to the fourteenth

century; but perhaps no strong reason
for this could be given. I find, however,
in the Cancionero General, a 'romance
viejo,' beginning with two lines of the
Conde de Alarcos, continued on another
subject. It was not uncommon to build
romances on the stocks of old ones, taking
only the first lines; several other instances occur among those in the Cancionero, which are not numerous.

sional vigour and spirit.[g] This poetry is in that irregular
Alexandrine measure, which, as has been observed, arose
out of the Latin pentameter. It gave place in the fifteenth
century to a dactylic measure, called *versos de arte mayor*,
generally of eleven syllables, the first, fourth, seventh, and
tenth being accented, but subject to frequent licences,
especially that of an additional short syllable at the beginning of the line. But the favourite metre in lyric songs and
romances was the redondilla, the type of which was a line of
four trochees, requiring, however, alternately, or at the end
of a certain number, one deficient in the last syllable, and
consequently throwing an emphasis on the close. By this
a poem was sometimes divided into short stanzas, the termination of which could not be mistaken by the ear. It is no
more, where the lines of eight and seven syllables alternate,
than that English metre with which we are too familiar to
need an illustration. Bouterwek has supposed that this
alternation, which is nothing else than the trochaic verse of
Greek and Latin poetry, was preserved traditionally in Spain
from the songs of the Roman soldiers. But it seems by
some Arabic lines which he quotes, in common characters,
that the Saracens had the line of four trochees, which, in all
languages where syllables are strongly distinguished in time
and emphasis, has been grateful to the ear. No one can
fail to perceive the sprightliness and grace of this measure,
when accompanied by simple melody. The lighter poetry
of the southern nations is always to be judged with some
regard to its dependence upon a sister art. It was not
written to be read, but to be heard; and to be heard in the
tones of song, and with the notes of the lyre or the guitar.
Music is not at all incapable of alliance with reasoning or
descriptive poetry; but it excludes many forms which either
might assume, and requires a rapidity as well as intenseness
of perception, which language cannot always convey. Hence
the poetry designed for musical accompaniment is sometimes
unfairly derided by critics, who demand what it cannot pretend to give; but it is still true, that, as it cannot give all

---

[g] [This has been the opinion of Mr.
Southey, and, I believe, of others. But
Masdeu, Hist. critica de España, vol. xx.
p. 321, says that the greatest antiquity
which can be given to the poem of the
Cid is the thirteenth century. It is as-
cribed, according to him, to one Pedro
Abad, of the church of Seville.—1842.]

which metrical language is able to afford, it is not poetry of
the very highest class.

42. The Castilian language is rich in perfect rhymes.
Consonant   But in their lighter poetry the Spaniards frequently
and assonant
rhymes.   contented themselves with *assonances*, that is, with
the correspondence of final syllables, wherein the vowel alone
was the same, though with different consonants, as *duro* and
humo, boca and *cosa*.   These were often intermingled with
perfect or consonant rhymes.   In themselves, unsatisfactory
as they may seem at first sight to our prejudices, there can
be no doubt but that the assonances contained a musical
principle, and would soon give pleasure to and be required
by the ear.   They may be compared to the alliteration so
common in the northern poetry, and which constitutes almost
the whole regularity of some of our oldest poems.   But
though assonances may seem to us an indication of a rude
stage of poetry, it is remarkable that they belong chiefly to
the later period of Castilian lyric poetry, and that consonant
rhymes, frequently with the recurrence of the same syllable,
are reckoned, if I mistake not, a presumption of the antiquity
of a romance.[h]

43. An analogy between poetry and music, extending
Nature of   beyond the mere laws of sound, has been ingeniously
the glosa.   remarked by Bouterwek in a very favourite species
of Spanish composition, the *glosa*.   In this a few lines,
commonly well known and simple, were glossed, or para-
phrased, with as much variety and originality as the poet's
ingenuity could give, in a succession of stanzas, so that the
leading sentiment should be preserved in each, as the subject
of an air runs through its variations.   It was often contrived
that the chief words of the glossed lines should recur
separately in the course of each stanza.   The two arts being
incapable of a perfect analogy, this must be taken as a
general one; but it was necessary that each stanza should
be conducted so as to terminate in the lines, or a portion of
them, which form the subject of the gloss.[i]   Of these arti-

---

[h] Bouterwek's Introduction. Velasquez, in Dieze's German translation,
p. 288. The assonance is peculiar to the
Spaniards. [But it is said by M. Raynouard, that assonances are common in
the earliest French poetry. Journal des
Savans, July, 1833.—1842.]
  [i] Bouterwek, p. 118.

ficial, though doubtless, at the time, very pleasing compositions, there is nothing, as far as I know, to be found
beyond the peninsula;[k] though, in a general sense, it may be
said, that all lyric poetry, wherein a burthen or repetition
of leading verses recurs, must originally be founded on the
same principle, less artfully and musically developed. The
burthen of a song can only be an impertinence, if its sentiment does not pervade the whole.

44. The Cancionero General, a collection of Spanish
poetry written between the age of Juan de la Mena, The Cancio-
near the beginning of the fifteenth century, and its nero General.
publication by Castillo in 1517, contains the productions of
one hundred and thirty-six poets, as Bouterwek says; and in
the edition of 1520 I have counted one hundred and thirty-
nine. There is also much anonymous. The volume is in
two hundred and three folios, and includes compositions
by Villena, Santillana, and the other poets of the age of
John II., besides those of later date. But I find also the
name of Don Juan Manuel, which, if it means the celebrated
author of the Conde Lucanor, must belong to the fourteenth
century, though the preface of Castillo seems to confine his
collection to the age of Mena.[m] A small part only are strictly
love songs (canciones); but the predominant sentiment of
the larger portion is amatory. Several romances occur in
this collection; one of them is Moorish, and, perhaps, older
than the capture of Granada; but it was long afterwards
that the Spanish romancers habitually embellished their
fictions with Moorish manners. These romances, as in the
above instance, were sometimes glosed, the simplicity of
the ancient style readily lending itself to an expansion of
the sentiment. Some that are called romances contain no
story; as the Rosa Fresca and the Fonte Frida, both of
which will be found in Bouterwek and Sismondi.

---

[k] They appear with the name Grosas
in the Cancioneiro Geral of Resende;
and there seems, as I have observed
already, to be something much of the
same kind in the older Portuguese
collection of the thirteenth century.

[m] Don Juan Manuel, a prince descended from Ferdinand III., was the
most accomplished man whom Spain produced in his age. One of the earliest
specimens of Castilian prose, El Conde
Lucanor, places him high in the literature of his country. It is a moral fiction, in which, according to the custom
of novelists, many other tales are interwoven. 'In every passage of the
book,' says Bouterwek, 'the author
shows himself a man of the world and
an observer of human nature.'

45. ' Love songs,' says Bouterwek, ' form by far the prin-
Bouterwek's character of Spanish songs. cipal part of the old Spanish cancioneros. To read them regularly through would require a strong passion for compositions of this class, for the monotony of the authors is interminable. To extend and spin out a theme as long as possible, though only to seize a new modificaton of the old ideas and phrases, was, in their opinion, essential to the truth and sincerity of their poetic effusions of the heart. That loquacity, which is an heredi-tary fault of the Italian canzone, must also be endured in perusing the amatory flights of the Spanish redondillas, while in them the Italian correctness of expression would be looked for in vain. From the desire, perhaps, of relieving their monotony by some sort of variety, the authors have indulged in even more witticisms and plays of words than the Italians, but they also sought to infuse a more emphatic spirit into their compositions than the latter. The Spanish poems of this class exhibit, in general, all the poverty of the compositions of the troubadours, but blend with the simplicity of these bards the pomp of the Spanish national style in its utmost vigour. This resemblance to the troubadour songs was not, however, produced by imitation ; it arose out of the spirit of romantic love, which at that period, and for several preceding cen-turies, gave to the south of Europe the same feeling and taste. Since the age of Petrarch this spirit had appeared in classical perfection in Italy. But the Spanish amatory poets of the fifteenth century had not reached an equal degree of cultiva-tion ; and the whole turn of their ideas required rather a passionate than a tender expression. The sighs of the lan-guishing Italians became cries in Spain. Glowing passion, despair, and violent ecstasy were the soul of the Spanish love songs. The continually recurring picture of the contest between reason and passion is a peculiar characteristic of these songs. The Italian poets did not attach so much import-ance to the triumph of reason. The rigidly moral Spaniard was, however, anxious to be wise even in the midst of his folly. But this obtrusion of wisdom in an improper place frequently gives an unpoetical harshness to the lyric poetry of Spain, in spite of all the softness of its melody.'[n]

---

[n] Vol. i. p. 109.

46. It was in the reign of John II., king of Castile from
1407 to 1454, that this golden age of lyric poetry
commenced.[o] A season of peace and regularity, a   John II.
monarchy well limited, but no longer the sport of domineering families, a virtuous king, a minister too haughty and
ambitious, but able and resolute, were encouragements to
that light strain of amorous poetry which a state of ease
alone can suffer mankind to enjoy. And Portugal, for the
whole of this century, was in as flourishing a condition as
Castile during this single reign. But we shall defer the
mention of her lyric poetry, as it seems chiefly to be of a later
date. In the court of John II. were found three men, whose
names stand high in the early annals of Spanish   Poets of his
poetry, —the marquises of Villena and Santillana,   court.
and Juan de Mena. But, except for their zeal in the cause
of letters, amidst the dissipations of a court, they have no
pretensions to enter into competition with some of the
obscure poets to whom we owe the romances of chivalry.
A desire, on the contrary, to show needless learning, and to
astonish the vulgar by an appearance of profundity, so often
the bane of poetry, led them into prosaic and tedious details,
and into affected refinements.[p]

47. Charles, duke of Orleans, long prisoner in England
after the battle of Agincourt, was the first who   Charles,
                                                   duke of
gave polish and elegance to French poetry. In a   Orleans.
more enlightened age, according to Goujet's opinion, he
would have been among their greatest poets.[q] Except a
little allegory in the taste of his times, he confined himself
to the kind of verse called rondeaux, and to slight amatory
poems, which, if they aim at little, still deserve the praise of
reaching what they aim at. The easy turns of thought, and
graceful simplicity of style, which these compositions re-

---

[o] Velasquez, pp. 165, 442 (in Dieze),
mentions, what has escaped Bouterwek,
a more ancient Cancionero than that of
Castillo, compiled in the reign of John
II., by Juan Alfonso de Baena, and
hitherto unpublished. As it is entitled
Cancionero de Poetas antiguos, it may
be supposed to contain some earlier
than the year 1400. I am inclined to
think, however, that few would be
found to ascend much higher. I do not
find the name of Don Juan Manuel,
which occurs in the Cancionero of Castillo. A copy of this manuscript Cancionero of Baena was lately sold (1836),
among the MSS. of Mr. Heber, and
purchased for 120*l.* by the King of the
French.

[p] Bouterwek, p. 78.

[q] Goujet, Bibliothèque française, ix.
233.

quire, came spontaneously to the duke of Orleans. Without as much humour as Clement Marot long afterwards displayed, he is much more of a gentleman, and would have been in any times, if not quite what Goujet supposes, a great poet, yet the pride and ornament of the court.[r]

48. The English language was slowly refining itself, and growing into general use. That which we sometimes call pedantry and innovation, the forced introduction of French words by Chaucer, though hardly more by him than by all his predecessors who translated our neighbour's poetry, and the harsh Latinisms that began to appear soon afterwards, has given English a copiousness and variety which perhaps no other language possesses. But as yet there was neither thought nor knowledge sufficient to bring out its capacities. After the death of Chaucer, in 1400, a dreary blank of long duration occurs in our annals. The poetry of Hoccleve is wretchedly bad, abounding with pedantry, and destitute of all grace or spirit.[s] Lydgate, the monk of Bury, nearly of the same age, prefers doubtless a higher claim to respect. An easy versifier, he served to make poetry familiar to the many, and may sometimes please the few. Gray, no light authority, speaks more favourably of Lydgate than either Warton or Ellis, or than the general complexion of his poetry would induce most readers to do.[t] But great poets have often the taste to discern, and the candour to acknowledge, those beauties which are latent amidst the tedious dulness of their humbler brethren. Lydgate, though probably a man of inferior powers of mind to Gower, has more of the minor qualities of a poet ; his lines have sometimes more spirit, more humour, and he describes with more graphic minuteness. But his diffuseness becomes

English poetry.

Lydgate.

---

[r] The following very slight vaudeville will show the easy style of the duke of Orleans. It is curious to observe how little the manner of French poetry, in such productions, has been changed since the fifteenth century.

> Petit mercier, petit panier :
> Pourtant si je n'ai marchandise
> Qui soit du tout à votre guise,
> Ne blâmez pour ce mon mestier,
> Je gagne denier à denier ;
> C'est loin du trésor de Venise.
>
> Petit mercier, petit panier,
> Et tandis qu'il est jour, ouvrier,

> Le temps perds, quand à vous devise,
> Je vais parfaire mon emprise,
> Et parmi les rues crier :
> Petit mercier, petit panier.

(Recueil des Anciens Poètes français, ii. 196.)

[s] Warton, ii. 348.

[t] Ibid. 361–407. Gray's works, by Mathias, ii. 55–73. These remarks on Lydgate show what the history of English poetry would have been in the hands of Gray, as to sound and fair criticism.

generally feeble and tedious ; the attention fails in the school-boy stories of Thebes and Troy ; and he had not the judgment to select and compress the prose narratives from which he commonly derived his subject. It seems highly probable that Lydgate would have been a better poet in satire upon his own times, or delineation of their manners ; themes which would have gratified us much more than the fate of princes. The King's Quair, by James I. of Scotland, is a long allegory, polished and imagi- native, but with some of the tediousness usual in such productions. It is uncertain whether he or a later sovereign, James V., were the author of a lively comic poem, Christ's Kirk o' the Green; the style is so provincial, that no Eng- lishman can draw any inference as to its antiquity. It is much more removed from our language than the King's Quair. Whatever else could be mentioned as deserving of praise is anonymous and of uncertain date. It seems to have been early in the fifteenth century that the ballad of our northern minstrels arose. But none of these that are extant could be placed with much likelihood so early as 1440.[u]

James I. of Scotland.

49. We have thus traced in outline the form of European literature, as it existed in the middle ages and in the first forty years of the fifteenth century. The result must be to convince us of our great obliga- tions to Italy for her renewal of classical learning. What might have been the intellectual progress of Europe if she had never gone back to the fountains of Greek and Roman genius, it is impossible to determine ; certainly nothing in the fourteenth and fifteenth centuries gave prospect of a very abundant harvest. It would be difficult to find any man of high reputation in modern times who has not reaped benefit, directly or through others, from the revival of an- cient learning. We have the greatest reason to doubt

Restoration of classical learning due to Italy.

---

[u] Chevy Chase seems to be the most ancient of those ballads that has been preserved. It may possibly have been written while Henry VI. was on the throne, though a late critic would bring it down to the reign of Henry VIII. Brydges' British Bibliography, iv. 97. The style is often fiery, like the old war songs, and much above the feeble, though natural and touching, manner of the later ballads. One of the most remarkable circumstances about this celebrated lay is, that it relates a totally fictitious event with all historical particularity, and with real names. Hence it was probably not composed while many remembered the days of Henry IV., when the fray of Chevy Chase is feigned to have occurred.

whether, without the Italians of these ages, it would ever
have occurred. The trite metaphors of light and darkness,
of dawn and twilight, are used carelessly by those who
touch on the literature of the middle ages, and suggest by
analogy an uninterrupted progression, in which learning,
like the sun, has dissipated the shadows of barbarism. But
with closer attention it is easily seen that this is not a
correct representation; that taking Europe generally, far
from being in a more advanced stage of learning at the
beginning of the fifteenth century than two hundred years
before, she had, in many respects, gone backwards, and gave
little sign of any tendency to recover her ground. There
is, in fact, no security, as far as the past history of mankind
assures us, that any nation will be uniformly progressive in
science, arts, and letters; nor do I perceive, whatever may
be the current language, that we can expect this with much
greater confidence of the whole civilised world.

50. Before we proceed to a more minute and chronological history, let us consider for a short time some of the
prevailing strains of sentiment and opinion which shaped
the public mind at the close of the mediæval period.

51. In the early European poetry, the art sedulously
Character of cultivated by so many nations, we are struck by
classical
poetry lost. characteristics that distinguish it from the remains
of antiquity, and belong to social changes which we should
be careful to apprehend. The principles of discernment
as to works of imagination and sentiment, wrought up in
Greece and Rome by a fastidious and elaborate criticism,
were of course effaced in the total oblivion of that literature
to which they had been applied. The Latin language, no
longer intelligible except to a limited class, lost that adaptation to popular sentiment which its immature progeny had
not yet attained. Hence, perhaps, or from some other
cause, there ensued, as has been shown in the last chapter,
a kind of palsy of the inventive faculties, so that we cannot
discern for several centuries any traces of their vigorous
exercise.

52. Five or six new languages, however, besides the
ancient German, became gradually flexible and copious
enough to express thought and emotion with more preci-

sion and energy; metre and rhyme gave poetry its form; a new European literature was springing up, New schools fresh and lively, in gay raiment, by the side of that of criticism decrepit Latinity, which rather ostentatiously wore languages. its threadbare robes of more solemn dignity than becoming grace. But in the beginning of the fifteenth century, the revival of ancient literature among the Italians seemed likely to change again the scene, and threatened to restore a standard of critical excellence by which the new Europe would be disadvantageously tried. It was soon felt, if not recognised in words, that what had delighted Europe for some preceding centuries depended upon sentiments fondly cherished, and opinions firmly held, but foreign, at least in the forms they presented, to the genuine spirit of antiquity. From this time we may consider as beginning to stand opposed to each other two schools of criticism, latterly called the classical and romantic; names which should not be understood as absolutely exact, but, perhaps, rather more apposite in the period to which these pages relate than in the nineteenth century.

53. War is a very common subject of fiction, and the warrior's character is that which poets have ever Effect of delighted to portray. But the spirit of chivalry, chivalry on nourished by the laws of feudal tenure and limited monarchy, by the rules of honour, courtesy, and gallantry, by ceremonial institutions and public shows, had rather artificially modified the generous daring which always forms the basis of that character. It must be owned that the heroic ages of Greece furnished a source of fiction not unlike those of romance; that Perseus, Theseus, or Hercules answer pretty well to knights errant, and that many stories in the poets are in the very style of Amadis or Ariosto. But these form no great part of what we call classical poetry; though they show that the word, in its opposition to the latter style, must not be understood to comprise everything that has descended from antiquity. Nothing could less resemble the peculiar form of chivalry than Greece in the republican times, or Rome in any times.

54. The popular taste had been also essentially affected by changes in social intercourse, rendering it more studiously

and punctiliously courteous, and especially by the homage

Effect of
gallantry
towards
women.
due to women under the modern laws of gallantry. Love, with the ancient poets, is often tender, sometimes virtuous, but never accompanied by a sense of deference or inferiority. This elevation of the female sex through the voluntary submission of the stronger, though a remarkable fact in the philosophical history of Europe, has not, perhaps, been adequately developed. It did not originate, or at least very partially, in the Teutonic manners, from which it has sometimes been derived. The love-songs again, and romances of Arabia, where others have sought its birthplace, display, no doubt, a good deal of that rapturous adoration which distinguishes the language of later poetry, and have, perhaps, in some measure, been the models of the Provençal troubadours; yet this seems rather consonant to the hyperbolical character of oriental works of imagination, than to a state of manners where the usual lot of women is seclusion, if not slavery. The late editor of Warton has thought it sufficient to call 'that reverence and adoration of the female sex which has descended to our own times, the offspring of the Christian dispensation.'[x] But until it can be shown that Christianity establishes any such principle, we must look a little farther down for its origin.

55. Without rejecting, by any means, the influence of these collateral and preparatory circumstances, we might ascribe more direct efficacy to the favour shown towards women in succession to lands, through inheritance or dower, by the later Roman law, and by the customs of the northern nations; to the respect which the clergy paid them (a subject which might bear to be more fully expanded); but, above all, to the gay idleness of the nobility, consuming the intervals of peace in festive enjoyments. In whatever country the charms of high-born beauty were first admitted to grace the banquet or give brilliancy to the tournament,—in whatever country the austere restraints of jealousy were most completely laid aside,—in whatever country the coarser, though often more

Its probable origin.

---

[x] Preface, p. 123.

virtuous, simplicity of unpolished ages was exchanged for winning and delicate artifices,—in whatever country, through the influence of climate or polish, less boisterousness and intemperance prevailed,—it is there that we must expect to find the commencement of so great a revolution in society.

56. Gallantry, in this sense of a general homage to the fair, a respectful deference to woman, independent of personal attachment, seems to have first become a perceptible element of European manners in the south of France, and, probably, not later than the end of the tenth century;[y] it was not at all in unison with the rough habits of the Carlovingian Franks or of the Anglo-Saxons. There is little or, as far as I know, nothing of it in the poem of Beowulf, or in that upon Attila, or in the oldest Teutonic fragments, or in the Nibelungen Lied;[z] love may appear as a natural passion, but not as a conventional idolatry. It appears, on the other hand, fully developed in the sentiments as well as the usages of northern France, when we look at the tales of the court of Arthur, which Geoffrey of Monmouth gave to the world about 1128. Whatever may be thought of the foundation of this famous romance, whatever of legendary tradition

It is not shown in old Teutonic poetry; but appears in the stories of Arthur.

---

[y] It would be absurd to assign an exact date for that which in its nature must be gradual. I have a suspicion, that sexual respect, though not with all the refinements of chivalry, might be traced earlier in the south of Europe than the tenth century; but it would require a long investigation to prove this.

A passage, often quoted, of Radulphus Glaber, on the affected and effeminate manners, as he thought them, of the southern nobility who came in the train of Constance, daughter of the count of Toulouse, on her marriage with Robert, King of France, in 999, indicates that the roughness of the Teutonic character, as well, perhaps, as some of its virtues, had yielded to the arts and amusements of peace. It became a sort of proverb; Franci ad bella, Provinciales ad victualia. Eichhorn, Allg. Gesch. i. Append. 73. The social history of the tenth and eleventh centuries is not easily recovered. We must judge from probabilities founded on single passages, and on the general tone of civil history. The kingdom of Arles was more tranquil than the rest of France.

[z] Von eigentlicher Galanterie ist in dem Nibelungen Lied wenig zu finden, von christlichen Mysticismus fast gar nichts. Bouterwek, ix. 147. I may observe that the positions in the text, as to the absence of gallantry in the old Teutonic poetry, are borne out by every other authority; by Weber, Price, Turner, and Eichhorn. The last writer draws rather an amusing inference as to the want of politeness towards the fair sex, from the frequency of abductions in Teutonic and Scandinavian story, which he enumerates. Allg. Gesch. i. 37. App. p. 37. [We might appeal also to the very curious old German poems on Hildebrand, perhaps of the eighth century, published by the Grimms at Cassel in 1812. They exhibit chivalry without its gallantry. Some account of them may be found in Roquefort, p. 51, or in Bouterwek. --1812.]

he may have borrowed from Wales or Britany, the position that he was merely a faithful translator appears utterly incredible.[a] Besides the numerous allusions to Henry I. of England, and to the history of his times, which Mr. Turner and others have indicated, the chivalrous gallantry, with which alone we are now concerned, is not characteristic of so rude a people as the Welsh or Armoricans. Geoffrey is almost our earliest testimony to these manners; and this gives the chief value to his fables. The crusades were probably the great means of inspiring an uniformity of conventional courtesy into the European aristocracy, which still constitutes the common character of gentlemen; but it may have been gradually wearing away their national peculiarities for some time before.

57. The condition and the opinions of a people stamp a character on its literature; while that literature powerfully reacts upon and moulds afresh the national temper from which it has taken its distinctive type. This is remarkably applicable to the romances of chivalry. Some have even believed that chivalry itself, in the fulness of proportion ascribed to it by these works, had never existence beyond their pages; others, with more probability, that it was heightened and preserved by their influence upon a state of society which had given them birth. A considerable difference is perceived between the metrical romances, contemporaneous with, or shortly subsequent to, the crusades, and those in prose after the middle of the fourteenth century. The former are more fierce, more warlike, more full of abhorrence of infidels; they display less of punctilious courtesy, less of submissive deference to woman, less of absorbing and passionate love, less of voluptuousness and luxury; their superstition has more of interior belief and less of ornamental machinery than those to which Amadis de Gaul and other heroes of the later cycles of romance furnished a model. The one reflect, in a tolerably faithful mirror, the rough customs of the feudal aristocracy in their original freedom, but partially

Romances of chivalry of two kinds.

---

[a] See, in Mr. Turner's Hist. of England, iv. 256–269, two dissertations on the romantic histories of Turpin and of Geoffrey, wherein the relation between the two, and the motives with which each was written, seem irrefragably demonstrated.

modified by the gallant and courteous bearing of France; the others represent to us, with more of licensed deviation from reality, the softened features of society, in the decline of the feudal system through the cessation of intestine war, the increase of wealth and luxury, and the silent growth of female ascendancy. This last again was, no doubt, promoted by the tone given to manners through romance; the language of respect became that of gallantry; the sympathy of mankind was directed towards the success of love; and, perhaps, it was thought that the sacrifices which this laxity of moral opinion cost the less prudent of the fair were but the price of the homage that the whole sex obtained.

58. Nothing, however, more showed a contrast between the old and the new trains of sentiments in points of taste than the difference of religion. It would be untrue to say that ancient poetry is entirely wanting in exalted notions of the Deity; but they are rare in comparison with those which the Christian religion has inspired into very inferior minds, and which, with more or less purity, pervaded the vernacular poetry of Europe. They were obscured in both periods by an enormous superstructure of mythological machinery, but so different in names and associations, though not always in spirit, or even in circumstances, that those who delighted in the fables of Ovid usually scorned the Golden Legend of James de Voragine, whose pages were turned over with equal pleasure by a credulous multitude, little able to understand why any one should relish heathen stories which he did not believe. The modern mythology, if we may include in it the saints and devils, as well as the fairy and goblin armies, which had been retained in service since the days of paganism, is so much more copious and so much more easily adapted to our ordinary associations than the ancient, that this has given an advantage to the romantic school in their contention, which they have well known how to employ and to abuse. *Effect of difference of religion upon poetry.*

59. Upon these three columns—chivalry, gallantry, and religion—repose the fictions of the middle ages, especially those usually designated as romances. *General tone of romance.* These, such as we now know them, and such as display

the characteristics above mentioned, were originally metrical, and chiefly written by natives of the north of France. The English and Germans translated or imitated them. A new era of romance began with the Amadis de Gaul, derived, as some have thought, but upon insufficient evidence, from a French metrical original, but certainly written in Portugal, though in the Castilian language, by Vasco de Lobeyra, whose death is generally fixed in 1325.[b] This romance is in prose; and though a long interval seems to have elapsed before those founded on the story of Amadis began to multiply, many were written in French during the latter part of the fourteenth and the fifteenth centuries, derived from other legends of chivalry, which became the popular reading, and superseded the old metrical romances, already somewhat obsolete in their forms of language.[c]

60. As the taste of a chivalrous aristocracy was naturally delighted with romances, that not only led the imagination through a series of adventures, but presented a mirror of sentiments, to which they themselves pretended, so that of mankind in general found its gratification, sometimes in tales of home growth, or transplanted from the East, whether serious or amusing, such as the Gesta Romanorum, the Dolopathos, the Decameron (certainly the most celebrated and best written of these inventions), the Pecorone; sometimes in historical ballads or in moral fables, a favourite style of composition, especially with the Teutonic nations; sometimes, again, in legends of saints and the popular demonology of the age. The experience and sagacity, the moral sentiments, the invention and fancy of many obscure centuries may be discerned more fully and favourably in these various fictions than in their elaborate treatises. No one of the European nations stand so high in this respect as the German; their ancient tales

Popular moral fictions.

---

[b] Bouterwek, Hist. of Spanish Literature, p. 48.

[c] The oldest prose romance, which also is partly metrical, appears to be Tristan of Leonois, one of the cycle of the round table, written or translated by Lucas de Gast, about 1170. Roquefort État de la Poésie française, p. 147. [Several romances in prose are said in Hist. litt. de la France, xvi. 170, 177, to be older than the close of the thirteenth century. Those relating to Arthur and the round table are esteemed of an earlier date than such as have Charlemagne for their hero. Most of these romances in prose are taken from metrical romances.—1842.]

have a raciness and truth which has been only imitated by others. Among the most renowned of these we must place the story of Reynard the Fox, the origin of which, long sought by literary critics, recedes, as they prolong the inquiry, into greater depths of antiquity. It was supposed to be written, or at least first published, in German rhyme, by Henry of Alkmaar, in 1498; but earlier editions, in the Flemish language, have since been discovered.[d] It has been found written in French verse by Jaquemars Gielée, of Lille, near the end, and in French prose by Peter of St. Cloud, near the beginning, of the thirteenth century. Finally, the principal characters are mentioned in a Provençal song by Richard Cœur de Lion.[e] But though we thus bring the story to France, where it became so popular as to change the very name of the principal animal, which was always called goupil (vulpes) till the fourteenth century, when it assumed, from the hero of the tale, the name of Renard,[f] there seems every reason to believe that it is of German origin; and, according to a conjecture, once thought probable, a certain Reinard of Lorraine, famous for his vulpine qualities in the ninth century, suggested the name to some unknown fabulist of the empire. But Raynouard, and, I believe, Grimm, have satisfactorily refuted this hypothesis.[g]

61. These moral fictions, as well as more serious productions, in what may be called the ethical literature of the middle ages, towards which Germany contributed a large share, speak freely of the vices of the great. But they deal with them as men responsible to

Exclusion of politics from literature.

---

[d] [I have been reminded, that Caxton's 'Historye of Reynard the Foxe' was published in 1481.—1847.]

[e] Recueil des Anciens Poètes, i. 21. M. Raynouard observes that the Troubadours, and, first of all, Richard Cœur de Lion, have quoted the story of Renard, sometimes with allusions not referable to the present romance. Journal des Sav. 1826, p. 340. A great deal has been written about this story; but I shall only quote Bouterwek, ix. 347; Heinsius, iv. 104; and the Biographie universelle, arts. Gielée, Alkmaar.

[f] Something like this nearly happened in England: bears have had a narrow

escape of being called only bruins, from their representative in the fable.

[g] [Journal des Savans, July, 1834. Raynouard, in reviewing a Latin poem, Reinardus Vulpis, published at Stutgard in 1832, and referred by its editor to the ninth century, shows that the allegorical meaning ascribed to the story is not in the slightest degree confirmed by real facts, or the characters of the parties supposed to be designed. The poem he places in the twelfth or thirteenth century, rather than the ninth; and there can be no doubt whatever that he is right with any one who is conversant with the Latin versification of the two periods.—1842.]

God, and subject to natural law, rather than as members
of a community. Of political opinions, properly so called,
which have in later times so powerfully swayed the conduct
of mankind, we find very little to say in the fifteenth century. In so far as they were not merely founded on temporary circumstances, or at most on the prejudices connected
with positive institutions in each country, the predominant associations that influenced the judgment were derived from respect for birth, of which opulence was as yet
rather the sign than the substitute. This had long been,
and long continued to be, the characteristic prejudice of
European society. It was hardly ever higher than in the
fifteenth century, when heraldry, the language that speaks
to the eye of pride, and the science of those who despise
every other, was cultivated with all its ingenious pedantry
and every improvement in useful art, every creation in
inventive architecture, was made subservient to the grandeur of an elevated class in society. The burghers, in those
parts of Europe which had become rich by commerce, emulated in their public distinctions, as they did ultimately in
their private families, the ensigns of patrician nobility.
This prevailing spirit of aristocracy was still but partially
modified by the spirit of popular freedom on one hand, or of
respectful loyalty on the other.

62. It is far more important to observe the disposition
Religious
opinions.
of the public mind in respect of religion, which
not only claims to itself one great branch of literature, but exerts a powerful influence over almost every
Attacks on
the church.
other. The greater part of literature in the middle
ages, at least from the twelfth century, may be
considered as artillery levelled against the clergy : I do not
say against the church, which might imply a doctrinal
opposition by no means universal. But if there is one
theme upon which the most serious as well as the lightest,
the most orthodox as the most heretical writers are united,
it is ecclesiastical corruption. Divided among themselves,
the secular clergy detested the regular ; the regular monks
satirised the mendicant friars, who, in their turn, after
exposing both to the ill-will of the people, incurred a double
portion of it themselves. In this most important respect,

therefore, the influence of mediæval literature was powerful towards change. But it rather loosened the associations of ancient prejudice, and prepared mankind for revolutions of speculative opinion, than brought them forward.

63. It may be said in general, that three distinct currents of religious opinion are discernible on this side of the Alps in the first part of the fifteenth century. 1. The high pretensions of the Church of Rome to a sort of moral, as well as theological, infallibility, and to a paramount authority even in temporal affairs, when she should think fit to interfere with them, were maintained by a great body in the monastic and mendicant orders, and had still, probably, a considerable influence over the people in most parts of Europe. 2. The Councils of Constance and Basle, and the contentions of the Gallican and German churches against the encroachments of the holy see, had raised up a strong adverse party, supported occasionally by the government, and more uniformly by the temporal lawyers and other educated laymen. It derived, however, its greatest force from a number of sincere and earnest persons, who set themselves against the gross vices of the time, and the abuses grown up in the church through self-interest or connivance. They were disgusted also at the scholastic systems, which had turned religion into a matter of subtle dispute, while they laboured to found it on devotional feeling and contemplative love. The mystical theology, which, from seeking the illuminating influence and piercing love of the Deity, often proceeded onward to visions of complete absorption in his essence, till that itself was lost, as in the East, from which this system sprang, in an annihilating pantheism, had never wanted, and can never want, its disciples. Some, of whom Bonaventura is the most conspicuous, opposed its enthusiastic emotions to the icy subtilties of the schoolmen. Some appealed to the hearts of the people in their own language. Such was Tauler, whose sermons were long popular and have often been printed; and another was the unknown author of the German Theology, a favourite work with Luther, and known by the Latin version of Sebastian Castalio. Such, too, were Gerson and Clemangis, and such

Three lines of religious opinion in fifteenth century.

were the numerous brethren who issued from the college of Deventer.[h] One, doubtless of this class, whenever he may Treatise De have lived, was author of the celebrated treatise De Imitatione Christi. Imitatione Christi (a title which has been transferred from the first chapter to the entire work), commonly ascribed to Thomas von Kempen or à Kempis, one of the Deventer society, but the origin of which has been, and will continue to be, the subject of strenuous controversy. Besides Thomas à Kempis, two candidates have been supported by their respective partisans; John Gerson, the famous chancellor of the university of Paris, and John Gersen, whose name appears in one manuscript, and whom some contend to have been abbot of a monastery at Vercelli in the thirteenth century, while others hold him an imaginary being, except as a misnomer of Gerson. Several French writers plead for their illustrious countryman, and especially M. Gence, one of the last who has revived the controversy; while the German and Flemish writers, to whom the Sorbonne acceded, have always contended for Thomas à Kempis, and Gersen has had the respectable support of Bellarmin, Mabillon, and most of the Benedictine order.[i]

---

[h] Eichhorn, vi. 1–136, has amply and well treated the theological literature of the fifteenth century. Mosheim is less satisfactory, and Milner wants extent of learning; yet both will be useful to the English reader. Eichhorn seems well acquainted with the mystical divines, in p. 97 et post.

[i] I am not prepared to state the external evidence upon this keenly debated question with sufficient precision. In a few words, it may, I believe, be said, that in favour of Thomas à Kempis has been alleged the testimony of many early editions bearing his name, including one about 1471, which appears to be the first, as well as a general tradition from his own time, extending over most of Europe, which has led a great majority, including the Sorbonne itself, to determine the cause in his favour. It is also said that a manuscript of the treatise De Imitatione bears these words at the conclusion : Finitus et completus per manum Thomæ de Kempis, 1441 ; and that in this manuscript are so many erasures and alterations, as give it the appearance of his original autograph. Against

Thomas à Kempis it is urged, that he was a professed calligrapher or copyist for the college of Deventer; that the Chronicle of St. Agnes, a contemporary work, says of him : Scripsit Bibliam nostram totaliter, et multos alios libros pro domo et pro pretio ; that the entry above mentioned is more like that of a transcriber than of an author ; that the same chronicle makes no mention of his having written the treatise De Imitatione, nor does it appear in an early list of works ascribed to him.   For Gerson are brought forward a great number of early editions in France, and still more in Italy, among which is the first that bears a date, (Venice, 1483,) both in the fifteenth and sixteenth centuries; and some other probabilites are alleged.   But this treatise is not mentioned in a list of his writings given by himself.   As to Gersen, his claim seems to rest on a manuscript of great antiquity, which ascribes it to him, and indirectly on all those manuscripts which are asserted to be older than the time of Gerson and Thomas à Kempis. But, as I have before observed, I do not profess to give a full view of the external

The book itself is said to have gone through 1800 editions, and has probably been more read than any one work after the Scriptures.   3.   A third religious party consisted of the avowed or concealed heretics, some disciples of the older sectaries, some of Wicliffe or Huss, resembling the school of Gerson and Gerard Groot in their earnest piety, but drawing a more decided line of separation between themselves and the ruling power, and ripe for a more complete reformation than the others were inclined to desire.   It is not possible, however, for us to pronounce on all the shades of opinion that might be secretly cherished in the fifteenth century.

64. Those of the second class were, perhaps, comparatively

---

evidence, of which I possess but a superficial knowledge.

From the book itself, two remarks, which I do not pretend to be novel, have suggested themselves to me. 1. The Gallicisms or Italicisms are very numerous, and strike the reader at once ; such as Scientia sine timore Dei quid importat ?—Resiste in principio inclinationi tuæ—Vigilia serotina—Homo passionatus—Vivere cum nobis contrariantibus —Timoratior in cunctis actibus—Sufferentia crucis. It seems strange that these barbarous adaptations of French or Italian should have occurred to any one whose native language was Dutch ; unless it can be shown, that through St. Bernard, or any other ascetic writer, they had become naturalised in religious style. 2. But, on the other hand, it seems impossible to resist the conviction, that the author was an inhabitant of a monastery, which was not the case with Gerson, originally a secular priest at Paris, and employed for many years in active life, as chancellor of the university and one of the leaders of the Gallican church. The whole spirit breathed by the treatise De Imitatione Christi is that of a solitary ascetic:—Vellem me pluries tacuisse et inter homines non fuisse.— Sed quare tam libenter loquimur, et invicem fabulamur, cum raro sine læsione conscientiæ ad silentium redimus.— Cella continuata dulcescit, et male custodita tædium generat. Si in principio conversionis tuæ bene eam incolueris et custodieris, erit tibi posthac dilecta, amica, et gratissimum solatium.

As the former consideration seems to

exclude Thomas à Kempis, so the latter is unfavourable to the claims of Gerson. It has been observed, however, that in one passage, l. i. c. 24, there is an apparent allusion to Dante ; which, if intended, must put an end to Gersen, abbot of Vercelli, whom his supporters place in the first part of the thirteenth century. But the allusion is not indisputable. Various articles in the Biographie universelle, from the pen of M. Gence, maintain his favourite hypothesis; and M. Daunou, in the Journal des Savans for 1826, and again in the volume for 1827, espouses the same cause, and even says, Nous ne nous arrêterons point à ce qui regarde Thomas à Kempis, à qui cet ouvrage n'est plus guère attribué aujourd'hui, p. 631. But *aujourd'hui* must be interpreted rather literally, if this be correct. This is in the review of a defence of the pretensions of Gersen, by M. Gregory, who adduces some strong reasons to prove that the work is older than the fourteenth century.

This book contains great beauty and heart-piercing truth in many of its detached sentences, but places its rule of life in absolute seclusion from the world, and seldom refers to the exercise of any social or even domestic duty. It has naturally been less a favourite in Protestant countries, both from its monastic character, and because those who incline towards Calvinism do not find in it the phraseology to which they are accustomed. The translations are very numerous, but there seems to be an inimitable expression in its concise and energetic, though barbarous Latin.

rare at this time in Italy, and those of the third much more
so. But the extreme superstition of the popular
creed, the conversation of Jews and Mahometans,
the unbounded admiration of pagan genius and virtue, the
natural tendency of many minds to doubt and to perceive
difficulties, which the schoolmen were apt to find everywhere,
and nowhere to solve, joined to the irreligious spirit of the
Aristotelian philosophy, especially as modified by Averroes,
could not but engender a secret tendency towards infidelity,
the course of which may be traced with ease in the writings
of those ages. Thus the tale of the three rings in Boccace,
whether original or not, may be reckoned among the sports
of a sceptical philosophy. But a proof, not less decisive,
that the blind faith we ascribe to the middle ages was by no
means universal, results from the numerous vindications
of Christianity written in the fifteenth century. Eichhorn,
after referring to several passages in the works of Petrarch,
mentions defences of religion by Marsilius Ficinus, Alfonso
de Spina, a converted Jew, Savonarola, Æneas Sylvius, Picus
of Mirandola. He gives an analysis of the first, which, in
its course of argument, differs little from modern apologies
of the same class.[k]

65. These writings, though by men so considerable as
most of those he has named, are very obscure at
present; but the treatise of Raimond de Sebonde
is somewhat better known, in consequence of the chapter in
Montaigne entitled an apology for him. Montaigne had
previously translated into French the Theologia Naturalis
of this Sebonde, professor of medicine at Barcelona in the
early part of the fifteenth century. This has been called by
some the first regular system of natural theology; but, even
if nothing of that kind could be found in the writings of the
schoolmen, which is certainly not the case, such an appellation, notwithstanding the title, seems hardly due to Sebonde's
book, which is intended, not so much to erect a fabric of
religion independent of revelation, as to demonstrate the
latter by proofs derived from the order of nature.

66. Dugald Stewart, in his first dissertation prefixed to

---

[k] Vol. vi. p. 24.

the Encyclopædia Britannica, observes, that 'the principal aim of Sebonde's book, according to Montaigne, His views misunderstood. is to show that Christians are in the wrong to make human reasoning the basis of their belief, since the object of it is only conceived by faith, and by a special inspiration of the divine grace.' I have been able to ascertain that the excellent author was misled in this passage by confiding in a translation of Montaigne, which he took in a wrong sense. Far from such being the aim of Sebonde, his book is wholly devoted to the rational proofs of religion; and what Stewart has taken for a proposition of Sebonde himself, is merely an objection which, according to Montaigne, some were apt to make against his mode of reasoning. The passage is so very clear that every one who looks at Montaigne (l. ii. c. 12) must instantaneously perceive the oversight which the translator, or rather Stewart, has made; or he may satisfy himself by the article on Sebonde in Bayle.[m]

67. The object of Sebonde's book, according to himself, is to develope those truths as to God and man, which His real object. are latent in nature, and through which the latter may learn everything necessary; and especially may understand Scripture, and have an infallible certainty of its truth. This science is incorporate in all the books of the doctors of the church, as the alphabet is in their words. It is the first science, the basis of all others, and requiring no other to be previously known. The scarcity of the book will justify an extract, which, though in very uncouth Latin, will serve to give a notion of what Sebonde really aimed at; but he labours with a confused expression, arising partly from the vastness of his subject.[n]

---

[m] [The translation used by Stewart may not have been that by Cotton, but one published in 1776, which professes to be original. It must be said that if he had been more attentive, the translation could not have misled him.— 1842.]

[n] Duo sunt libri nobis data a Deo: scilicet liber universitatis creaturarum, sive liber naturæ, et alius est liber sacræ scripturæ. Primus liber fuit datus homini a principio, dum universitas rerum fuit condita, quoniam quælibet creatura non est nisi quædam litera digito Dei scripta, et ex pluribus creaturis sicut ex pluribus literis componitur liber. Ita componitur liber creaturarum, in quo libro etiam continetur homo ; et est principalior litera ipsius libri. Et sicut literæ et dictionis factæ ex literis important et includunt scientiam et diversas significationes et mirabiles sententias : ita conformiter ipsæ creaturæ simul conjunctæ et ad invicem comparatæ important et

68. Sebonde seems to have had floating in his mind, as this extract will suggest, some of those theories as to the correspondence of the moral and material world, which were afterwards propounded, in their cloudy magnificence, by the Theosophists of the next two centuries. He undertakes to prove the Trinity from the analogy of nature. His argument is ingenious enough, if not quite of orthodox tendency, being drawn from the scale of existence, which must lead us to a being immediately derived from the First Cause. He proceeds to derive other doctrines of Christianity from principles of natural reason; and after this, which occupies about half a volume of 779 closely printed pages, he comes to direct proofs of revelation: first, because God, who does all for his own honour, would not suffer an impostor to persuade the world that he was equal to God, which Mahomet never pretended; and afterwards by other arguments more or less valid or ingenious.

Nature of his arguments.

---

significant diversas significationes et sententias, et continent scientiam homini necessariam. Secundus autem liber scripturæ datus est homini secundo, et hoc in defectu primi libri ; eo quia homo nesciebat in primo legere, qui erat cæcus ; sed tamen primus liber creaturarum est omnibus communis, quia solum clerici legere sciunt in eo [i. e. secundo].

Item primus liber, scilicet naturæ, non potest falsificari, nec deleri, neque false interpretari ; ideo hæretici non possunt eum false intelligere, nec aliquis potest in eo fieri hæreticus. Sed secundus potest falsificari et false interpretari et male intelligi. Attamen uterque liber est ab eodem, quia idem Dominus et creaturas condidit, et sacram Scripturam revelavit. Et ideo conveniunt ad invicem, et non contradicit unus alteri, sed tamen primus est nobis connaturalis, secundus supernaturalis. Præterea cum homo sit naturaliter rationalis, et susceptibilis disciplinæ et doctrinæ ; et cum naturaliter a sua creatione nullam habeat actu doctrinam neque scientiam, sit tamen aptus ad suscipiendum eam ; et cum doctrina et scientia sine libro, in quo scripta sit, non possit haberi, convenientissimum fuit, ne frustra homo esset capax doctrinæ et scientiæ, quod divina scientia homini librum creaverit, in quo

per se et sine magistro possit studere doctrinam necessariam ; propterea hoc totum istum mundum visibilem sibi creavit, et dedit tanquam librum proprium et naturalem et infallibilem, Dei digito scriptum, ubi singulæ creaturæ quasi literæ sunt, non humano arbitrio sed divino juvante judicio ad demonstrandum homini sapientiam et doctrinam sibi necessariam ad salutem. Quam quidem sapientiam nullus potest videre, neque legere per se in dicto libro semper aperto, nisi fuerit a Deo illuminatus et a peccato originali mundatus. Et ideo nullus antiquorum philosophorum paganorum potest legere hanc scientiam, quia erant excæcati quantum ad propriam salutem, quamvis in dicto libro legerunt aliquam scientiam, et omnem quam habuerunt ab eodem contraxerunt ; sed veram sapientiam quæ ducit ad vitam æternam, quamvis fuerat in eo scripta, legere non potuerunt.

Ista autem scientia non est aliud, nisi cogitare et videre sapientiam scriptam in creaturis, et extrahere ipsam ab illis, et ponere in animâ, et videre significationem creaturarum. Et sic comparando ad aliam et conjungere sicut dictionem dictioni, et ex tali conjunctione resultat sententia et significatio vera, dum tamen sciat homo intelligere et cognoscere.

69. We shall now adopt a closer and more chronological arrangement than before, ranging under each decennial period the circumstances of most importance in the general history of literature, as well as the principal books published within it.   This course we shall pursue till the channels of learning become so various, and so extensively diffused through several kingdoms, that it will be found convenient to deviate in some measure from so strictly chronological a form, in order to consolidate better the history of different sciences, and diminish, in some measure, what can never wholly be removed from a work of this nature, the confusion of perpetual change of subject.

CHAPTER III.

ON THE LITERATURE OF EUROPE FROM 1440 TO THE CLOSE OF THE FIFTEENTH CENTURY.

SECT. I.   1440—1450.

Classical Literature in Italy—Nicolas V.—Laurentius Valla.

1. THE reader is not to consider the year 1440 as a marked

The year 1440 not chosen as an epoch. epoch in the annals of literature. It has sometimes been treated as such by those who have referred the inventing of printing to this particular era. But it is here chosen as an arbitrary line, nearly coincident with the complete development of an ardent thirst for classical, and especially Grecian, literature in Italy, as the year 1400 was with its first manifestation.

2. No very conspicuous events belong to this decennial

Continual progress of learning. period. The spirit of improvement, already so powerfully excited in Italy, continued to produce the same effects in rescuing ancient manuscripts from the chances of destruction, accumulating them in libraries, making translations from the Greek, and by intense labour in the perusal of the best authors, rendering both their substance and their language familiar to the Italian scholar. The patronage of Cosmo de' Medici, Alfonso king of Naples, and Nicolas of Este, has already been mentioned. Lionel, successor of the last prince, was by no means inferior to him in love of letters. But they had no patron so important as Nicolas V. (Thomas of Sarzana), who became pope in 1447;

Nicholas V. nor has any later occupant of his chair, without excepting Leo X., deserved equal praise as an encourager of learning. Nicolas founded the Vatican

library, and left it, at his death in 1455, enriched with
5000 volumes; a treasure far exceeding that of any other
collection in Europe. Every scholar who needed maintenance, which was of course the common case, found it at the
court of Rome; innumerable benefices all over Christendom,
which had fallen into the grasp of the holy see, and frequently
required of their incumbents, as is well known, neither residence, nor even the priestly character, affording the means
of generosity, which have seldom been so laudably applied.
Several Greek authors were translated into Latin by direction
of Nicolas V., among which are the history of Diodorus
Siculus, and Xenophon's Cyropædia, by Poggio,[a] who still
enjoyed the office of apostolical secretary, as he had under
Eugenius IV., and with still more abundant munificence on
the part of the Pope; Herodotus and Thucydides by Valla,
Polybius by Perotti, Appian by Decembrio, Strabo by
Gregory of Tiferno and Guarino of Verona, Theophrastus by
Gaza, Plato de Legibus, Ptolemy's Almagest, and the Præpa-
ratio Evangelica of Eusebius, by George of Trebizond.[b]
These translations, it has been already observed, will not
bear a very severe criticism, but certainly there was an
extraordinary cluster of learning round the chair of this
excellent pope.

3. Corniani remarks, that if Nicolas V., like some
popes, had raised a distinguished family, many Justice due
to his cha-
pens would have been employed to immortalise racter.
him; but not having surrounded himself with relations,
his fame has been much below his merits. Gibbon, one of
the first to do full justice to Nicolas, has made a similar
observation. How striking the contrast between this pope
and his famous predecessor Gregory I., who, if he did not

---

[a] This translation of Diodorus has
been ascribed by some of our writers,
even since the error has been pointed out,
to John Free, an Englishman, who had
heard the lectures of the younger Guarini in Italy. Quod opus, Leland observes, Itali Poggio vanissime attribuunt
Florentino. De Scriptoribus Britann.,
p. 462. But it bears the name of Poggio
in the two editions, printed in 1472 and
1493; and Leland seems to have been
deceived by some one who had put Free's

name on a manuscript of the translation.
Poggio, indeed, in his preface, declares
that he undertook it by command of
Nicolas V. See Niceron, ix. 158; Zeno,
Dissertazioni Vossiane, i. 41; Ginguéné,
iii. 245. Pits follows Leland in ascribing a translation of Diodorus to Free,
and quotes the first words: thus, if it still
should be suggested that this may be a
different work, there are the means of
proving it.
[b] Heeren, p. 72.

burn and destroy heathen authors, was at least anxious to
discourage the reading of them! These eminent men, like
Michael Angelo's figures of Night and Morning, seem to
stand at the two gates of the middle ages, emblems and
heralds of the mind's long sleep, and of its awakening.

4. Several little treatises by Poggio, rather in a moral than
Poggio on political strain, display an observing and intelligent
the ruins of
Rome. mind. Such are those on nobility, and on the un-
happiness of princes. For these, which were written before
1440, the reader may have recourse to Shepherd, Corniani,
or Ginguéné. A later essay, if we may so call it, on the
vicissitudes of fortune, begins with rather an interesting
description of the ruins of Rome. It is an enumeration
of the more conspicuous remains of the ancient city; and
we may infer from it that no great devastation or injury has
taken place since the fifteenth century. Gibbon has given
an account of this little tract, which is not, as he shows, the
earliest on the subject. Poggio, I will add, seems not to
have known some things with which we are familiar, as the
Cloaca Maxima, the fragments of the Servian wall, the
Mamertine prison, the temple of Nerva, the Giano Quadri-
fronte; and by some odd misinformation, believes that the
tomb of Cecilia Metella, which he had seen entire, was afterwards destroyed.[c] This leads to a conjecture that the treatise
was not finished during his residence at Rome, and consequently not within the present decennium.

5. In the fourth book of this treatise De Varietate Fortunæ,
Account of Poggio has introduced a remarkable narration of
the East by
Conti. travels by a Venetian, Nicolo di Conti, who in 1419
had set off from his country, and, after passing many years
in Persia and India, returned home in 1444. His account of
those regions, in some respects the earliest on which reliance
could be placed, will be found, rendered into Italian from a
Portuguese version of Poggio, in the first volume of Ramusio.
That editor seems not to have known that the original was
in print.

6. A far more considerable work by Laurentius Valla, on
the graces of the Latin language, is rightly, I believe,

---

[c] Ad calcem postea majore ex parte exterminatum.

placed within this period; but it is often difficult to determine the dates of books published before the inven- Laurentius
Valla.
tion of printing. Valla, like Poggio, had also
earned the favour of Alfonso, but, unlike him, had forfeited
that of the court of Rome. His character was very irascible
and overbearing, a fault too general with the learned of the
fifteenth century; but he may, perhaps, be placed at the
head of the literary republic at this time; for if inferior to
Poggio, as probably he was, in vivacity and variety of genius,
he was undoubtedly above him in what was then most valued
and most useful, grammatical erudition.

7. Valla began with an attack on the court of Rome in
his declamation against the donation of Constan- His attack
on the court
of Rome.
tine. Some have in consequence reckoned him
among the precursors of Protestantism; while others have
imputed to the Roman see, that he was pursued with its
hostility for questioning that pretended title to sovereignty.
But neither of these representations is just. Valla confines
himself altogether to the temporal principality of the pope;
but as to this, his language must be admitted to have been so
abusive, as to render the resentment of the court of Rome
not unreasonable.[d]

8. The more famous work of Valla, De Elegantiis La-
tinæ Linguæ, begins with too arrogant an assump- His treatise
on the Latin
language.
tion. 'These books,' he says, 'will contain
nothing that has been said by any one else. For many
ages past, not only no man has been able to speak Latin,
but none have understood the Latin they read: the studious of philosophy have had no comprehension of the

---

[d] A few lines will suffice as a specimen. O Romani pontifices, exemplum
facinorum omnium cæteris pontificibus,
et improbissimi scribæ et pharisæi, qui
sedetis super cathedram Moysi, et opera
Dathan et Abyron facitis, itane vesti-
menta apparatûs, pompa equitatûs, omnis denique vita Cæsaris, vicarium Christi
decebit? The whole tone is more like
Luther's violence, than what we should
expect from an Italian of the fifteenth
century. But it is with the ambitious
spirit of aggrandisement as temporal
princes, that he reproaches the pontiffs;
nor can it be denied, that Martin and
Eugenius had given provocation for his

invective. Nec amplius horrenda vox
audiatur, partes contra ecclesiam; ecclesia contra Perusinos pugnat, contra Bo-
nonienses. Non contra Christianos pugnat ecclesia, sed papa. Of the papal
claim to temporal sovereignty by pre-
scription, Valla writes indignantly. Præscripsit Romana ecclesia; o imperiti, o
divini juris ignari. Nullus quantumvis
annorum numerus verum abolere titu-
lum potest. Præscripsit Romana ecclesia. Tace, nefaria lingua. Præscrip-
tionem quæ fit de rebus mutis atque
irrationalibus, ad hominem transfers;
cujus quo diuturnior in servitute pos-
sessio, eo detestabilior.

philosophers, the advocates of the orators, the lawyers of the jurists, the general scholar of any writers of antiquity.' Valla, however, did at least incomparably more than any one who had preceded him ; and it would probably appear that a great part of the distinctions in Latin syntax, inflexion, and synonymy, which our best grammars contain, may be traced to his work. It is to be observed, that he made free use of the ancient grammarians, so that his vaunt of originality must be referred to later times. Valla is very copious as to synonyms, on which the delicate, and even necessary understanding of a language mainly depends. If those have done most for any science who have carried it farthest from the point whence they set out, philology seems to owe quite as much to Valla as to any one who has come since. The treatise was received with enthusiastic admiration, continually reprinted, honoured with a paraphrase by Erasmus, commented, abridged, extracted, and even turned into verse.[e]

9. Valla, however, self-confident and of no good temper, in censuring the language of others, fell not unfrequently into mistakes of his own. Vives and Budæus, coming in the next century, and in a riper age of philology, blame the hypercritical disposition of one who had not the means of pronouncing negatively on Latin words and phrases, from his want of sufficient dictionaries; his fastidiousness became what they call superstition, imposing captious scruples and unnecessary observances on himself and the world.[f] And of this species of superstition, there has been much since his time in philology.

Its defects.

10. Heeren, one of the few who have, in modern times, spoken of this work from personal knowledge, and with sufficient learning, gives it a high character. 'Valla was without doubt the best acquainted with Latin

Heeren's praise of it.

---

[e] Corniani, ii. 221. The editions of Valla de Elegantiis, recorded by Panzer, are twenty-eight in the fifteenth century-beginning in 1471, and thirty-one in the first thirty-six years of the next.

[f] Vives de tradendis disciplinis, i. 478. Budæus observes : —Ego Laurentium Vallensem, egregii spiritus virum, existimo sæculi sui imperitia offensum primum Latine loquendi consuetudinem constituere summa religione institisse ; deinde judicii cerimonia singulari, cum profectus quoque diligentiam æquasset, in eam superstitionem sensim delapsum esse, ut et sese ipse et alios captiosis observationibus scribendique legibus obligaret. Commentar. in Ling. Græc. p. 26, (1529.) But sometimes, perhaps, Valla is right, and Budæus wrong in censuring him.

of any man in his age; yet, no pedantic Ciceronian, he had studied all the classical writers of Rome. His Elegantiæ is a work on grammar; it contains an explanation of refined turns of expression, especially where they are peculiar to Latin; displaying not only an exact knowledge of that tongue, but often also a really philosophical study of language in general. In an age when nothing was so much valued as a good Latin style, yet when the helps, of which we now possess so many, were all wanting, such a work must obtain a great success, since it relieved a necessity which every one felt.'[g]

11. We have to give this conspicuous scholar a place in another line of criticism, that on the text and interpretation of the New Testament. His annotations are the earliest specimen of explanations founded on the original language. In the course of these he treats the Vulgate with some severity. But Valla is said to have had but a slight knowledge of Greek;[h] and it must also be owned, that with all his merit as a Latin critic, he wrote indifferently, and with less classical spirit than his adversary Poggio. The invectives of these against each other do little honour to their memory, and are not worth recording in this volume, though they could not be omitted in a legitimate history of the Italian scholars.

Valla's annotations on the New Testament.

Sect. II.   1450—1460.

Greeks in Italy—Invention of Printing.

12. The capture of Constantinople in 1453 drove a few learned Greeks, who had lingered to the last amidst the crash of their ruined empire, to the hospitable and admiring Italy. Among these have been

Fresh arrival of Greeks in Italy.

---

[g] P. 220.

[h] Annis abhinc ducentis Herodotum et Thucydidem Latinis literis exponebat Laurentius Valla, in ea bene et eleganter dicendi copia, quam totis voluminibus explicavit, inelegans tamen, et pæne barbarus, Græcis ad hoc literis leviter tinctus, ad auctorum sententias parum attentus, oscitans sæpe, et alias res agens, fidem apud eruditos decoxit. Huet de claris Interpretibus, apud Blount. Daunou, however, in the Biographie universelle, art. Thucydides, asserts that Valla's translation of that historian is generally faithful. This would show no inconsiderable knowledge of Greek for that age.

reckoned Argyropulus and Chalcondyles, successively teachers of their own language; Andronicus Callistus, who is said to have followed the same profession both there and at Rome; and Constantine Lascaris, of an imperial family, whose lessons were given for several years at Milan, and afterwards at Messina. It seems, however, to be proved that Argyropulus had been already for several years in Italy.[i]

13. The cultivation of Greek literature gave rise about Platonists this time to a vehement controversy, which had and Aristote- lians. some influence on philosophical opinions in Italy. Gemistus Pletho, a native of the Morea, and one of those who attended the council of Florence in 1439, being an enthusiastic votary of the Platonic theories in metaphysics and natural theology, communicated to Cosmo de' Medici part of his own zeal; and from that time the citizens of Florence formed a scheme of establishing an academy of learned men, to discuss and propagate the Platonic system. This seems to have been carried into effect early in the present decennial period.

14. Meantime, a treatise by Pletho, wherein he not only Their con- extolled the Platonic philosophy, which he mingled, troversy. as was then usual, with that of the Alexandrian school, and of the spurious writings attributed to Zoroaster and Hermes, but inveighed without measure against Aristotle and his disciples, had aroused the Aristotelians of Greece, where, as in Western Europe, their master's authority had long prevailed. It seems not improbable that the Platonists were obnoxious to the orthodox party for sacrificing their own church to that of Rome; and there is also some ground for ascribing a rejection of Christianity to Pletho. The dispute, at least, began in Greece, where Pletho's treatise met with an angry opponent in Gennadius, patriarch of Constantinople.[k] It soon spread to Italy;

---

[i] Hody, Tiraboschi, Roscoe.

[k] Pletho's death, in an extreme old age, is fixed by Brucker, on the authority of George of Trebizond, before the capture of Constantinople. A letter, indeed, of Bessarion, in 1462 (Mém. de l'Acad. des Inscript., vol. ii.), seems to imply that he was then living; but this cannot have been the case. Gennadius, his enemy, abdicated the patriarchate of Constantinople in 1458, having been raised to it in 1453. The public burning of Pletho's book was in the intermediate time; and it is agreed that this was done after his death.

Theodore Gaza embracing the cause of Aristotle with temper and moderation, and George of Trebizond, a far inferior man, with invectives against the Platonic philosophy and its founder. Others replied in the same tone; and whether from ignorance or from rudeness, this controversy appears to have been managed as much with abuse of the lives and characters of two philosophers, dead nearly two thousand years, as with any rational discussion of their tenets. Both sides, however, strove to make out, what in fact was the ultimate object, that the doctrine they maintained was more consonant to the Christian religion than that of their adversaries. Cardinal Bessarion, a man of solid and elegant learning, replied to George of Trebizond in a book entitled Adversus Calumniatorem Platonis; one of the first books that appeared from the Roman press, in 1470. This dispute may possibly have originated, at least in Greece, before 1450; and it was certainly continued beyond 1460, the writings both of George and Bessarion appearing to be rather of later date.[n]

15. Bessarion himself was so far from being as unjust towards Aristotle as his opponent was towards Plato, that he translated his metaphysics. That philosopher, though almost the idol of the schoolmen, lay still in some measure under the ban of the church, which had very gradually removed the prohibition she laid on his writings in the beginning of the thirteenth century. Nicolas V. first permitted them to be read without restriction in the universities.[o]

16. Cosmo de' Medici selected Marsilius Ficinus, as a youth of great promise, to be educated in the mysteries of Platonism, that he might become the chief Marsilius Ficinus. and preceptor of the new academy; nor did the devotion of the young philosopher fall short of the patron's hope.

---

[m] Hody, p. 79, doubts whether Gaza's vindication of Aristotle were not merely verbal, in conversation with Bessarion; which is however implicitly contradicted by Boivin and Tiraboschi, who assert him to have written against Pletho. The comparison of Plato and Aristotle by George of Trebizond was published at Venice in 1523, as Heeren says on the authority of Fabricius.

[n] The best account, and that from which later writers have freely borrowed, of this philosophical controversy, is by Boivin, in the second volume of the Memoirs of the Academy of Inscriptions, p. 15. Brucker, iv. 40, Buhle, ii. 107, and Tiraboschi, vi. 303, are my other authorities.

[o] Launoy de varia Aristotelis Fortuna in Academia Parisiensi, p. 44.

Ficinus declares himself to have profited as much by the conversation of Cosmo as by the writings of Plato; but this is said in a dedication to Lorenzo, and the author has not, on other occasions, escaped the reproach of flattery. He began as early as 1456, at the age of twenty-three, to write on the Platonic philosophy; but being as yet ignorant of Greek, prudently gave way to the advice of Cosmo and Landino, that he should acquire more knowledge before he imparted it to the world.[p]

17. The great glory of this decennial period is the inven-
Invention of   tion of printing, or at least, as all must allow, its
printing.   application to the purposes of useful learning. The reader will not expect a minute discussion of so long and unsettled a controversy as that which the origin of this art has furnished. For those who are little conversant with the subject, a very few particulars may be thought necessary.

18. About the end of the fourteenth century, we find a
Block books.   practice of taking impressions from engraved blocks
of wood; sometimes for playing-cards, which were not generally used long before that time, sometimes for rude cuts of saints.[q] The latter were frequently accompanied by a few lines of letter cut in the block. Gradually entire pages were impressed in this manner; and thus began what are called block books, printed in fixed characters, but never exceeding a very few leaves. Of these there exist nine or ten, often reprinted, as it is generally thought, between 1400 and 1440.[r] In using the word printed, it is of course not intended to prejudice the question as to the real art of printing. These block books seem to have been all executed in the Low Countries. They are said to have been followed by several editions of the short grammar of Donatus.[s] These also were printed in Holland. This mode of printing from blocks of wood has been practised in China from time immemorial.

19. The invention of printing, in the modern sense, from

---

[p] Brucker, iv. 50. Roscoe.

[q] Heinekke and others have proved that playing-cards were known in Germany as early as 1299; but these were probably painted. Lambinet, Origines de l'Imprimerie. Singer's History of Playing-Cards. The earliest cards were on parchment.

[r] Lambinet, Singer, Ottley, Dibdin, &c.

[s] Lambinet.

moveable letters, has been referred by most to Guten- Gutenberg
berg, a native of Mentz, but settled at Strasburg. Gutenberg
and Costar's
He is supposed to have conceived the idea before claims.
1440, and to have spent the next ten years in making
attempts at carrying it into effect, which some assert
him to have done in short fugitive pieces, actually printed
from his moveable wooden characters before 1450. But of
the existence of these there seems to be no evidence.[t]
Gutenberg's priority is disputed by those who deem Lawrence
Costar of Haarlem the real inventor of the art. According
to a tradition, which seems not to be traced beyond the
middle of the sixteenth century, but resting afterwards upon
sufficient testimony to prove its local reception, Costar substituted moveable for fixed letters as early as 1430 ; and
some have believed that a book called Speculum humanæ
Salvationis, of very rude wooden characters, proceeded from
the Haarlem press before any other that is generally recognised.[u] The tradition adds that, an unfaithful servant
having fled with the secret, set up for himself at Strasburg or
Mentz ; and this treachery was originally ascribed to
Gutenberg or Fust, but seems, since they have been manifestly
cleared of it, to have been laid on one Gensfleisch, reputed to
be the brother of Gutenberg.[x] The evidence, however, as to
this is highly precarious ; and even if we were to admit the
claims of Costar, there seems no fair reason to dispute that
Gutenberg might also have struck out an idea, which surely
did not require any extraordinary ingenuity, and left the
most important difficulties to be surmounted, as they undeni-
ably were, by himself and his coadjutors.[y]

20. It is agreed by all, that about 1450, Gutenberg, having
gone to Mentz, entered into partnership with Fust, Progress
a rich merchant of that city, for the purpose of of the inven-
tion.
carrying the invention into effect, and that Fust supplied

---

[t] Mémoires de l'Acad. des Inscript.,
xvii. 762. Lambinet, p. 113.

[u] In Mr. Ottley's History of Engraving, the claims of Costar are strongly
maintained, though chiefly on the authority of Meerman's proofs, which go to
establish the local tradition. But the
evidence of Ludovico Guicciardini is an
answer to those who treat it as a forgery

of Hadrian Junius. Santander, Lambinet, and most recent investigators, are
for Mentz against Haarlem.

[x] Gensfleisch seems to have been the
name of that branch of the Gutenberg
family to which the inventor of printing
belonged. Biogr. univ., art. Gutenberg.

[y] Lambinet, p. 315.

him with considerable sums of money. The subsequent steps
are obscure. According to a passage in the Annales
Hirsargienses of Trithemius, written sixty years afterwards,
but on the authority of a grandson of Peter Schæffer, their
assistant in the work, it was about 1452 that the latter
brought the art to perfection, by devising an easier mode of
casting types.[z] This passage has been interpreted, according
to a lax construction, to mean, that Schæffer invented the
method of casting types in a matrix; but seems more strictly
to intimate, that we owe to him the great improvement in
letter-casting, namely, the punches of engraved steel, by
which the matrices or moulds are struck, and without which,
independent of the economy of labour, there could be no
perfect uniformity of shape. Upon the former supposition,
Schæffer may be reckoned the main inventor of the art of
printing; for moveable wooden letters, though small books
may possibly have been printed by means of them, are so
inconvenient, and letters of cut metal so expensive, that few
great works were likely to have passed through the press till
cast types were employed. Van Praet, however, believes the
Psalter of 1457 to have been printed from wooden characters;
and some have conceived letters of cut metal to have been
employed both in that and in the first Bible. Lambinet,
who thinks 'the essence of the art of printing is in the engraved punch,' naturally gives the chief credit to Schæffer;[a]
but this is not the more usual opinion.

21. The earliest book, properly so called, is now generally
First printed believed to be the Latin Bible, commonly called the
Bible. Mazarin Bible, a copy having been found, about the
middle of the last century, in Cardinal Mazarin's library at
Paris.[b] It is remarkable that its existence was unknown

---

[z] Petrus Opilio de Gernsheim, tunc
famulus inventoris primi Joannis Fust,
homo ingeniosus et prudens, faciliorem
modum fundendi characteras excogitavit,
et artem, ut nunc est, complevit. Lambinet, i. 101. See Daunou contra. Id.
417.

[a] ii. 213. In another place, he divides the praise better : Gloire donc à
Gutenberg, qui, le premier, conçut l'idée
de la typographie, en imaginant la mo-

bilité des caractères, qui en est l'âme;
gloire à Fust, qui en fit usage avec lui,
et sans lequel nous ne jouirions peut-
être pas de ce bienfait ; gloire à Schæffer,
à qui nous devons tout le mécanisme,
et toutes les merveilles de l'art. i. 119.
[b] The Cologne Chronicle says, Anno
Domini 1450, qui jubilæus erat, cœptum
est imprimi, primusque liber, qui excu-
debatur, biblia fuere Latina.

before; for it can hardly be called a book of very extraordinary scarcity, nearly twenty copies being in different libraries, half of them in those of private persons in England.[c] No date appears in this Bible, and some have referred its publication to 1452, or even to 1450, which few perhaps would at present maintain; while others have thought the year 1455 rather more probable.[d] In a copy belonging to the Royal Library at Paris, an entry is made, importing that it was completed in binding and illuminating at Mentz, on the feast of the Assumption (Aug. 15), 1456. But Trithemius, in the passage above quoted, seems to intimate that no book had been printed in 1452; and, considering the lapse of time that would naturally be employed in such an undertaking during the infancy of the art, and that we have no other printed book of the least importance to fill up the interval till 1457, and also that the binding and illuminating the above-mentioned copy is likely to have followed the publication at no great length of time, we may not err in placing its appearance in the year 1455, which will secure its hitherto unimpeached priority in the records of bibliography.[e]

22. It is a very striking circumstance, that the high-minded inventors of this great art tried at the very outset so bold a flight as the printing an entire Bible, and executed it with astonishing success. It was Minerva leaping on earth in her divine strength and radiant armour, ready at the moment of her nativity to subdue and destroy her enemies. The Mazarin Bible is printed, some copies on vellum, some on paper of choice quality, with strong, black, and tolerably handsome characters, but with some want of uniformity, which has led, perhaps unreason-

Beauty of the book.

---

[c] Bibliotheca Sussexiana, i. 293, (1827). The number there enumerated is eighteen; nine in public, and nine in private libraries; three of the former, and all the latter, English.

[d] Lambinet thinks it was probably not begun before 1453, nor published till the end of 1455: i. 130. See, on this Bible, an article by Dr. Dibdin in Valpy's Classical Journal, No. 8, which collects the testimonies of his predecessors.

[e] It is very difficult to pronounce on the methods employed in the earliest books, which are almost all controverted.

This Bible is thought by Fournier, himself a letter-founder, to be printed from wooden types; by Meerman, from types cut in metal; by Heinekke and Daunou from cast types, which is most probable. Lambinet, i. 417. Daunou does not believe that any book was printed with types cut either in wood or metal; and that, after block books, there were none but with cast letters like those now in use, invented by Gutenberg. perfected by Schæffer, and first employed by them and Fust in the Mazarin Bible. Id., p. 423.

ably, to a doubt whether they were cast in a matrix. We
may see in imagination this venerable and splendid volume
leading up the crowded myriads of its followers, and implor-
ing, as it were, a blessing on the new art, by dedicating its
first fruits to the service of Heaven.

23. A metrical exhortation, in the German language, to
take arms against the Turks, dated in 1454, has
been retrieved in the present century. If this date
unequivocally refers to the time of printing, which does not
seem a necessary consequence, it is the earliest loose sheet
that is known to be extant. It is said to be in the type of
what is called the Bamberg Bible, which we shall soon have
to mention. Two editions of Letters of Indulgence from
Nicholas V., bearing the date of 1454, are extant in single
printed sheets, and two more editions of 1455;[f] but it has
justly been observed that, even if published before the Mazarin Bible, the printing of that great volume must have
commenced long before. An almanac for the year 1457 has
also been detected; and as fugitive sheets of this kind are
seldom preserved, we may justly conclude that the art or
printing was not dormant, so far as these light productions
are concerned. A Donatus, with Schæffer's name, but no
date, may or may not be older than a Psalter published in
1457 by Fust and Schæffer (the partnership with Gutenberg
having been dissolved in November, 1455, and having led to
a dispute and litigation) with a colophon or notice subjoined
in the last page, in these words :—

Psalmorum codex venustate capitalium decoratus, rubri-
cationibusque sufficienter distinctus, adinventione artificiosa
imprimendi ac caracterizandi, absque calami ulla exaratione
sic effigiatus, et ad cnsebiam Dei industrie est summatus.
Per Johannem Fust, ci em Moguntinum, et Petrum Schæffer
de Gernsheim, anno Domini millesimo cccclvii. In vigilia
Assumptionis.[g]

Marginal note: Early printed sheets.

<hr />

[f] Brunet, Supplément au Manuel du
Libraire. It was not known till lately
that more than one edition out of these
four was in existence. Santander thinks
their publication was after 1460. Dict.
bibliographique du 15me siècle, i. 92.
But this seems improbable, from the
transitory character of the subject. He
argues from a resemblance in the letters
to those used by Fust and Schæffer in
the Durandi Rationale of 1459.

[g] Dibdin's Bibliotheca Spenceriana.
Biogr. univ.: Gutenberg, &c. In this
edition of Donatus, the method of
printing is also mentioned: Explicit
Donatus arte nova imprimendi seu carac-

A colophon, substantially similar, is subjoined to several of the Fustine editions. And this seems hard to reconcile with the story that Fust sold his impressions at Paris, as late as 1463, for manuscripts.

24. Another Psalter was printed by Fust and Schæffer with similar characters in 1459; and in the same year, Durandi Rationale, a treatise on the liturgi- Psalter of 1459. Other early books. cal offices of the Church; of which Van Praet says, that it is perhaps the earliest with cast types to which Fust and Schæffer have given their name and a date.[h] The two Psalters he conceives to have been printed from wood. But this would be disputed by other eminent judges.[i] In 1460, a work of considerable size, the Catholicon of Balbi, came out from an opposition press, established at Mentz by Gutenberg. The Clementine Constitutions, part of the canon law, were also printed by him in the same year.

25. These are the only monuments of early typography acknowledged to come within the present decen- Bible of Pfister. nium. A Bible without a date, supposed by most to have been printed by Pfister at Bamberg, though ascribed by others to Gutenberg himself, is reckoned by good judges certainly prior to 1462, and, perhaps, as early as 1460. Daunou and others refer it to 1461. The antiquities of typography, after all the pains bestowed upon them, are not unlikely to receive still further elucidation in the course of time.

26. On the 19th of January, 1458, as Crevier, with a minuteness becoming the subject, informs us, the Greek first taught at Paris. university of Paris received a petition from Gregory, a native of Tiferno, in the kingdom of Naples, to be appointed teacher of Greek. His request was granted, and a salary of one hundred crowns assigned to him, on condition that he should teach gratuitously, and deliver two lectures every day, one on the Greek language, and the other

---

erizandi per Petrum de Gernsheim in urbe Moguntina effigiatus. Lambinet considers this and the Bible to be the first specimens of typography; for he doubts the Literæ Indulgentiarum, though probably with no cause.

[h] Lambinet, i. 154.
[i] Lambinet, Dibdin. The former thinks the inequality of letters observed in the Psalter of 1457 may proceed from their being cast in a matrix of plaster or clay, instead of metal.

on the art of rhetoric.[k] From this auspicious circumstance Crevier deduces the restoration of ancient literature in the university of Paris, and consequently in the kingdom of France. For above two hundred years the scholastic logic and philosophy had crushed polite letters. No mention is made of rhetoric, that is, of the art that instructs in the ornaments of style, in any statute or record of the university since the beginning of the thirteenth century. If the Greek language, as Crevier supposes, had not been wholly neglected, it was, at least, so little studied, that entire neglect would have been practically the same.

27. This concession was perhaps unwillingly made, and, as frequently happens in established institutions, it left the prejudices of the ruling party rather stronger than before. The teachers of Greek and rhetoric were specially excluded from the privileges of regency by the faculty of arts. These branches of knowledge were looked upon as unessential appendages to a good education; but a bigoted adherence to old systems, and a lurking reluctance that the rising youth should become superior in knowledge to ourselves, were no peculiar evil spirits that haunted the university of Paris, though none ever stood more in need of a thorough exorcism. For many years after this time, the Greek and Latin languages were thus taught by permission, and with very indifferent success.

Leave unwillingly granted.

28. Purbach, or Peurbach, native of a small Austrian town of that name, has been called the first restorer of mathematical science in Europe. Ignorant of Greek, and possessing only a bad translation of Ptolemy, lately made by George of Trebizond,[m] he yet was able to explain the rules of physical astronomy and the theory of the planetary motions far better than his predecessors. But his chief merit was in the construction of trigonometrical tables. The Greeks had introduced the sexagesimal division, not only of the circle, but of the radius, and calculated

Purbach: his mathematical discoveries.

---

[k] Crevier, Hist. de l'Univ. de Paris, iv. 243.

[m] Montucla, Biogr. univ. It is however certain, and is admitted by Delambre, the author of this article in the Biog. univ., that Purbach made considerable progress in abridging and explaining the text of this translation, which, if ignorant of the original, he must have done by his mathematical knowledge. Kästner, ii. 521.

chords according to this scale. The Arabians, who about the ninth century first substituted the sine, or half chord of the double arch, in their tables, preserved the same graduation. Purbach made one step towards a decimal scale, which the new notation by Arabic numerals rendered highly convenient, by dividing the radius, or sinus totus, as it was then often called, into 600,000 parts, and gave rules for computing the sines of arcs ; which he himself also calculated, for every minute of the quadrant, as Delambre and Kästner think, or for every ten minutes, according to Gassendi and Hutton, in parts of this radius. The tables of Albaten the Arabian geometer, the inventor, as far as appears, of sines, had extended only to quarters of a degree.[n]

29. Purbach died young, in 1461, when, by the advice of Cardinal Bessarion, he was on the point of setting out for Italy, in order to learn Greek. His mantle descended on Regiomontanus, a disciple, who went beyond his master, though he has sometimes borne away his due credit. A mathematician rather earlier than Purbach was Nicolas Cusanus, raised to the dignity of cardinal in 1448. He was by birth a German, and obtained a considerable reputation for several kinds of knowledge.[o] But he was chiefly distinguished for the tenet of the earth's motion, which, however, according to Montucla, he proposed only as an ingenious hypothesis. Fioravanti, of Bologna, is said, on contemporary authority, to have removed, in 1455, a tower with its foundation to a distance of several feet, and to have restored to the perpendicular one at Cento seventy-five feet high, which had swerved five feet.[p]

Other mathematicians.

---

[n] Montucla, Hist. des Mathématiques, i. 539. Hutton's Mathematical Dictionary, and his Introduction to Logarithms. Gassendi, Vita Purbachii. Biogr. univ.: Peurbach (by Delambre). Kästner, Geschichte der Mathematik, i. 529–543, 572; ii. 319. Gassendi twice gives 6,000,000 for the parts of Purbach's radius. None of these writers seem comparable in accuracy to Kästner.

[o] A work upon statics, or rather upon the weight of bodies in water, by Cusanus, seems chiefly remarkable, as it shows both a disposition to ascertain physical truths by experiment, and an extraordinary misapprehension of the results. See Kästner, ii. 122. It is published in an edition of Vitruvius, Strasburg, 1550.

[p] Tiraboschi. Montucla, Biogr. univ.

Sect. III.   1460—1470.

Progress of Art of Printing—Learning in Italy and rest of Europe.

30. The progress of that most important invention, which
Progress of illustrated the preceding ten years, is the chief
printing in
Germany. subject of our consideration in the present. Many
books, it is to be observed, even of the superior class, were
printed, especially in the first thirty years after the invention of the art, without date of time or place ; and this was,
of course, more frequently the case with smaller or fugitive
pieces. A catalogue, therefore, of books that can be certainly referred to any particular period must always be very
defective. A collection of fables in German was printed at
Bamberg in 1461, and another book in 1462, by Pfister, at
the same place.[q] The Bible which bears his name has been
already mentioned. In 1462 Fust published a Bible, commonly called the Mentz Bible, and which passed for the
earliest till that in the Mazarin library came to light. But
in the same year, the city having been taken by Adolphus
count of Nassau, the press of Fust was broken up, and his
workmen, whom he had bound by an oath to secresy, dispersed themselves into different quarters. Released thus,
as they seem to have thought, from their obligation, they
exercised their skill in other places. It is certain, that the
art of printing, soon after this, spread into the towns near
the Rhine ; not only Bamberg, as before mentioned, but
Cologne, Strasburg, Augsburg, and one or two more places,
sent forth books before the conclusion of these ten years.
Nor was Mentz altogether idle, after the confusion occasioned
by political events had abated. Yet the whole number of
books printed with dates of time and place, in the German
empire, from 1461 to 1470, according to Panzer, was only
twenty-four ; of which five were Latin, and two German,
Bibles. The only known classical works are two editions of
Cicero de Officiis, at Mentz, in 1465 and 1466, and another
about the latter year at Cologne by Ulric Zell ; perhaps too
the treatise de Finibus, and that de Senectute, at the same

---

[q] Lambinet.

place. There is also reason to suspect that a Virgil, a Valerius Maximus, and a Terence, printed by Mentelin at Strasburg, without a date, are as old as 1470; and the same has been thought of one or two editions of Ovid de Arte Amandi by Zell of Cologne. One book, Joannis de Turrecremata Explanatio in Psalterium, was printed by Zainer at Cracow, in 1465. This is remarkable, as we have no evidence of the Polish press from that time till 1500. Several copies of this book are said to exist in Poland; yet doubts of its authenticity have been entertained. Zainer settled soon afterwards at Augsburg.[r]

31. It was in 1469 that Ulrick Gering, with two more who had been employed as pressmen by Fust at Mentz, were induced by Fichet and Lapierre, rectors of the Sorbonne, to come to Paris, where several books were printed in 1470 and 1471. The epistles of Gasparin of Barziza appear, by some verses subjoined, to have been the earliest among these.[s] Panzer has increased to eighteen the list of books printed there before the close of 1472.[t]

Introduced into France.

32. But there seem to be unquestionable proofs that a still earlier specimen of typography is due to an English printer, the famous Caxton. His Recueil des Histoires de Troye appears to have been printed during the life of Philip duke of Burgundy, and consequently before June 15, 1467. The place of publication, certainly within the duke's dominions, has not been conjectured. It is, therefore, by several years the earliest printed book in the French language.[u] A Latin speech by Russell, ambassador of Edward IV. to Charles of Burgundy, in 1469, is the next publication of Caxton. This was also printed in the Low Countries.[x]

Caxton's first works.

33. A more splendid scene was revealed in Italy. Sweynheim and Pannartz, two workmen of Fust, set up a press,

---

[r] Panzer, Annales Typographici. Biographie universelle : Zainer.

[s] The last four of these lines are the following :—

Primos ecce libros quos hæc industria finxit,
Francorum in terris, ædibus atque tuis.
Michael, Udalricus, Martinusque magistri
Hos impresserunt, et facient alios.

[t] See Gresswell's Early Parisian Press.

[u] [I am obliged to a correspondent for reminding me, that the Recueil des Histoires de Troye, though printed, and afterwards translated, by Caxton, was written by Raoul le Fèvre.—1847.]

[x] Dibdin's Typographical Antiquities. This is not noticed in the Biographie universelle, nor in Brunet; an omission hardly excusable.

doubtless with encouragement and patronage, at the monas-
Printing tery of Subiaco in the Apennines, a place chosen, either
exercised in
Italy. on account of the numerous manuscripts it contained,
or because the monks were of the German nation ; and hence
an edition of Lactantius issued in October, 1465, which one,
no longer extant, of Donatus's little grammar is said to have
preceded. An edition of Cicero de Officiis, without a date,
is referred by some to the year 1466. In 1467, after printing
Augustin de Civitate Dei and Cicero de Oratore, the two
Germans left Subiaco for Rome, where they sent forth not
less than twenty-three editions of ancient Latin authors
before the close of 1470. Another German, John of Spire,
established a press at Venice in 1469, beginning with Cicero's
Epistles. In that and the next year, almost as many
classical works were printed at Venice as at Rome, either by
John and his brother Vindelin, or by a Frenchman, Nicolas
Jenson. Instances are said to exist of books printed by
unknown persons at Milan, in 1469 ; and in 1470, Zarot, a
German, opened there a fertile source of typography, though
but two Latin authors were published that year. An edition
of Cicero's Epistles appeared also in the little town of Foligno. The whole number of books that had issued from
the press in Italy at the close of that year amounts, according to Panzer, to eighty-two ; exclusive of those
which have no date, some of which may be referable to this
period.

34. Cosmo de' Medici died in 1464. But the happy
Lorenzo de'
Medici. impulse he had given to the restoration of letters
was not suspended; and in the last year of the
present decad, his wealth and his influence over the republic
of Florence had devolved on a still more conspicuous character, his grandson Lorenzo, himself worthy, by his literary
merits, to have done honour to any patron, had not a more
prosperous fortune called him to become one.

35. The epoch of Lorenzo's accession to power is distin-
Italian
poetry of
fifteenth
century. guished by a circumstance hardly less honourable
than the restoration of classical learning,—the revival of native genius in poetry, after the slumber
of near a hundred years. After the death of Petrarch, many
wrote verses, but none excelled in the art ; though Muratori

has praised the poetry down to 1400, especially that of Giusto di Conti, whom he does not hesitate to place among the first poets of Italy.[y] But that of the fifteenth century is abandoned by all critics as rude, feeble, and ill expressed. The historians of literature scarcely deign to mention a few names, or the editors of selections to extract a few sonnets. The romances of chivalry in rhyme, Buovo d'Antona, la Spagna, l'Ancroja, are only deserving to be remembered as they led in some measure to the great poems of Boiardo and Ariosto. In themselves they are mean and prosaic. It is vain to seek a general cause for this sterility in the cultivation of Latin and Greek literature, which we know did not obstruct the brilliancy of Italian poetry in the next age. There is only one cause for the want of great men in any period;—nature does not think fit to produce them. They are no creatures of education and circumstance.

36. The Italian prose literature of this interval from the age of Petrarch would be comprised in a few volumes. Some historical memoirs may be found *Italian prose of same age.* in Muratori, but far the chief part of his collection is in Latin. Leonard Aretin wrote lives of Dante and Petrarch in Italian, which, according to Corniani, are neither valuable for their information nor for their style. The Vita Civile of Palmieri seems to have been written some time after the middle of the fifteenth century; but of this Corniani says, that having wished to give a specimen, on account of the rarity of Italian in that age, he had abandoned his intention, finding that it was hardly possible to read two sentences in the Vita Civile without meeting some barbarism or incorrectness. The novelists Sacchetti and Ser Giovanni, author of the Pecorone, who belong to the end of the fourteenth century, are read by some; their style is familiar and idiomatic; but Crescimbeni praises that of the former. Corniani bestows some praise on Passavanti and Pandolfini; the first a religious writer, not much later than Boccaccio; the latter a noble Florentine, author of a moral dialogue in the beginning of the fifteenth century. Filelfo, among his voluminous productions, has an Italian commen-

---

[y] Muratori della perfetta poesia, p. 193.   Bouterwek, Gesch. der Ital. Poesie, i. 216.

tary on Petrarch, of which Corniani speaks very slightingly. The commentary of Landino on Dante is much better esteemed ; but it was not published till 1481.

37. It was on occasion of a tournament, wherein Lo-

Giostra of Politian.

renzo himself and his brother Julian had appeared in the lists, that poems were composed by Luigi Pulci, and by Politian, then a youth, or rather a boy, the latter of which displayed more harmony, spirit, and imagination, than any that had been written since the death of Petrarch.[a] It might thus be seen, that there was no real incompatibility between the pursuits of ancient literature and the popular language of fancy and sentiment; and that, if one gave chastity and elegance of style, a more lively and natural expression of the mind could best be attained by the other

38. This period was not equally fortunate for the learned

Paul II. persecutes the learned.

in other parts of Italy. Ferdinand of Naples, who came to the throne in 1458, proved no adequate represeniative of his father Alfonso. But at Rome they encountered a serious calamity. A few zealous scholars, such as Pomponius Lætus, Platina, Callimachus Experiens, formed an academy in order to converse together on subjects of learning, and communicate to each other the results of their private studies. Dictionaries, indexes, and all works of compilation being very deficient, this was the best substitute for the labour of perusing the whole body of Latin antiquity. They took Roman names ; an innocent folly, long after practised in Europe. The pope, however, Paul II., thought fit, in 1468, to arrest all this society on charges of conspiracy against his life, for which there was certainly no foundation, and of setting up Pagan superstitions against Christianity, of which, in this instance, there seems to have been no proof. They were put to the torture

---

[a] Extracts from this poem will be found in Roscoe's Lorenzo, and in Sismondi, Littérature du Midi, ii. 43, who praises it highly, as the Italian critics have done, and as by the passages quoted it seems well to deserve. Roscoe supposes Politian to be only fourteen years old when he wrote the Giostra di Giuliano. But the lines he quotes allude to Lorenzo as chief of the republic, which could not be said before the death of Pietro in December, 1469. If he wrote them at sixteen, it is extraórdinary enough ; but these two years make an immense difference. Ginguéné is of opinion, that they do not allude to the tournament of 1468, but to one in 1473.

and kept in prison a twelvemonth; when the tyrant, who
is said to have vowed this in his first rage set them all at
liberty; but it was long before the Roman academy recovered any degree of vigour.[b]

39. We do not discover as yet much substantial encouragement to literature in any country on this side the
Alps, with the exception of one where it was least to be anticipated.   Mathias Corvinus, king of Hungary, from his
accession in 1458 to his death in 1490, endea- Mathias
voured to collect round himself the learned of Italy, Corvinus.
and to strike light into the midst of the depths of darkness
that encompassed his country.   He determined, therefore,
to erect an university, which, by the original plan, was to
have been in a distinct city; but the Turkish wars compelled him to fix it at Buda.   He availed himself of the
dispersion of libraries after the capture of Constantinople
to purchase Greek manuscripts, and employed four transcribers at Florence, besides thirty at Buda, to enrich his
collection.   Thus, at his death, it is said that the
royal library at Buda contained 50,000 volumes; His library.
a number that appears wholly incredible.[c]   Three hundred
ancient statues are reported to have been placed in the same
repository.   But when the city fell into the hands of the
Turks in 1527, these noble treasures were dispersed, and in
great measure destroyed.   Though the number of books, as
is just observed, must have been exaggerated, it is possible
that neither the burning of the Alexandrian library by
Omar, if it ever occurred, nor any other single calamity
recorded in history, except the two captures of Constantinople itself, has been more fatally injurious to literature;
and, with due regard to the good intentions of Mathias
Corvinus, it is deeply to be regretted that the inestimable
relics once rescued from the barbarian Ottomans should

---

[b] Tiraboschi, vi. 93.   Ginguéné.
Brucker. Corniani, ii. 280. This writer,
inferior to none in his acquaintance with
the literature of the fifteenth century,
but, though not an ecclesiastic, always
favourable to the court of Rome, seems
to strive to lay the blame on the im-
prudence of Platina.

[c] The library collected by Nicolas V.
contained only 5000 manuscripts. The
volumes printed in Europe before the
death of Corvinus would probably be
reckoned highly at 15,000.   Heeren suspects the number 50,000 to be hyperbolical; and in fact there can be no
doubt of it.

have been accumulated in a situation of so little security against their devastating arms.[d]

40. England under Edward IV. presents an appearance, Slight signs in the annals of publication, about as barren as of literature in England. under Edward the Confessor; there is, I think, neither in Latin nor in English, a single book that we can refer to this decennial.[e] Yet we find a few symptoms, not to be overlooked, of the incipient regard to literature. Leland enumerates some Englishmen who travelled to Italy, perhaps before 1460, in order to become disciples of the younger Guarini at Ferrara : Robert Fleming, William Gray, bishop of Ely, John Free, John Gunthorpe, and a very accomplished nobleman, John Tiptoft, earl of Worcester. It is but fairness to give credit to these men for their love of learning, and to observe, that they preceded any whom we could mention on sure grounds either in France or Germany. We trace, however, no distinct fruits from their acquisitions. But, though very few had the means of attaining that on which we set a high value in literature, the mere rudiments of grammatical learning were communicated to many. Nor were munificent patrons, testators, in the words of Burke, to a posterity which they embraced as their own, wanting in this latter period of the middle ages. William of Wykeham, chancellor of England under Richard II., and bishop of Winchester, founded a school in that city, and a college at Oxford in connection with it, in 1373.[f] Henry VI., in imitation of him, became the founder of Eton School, and of King's College, Cambridge, about 1442.[g] In each of these schools seventy boys, and in each college seventy fellows and scholars, are maintained by these princely endowments.

---

[d] Brucker, Roscoe, Gibbon. Heeren, p. 173, who refers to several modern books expressly relating to the fate of this library. Part of it, however, found its way to that of Vienna.

[e] The university of Oxford, according to Wood, as well as the church generally, stood very low about this time : the grammar schools were laid aside ; degrees were conferred on undeserving persons for money. A.D. 1455, 1466. He had previously mentioned those schools as kept up in the university under the superintendence of masters of arts. A.D. 1442. But the statutes of Magdalen College, founded in the reign of Edward, provide for a certain degree of learning. —Chandler's Life of Waynflete, p. 200.

[f] Lowth's Life of Wykeham. He permits in his statutes a limited number of sons of gentlemen (gentilium) to be educated in his school. Chandler's Life of Waynflete, p. 5.

[g] Waynflete became the first head master of Eton in 1442. Chandler, p. 26.

It is unnecessary to observe, that they are still the amplest, as they are much the earliest, foundations for the support of grammatical learning in England.   What could be taught in these, or any other schools at this time, the reader has been enabled to judge; it must have been the Latin language, through indifferent books of grammar, and with the perusal of very few heathen writers of antiquity.   In the curious and unique collection of the Paston Letters we find one from a boy at Eton in 1468, wherein he gives two Latin verses, not very good, of his own composition.[h]   I am sensible that the mention of such a circumstance may appear trifling, especially to foreigners: but it is not a trifle to illustrate by any fact the gradual progress of knowledge among the laity; first in the mere elements of reading and writing, as we did in a former chapter; and now, in the fifteenth century, in such grammatical instruction as could be imparted.   This boy of the Paston family was well born, and came from a distance; nor was he in training for the church, since he seems by this letter to have had marriage in contemplation.

41. But the Paston letters are, in other respects, an important testimony to the progressive condition of society, and come in as a precious link in the chain Paston Letters. of the moral history of England, which they alone in this period supply.   They stand indeed singly, as far as I know, in Europe; for though it is highly probable that in the archives of Italian families, if not in France or Germany, a series of merely private letters equally ancient may be concealed, I do not recollect that any have been published. They are all written in the reigns of Henry VI. and Edward IV., except a few as late as Henry VII., by different members of a wealthy and respectable, but not noble, family; and are, therefore, pictures of the life of the English gentry in that age.[i]   We are merely concerned with their evidence

---

[h] Vol. i. p. 301. Of William Paston, author of these lines, it is said, some years before, that he had "gone to school to a Lombard called Karol Giles, to learn and to be read in poetry, or else in French.   He said, that he would be as glad and as fain of a good book of French or of poetry as my master Falstaff would

be to purchase a fair manor." p. 173. (1459.)

[i] This collection is in five quarto volumes, and has become scarce.   The length has been doubled by an injudicious proceeding of the editor, in printing the original orthography and abbreviations of the letters on each left-hand

as to the state of literature. And this upon the whole is more favourable than, from the want of authorship in those reigns, we should be led to anticipate. It is plain that several members of the family, male and female, wrote not only grammatically, but with a fluency and facility, an epistolary expertness, which implies the habitual use of the pen. Their expression is much less formal and quaint than that of modern novelists, when they endeavour to feign the familiar style of ages much later than the fifteenth century. Some of them mix Latin with their English, very bad, and probably for the sake of concealment; and Ovid is once mentioned as a book to be sent from one to another.[k] It appears highly probable, that such a series of letters, with so much vivacity and pertinence, would not have been written by any family of English gentry in the reign of Richard II., and much less before. It is hard to judge from a single case; but the letter of Lady Pelham, quoted in the first chapter of this volume, is ungrammatical and unintelligible. The seed, therefore, was now rapidly germinating beneath the ground; and thus we may perceive that the publication of books is not the sole test of the intellectual advance of a people. I may add, that although the middle of the fifteenth century was the period in which the fewest books were written, a greater number, in the opinion of experienced judges, were transcribed in that than in any former age; a circumstance easily accounted for by the increased use of linen paper.

42. It may be observed here, with reference to the state of learning generally in England down to the age immediately preceding the Reformation, that Leland, in the fourth volume of his Collectanea, has given several lists of books in colleges and monasteries, which do not by any means warrant the supposition of a tolerable

page, and a more legible modern form on the right. As orthography is of little importance, and abbreviations of none at all, it would have been sufficient to have given a single specimen.

[k] "As to Ovid de arte amandi, I shall send him you next week, for I have him not now ready." iv. 175. This was between 1463 and 1469, according to the editor. We do not know positively of any edition of Ovid de arte amandi so early; but Zell of Cologne is supposed to have printed one before 1470, as has been mentioned above. Whether the book to be sent were in print, or manuscript, must be left to the sagacity of critics.

acquaintance with ancient literature. We find, however, some of the recent translations made in Italy from Greek authors. The clergy, in fact, were now retrograding, while the laity were advancing; and when this was the case, the ascendancy of the former was near its end.

43. I have said that there was not a new book written within these ten years. In the days of our fathers it would have been necessary at least to mention as a forgery the celebrated poems attributed to Thomas Rowley. But, probably, no one person living believes in their authenticity; nor should I have alluded to so palpable a fabrication at all, but for the curious circumstance that a very similar trial of literary credulity has not long since been essayed in France. A gentleman of the name of Surville published a collection of poems, alleged to have been written by Clotilde de Surville, a poetess of the fifteenth century. The muse of the Ardèche warbled her notes during a longer life than the monk of Bristow; and having sung the relief of Orleans by the Maid of Arc in 1429, lived to pour her swanlike chant on the battle of Fornova in 1495. Love, however, as much as war, is her theme; and it was a remarkable felicity that she rendered an ode of her prototype Sappho into French verse, many years before any one else in France could have seen it. But having, like Rowley, anticipated too much the style and sentiments of a later period, she has, like him, fallen into the numerous ranks of the dead who never were alive.[m]

Marginal notes: Rowley. / Clotilde de Surville.

---

[m] Auguis, Recueil des Poètes, vol. ii. Biogr. univ.: Surville. Villemain, Cours de Littérature, vol. ii. Sismondi, Hist. des Français, xiii. 593. The forgery is by no means so gross as that of Chatterton; but, as M. Sismondi says, "We have only to compare Clotilde with the duke of Orleans, or Villon." The following lines, quoted by him, will give the reader a fair specimen:—

Suivons l'amour, tel en soit le danger ;
Cy nous attend sur lits charmans de mousse.

A des rigueurs ; qui voudroit s'en venger ?
Qui (même alors que tout désir s'émousse)
Au prix fatal de ne plus y songer ?
Règne sur moi, cher tyran, dont les armes
Ne me sauroient porter coups trop puissans !
Pour m'épargner n'en crois onc à mes larmes ;
Sont de plaisir, tant plus auront de charmes
Tes dards aigus, que seront plus cuisans.

It has been justly remarked, that the extracts from Clotilde in the Recueil des anciens Poètes occupy too much space, while the genuine writers of the fifteenth century appear in very scanty specimens.

SECT. IV.   1471—1480.

The same Subjects continued—Lorenzo de' Medici—Physical Controversy—
Mathematical Sciences.

44. THE books printed in Italy during these ten years
Number of
books print-
ed in Italy. amount, according to Panzer, to 1,297; of which
23 are editions of ancient classical authors. Books
without dates are of course not included; and the list must
not be reckoned complete as to others.

45. A press was established at Florence by Lorenzo, in
which Cennini, a goldsmith, was employed; the first
printer, except Caxton and Jenson, who was not a German.
Virgil was published in 1471. Several other Italian cities
began to print in this period. The first edition of Dante
issued from Foligno in 1472; it has been improbably as
well as erroneously, referred to Mentz. Petrarch had been
published in 1470, and Boccace in 1471. They were reprinted several times before the close of this decad.

46. No one had attempted to cast Greek types in sufficient
First Greek
printed. number for an entire book; though a few occur in
the early publications by Sweynheim and Pan-
nartz;[n] while in those printed afterwards at Venice, Greek
words are inserted by the pen; till, in 1476, Zarot of Milan
had the honour of giving the Greek grammar of Constantine Lascaris to the world.[o] This was followed in 1480 by
Craston's Lexicon, a very imperfect vocabulary; but which
for many years continued to be the only assistance of the
kind to which a student could have recourse. The author
was an Italian.

---

[n] Greek types first appear in a treatise
of Jerome, printed at Rome in 1468.
Heeren, from Panzer.

[o] Lascaris Grammatica Græca, Me-
diolani ex recognitione Demetrii Cretensis per Dionysium Paravisinum, 4to.
The characters in this rare volume are
elegant and of a moderate size. The
earliest specimens of Greek printing consist of detached passages and citations;
found in a very few of the first printed
copies of Latin authors, such as the Lactantius of 1465, the Aulus Gellius and
Apuleius of Sweynheim and Pannartz,
1469, and some works of Bessarion about
the same time. In all these it is remarkable that the Greek typography is legibly
and creditably executed, whereas the
Greek introduced into the Officia et Para-
doxa of Cicero, Milan, 1474, by Zarot, is
so deformed as to be scarcely legible. I
am indebted for the whole of this note to
Gresswell's Early Parisian Greek Press,
i. 1.

47. Ancient learning is to be divided into two great departments; the knowledge of what is contained in the $\quad$ Study of
works of Greek and Roman authors, and that of the $\quad$ antiquities.
matériel, if I may use the word, which has been preserved in a
bodily shape, and is sometimes known by the name of antiquities. Such are buildings, monuments, inscriptions, coins,
medals, vases, instruments, which, by gradual accumulation,
have thrown a powerful light upon ancient history and literature. The abundant riches of Italy in these remains could
not be overlooked as soon as the spirit of admiration for all
that was Roman began to be kindled. Petrarch himself
formed a little collection of coins ; and his contemporary Past-
rengo was the first who copied inscriptions; but in the early
part of the fifteenth century her scholars and her patrons of
letters began to collect the scattered relics which almost
every region presented to them.[p] Niccolo Niccoli, according
to the funeral oration of Poggio, possessed a series of medals,
and even wrote a treatise in Italian, correcting the common
orthography of Latin words, on the authority of inscriptions
and coins. The love of collection increased from this time ;
the Medici and other rich patrons of letters spared no expense
in accumulating these treasures of the antiquary. Ciriacus
of Ancona, about 1440, travelled into the East in order to
copy inscriptions ; but he was naturally exposed to deceive
himself and to be deceived ; nor has he escaped the suspicion
of imposture, or at least of excessive credulity.[q]

48. The first who made his researches of this kind collectively known to the world was Biondo Flavio, $\quad$ Works on
or Flavio Biondo,—for the names may be found in $\quad$ that subject.
a different order, but more correctly in the first [r]—secretary
to Eugenius IV., and to his successors. His long residence
at Rome inspired him with the desire, and gave him the
opportunity, of describing her imperial ruins. In a work,

---

[p] Tiraboschi, vols. v. and vi. Andrès,
ix. 196.

[q] Tiraboschi. Andrès, ix. 199. Ci-
riaco has not wanted advocates : some of
the inscriptions he was accused of having
forged have turned out to be authentic ;
and it is presumed in his favour, that
others which do not appear may have
perished since his time. Biogr. univ. :

Cyriaque. One that rests on his authority is that which is supposed to record the persecution of the Christians in
Spain under Nero. See Lardner's Jewish
and Heathen Testimonies, vol. i., who,
though by no means a credulous critic,
inclines to its genuineness.

[r] Zeno, Dissertazioni Vossiane, i. 229.

dedicated to Eugenius IV., who died in 1447, but not printed till 1471, entitled, Romæ Instauratæ libri tres, he describes, examines, and explains, by the testimonies of ancient authors, the numerous monuments of Rome. In another, Romæ Triumphantis libri decem, printed about 1472, he treats of the government, laws, religion, ceremonies, military discipline, and other antiquities of the republic. A third work, compiled at the request of Alfonso king of Naples, and printed in 1474, called Italia Illustrata, contains a description of all Italy, divided into its ancient fourteen regions. Though Biondo Flavio was almost the first to hew his way into the rock, which should cause his memory to be respected, it has naturally happened, that his works being imperfect and faulty, in comparison with those of the great antiquaries of the sixteenth century, they have not found a place in the collection of Grævius, and are hardly remembered by name.[s]

49. In Germany and the Low Countries the art of printing Publications began to be exercised at Deventer, Utrecht, Louvain, in Germany. Basle, Ulm, and other places, and in Hungary at Buda. We find however, very few ancient writers; the whole list of what can pass for classics being about thirteen. One or two editions of parts of Aristotle in Latin, from translations lately made in Italy, may be added. Yet it was not the length of manuscripts that discouraged the German printers ; for besides their editions of the Scriptures, Mentelin of Strasburg published, in 1473, the great Encyclopædia of Vincent of Beauvais, in ten volumes folio, generally bound in four; and, in 1474, a similar work of Berchorius, or Berchœur, in three other folios. The contrast between these labours and those of his Italian contemporaries is very striking.

50. Florus and Sallust were printed at Paris early in this In France. decad, and twelve more classical authors at the same place before its termination. An edition of Cicero

A superior treatise of the same age on the antiquities of the Roman city is by Bernard Rucellai (de urbe Româ, in Rer. Ital. Script. Florent. vol ii.). But it was not published before the eighteenth century. Rucellai wrote some historical works in a very good Latin style, and was distinguished also in the political revolutions of Florence. After the death of Lorenzo, he became the protector of the Florentine academy, for the members of which he built a palace with gardens. Corniani, iii. 143. Biog. univ. : Rucellai.

ad Herennium appeared at Angers in 1476, and one of Horace at Caen in 1480. The press of Lyons also sent forth several works, but none of them classical. It has been said by French writers that the first book printed in their language is Le Jardin de Dévotion, by Colard Mansion of Bruges, in 1473. This date has been questioned in England; but it is of the less importance, as we have already seen that Caxton's Recueil des Histoires de Troye has the clear priority. Le Roman de Baudouin comte de Flandres, Lyon, 1474, seems to be the earliest French book printed in France. In 1476, Les grands Chroniques de St. Denis, an important and bulky volume, appeared at Paris.

51. We come now to our own Caxton, who finished a translation into English of the Recueil des Histoires de Troye, by order of Margaret duchess of Burgundy, at Cologne, in September, 1471. It was probably printed there the next year.[t] But soon afterwards he came to England with the instruments of his art; and his Game of Chess, a slight and short performance, referred to 1474, though without a date, is supposed to have been the first specimen of English typography.[u] In almost every year from this time to his death in 1483, Caxton continued to publish those volumes which are the delight of our collectors. The earliest of his editions bearing a date in England, is the 'Dictes and Sayings,' a translation by Lord Rivers from a Latin compilation, and published in 1477. In a literary history it should be observed, that the Caxton publications are more adapted to the general than the learned reader, and indicate, upon the whole, but a low state of knowledge in England. A Latin translation, however, of Aristotle's Ethics was printed at Oxford in 1479.

52. The first book printed in Spain was on the very subject

In England, by Caxton.

---

[t] This book at the duke of Roxburghe's famous sale brought 1,060*l*.

[u] The Expositio Sancti Hieronymi, of which a copy, in the public library at Cambridge, bears the date of Oxford, 1468, on the title-page, is now generally given up. It has been successfully contended by Middleton, and lately by Mr. Singer, that this date should be 1478; the numeral letter x having been casu-ally omitted. Several similar instances occur in which a pretended early book has not stood the keen eye of criticism : as the Decor Puellarum, ascribed to Nicolas Jenson of Venice, in 1461, for which we should read 1471; a cosmography of Ptolemy with the date of 1462; a book appearing to have been printed at Tours in 1467, &c.

we might expect to precede all others, the Conception of
the Virgin. It should be a very curious volume,
In Spain.   being a poetical contest on that sublime theme by
thirty-six poets, four of whom had written in Spanish, one
in Italian, and the rest in Provençal or Valencian. It appeared at Valencia in 1474. A little book on grammar
followed in 1475, and Sallust was printed the same year.
In that year printing was also introduced at Barcelona and
Saragossa, in 1476 at Seville, in 1480 at Salamanca and
Burgos.

53. A translation of the Bible by Malerbi, a Venetian,
Translations   was published in 1471, and two other editions of
of Scripture. that, or a different version, the same year. Eleven
editions are enumerated by Panzer in the fifteenth century.
The German translation has already been mentioned; it was
several times reprinted in this decad ; one in Dutch appeared
in 1477, one in the Valencian language, at that city, in
1478 ;ˣ the New Testament was printed in Bohemian, 1475,
and in French, 1477 ; the earliest French translation of the
Old Testament seems to be about the same date. The reader
will of course understand, that all these translations were
made from the Vulgate Latin. It may naturally seem remarkable, that not only at this period, but down to the
Reformation, no attempt was made to render any part of the
Scriptures public in English. But, in fact, the ground was
thought too dangerous by those in power. The translation
of Wicliffe had taught the people some comparisons between
the worldly condition of the first preachers of Christianity
and their successors, as well as some other contrasts, which
it was more expedient to avoid. Long before the invention
of printing it was enacted, in 1408, by a constitution of
Archbishop Arundel in convocation, that no one should
thereafter ' translate any text of Holy Scripture into English,
by way of a book, or little book or tract; and that no book
should be read that was composed lately in the time of
John Wicliffe, or since his death.' Scarcely any of Caxton's
publications are of a religious nature.

ˣ This edition was suppressed or destroyed ; no copy is known to exist; but
there is preserved a final leaf containing
the names of the translator and printer.

M'Crie's Reformation in Spain, p. 192.
Andrès says (xix. 154) that this translation was made early in the fifteenth
century, with the approbation of divines.

54. It would have been strange if Spain, placed on the genial shores of the Mediterranean, and intimately Revival of literature in Spain. connected through the Aragonese kings with Italy, had not received some light from that which began to shine so brightly. Her progress, however, in letters was but slow. Not but that several individuals are named by compilers of literary biography in the first part of the fifteenth century, as well as earlier, who are reputed to have possessed a knowledge of languages, and to have stood at least far above their contemporaries. Alfonsus Tostatus passes for the most considerable ; his writings are chiefly theological, but Andrès praises his commentary on the Chronicle of Eusebius, at least as a bold essay ;[y] contending also that learning was not deficient in Spain during the fifteenth century, though he admits that the rapid improvements made at its close, and about the beginning of the next age, were due to Lebrixa's public instructions at Seville and Salamanca. Several translations were made from Latin authors into Spanish, which, however, is not of itself any great proof of peninsular learning. The men to whom Spain chiefly owes the advancement of useful learning, and who should not be defrauded of their glory, were Arias Barbosa, a scholar of Politian, and the more renowned, though not more learned or more early propagator of Grecian literature, Antonio of Lebrixa, whose name was latinised into Nebrissensis, by which he is commonly known. Of Arias, who unaccountably has no place in the Biographie universelle, Nicolas Antonio gives a very high character.[z] He taught the Greek language at Salamanca probably about this time. But his writings are not at all numerous. For Lebrixa, instead of compiling from other sources, I shall transcribe what Dr. M'Crie has said with his usual perspicuous brevity.

---

[y] ix. 151.

[z] In quo Antonium Nebrissensem socium habuit, qui tamen quicquid usquam Græcarum literarum apud Hispanos esset, ab uno Aria emanâsse in præfatione suarum Introductionum Grammaticarum ingenue affirmavit. His duobus amplissimum illud gymnasium, indeque Hispania tota debet barbariei, quæ longo apud nos bellorum dominatu in immensum creverat, extirpationem, bonarumque omnium disciplinarum divitias. Quas Arias noster ex antiquitatis penu per vicennium integrum auditoribus suis larga et locuplete vena communicavit, in poetica facultate Græcanicaque doctrina Nebrissense melior, a quo tamen in varia multiplicique doctrina superabatur. Bibl. Vetus.

55. 'Lebrixa, usually styled Nebrissensis, became to Spain
Character what Valla was to Italy, Erasmus to Germany, or
of Lebrixa. Budæus to France. After a residence of ten years
in Italy, during which he had stored his mind with various
kinds of knowledge, he returned home, in 1473, by the advice
of the younger Philelphus and Hermolaus Barbarus, with the
view of promoting classical literature in his native country.
Hitherto the revival of letters in Spain was confined to a few
inquisitive individuals, and had not reached the schools and
universities, whose teachers continued to teach a barbarous
jargon under the name of Latin, into which they initiated
the youth by means of a rude system of grammar, rendered
unintelligible in some instances, by a preposterous intermixture of the most abstruse questions in metaphysics. By
the lectures which he read in the universities of Seville,
Salamanca, and Alcalá, and by the institutes which he
published on Castilian, Latin, Greek, and Hebrew grammar,
Lebrixa contributed in a wonderful degree to expel barbarism
from the seats of education, and to diffuse a taste for elegant
and useful studies among his countrymen. His improvements were warmly opposed by the monks, who had engrossed
the art of teaching, and who, unable to bear the light themselves, wished to prevent all others from seeing it; but,
enjoying the support of persons of high authority, he disregarded their selfish and ignorant outcries. Lebrixa continued
to an advanced age to support the literary reputation of
his native country.' [a]

56. This was the brilliant era of Florence, under the
Library of supremacy of Lorenzo de' Medici. The reader is pro-
Lorenzo. bably well acquainted with this eminent character,
by means of a work of extensive and merited reputation.
The Laurentian library, still consisting wholly of manuscripts, though formed by Cosmo, and enlarged by his son
Pietro, owed not only its name, but an ample increase of its
treasures, to Lorenzo, who swept the monasteries of Greece
through his learned agent, John Lascaris. With that true

---

[a] M'Crie's Hist of Reformation in
Spain, p. 61. It is probable that Le
brixa's exertions were not very effectual
in the present decennium, nor perhaps
in the next, but his Institutiones Grammaticæ, a very scarce book, were printed
at Seville in 1481.

love of letters which scorns the monopolising spirit of possession, Lorenzo permitted his manuscripts to be freely copied for the use of other parts of Europe.

57. It was an important labour of the learned at Florence to correct, as well as elucidate, the text of their Classics corrected and manuscripts, written generally by ignorant and explained. careless monks, or trading copyists (though the latter probably had not much concern with ancient writers), and become almost wholly unintelligible through the blunders of these transcribers.[b] Landino, Merula, Calderino, and Politian were the most indefatigable in this line of criticism during the age of Lorenzo. Before the use of printing fixed the text of a whole edition—one of the most important of its consequences—the critical amendments of these scholars could only be made useful through their oral lectures. And these appear frequently to have been the foundation of the valuable, though rather prolix, commentaries we find in the old editions. Thus those of Landino accompany many editions of Horace and Virgil, forming, in some measure, the basis of all interpretative annotations on those poets. Landino in these seldom touches on verbal criticisms; but his explanations display a considerable reach of knowledge. They are founded, as Heeren is convinced, on his lectures, and consequently give us some notion of the tone of instruction. In explaining the poets, two methods were pursued, the grammatical and the moral, the latter of which consisted in resolving the whole sense into allegory. Dante had given credit to a doctrine, orthodox in this age and long afterwards, that every great poem must have a hidden meaning.[c]

58. The notes of Calderino, a scholar of high fame, but infected with the common vice of arrogance, are Character of found with those of Landino in the early editions of Lorenzo. Virgil and Horace. Regio commented upon Ovid, Omnibonus Leonicenus upon Lucan, both these upon Quintilian, many upon Cicero.[d] It may be observed, for the sake of chronological exactness, that these labours are by no means

---

[b] Meiners, Vergleich. der Sitten, iii. [c] Heeren, pp. 241, 287.
108. Heeren, p. 293. [d] Id. 297.

confined, even principally, to this decennial period. They
are mentioned in connexion with the name of Lorenzo de'
Medici, whose influence over literature extended from 1470
to his death in 1492. Nor was mere philology the sole or
the leading pursuit to which so truly noble a mind accorded
its encouragement. He sought in ancient learning something more elevated than the narrow, though necessary, researches of criticism. In a villa overhanging the towers of
Florence, on the steep slope of that lofty hill crowned by the
mother city, the ancient Fiesole, in gardens which Tully
might have envied, with Ficino, Landino, and Politian at
his side, he delighted his hours of leisure with the beautiful
visions of Platonic philosophy, for which the summer still-
ness of an Italian sky appears the most congenial accompaniment.

59. Never could the sympathies of the soul with outward
Prospect from nature be more finely touched; never could more
his villa at
Fiesole. striking suggestions be presented to the philosopher
and the statesman. Florence lay beneath them; not with
all the magnificence that the later Medici have given her,
but, thanks to the piety of former times, presenting almost
as varied an outline to the sky. One man, the wonder of
Cosmo's age, Brunelleschi, had crowned the beautiful city
with the vast dome of its cathedral; a structure unthought
of in Italy before, and rarely since surpassed. It seemed,
amidst clustering towers of inferior churches, an emblem of
the Catholic hierarchy under its supreme head; like Rome
itself, imposing, unbroken, unchangeable, radiating in equal
expansion to every part of the earth, and directing its con-
vergent curves to heaven. Round this were numbered, at
unequal heights, the Baptistery, with its gates, as Michael
Angelo styled them, worthy of Paradise; the tall and richly
decorated belfry of Giotto; the church of the Carmine, with
the frescoes of Masaccio; those of Santa Maria Novella (in
the language of the same great man), beautiful as a bride;
of Santa Croce, second only in magnificence to the cathedral,
of St. Mark, and of San Spirito, another great monument of
the genius of Brunelleschi; the numerous convents that rose
within the walls of Florence, or were scattered immediately
about them. From these the eye might turn to the trophies

of a republican government that was rapidly giving way before
the citizen-prince who now surveyed them; the Palazzo
Vecchio, in which the signiory of Florence held their councils, raised by the Guelf aristocracy, the exclusive, but not
tyrannous faction that long swayed the city; or the new
and unfinished palace which Brunelleschi had designed for
one of the Pitti family, before they fell, as others had already
done, in the fruitless struggle against the house of Medici;
itself destined to become the abode of the victorious race,
and to perpetuate, by retaining its name, the revolutions
that had raised them to power.

60. The prospect, from an elevation, of a great city in its
silence, is one of the most impressive, as well as beautiful,
we ever behold. But far more must it have brought home
thoughts of seriousness to the mind of one who, by the force
of events, and the generous ambition of his family and his
own, was involved in the dangerous necessity of governing
without the right, and, as far as might be, without the semblance of power; one who knew the vindictive and unscrupulous hostility which, at home and abroad, he had to
encounter. If thoughts like these could bring a cloud over
the brow of Lorenzo, unfit for the object he sought in that
retreat, he might restore its serenity by other scenes which
his garden commanded. Mountains bright with various
hues, and clothed with wood, bounded the horizon, and, on
most sides, at no great distance; but embosomed in these were
other villas and domains of his own : while the level country
bore witness to his agricultural improvements, the classic
diversion of a statesman's cares. The same curious spirit
which led him to fill his garden at Careggi with exotic
flowers of the East, the first instance of a botanical collection
in Europe, had introduced a new animal from the same
regions. Herds of buffaloes, since naturalised in Italy, whose
dingy hide, bent neck, curved horns, and lowering aspect,
contrasted with the greyish hue and full mild eye of the
Tuscan oxen, pastured in the valley, down which the yellow
Arno steals silently through its long reaches to the sea.[e]

---

e Talia Fæsuleo lentus meditabar in antro,
Rure suburbano Medicum, qua mons sacer
urbem
Mæoniam, longique volumina despicit Arni ;

Qua bonus hospitium felix placidamque qui-
etem
Indulget Laurens.

Politiani Rusticus.

61. The Platonic academy, which Cosmo had planned

Platonic academy. came to maturity under Lorenzo. The academicians were divided into three classes :—the patrons (mecenati), including the Medici; the hearers (ascoltatori, probably from the Greek word ἀκρόαται) ; and the novices, or disciples, formed of young aspirants to philosophy. Ficino presided over the whole. Their great festival was the 13th of November, being the anniversary of the birth and death of Plato. Much of absurd mysticism, much of frivolous and mischievous superstition, was mingled with their speculations.[f]

62. The Disputationes Camaldulenses of Landino were

Disputationes Camaldulenses of Landino. published during this period, though, perhaps, written a little sooner. They belong to a class prominent in the literature of Italy in this and the succeeding century; disquisitions on philosophy in the form of dialogue, with more solicitude to present a graceful delineation of virtue, and to kindle a general sympathy for moral beauty, than to explore the labyrinths of theory, or even to lay down clear and distinct principles of ethics. The writings of Plato and Cicero, in this manner, had shown a track, in which their idolaters, with distant and hesitating steps, and more of reverence than emulation, delighted to tread. These disputations of Landino, in which, according to the beautiful patterns of ancient dialogue, the most honoured names of the age appear—Lorenzo and his brother Julian; Alberti, whose almost universal genius is now best known by his architecture; Ficino, and Landino himself— turn upon a comparison between the active and contempla-

---

And let us from the top of Fiesole,
Whence Galileo's glass by night observed
The phases of the moon, look round below
On Arno's vale, where the dove-coloured steer
Is ploughing up and down among the vines,
While many a careless note is sung aloud,
Filling the air with sweetness—and on thee,
Beautiful Florence, all within thy walls,
Thy groves and gardens, pinnacles and towers,
Drawn to our feet.

It is hardly necessary to say that these lines are taken from my friend Mr. Rogers's Italy, a poem full of moral and descriptive sweetness, and written in the chastened tone of fine taste. With respect to the buffaloes, I have no

other authority than these lines of Politian, in his poem of Ambra on the farm of Lorenzo at Poggio Cajano:

Atque aliud nigris missum, quis credat ? ab Indis,
Ruminat insuetas armentum discolor herbas.

But I must own, that Buffon tells us, though without quoting any authority, that the buffalo was introduced into Italy as early as the seventh century. I did not take the trouble of consulting Aldrovandus, who would perhaps have confirmed him—especially as I have a better opinion of my readers than to suppose they would care about the matter.

[f] Roscoe, Corniani.

tive life of man, to the latter of which it seems designed to give the advantage, and are saturated with the thoughtful spirit of Platonism.[g]

63. Landino was not, by any means, the first who had tried the theories of ancient philosophy through the feigned warfare of dialogue. Valla, intrepid Philosophical dialogues. and fond of paradox, had vindicated the Epicurean ethics from the calumnious or exaggerated censure frequently thrown upon them, contrasting the true methods by which pleasure should be sought with the gross notions of the vulgar. Several other writings of the same description, either in dialogue or regular dissertation, belong to the fifteenth century, though not always published so early, such as Franciscus Barbarus de re uxoria, Platina de falso et vero bono, the Vita Civile of Palmieri, the moral treatises of Poggio, Alberti, Pontano, and Matteo Bosso, concerning some of which little more than the names are to be learned from literary history, and which it would not, perhaps, be worth while to mention, except as collectively indicating a predilection for this style which the Italians long continued to display.[h]

64. Some of these related to general criticism, or to that of single authors. My knowledge of them is chiefly limited to the dialogue of Paulus Cortesius de ho- Paulus Cortesius. minibus doctis, written, I conceive, about 1490; no unsuccessful imitation of Cicero de claris oratoribus, from which indeed modern Latin writers have always been accustomed to collect the discriminating phrases of criticism. Cortesius, who was young at the time of writing this dialogue, uses an elegant, if not always a correct Latinity; characterising agreeably, and with apparent taste, the authors of the fifteenth century. It may be read in conjunction with the Ciceronianus of Erasmus, who, with no knowledge, perhaps, of Cortesius, has gone over the same ground in rather inferior language.

---

[g] Corniani and Roscoe have given this account of the Disputationes Camaldulenses. I have no direct acquaintance with the book.

[h] Corniani is much fuller than Tira-boschi on these treatises. Roscoe seems to have read the ethical writings of Matteo Bosso (Life of Leo X. c. xx.), but hardly adverts to any of the rest I have named. Some of them are very scarce.

65. It was about the beginning of this decad that a few
Schools in
Germany. Germans and Netherlanders, trained in the college
of Deventer, or that of Zwoll, or of St. Edward's
near Groningen, were roused to acquire that extensive knowledge of the ancient languages which Italy as yet exclusively
possessed. Their names should never be omitted in any
remembrance of the revival of letters; for great was their
influence upon the subsequent times. Wessel of Groningen,
one of those who contributed most steadily towards the
purification of religion, and to whom the Greek and Hebrew
languages are said, but probably on no solid grounds, to
have been known, may be reckoned in this class. But
others were more directly engaged in the advancement of
literature. Three schools, from which issued the most conspicuous ornaments of the next generation, rose under
masters, learned for that time, and zealous in the good
cause of instruction. Alexander Hegius became, about
1475, rector of that at Deventer, where Erasmus received
his early education.[i] Hegius was not wholly ignorant of
Greek, and imparted the rudiments of it to his illustrious
pupil. I am inclined to ascribe the publication of a very
rare and curious book, the first endeavour to print Greek on
this side of the Alps, to no other person than Hegius.[k]

---

[i] Heeren, p. 149, says that Hegius
began to preside over the school of Deventer in 1480; but I think the date in
the text is more probable, as Erasmus
left it at the age of fourteen, and was
certainly born in 1465. Though Hegius
is said to have known but little Greek, I
find in Panzer the title of a book by him,
printed at Deventer in 1501, de Utilitate
Linguæ Græcæ.
  The life of Hegius in Melchior Adam
is interesting. Primus hic in Belgio
literas excitavit, says Revius, in Daventria Illustrata, p. 130. Mihi, says Erasmus, admodum adhuc puero contigit uti
præceptore hujus discipulo Alexandro
Hegio Westphalo, qui ludum aliquando
celebrem oppidi Daventriensis modera-
batur, in quo nos olim admodum pueri
utriusque linguæ prima didicimus elementa. Adag. Chil. i. cent. iv. 39. In
another place he says of Hegius: Ne hic
quidem Græcarum literarum omnino ig-
narus est. Epist. 411, in Appendice.

Erasmus left Deventer at the age of fourteen; consequently in 1479 or 1480, as
he tells us in an epistle, dated 17th Apr.
1519.
  [k] This very rare book, unnoticed by
most bibliographers, is of some importance in the history of literature. It is
a small quarto tract, entitled Conjuga-
tiones verborum Græcæ, Daventriæ
noviter extremo labore collectæ et impressæ. No date or printer's name appears. A copy is in the British Museum,
and another in Lord Spencer's library.
It contains nothing but the word τύπτω
in all its voices and tenses, with Latin
explanations in Gothic letters. The
Greek types are very rude, and the characters sometimes misplaced. It must, I
should presume, seem probable to every
one who considers this book, that it is
of the fifteenth century, and consequently older than any known Greek on
this side of the Alps; which of itself
should render it interesting in the eyes

Louis Dringeberg founded, not perhaps before 1480, a still more distinguished seminary at Schelstadt in Alsace. Here the luminaries of Germany in a more advanced stage of

of bibliographers and of every one else. But fully disclaiming all such acquaintance with the technical science of typographical antiquity, as to venture any judgment founded on the appearance of a particular book, or on a comparison of it with others, I would, on other grounds, suggest the probability that this little attempt at Greek grammar issued from the Deventer press about 1480. It appears clear that whoever "collected with extreme labour" these forms of the verb τύπτω, had never been possessed of a Greek and Latin grammar. For would it not be absurd to use such expressions about a simple transcription? Besides which, the word is not only given in an arrangement different from any I have ever seen, but with a non-existent form of participle, τετυψάμενος for τυψάμενος, which could not surely have been found in any prior grammar. Now the grammar of Lascaris was published with a Latin translation by Craston in 1480. It is indeed highly probable that this book would not reach Deventer immediately after its impression; but it does seem as if there could not long have been any extreme difficulty in obtaining a correct synopsis of the verb τύπτω.

We have seen that Erasmus, about 1477, acquired a very slight tincture of Greek under Alexander Hegius at Deventer. And here, as he tells us, he saw Agricola, returning probably from Italy to Groningen. Quem mihi puero, ferme duodecim annos nato, Daventriæ videre contigit, nec aliud contigit. (Jortin, ii. 416.) No one could be so likely as Hegius to attempt a Greek grammar; nor do we find that his successors in that college were men as distinguished for learning as himself. But in fact at a later time it could not have been so incorrect. We might perhaps conjecture that he took down these Greek tenses from the mouth of Agricola, since we must presume oral communication rather than the use of books. Agricola, repeating from memory, and not thoroughly conversant with the language, might have given the false participle τετυψά-μενος. The tract was probably printed by Pafroet, some of whose editions bear as early a date as 1477. It has long been

extremely scarce; for Revius does not include it in the list of Pafroet's publications which he has given in Daventria Illustrata, nor will it be found in Panzer. Beloe was the first to mention it in his Anecdotes of Scarce Books; and it is referred by him to the fifteenth century; but apparently without his being aware that there was anything remarkable in that antiquity. Dr. Dibdin, in Bibliotheca Spenceriana, has given a fuller account; and from him Brunet has inserted it in the Manuel de Libraire. Neither Beloe nor Dibdin seems to have known that there is a copy in the Museum; they speak only of that belonging to Lord Spencer.

If it were true that Reuchlin, during his residence at Orleans, had published, as well as compiled, a Greek grammar, we should not need to have recourse to the hypothesis of this note, in order to give the antiquity of the present decad to Greek typography. Such a grammar is asserted by Meiners, in his Life of Reuchlin, to have been printed at Poitiers; and Eichhorn positively says, without reference to the place of publication, that Reuchlin was the first German who published a Greek grammar. (Gesch. der Litt. iii. 275.) Meiners, however, in a subsequent volume (iii. 10), retracts this assertion, and says it has been proved that the Greek grammar of Reuchlin was never printed. Yet I find in the Bibliotheca Universalis of Gesner: Joh. Capnio [Reuchlin] scripsit de diversitate quatuor idiomatum Græcæ linguæ lib. i. No such book appears in the list of Reuchlin's works in Niceron, vol. xxv., nor in any of the bibliographies. If it ever existed, we may place it with more probability at the very close of this century, or at the beginning of the next.

[The learned Dr. West of Dublin informed me that Reuchlin, in a dedication of a Commentary on the Seven Penitential Psalms in 1512, mentions a work that he had published on the Greek grammar, entitled Micropædia. There seems no reason to suppose that it was earlier than the time at which I have inclined to place it.—1842.]

learning, Conrad Celtes, Bebel, Rhenanus, Wimpheling,
Pirckheimer, Simler, are said to have imbibed their knowledge.[m] The third school was at Munster; and over this
Rodolph Langius presided, a man not any way inferior to the
other two, and of more reputation as a Latin writer, especially as a poet. The school of Munster did not come under
the care of Langius till 1483, or perhaps rather later; and
his strenuous exertions in the cause of useful and polite
literature against monkish barbarians extended into the
next century. But his life was long : the first, or nearly
such, to awaken his countrymen, he was permitted to behold
the full establishment of learning, and to exult in the dawn
of the Reformation. In company with a young man of
rank and equal zeal, Maurice count of Spiegelberg, who
himself became the provost of a school at Emmerich,
Langius visited Italy, and as Meiners supposes, though, I
think, upon uncertain grounds, before 1460. But not long
afterwards, a more distinguished person than any we have
mentioned, Rodolph Agricola of Groningen, sought in that
more genial land the taste and correctness which no Cisalpine nation could supply. Agricola passed several years of
this decad in Italy. We shall find the effects of his example
in the next.[n]

66. Meantime a slight impulse seems to have been given
to the university of Paris, by the lessons of George
Tifernas ; and from some disciples of his, Reuchlin,
a young German of great talents and celebrity, acquired,
probably about the year 1470, the first elements of the
Greek language. This knowledge he improved by the lessons of a native Greek, Andronicus Cartoblacas, at Basle.
In that city he had the good fortune, rare on this side of
the Alps, to find a collection of Greek manuscripts, left
there at the time of the council by a Cardinal Nicolas of
Ragusa. By the advice of Cartoblacas, he taught Greek
himself at Basle. After the lapse of some years, Reuchlin went
again to Paris, and found a new teacher George Hermony-

Study of Greek at Paris.

---

[m] Eichhorn, iii. 231. Meiners, ii. 369.
Eichhorn carelessly follows a bad authority in counting Reuchlin among these
pupils of the Schelstadt school.

[n] See Meiners, vol. ii., Eichhorn, and
Heeren, for the revival of learning in
Germany ; or something may be found
in Brucker.

mus of Sparta, who had settled there about 1472. From
Paris he removed to Orleans and Poitiers.[o]

67. The classical literature which delighted Reuchlin and
Agricola was disregarded as frivolous by the wise
of that day in the university of Paris; but they
were much more keenly opposed to innovation and
heterodoxy in their own peculiar line, the scholastic metaphysics. Most have heard of the long controversies between
the Realists and Nominalists concerning the nature of universals, or the genera and species of things. The first, with
Plato, and, at least as has been generally held, Aristotle,
maintained their objective or external reality; either, as it
was called, *ante rem*, as eternal archetypes in the Divine
Intelligence, or *in re*, as forms inherent in matter; the
second, with Zeno, gave them only a subjective existence as
ideas conceived by the mind, and have hence in later times
acquired the name of Conceptualists.[p] Roscelin, the first
of the modern Nominalists, went farther than this, and
denied, as Hobbes, and Berkeley, with many others, have
since done, all universality except to words and propositions.
Abelard, who inveighs against the doctrine of Roscelin, as
false logic and false theology, and endeavours to confound
it with the denial of any objective reality even in singular
things,[q] may be esteemed the restorer of the Conceptualist
school. We do not know his doctrines, however, by his
own writings, but by the testimony of John of Salisbury,
who seems not well to have understood the subject. The
words Realist and Nominalist came into use about the
end of the twelfth century. But in the next, the latter party

Marginal note: Controversy of Realists and Nominalists.

---

[o] Meiners, i. 49. Besides Meiners,
Brucker, iv. 358, as well as Heeren,
have given pretty full accounts of Reuchlin ; and a good life of him will be found
in the 25th volume of Niceron : but the
Epistolæ ad Reuchlinum throw still
more light on the man and his contemporaries.

[p] I am chiefly indebted for the facts in
the following paragraphs to a dissertation by Meiners, in the Transactions of
the Göttingen Academy, vol. xii.

[q] Hic sicut pseudo-dialecticus, ita
pseudo-christianus—ut eo loco quo dicitur, Dominus partem piscis assi come-
disse partem hujus vocis, quæ est piscis

assi, non partem rei intelligere cogatur.
Meiners, p. 27. This may serve to show
the cavilling tone of scholastic disputes;
and Meiners may well say, Quicquid
Roscelinus peccavit, non adeo tamen in-
sanisse pronuntiandum est, ut Abelardus
illum fecisse invidiose fingere sustinuit.
[M. Cousin has nevertheless proved,
from a passage in some lately discovered
manuscripts of Abelard, that he had
really learned under Roscelin. This
had been asserted by Otho of Frisingen,
but doubted on account of a supposed
incompatibility of dates. Fragmens
philosophiques, vol. iv. p. 57.—1853.]

by degrees disappeared; and the great schoolmen, Aquinas
and Scotus, in whatever else they might disagree, were
united on the Realist side. In the fourteenth century
William Ockham revived the opposite hypothesis with considerable success. Scotus and his disciples were
the great maintainers of Realism. If there were no
substantial forms, he argued, that is, nothing real, which
determines the mode of being in each individual, men and
brutes would be of the same substance; for they do not differ
as to matter, nor can extrinsic accidents make a substantive
difference. There must be a substantial form of a horse,
another of a lion, another of a man. He seems to have held
the immateriality of the soul, that is, the substantial form of
man. But no other form, he maintained, can exist without
matter naturally, though it may supernaturally by the
power of God. Socrates and Plato agree more than Socrates
and an ass. They have, therefore, something in common,
which an ass has not. But this is not numerically the
same; it must, therefore, be something universal, namely,
human nature.[r]

68. These reasonings, which are surely no unfavourable
specimen of the subtle philosopher (as Scotus was
called), were met by Ockham with others which sometimes appear more refined and obscure. He confined reality
to objective things, denying it to the host of abstract entities
brought forward by Scotus. He defines a universal to be
'a particular intention (meaning probably idea or conception) of the mind itself, capable of being predicated of many
things, not for what it properly is itself, but for what those
things are; so that, in so far as it has this capacity, it is
called universal, but inasmuch as it is one form really
existing in the mind, it is called singular.'[s] I have not examined the writings of Ockham, and am unable to determine
whether his Nominalism extends beyond that of Berkeley
or Stewart, which is generally asserted by the modern

Scotus.

Ockham

---

[r] Meiners, p. 39.

[s] Unam intentionem singularem ipsius
animæ, natam prædicari de pluribus, non
pro se, sed pro ipsis rebus; ita quod per
hoc, quod ipsa nata est prædicari de pluribus, non pro se sed pro illis pluribus,
illa dicitur universalis; propter hoc autem, quod est una forma existens realiter
in intellectu, dicitur singulare. p. 42.

inquirers into scholastic philosophy; that is, whether it amounts to Conceptualism; the foregoing definition, as far as I can judge, might have been given by them.[t]

69. The later Nominalists of the scholastic period, Buridan, Biel, and several others mentioned by the historians of philosophy, took all their reasonings from the storehouse of Ockham. His doctrine was prohibited at Paris by pope John XXII., whose theological opinions, as well as secular encroachments, he had opposed. All masters of arts were bound by oath never to teach Ockhamism. But after the pope's death the university condemned a tenet of the Realists, that many truths are eternal, which are not God; and went so far towards the Nominalist theory, as to determine that our knowledge of things is through the medium of words.[u] Peter d'Ailly, Gerson, and other principal men of their age, were Nominalists; the sect was very powerful in Germany, and may be considered, on the whole, as prevalent in this century. The Realists, however, by some management gained the ear of Louis XI., who, by an ordinance in 1473, explicitly approves the doctrines of the great Realist philosophers, condemns that of Ockham and his disciples, and forbids it to be taught, enjoining the books of the Nominalists to be locked up from public perusal, and all present as well as future graduates in the university to swear to the observation of this ordinance. The prohibition, nevertheless, was repealed in 1481; the guilty books set free from their chains, and the hypothesis of the Nominalists virtually permitted to be held, amidst the acclamations of the university, and especially one of its four nations, that of Germany. Some of their party had, during this persecution, taken refuge in that empire and in England, both friendly to their cause; and this metaphysical contention of the fifteenth century suggests and typifies the great religious convulsion of the next. The weight of ability, during this later and less flourishing period of scholastic philosophy, was on the Nominalist side; and though nothing in the Reformation was imme-

Margin notes: Nominalists in University of Paris.

---

[t] [The definition seems hardly such as Berkeley would have given; it plainly recognises a general conception existing in the mind.—1847.]

[u] Meiners, p. 45: Scientiam habemus de rebus, sed mediantibus terminis.

diately connected with their principle, this metaphysical sect facilitated in some measure its success.

70. We should still look in vain to England for either Low state of learning or native genius. The reign of Edward learning in England. IV. may be reckoned one of the lowest points in our literary annals. The universities had fallen in reputation and in frequency of students; where there had been thousands, according to Wood, there was not now one; which must be understood as an hyperbolical way of speaking. But the decline of the universities, frequented as they had been by indigent vagabonds withdrawn from useful labour, and wretched as their pretended instruction had been, was so far from an evil in itself, that it left clear the path for the approaching introduction of real learning. Several colleges were about this time founded at Oxford and Cambridge, which, in the design of their munificent founders, were to become, as they have done, the instruments of a better discipline than the barbarous schoolmen afforded. We have already observed, that learning in England was like seed fermenting in the ground through the fifteenth century. The language was becoming more vigorous, and more capable of giving utterance to good thoughts, as some translations from Caxton's press show, such as the Dicts of Philosophers by Lord Rivers. And perhaps the best exercise for a school-boy people is that of school-boys. The poetry of two Scotsmen, Henryson and Mercer, which is not without merit, may be nearly referred to the present decad.[x]

71. The progress of mathematical science was regular, though not rapid. We might have mentioned before Mathematics the gnomon erected by Toscanelli in the cathedral at Florence, which is referred to 1468; a work, it has been said, which, considering the times, has done as much honour to his genius as that so much renowned at Bologna to Cassini.[y] The greatest mathematician of the fifteenth cen-

---

[x] Campbell's Specimens of British Poets, vol. i.

[y] This gnomon of Florence is by much the loftiest in Europe. It would be no slight addition to the glory of Toscanelli if we should suppose him to have suggested the discovery of a passage westward to the Indies in a letter to Columbus, as his article in the Biographie universelle seems to imply. But more accurate expressions of Tiraboschi, referring to the correspondence between these great men, leave Columbus in possession of the original idea, at least con-

tury, Muller, or Regiomontanus, a native of Konigsberg, or Konigshoven, a small town in Franconia, Regiomontanus. whence he derived his latinised appellation, died prematurely, like his master, Purbach, in 1476. He had begun at the age of fifteen to assist the latter in astronomical observations; and having, after Purbach's death, acquired a knowledge of Greek in Italy, and devoted himself to the ancient geometers, after some years spent with distinction in that country, and at the court of Matthias Corvinus, he settled finally at Nuremberg; where a rich citizen, Bernard Walther, both supplied the means of accurate observations, and became the associate of his labours.[x] Regiomontanus died at Rome, whither he had been called to assist in rectifying the calendar. Several of his works were printed in this decad, and among others his ephemerides, or calculations of the places of the sun and moon, for the ensuing thirty years; the best, though not strictly the first, that had been made in Europe.[a] His more extensive productions did not appear till afterwards; and the treatise on triangles, the most celebrated of them, not till 1533. The solution of the more difficult cases, both in plane and spherical trigonometry, is found in this work; and with the exception of what the science owes to Napier, it may be said that it advanced little for more than two centuries after the age of Regiomontanus. Purbach had computed a table of sines to a radius of 600,000 parts. Regiomontanus, ignorant, as has been thought, which appears very strange, of

---

currently with the Florentine astronomer, though the latter gave him strong encouragement to persevere in his undertaking. Toscanelli, however, had, on the authority of Marco Polo, imbibed an exaggerated notion of the distance eastward to China; and consequently believed, as Columbus himself did, that the voyage by the west to that country would be far shorter than, if the continent of America did not intervene, it could have been. Tiraboschi, vi. 189, 207. Roscoe's Leo X. ch. 20.

[x] Walther was more than a patron of science, honourable as that name was. He made astronomical observations, worthy of esteem relatively to the age. Montucla, i. 545. It is to be regretted

that Walther should have diminished the credit due to his name by withholding from the public the manuscripts of Regiomontanus, which he purchased after the latter's death; so that some were lost by the negligence of his own heirs, and the rest remained unpublished till 1533.

[a] Gassendi, Vita Regiomontani. He speaks of them himself, as quas vulgo vocant almanach; and Gassendi says, that some were extant in manuscript at Paris, from 1442 to 1472. Those of Regiomontanus contained eclipses, and other matters not in former almanacs.

[b] Hutton's Logarithms, Introduction, p. 3.

his master's labours, calculated them to 6,000,000 parts. But perceiving the advantages of a decimal scale, he has given a second table, wherein the ratio of the sines is computed to a radius of 10,000,000 parts, or, as we should say, taking the radius as unity, to seven places of decimals. He subjoined what he calls Canon Fæcundus, or a table of tangents, calculating them, however, only for entire degrees to a radius of 100,000 parts.[c] It has been said, that Regiomontanus was inclined to the theory of the earth's motion, which indeed Nicolas Cusanus had already espoused.

72. Though the arts of delineation do not properly come within the scope of this volume, yet so far as they are directly instrumental to science, they ought not to pass unregarded. Without the tool that presents figures to the eye, not the press itself could have diffused an adequate knowledge either of anatomy or of natural history. As figures cut in wooden blocks gave the first idea of letter-printing, and were for some time associated with it, an obvious invention, when the latter art became improved, was to arrange such blocks together with types in the same page. We find accordingly, about this time, many books adorned or illustrated in this manner ; generally with representations of saints, or other ornamental delineations not of much importance; but in a few instances with figures of plants and animals, or of human anatomy. The Dyalogus creaturarum moralizatus, of which the first edition was published at Gouda, 1480, seems to be nearly, if not altogether, the earliest of these. It contains a series of fables with rude woodcuts, in little more than outline. A second edition, printed at Antwerp in 1486, repeats the same cuts, with the addition of one representing a church, which is really elaborate.[d]

Arts of delineation.

73. The art of engraving figures on plates of copper was

---

[c] Kästner, i. 557.

[d] Both these editions are in the British Museum. In the same library is a copy of the exceedingly scarce work, Ortus Sanitatis. Mogunt. 1491. The colophon, which may be read in De Bure (Sciences, No. 1554), takes much credit for the carefulness of the delineations. The wooden cuts of the plants, especially, are as good as we usually find in the sixteenth century ; the form of the leaves and character of the plant are generally well preserved. The animals are also tolerably figured, though with many exceptions, and, on the whole, fall short of the plants. The work itself is a compilation from the old naturalists, arranged alphabetically.

nearly coëval with that of printing, and is due either to Thomas Finiguerra about 1460, or to some German about the same time. It was not a difficult step to apply this invention to the representation of geographical maps; and this we owe to Arnold Buckinck, an associate of the printer Sweynheim. His edition of Ptolemy's geography appeared at Rome in 1478. These maps are traced from those of Agathodæmon in the fifth century; and it has been thought that Buckinck profited by the hints of Donis, a German monk, who himself gave two editions of Ptolemy not long afterwards at Ulm.[e] The fifteenth century had already witnessed an increasing attention to geographical delineations. The libraries of Italy contain several unpublished maps, of which that by Fra Mauro, a monk of the order of Camaldoli, now in the convent of Murano, near Venice, is the most celebrated.[f] Two causes, besides the increase of commerce and the gradual accumulation of knowledge had principally turned the

Maps.

Geography.

---

[e] Biogr. univ.: Buckinck, Donis.

[f] Andrès, ix. 88. Corniani, iii. 162. [A better account of this celebrated map was given in the seventh volume of the Annales Camaldulenses, p. 252 (1762); and Cardinal Zurla published in 1806 Il Mappamondo di Fra Mauro Camaldolense illustrato. A fine copy of this map, taken from the original at Murano, about forty years since, is in the British Museum; there is also one in a Portuguese convent, supposed to have been made by Fra Mauro himself in 1459, for the use of Alfonso V., king of Portugal. Fra Mauro professes not to have followed Ptolemy in all things, but to have collected information from travellers; investigando per molti anni, e practicando cum persone degne di fede, le qual hano veduto ad occhio quelo, que qui suso fedelmente demostro. It appears, however, to me, that he has been chiefly indebted to Marco Polo, who had contributed a vast stock of names, to which the geographer was to annex locality in the best manner he could. Very little relating to Asia or Africa will be found in the Murano map which may not be traced to this source. It does not indeed appear manifest that Polo was aquainted with the termination of

the African coast; but that had been so often asserted, that we cannot feel surprised when we find, in Fra Mauro's map, the sea rolling round the Cape of Good Hope, though the form of that part of the continent is ill delineated.

The marginal entries of this map are not unworthy of attention. One of them attributes the tides to the attraction of the moon, but not on any philosophical principle. He speaks of spring and neap tides as already known, which indeed must have been the case, after the experience of navigators reached beyond the Mediterranean, but says that no one had explained their cause. Zurla, or some one whom he quotes, exaggerates a little the importance of what Fra Mauro has said about the tides, which is mixed up with great error; and loosely talks about an anticipation of Newton. Upon the whole, although this map is curious and interesting, something more has been said of it than it deserves by the author of Annales Camaldulenses: Mauro itaque Camaldulensi m onacho ea gloria jure merito tribuenda erat, ut non parum tabulis suis geographicis juverit ad tentandas expeditiones in terras incognitas, quod postea præstitum erat ab Lusitanis.—1842.]

thoughts of many towards the figure of the earth on which they trod. Two translations, one of them by Emanuel Chrysoloras, had been made early in the century, from the cosmography of Ptolemy ; and from his maps the geographers of Italy had learned the use of parallels and meridians, which might a little, though inadequately, restrain their arbitrary admeasurements of different countries.[g] But the real discoveries of the Portuguese on the coast of Africa, under the patronage of Don Henry, were of far greater importance in stimulating and directing enterprise. In the academy founded by that illustrious prince, nautical charts were first delineated in a method more useful to the pilot, by projecting the meridians in parallel right lines,[h] instead of curves on the surface of the sphere. This first step in hydrographical science entitles Don Henry to the name of its founder. And though these early maps and charts of the fifteenth century are to us but a chaos of error and confusion, it was on them that the patient eye of Columbus had rested through long hours of meditation, while strenuous hope and unsubdued doubt where struggling in his soul.

Sect. V. 1480—1490.

Great Progress of Learning in Italy—Italian Poetry—Pulci—Metaphysical Theology—Ficinus—Picus of Mirandola—Learning in Germany—Early European Drama—Alberti and Leonardo da Vinci.

74. The press of Italy was less occupied with Greek for several years than might have been expected. But Greek printed in Italy. the number of scholars was still not sufficient to repay the expenses of impression, The Psalter was published in Greek twice at Milan in 1481, once at Venice in 1486. Craston's Lexicon was also once printed, and the grammar of Lascaris several times. The first classical work the printers ventured upon, was Homer's Battle of Frogs and Mice, published at Venice in 1486 or according to some, at Milan in 1485 ; the priority of the two editions being disputed. But in 1488, under the munificent patronage of Lorenzo, and by

      g Andrès, 86.   h Id. 83.

the care of Demetrius of Crete, a complete edition of Homer issued from the press of Florence. This splendid work closes our catalogue for the present.[i]

75. The first Hebrew book, Jarchi's commentary on the Pentateuch, had been printed by some Jews at Reggio in Calabria, as early as 1475. In this period a press was established at Soncino, where the Pentateuch was published in 1482, the greater prophets in 1486, and the whole Bible in 1488. But this was intended for themselves alone. What little instruction in Hebrew had anywhere hitherto been imparted to Christian scholars, was only oral. The commencement of Hebrew learning, properly so called, was not till about the end of the century, in the Franciscan monasteries of Tubingen and Basle. Their first teacher, however, was an Italian, by name Raimondi.[k]

Hebrew printed.

76. To enumerate every publication that might scatter a gleam of light on the progress of letters in Italy, or to mention every scholar who deserves a place in biographical collections, or in an extended history of literature, would crowd these pages with two many names. We must limit ourselves to those best deserving to be had in remembrance. In 1480, according to Meiners, or, as Heeren says, in 1483, Politian was placed in the chair of Greek and Latin eloquence at Florence; a station perhaps the most conspicuous and the most honourable which any scholar could occupy. It is beyond controversy, that he stands at the head of that class in the fifteenth century. The envy of some of his contemporaries attested his superiority. In 1489, he published his once celebrated Miscellanea, consisting of one hundred observations illustrating passages of Latin authors, in the desultory manner of Aulus Gellius, which is certainly the easiest and perhaps the most agreeable method of conveying information. They are sometimes grammatical; but more frequently relate to obscure (at that time) customs or mythological allusions. Greek quotations occur not seldom, and the author's command of classical literature seems considerable. Thus he explains, for in-

Miscellanies of Politian.

---

[i] See Maittaire's character of this edition quoted in Roscoe's Leo X., ch. 21.

[k] Eichhorn, ii. 562.

stance, the crambe repetita of Juvenal by a proverb mentioned in Suidas, δὶς κράμβη θάνατος : κράμβη being a kind
of cabbage, which, when boiled a second time, was of course
not very palatable, This may serve to show the extent of
learning which some Italian scholars had reached through
the asistance of the manuscripts collected by Lorenzo. It is
not improbable that no one in England at that time had
heard the name of Suidas. Yet the imperfect knowledge
of Greek which these early writers possessed, is shown when
they attempt to write it. Politian has some verses in his
Miscellanea, but very bald and full of false quantities. This
remark we may have occasion to repeat; for it is applicable
to much greater names in philology than his.[m]

77. The Miscellanies, Heeren says, were then considered
Their character, by Heeren. an immortal work; it was deemed an honour to be
mentioned in them, and those who missed this made
it a matter of complaint. If we look at them now, we are
astonished at the different measure of glory in the present
age. This book probably sprang out of Politian's lectures.
He had cleared up in these some difficult passages, which
had led him on to further inquiries. Some of his explanations might probably have arisen out of the walks and rides
that he was accustomed to take with Lorenzo, who had
advised the publication of the Miscellanies. The manner
in which these explanations are given, the light, yet solid
mode of handling the subjects, and their great variety, give
in fact a charm to the Miscellanies of Politian which few
antiquarian works possess. Their success is not wonderful.
They were fragments, and chosen fragments, from the
lectures of the most celebrated teacher of that age, whom
many had heard, but still more had wished to hear,
Scarcely had a work appeared in the whole fifteenth century, of which so vast expectations had been entertained,
and which was received with such curiosity.[n] The very

[m] Meiners has praised Politian's Greek,
verses, but with very little skill in such
matters, p. 214. The compliments he
quotes from contemporary Greeks, non
esse tam Atticas Athenas ipsas, may not
have been very sincere, unless they
meant *esse* to be taken in the present
tense. These Greeks, besides, knew but
little of their metrical language.

[n] Heeren, p. 263. Meiners, Lebensbeschreibungen, &c., has written the life
of Politian, ii. 111-220, more copiously
than any one that I have read. His character of the Miscellanies is in p. 136.

fault of Politian's style, as it was that of Hermolaus Barbarus, his affected intermixture of obsolete words, for which it is necessary in almost every page of his Miscellanies to consult the dictionary, would, in an age of pedantry, increase the admiration of his readers.[o]

78. Politian was the first that wrote the Latin language with much elegance; and while every other early translator from the Greek has incurred more or less of censure at the hands of judges whom better learning had made fastidious, it is agreed by them that his Herodian has all the spirit of his original, and frequently excels it.[p] Thus we perceive that the age of Poggio, Filelfo, and Valla was already left far behind by a new generation; these had been well employed as the pioneers of ancient literature, but for real erudition and taste we must descend to Politian, Christopher Landino, and Hermolaus Barbarus.[q]

His version of Herodian.

79. The Cornucopia sive linguæ Latinæ Commentarii, by Nicolas Perotti, bishop of Siponto, suggests rather more by its title than the work itself seems to warrant. It is a copious commentary upon part of Martial; in which he takes occasion to explain a vast many Latin words, and has been highly extolled by Morhof, and by writers quoted in Baillet and Blount. To this commentary is appended an alphabetical index of words, which rendered it a sort of dictionary for the learned reader. Perotti lived a little before this time; but the first edition seems to have been in 1489. He also wrote a small Latin grammar, frequently reprinted in the fifteenth century, and was an indifferent translator of Polybius.[r]

Cornucopia of Perotti.

---

[o] Meiners, pp. 155, 209. In the latter passage Meiners censures, with apparent justice, the affected words of Politian, some of which he did not scruple to take from such writers as Apuleius and Tertullian, with an inexcusable display of erudition at the expense of good taste.

[p] Huet. apud Blount in Politiano.

[q] Meiners, Roscoe, Corniani, Heeren, and Gresswell's Memoirs of early Italian Scholars, are the best authorities to whom the reader can have recourse for the character of Politian, besides his own works. I think, however, that Heeren has hardly done justice to Politian's poetry. Tiraboschi is unsatisfactory. Blount, as usual, collects the suffrages of the sixteenth century.

[r] Heeren, 272. Morhof, i. 821, who calls Perotti the first compiler of good Latin, from whom those who followed have principally borrowed. See also Baillet and Blount for testimonies to Perotti.

80. We have not thought it worth while to mention the
Latin poetry Latin poets of the fourteenth and fifteenth centuries.
of Politian. They are numerous, and somewhat rude, from
Petrarch and Boccace to Maphæus Vegius, the continuator
of the Æneid in a thirteenth book, first printed in 1471,
and very frequently afterwards. This is, probably, the best
versification before Politian. But his Latin poems display
considerable powers of description, and a strong feeling
of the beauties of Roman poetry. The style is imbued
with these, not too ambitiously chosen, nor in the manner called centonism, but so as to give a general elegance
to the composition, and to call up pleasing associations in
the reader of taste. This, indeed, is the common praise of
good versifiers in modern Latin, and not peculiarly appropriate to Politian, who is inferior to some who followed,
though to none, as I apprehend, that preceded in that numerous fraternity. His ear is good, and his rhythm, with
a few exceptions, musical and Virgilian. Some defects are
nevertheless worthy of notice. He is often too exuberant,
and apt to accumulate details of description. His words,
unauthorised by any legitimate example, are very numerous; a fault in some measure excusable by the want of
tolerable dictionaries; so that the memory was the only
test of classical precedent. Nor can we deny that Politian's
Latin poetry is sometimes blemished by affected and effeminate expressions, by a too studious use of repetitions, and
by a love of diminutives, according to the fashion of his
native language, carried beyond all bounds that correct
Augustan Latinity could possibly have endured. This last
fault, and to a man of good taste it is an unpleasing one,
belongs to a great part of the lyrical and even elegiac
writers in modern Latin. The example of Catullus would
probably have been urged in excuse; but perhaps Catullus
went farther than the best judges approved; and nothing in
his poems can justify the excessive abuse of that effeminate
grace, what the stern Persius would have called ' summa
delumbe saliva,' which pervades the poetry both of Italian
and Cisalpine Latinists for a long period. On the whole,
Politian, like many of his followers, is calculated to delight

and mislead a schoolboy, but may be read with pleasure by a man.[s]

81. Amidst all the ardour for the restoration of classical literature in Italy, there might seem reason to ap- Italian prehend that native originality would not meet its poetry of Lorenzo. due reward, and even that the discouraging notion of a degeneracy in the powers of the human mind might come to prevail. Those who annex an exaggerated value to correcting an unimportant passage in an ancient author, or, which is much the same, interpreting some worthless inscription, can hardly escape the imputation of pedantry; and doubtless this reproach might justly fall on many of the learned in that age, as, with less excuse, it has often done upon their successors. We have already seen that, for a hundred years, it was thought unworthy a man of letters, even though a poet, to write in Italian; and Politian, with his great patron Lorenzo, deserves no small honour for having disdained the false vanity of the philologers. Lorenzo stands at the head of the Italian poets of the fifteenth century in the sonnet as well as in the light lyrical composition. His predecessors, indeed, were not likely to remove the prejudice against vernacular poetry. Several of his sonnets appear, both for elevation and elegance of style, worthy of comparison with those of the next age. But perhaps his most original claim to the title of a poet is founded upon the Canti Carnascialeschi, or carnival songs, composed for the popular shows on festivals. Some of these, which are collected in a volume printed in 1558, are by Lorenzo, and display a union of classical grace and imitation with the native raciness of Florentine gaiety.[t]

82. But at this time appeared a poet of a truly modern school, in one of Lorenzo's intimate society, Luigi Pulci. Pulci. The first edition of his Morgante Maggiore, containing twenty-three cantos, to which five were subse-

---

[s] The extracts from Politian, and other Latin poets of Italy, by Pope, in the two little volumes entitled Poemata Italorum, are extremely well chosen, and give a just measure of most of them.

[t] Corniani. Roscoe. Crescimbeni

(della volgar Poesia, ii. 324) strongly asserts Lorenzo to be the restorer of poetry, which had never been more barbarous than in his youth. But certainly the Giostra of Politian was written while Lorenzo was young.

quently added, was published at Venice in 1481. The taste of the Italians has always been strongly inclined to extravagant combinations of fancy, caprices rapid and sportive as the animal from which they take their name. The susceptible and versatile imaginations of that people, and their habitual cheerfulness, enable them to render the serious and terrible instrumental to the ridiculous, without becoming, like some modern fictions, merely hideous and absurd.

83. The Morgante Maggiore was evidently suggested by Character of some long romances written within the preceding Morgante Maggiore. century in the octave stanza, for which the fabulous chronicle of Turpin, and other fictions wherein the same real and imaginary personages had been introduced, furnished the materials. Under pretence of ridiculing the intermixture of sacred allusions with the romantic legends, Pulci carried it to an excess which, combined with some sceptical insinuations of his own, seems clearly to display an intention of exposing religion to contempt.[u] As to the heroes of his romance, there can be, as it seems, no sort of doubt, that he designed them for nothing else than the butts of his fancy; that the reader might scoff at those whom duller poets had held up to admiration. It has been a question among Italian critics, whether the poem of Pulci is to be reckoned burlesque.[v]

---

[u] The story of Meridiana, in the eighth canto, is sufficient to prove Pulci's irony to have been exercised on religion. It is well known to the readers of the Morgante. It has been alleged in the Biographie universelle, that he meant only to turn into ridicule ' ces muses mendiantes du 14me siècle,' the authors of la Spagna or Buovo d'Antona, who were in the habit of beginning their songs with scraps of the liturgy, and even of introducing theological doctrines in the most absurd and misplaced style. Pulci has given us much of the latter, wherein some have imagined that he had the assistance of Ficinus.

[v] This seems to have been an old problem in Italy (Corniani, ii. 302); and the gravity of Pulci has been maintained of late by such respectable authorities as Foscolo and Panizzi. Ginguéné, who does not go this length, thinks the death of Orlando, and his last prayer, both

pathetic and sublime. I can see nothing in it but the systematic spirit of parody which we find in Pulci. But the lines on the death of Forisena, in the fourth canto, are really graceful and serious. The following remarks on Pulci's style come from a more competent judge than myself :

' There is something harsh in Pulci's manner, owing to his abrupt transition from one idea to another, and to his carelessness of grammatical rules. He was a poet by nature, and wrote with ease, but he never cared for sacrificing syntax to meaning; he did not mind saying anything incorrectly, if he were but sure that his meaning would be guessed. The rhyme very often compels him to employ expressions, words, and even lines which frequently render the sense obscure and the passage crooked, without producing any other effect than that of destroying a fine stanza. He has

This may seem to turn on the definition, though I do not see what definition could be given, consistently with the use of language, that would exclude it ; it is intended as a caricature of the poetical romances, and might even seem by anticipation a satirical, though not ill-natured, parody on the Orlando Furioso. That he meant to excite any other emotion than laughter cannot, as it seems, be maintained ; and a very few stanzas of a more serious character, which may rarely be found, are not enough to make an exception to his general design. The Morgante was to the poetical romances of chivalry what Don Quixote was to their brethren in prose.

84. A foreigner must admire the vivacity of the narrative, the humorous gaiety of the characters, the adroitness of the satire. But the Italians, and especially the Tuscans, delight in the raciness of Pulci's Florentine idiom, which we cannot equally relish. He has not been without influence on men of more celebrity than himself. In several passages of Ariosto, especially the visit of Astolfo to the moon, we trace a resemblance not wholly fortuitous. Voltaire, in one of his most popular poems, took the dry archness of Pulci, and exaggerated the profaneness, superadding the obscenity from his own stores. But Mr. Frere, with none of these two ingredients in his admirable vein of humour, has come, in the War of the Giants, much closer to the Morgante Maggiore than any one else.

85. The Platonic academy, in which the chief of the Medici took so much delight, did not fail to reward Platonic his care. Marsilius Ficinus, in his Theologica Pla- theology of Ficinus. tonica (1482), developed a system chiefly borrowed from the later Platonists of the Alexandrian school, full of delight to the credulous imagination, though little appealing to the reason, which, as it seemed remarkably to coincide in some respects with the received tenets of the church, was connived at in a few reveries, which could not so well bear the test of

---

no similes of any particular merit, nor does he stand eminent in description. His verses almost invariably make sense taken singly, and convey distinct and separate ideas. Hence he wants that richness, fulness, and smooth flow of diction, which is indispensable to an epic poet, and to a noble description or comparison. Occasionally, when the subject admits of a powerful sketch which may be presented with vigour and spirit by a few strokes boldly drawn, Pulci appears to a great advantage.' —Panizzi on romantic poetry of Italians, in the first volume of his Orlando Innamorato, p. 298.

an orthodox standard. He supported his philosophy by a translation of Plato into Latin, executed by the direction of Lorenzo, and printed before 1490. Of this translation Buhle has said, that it has been very unjustly reproached with want of correctness; it is, on the contrary, perfectly conformable to the original, and has even, in some passages, enabled us to restore the text; the manuscripts used by Ficinus, I presume, not being in our hands. It has also the rare merit of being at once literal, perspicuous, and in good Latin.[x]

86. But the Platonism of Ficinus was not wholly that of the master. It was based on the emanation of the human soul from God, and its capacity of reunion by an ascetic and contemplative life; a theory perpetually reproduced in various modifications of meaning, and far more of words. The nature and immortality of the soul, the functions and distinguishing characters of angels, the being and attributes of God, engaged the thoughtful mind of Ficinus. In the course of his high speculations he assailed a doctrine, which, though rejected by Scotus and most of the schoolmen, had gained much ground among the Aristotelians, as they deemed themselves, of Italy; a doctrine first held by Averroes—that there is one common intelligence, active, immortal, indivisible, unconnected with matter, the soul of human kind; which is not in any one man, because it has no material form, but which yet assists in the rational oper- ations of each man's personal soul, and from those operations, which are all conversant with particulars, derives its own knowledge of universals. Thus, if I understand what is meant, which is rather subtle, it might be said, that as in the common theory particular sensations furnish means to the soul of forming general ideas, so, in that of Averroes, the ideas and judgments of separate human souls furnish col- lectively the means of that knowledge of universals, which the one great soul of mankind alone can embrace. This was a theory built, as some have said, on the bad Arabic version of Aristotle which Averroes used. But, whatever might have

Marginal note: Doctrine of Averroes on the soul.

---

[x] Hist. de la Philosophie, vol. ii. The fullest account of the philosophy of Ficinus has been given by Buhle. Those who seek less minute information may have recourse to Brucker or Cor- niani; or, if they are content with still less, to Tiraboschi, Roscoe, Heeren, or the Biographie universelle.

first suggested it to the philosopher of Cordova, it seems little else than an expansion of the Realist hypothesis, urged to a degree of apparent paradox. For if the human soul, as an universal, possess an objective reality, it must surely be intelligent; and, being such, it may seem no extravagant hypothesis, though one incapable of that demonstration we now require in philosophy, to suppose that it acts upon the subordinate intelligences of the same species, and receives impressions from them. By this also they would reconcile the knowledge we were supposed to possess of the reality of universals, with the acknowledged impossibility, at least in many cases, of representing them to the mind.

87. Ficinus is the more prompt to refute the Averroists, that they all maintained the mortality of the par- *Opposed by* ticular soul, while it was his endeavour, by every *Ficinus.* argument that erudition and ingenuity could supply, to prove the contrary. The whole of his Platonic Theology appears a beautiful, but too visionary and hypothetical, system of theism, the ground-works of which lay deep in the meditations of ancient oriental sages. His own treatise, of which a very copious account will be found in Buhle, soon fell into oblivion; but it belongs to a class of literature, which, in all its extension, has, full as much as any other, engaged the human mind.

88. The thirst for hidden knowledge, by which man is distinguished from brutes, and the superior races of *Desire of* men from savage tribes, burns generally with more *man to explore* intenseness in proportion as the subject is less defi- *mysteries.* nitely comprehensible, and the means of certainty less attainable. Even our own interest in things beyond the sensible world does not appear to be the primary or chief source of the desire we feel to be acquainted with them; it is the pleasure of belief itself, of associating the conviction of reality with ideas not presented by sense; it is sometimes the necessity of satisfying a restless spirit, that first excites our endeavour to withdraw the veil that conceals the mystery of our being. The few great truths in religion that reason discovers, or that an explicit revelation deigns to communicate, sufficient as they may be for our practical good, have proved to fall very short of the ambitious curiosity of man. They

leave so much imperfectly known, so much wholly unexplored, that in all ages he has never been content without trying some method of filling up the void. These methods have often led him to folly, and weakness, and crime. Yet as those who want the human passions, in their excess the great fountains of evil, seem to us maimed in their nature, so an indifference to this knowledge of invisible things, or a premature despair of attaining it, may be accounted an indication of some moral or intellectual deficiency, some scantness of due proportion in the mind.

89. The means to which recourse has been had to enlarge

Various methods employed. the boundaries of human knowledge in matters relating to the Deity, or to such of his intelligent creatures as do not present themselves in ordinary objectiveness to our senses, have been various, and may be dis-

Reason and inspiration. tributed into several classes. Reason itself, as the most valuable, though not the most frequent in use, may be reckoned the first. Whatever deductions have suggested themselves to the acute, or analogies to the observant, mind, whatever has seemed the probable interpretation of revealed testimony, is the legitimate province of a sound and rational theology. But so fallible appears the reason of each man to others, and often so dubious are its inferences to himself, so limited is the span of our faculties, so incapable are they of giving more than a vague and conjectural probability, where we demand most of definiteness and certainty, that few, comparatively speaking, have been content to acquiesce even in their own hypotheses upon no other grounds than argument has supplied. The uneasiness that is apt to attend suspense of belief has required, in general, a more powerful remedy. Next to those who have solely employed their rational faculties in theology, we may place those who have relied on a supernatural illumination. These have nominally been many; but the imagination, like the reason, bends under the incomprehensibility of spiritual things; a few excepted, who have become founders of sects, and lawgivers to the rest, the mystics fell into a beaten track, and grew mechanical even in their enthusiasm.

90. No solitary and unconnected meditations, however, either of the philosopher or the mystic, could furnish

a sufficiently extensive stock of theological faith for the multitude, who, by their temper and capacities, were more prone to take it at the hands of others than choose any tenets for themselves. They looked, there- fore, for some authority upon which to repose ; and instead of builders, became as it were occupants of mansions pre- pared for them by more active minds. Among those who acknowledge a code of revealed truths, the Jews, Christians, and Mahometans, this authority has been sought in largely expansive interpretations of their sacred books; either of positive obligation, as the decisions of general councils were held to be, or at least of such weight as a private man's reason, unless he were of great name himself, was not per- mitted to contravene. These expositions, in the Christian church, as well as among the Jews, were frequently allego- rical; a hidden stream of esoteric truth was supposed to flow beneath all the surface of Scripture ; and every text germinated, in the hands of the preacher, into meanings far from obvious, but which were presumed to be not undesigned. This scheme of allegorical interpretation began among the earliest fathers, and spread with perpetual expansion through the middle ages.[y] The Reformation swept most of it away ; but it has frequently revived in a more partial manner. We mention it here only as one great means of enabling men to believe more than they had done, of communicating to them what was to be received as divine truths, not additional to Scripture, because they were concealed in it, but such as the church could only have learned through her teachers.

Extended inferences from sacred books.

91. Another large class of religious opinions stood on a somewhat different footing. They were, in a pro- per sense, according to the notions of those times, revealed from God ; though not in the sacred writings which were the chief depositories of his word. Such were the re- ceived traditions in each of the three great religions, some- times absolutely infallible, sometimes, as in the former case, of interpretations, resting upon such a basis of authority, that no one was held at liberty to withhold his assent. The Jewish traditions were of this kind ; and the Mahometans

Confidence in traditions.

---

[y] Fleury (5me discours), xvii. 37. Mosheim, passim.

have trod in the same path. We may add to these the
legends of saints: none, perhaps, were positively enforced
as of faith; but a Franciscan was not to doubt the inspiration and miraculous gifts of his founder. Nor was there
any disposition in the people to doubt of them; they filled
up with abundant measure the cravings of the heart and
fancy, till, having absolutely palled both by excess, they
brought about a kind of re-action, which has taken off much
of their efficacy.

92. Francis of Assisi may naturally lead us to the last
Confidence in mode in which the spirit of theological belief mani-
individuals
as inspired. fested itself; the confidence in a particular man,
as the organ of a special divine illumination. But
though this was fully assented to by the order he instituted,
and probably by most others, it cannot be said that Francis
pretended to set up any new tenets, or enlarge, except by
his visions and miracles, the limits of spiritual knowledge.
Nor would this, in general, have been a safe proceeding in
the middle ages. Those who made a claim to such light
from heaven as could irradiate what the church had left
dark seldom failed to provoke her jealousy. It is, therefore,
in later times, and under more tolerant governments, that we
shall find the fanatics, or impostors, whom the multitude has
taken for witnesses of divine truth, or at least for interpreters
of the mysteries of the invisible world.

93. In the class of traditional theology, or what might be
Jewish   called complemental revelation, we must place the
Cabbala.   Jewish Cabbala. This consisted in a very specific and
complex system, concerning the nature of the Supreme Being,
the emanation of various orders of spirits in successive links
from his essence, their properties and characters. It is
evidently one modification of the oriental philosophy, borrowing little from the Scriptures, at least through any natural
interpretation of them, and the offspring of the Alexandrian
Jews, not far from the beginning of the Christian era. They
referred it to a tradition from Esdras, or some other eminent
person, on whom they fixed as the depositary of an esoteric
theology communicated by divine authority. The Cabbala
was received by the Jewish doctors in the first centuries after
the fall of their state; and after a period of long duration, as

remarkable for the neglect of learning in that people as in the Christian world, it revived again in that more genial season, the eleventh and twelfth centuries, when the brilliancy of many kinds of literature among the Saracens of Spain excited their Jewish subjects to emulation. Many conspicuous men illustrate the Hebrew learning of those and the succeeding ages. It was not till now, about the middle of the fifteenth century, that they came into contact with the Christians in theological philosophy. The Platonism of Ficinus, derived, in great measure, from that of Plotinus and the Alexandrian school, was easily connected, by means especially of the writings of Philo, with the Jewish orientalism, sisters as they were of the same family. Several forgeries in celebrated names, easy to effect and sure to deceive, had been committed in the first ages of Christianity by the active propagators of this philosophy. Hermes Trismegistus and Zoroaster were counterfeited in books which most were prone to take for genuine, and which it was not then easy to refute on critical grounds. These altogether formed a huge mass of imposture, or, at best, of arbitrary hypothesis, which, for more than a hundred years after this time, obtained an undue credence, and consequently retarded the course of real philosophy in Europe.[z]

94. They never gained over a more distinguished proselyte, or one whose credulity was more to be regret-　Picus of
ted, than a young man who appeared at Florence　Mirandola.
in 1485, John Picus of Mirandola. He was then twenty-two years old, the younger son of an illustrious family, which held that little principality as an imperial fief. At the age of fourteen he was sent to Bologna, that he might study the canon law, with a view to the ecclesiastical profession ; but after two years he felt an inexhaustible desire for more elevated, though less profitable, sciences. He devoted the next six years to the philosophy of the schools, in the chief universities of Italy and France ; whatever disputable subtleties the metaphysics and theology of that age could supply, became familiar to his mind ; but to these he added a knowledge of the Hebrew and other eastern languages, a

---

[z] Brucker, vol. ii. Buhle, ii. 316. Meiners, Vergl. der Sitten, iii. 277.

power of writing Latin with grace, and of amusing his leisure
with the composition of Italian poetry. The natural genius
of Picus is well shown, though in a partial manner, by a
letter which will be found among those of Politian, in
answer to Hermolaus Barbarus. His correspondent had
spoken with the scorn, and almost bitterness, usual with
philologers, of the Transalpine writers, meaning chiefly the
schoolmen, for the badness of their Latin. The young
scholastic answered, that he had been at first disheartened
by the reflection that he had lost six years' labour; but considered afterwards that the barbarians might say something
for themselves, and puts a very good defence in their
mouths; a defence which wants nothing but the truth of
what he is forced to assume, that they had been employing
their intellects upon things instead of words. Hermolaus
found, however, nothing better to reply than the compliment,
that Picus would be disavowed by the schoolmen for defending them in so eloquent a style.[a]

95. He learned Greek very rapidly, probably after his
His credulity
in the Cab-
bala. coming to Florence. And having been led, through
Ficinus, to the study of Plato, he seems to have
given up his Aristotelian philosophy for theories more congenial to his susceptible and credulous temper. These led
him onwards to wilder fancies. Ardent in the desire of
knowledge, incapable, in the infancy of criticism, to discern
authentic from spurious writings, and perhaps disqualified,

---

[a] The letter of Hermolaus is dated
Apr. 1485. He there says, after many
compliments to Picus himself: Nec
enim inter autores Latinæ linguæ numero Germanos istos et Teutonas qui ne
viventes quidem vivebant, nedum ut ex-
tincti vivant, aut si vivunt, vivunt in
pœnam et contumeliam. The answer of
Picus is dated in June. A few lines
from his pleading for the schoolmen will
exhibit his ingenuity and elegance. Admirentur nos sagaces in inquirendo, cir-
cumspectos in explorando, subtiles in
contemplando, in judicando graves, im-
plicitos in vinciendo, faciles in enodando.
Admirentur in nobis brevitatem styli,
fœtam rerum multarum atque magna-
rum, sub expositis verbis remotissimas
sententias, plenas quæstionum, plenas so-

lutionum, quam apti sumus, quam bene
instructi ambiguitates tollere, scrupos di-
luere, involuta evolvere, flexanimis syl-
logismis et infirmare falsa et vera confir-
mare. Viximus celebres, o Hermolae, et
posthac vivemus, non in scholis gram-
maticorum et pædagogiis, sed in philosophorum coronis, in conventibus sapien-
tum, ubi non de matre Andromaches,
non de Niobes filiis, atque id genus levi-
bus nugis, sed de humanarum divina-
rumque rerum rationibus agitur et dis-
putatur. In quibus meditandis, inqui-
rendis, et enodandis, ita subtiles acuti
acresque fuimus, ut anxii quandoque
nimium et morosi fuisse forte videamur,
si modo esse morosus quispiam aut
curiosus nimio plus in indagando veritate
potest. Polit. Epist. lib. 9.

by his inconceivable rapidity in apprehending the opinions
of others, from judging acutely of their reasonableness,
Picus of Mirandola fell an easy victim to his own enthusiasm
and the snares of fraud. An impostor persuaded him to purchase fifty Hebrew manuscripts, as having been composed
by Esdras, and containing the most secret mysteries of the
Cabbala. 'From this time,' says Corniani, 'he imbibed more
and more such idle fables, and wasted in dreams a genius
formed to reach the most elevated and remote truths.' In
these spurious books of Esdras, he was astonished to find, as
he says, more of Christianity than Judaism, and trusted them
the more confidently for the very reason that demonstrates
their falsity.[b]

96. Picus, about the end of 1486, repaired to Rome, and
with permission of Innocent VIII. propounded his His literary
famous nine hundred theses, or questions, logical, ances.
ethical, mathematical, physical, metaphysical, theological,
magical, and cabbalistical; upon every one of which he offered to dispute with any opponent. Four hundred of these
propositions were from philosophers of Greece or Arabia, from
the schoolmen, or from the Jewish doctors; the rest were
announced as his own opinions, which, saving the authority
of the church, he was willing to defend.[c] There was some
need of this reservation; for several of his theses were ill-
sounding, as it was called, in the ears of the orthodox. They
raised a good deal of clamour against him; and the high
rank, brilliant reputation, and obedient demeanour of Picus
were all required to save him from public censure, or more
serious animadversions. He was compelled, however, to
swear that he would adopt such an exposition of his theses
as the pope should set forth. But as this was not done, he
published an apology, especially vindicating his employment
of cabbalistical and magical learning. This excited fresh
attacks, which in some measure continued to harass him, till,
on the accession of Alexander VI. to the papal chair, he was
finally pronounced free from blamable intention. He had
meantime, as we may infer from his later writings, receded
from some of the bolder opinions of his youth. His mind

---

[c] Corniani, iii. 63. Meiners, Lebens-   21. Tiraboschi, vii. 325.
beschreibungen berühmter Männer, ii.   [c] Meiners, p. 14.

became more devout, and more fearful of deviating from the
church.   On his first appearance at Florence, uniting rare
beauty with high birth and unequalled renown, he had been
much sought by women, and returned their love.   But at the
age of twenty-five he withdrew himself from all worldly dis-
traction, destroying, as it is said, his own amatory poems, to
the regret of his friends.[d]   He now published several works
of which the Heptaplus is a cabbalistic exposition of the first
chapter of Genesis.   It is remarkable that, with his excessive
tendency to belief, he rejected altogether, and confuted in a
distinct treatise, the popular science of astrology, in which
men so much more conspicuous in philosophy have trusted.
But he had projected many other undertakings of vast extent;
an allegorical exposition of the New Testament, a defence of
the Vulgate and Septuagint against the Jews, a vindication
of Christianity against every species of infidelity and heresy;
and finally, a harmony of philosophy, reconciling the apparent inconsistencies of all writers, ancient and modern, who
deserved the name of wise, as he had already attempted by
Plato and Aristotle.   In these arduous labours he was cut off
by a fever at the age of thirty-one, in 1494, on the very day
that Charles VIII. made his entry into Florence.   A man, so
justly called the phœnix of his age, and so extraordinarily
gifted by nature, ought not to be slightly passed over, though
he may have left nothing which we could read with advantage.
If we talk of the admirable Crichton, who is little better than
a shadow, and lives but in panegyric, so much superior and
more wonderful a person as John Picus of Mirandola should
not be forgotten.[e]

97. If, leaving the genial city of Florence, we are to judge
State of of the state of knowledge in our Cisalpine regions,
learning in
Germany.   and look at the books it was thought worth while to
publish, which seems no bad criterion, we shall rate but lowly
their proficiency in the classical literature so much valued in

---

[d] Meiners, p. 10.

[e] The long biography of Picus in
Meiners is in great measure taken from
a life written by his nephew, John Francis Picus, count of Mirandola, himself a
man of great literary and philosophical
reputation in the next century.   Meiners
has made more use of this than any one

else; but much will be found concerning
Picus, from this source, and from his
own works, in Brucker, Buhle, Corniani,
and Tiraboschi.   The epitaph on Picus
by Hercules Strozza is, I believe, in the
church of St. Mark :—

Joannes jacet hic Mirandola ; cætera nôrunt
    Et Tagus et Ganges ; forsan et Antipodes.

Italy. Four editions, and those chiefly of short works, were printed at Deventer, one at Cologne, one at Louvain, five perhaps at Paris, two at Lyons.[f] But a few undated books might, probably, be added. Either, therefore, the love of ancient learning had grown colder, which was certainly not the case, or it had never been strong enough to reward the labour of the too sanguine printers. Yet it was now striking root in Germany. The excellent schools of Munster and Schelstadt were established in some part of this decad ; they trained those who were themselves to become instructors ; and the liberal zeal of Langius extending beyond his immediate disciples, scarce any Latin author was published in Germany of which he did not correct the text.[g] The opportunities he had of doing so were not, as has been just seen, so numerous in this period as they became in the next. He had to withstand a potent and obstinate faction. The mendicant friars of Cologne, the head-quarters of barbarous superstition, clamoured against his rejection of the old school-books, and the entire reform of education. But Agricola addresses his friend in sanguine language : Agricola.
' I entertain the greatest hope from your exertions, that we shall one day wrest from this insolent Italy her vaunted glory of pre-eminent eloquence; and redeeming ourselves from the opprobrium of ignorance, barbarism, and incapacity of expression, which she is ever casting upon us, may show our Germany so deeply learned, that Latium itself shall not be more Latin than she will appear.'[h] About 1482, Agricola was invited to the court of the elector palatine at Heidelberg. He seems not to have been engaged in public instruction, but passed the remainder of his life, unfortunately too short, for he died in 1485, in diffusing and promoting a taste for literature among his contemporaries. No German wrote in so pure a style, or possessed so large a portion of classical learning. Vives places him in dignity and grace of language even above

---

[f] Panzer.

[g] Meiners, Lebensbesch. ii. 328. Eichhorn, iii. 231-239.

[h] Unum hoc tibi affirmo, ingentem de te concipio fiduciam, summamque in spem adducor, fore aliquando, ut priscam insolenti Italiæ, et propemodum occupatam bene dicendi gloriam extorquea-

mus ; vindicemusque nos, et ab ignavia, qua nos barbaros, indoctosque et elingues, et si quid est his incultius, esse nos jactitant, exsolvamus, futuramque tam doctam et literatam Germaniam nostram, ut non Latinius vel ipsum sit Latium. This is quoted by Heeren, p. 154, and Meiners, ii. 329.

Politian and Hermolaus.[i] The praises of Erasmus, as well as of the later critics, if not so marked, are very freely bestowed. His letters are frequently written in Greek; a fashion of those who could follow it; and, as far as I have attended to them, seem equal in correctness to some from men of higher name in the next age.

98. The immediate patron of Agricola, through whom he was invited to Heidelberg, was John Camerarius, of the house of Dalberg, bishop of Worms, and chancellor of the Palatinate. He contributed much himself to the cause of letters in Germany; especially if he is to be deemed the founder, as probably he should be, of an early academy, the Rhenish Society, which, we are told, devoted its time to Latin, Greek, and Hebrew criticism, astronomy, music, and poetry; not scorning to relax their minds with dances and feasts, nor forgetting the ancient German attachment to the flowing cup.[k] The chief seat of the Rhenish Society was at Heidelberg; but it had associate branches in other parts of Germany, and obtained imperial privileges. No member of this academy was more conspicuous than Conrad Celtes, who has sometimes been reckoned its founder, which, from his youth, is hardly probable, and was, at least, the chief instrument of its subsequent extension. He was

Rhenish academy.

---

[i] Vix et hac nostra et patrum memoria fuit unus atque alter dignior, qui multum legeretur, multumque in manibus haberetur, quam Radulphus Agricola Frisius; tantum est in ejus operibus ingenii, artis, gravitatis, dulcedinis, eloquentiæ, eruditionis; at is paucissimis noscitur, vir non minus, qui ab hominibus cognosceretur, dignus quam Politianus, vel Hermolaus Barbarus, quos mea quidem sententia, et majestate et suavitate dictionis non æquat modo, sed etiam vincit. Vives, Comment. in Augustin. (apud Blount, Censura Auctorum, sub nomine Agricola.)

Agnosco virum divini pectoris, eruditionis reconditæ, stylo minime vulgari, solidum, nervosum, elaboratum, compositum. In Italia summus esse poterat, nisi Germaniam prætulisset. Erasmus in Ciceroniano. He speaks as strongly in many other places. Testimonies to the merits of Agricola from Huet,

Vossius, and others, are collected by Bayle, Blount, Baillet, and Niceron. Meiners has written his life, ii. pp. 332–363; and several of his letters will be found among those addressed to Reuchlin, Epistolæ ad Reuchlinum; a collection of great importance for this portion of literary history.

[k] Studebant eximia hæc ingenia Latinorum, Græcorum, Ebræorumque scriptorum lectioni, cum primis criticæ; astronomiam et artem musicam excolebant. Poesin atque jurisprudentiam sibi habebant commendatam; imo et interdum gaudia curis interponebant. Nocturno nimirum tempore, defessi laboribus, ludere solebant, saltare, jocari cum mulierculis, epulari, ac more Germanorum inveterato strenue potare. (Jugler, Hist. litteraria, p. 1993, vol. iii.) The passage seems to be taken from Ruprecht, Oratio de Societate Litteraria Rhenana, Jenæ, 1752, which I have not seen.

indefatigable in the vineyard of literature, and, travelling to different parts of Germany, exerted a more general influence than Agricola himself. Celtes was the first from whom Saxony derived some taste for learning. His Latin poetry was far superior to any that had been produced in the empire; and for this, in 1487, he received the laurel crown from Frederick III.[m]

99. Reuchlin, in 1482, accompanied the duke of Wirtemberg on a visit to Rome. He thus became acquainted with the illustrious men of Italy, and convinced them of his own pretensions to the name of a scholar. The old Constantinopolitan Argyropulus, on hearing him translate a passage of Thucydides, exclaimed, ' Our banished Greece has now flown beyond the Alps.' Yet Reuchlin, though from some other circumstances of his life a more celebrated, was not probably so learned or so accomplished a man as Agricola; he was withdrawn from public tuition by the favour of several princes, in whose courts he filled honourable offices; and, after some years more, he fell unfortunately into the same seducing error as Picus of Mirandola, and sacrificed his classical pursuits for the Cabbalistic philosophy.

Reuchlin.

100. Though France contributed little to the philologer, several books were now published in French. In the Cent Nouvelles Nouvelles, 1486, a slight improvement in polish of language is said to be discernible.[n] The poems of Villon are rather of more importance. They were first published in 1489; but many of them had been written thirty years before. Boileau has given Villon credit for being the first who cleared his style from the rudeness and redundancy of the old romancers.[o] But this praise, as some have observed, is more justly due to the duke of Orleans, a man of full as much talent as Villon, with a finer taste. The poetry of the latter, as might be expected from a life of dissoluteness and roguery, is often low and coarse; but he seems by no

French language and poetry.

---

[m] Jugler, ubi supra. Eichhorn, ii. 557. Heeren, p. 160. Biogr. universelle, arts. Celtes, Dalberg, Trithemius.

[n] Essai du C. François de Neufchâteau sur les meilleurs ouvrages en prose; prefixed to Œuvres de Pascal (1819), i.

p. cxx.

[o] Villon fut le premier dans des siècles grossiers

Débrouiller l'art confus de nos vieux romanciers.

Art poétique, l. i, v. 117.

means incapable of a moral strain, not destitute of terseness
and spirit. Martial d'Auvergne, in his Vigiles de la Mort
de Charles VII., which, from its subject, must have been
written soon after 1460, though not printed till 1490, displays,
to judge from the extracts in Goujet, some compass of imagination.[p] The French poetry of this age was still full of
allegorical morality, and had lost a part of its original
raciness. Those who desire an acquaintance with it may
have recourse to the author just mentioned, or to Bouterwek ;
and extracts, though not so copious as the title promises,
will be found in the Recueil des anciens Poètes français.

101. The modern drama of Europe is derived, like its
European poetry, from two sources, the one ancient or classical,
drama. the other mediæval ; the one an imitation of Plautus
and Seneca, the other a gradual refinement of the rude scenic
performances, denominated miracles, mysteries, or moralities.

Latin. Latin plays upon the former model, a few of which
are extant, were written in Italy during the fourteenth and fifteenth centuries, and sometimes represented,
either in the universities, or before an audience of ecclesiastics and others who could understand them.[q] One of
these, the Catinia of Secco Polentone, written about the
middle of the fifteenth century, and translated by a son of
the author into the Venetian dialect, was printed in 1482.
This piece, however, was confined to the press.[r] Sabellicus,
as quoted by Tiraboschi, has given to Pomponius Lætus the
credit of having re-established the theatre at Rome, and
caused the plays of Plautus and Terence, as well as some
more modern, which we may presume to have been in Latin,
to be performed before the pope, probably Sixtus IV. And
James of Volterra, in a diary published by Muratori, expressly
mentions a History of Constantine represented in the papal
palace during the carnival of 1484.[s] In imitation of Italy,
but perhaps a little after the present decennial period,
Reuchlin brought Latin plays of his own composition before
a German audience. They were represented by students of

---

[p] Goujet, Bibliothèque française,   [r] Tiraboschi, p. 201.
vol. x.   [s] Id. p. 204.
[q] Tiraboschi, vii. 200.

Heidelberg. An edition of his Progymnasmata Scenica, containing some of these comedies, was printed in 1498. It has been said that one of them is taken from the French farce Maître Patelin;[t] while another, entitled Sergius, according to Warton, flies a much higher pitch, and is a satire on bad kings and bad ministers; though, from the account of Meiners, it seems rather to fall on the fraudulent arts of the monks.[u] The book is very scarce, and I have never seen it. Conrad Celtes, not long after Reuchlin, produced his own tragedies and comedies in the public halls of German cities. It is to be remembered, that the oral Latin language might at that time be tolerably familiar to a considerable audience in Germany.

102. The Orfeo of Politian has claimed precedence as the earliest represented drama, not of a religious nature, Orfeo of in a modern language. This was written by him in Politian. two days, and acted before the court of Mantua in 1483. Roscoe has called it the first example of the musical drama, or Italian opera; but though he speaks of this as agreed by general consent, it is certain that the Orfeo was not designed for musical accompaniment, except, probably, in the songs and choruses.[v] According to the analysis of the fable in Ginguéné, the Orfeo differs only from a legendary mystery by substituting one set of characters for another; and it is surely by an arbitrary definition that we pay it the compliment upon which the modern historians of literature seem to have agreed. Several absurdities which appear in the first edition are said not to exist in the original manuscripts from which

---

[t] Gresswell's Early Parisian Press, p. 124; quoting La Monnoye. This seems to be confirmed by Meniers, i. 63. [It has been suggested to me by Dr. West, that the Progymnasmata Scenica is the title of a single comedy, namely, that which is taken from Maître Patelin. Meiners, vol. i. p. 63, seems to confirm this.

Some extracts from the Sergius, for which I am indebted to the same obliging correspondent, lead me to conclude that the satire is more general than the account of that play by Meiners had implied; and that priests or monks come in only for a share in it.—1842.]

[u] Warton, iii. 203. Meiners, i. 62. The Sergius was represented at Heidelberg about 1497.

[v] Burney (Hist. of Music, iv. 17) seems to countenance this; but Tiraboschi does not speak of musical accompaniment to the Orfeo; and Corniani only says: Alcuni di essi sembrano dall' autor destinati ad accoppiarsi colla musica. Tali sono i canzoni e i cori alla greca. Probably Roscoe did not mean all that his words imply; for the origin of recitative, in which the essence of the Italian opera consists, more than a century afterwards, is matter of notoriety.

the Orfeo has been reprinted.[x] We must give the next place
to a translation of the Menæchmi of Plautus, acted at Ferrara
in 1486, by order of Ercole I., and, as some have thought,
his own production, or to some original plays said to have
been performed at the same brilliant court in the following
years.[y]

103. The less regular, though in their day not less interest-
Origin of
dramatic
mysteries. ing, class of scenical stories, commonly called mysteries, all of which related to religious subjects, were
never in more reputation than at this time. It is impossible
to fix their first appearance at any single era, and the inquiry
into the origin of dramatic representation must be very
limited in its subject, or perfectly futile in its scope. All
nations, probably, have at all times, to a certain extent,
amused themselves both with pantomimic and oral representation of a feigned story; the sports of children are seldom
without both ; and the exclusive employment of the former,
instead of being a first stage of the drama, as has sometimes been assumed, is rather a variety in the course of its
progress.

104. The Christian drama arose on the ruins of the heathen
Their early
stage. theatre : it was a natural substitute of real sympathies for those which were effaced and condemned.
Hence we find Greek tragedies on sacred subjects almost as
early as the establishment of the church, and we have testimonies to their representation at Constantinople. Nothing
of this kind being proved with respect to the west of Europe
in the dark ages, it has been conjectured, not improbably,
though without necessity, that the pilgrims, of whom great
numbers repaired to the East in the eleventh century, might
have obtained notions of scenical dialogue, with a succession
of characters, and with an ornamental apparatus, in which
theatrical representation properly consists. The earliest
mention of them, it has been said, is in England. Geoffrey,
afterwards abbot of St. Alban's, while teaching a school at

---

[x] Tiraboschi, vii. 216. Ginguéné, iii.
514. Andrès, v. 125, discussing the
history of the Italian and Spanish theatres, gives the precedence to the Orfeo,
as a represented play, though he conceives the first act of the Celestina to
have been written and well known not
later than the middle of the fifteenth
century.

[y] Tiraboschi vii. 203, et post. Roscoe, Leo X., ch. ii. Ginguéné, vi. 18.

Dunstable, caused one of the shows vulgarly called miracles, on the story of St. Catherine, to be represented in that town. Such is the account of Matthew Paris, who mentions the circumstance incidentally, in consequence of a fire that ensued. This must have been within the first twenty years of the twelfth century.[x] It is not to be questioned, that Geoffrey, a native of France, had some earlier models in his own country. Le Bœuf gives an account of a mystery written in the middle of the preceding century, wherein Virgil is introduced among the prophets that come to adore the Saviour ; doubtless in allusion to the fourth eclogue.

105. Fitz-Stephen, in the reign of Henry II., dwells on the sacred plays acted in London, representing the miracles or passions of martyrs. They became very common by the names of mysteries or miracles, both in England and on the Continent, and were not only exhibited within the walls of convents, but upon public occasions and festivals for the amusement of the people. It is probable, however, that the performers for a long time were always ecclesiastics. The earlier of these religious dramas were in Latin. A Latin farce on St. Nicolas exists, older than the thirteenth century.[a] It was slowly that the modern languages were employed ; and perhaps it might hence be presumed, that the greater part of the story was told through pan- *(margin note: Extant English mysteries.)*

---

[x] Mat. Paris, p. 1007 (edit. 1684). See Warton's 34th section (iii. 193–233) for the early drama, and Beauchamps, Hist. du Théâtre français, vol. i., or Bouterwek, v. 95–117, for the French in particular; Tiraboschi, ubi supra, or Riccoboni, Hist. du Théâtre italien, for that of Italy.

[It is not sufficient, in order to prove the continuity of dramatic representation through the dark ages, that we should possess a few poetical dialogues in Latin, or even entire plays, like those of Hroswitha, abbess of Gandersaen, in the 10th century. A modern French writer calls one of her sacred comedies " Un des chaînons le plus brillant, peut-être, et le plus pur de cette série non interrompue d'œuvres dramatiques, jusqu'ici trop peu étudiées, qui lient le théâtre païen, expirant vers le cinquième siècle, au théâtre moderne, renaissant dans presque toutes les contrées de l'Europe

vers la fin du treizième siècle."—Quotation in Jubinal, Mystères inédits du Quinzième Siècle, Paris, 1837, p. 9. But we have no sort of evidence that the dramas of Hroswitha were represented, nor is it by any means probable that they were. Until the new languages, which alone the people understood, were employed in popular writings, the stage must have been silent. In the mystery of the Wise and Foolish Virgins, we find both Latin and Provençal. This, therefore, is an evidence of transition ; and whether as old as the 11th century, or a little later, may stand at the head of European dramatic literature. Several others, however, are referred by late French antiquaries to the same age, and have been published by M. Monmerqué.—1847.]

[a] Journal des Savans, 1828, p. 297. These farces, according to M. Raynouard, were the earliest dramatic representations, and gave rise to the mysteries.

tomime. But as this was unsatisfactory, and the spectators
could not always follow the fable, there was an obvious
inducement to make use of the vernacular language. The
most ancient specimens appear to be those which Le Grand
d'Aussy found among the compositions of the Trouveurs. He
has published extracts from three; two of which are in the
nature of legendary mysteries; while the third, which is far
more remarkable, and may possibly be of the following century, is a pleasing pastoral drama, of which there seem to
be no other instances in the mediæval period.[b] Bouterwek
mentions a fragment of a German mystery, near the end of
the thirteenth century.[c] Next to this it seems that we should
place an English mystery called 'The Harrowing of Hell.'
'This,' its editor observes, 'is believed to be the most
ancient production in a dramatic form in our language. The
manuscript from which it is now printed is on vellum, and is
certainly as old as the reign of Edward III., if not older. It
probably formed one of a series of performances of the same
kind, founded upon Scripture history.' It consists of a prologue, epilogue, and intermediate dialogue of nine persons,
Dominus, Sathan, Adam, Eve, &c. Independently of the
alleged age of the manuscript itself, the language will hardly
be thought later than 1350.[d] This, however, seems to stand
at no small distance from any extant work of the kind.
Warton having referred the Chester mysteries to 1327, when
he supposes them to have been written by Ranulph Higden,
a learned monk of that city, best known as the author of the
Polychronicon, Roscoe positively contradicts him, and denies
that any dramatic composition can be found in England
anterior to the year 1500.[e] Two of these Chester mysteries

---

[b] Fabliaux, ii. 119.

    [c] ix. 265. The 'Tragedy of the Ten
Virgins' was acted at Eisenach in 1322.
This is evidently nothing but a mystery.
Weber's Illustrations of Northern Poe-
try, p. 19. [A drama of the Wise and
Foolish Virgins, written in a mixture of
Latin and Romance, and ascribed by Le
Bœuf to the eleventh century, has been
published by Raynouard. See Journal
des Savans, June 1836, p. 366, for this
early mystery.—1842.]

    [d] Mr. Collier has printed twenty-five

copies (why veteris tam parcus aceti?) of
this very curious record of the ancient
drama. I do not know that any other in
Europe of that early age has yet been
given to the press.

    [The Harrowing of Hell has since
been published by Mr. Halliwell. In
the Théâtre français du Moyen Âge,
1839, M. Michel has published several
French mysteries or miracle plays of
the 14th century, or perhaps earlier.—
1847.]

    [e] Lorenzo de' Medici, i. 299. Roscoe

have been since printed; but notwithstanding the very respectable authorities which assign them to the fourteenth century, I cannot but consider the language in which we now read them not earlier, to say the least, than the middle of the next. It is possible that they have in some degree been modernised. Mr. Collier has given an analysis of our own extant mysteries, or, as he prefers to call them, Miracle-plays.[f] There does not seem to be much dramatic merit, even with copious indulgence, in any of them; and some, such as the two Chester mysteries, are in the lowest style of buffoonery; yet they are not without importance in the absolute sterility of English literature during the age in which we presume them to have been written, the reigns of Henry VI. and Edward IV.

106. The fourteenth and fifteenth centuries were fertile of these religious dramas in many parts of Europe. They were frequently represented in Germany, but more in Latin than the mother-tongue. The French Scriptural theatre, whatever may have been previously exhibited, seems not to be traced in permanent existence beyond the last years of the fourteenth century.[g] It was about 1400, according to Beauchamps, or some years before, as the authorities quoted by Bouterwek imply, that the Confrairie de la Passion de N. S. was established as a regular body of actors at Paris.[h] They are said to have taken their name from the mystery of the passion, which in fact represented the whole life of our Lord from his baptism, and was divided into several days. In pomp of show they far excelled our English mysteries, in which few persons appeared, and the scenery was simple. But in the mystery of the passion,

First French theatre.

---

thinks there is reason to conjecture that the Miracle-play acted at Dunstable was in dumb show; and assumes the same of the 'grotesque exhibitions' known by the name of the Harrowing of Hell. In this we have just seen that he was mistaken, and probably in the former.

[f] Hist. of English Dramatic Poetry, vol. ii. The Chester mysteries were printed for the Roxburghe Club, by my friend Mr. Markland; and what are called the Townley mysteries are announced for publication (1836). [They

have since appeared. 1842.]

[g] [The mystery of St. Crispin and St. Crispinien, published about 1836, is reviewed by Raynouard in the Journal des Savans for that year. He seems to assign no date to this mystery; but it is clear that similar dramas were represented long before the end of the fourteenth century. But not perhaps on a permanent theatre.—1842.]

[h] Beauchamps, Recherches sur le Théâtre français, Bouterwek, v. 96.

eighty-seven characters were introduced in the first day; heaven, earth, and hell combined to people the stage; several scenes were written for singing, and some for choruses. The dialogue, of which I have only seen the few extracts in Bouterwek, is rather similar to that of our own mysteries, though less rude, and with more efforts at a tragic tone.[i]

107. The mysteries, not confined to Scriptural themes, Theatrical machinery. embraced those which were hardly less sacred and trustworthy in the eyes of the people, the legends of saints. These afforded ample scope for the gratification which great part of mankind seem to take in witnessing the endurance of pain. Thus, in one of these Parisian mysteries, St. Barbara is hung up by the heels on the stage ; and after uttering her remonstrances in that unpleasant situation, is torn with pincers and scorched with lamps before the audience. The decorations of this theatre must have appeared splendid. A large scaffolding at the back of the stage displayed heaven above and hell below, between which extended the world, with representations of the spot where the scene lay. Nor was the machinist's art unknown. An immense dragon, with eyes of polished steel, sprang out from hell, in a mystery exhibited at Metz in the year 1437, and spread his wings so near to the spectators, that they were all in consternation.[k] Many French mysteries, chiefly without date of the year, are in print, and probably belong, typographically speaking, to the present century.[m] One bears, according to Brunet, the date of 1484. These may, however, have been written long before their publication. Beauchamps has given a list of early mysteries and moralities in the French language, beginning near the end of the fourteenth century.

108. The religious drama was doubtless full as ancient in Italian religious dramas. Italy as in any other country; it was very congenial to a people whose delight in sensible objects is so intense. It did not supersede the extemporaneous performances, the mimi and histriones, who had probably never intermitted their sportive licence since the days of their

[i] Bouterwek, p. 100.   [m] Brunet, Manuel du Libraire.
[k] Ib. pp. 100–106.

Oscan fathers, and of whom we find mention, sometimes
with severity, sometimes with toleration, in ecclesiastical
writers,[n] but it came into competition with them; and thus
may be said to have commenced in the thirteenth century a
war of regular comedy against the lawless savages of the
stage, which has only been terminated in Italy within very
recent recollection.   We find a society del Gonfalone established at Rome in 1264, the statutes of which declare, that it
is designed to represent the passion of Jesus Christ.[o] Lorenzo
de' Medici condescended to publish a drama of this kind on
the martyrdom of two saints; and a considerable collection
of similar productions during the fifteenth century was in the
possession of Mr. Roscoe.[p]

109. Next to the mysteries came the kindred class, styled
moralities. But as these belong more peculiarly to the
next century, both in England and France, though
they began about the present time, we may better reserve
them for that period.   There is still another species of dramatic composition, what may be called the farce,
not always very distinguishable from comedy, but
much shorter, admitting more buffoonery without reproach,
and more destitute of any serious or practical end.   It may
be reckoned a middle link between the extemporaneous
effusions of the mimes and the legitimate drama.   The
French have a diverting piece of this kind, Maître Patelin,
ascribed to Pierre Blanchet, and first printed in 1490.   It
was restored to the stage, with much alteration, under the
name of l'Avocat Patelin, about the beginning of the last
century; and contains strokes of humour which Molière
would not have disdained.[q] Of these productions there were
not a few in Germany, called Fastnachtsspiele, or Carnival
plays, written in the licence which that season has generally

Moralities.

Farces.

---

[n] Thomas Aquinas mentions the his-
trionatûs ars, as lawful if not abused.
Antonin of Florence does the same.
Riccoboni, i. 23.

[o] Riccoboni.   Tiraboschi, however,
v. 376, disputes the antiquity of any
scenical representations truly dramatic
in Italy: in which he seems to be mistaken.

[p] Life of Lorenzo, i. 402.

[q] The proverbial expression for quitting a digression, Revenons à nos mou-
tons, is taken from this farce; which is
at least short, and as laughable as most
farces are.   It seems to have been written not long before its publication.   See
Pasquier, Recherches de la France, l.
viii. c. 59; Biogr. univ., Blanchet; and
Bouterwek, v. 118.

permitted. They are scarce, and of little value. The most
remarkable is the Apotheosis of Pope Joan, a tragi-comic
legend, written about 1480.[r]

110. Euclid was printed for the first time at Venice in
Mathema-   1482; the diagrams in this edition are engraved on
tical works. copper, and remarkably clear and neat.[s] The translation is that of Campanus from the Arabic. The cosmography
of Ptolemy, which had been already twice published in Italy,
appeared the same year at Ulm, with maps by Donis, some
of them traced after the plans drawn by Agathodæmon, some
modern; and it was reprinted, as well as Euclid, at the same
place in 1486. The tables of Regiomontanus were printed
both at Augsburg and Venice in 1490. We may take this
occasion of introducing two names which do not exclusively
belong to the exact sciences, nor to the present period.

111. Leo Baptista Alberti was a man, who, if measured
Leo Baptista by the universality of his genius, may claim a place
Alberti.   in the temple of glory he has not filled; the author
of a Latin comedy, entitled Philodoxios, which the younger
Aldus Manutius afterwards published as the genuine work
of a supposed ancient Lepidus; a moral writer in the various
forms of dialogue, dissertation, fable, and light humour; a
poet, extolled by some, though not free from the rudeness of
his age; a philosopher of the Platonic school of Lorenzo; a
mathematician and inventor of optical instruments; a painter
and the author of the earliest modern treatise on painting;
a sculptor, and the first who wrote about sculpture; a musi-
cian, whose compositions excited the applause of his contemporaries; an architect of profound skill, not only displayed
in many works, of which the church of Saint Francis at
Rimini is the most admired,[t] but in a theoretical treatise,
De re ædificatoriâ, published posthumously in 1485. It has

---

[r] Bouterwek, Gesch. der Deutschen
Poesie, ix. 357–367. Heinsius, Lehrbuch der Sprachwissenschaft, iv. 125.

[s] A beautiful copy of this edition,
presented to Mocenigo. doge of Venice, is
in the British Museum. The diagrams,
especially those which represent solids,
are better than in most of our modern
editions of Euclid. I will take this opportunity of mentioning, that the earliest book in which engravings are found,

is the edition of Dante by Landino, pub-
lished at Florence in 1481. See Brunet,
Manuel du Libraire, Dibdin's Bibl.
Spencer, &c.

[t] [Let me add that of St. Andrew at
Mantua, worthy of comparison with the
best of the 16th century, and free from
the excessive decoration by which they
often lose sight both of pure taste and
religious effect.—1847.]

been called the only work on architecture which we can place on a level with that of Vitruvius, and by some has been preferred to it. Alberti had deeply meditated the remains of Roman antiquity, and endeavoured to derive from them general theorems of beauty, variously applicable to each description of buildings.[u]

112. This great man seems to have had two impediments to his permanent glory : one, that he came a few years too soon into the world, before his own language was become polished, and before the principles of taste in art had been wholly developed ; the other, that, splendid as was his own genius, there were yet two men a little behind, in the presence of whom his star has paled ; men, not superior to Alberti in universality of mental powers, but in their transcendency and command over immortal fame. Many readers will have perceived to whom I allude—Leonardo da Vinci and Michael Angelo.

113. None of the writings of Leonardo were published till more than a century after his death ; and, indeed, the most remarkable of them are still in manuscript. We cannot, therefore, give him a determinate place under this rather than any other decennium ; but as he was born in 1452, we may presume his mind to have been in full expansion before 1490. His Treatise on Painting is known as a very early disquisition on the rules of the art. But his greatest literary distinction is derived from those short fragments of his unpublished writings that appeared not many years since ; and which, according, at least, to our common estimate of the age in which he lived, are more like revelations of physical truths vouchsafed to a single mind, than the superstructure of its reasoning upon any established basis. The discoveries which made Galileo, and Kepler, and Mæstlin, and Maurolycus, and Castelli, and other names illustrious, the system of Copernicus, the very theories of recent geologers, are anticipated by Da Vinci, within the compass of a few pages, not perhaps in the most precise language, or on the most conclusive reasoning, but so as to strike us with something like the awe of præternatural know-

Leonardo da Vinci.

---

[n] Corniani, ii. 160. Tiraboschi, vii. 360.

ledge. In an age of so much dogmatism, he first laid down the grand principle of Bacon, that experiment and observation must be the guides to just theory in the investigation of nature. If any doubt could be harboured, not as to the right of Leonardo da Vinci to stand as the first name of the fifteenth century, which is beyond all doubt, but as to his originality in so many discoveries, which, probably, no one man, especially in such circumstances, has ever made, it must be on an hypothesis, not very untenable, that some parts of physical science had already attained a height which mere books do not record. The extraordinary works of ecclesiastical architecture in the middle ages, especially in the fifteenth century, as well as those of Toscanelli and Fioravanti, which we have mentioned, lend some countenance to this opinion. Leonardo himself speaks of the earth's annual motion, in a treatise that appears to have been written about 1510, as the opinion of many philosophers in his age.[v]

---

[v] The manuscripts of Leonardo da Vinci, now at Paris, are the justification of what has been said in the text. A short account of them was given by Venturi, who designed to have published a part; but, having relinquished that intention, the fragments he has made known are the more important. As they are very remarkable, and not, I believe, very generally known, I shall extract a few passages from his Essai sur les Ouvrages physico-mathématiques de Léonard de Vinci. Paris, 1797.

En mécanique, Vinci connaissait, entr'autres choses : 1. La théorie des forces appliquées obliquement au bras du levier ; 2. La résistance respective des poutres ; 3. Les loix du frottement données ensuite par Amontons ; 4. L'influence du centre de gravité sur les corps en repos ou en mouvement ; 5. L'application du principe des vitesses virtuelles à plusieurs cas que la sublime analyse a porté de nos jours à sa plus grande généralité. Dans l'optique il décrivit la chambre obscure avant Porta, il expliqua avant Maurolycus la figure de l'image du soleil dans un trou de forme anguleuse ; il nous apprend la perspective aérienne, la nature des ombres colorées, les mouvemens de l'iris, les effets de la durée de l'impression visible, et plusieurs

autres phénomènes de l'œil qu'on ne rencontre point dans Vitellion. Enfin non-seulement Vinci avait remarqué tout ce que Castelli a dit un siècle après lui sur le mouvement des eaux ; le premier me paraît même dans cette partie supérieure de beaucoup à l'autre, que l'Italie cependant a regardé comme le fondateur de l'hydraulique.

Il faut donc placer Léonard à la tête de ceux qui se sont occupés des sciences physico-mathématiques, et de la vraie méthode d'étudier parmi les modernes. p. 5.

The first extract Venturi gives is entitled, On the descent of heavy bodies combined with the rotation of the earth. He here assumes the latter, and conceives that a body falling to the earth from the top of a tower would have a compound motion, in consequence of the terrestrial rotation. Venturi thinks that the writings of Nicolas de Cusa had set men on speculating concerning this before the time of Copernicus.

Vinci had very extraordinary lights as to mechanical motions. He says plainly that the time of descent on inclined planes of equal height is as their length: that a body descends along the arc of a circle sooner than down the cord, and that a body descending an inclined plane

Sect. VI. 1491—1500.

State of Learning in Italy—Latin and Italian Poets—Learning in France and England—Erasmus—Popular Literature and Poetry—Other Kinds of Literature—General Literary Character of Fifteenth Century—Book-trade, its Privileges and Restraints.

114. The year 1494 is distinguished by an edition of Musæus, generally thought the first work from the press established

---

will re-ascend with the same velocity as if it had fallen down the height. He frequently repeats, that every body weighs in the direction of its movement, and weighs the more in the ratio of its velocity; by weight evidently meaning what we call force. He applies this to the centrifugal force of bodies in rotation: Pendant tout ce temps elle pèse sur la direction de son mouvement.

Lorsqu'on employe une machine quelconque pour mouvoir un corps grave, toutes les parties de la machine qui ont un mouvement égal à celui du corps grave ont une charge égale au poids entier du même corps. Si la partie qui est le moteur a, dans le même temps, plus de mouvement que le corps mobile, elle aura plus de puissance que le mobile; et cela d'autant plus qu'elle se mouvra plus vîte que le corps même. Si la partie qui est le moteur a moins de vîtesse que le mobile, elle aura d'autant moins de puissance que ce mobile. If in this passage there is not the perfect luminousness of expression we should find in the best modern books, it seems to contain the philosophical theory of motion as unequivocally as any of them.

Vinci had a better notion of geology than most of his contemporaries, and saw that the sea had covered the mountains which contained shells: Ces coquillages ont vécu dans le même endroit lorsque l'eau de la mer le recouvrait. Les bancs, par la suite des temps, ont été recouverts par d'autres couches de limon de différentes hauteurs; ainsi, les coquilles ont été enclavées sous le bourbier amoncelé au dessus, jusqu'à sortir de l'eau. He seems to have had an idea of the elevation of the continents, though he gives an unintelligible reason for it.

He explained the obscure light of the unilluminated part of the moon by the reflection of the earth, as Mæstlin did long after. He understood the camera obscura, and describes its effect. He perceived that respirable air must support flame : Lorsque l'air n'est pas dans un état propre à recevoir la flamme, il n'y peut vivre ni flamme ni aucun animal terrestre ou aérien. Aucun animal ne peut vivre dans un endroit où la flamme ne vit pas.

Vinci's observations on the conduct of the understanding are also very much beyond his time. I extract a few of them.

Il est toujours bon pour l'entendement d'acquérir des connaissances quelles qu'elles soient; on pourra ensuite choisir les bonnes et écarter les inutiles.

L'interprète des artifices de la nature, c'est l'expérience. Elle ne se trompe jamais; c'est notre jugement qui quelquefois se trompe lui-même parce qu'il s'attend à des effets auxquels l'expérience se refuse. Il faut consulter l'expérience, en varier les circonstances jusqu'à ce que nous en ayons tiré des règles générales; car c'est elle qui fournit les vraies règles. Mais à quoi bon ces règles, me direz-vous? Je réponds qu'elles nous dirigent dans les recherches de la nature et les opérations de l'art. Elles empêchent que nous ne nous abusions nous-mêmes ou les autres, en nous promettant des résultats que nous ne saurions obtenir.

Il n'y a point de certitude dans les sciences où on ne peut pas appliquer quelque partie des mathématiques, ou qui n'en dépendent pas de quelque manière.

Dans l'étude des sciences qui tiennent aux mathématiques, ceux qui ne consultent pas la nature, mais les auteurs, ne sont pas les enfans de la nature; je dirais qu'ils n'en sont que les petits fils : elle seule, en effet, est le maître des vrais

at Venice by Aldus Manutius, who had settled there in 1489.[x]
Aldine Greek editions. In the course of about twenty years, with some
interruption, he gave to the world several of the
principal Greek authors; and though, as we have seen, not
absolutely the earliest printer in that language, he so far
excelled all others in the number of his editions, that he
may be justly said to stand at the head of the list. It is
right, however, to mention that Zarot had printed Hesiod
and Theocritus in one volume, and also Isocrates, at Milan,
in 1493; that the Anthologia appeared at Florence in 1494;
Lucian and Apollonius Rhodius in 1496; the Lexicon of
Suidas at Milan in 1499. About fifteen editions of Greek
works, without reckoning Craston's Lexicon and several
grammars, had been published before the close of the century.[y] The most remarkable of the Aldine editions are the
Aristotle, in five volumes, the first bearing the date of 1495,
the last of 1498, and nine plays of Aristophanes in the latter

---

génies. Mais voyez la sottise! on se
moque d'un homme qui aimera mieux
apprendre de la nature elle-même, que
des auteurs, qui n'en sont que les clercs.
Is not this the precise tone of Lord Bacon?

Vinci says in another place : Mon des-
sein est de citer d'abord l'expérience,
et de démontrer ensuite pourquoi les
corps sont contraints d'agir de telle manière. C'est la méthode qu'on doit observer dans les recherches des phénomènes de la nature. Il est bien vrai que
la nature commence par le raisonnement,
et finit par l'expérience ; mais n'importe,
il nous faut prendre la route opposée :
comme j'ai dit, nous devons commencer
par l'expérience, et tâcher par son moyen
d'en découvrir la raison.

He ascribes the elevation of the equa-
torial waters above the polar to the heat
of the sun : Elles entrent en mouvement
de tous les côtés de cette éminence
aqueuse pour rétablir leur sphéricité
parfaite. This is not the true cause of
the elevation, but by what means could
he know the fact ?

Vinci understood fortification well, and
wrote upon it. Since in our time, he
says, artillery has four times the power
it used to have, it is necessary that the
fortification of towns should be strengthened in the same proportion. He was
employed on several great works of en-

gineering. So wonderful was the variety of power in this miracle of nature.
For we have not mentioned that his Last
Supper, at Milan, is the earliest of the
great pictures in Italy, and that some
productions of his easel vie with those of
Raphael. His only published work, the
Treatise on Painting, does him injustice ;
it is an ill-arranged compilation from
several of his manuscripts. That the
extraordinary works, of which this note
contains an account, have not been published entire and in their original language, is much to be regretted by all
who know how to venerate so great a
genius as Leonardo da Vinci.

[x] The Erotemata of Constantine Lascaris, printed by Aldus, bears date Feb.
1494, which seems to mean 1495. But
the Musæus has no date, nor the Galeo-
myomachia, a Greek poem by one Theo-
dorus Prodromus. Renouard, Hist. de
l'Imprimerie des Aldes.

[y] The Grammar of Urbano Valeriano
was first printed in 1497. It is in Greek
and Latin, and of extreme rarity. Roscoe (Leo X., ch. xi.) says, 'it was received with such avidity that Erasmus,
on enquiring for it in the year 1499,
found that not a copy of this impression
remained unsold.' I have given, a little
below, a different construction to these
words of Erasmus.

year. In this Aristophanes, and perhaps in other editions of this time, Aldus had fortunately the assistance of Marcus Musurus, one of the last, but by no means the least eminent, of the Greeks who transported their language to Italy. Musurus was now a public teacher at Padua. John Lascaris, son, perhaps, of Constantine, edited the Anthologia at Florence. It may be doubted whether Italy had as yet produced any scholar, unless it were Varino, more often called Phavorinus, singly equal to the task of superintending a Greek edition. His Thesaurus Cornucopiæ, a collection of thirty-four grammatical tracts in Greek, printed 1496, may be an exception. The Etymologicum Magnum, Venice, 1499, being a lexicon with only Greek explanations, is supposed to be chiefly due to Musurus. Aldus had printed Craston's Lexicon in 1497, with the addition of an index; this has often been mistaken for an original work.[z]

115. The state of Italy was not so favourable as it had been to the advancement of philosophy. After the expulsion of the Medici from Florence, in 1494, the Platonic academy was broken up; and that philosophy never found again a friendly soil in Italy, though Ficinus had endeavoured to keep it up by a Latin translation of Plotinus. Aristotle and his followers began now to regain the ascendant. Perhaps it may be thought that even polite letters were not so flourishing as they had been; no one at least yet appeared to fill the place of Hermolaus Barbarus, who died in 1493, or Politian, who followed him the next year. *Decline of learning in Italy.*

116. Hermolaus Barbarus was a noble Venetian, whom Europe agreed to place next to Politian in critical learning, and to draw a line between them and any third name. 'No time, no accident, no destiny,' says an enthusiastic scholar of the next age, 'will ever efface their remembrance from the hearts of the learned.'[a]   Erasmus *Hermolaus Barbarus.*

---

[z] Renouard. Roscoe's Leo X., ch. xi.

[a] Habuit nostra hæc ætas bonarum literarum proceres duos, Hermolaum Barbarum atque Angelum Politianum: Deum immortalem! quam acri judicio, quanta facundia, quanta linguarum, quanta disciplinarum omnium scientia præditos! Hi Latinam linguam jampri- dem squalentem et multa barbariei rubigine exesam, ad pristinum revocare nitorem conati sunt, atque illis suus profecto conatus non infeliciter cessit, suntque illi de Latina lingua tam bene meriti, quam qui ante eos optimi meriti fuere. Itaque immortalem sibi gloriam, immortale decus paraverunt, manebit-

calls him a truly great and divine man. He filled many
honourable offices for the republic; but lamented that they
drew him away from that learning for which he says he was
born, and to which alone he was devoted.[b] Yet Hermolaus
is but faintly kept in mind at the present day. In his Latin
style, with the same fault as Politian, an affectation of obsolete
words, he is less flexible and elegant. But his chief merit
was in the restoration of the text of ancient writers. He
boasts that he had corrected above five thousand passages in
Pliny's natural history, and more than three hundred in the
very brief geography of Pomponius Mela. Hardouin, however, charges him with extreme rashness in altering passages
he did not understand. The pope had nominated Hermolaus
to the greatest post in the Venetian church, the patriarchate
of Aquileia; but his mortification at finding that the senate
refused to concur in the appointment is said to have hastened
his death.[c]

117. A Latin poet once of great celebrity, Baptista Mantuan, seems to fall within this period as fitly as any

Mantuan.

other, though several of his poems had been separately printed before, and their collective publication was
not till 1513. Editions recur very frequently in the bibliography of Italy and Germany. He was, and long continued
to be, the poet of school-rooms. Erasmus says, that he would
be placed by posterity not much below Virgil;[d] and the
marquis of Mantua, anticipating this suffrage, erected their
statues side by side. Such is the security of contemporary
compliments! Mantuan has long been utterly neglected,
and does not find a place in most selections of Latin poetry.
His Eclogues and Silvæ are said to be the least bad of his
numerous works. He was among the many assailants of the
church, or at least the court, of Rome; and this animosity
inspired him with some bitter, or rather vigorous, invectives.

---

que semper in omnium eruditorum pec-
toribus consecrata Hermolai et Politiani
memoria, nullo ævo, nullo casu, nullo
fato abolenda. Brixeus Erasmo in Erasm.
Epist. ccxii.

[b] Meiners, ii. 200.

[c] Bayle. Niceron, vol. xiv. Tiraboschi, vii. 152. Corniani, iii. 197.
Heeren, p. 274

[d] Et nisi me fallit augurium, erit, erit
aliquando Baptista suo concive gloriâ
celebritateque non ita multo inferior, simul invidiam anni detraxerint. Append.
ad Erasm. Epist. cccxcv. (edit. Lugd.)
It is not conceivable that Erasmus meant
this literally; but the drift of the letter
is to encourage the reading of Christian
poets.

But he became afterwards a Carmelite friar.[e] Marullus, a
Greek by birth, has obtained a certain reputation for his
Latin poems, which are of no great value.

118. A far superior name is that of Pontanus, to whom,
if we attend to some critics, we must award the palm   Pontanus.
above all Latin poets of the fifteenth century. If
I might venture to set my own taste against theirs, I should
not agree to his superiority over Politian. His hexameters
are by no means deficient in harmony, and may perhaps be
more correct than those of his rival, but. appear to me less
pleasing and poetical. His lyric poems are like too much
modern Latin, in a tone of languid voluptuousness, and ring
changes on the various beauties of his mistress, and the
sweetness of her kisses. The few elegies of Pontanus, among
which that addressed to his wife, on the prospect of peace, is
the best known, fall very short of the admirable lines of
Politian on the death of Ovid. Pontanus wrote some moral
and political essays in prose, which are said to be full of just
observations and sharp satire on the court of Rome, and
written in a style which his contemporaries regarded with
admiration. They were published in 1490. Erasmus, though
a parsimonious distributor of praise to the Italians, has
acknowledged their merit in the Ciceronianus.[f]

119. Pontanus presided at this time over the Neapolitan
academy, a dignity which he had attained upon the   Neapolitan
death of Beccatelli, in 1471. This was, after the   academy.
decline of the Roman and the Florentine academies, by far
the most eminent re-union of literary men in Italy; and
though it was long conspicuous, seems to have reached its

---

[e] Corniani, iii. 148.   Niceron, vol.
xxvii. Such of Mantuan's eclogues as
are printed in Carmina illustrium Poetarum Italorum, Florent. 1719, are but
indifferent. I doubt, however, whether
that voluminous collection has been
made with much taste; and his satire on
the see of Rome would certainly be excluded, whatever might be its merit.
Corniani has given an extract, better
than what I have seen of Mantuan.

[f] Roscoe, Leo X., ch. ii. and xx.
Niceron, vol. viii. Corniani. Tiraboschi.
Pontanus cum illa quatuor complecti
summa cura conatus sit, nervum dico,

numeros, candorem, venustatem, profecto est omnia consecutus. Quintum
autem illud quod est horum omnium
veluti vita quædam, modum intelligo,
penitus ignoravit.   Aiunt Virgilium
cum multos versus matutino calore
effudisset, pomeridianis horis novo judicio solitum ad paucorum numerum revocare.   Contra quidem Pontano eve-
nisse arbitror. Quæ prima quaque in-
ventione arrisissent, iis plura postea,
dum recognosceret, addita, atque ipsis
potius carminibus, quam sibi pepercisse.
Scaliger de re poetica (apud Blount).

highest point in the last years of this century, under the
patronage of the mild Frederic of Aragon, and during that
transient calm which Naples was permitted to enjoy between
the invasions of Charles VIII. and Louis XII. That city
and kingdom afforded many lovers of learning and poetry;
some of them in the class of its nobles; each district being,
as it were, represented in this academy by one or more of its
distinguished residents. But other members were associated
from different parts of Italy; and the whole constellation of
names is still brilliant, though some have grown dim by time.
The house of Este, at Ferrara, were still the liberal patrons
of genius; none more eminently than their reigning marquis,
Hercules I. And not less praise is due to the families who
held the principalities of Urbino and Mantua.[g]

120. A poem now appeared in Italy, well deserving of
Boiardo.   attention for its own sake, but still more so on ac-
             count of the excitement and direction it gave to one
of the most famous poets that ever lived. Matteo Maria
Boiardo, count of Scandiano, a man esteemed and trusted
at the court of Ferrara, amused his leisure in the publication of a romantic poem, for which the stories of Charlemagne and his paladins, related by one who assumed the
name of Turpin, and already woven into long metrical nar-
rations, current at the end of the fourteenth and during the
fifteenth century in Italy, supplied materials, which are
almost lost in the original inventions of the author. The
first edition of this poem is without date, but probably in
1495. The author, who died the year before, left it unfinished at the ninth canto of the third book. Agostini, in
1516, published a continuation, indifferently executed, in
three more books; but the real complement of the Innamorato is the Furioso.[b] The Orlando Innamorato of Boiardo
has hitherto not received that share of renown which seems
to be its due: overpowered by the splendour of Ariosto's
poem, and almost set aside in its original form by the improved edition or remaking (rifaccimento), which Berni

---

[g] Roscoe's Leo X., ch. ii. This contains an excellent account of the state of
literature in Italy about the close of the

century.
[b] Fontanini, dell' eloquenza Italiana,
edit. di Zeno, p. 270.

afterwards gave, it has rarely been sought or quoted, even in Italy.[c]

121. The style is uncouth and hard; but with great defects of style, which should be the source of perpetual delight, no long poem will be read; and it has been observed by Ginguéné with some justice, that Boiardo's name is better remembered, though his original poem may have been more completely neglected, through the process to which Berni has subjected it. In point of novel invention and just keeping of character, especially the latter, he has not been surpassed by his illustrious follower Ariosto; and whatever of this we find in the Orlando Innamorato is due to Boiardo alone; for Berni has preserved the sense of almost every stanza. The imposing appearance of Angelica at the court of Charlemagne, in the first canto, opens the poem with a splendour rarely equalled, with a luxuriant fertility of invention, and with admirable art; judiciously presenting the subject in so much singleness, that amidst all the intricacies and episodes of the story, the reader never forgets the incomparable princess of Albracca. The latter city, placed in that remote Cathay which Marco Polo had laid open to the range of fancy, and its siege by Agrican's innumerable cavalry, are creations of Boiardo's most inventive mind. Nothing in Ariosto is conceived so nobly, or so much in the true genius of romance. Castelvetro asserts that the names Gradasso, Mandricardo, Sobrino, and others, which Boiardo has given to his imaginary characters, belonged to his own peasants of Scandiano; and some have improved upon this by assuring us, that those who take the pains to ascertain the fact, may still find the representatives of these sonorous heroes at the plough, which, if the story were true, ought to be the case.[d] But we may give him credit for talent enough

Character of his poem.

---

[c] See my friend Mr. Panizzi's excellent introduction to his edition of the Orlando Innamorato. This poem had never been reprinted since 1544; so much was Roscoe deceived in fancying that 'the simplicity of the original has caused it to be preferred to the same work, as altered or reformed by Francesco Berni.'   Life of Leo X., ch. ii.

[d] Camillo Pellegrino, in his famous controversy with the Academy of Florence on the respective merits of Ariosto and Tasso, having asserted this, they do not deny the fact, but say it stands on the authority of Castelvetro.   Opere di Tasso, 4to. ii. 94.   The critics held rather a pedantic doctrine; that though the names of private men may be feigned, the poet has no right to introduce kings unknown to history, as this

to invent those appellations; he hardly found an Albracca
on his domains; and those who grudge him the rest, acknowledge that, in a moment of inspiration, while hunting, the
name of Rodomont occurred to his mind.   We know how
finely Milton, whose ear pursued, almost to excess, the pleasure
of harmonious names, and who loved to expatiate in these
imaginary regions, has alluded to Boiardo's poem in the
Paradise Regained.   The lines are perhaps the most musical he has ever produced :—

> Such forces met not, nor so wide a camp,
> When Agrican with all his northern powers
> Besieged Albracca, as romances tell,
> The city of Gallaphron, from thence to win
> The fairest of her sex Angelica.
> His daughter, sought by many prowest knights,
> Both paynim and the peers of Charlemagne.[e]

122. The Mambriano of Francesco Bello, surnamed il
Francisco   Cieco, another poem of the same romantic class,
Bello.   was published posthumously in 1497.   Apostolo
Zeno, as quoted by Roscoe, attributes the neglect of the
Mambriano to its wanting an Ariosto to continue its subject,
or a Berni to reform its style.[f]   But this seems a capricious opinion.   Bello composed it at intervals to amuse the
courtiers of the marquis of Mantua.   The poem, therefore,
wants unity.   'It is a re-union,' says Mr. Panizzi, ' of detached tales, without any relation to each other, except in
so far as most of the same actors are before us.'[g]   We may
perceive by this, how little a series of rhapsodies, not directed
by a controlling unity of purpose, even though the work of
a single man, are likely to fall into a connected poem.
But that a long poem, such as the greatest and most ancient
of all, of singular coherence and subordination of parts to
an end, should be framed from the random and insulated
songs of a great number of persons, is almost as incredible
as that the annals of Ennius, to use Cicero's argument

---

destroys the probability required for   p. 360. He does not highly praise the
his fiction.   poem, of which he gives an analysis
  [e] Book iii.   [f] Leo X., ch. ii.   with extracts. See too Ginguéné, vol.
  [g] Panizzi's Introduction to Boiardo,   iv.

against the fortuitous origin of the world, should be formed by shaking together the letters of the alphabet.

123. Near the close of the fifteenth century we find a great increase of Italian poetry, to which the pa- Italian poetry
tronage and example of Lorenzo had given encou- near the end
ragement. It is not easy to place within such tury. of the cen-
narrow limits as a decennial period the names of writers whose productions were frequently not published, at least collectively, during their lives. Serafino d'Aquila, born in 1466, seems to fall, as a poet, within this decad; and the same may be said of Tibaldeo and Benivieni. Of these the first is perhaps the best known; his verses are not destitute of spirit, but extravagance and bad taste deform the greater part.[h] Tibaldeo unites false thoughts with rudeness and poverty of diction. Benivieni, superior to either of these, is reckoned by Corniani a link between the harshness of the fifteenth and the polish of the ensuing century. The style of this age was far from the grace and sweetness of Petrarch; forced in sentiment, low in choice of words, deficient in harmony, it has been condemned by the voice of all Italian critics.[i]

124. A greater activity than before was now perceptible in the literary spirit of France and Germany. It Progress of
was also regularly progressive. The press of Paris learning in
gave twenty-six editions of ancient Latin authors, Germany. France and
nine of which were in the year 1500. Twelve were published at Lyons. Deventer and Leipsic, especially the latter, which now took a lead in the German press, bore a part in this honourable labour; a proof of the rapid and extensive influence of Conrad Celtes on that part of Germany. It is to be understood that a very large proportion, or nearly the whole, of the Latin editions printed in Germany were for the use of schools.[k] We should be warranted

[h] Bouterwek, Gesch. der Ital. Poesie, i. 321. Corniani.

[i] Corniani. Muratori, della perfetta Poesia. Crescimbeni, Storia della volgar Poesia.

[k] A proof of this may be found in the books printed at Deventer from 1491 to 1500. They consisted of Virgil's Bucolics three times, Virgil's Georgics twice, and the eclogues of Calpurnius once, or perhaps twice. At Leipsic the list is much longer, but in great measure of the same kind; single treatises of Seneca or Cicero, or detached parts of Virgil, Horace, Ovid, sometimes very short, as the Culex or the Ibis, form, with not many exceptions, the Cisalpine classical bibliography of the fifteenth century.

in drawing an inference as to the progress in literary instruction in these countries from the increase in the number
of publications, small as that number still is, and trifling as
some of them may appear.   It may be accounted for by
the gradual working of the schools at Munster and other
places, which had now sent out a race of pupils well fitted
to impart knowledge in their turn to others; and by the
patronage of some powerful men, among whom the first
place, on all accounts, is due to the emperor Maximilian.
Nothing was so likely to contribute to the intellectual improvement of Germany as the public peace of 1495, which
put an end to the barbarous customs of the middle ages,
not unaccompanied by generous virtues, but certainly as
incompatible with the steady cultivation of literature, as
with riches and repose.   Yet there seems to be no proof
that the Greek language had obtained much more attention; no book connected with it is recorded to have been
printed, and I do not find mention that it was taught, even
superficially, in any university or school, at this time, though
it might be conjectured without improbability.   Reuchlin
had now devoted his whole thoughts to cabbalistic philosophy, and the study of Hebrew; and Eichhorn, though
not unwilling to make the most of early German learning,
owns that, at the end of the century, no other person had
become remarkable for a skill in Greek.[m]

125. Two men, however, were devoting incessant labour to
the acquisition of that language at Paris, for whom was re-

---

[m] Eichhorn, iii. 236. This section in
Eichhorn is valuable, but exhibits some
want of precision.

Reuchlin had been very diligent in
purchasing Greek manuscripts. But
these were very scarce, even in Italy. A
correspondent of his, Streler by name,
one of the young men who went from
Germany to Florence for education, tells
him, in 1491 ; Nullos libros Græcos hic
venales reperio : and again, de Græcis
libris coemendis hoc scias ; fui penes
omnes hic librarios, nihil horum prorsus
reperio. Epist. ad Reuchl. (1562), fol. 7.
In fact, Reuchlin's own library was so
large as to astonish the Italian scholars
when they saw the catalogue, who plainly
owned they could not procure such books

themselves. They had of course been
originally purchased in Italy, unless we
suppose some to have been brought by
way of Hungary.

It is not to be imagined that the libraries of ordinary scholars were to be compared with that of Reuchlin, probably
more opulent than most of them. The
early printed books of Italy, even the
most indispensable, were very scarce, at
least in France. A Greek grammar was
a rarity at Paris in 1499. Grammaticen
Græcam, says Erasmus to a correspondent, summo studio vestigavi, ut emptam
tibi mitterem, sed jam utraque divendita
fuerat, et Constantini quæ dicitur, quæ-
que Urbani. Epist. lix. See too Epist.
lxxiii.

served the glory of raising the knowledge of it in Cisalpine
Europe to a height which Italy could not attain.   Erasmus;
These were Erasmus and Budæus. The former, who
had acquired as a boy the mere rudiments of Greek under
Hegius at Deventer, set himself in good earnest to that
study about 1499, hiring a teacher at Paris, old Hermonymus of Sparta, of whose extortion he complains; but he was
little able to pay anything; and his noble endurance of pri-
vations for the sake of knowledge deserved the high reward
of glory that it received. 'I have given my whole soul,' he
says, 'to Greek learning, and as soon as I get any   his diligence.
money I shall first buy Greek books and then
clothes.'[n] 'If any new Greek book comes to hand, I would
rather pledge my cloak than not obtain it; especially if it be
religious, such as a psalter or a gospel.'[c]   It will be remembered, that the books of which he speaks must have been
frequently manuscripts.

126. Budæus, in his proper name Budé, nearly of the same
age as Erasmus, had relinquished every occupation   Budæus; his
for intense labour in literature. In an interesting   early studies.
letter, addressed to Cuthbert Tunstall in 1517, giving an
account of his own early studies, he says that he learned
Greek very ill from a bad master at Paris in 1491. This was
certainly Hermonymus, of whom Reuchlin speaks more favourably; but he was not quite so competent a judge.[p] Some
years afterwards Budæus got much better instruction; 'ancient literature having derived within a few years great improvement in France by our intercourse with Italy, and by
the importation of books in both the learned languages.'
Lascaris, who now lived at the court of Charles VIII., having

---

[n] Epist, xxix.   [o] Epist. lviii.

[p] Hody (de Græcis illustribus, p. 238)
thinks that the master of Budæus could
not have been Hermonymus; probably
because the praise of Reuchlin seemed
to him incompatible with the contemptuous language of Budæus. But Erasmus is very explicit on this subject.
Ad Græcas literas utcunque puero de-
gustatas jam grandior redii; hoc est,
annos natus plus minus triginta, sed tum
cum apud nos nulla Græcorum codicum
esset copia, neque minor penuria doctorum. Lutetiæ tantum unus Georgius

Hermonymus Græcè balbutiebat; sed
talis, ut neque potuisset docere si voluisset, neque voluisset si potuisset. Itaque
coactus ipse mihi præceptor esse, &c.
(A.D. 1524), I transcribe from Jortin, ii.
419.   Of Hermonymus, it is said by
Beatus Rhenanus, in a letter to Reuchlin, that he was non tam doctrina quam
patria clarus. (Epist. ad Reuchl. fol. 52.)
Roy, in his life of Budæus, says, that
the latter having paid Hermonymus
500 gold pieces and read Homer and
other books with him, nihilo doctior est
factus.

returned with him from the Neapolitan expedition, gave
Budæus some assistance, though not, according to the latter's
biographer, to any great extent.

127. France had as yet no writer of Latin, who could be
Latin not well written in France. endured in comparison with those of Italy. Robert
Gaguin praises Fichet, rector of the Sorbonne, as
learned and eloquent, and the first who had taught many to
employ good language in Latin. The more certain glory of
Fichet is to have introduced the art of printing into France.
Gaguin himself enjoyed a certain reputation for his style, and
his epistles have been printed. He possessed, at least, what
is more important, a love of knowledge, and an elevated way
of thinking. But Erasmus says of him, that ' whatever he
might have been in his own age, he would now scarcely be
reckoned to write Latin at all.' If we could rely on a pane-
gyrist of Faustus Andrelinus, an Italian who came about
1489 to Paris, and was authorised, in conjunction with one
Balbi, and with Cornelio Vitelli, to teach in the university,[q]
he was the man who brought polite literature into France,
and changed its barbarism for classical purity. But Andrelinus, who is best known as a Latin poet of by no means a
high rank, seems not to merit this commendation. Whatever
his capacities of teaching may have been, we have little evidence of his success. Yet the number of editions of Latin
authors published in France during this decad proves some
diffusion of classical learning ; and we must admit the circumstance to be quite decisive of the inferiority of England.

128. A gleam of light, however, now broke out there. We
Dawn of Greek learn- ing in Eng- land. have seen already that a few, even in the last years
of Henry VI., had overcome all obstacles in order to
drink at the fountain-head of pure learning in Italy.
One or two more names might be added for the intervening
period ; Milling, abbot of Westminster, and Selling, prior of
a convent at Canterbury.[r] It is reported by Polydore Virgil,

---

[q] This I find quoted in Bettinelli,
Risorgimento d' Italia, i. 250. See also
Bayle, and Biogr. univ. art. Andrelini.
They were only allowed to teach for one
hour in the evening, the jealousy of the
logicians not having subsided. Crevier,
iv. 439.

[r] Warton, iii. 247. Johnson's Life
of Linacre, p. 5. This is mentioned on
Selling's monument now remaining in
Canterbury Cathedral :—

Doctor theologus Selling Græca atque Latina
Lingua perdoctus.

Selling, however, did not go to Italy

and is proved by Wood, that Cornelio Vitelli, an Italian, came to Oxford about 1488, in order to give that most barbarous university some notion of what was going forward on the other side of the Alps; and it has been probably conjectured, or rather may be assumed, that he there imparted the rudiments of Greek to William Grocyn.[s] It is certain, at least, that Grocyn had acquired some insight into that language before he took a better course, and, travelling into Italy, became the disciple of Chalcondyles and Politian. He returned home in 1491, and began to communicate his acquisitions, though chiefly to deaf ears, teaching in Exeter College at Oxford. A diligent emulator of Grocyn, but some years younger, and like him, a pupil of Politian and Hermolaus, was Thomas Linacre, a physician; but though a first edition of his translation of Galen has been supposed to have been printed at Venice in 1498, it seems to be ascertained that none preceded that of Cambridge in 1521. His only contribution to literature in the fifteenth century was a translation of the very short mathematical treatise of Proclus on the sphere, published in a volume of ancient writers on astronomy, by Aldus Manutius, in 1499.[t]

129. Erasmus paid his first visit to England in 1497, and was delighted with everything that he found, espe- Erasmus cially at Oxford. In an epistle dated Dec. 5th, after England. praising Grocyn, Colet, and Linacre to the skies, he says of Thomas More, who could not then have been eighteen years old, 'What mind was ever framed by nature more gentle,

---

till after 1480, far from returning in 1460, as Warton has said with his usual indifference to anachronisms.

[s] Polydore says nothing about Vitelli's teaching Greek, though Knight, in his Life of Colet, translates bonæ literæ, 'Greek and Latin.' But the following passages seem decisive as to Grocyn's early studies in the Greek language. Grocinus, qui prima Græcæ et Latinæ linguæ rudimenta in Britannia hausit, mox solidiorem iisdem operam sub Demetrio Chalcondyle et Politiano præceptoribus in Italia hausit. Lilly, Elogia virorum doctorum, in Knight's Life of Colet, p. 24. And Erasmus as positively: Ipse Grocinus, cujus exemplum affers, nonne primum in Anglia Græcæ

linguæ rudimenta didicit? Post in Italiam profectus audivit summos viros, sed interim lucro fuit illa prius a qualibuscunque didicisse. Epist. ccclxiii. Whether the *qualescunque* were Vitelli or any one else, this can leave no doubt as to the existence of some Greek instruction in England before Grocyn; and as no one can be suggested, so far as appears, except Vitelli, it seems reasonable to fix upon him as the first preceptor of Grocyn. Vitelli had returned to Paris in 1489, and taught in the university, as has just been mentioned; so that he could have little time, if Polydore's date of 1488 be right, for giving much instruction at Oxford.

[t] Johnson's Life of Linacre, p. 152.

more pleasing, more gifted?—It is incredible what a treasure
of old books is found here far and wide. There is so much
erudition, not of a vulgar and ordinary kind, but recondite,
accurate, ancient, both Latin and Greek, that you would not
seek anything in Italy, but the pleasure of travelling.'ᵘ But
this letter is addressed to an Englishman, and the praise is
evidently much exaggerated; the scholars were few, and not
more than three or four could be found, or at least could now
be mentioned, who had any tincture of Greek,—Grocyn,
Linacre, William Latimer, who, though an excellent scholar,
never published anything, and More, who had learned at
Oxford under Grocyn.ˣ It should here be added, that in
1497, Terence was printed by Pynson, being the first edition
of a strictly classical author in England; though Boethius had
already appeared with Latin and English on opposite pages.

130. In 1500 was printed at Paris the first edition of
He publishes Erasmus's Adages, doubtless the chief prose work
his Adages. of this century beyond the limits of Italy; but this
edition should, if possible, be procured, in order to judge with
chronological exactness of the state of literature; for as his
general knowledge of antiquity, and particularly of Greek,
which was now very slender, increased, he made vast additions. The Adages, which were now about eight hundred,
amounted in his last edition to 4151; not that he could find
so many which properly deserve that name, but the number
is made up by explanations of Latin and Greek idioms, or
even of single words. He declares himself, as early as 1504,
ashamed of the first edition of his Adages, which already
seemed meagre and imperfect.ʸ Erasmus had been preceded

ᵘ Thomæ Mori ingenio quid unquam
finxit natura vel mollius, vel dulcius, vel
felicius ? . . . Mirum est dictu, quam hic
passim, quam dense veterum librorum
seges efflorescat . . . tantum eruditionis
non illius protritæ ac trivialis, sed reconditæ, exactæ, antiquæ, Latinæ Græcæ-
que, ut jam Italiam nisi visendi gratia
non multum desideres. Epist. xiv.

ˣ A letter of Colet to Erasmus from
Oxford, in 1497, is written in the style
of a man who was conversant with the
best Latin authors. Sir Thomas More's
birth has not been placed by any biographer earlier than 1480.

It has been sometimes asserted, on the
authority of Antony Wood, that Erasmus
taught Greek at Oxford; but there is no
foundation for this, and in fact he did not
know enough of the language. Knight,
on the other hand, maintains that he
learned it there under Grocyn and Linacre; but this rests on no evidence; and
we have seen that he gives a different account of his studies in Greek. Life of
Erasmus, p. 22.

ʸ Epist. cii. : jejunum atque inops
videri cœpit, posteaquam Græcos colui
auctores.

in some measure by Polydore Virgil, best known as the historian of this country, where he resided many years as collector of papal dues. He published a book of Adages, which must have been rather a juvenile, and is a superficial production, at Venice in 1498.

131. The Castilian poets of the fifteenth century have been collectively mentioned on a former occasion. Bouterwek refers to the latter part of this age most Romantic
ballads of
Spain. of the romances which turn upon Saracen story, and the adventures of 'knights of Granada, gentlemen, though Moors.' Sismondi follows him without, perhaps, much reflection, and endeavours to explain what he might have doubted. Fear, he thinks, having long ceased in the bosoms of the Castilian Christians, even before conquest had set its seal to their security, hate, the child of fear, had grown feebler; and the romancers felt themselves at liberty to expatiate in the rich field of Mohammedan customs and manners. These had already exercised a considerable influence over Spain. But this opinion seems hard to be supported; nor do I find that the Spanish critics claim so much antiquity for the Moorish class of romantic ballads. Most of them, it is acknowledged, belong to the sixteenth, and some to the seventeenth century; and the internal evidence is against their having been written before the Moorish wars had become matter of distant tradition. We shall therefore take no notice of the Spanish romance-ballads till we come to the age of Philip II., to which they principally belong.[z]

132. Bouterwek places in this decad the first specimens of the pastoral romance which the Castilian language Pastoral
romances. affords.[a] But the style is borrowed from a neighbouring part of the peninsula, where this species of fiction seems to have been indigenous. The Portuguese nation cultivated poetry as early as the Castilian; and we have seen that some is extant of a date anterior to the fourteenth century. But to the heroic romance they seem to have paid no regard; we do not find that it ever existed among them. Love chiefly occupied the Lusitanian muse; and to trace that

---

[z] Bouterwek, p. 121. Sismondi, iii. 222. Romances Moriscos, Madr. 1828.
[a] P. 123.

passion through all its labyrinths, to display its troubles in
a strain of languid melancholy, was the great aim of every
poet. This led to the invention of pastoral romances, founded
on the ancient traditions as to the felicity of shepherds and
their proneness to love, and rendered sometimes more interesting for the time by the introduction of real characters
and events under a slight disguise.[b]   This artificial and effeminate sort of composition, which, if it may now and then
be not unpleasing, cannot fail to weary the modern reader by
its monotony, is due to Portugal, and having been adopted in
languages better known, became for a long time highly popular in Europe.

133. The lyrical poems of Portugal were collected by
Portuguese Garcia de Resende, in the Cancioneiro Geral, pub-
lyric poetry. lished in 1516. Some few of these are of the fourteenth century, for we find the name of king Pedro, who died
in 1369. Others are by the Infant Don Pedro, son of John I.,
in the earlier part of the fifteenth. But a greater number
belong nearly to the present or preceding decad, or even to
the ensuing age, commemorating the victories of the Portuguese in Asia. This collection is of extreme scarcity ; none
of the historians of Portuguese literature have seen it. Bouterwek and Sismondi declare that they have caused search
to be made in various libraries of Europe without success.
There is, however, a copy in the British Museum ; and M.
Raynouard has given a short account of one that he had seen
in the Journal des Savans for 1826. In this article he observes, that the Cancioneiro is a mixture of Portuguese
and Spanish pieces.   I believe, however, that very little
Spanish will be found, with the exception of the poems of
the Infante Pedro, which occupy some leaves. The whole
number of poets is but one hundred and thirty-two, even if
some names do not occur twice ; which I mention, because it
has been erroneously said to exceed considerably that of the
Spanish Cancioneiro. The volume is in folio, and contains two
hundred and twenty-seven leaves.   The metres are those
usual in Spanish ; some *versos de arte mayor* ; but the greater
part in trochaic redondillas. I observed no instance of the

---

[b] Bouterwek's Hist. of Portuguese Literature, p. 43.

assonant rhyme; but there are several glosses, or, in the Portuguese word, *grosas*.[c] The chief part is amatory; but there are lines on the death of kings, and other political events.[d]

134. The Germans, if they did not as yet excel in the higher department of typography, were by no means German negligent of their own great invention. The books, popular books. if we include the smallest, printed in the empire between 1470 and the close of the century, amount to several thousand editions. A large proportion of these were in their own language. They had a literary public, as we may call it, not merely in their courts and universities, but in their respectable middle class, the burghers of the free cities, and, perhaps, in the artisans whom they employed. Their reading was almost always with a serious end; but no people so successfully cultivated the art of moral and satirical fable. These, in many instances, spread with great favour through Cisalpine Europe. Among the works of this kind, in the fifteenth century, two deserve mention; the Eulenspiegel, popular afterwards in England by the name of Howleglass, and a superior and better known production, the Narrenschiff, or Ship of Fools, by Sebastian Brandt of Strasburg, the first edition of which is referred by Brunet to the year 1494. The Latin translation, which bears the title of 1488 in an edition printed at Lyons, ought to be placed, according to the same bibliographer, ten years later, a numeral letter having probably been omitted. It was translated into English by Barclay, and published early in 1509. It is a metrical satire on the follies of every class, and may possibly have suggested to Erasmus his Encomium Moriæ. But the idea was not absolutely new; the theatrical company established at Paris, under the name of Enfans de Sans Souci, as well as the ancient office of jester or fool in our courts and castles, implied the same principle of satirising mankind with ridicule so general, that every man should feel more

---

[c] Bouterwek, p. 30, has observed that the Portuguese employ the *glosa*, calling it *volta*. The word in the Cancioneiro is *grosa*.

[d] A manuscript collection of Portuguese lyric poetry of the fifteenth century belonged to Mr. Heber, and was sold to Messrs. Payne and Foss. It would probably be found on comparison to contain many of the pieces in the Cancioneiro Geral, but it is not a copy of it.

pleasure from the humiliation of his neighbours, than pain
from his own. Brandt does not show much poetical talent;
but his morality is clear and sound; he keeps the pure and
right-minded reader on his side; and in an age when little
better came into competition, his characters of men, though
more didactic than descriptive, did not fail to please. The
influence such books of simple fiction and plain moral would
possess over a people, may be judged by the delight they
once gave to children, before we had learned to vitiate the
healthy appetite of ignorance by premature refinements and
stimulating variety.[e]

135. The historical literature of this century presents very
Historical
works. little deserving of notice. The English writers of
this class are absolutely contemptible; and if some
annalists of good sense and tolerable skill in narration may
be found on the continent, they are not conspicuous enough
to arrest our regard in a work which designedly passes over
that department of literature, so far as it is merely conversant with particular events. But the memoirs of Philip de
Philip de
Comines. Comines, which, though not published till 1529,
must have been written before the close of the
fifteenth century, are not only of a higher value, but almost
make an epoch in historical literature. If Froissart, by his
picturesque descriptions and fertility of historical *invention*,
may be reckoned the Livy of France, she had her Tacitus in
Philip de Comines. The intermediate writers, Monstrelet
and his continuators, have the merits of neither, certainly not
of Comines. He is the first modern writer (or, if there had
been any approach to an exception among the Italians, it has
escaped my recollection) who in any degree has displayed
sagacity in reasoning on the characters of men, and the consequences of their actions, or who has been able to generalise
his observation by comparison and reflection. Nothing of
this could have been found in the cloister; nor were the philologers of Italy equal to a task which required capacities and
pursuits very different from their own. An acute understanding and much experience of mankind gave Comines this
superiority; his life had not been spent over books; and he is

---

[e] Bouterwek, ix. 332–354, v. 113.   Heinsius, iv. 113.   Warton, iii. 74.

consequently free from that pedantic application of history which became common with those who passed for political reasoners in the next two centuries. Yet he was not ignorant of former times; and we see the advantage of those translations from antiquity, made during the last hundred years in France, by the use to which he turned them.

136. The earliest printed treatise of algebra, till that of Lionardo Fibonacci was lately given to the press, was published in 1494, by Luca Pacioli di Borgo, *Algebra.* a Franciscan, who taught mathematics in the university of Milan. This book is written in Italian, with a mixture of the Venetian dialect, and with many Latin words. In the first part, he explains the rules of commercial arithmetic in detail, and is the earliest Italian writer who shows the principles of Italian book-keeping by double entry. Algebra he calls l' arte maggiore, detta dal volgo la regola de la cosa, over alghebra e almacabala, which last he explains by restauratio et oppositio. The known number is called *n°* or *numero*; *co.* or *cosa* stands for the unknown quantity; whence algebra was sometimes called the cossic art. In the early Latin treatises *Res* is used, or *R.*, which is an approach to literal expression. The square is called *censo* or *ce.*; the cube, *cubo* or *cu.*; *p.* and *m.* stand for *plus* and *minus.* Thus 3*co. p.* 4*ce. m.* 5*cu. p.* 2*ce.ce m.* 6*n°* would have been written for what would now be expressed $3x + 4x^2 - 5x^3 + 2x^4 - 6$. Luca di Borgo's algebra goes as far as quadratic equations; but though he had very good notions on the subject, it does not appear that he carried the science much beyond the point where Leonard Fibonacci had left it three centuries before. And its principles were already familiar to mathematicians; for Regiomontanus, having stated a trigonometrical solution in the form of a quadratic equation, adds, quod restat, præcepta artis edocebunt. Luca di Borgo perceived, in a certain sense, the applicability of algebra to geometry, observing, that the rules as to surd roots are referable to incommensurable magnitudes.[f]

---

[f] Montucla. Kästner. Cossali. Hutton's Mathem. Dict., art. Algebra. The last writer, and perhaps the first, had never seen the book of Luca Pacioli.

Mr. Colebrooke, in his Indian Algebra, has shown that the Hindoos carried that

137. This period of ten years, from 1490 to 1500, will
Events from 1490 to 1500. ever be memorable in the history of mankind. It
is here that we usually close the long interval be-
tween the Roman world and this our modern Europe, denominated the Middle Ages. The conquest of Granada,
which rendered Spain a Christian kingdom ; the annexation
of the last great fief of the French crown, Britany, which
made France an entire and absolute monarchy ; the public
peace of Germany ; the invasion of Naples by Charles VIII.,
which revealed the weakness of Italy, while it communicated her arts and manners to the Cisalpine nations, and
opened the scene of warfare and alliances which may be
deduced to the present day; the discovery of two worlds
by Columbus and Vasco de Gama, all belong to this decad.
But it is not, as we have seen, so marked an era in the
progression of literature.

138. In taking leave of the fifteenth century, to which
Close of fifteenth century. we have been used to attach many associations of
reverence, and during which the desire of know-
ledge was, in one part of Europe, more enthusiastic and
universal than perhaps it has since ever been, it is natural
to ask ourselves, what harvest had already rewarded their
zeal and labour, what monuments of genius and erudition
still receive the homage of mankind ?

139. No very triumphant answer can be given to this
Its literature nearly neglected. interrogation. Of the books then written, how few
are read ! Of the men then famous, how few are
familiar in our recollection ! Let us consider what Italy
itself produced of any effective tendency to enlarge the
boundaries of knowledge, or to delight the taste and fancy.
The treatise of Valla on Latin grammar, the miscellaneous
observations of Politian on ancient authors, the commentaries of Landino and some other editors, the Platonic
theology of Ficinus, the Latin poetry of Politian and Pontanus, the light Italian poetry of the same Politian and Lorenzo de' Medici, the epic romances of Pulci and Boiardo.
Of these, Pulci alone, in an original shape, is still read in

---

science considerably farther than either
the Greeks or the Arabians (though he
thinks they may probably have derived
their notions of the science from the
former), anticipating some of the discoveries of the sixteenth century.

Italy, and by some lovers of that literature in other countries, and the Latin poets by a smaller number. If we look on the other side of the Alps, the catalogue is much shorter, or rather does not contain a single book, except Philip de Comines, that enters into the usual studies of a literary man. Froissart hardly belongs to the fifteenth century, his history terminating about 1400. The first undated edition, with a continuation by some one to 1498, was printed between that time and 1509, when the second appeared.

140. If we come to inquire what acquisitions had been made between the years 1400 and 1500, we shall find that, in Italy, the Latin language was now written by some with elegance, and by most with tolerable exactness and fluency; while, out of Italy, there had been, perhaps, a corresponding improvement, relatively to the point from which they started; the flagrant barbarisms of the fourteenth century having yielded before the close of the next to a more respectable, though not an elegant or exact kind of style. Many Italians had now some acquaintance with Greek, which in 1400 had been hardly the case with any one; and the knowledge of it was of late beginning to make a little progress in Cisalpine Europe. The French and English languages were become what we call more polished, though the difference in the former seems not to be very considerable. In mathematical science, and in natural history, the ancient writers had been more brought to light, and a certain progress had been made by diligent, if not very inventive, philosophers. We cannot say that metaphysical or moral philosophy stood higher than it had done in the time of the schoolmen. The history of Greece and Rome, and the antiquities of the latter, were, of course, more distinctly known after so many years of attentive study bestowed on their principal authors; yet the acquaintance of the learned with those subjects was by no means exact or critical enough to save them from gross errors, or from becoming the dupes of any forgery. A proof of this was furnished by the impostures of Annius of Viterbo, who, having published large fragments of Megasthenes, Berosus, Manetho, and a great many more lost historians, as having been discovered by himself, obtained full credence at the

[marginal note:] Summary of its acquisitions.

time, which was not generally withheld for too long a period afterwards, though the forgeries were palpable to those who had made themselves masters of genuine history.[g]

141. We should therefore, if we mean to judge accu-
Their imper- rately, not over-value the fifteenth century, as one in
fection. which the human mind advanced with giant strides in the kingdom of knowledge. General historians of lite-rature are apt to speak rather hyperbolically in respect of men who rose above their contemporaries; language fre-quently just, in relation to the vigorous intellects and ardent industry of such men, but tending to produce an exaggerated estimate of their absolute qualities. But the question is at present not so much of men, as of the average or general proficiency of nations. The catalogues of printed books in the common bibliographical collections afford, not quite a gauge of the learning of any particular period, but a reason-able presumption, which it requires a contrary evidence to rebut. If these present us very few and imperfect editions of books necessary to the progress of knowledge, if the works most in request appear to have been trifling and igno-rant productions, it seems as reasonable to draw an in-ference one way from these scanty and discreditable lists, as on the other hand we hail the progressive state of any branch of knowledge from the redoubled labours of the press, and the multiplication of useful editions. It is true that the deficiency of one country might be supplied by im-portation from another; and some cities, especially Paris, had acquired a typographical reputation somewhat dispro-portioned to the local demand for books; but a considerable increase of readers would naturally have created a press, or multiplied its operations, in any country of Europe.

142. The bibliographies, indeed, even the best and latest,
Number of are always imperfect; but the omissions, after the
books
printed. immense pains bestowed on the subject, can hardly be such as to affect our general conclusions. We will there-

---

[g] Annius of Viterbo did not cease to have believers after this time. See Blount, Niceron, vol. ii., Corniani, iii. 131, and his article in Biographie uni-verselle. Apostolo Zeno and Tiraboschi have imputed less fraud than credulity to Annius, but most have been of another opinion; and it is unimportant for the purpose of the text.

fore illustrate the literary history of the fifteenth century
by a few numbers taken from the typographical annals of
Panzer, which might be corrected in two ways: first, by
adding editions since brought to light, or, secondly, by
striking out some inserted on defective authority; a kind of
mistake which tends to compensate the former. The books
printed at Florence down to 1500 are 300; at Milan, 629;
at Bologna, 298; at Rome, 925; at Venice, 2835; fifty
other Italian cities had printing presses in the fifteenth century.[h] At Paris, che number of books is 751; at Cologne,
530; at Nuremberg, 382; at Leipsic, 351; at Basle, 320;
at Strasburg, 526; at Ausburg, 256; at Louvain, 116;
at Mentz, 134; at Deventer, 169. The whole number
printed in England appears to be 141; whereof 130 at
London and Westminster; seven at Oxford; four at St.
Alban's. Cicero's works were first printed entire by Minu-
tianus, at Milan, in 1498; but no less than 291 editions of
different portions appeared in the century. Thirty-seven
of these bear date on this side of the Alps; and forty-five
have no place named. Of ninety-five editions of Virgil,
seventy are complete; twenty-seven are Cisalpine, and four
bear no date. On the other hand, only eleven out of fifty-
seven editions of Horace contain all his works. It has
been already shown, that most editions of classics printed
in France and Germany are in the last decennium of the
century.

143. The editions of the Vulgate registered in Panzer
are ninety-one, exclusive of some spurious or suspected.
Next to theology, no science furnished so much occupation
to the press as the civil and canon laws. The editions of
the Digest and Decretals, or other parts of those systems of
jurisprudence, must amount to some hundreds.

144. But while we avoid, for the sake of truth, any
undue exaggeration of the literary state of Europe Advantages
at the close of the fifteenth century, we must even already
reaped from
more earnestly deprecate the hasty prejudice, that printing.
no good had been already done by the culture of classical

---

[h] I find this in Heeren, p. 127, for I have not counted the number of cities in
Panzer.

learning, and by the invention of printing. Both were of inestimable value, even where their immediate fruits were not clustering in ripe abundance. It is certain that much more than ten thousand editions of books or pamphlets (a late writer says fifteen thousand[1]) were printed from 1470 to 1500. More than half the number appeared in Italy. All the Latin authors, hitherto painfully copied by the scholar, or purchased by him at inconvenient cost, or borrowed for a time from friends, became readily accessible, and were printed, for the most part, if not correctly, according to our improved criticism, yet without the gross blunders of the ordinary manuscripts. The saving of time which the art of printing has occasioned can hardly be too highly appreciated. Nor was the Cisalpine press unserviceable in this century, though it did not pour forth so much from the stores of ancient learning. It gave useful food, and such as the reader could better relish and digest. The historical records of his own nation, the precepts of moral wisdom, the regular metre that pleased the ear and supplied the memory, the fictions that warmed the imagination, and sometimes ennobled or purified the heart, the repertories of natural phenomena, mingled as truth was on these subjects, and on all the rest, with error, the rules of civil and canon law that guided the determinations of private right, the subtle philosophy of the scholastics, were laid open to his choice, while his religious feelings might find their gratification in many a treatise of learned doctrine, according to the received creed of the church, in many a legend on which a pious credulity delighted to rely, in the devout aspirations of holy ascetic men; but, above all, in the Scriptures themselves, either in the Vulgate Latin, which had by use acquired the authority of an original text, or in most of the living languages of Europe.

145. We shall conclude this portion of literary history

---

[1] Santander, Dict. bibliogr. du 15me Siècle. I do not think so many would be found in Panzer. I have read somewhere that the library of Munich claims to possess 20,000 Incunabula, or books of the fifteenth century; a word lately so applied in Germany. But unless this comprehends many duplicates, it seems a little questionable, even understanding it of volumes. Books were not in general so voluminous in that age as at present.

with a few illustrations of what a German writer calls
'the exterior being of books,'[k] for which I do not Trade of
find an equivalent in English idiom. The trade of bookselling.
bookselling seems to have been established at Paris and at
Bologna in the twelfth century; the lawyers and universities
called it into life.[1] It is very improbable that it existed in
what we properly call the dark ages. Peter of Blois mentions a book which he had bought of a public dealer (a
quodam publico mangone librorum). But we do not find,
I believe, many distinct accounts of them till the next age.
These dealers were denominated Stationarii, perhaps from
the open stalls at which they carried on their business,
though statio is a general word for a shop in low Latin.[m]
They appear, by the old statutes of the university of Paris,
and by those of Bologna, to have sold books upon commission; and are sometimes, though not uniformly, distinguished from the Librarii; a word which, having originally
been confined to the copyists of books, was afterwards applied to those who traded in them.[n] They sold parchment
and other materials of writing, which with us, though, as
far as I know, nowhere else, have retained the name of
stationery, and naturally exercised the kindred occupations
of binding and decorating. They probably employed transcribers : we find at least that there was a profession of
copyists in the universities and in large cities; and by
means of these, before the invention of printing, the necessary books of grammar, law, and theology were multiplied
to a great extent for the use of students; but with much
incorrectness, and far more expense than afterwards. That
invention put a sudden stop to their honest occupation.
But whatever hatred they might feel towards the new art,
it was in vain to oppose its reception: no party could be
raised in the public against so manifest and unalloyed a
benefit; and the copyists, grown by habit fond of books,

---

[k] Aeusseres Bücherwesen.   Savigny,
iii. 532.
[1] Hist. litt. de la France, ix. 142.
[m] Du Cange, in voc.
[n] The Librarii were properly those

who transcribed new books; the Anti-
quarii, old ones. This distinction is as
old as Cassiodorus ; but doubtless it was
not strictly observed in later times. Muratori, Dissert. 43. Du Cange.

frequently employed themselves in the somewhat kindred labour of pressmen.[o]

146. The first printers were always booksellers, and sold Books sold their own impressions. These occupations were by printers. not divided till the early part of the sixteenth century.[p] But the risks of sale, at a time when learning was by no means general, combined with the great cost of production, paper and other materials being very dear, rendered this a hazardous trade. We have a curious petition of Sweynheim and Pannartz to Sixtus IV. in 1472, wherein they complain of their poverty, brought on by printing so many works, which they had not been able to sell. They state the number of impressions of each edition. Of the classical authors they had generally printed 275; of Virgil and the philosophical works of Cicero, twice that number. In theological publications the usual number of copies had also been 550. The whole number of copies printed was 12,475.[q] It is possible that experience made other printers more discreet in their estimation of the public demand. Notwithstanding the casualties of three centuries, it seems, from the great scarcity of these early editions which has long existed, that the original circulation must have been much below the number of copies printed, as indeed the complaint of Sweynheim and Pannartz shows.[r]

147. The price of books was diminished by four-fifths Price of after the invention of printing. Chevillier gives books. some instances of a fall in this proportion. But not content with such a reduction, the university of Paris proceeded to establish a tariff, according to which every edition

---

[o] Crevier, ii. 66, 130, et alibi. Du Cange, in voc. Stationarii, Librarii. Savigny, iii. 532–548. Chevillier, 302. Eichhorn, ii. 531. Meiners, Vergleich. der Sitten, ii. 539. Gresswell's Parisian Press, p. 8.

The Parliament of Paris, on the petition of the copyists, ordered some of the first printed books to be seized. Lambinet calls this superstition; it was more probably false compassion, and regard for existing interests, combined with dislike of all innovation. Louis XI., however, who had the merit of esteeming literature, evoked the process

to the council of state, who restored the books. Lambinet, Hist. de l'Imprimerie, p. 172.

[p] Conversations-Lexicon, art. Buchhandlung.

[q] Maittaire. Lambinet, p. 166. Beckmann, iii 119, erroneously says that this was the number of volumes remaining in their warehouses.

[r] Lambinet says that the number of impressions did not 'generally exceed three hundred (p. 197). Even this seems large, compared with the present scarcity of books unlikely to have been destroyed by careless use.

was to be sold, and seems to have set the prices very low. This was by virtue of the prerogatives they exerted, as we shall soon find, over the book-trade of the capital. The priced catalogues of Colinæus and Robert Stephens are extant, relating, of course, to a later period than the present; but we shall not return to the subject. The Greek Testament of Colinæus was sold for twelve sous, the Latin for six. The folio Latin Bible, printed by Stephens in 1532, might be had for one hundred sous, a copy of the Pandects for forty sous, a Virgil for two sous and six deniers; a Greek grammar of Clenardus for two sous; Demosthenes and Æschines, I know not what edition, for five sous. It would of course be necessary, before we could make any use of these prices, to compare them with that of corn.[a]

148. The more usual form of books printed in the fifteenth century is in folio. But the Psalter of 1457, and the Donatus of the same year, are in quarto; and this size is not uncommon in the early Italian editions of classics. The disputed Oxford book of 1468, Sancti Jeronymi Expositio, is in octavo, and would, if genuine, be the earliest specimen of that size; which may perhaps furnish an additional presumption against the date. It is at least, however, of 1478, when the octavo form, as we shall immediately

Form of books.

---

[a] Chevillier, Origines de l'Imprimerie de Paris, p. 370 et seqq. In the preceding pages he mentions what I should perhaps have introduced before, that a catalogue of the books in the Sorbonne, in 1292, contains above 1,000 volumes, which were collectively valued at 3,812 livres, 10 sous, 8 deniers. In a modern English book on literary antiquities, this is set down 3,812*l.* 10*s.* 8*d.*, which is a happy way of helping the reader.

Lambinet mentions a few prices of early books, which are not trifling. The Mentz Bible of 1462 was purchased in 1470 by a bishop of Angers for forty gold crowns. An English gentleman paid eighteen gold florins, in 1481, for a missal: upon which Lambinet makes a remark:—Mais on a toujours fait payer plus cher aux Anglais qu'aux autres nations (p. 198). The florin was worth about four francs of present money, equivalent at least to twenty-four in command of commodities. The crown

was worth rather more.

Instances of an almost incredible price of manuscripts are to be met with in Robertson and other common authors. It is to be remembered that a particular book might easily bear a monopoly price; and that this is no test of the cost of those which might be multiplied by copying. ["En général nous pourrions dire que le prix moyen d'un volume in-folio d'alors [au 14ᵐᵉ siècle] équivalait à celui des choses qui coûteraient aujourd'hui quatre à cinq cents francs." Hist. litt. de la France, xvi. 39. But this supposes illuminations or other costly ornaments. The price of law-books, such as Savigny has collected, was very much lower; and we may conclude the same of all ordinary manuscripts. Mr. Maitland, in his Letters on the Dark Ages, p. 61, has animadverted with his usual sharpness on Robertson for too hasty a generalization. —1847.]

see, was of the rarest occurrence. Maittaire, in whom alone
I have had the curiosity to make this search, which would
be more troublesome in Panzer's arrangement, mentions a
book printed in octavo at Milan in 1470; but the existence
of this, and of one or two more that follow, seems equivocal;
and the first on which we can rely is the Sallust, printed at
Valencia in 1475. Another book of that form, at Treviso,
occurs in the same year, and an edition of Pliny's epistles
at Florence in 1478. They become from this time gradually more common; but even at the end of the century
form rather a small proportion of editions. I have not observed that the duodecimo division of the sheet was adopted
in any instance. But it is highly probable that the volumes
of Panzer furnish means of correcting these little notices,
which I offer as suggestions to persons more erudite in such
matters. The price and convenience of books are evidently
not unconnected with their size.

149. Nothing could be less unreasonable than that the
Exclusive printer should have a better chance of indemnify-
privileges. ing himself and the author, if in those days the
author, as probably he did, hoped for some lucrative return
after his exhausting drudgery, by means of an exclusive
privilege. The senate of Venice granted an exclusive privilege for five years to John of Spire in 1469, for the first
book printed in the city, his edition of Cicero's epistles.[t]
But I am not aware that this extended to any other work.
And this seems to have escaped the learned Beckmann,
who says, that the earliest instance of protected copyright
on record appears to be in favour of a book insignificant
enough, a missal for the church of Bamberg, printed in
1490. It is probable that other privileges of an older date
have not been found. In 1491, one occurs at the end of a
book printed at Venice, and five more at the same place
within the century; the Aristotle of Aldus being one of
the books: one also is found at Milan. These privileges
are always recited at the end of the volume. They are,
however, very rare in comparison with the number of books
published, and seem not accorded by preference to the
most important editions.[u]

---

[t] Tiraboschi, vi. 139.　　　　[u] Beckmann's Hist. of Inventions, iii. 109.

150. In these exclusive privileges, the printer was forced
to call in the magistrate for his own benefit. But
there was often a different sort of interference by
the civil power with the press. The destruction
of books, and the prohibition of their sale, had not been
unknown to antiquity; instances of it occur in the free
republics of Athens and Rome; but it was naturally more
frequent under suspicious despotisms, especially when to
the jealousy of the state was superadded that of the church,
and novelty, even in speculation, became a crime.[x] Ignorance came on with the fall of the empire, and it was unnecessary to guard against the abuse of an art which very
few possessed at all. With the first revival of letters in
the eleventh and twelfth centuries sprang up the reviving
shoots of heretical freedom; but with Berenger and Abelard came also the jealousy of the church, and the usual
exertion of the right of the strongest. Abelard was censured by the council of Soissons in 1121, for suffering
copies of his book to be taken without the approbation of
his superiors, and the delinquent volumes were given to the
flames. It does not appear, however, that any regulation
on this subject had been made.[y] But when the sale of
books became the occupation of a class of traders, it was
deemed necessary to place them under restraint. Those of
Paris and Bologna, the cities, doubtless, where the greatest
business of this kind was carried on, came altogether into
the power of the universities. It is proved by various statutes of the university of Paris, originating, no doubt, in
some authority conferred by the crown, and bearing date
from the year 1275 to 1403, that booksellers were appointed
by the university, and considered as its officers, probably
matriculated by entry on her roll; that they took an oath
renewable at her pleasure, to observe her statutes and regulations; that they were admitted upon security, and with
testimonials to their moral conduct; that no one could sell
books in Paris without this permission; that they could ex-
pose no book to sale without communication with the university, and without its approbation; that the university
fixed the prices, according to the tariff of four sworn book-

Power of
universities
over book-
selling.

---

[x] Beckmann's Hist. of Inventions, iii. 93.   [y] Hist. litt. de la France, ix. 28.

sellers, at which books should be sold, or lent to the scholars;
that a fine might be imposed for incorrect copies ; that the
sellers were bound to fix up in their shops a priced catalogue
of their books, besides other regulations of less importance.
Books deemed by the university unfit for perusal were sometimes burned by its order.[z] Chevillier gives several prices
for lending books (pro exemplari concesso scholaribus) fixed
about 1303. The books mentioned are all of divinity, philosophy, or canon law ; on an average, the charge for about
twenty pages was a sol. The university of Toulouse exercised the same authority ; and Albert III., archduke of
Austria, founding the university of Vienna about 1384,
copied the statutes of Paris in this control over bookselling
as well as in other respects.[a] The stationarii of Bologna
were also bound by oath, and gave sureties to fulfil their
duties towards the university; one of these was, to keep
by them copies of books to the number of one hundred and
seventeen, for the hire of which a price was fixed.[b] By
degrees, however, a class of booksellers grew up at Paris,
who took no oath to the university, and were consequently not
admitted to its privileges, being usually poor scholars, who
were tolerated in selling books of low price. These were of
no importance, till the privileged, or sworn traders, having
been reduced by a royal ordinance of 1488 to twenty-four,
this lower class silently increased, and at length the practice of taking an oath to the university fell into disuse.[c]

151. The vast and sudden extension of the means of
communicating and influencing opinion which the
discovery of printing afforded did not long remain
unnoticed. Few have temper and comprehensive
views enough not to desire the prevention by force of
that which they reckon detrimental to truth and right.
Hermolaus Barbarus, in a letter to Merula, recommends
that, on account of the many trifling publications which
took men off from reading the best authors, nothing should
be printed without the approbation of competent judges.[d]

Restraints on sale of printed books.

---

[z] Chevillier, Origines de l'Imprimerie
de Paris, p. 302 et seqq. Crevier, ii. 66.
  [a] Chevillier, Origines de l'Imprimerie
de Paris, p. 302 et seqq.

[b] Savigny, iii. 540.
[c] Chevillier, 334- 351.
[d] Beckmann, iii. 98.

The governments of Europe cared little for what seemed an evil to Hermolaus. But they perceived that, especially in Germany, a country where the principles that were to burst out in the Reformation were evidently germinating in this century, where a deep sense of the corruptions of the Church pervaded every class, that incredible host of popular religious tracts, which the Rhine and Neckar poured forth like their waters, were of no slight danger to the two powers, or at least the union of the two, whom the people had so long obeyed. We find, therefore, an instance in 1480, of a book called Nosce teipsum, printed at Heidelberg, with the approving testimonies of four persons, who may be presumed, though it is not stated, to have been appointed censors on that occasion.[e] Two others, one of which is a Bible, have been found printed at Cologne in 1479; in the subscription to which, the language of public approbation by the university is more express. The first known instance, however, of the regular appointment of a censor on books is in the mandate of Berthold, archbishop of Mentz, in 1486. 'Notwithstanding,' he begins, 'the facility given to the acquisition of science by the divine art of printing, it has been found that some abuse this invention, and convert that which was designed for the instruction of mankind to their injury. For books on the duties and doctrines of religion are translated from Latin into German, and circulated among the people, to the disgrace of religion itself; and some have even had the rashness to make faulty versions of the canons of the Church into the vulgar tongue, which belong to a science so difficult, that it is enough to occupy the life of the wisest man. Can such men assert, that our German language is capable of expressing what great authors have written in Greek and Latin on the high mysteries of the Christian faith, and on general science? Certainly it is not; and hence they either invent new words, or use old ones in erroneous senses; a thing especially dangerous in sacred Scripture. For who will admit that men without learning, or women, into whose hands

<hr>

[e] Beckmann, iii. 99.

these translations may fall, can find the true sense of the
gospels, or of the epistles of St. Paul? much less can they
enter on questions which, even among catholic writers, are
open to subtle discussion. But since this art was first discovered in this city of Mentz, and we may truly say by
divine aid, and is to be maintained by us in all its honour,
we strictly forbid all persons to translate, or circulate when
translated, any books upon any subject whatever from the
Greek, Latin, or any other tongue into German, until,
before printing, and again before their sale, such translations
shall be approved by four doctors herein named, under penalty of excommunication, and of forfeiture of the books, and
of one hundred golden florins to the use of our exchequer.' [f]

152. I have given the substance of this mandate rather
Effect of   at length, because it has a considerable bearing
printing on   on the preliminary history of the Reformation, and
the Reform-
ation.   yet has never, to my knowledge, been produced
with that view. For it is obvious that it was on account
of religious translations, and especially those of the Scripture, which had been very early printed in Germany, that
this alarm was taken by the worthy archbishop. A bull
of Alexander VI., in 1501, reciting that many pernicious
books had been printed in various parts of the world, and
especially in the provinces of Cologne, Mentz, Treves, and
Magdeburg, forbids all printers in these provinces to publish any books without the licence of the archbishops or
their officials.[g] We here perceive the distinction made
between these parts of Germany and the rest of Europe,
and can understand their ripeness for the ensuing revolution. We perceive, also, the vast influence of the art of
printing upon the Reformation. Among those who have
been sometimes enumerated as its precursors, a place
should be left for Schœffer and Gutenberg; nor has this
always been forgotten.[h]

---

[f] Beckmann, iii. 101, from the fourth
volume of Guden's Codex diplomaticus.
The Latin will be found in Beckmann.
[g] Beckmann, iii. 106.

[h] Gerdes, in his Hist. Evangel. Re-
formati, who has gone very laboriously
into this subject, justly dwells on the
influence of the art of printing.

CHAPTER IV.

ON THE LITERATURE OF EUROPE FROM 1500 TO 1520.

Sect. I.   1501—1510.

Classical Learning of Italy in this Period—Of France, Germany, and England—Works of Polite Literature in Languages of Italy, Spain, and England.

1. The new century did not begin very auspiciously for the literary credit of Italy.   We may, indeed, Decline of consider the whole period between the death of learning in Italy. Lorenzo in 1492, and the pontificate of his son in 1513, as less brilliant than the two ages which we connect with their names.   But when measured by the labours of the press, the last ten years of the fifteenth century were considerably more productive than any which had gone before. In the present decad a striking decline was perceptible. Thus, in comparing the numbers of books printed in the chief towns of Italy, we find—

	1491—1500	1501—1510
Florence	179	47
Rome	460	41
Milan	228	99
Venice	1491	536 [a]

Such were the fruits of the ambition of Ferdinand and of Louis XII., and the first interference of strangers with the liberties of Italy.   Wars so protracted within the bosom of a country, if they do not prevent the growth of original genius, must yet be unfavourable to that secondary, but

---

[a] Panzer.

more diffused excellence, which is nourished by the wealth
of patrons and the tranquillity of universities. Thus, the
gymnasium of Rome, founded by Eugenius IV., but lately
endowed and regulated by Alexander VI., who had established it in a handsome edifice on the Quirinal hill, was
despoiled of its revenues by Julius II., who, with some
liberality towards painters, had no regard for learning;
and this will greatly account for the remarkable decline in
the typography of Rome. Thus, too, the Platonic school
at Florence soon went to decay after the fall of the Medici,
who had fostered it; and even the rival philosophy which
rose upon its ruins, and was taught at the beginning of this
century with much success at Padua by Pomponatius,
according to the original principles of Aristotle, and by
two other professors of great eminence in their time, Nifo
and Achillini, according to the system of Averroes, could
not resist the calamities of war: the students of that university were dispersed in 1509, after the unfortunate defeat
of Ghiaradadda.

2. Aldus himself left Venice in 1506, his effects in the
territory having been plundered, and did not open
his press again until 1512, when he entered into
partnership with his father-in-law, Andrew Asola. He
had been actively employed during the first years of the
century. He published Sophocles, Herodotus, and Thucydides in 1502, Euripides and Herodian in 1503, Demosthenes in 1504. These were important accessions to
Greek learning, though so much remained behind. A
circumstance may be here mentioned, which had so much
influence in facilitating the acquisition of knowledge, that
it renders the year 1501 a sort of epoch in literary history. He that year not only introduced a new Italian
character, called Aldine, more easily read perhaps than
his Roman letters, which are somewhat rude; but, what
was of more importance, began to print in a small octavo
or duodecimo form, instead of the cumbrous and expensive
folios that had been principally in use. Whatever the
great of ages past might seem to lose by this indignity,
was more than compensated in the diffused love and
admiration of their writings. 'With what pleasure,' says

Press of Aldus.

M. Renouard, 'must the studious man, the lover of letters, have beheld these benevolent octavos, these Virgils and Horaces contained in one little volume, which he might carry in his pocket while travelling or in a walk; which besides cost him hardly more than two of our francs, so that he could get a dozen of them for the price of one of those folios that had hitherto been the sole furniture of his library! The appearance of these correct and well printed octavos ought to be as much remarked as the substitution of printed books for manuscripts itself.'[b] We have seen above, that not only small quartos, nearly as portable perhaps as octavos, but the latter form also, had been coming into use towards the close of the fifteenth century, though, I believe, it was sparingly employed for classical authors.

3. It was about 1500 that Aldus drew together a few scholars into a literary association, called Aldi Neacademia. Not only amicable discussions, but *His academy.* the choice of books to be printed, of manuscripts and various readings, occupied their time, so that they may be considered as literary partners of the noble-minded printer. This academy was dispersed by the retirement of Aldus from Venice, and never met again.[c]

4. The first edition of Calepio's Latin Dictionary, which though far better than one or two obscure books that preceded it, and enriched by plundering the *Dictionary of Calepio.* stores of Valla and Perotti, was very defective, appeared at Reggio in 1502.[d] It was so greatly augmented by subsequent improvers, that *calepin* has become a name in French for any voluminous compilation. This dictionary was not only of Latin and Italian, but several other languages; and these were extended in the Basle edition of 1581 to eleven. It is still, if not the best, the most complete polyglott lexicon for the European languages. Ca-

---

[b] Renouard, Hist. de l'Imprimerie des Aldes. Roscoe's Leo X., ch. ii.

[c] Tiraboschi. Roscoe. Renouard. Scipio Forteguerra, who latinised his name into Carteromachus, was secretary to this society, and among its most distinguished members. He was celebrated in his time for a discourse, De Laudibus Literarum Græcarum, reprinted by Henry Stephens in his Thesaurus. Biogr. univ., Forteguerra.

[d] Brunet. Tiraboschi (x. 383) gives some reason to suspect that there may have been an earlier edition.

lepio, however moderate might be his erudition, has just
claim to be esteemed one of the most effective instruments
in the restoration of the Latin language in its purity to
general use; for though some had by great acuteness and
diligence attained a good style in the fifteenth century,
that age was looked upon in Italy itself as far below the
subsequent period.[e]

5. We may read in Panzer the titles of 325 books printed
Books during these ten years at Leipsic, 60 of which are
printed in Germany, classical, but chiefly as before, small school-books;
14 out of 214 at Cologne, 10 out of 208 at Strasburg, 1
out of 84 at Basle, are also classical; but scarcely any
books whatever appear at Louvain. One printed at Erfurt
in 1501 deserves some attention. The title runs ' Εισαγωγη
προς των γραμματων 'Ελληων, Elementale Introductorium
in idioma Græcanicum,' with some more words. Panzer
observes : 'This Greek grammar, published by some unknown person, is undoubtedly the first which was published in Germany since the invention of printing.' In
this, however, as has already been shown, he is mistaken;
unless we deny to the book printed at Deventer the name
of a grammar. But Panzer was not acquainted with it.
This seems to be the only attempt at Greek that occurs in
Germany during this decad; and it is unnecessary to comment on the ignorance which the gross solecism in the title
displays.[f]

6. Paris contributed in ten years 430 editions, thirty-
First Greek two being of Latin classics. And in 1507 Giles
press at Paris. Gourmont, a printer of that city, assisted by the
purse of Francis Tissard, had the honour of introducing the

---

* Calepio is said by Morhof and Baillet to have copied Perotti's Cornucopia
almost entire. Sir John Elyot long before had remarked : ' Calepin nothing
amended, but rather appaired that which
Perottus had studiously gathered.' But
the Cornucopia was not a complete dictionary. It is generally agreed that
Calepio was an indifferent scholar, and
that the first editions of his dictionary
are of no great value. Nor have those
who have enlarged it done so with ex-

actness, or with selection of good Latinity.
Even Passerat, the most learned of them,
has not extirpated the unauthorised
words of Calepio. Baillet, Jugemens
des Savans, ii. 44. ·
Several bad dictionaries, abridged from
the Catholicon, appeared near the end of
the fifteenth century, and at the beginning of the next. Du Cange, præfat. in
Glossar. p. 47.
[f] Panzer, vi. 494. We find, however,
a tract by Hegius—De Utilitate Linguæ

Greek language on this side, as we may say of the Alps; for the trifling exceptions we have mentioned scarcely affect his priority. Greek types had been used in a few words by Badius Ascensius, a learned and meritorious Parisian printer, whose publications began about 1498. They occur in his edition (1505) of Valla's Annotations on the Greek Testament.[g] Four little books, namely, a small miscellaneous volume, preceded by an alphabet, the Works and Days of Hesiod, the Frogs and Mice of Homer, and the Erotemata or Greek grammar of Chrysoloras, to which four a late writer has added an edition of Musæus, were the first fruits of Gourmont's press. Aleander, a learned Italian, who played afterwards no inconsiderable part in the earlier period of the Reformation, came to Paris in 1508, and received a pension from Louis XII.[h] He taught Greek there, and perhaps Hebrew. Through his care, besides a Hebrew and Greek alphabet in 1508, Gourmont printed some of the moral works of Plutarch in 1509.

7. We learn from a writer of the most respectable authority, Camerarius, that the elements of Greek were already taught to boys in some parts of Ger- *Early studies of Melanchthon.*

Græcæ, printed at Deventer in 1501; but whether it contains Greek characters or not, must be left to conjecture. Lambinet says, that Martens, a Flemish printer, employed Greek types in quotations as early as 1501 or 1502.

[g] Chevillier, Origines de l Imprimerie de Paris, p. 246. Gresswell's View of early Parisian Greek Press, i. 15. Panzer, according to Mr. Gresswell, has recorded nearly 400 editions from the press of Badius. They include almost every Latin classic, usually with notes. He also printed a few Greek authors. See also Bayle and Biogr. univ. The latter refers the first works from the Parisian press of Badius to 1511, but probably by misprint. Badius had learned Greek at Ferrara. If Bayle is correct, he taught it at Lyons before he set up his press at Paris, which is worthy of notice; but he gives no authority, except for the fact of his teaching in the former city, which might not be the Greek language. It is said, however, that he came to Paris in order to give instruction

in Greek about 1499. Bayle, art. Badius, note H. It is said in the Biographie universelle, that Denys le Fevre taught Greek at Paris in 1504, when only sixteen years old: but the story seems apocryphal.

[h] Aleander was no favourite with Erasmus, and Luther utters many invectives against him. He was a strenuous supporter of all things as they were in the church, and would have presided in the Council of Trent as legate of Paul III., who had given him a cardinal's hat, if he had not been prevented by death.

It is fair to say of Aleander, that he was the friend of Sadolet. In a letter of that excellent person to Paul III., he praises Aleander very highly, and requests for him the hat, which the pope in consequence bestowed. Sadolet, Epist. l. xii. See, for Aleander, Bayle; Sleidan, Hist. de la Réformation, l. ii. and iii.; Roscoe's Leo X., ch. xxi.; Jortin's Erasmus, passim.

many.[i]   About 1508, Reuchlin, on a visit to George
Simler, a schoolmaster in Hesse, found a relation of his
own, little more than ten years old, who, uniting extraordinary quickness with thirst for learning, had already
acquired the rudiments of that language ; and presenting
him with a lexicon and grammar, precious gifts in those
times, changed his German name, Schwartzerd, to one of
equivalent meaning and more classical sound, Melanchthon.
He had himself set the example of assuming a name of
Greek derivation, being almost as much known by the
name of Capnio as by his own.   And this pedantry, which
continued to prevail for a century and a half afterwards,
might be excused by the great uncouthness of many German,
not to say French and English, surnames in their Latinised forms.   Melanchthon, the precocity of his youth being
followed by a splendid maturity, became not only one of
the greatest lights of the Reformation, but, far above all
others, the founder of general learning in Germany.[k]

8. England seems to have been nearly stationary in academical learning during the unpropitious reign
of Henry VII.[l]   But just hopes were entertained
from the accession of his son in 1509, who had received in
some degree a learned education.   And the small knot of

Learning in England.

---

[i] Jam enim pluribus in locis melius
quam dudum pueritia institui et doctrina
in scholis usurpari politior, quod et
bonorum autorum scripta in manus
tenerentur, et elementa quoque linguæ
Græcæ alicubi proponerentur ad discen-
dum, cum seniorum admiratione maxima, et ardentissima cupiditate juniorum,
cujus utriusque tum non tam judicium
quam novitas causa fuit. Simlerus, qui
postea ex primario grammatico eximius
jurisconsultus factus est, initio hanc
doctrinam non vulgandam aliquantisper
arbitrabatur. Itaque Græcarum literarum scholam explicabat aliquot discipulis suis privatim, quibus dabat hanc
operam peculiarem, ut quos summopere
diligeret. Camerarius, Vita Melanchthonis. I find also, in one of Melanchthon's own epistles, that he learned
the Greek grammar from George Simler. Epist. Melanchth. p. 351 (edit.
1647).

[k] Camerarius. Meiners, i. 73. The

Biographie universelle, art. Melanchthon, calls him nephew of Reuchlin :
but this seems not to be the case ;
Camerarius only says, that their families
were connected quadam cognationis ne-
cessitudine.

[l] 'The schools were much frequented
with quirks and sophistry. All things,
whether taught or written, seemed to be
trite and inane. No pleasant streams of
humanity or mythology were gliding
among us ; and the Greek language, from
whence the greater part of knowledge is
derived, was at a very low ebb, or in a
manner forgotten.' Wood's Annals of
Oxford, A.D. 1508. The word 'forgotten' is improperly applied to Greek,
which had never been known. In this
reign, but in what part of it does not appear, the university of Oxford hired an
Italian, one Caius Auberinus, to compose
the public orations and epistles, and to
explain Terence in the schools. Warton,
ii. 420, from MS. authority.

excellent men, united by zeal for improvement, Grocyn, Linacre, Latimer, Fisher, Colet, More, succeeded in bringing over their friend Erasmus to teach Greek at Cambridge, in 1510. The students, he says, were too poor to pay him anything, nor had he many scholars.[m] His instruction was confined to the grammar. In the same year Colet, Dean of St. Paul's founded there a school, and published a Latin grammar. Five or six little works of the kind had already appeared in England.[n] These trifling things are mentioned to let the reader take notice that there is nothing more worthy to be named. Twenty-six books were printed at London during this decad. Among these Terence in 1504, but no other Latin author of classical name. The difference in point of learning between Italy and England was at least that of a century; that is, the former was as much advanced in knowledge of ancient literature in 1400 as the latter was in 1500.

9. It is plain, however, that on the continent of Europe, though no very remarkable advances were made in *Erasmus and* these ten years, learning was slowly progressive, *Budæus.* and the men were living who were to bear fruit in due season. Erasmus republished his Adages with such great additions as rendered them almost a new work; while Budæus, in his Observations upon the Pandects, gave the first example of applying philological and historical literature to the illustration of Roman law, by which others, with more knowledge of jurisprudence than he possessed, were in the next generation signally to change the face of that science.

10. The eastern languages began now to be studied, though with very imperfect means. Hebrew had *Study of* been cultivated in the Franciscan monasteries of *eastern languages.* Tubingen and Basle before the end of the last century.

---

[m] Hactenus prælegimus Chrysoloræ grammaticam, sed paucis; fortassis frequentiori auditorio Theodori grammaticam auspicabimur. Ep. cxxiii. (16th Oct. 1511.)

[n] Wood talks of Holt's Lac Puerorum, published in 1497, as if it had made an epoch in literature. It might be superior to any grammar we already possessed.

[The syntax in Lilly's grammar, which has been chiefly in use with us (under that or other names), was much altered by Erasmus, at Colet's desire: sic emendaram, ut pleraque mutarem. It was published anonymously. This syntax is admired for conciseness and perspicuity. —1842.]

The first grammar was published by Conrad Pellican in 1503. Eichhorn calls it an evidence of the deficiencies of his knowledge, though it cost him incredible pains. Reuchlin gave a better, with a dictionary, in 1506, which, enlarged by Munster, long continued to be a standard book. A Hebrew psalter, with three Latin translations, and one in French was published in 1509 by Henry Stephens, the progenitor of a race illustrious in typographical and literary history. Petrus de Alcalá, in 1506, attempted an Arabic vocabulary, printing the words in Roman letter.[o]

11. If we could trust an article in the Biographie uni-

Dramatic works. verselle, a Portuguese, Gil Vicente, deserves the high praise of having introduced the regular drama into Europe, the first of his pieces having been represented at Lisbon at 1504.[p] But, according to the much superior authority of Bouterwek, Gil Vicente was a writer in the old national style of Spain and Portugal; and his early compositions are Autos, or spiritual dramas; totally unlike any regular plays, and rude both in design and execution. He became, however, a comic writer of great reputation among his countrymen at a later period, but in the same vein of uncultivated genius, and not before Machiavel and Ariosto had established their dramatic renown. The Calandra of Bibbiena, afterwards a cardinal, was represented at Venice in 1508, though not published till 1524. An analysis of this play will be found in Ginguéné; it bears only a general resemblance to the Menæchmi of Plautus. Perhaps the Calandra may be considered as the earliest modern comedy, or at least the earliest that is known to be extant; for its five acts and intricate plot exclude the competition of Maître Patelin.[q]

---

[o] Eichhorn, ii. 562, 563; v. 609. Meiners's Life of Reuchlin, in Lebensbeschreibungen berühmter Männer, i. 68. A very few instances of Hebrew scholars in the fifteenth century might be found, besides Reuchlin and Picus of Mirandola. Tiraboschi gives the chief place among these to Giannozzo Manetti. vii. 123.

[p] Biogr. univ. art. Gil Vicente.

Another Life of the same dramatist in a later volume, under the title Vicente, seems designed to retract this claim. Bouterwek adverts to this supposed drama of 1504, which is an Auto on the festival of Corpus Christi, and of the simplest kind.

[q] Ginguéné, vi. 171. An earlier writer on the Italian theatre is in raptures with this play. 'The Greeks,

But there is a more celebrated piece in the Spanish language, of which it is probably impossible to determine Calisto and Melibœa. the date, the tragi-comedy, as it has been called, of Calisto and Melibœa. This is the work of two authors, one generally supposed to be Rodrigo Cota, who planned the story and wrote the first act; the other, Fernando de Rojas, who added twenty more acts to complete the drama. This alarming number does not render the play altogether so prolix as might be supposed, the acts being only what with us are commonly denominated scenes. It is, however, much beyond the limits of representation. Some have supposed Calisto and Melibœa to have been commenced by Juan de la Mena before the middle of the fifteenth century. But this, Antonio tells us, shows ignorance of the style belonging to that author and to his age. It is far more probably of the time of Ferdinand and Isabella; and as an Italian translation appears to have been published in 1514, we may presume that it was finished and printed in Spain about the present decad.[r]

12. Bouterwek and Sismondi have given some account of this rather remarkable dramatic work. But Its character. they hardly do it justice, especially the former, who would lead the reader to expect something very anomalous and extravagant. It appears to me that it is as regular and well contrived as the old comedies generally were: the action is simple and uninterrupted; nor can it be reckoned very extraordinary, that what Bouterwek calls the unities of time and place should be transgressed, when for the next two centuries they were never observed. Calisto and Melibœa was at least deemed so original and important an accession to literature, that it was naturalised in several languages. A very early imitation, rather than

---

Latins, and moderns have never made, and perhaps never will make, so perfect a comedy as the Calandra.' It is, in my opinion, the model of good comedy.' Riccoboni, Hist. du Théâtre italien, i. 148. This is much to say, and shows an odd taste, for the Calandra neither displays character nor excites interest.

[r] Antonio, Bibl. Hisp. Nova. Andrès,

v. 125. La Celestina, says the latter, certo contiene un fatto bene svolto, e spiegato con episodj verisimili e naturali, dipinge con verità i caratteri, ed esprime talora con calore gli affetti; e tutto questo a mio giudizio potrà bastare per darli il vanto d'essere stata la prima composizione teatrale scritta con eleganza e regolarità.

version, in English, appears to have been printed in 1530.[s]
A real translation, with the title Celestina (the name of a
procuress who plays the chief part in the drama, and by
which it has been frequently known), is mentioned by
Herbert under the year 1598. And there is another
translation, or second edition, in 1631, with the same title,
from which all my acquaintance with this play is derived.
Gaspar Barthius gave it in Latin, 1624, with the title,
Pornobosco-didascalus.[t] It was extolled by some as a salutary exposition of the effects of vice—

> Quo modo adolescentulæ
> Lenarum ingenia et mores possent noscere,—

and condemned by others as too open a display of it. Bouterwek has rather exaggerated the indecency of this drama,
which is much less offensive, unless softened in the translation, than in most of our old comedies. The style of the
first author is said to be more elegant than that of his continuator, but this is not very apparent in the English
version. The chief characters throughout are pretty well
drawn, and there is a vein of humour in some of the comic
parts.

13. The first edition of the works of a Spanish poet,
Juan de la Enzina, appeared in 1501, though they
were probably written in the preceding century.
Some of these are comedies, as one biographer calls them,
or rather, perhaps, as Bouterwek expresses it, ' sacred and
profane eclogues, in the form of dialogues, represented
before distinguished persons on festivals.' Enzina wrote
also a treatise on Castilian poetry, which, according to
Bouterwek, is but a short essay on the rules of metre.[u]

14. The pastoral romance, as was before mentioned,

---

[s] Dibdin's Typographical Antiquities.
Mr. Collier (Hist. of Dramatic Poetry,
ii. 408) has given a short account of this
production, which he says ' is not long
enough for a play, and could only have
been acted as an interlude.' It must
therefore be very different from the
original.
[t] Clément, Bibliothèque curieuse.

This translation is sometimes erroneously
named Porno-didascalus ; the title of
a very different book.
[u] Bouterwek. Biogr. univ., art. Enzina. The latter praises this work of
Enzina more highly, but whether from
equal knowledge I cannot say. The
dramatic compositions above mentioned
are most scarce.

began a little before this time in Portugal. An Italian writer of fine genius, Sannazzaro, adopted it in his Arcadia, of which the first edition was in 1502. Arcadia of Sannazzaro. Harmonious prose intermingled with graceful poetry, and with a fable just capable of keeping awake the attention, though it could never excite emotion, communicate a tone of pleasing sweetness to this volume. But we have been so much used to fictions of more passionate interest, that we hardly know how to accommodate ourselves to the mild languor of these early romances. A recent writer places the Arcadia at the head of Italian prose in that age. 'With a less embarrassed construction,' he says, ' than Boccaccio, and less of a servile mannerism than Bembo, the style of Sannazzaro is simple, flowing, rapid, harmonious. If it should seem now and then too florid and diffuse, this may be pardoned in a romance. It is to him, in short, rather than to Bembo, that we owe the revival of correctness and elegance in the Italian prose of the sixteenth century; and his style in the Arcadia would have been far more relished than that of the Asolani, if the originality of his poetry had not engrossed our attention.' He was the first who employed in any considerable degree the *sdrucciolo* verse, though it occurs before; but the difficulty of finding rhymes for it drives him frequently upon unauthorised phrases. He may also be reckoned the first who restored the polished style of Petrarch, which no writer of the fifteenth century had successfully emulated.[x]

15. The Asolani of Peter Bembo, a dialogue, the scene of which is laid at Asola, in the Venetian terri- Asolani of Bembo. tory, were published in 1505. They are disquisitions on love, tedious enough to our present apprehension,

---

[x] Salfi, Continuation de Ginguéné, x. 92. Corniani, iv. 12. Roscoe speaks of the Arcadia with less admiration, but perhaps more according to the feelings of the general reader. But I cannot altogether concur in his sweeping denunciation of poetical prose, 'that hermaphrodite of literature.' In many styles of composition, and none more than such as the Arcadia, it may be read with delight, and without wounding a rational taste. The French language, which is not well adapted to poetry, would have lost some of its most imaginative passages, with which Buffon, St.-Pierre, and others have enriched it, if a highly ornamented prose had been wholly proscribed; and we may say the same with equal truth of our own. It is another thing to condemn the peculiar style of poetry in writings that from their subject demand a very different tone.

but in a style so pure and polite, that they became the favourite reading among the superior ranks in Italy, where the coldness and pedantry of such dissertations were forgiven for their classical dignity and moral truth. The Asolani has been thought to make an epoch in Italian literature, though the Arcadia is certainly a more original and striking work of genius.

16. I do not find at what time the poems in the Scottish dialect by William Dunbar were published; but ' The Thistle and the Rose,' on the marriage of James IV. with Margaret of England in 1503, must be presumed to have been written very little after that time. Dunbar, therefore, has the honour of leading the vanguard of British poetry in the sixteenth century. His allegorical poem, The Golden Targe, is of a more extended range, and displays more creative power. The versification of Dunbar is remarkably harmonious and exact for his age; and his descriptions are often very lively and picturesque. But it must be confessed that there is too much of sunrise and singing-birds in all our mediæval poetry; a note caught from the French and Provençal writers, and repeated to satiety by our own. The allegorical characters of Dunbar are derived from the same source. He belongs, as a poet, to the school of Chaucer and Lydgate.[y]

Dunbar.

17. The first book upon anatomy, since that of Mundinus, was by Zerbi of Verona, who taught in the University of Padua in 1495. The title is, Liber anatomiæ corporis humani et singulorum membrorum illius, 1503. He follows in general the plan of Mundinus, and his language is obscure, as well as full of inconvenient abbreviations; yet the germ of discoveries that have crowned later anatomists with glory is sometimes perceptible in Zerbi; among others, that of the Fallopian tubes.[z]

Anatomy of Zerbi.

18. We now, for the first time, take relations of voyages into our literary catalogue. During the fifteenth century, though the old travels of Marco Polo

Voyages of Cadamosto.

---

[y] Warton, iii. 90. Ellis (Specimens, i. 377) strangely calls Dunbar ' the greatest poet that Scotland has produced.' Pinkerton places him above

Chaucer and Lydgate. Chalmers's Biogr. Dict.

[z] Portal, Hist. de l'Anatomie. Biogr. univ., art, Zerbi.

had been printed several times, and in different languages, and even those of Sir John Mandeville once; though the Cosmography of Ptolemy had appeared in not less than seven editions, and generally with maps, few, if any, original descriptions of the kingdoms of the world had gratified the curiosity of modern Europe. But the stupendous discoveries that signalised the last years of that age could not long remain untold. We may, however, give perhaps the first place to the voyages of Cadamosto, a Venetian, who, in 1455, under the protection of Prince Henry of Portugal, explored the western coast of Africa, and bore a part in discovering its two great rivers, as well as the Cape de Verde islands. 'The relation of his voyages,' says a late writer, 'the earliest of modern travels, is truly a model, and would lose nothing by comparison with those of our best navigators. Its arrangement is admirable, its details are interesting, its descriptions clear and precise.'[a] These voyages of Cadamosto do not occupy more than thirty pages in the collection of Ramusio, where they are reprinted. They are said to have first appeared at Vicenza in 1507, with the title Prima navigazione per l' oceano alle terre de' negri della bassa Ethiopa di Luigi Cadamosto. It is supposed, however, by Brunet, that no separate account of Cadamosto's voyage exists earlier than 1519, and that this of 1507 is a confusion with the next book. This was a still more important production, announcing the great discoveries that Americo Vespucci was suffered to wrest, at least in name, from a more illustrious though ill-requited Italian : Mondo nuovo, e pessi nuovamente ritrovati da Alberico Vesputio Florentino intitolati. Vicenza, 1507. But this includes the voyage of Cadamosto. It does not appear that any earlier work on America had been published; but an epistle of Columbus himself, de insulis Indiæ nuper inventis, was twice printed about 1493 in Germany, and probably in other countries; and a few other brief notices of the recent discovery are to be traced. We find also in 1508 an account of the Portuguese in the

---

[a] Biogr. univ. art. Cadamosto.

East, which, being announced as a translation from the native language into Latin, may be presumed to have appeared before.[b]

SECT. II.   1511—1520.

Age of Leo X.—Italian Dramatic Poetry—Classical Learning, especially Greek, in France, Germany, and England—Utopia of More—Erasmus—His Adages—Political Satire contained in them—Opposition of the Monks to Learning—Antipathy of Erasmus to them—Their Attack on Reuchlin—Origin of Reformation—Luther—Ariosto—Character of the Orlando Furioso—Various Works of Amusement in modern Languages—English Poetry—Pomponatius—Raymond Lully.

19. LEO X. became pope in 1513. His chief distinction, no doubt, is owing to his encouragement of the arts, or, more strictly, to the completion of those splendid labours of Raffaelle under his pontificate, which had been commenced by his predecessor. We have here only to do with literature; and in the promotion of this he certainly deserves a much higher name than any former pope, except Nicolas V., who, considering the difference of the times, and the greater solidity of his own character, as certainly stands far above him. Leo began by placing men of letters in the most honourable stations of his court. There were two, Bembo and Sadolet, who had by common confession reached a consummate elegance of style, in comparison of which the best productions of the last age seemed very imperfect. They were made apostolical secretaries. Beroaldo, second of the name, whose father, though a more fertile author, was inferior to him in taste, was intrusted with the Vatican library. John Lascaris and Marcus Musurus were invited to reside at Rome;[c] and the pope, considering it, he says, no small

Leo X., his patronage of letters.

[b] See Brunet, Manuel du Libraire, arts. Itinerarium, Primo, Vespucci. [Also his Supplément au Manuel du Libraire, art. Vespucci. This last article corrects the former, and has enabled me to state M. Brunet's opinion more clearly than in my first edition.—1842.]

[c] John Lascaris, who is not to be con- founded with Constantine Lascaris, by some thought to be his father, and to whom we owe a Greek grammar, after continuing for several years under the patronage of Lorenzo at Florence, where he was editor of the Anthologia, or collection of epigrams, printed in 1494, on the fall of the Medici family entered the

part of his pontifical duty to promote the Latin literature, caused search to be made everywhere for manuscripts. This expression sounds rather oddly in his mouth: and the less religious character of Transalpine literature is visible in this as in everything else.

20. The personal taste of Leo was almost entirely directed towards poetry and the beauties of style. Roman gymnasium. This, Tiraboschi seems to hint, might cause the more serious learning of antiquity to be rather neglected. But there does not seem to be much ground for this charge. We owe to Leo the publication, by Beroaldo, of the first five books of the Annals of Tacitus, which had lately been found in a German monastery. It appears that in 1514 above one hundred professors received salaries in the Roman University or gymnasium, restored by the pope to its alienated revenues.[d] Leo seems to have founded a seminary distinct from the former, under the superintendence of Lascaris, for the sole study of Greek, and to have brought over young men as teachers from Greece. In this academy a Greek press was established, where the scholiasts on Homer were printed in 1517.[e]

21. Leo was a great admirer of Latin poetry; and in

---

service of Charles VIII., and lived many years at Paris. He was afterwards employed by Louis XII. as minister at Venice. After a residence of some duration at Rome, he was induced by Francis I. in 1518 to organise the literary institutions designed by the king to be established at Paris. But these being postponed, Lascaris spent the remainder of his life partly in Paris, partly in Rome, and died in the latter city in 1535. Hody, de Græcis illustribus.

[d] We are indebted to Roscoe for publishing this list. But as the number of one hundred professors might lead us to expect a most comprehensive scheme, it may be mentioned that they consisted of four for theology, eleven for canon law, twenty for civil law, sixteen for medicine, two for metaphysics, five for philosophy (probably physics), two for ethics, four for logic, one for astrology (probably astronomy), two for mathematics, eighteen for rhetoric, three for Greek, and thirteen for grammar, in all a

hundred and one. The salaries are subjoined in every instance; the highest are among the medical professors; the Greek are also high. Roscoe, ii. 333, and Append. No. 89.

Roscoe remarks that medical botany was one of the sciences taught, and that it was the earliest instance. If this be right, Bonafede of Padua cannot have been the first who taught botany in Europe, as we read that he did in 1533. But in the roll of these Roman professors we only find that one was appointed ad declarationem simplicium medicinæ. I do not think this means more than the materia medica; we cannot infer that he lectured upon the plants themselves.

[e] Tiraboschi. Hody, p. 247. Roscoe, ch. 11. Leo was anticipated in his Greek editions by Chigi, a private Roman, who, with the assistance of Cornelio Benigno, and with Calliergus, a Cretan, for his printer, gave to the world two good editions of Pindar and Theocritus in 1515 and 1516.

his time the chief poets of Italy seem to have written seve-
Latin
poetry. ral of their works, though not published till afterwards. The poems of Pontanus, which naturally
belong to the fifteenth century, were first printed in 1513
and 1518; and those of Mantuan, in a collective form, about
the same time.

22. The Rosmunda of Rucellai, a tragedy in the Italian
Italian
tragedy. language, on the ancient regular model, was represented before Leo at Florence in 1515. It
was the earliest known trial of blank verse; but it is
acknowledged by Rucellai himself that the Sophonisba of
his friend Trissino, which is dedicated to Leo in the same
year, though not published till 1524, preceded and suggested his own tragedy.[f] The Sophonisba is strictly on
Sophonisba
of Trissino. the Greek model, divided only by the odes of the
chorus, but not into five portions or acts. The
speeches in this tragedy are sometimes too long, the style
unadorned, the descriptions now and then trivial. But in
general there is a classical dignity about the sentiments,
which are natural, though not novel; and the latter part,
which we should call the fifth act, is truly noble, simple,
and pathetic. Trissino was thoroughly conversant with
the Greek drama, and had imbibed its spirit: seldom has
Euripides written with more tenderness, or chosen a subject more fitted to his genius; for that of Sophonisba, in

---

[f] This dedication, with a sort of apology for writing tragedies in Italian,
will be found in Roscoe's Appendix, vol.
vi. Roscoe quotes a few words from
Rucellai's dedication of his poem,
L'Api, to Trissino, acknowledging the
latter as the inventor of blank verse.
Voi foste il primo, che questo modo di
scrivere, in versi materni, liberi delle
rime, poneste in luce. Life of Leo X.,
ch. 16. See also Ginguéné, vol. vi., and
Walker's Memoir on Italian tragedy,
as well as Tiraboschi. The earliest
Italian tragedy, which is also on the
subject of Sophonisba, by Galeotto del
Carretto, was presented to the Mar-
chioness of Mantua in 1502. But we
do not find that it was brought on the
stage; nor is it clear that it was printed
so early as the present decad. But an
edition of the Pamphila, a tragedy on

the story of Sigismunda, by Antonio da
Pistoja, was printed at Venice in 1508.
Walker, p. 11. Ginguéné has been
ignorant of this very curious piece, from
which Walker had given a few extracts,
in rhymed measures of different kinds.
Ginguéné indeed had never seen Walker's
book, and his own is the worse for it.
Walker was not a man of much vigour
of mind, but had some taste, and great
knowledge of his subject. This tragedy
is mentioned by Quadrio, iv. 58, with
the title Il Filostrato e Panfila, doi
amanti.

It may be observed, that notwithstanding the testimony of Rucellai himself above quoted, it is shown by Walker
(Appendix, No. 3) that blank verse had
been occasionally employed before Trissino.

which many have followed Trissino with inferior success, is wholly for the Greek school; it admits, with no great difficulty, of the chorus, and consequently of the unities of time and place. It must, however, always chiefly depend on Sophonisba herself; for it is not easy to make Masinissa respectable, nor has Trissino succeeded in attempting it. The long continuance of alternate speeches in single lines, frequent in this tragedy, will not displease those to whom old associations are recalled by it.

23. The Rosmunda falls, in my opinion, below the Sophonisba, though it is the work of a better poet; and perhaps in language and description it is superior. *Rosmunda of Rucellai.* What is told in narration, according to the ancient inartificial form of tragedy, is finely told; but the emotions are less represented than in the Sophonisba; the principal character is less interesting, and the story is unpleasing. Rucellai led the way to those accumulations of horrible and disgusting circumstances which deformed the European stage for a century afterwards. The Rosmunda is divided into five acts, but preserves the chorus. It contains imitations of the Greek tragedies, especially the Antigone, as the Sophonisba does of the Ajax and the Medea. Some lines in the latter, extolled by modern critics, are simply translated from the ancient tragedians.

24. Two comedies by Ariosto seem to have been acted about 1512, and were written as early as 1495, when he was but twenty-one years old, which enti- *Comedies of Ariosto.* tles him to the praise of having first conceived and carried into effect the idea of regular comedies, in imitation of the ancient, though Bibbiena had the advantage of first occupying the stage with his Calandra. The Cassaria and Suppositi of Ariosto are, like the Calandra, free imitations of the manner of Plautus, in a spirited and natural dialogue, and with that graceful flow of language which appears spontaneous in all his writings.[g]

25. The north of Italy still endured the warfare of

---

[g] Ginguéné, vi. 183, 218, has given a full analysis of these celebrated comedies. They are placed next to those of Machiavel by most Italian critics.

stranger armies : Ravenna, Novara, Marignan, attest the well-
Books printed in Italy. fought contention. Aldus, however, returning to
Venice in 1512, published many editions before his
death in 1516. Pindar, Plato, and Lysias first appeared in
1513, Athenæus in 1514, Xenophon, Strabo, and Pausanias
in 1516, Plutarch's Lives in 1517. The Aldine press then
continued under his father-in-law, Andrew Asola, but with
rather diminished credit. It appears that the works printed
during this period, from 1511 to 1520, were, at Rome 116,
at Milan 91, at Florence 133, and at Venice 511. This is,
perhaps, less than from the general renown of Leo's age
we should have expected. We may select, among the
Cælius Rhodiginus. original publications, the Lectiones Antiquæ of
Cælius Rhodiginus (1516), and a little treatise on
Italian grammar by Fortunio, which has no claim to notice
but as the earliest book on the subject.[h] The former,
though not the first, appears to have been by far the best
and most extensive collection hitherto made from the
stores of antiquity. It is now hardly remembered; but
obtained almost universal praise, even from severe critics,
for the deep erudition of its author, who, in a somewhat
rude style, pours forth explanations of obscure, and emendations of corrupted passages, with profuse display of
knowledge in the customs, and even philosophy of the
ancients, but more especially in medicine and botany.
Yet he seems to have inserted much without discrimination
of its value, and often without authority. A more perfect
edition was published in 1550, extending to thirty books
instead of sixteen.[i]

26. It may be seen that Italy, with all the lustre of
Greek print-ed in France and Ger-many. Leo's reputation, was not distinguished by any
very remarkable advance in learning during his
pontificate ; and I believe it is generally admitted
that the elegant biography of Roscoe, in making the public

---

[h] Regole grammaticali della volgar
lingua. (Ancona, 1516.) Questo libro
fuor di dubbio è stato il primo che si
videsse stampato, a darne insegnamenti
d' Italiana, non già eloquenza, ma lingua. Fontanini dell' eloquenza Italiana,
p. 5. Fifteen editions were printed
within six years ; a decisive proof of
the importance attached to the subject.
[i] Blount. Biogr. univ. art. Rhodiginus.

more familiar with the subject, did not raise the previous estimation of its hero and of his times. Meanwhile the Cisalpine regions were gaining ground upon their brilliant neighbour. From the Parisian press issued in these ten years eight hundred books; among which were a Greek Lexicon by Aleander, in 1512, and four more little grammatical works, with a short romance in Greek.[k] This is trifling indeed; but in the cities on the Rhine something more was done in that language. A Greek grammar, probably quite elementary, was published at Wittenberg in 1511; one at Strasburg in 1512,—thrice reprinted in the next three years. These were succeeded by a translation of Theodore Gaza's grammar by Erasmus, in 1516, by the Progymnasmata Græcæ Literaturæ of Luscinius, in 1517, and by the Introductiones in Linguam Græcam of Croke, in 1520. Isocrates and Lucian appeared at Strasburg in 1515; the first book of the Iliad next year, besides four smaller tracts;[n] several more followed before the end of the decad. At Basle the excellent printer Frobenius, an intimate friend of Erasmus, had established himself as early as 1491.[o] Besides the great edition of the New Testament by Erasmus, which issued from his press, we find, before the close of 1520, the Works and Days of Hesiod, the Greek Lexicon of Aldus, the Rhetoric and Poetics of Aristotle, the first two books of the Odyssey, and several grammatical treatises. At Cologne two or three small Greek pieces were printed in 1517. And Louvain, besides the Plutus of Aristophanes in 1518, and three or four others about the same time, sent forth in the year 1520 six Greek editions, among which were Lucian, Theocritus, and two tragedies of Euripides.[p] We may hence perceive, that the

---

[k] [It is said in Liron, Singularités historiques, i. 490, that one Cheradamus taught Greek at Paris about 1517, and published a Greek Lexicon there in 1523: Lexicon Græcum, cæteris omnibus aut in Italia aut Gallia Germaniave, antehac excusis multo locupletius, utpote supra tér mille additiones Basiliensi Lexico, A.D. 1522 apud Carionem impresso, adjectas. I do not find this Lexicon mentioned by Brunet or Watts. —1842.]

[n] These were published by Luscinius (Nachtigall), a native of Strasburg, and one of the chief members of the literary academy, established by Wimpheling in that city. Biogr. univ.

[o] Biogr. univ.

[p] The whole number of books, according to Panzer, printed from 1511 to 1520 at Strasburg, was 373; at Basle, 289; at Cologne, 120; at Leipsic, 462; at Louvain, 57. It may be worth while to remind the reader once more that these

Greek language now first became known and taught in Germany and in the Low Countries.

27. It is evident that these works were chiefly designed for students in the universities. But it is to be observed, that Greek literature was now much more cultivated than before. In France there were, indeed, not many names that could be brought forward; but Lefevre of Etaples, commonly called Faber Stapulensis, was equal to writing criticisms on the Greek Testament of Erasmus. He bears a high character among contemporary critics for his other writings, which are chiefly on theological and philosophical subjects; but it appears by his age that he must have come late to the study of Greek.[q] That difficult language was more easily mastered by younger men. Germany had already produced some deserving of remembrance. A correspondent of Erasmus, in 1515, writes to recommend Œcolampadius as 'not unlearned in Greek literature.'[r] Melanchthon was, even in his early youth, deemed competent to criticise Erasmus himself. At the age of sixteen, he lectured on the Greek and Latin authors of antiquity. He was the first who printed Terence as verse.[s] The library of this great scholar was, in 1835, sold in London, and was proved to be his own by innumerable marginal notes of illustration and correction. Beatus Rhenanus stands perhaps next to him as a scholar; and we may add the names of Luscinius, of Bilibald Pirckheimer, a learned senator of Nuremberg, who made several translations, and of Petrus Mosellanus, who became about 1518 lecturer in Greek at Leipsic.[t] He succeeded our distinguished countryman,

Greek scholars in these countries.

---

lists must be very defective as to the slighter class of publications, which have often perished to every copy. Panzer is reckoned more imperfect after 1500 than before. Biogr. universelle. In England, we find thirty-six by Pynson, and sixty-six by Wynkyn de Worde, within these ten years.

[q] Jortin's Erasmus, i. 92. Bayle, Fevre d'Etaples. Blount. Biogr. univ. Febure d'Etaples.

[r] Erasmus himself says afterwards, Œcolampadius satis novit Græcè, Latini sermonis rudior; quanquam ille magis

peccat indiligentia quam imperitia.

[s] Cox's Life of Melanchthon, p. 19. Melanchthon wrote Greek verse indifferently and incorrectly, but Latin with spirit and elegance; specimens of both are given in Dr. Cox's valuable biography.

[t] The lives and characters of Rhenanus, Pirckheimer, and Mosellanus will be found in Blount, Niceron, and the Biographie universelle; also in Gerdes's Historia evangel. Renov., Melchior Adam, and other less common books.

Richard Croke, a pupil of Grocyn, who had been invited to
Leipsic in 1514, with the petty salary of fifteen guilders, but
with the privilege of receiving other remuneration from his
scholars, and had the signal honour of first imbuing the
students of Northern Germany with a knowledge of that
language.[u] One or two trifling works on Greek grammar
were published by Croke during this decennium. Ceratinus,
who took his name, in the fanciful style of the times, from
his birthplace, Horn in Holland, was now professor of Greek
at Louvain ; and in 1525, on the recommendation of Erasmus,
became the successor of Mosellanus at Leipsic.[x] William
Cop, a native of Basle, and physician to Francis I., published in this period some translations from Hippocrates and
Galen.

28. Cardinal Ximenes about the beginning of the century founded a college at Alcalá, his favourite   Colleges at
university, for the three learned languages. This   Louvain.
example was followed by Jerome Busleiden, who by his
last testament, in 1516 or 1517, established a similar foundation at Louvain.[y] From this source proceeded many men
of conspicuous erudition and ability ; and Louvain, through
its Collegium trilingue, became in a still higher degree
than Deventer had been in the fifteenth century, not only
the chief seat of Belgian learning, but the means of diffusing it over parts of Germany. Its institution was resisted

---

[u] Crocus regnat in Academia Lipsi-
ensi, publicitus Græcas docens litteras.
Erasm. Epist. clvii. 5th June, 1514.
Eichhorn says, that Conrad Celtes and
others had taught Latin only, iii. 272.
Camerarius, who studied for three years
under Croke, gives him a very high character; qui primus putabatur ita docuisse
Græcam linguam in Germania, ut plane
perdisci illam posse, et quid momenti ad
omnem doctrinæ eruditionem atque cul-
tum hujus cognitio allatura esse videretur, nostri homines sese intelligere arbi-
trarentur. Vita Melanchthonis, p. 27 ;
and Vita Eobani Hessi, p. 4. He was received at Leipsic 'like a heavenly messen-
ger:' every one was proud of knowing
him, of paying whatever he demanded,
of attending him at any hour of the day
or night. Melanchthon apud Meiners,
i. 163. A pretty good life of Croke is

in Chalmers's Biographical Dictionary.
Bayle does not mention him. Croke
was educated at King's College, Cambridge, to which he went from Eton in
1506, and is said to have learned Greek
at Oxford from Grocyn, while still a
scholar of King's.

[x] Erasmus gives a very high character
of Ceratinus. Græcæ linguæ peritia su-
perat vel tres Mosellanos, nec inferior,
ut arbitror, Romanæ linguæ facundia.
Epist. DCCxxxvii. Ceratinus Græcanicæ
literaturæ tam exacte callens, ut vix
unum aut alterum habeat Italia quicum
dubitem hunc committere. Magnæ doctrinæ erat Mosellanus, spei majoris, et
amabam unicè hominis ingenium, nec
falso dicunt odiosas esse comparationes ;
sed hoc ipsa causa me compellit dicere,
longe alia res est. Epist. DCCxxxviii.

[y] Bayle, art. Busleiden.

by the monks and theologians, unyielding, though beaten, adversaries of literature.[z]

29. It cannot be said, that many yet on this side of the Alps wrote Latin well. Budæus is harsh and un-

Latin style in France.

polished; Erasmus fluent, spirited, and never at a loss to express his meaning; nor is his style much defaced by barbarous words, though by no means exempt from them; yet it seldom reaches a point of classical elegance. Francis Sylvius (probably Dubois), brother of a celebrated physician, endeavoured to inspire a taste for purity of style in the university of Paris. He had, however, acquired it himself late, for some of his writings are barbarous. The favourable influence of Sylvius was hardly earlier than 1520.[a] The writer most solicitous about his diction was Longolius (Christopher de Longueil, a native of Malines), the only true Ciceronian out of Italy; in which country, however, he passed so much time, that he is hardly to be accounted a mere Cisalpine. Like others of the Ciceronian denomination, he was more ambitious of saying common things well, than of producing what was intrinsically worthy of being remembered.

30. We have the imposing testimony of Erasmus him-

Greek scholars in England.

self, that neither France nor Germany stood so high about this period as England. That country, he says, so distant from Italy, stands next to it in the esteem of the learned. This, however, is written in 1524. About the end of the present decennial period we can produce a not very small number of persons possessing a competent acquaintance with the Greek tongue, more, perhaps, than could be traced in France, though all together might not weigh as heavy as Budæus alone. Such were Grocyn, the patriarch of English learning, who died in 1519; Linacre, whose translation of Galen, first printed in 1521, is one of the few in that age that escape censure for inelegance or incorrectness; Latimer, beloved and admired by his friends, but of whom we have no memorial in any writings of his own; More, known as a Greek scholar by epigrams of some

---

[z] Von der Hardt, Hist. Litt. Reformat.
[a] Bayle, art. Sylvius.

merit; [b] Lilly, master of St. Paul's school, who had acquired Greek at Rhodes, but whose reputation is better preserved by the grammars that bear his name; Lupsett, who is said to have learned from Lilly, and who taught some time at Oxford; Richard Croke, already named; Gerard Lister, a physician, to whom Erasmus gives credit for skill in the three languages; Pace and Tunstall, both men well known in the history of those times; Lee and Stokesley, afterwards bishops, the former of whom published Annotations on the Greek Testament of Erasmus at Basle in 1520, [c] and probably Gardiner; Clement, one of Wolsey's first lecturers at Oxford; [d] Brian, Wakefield, Bullock, Tyndale, and a few more whose names appear in Pits and Wood. We could not of course, without presumption, attempt to enumerate every person who at this time was not wholly unacquainted with the Greek language. Yet it would be an error, on the other hand, to make a large allowance for omissions; much less to conclude that every man who might enjoy some reputation

---

[b] The Greek verses of More and Lilly, Progymnasmata Mori et Lillii, were published at Basle, 1518. It is in this volume that the distich, about which some curiosity has been shown, is found; Inveni portum, spes et fortuna valete, &c. But it is a translation from an old Greek epigram.

Quid tandem non præstitisset admirabilis ista naturæ felicitas, si hoc ingenium instituisset Italia? si totum Musarum sacris vacasset? si ad justam frugem ac velut autumnum suum maturuisset? Epigrammata lusit adolescens admodum, ac pleraque puer; Britanniam suam nunquam egressus est, nisi semel atque iterum principis sui nomine legatione functus apud Flandros. Præter rem uxoriam, præter curas domesticas, præter publici muneris functionem et causarum undas, tot tantisque regni negotiis distrahitur, ut mireris esse otium vel cogitandi de libris. Epist. clxix. Aug. 1517. In the Ciceronianus he speaks of More with more discriminating praise, and the passage is illustrative of that just quoted.

[c] Erasmus does not spare Lee. Epist. ccxlviii. Quo uno nihilunquam adhuc terra produxit, nec arrogantius, nec virulentius, nec stultius. This was the tone

of the age towards any adversary, who was not absolutely out of reach of such epithets. In another place, he speaks of Lee as nuper Græcæ linguæ rudimentis initiatus. Ep. cccclxxxxi.

[d] Knight says (apud Jortin, i. 45) that Clement was the first lecturer at Oxford in Greek after Linacre, and that he was succeeded by Lupsett. And this seems, as to the fact that they did successively teach, to be confirmed by More. Jortin, ii. 396. But the Biographia Britannica, art. Wolsey, asserts that they were appointed to the chair ot rhetoric or humanity; and that Calpurnius, a native of Greece, was the first professor of the language. No authority is quoted by the editors; but I have found it confirmed by Caius in a little treatise De Pronuntiatione Græcæ et Latinæ Linguæ. Novit, he says, Oxoniensis schola, quemadmodum ipsa Græcia pronuntiavit, ex Matthæo Calpurnio Græco, quem ex Græciâ Oxoniam Græcarum literarum gratia perduxerat Thomas Wolseus, de bonis literis optime meritus cardinalis, cum non alia ratione pronuntiant illi, quam quâ, nos jam profitemur. Caius de pronunt. Græc. et Lat. Linguæ, edit. Jebb, p 228.

in a learned profession could in a later generation have passed for a scholar. Colet, for example, and Fisher, men as distinguished as almost any of that age, were unacquainted with the Greek tongue, and both made some efforts to attain it at an advanced age.[e] It was not till the year 1517 that the first Greek lecture was established at Oxford by Fox, bishop of Hereford, in his new foundation of Corpus Christi College. Wolsey, in 1519, endowed a regular professorship in the university. It was about the same year that Fisher, chancellor of the university of Cambridge, sent down Richard Croke, lately returned from Leipsic, to tread in the footsteps of Erasmus as teacher of Greek.[f] But this was in advance of our neighbours; for no public instruction in that language was yet given in France.

31. By the statutes of St. Paul's school, dated in 1518, the master is to be 'lerned in good and clene Latin literature, and also in Greke, iff such may be gotten.' Of the boys he says, 'I wolde they were taught always in good literature both Latin and Greke.' But it does not follow from hence that Greek was actually taught; and considering the want of lexicons and grammars, none of which, as we shall see, were published in England for many years afterwards, we shall be apt to think that little instruction could have been given.[g] This, however, is not conclu-

Mode of teaching in schools.

---

[e] Nunc dolor me tenet, says Colet in 1516, quod non didicerim Græcum sermonem, sine cujus peritia nihil sumus. From a later epistle of Erasmus, where he says, Colctus strenue Græcatur, it seems likely that he actually made some progress; but at his age it would not be very considerable. Latimer dissuaded Fisher from the attempt, unless he could procure a master from Italy, which Erasmus thought needless. Epist. ccclxiii. In an edition of his Adages, he says, Joannes Fischerus tres linguas ætate jam vergente non vulgari studio amplectitur, Chil. iv. cent. v. 1.

[f] Greek had not been neglected at Cambridge during the interval, according to a letter of Bullock (in Latin Bovillus) to Erasmus in 1516 from thence. Hic acriter incumbunt literis Græcis, optantque non mediocriter tuum adventum, et hi magnopere favent tuæ huic in Novum Testamentum editioni. It is

probable that Cranmer was a pupil of Croke; for in the deposition of the latter before Mary's commissioners in 1555, he says that he had known the archbishop thirty-six years, which brings us to his own first lectures at Cambridge. Todd's Life of Cranmer, ii. 449. But Cranmer may have known something of the language before, and is, not improbably, one of those to whom Bullock alludes.

[g] In a letter of Erasmus on the death of Colet in 1522, Epist. ccccxxxv. (and in Jortin's App. ii. 315), though he describes the course of education at St. Paul's school rather diffusely, and in a strain of high panegyric, there is not a syllable of allusion to the study of Greek. Pits, however, in an account of one William Horman, tells us that he was ad collegium Etonense studiorum causa missus, ubi avide haustis litteris humanioribus, *perceptisque Græcæ linguæ rudimentis*, dignus habitus est qui Canta-

sive, and would lead us to bring down the date of philological learning in our public seminaries much too low. The process of learning without books was tedious and difficult, but not impracticable for the diligent. The teacher provided himself with a lexicon which was in common use among his pupils, and with one of the grammars published on the Continent, from which he gave oral lectures, and portions of which were transcribed by each student. The books read in the lecture-room were probably copied out in the same manner, the abbreviations giving some facility to a cursive hand; and thus the deficiency of impressions was in some degree supplied, just as before the invention of printing. The labour of acquiring knowledge strengthened, as it always does, the memory; it excited an industry which surmounted every obstacle, and yielded to no fatigue; and we may thus account for that copiousness of verbal learning which some-times astonishes us in the scholars of the sixteenth century, and in which they seem to surpass the more exact philologers of later ages.

32. It is to be observed, that we rather extol a small number of men who have struggled against diffi- *Few classical works printed here.* culties, than put in a claim for any diffusion of literature in England, which would be very far from the truth. No classical works were yet printed, except four editions of Virgil's Bucolics, a small treatise of Seneca, the first book of Cicero's Epistles (the latter at Oxford in 1519), all merely of course for learners. We do not reckon Latin grammars. And as yet no Greek types had been employed. In the spirit of truth, we cannot quite take to ourselves the compliment of Erasmus; there must evidently have been a far greater diffusion of sound learning in Germany, where professors of Greek had for some time been established in all

---

brigiam ad altiores disciplinas destina-retur. Horman became Græcæ linguæ peritissimus, and returned, as head master, to Eton; quo tempore in litteris humanioribus scholares illic insigniter erudivit. He wrote several works, partly grammatical, of which Pits gives the titles, and died, *plenus dierum,* in 1535.

If we could depend on the accuracy of all this, we must suppose that Greek was taught at Eton so early, that one who acquired the rudiments of it in that school might die at an advanced age in 1535. But this is not to be received on Pits's authority. And I find, in Harwood's Alumni Etonenses, that Horman became head master as early as 1485; no one will readily believe that he could have learned Greek while at school; and the fact is, that he was not educated at Eton, but at Winchester.

the universities, and where a long list of men ardent in the
cultivation of letters could be adduced.[h] Erasmus had a
panegyrical humour towards his friends, of whom there were
many in England.

33. Scotland had, as might naturally be expected, par-
State of
learning in
Scotland. taken still less of Italian light than the south of
Britain. But the reigning king, contemporary with
Henry VII., gave proofs of greater good-will towards letters.
A statute of James IV., in 1496, enacts that gentlemen's
sons should be sent to school in order to learn Latin. Such
provisions were too indefinite for execution, even if the royal
authority had been greater than it was; but they serve to
display the temper of the sovereign. His natural son,
Alexander, on whom, at a very early age, he conferred the
archbishopric of St. Andrew's, was the pupil of Erasmus in
the Greek language. The latter speaks very highly of this
promising scion of the house of Stuart in one of his adages.[i]
But, at the age of twenty, he perished with his royal father
on the disastrous day of Flodden Field. Learning had made
no sensible progress in Scotland ; and the untoward circumstances of the next twenty years were far from giving it
encouragement. The translation of the Æneid by Gawin
Douglas, bishop of Dunkeld, though we are not at present
on the subject of poetry, may be here mentioned in connection with Scottish literature. It was completed about 1513,
though the earliest edition is not till 1553. 'This translation,' says Warton, 'is executed with equal spirit and
fidelity ; and is a proof that the Lowland Scotch and English
languages were now nearly the same. I mean the style of
composition, more especially in the glaring affectation of
anglicising Latin words. The several books are introduced
with metrical prologues, which are often highly poetical, and
show that Douglas's proper walk was original poetry.'
Warton did well to explain his rather startling expression,
that the Lowland Scotch and English languages were then
nearly the same ; for I will venture to say, that no Englishman, without guessing at every other word, could understand

---

[h] Such a list is given by Meiners, i.
154, of the supporters of Reuchlin, who
comprised all the real scholars of Germany : he enumerates sixty-seven, which
might doubtless be enlarged.
[i] Chil. ii. cent. v. 1.

the long passage which he proceeds to quote from Gawin Douglas. It is true that the differences consisted mainly in pronunciation, and consequently in orthography; but this is the great cause of diversity in dialect. The character of Douglas's original poetry seems to be that of the middle ages in general,—prolix, though sometimes animated, description of sensible objects.[k]

34. We must not leave England without mention of the only work of genius that she can boast in this age, the Utopia[m] of Sir Thomas More. Perhaps we scarcely appreciate highly enough the spirit and originality of this fiction, which ought to be considered with regard to the barbarism of the times, and the meagreness of preceding inventions. The Republic of Plato no doubt furnished More with the germ of his perfect society;[n] but it would be unreasonable to deny him the merit of having struck out the fiction of its real existence from his own fertile imagination; and it is manifest, that some of his most distinguished successors in the same walk of romance, especially Swift, were largely indebted to his reasoning as well as inventive talents. Those who read the Utopia in Burnet's translation may believe that they are in Brobdignag; so similar is the vein of satirical humour and easy language. If false and impracticable theories are found in the Utopia (and perhaps he knew them to be such), this is in a much greater degree true of the Platonic Republic; and they are more than compensated by the sense of justice and humanity that pervades it, and his bold censures on the vices of power. These are remarkable in a courtier of Henry VIII.; but, in the first years of Nero, the voice of Seneca was heard without resentment. Nor had Henry much to take to himself in the reprehension of parsimonious accumulation of wealth, which was meant for his father's course of government.

Utopia of More.

35. It is possible that some passages in the Utopia, which are neither philosophical nor compatible with just principles of morals, were thrown out as mere

Its inconsistency with his opinions.

---

[k] Warton, iii. 111.

[m] Utopia is named from a king Utopus. I mention this, because some have shown their learning by changing the word to Eutopia.

[n] [Perhaps this is at least doubtful; neither the Republic, nor the Laws, of Plato bear any resemblance to the Utopia.—1847.]

paradoxes of a playful mind; nor is it easy to reconcile his language as to the free toleration of religious worship with those acts of persecution which have raised the only dark cloud on the memory of this great man. He positively indeed declares for punishing those who insult the religion of others, which might be an excuse for his severity towards the early reformers. But his latitude as to the acceptability of all religions with God, as to their identity in essential principles, and as to the union of all sects in a common worship, could no more be made compatible with his later writings or conduct, than his sharp satire against the court of Rome for breach of faith, or against the monks and friars for laziness and beggary. Such changes, however, are very common, as we may have abundantly observed, in all seasons of revolutionary commotions. Men provoke these, sometimes in the gaiety of their hearts with little design, sometimes with more deliberate intention, but without calculation of the entire consequences, or of their own courage to encounter them. And when such men, like More, are of very quick parts, they are often found to be not over retentive of their opinions, and have little difficulty in abandoning any speculative notion, especially when, like those in the Utopia, it can never have had the least influence upon their behaviour. We may acknowledge, after all, that the Utopia gives us the impression of its having proceeded rather from a very ingenious than a profound mind; and this, apparently, is what we ought to think of Sir Thomas More. The Utopia is said to have been first printed at Louvain in 1516;° it certainly appeared at the close of the preceding year; but the edition of Basle in 1518, under the care of Erasmus, is the earliest that bears a date. It was greatly admired on the Continent;

° Of an undated edition, to which Panzer gives the name of editio princeps, there is a copy in the British Museum, and another was in Mr. Heber's library. Dibdin's Utopia, 1808, preface, cxi. It appears from a letter of Montjoy to Erasmus, dated 4th Jan. 1516, that he had received the Utopia, which must therefore have been printed in 1515; and it was reprinted once at least in 1516 or 1517. Erasm. Epist. cciii. ccv. Append. Ep. xliv. lxxix. ccli. et alibi. Panzer mentions one at Louvain in December, 1516. This volume by Dr. Dibdin is a reprint of Robinson's early and almost contemporary translation. That by Burnet, 1685, is more known, and I think it good. Burnet, and I believe some of the Latin editions, omit a specimen of the Utopian language, and some Utopian poetry; which probably was thought too puerile.

indeed there had been little or nothing of equal spirit and originality in Latin since the revival of letters.

36. The French themselves give Francis I. the credit of having been the father of learning in that country. Galland, in a funeral panegyric on that prince, asks if at his accession (in 1513) any one man in France could read Greek or write Latin. Now this is an absurd question, when we recollect the names of Budæus, Longolius, and Faber Stapulensis; yet it shows that there could have been very slender pretensions to classical learning in the kingdom. Erasmus, in his Ciceronianus, enumerates among French scholars, not only Budæus, Faber, and the eminent printer Jodocus Badius (a Fleming by birth), whom, in point of style, he seems to put above Budæus, but John Pin, Nicolas Berald, Francis Deloin, Lazarus Baif, and Ruel. This was however in 1529, and the list assuredly is not long. But as his object was to show that few men of letters were worthy of being reckoned fine writers, he does not mention Longueil, who was one; or whom, perhaps, he might omit, as being then dead.

Learning restored in France.

37. Budæus and Erasmus were now at the head of the literary world; and as the friends of each behaved rather too much like partisans, a kind of rivalry in public reputation began, which soon extended to themselves, and lessened their friendship. Erasmus seems to have been, in a certain degree, the aggressor; at least some of his letters to Budæas indicate an irritability, which the other, as far as appears, had not provoked. Budæus had published in 1514 an excellent treatise De Asse, the first which explained the denominations and values of Roman money in all periods of history.[p] Erasmus sometimes alludes to this with covert jealousy. It was set up by a party against his Adages, which he justly considered more full of original thoughts and extensive learning. But Budæus understood Greek better; he had learned it with prodigious labour, and probably about the same time with Erasmus, so that the comparison between them was not unnatural. The name of one is at present only retained by scholars, and that of the other

Jealousy of Erasmus and Budæus.

---

[p] Quod opus ejus, says Vives, in a letter to Erasmus (Ep. DCX.), Hermolaos omnes, Picos, Politianos, Gazas, Vallas cunctam Italiam pudefecit.

by all mankind; so different is contemporary and posthumous reputation. It is just to add that, although Erasmus had written to Budæus in far too sarcastic a tone,[q] under the smart of that literary sensitiveness which was very strong in his temper, yet when the other began to take serious offence, and to threaten a discontinuance of their correspondence, he made amends by an affectionate letter, which ought to have restored their good understanding. Budæus, however, who seems to have kept his resentments longer than his quickminded rival, continued to write peevish letters; and fresh circumstances arose afterwards to keep up his jealousy.[r]

38. Erasmus diffuses a lustre over his age, which no other Character of Erasmus. name among the learned supplies. The qualities which gave him this superiority were his quickness of apprehension, united with much industry, his liveliness of fancy, his wit and good sense. He is not a very profound thinker, but an acute observer; and the age for original thinking was hardly come. What there was of it in More produced little fruit. In extent of learning, no one perhaps was altogether his equal. Budæus, with more accurate scholarship, knew little of theology, and might be less ready perhaps in general literature than Erasmus. Longolius, Sadolet, and several others, wrote Latin far more ele-

---

[q] Epist. cc. I quote the numeration of the Leyden edition.

[r] Erasmi Epistolæ, passim. The publication of his Ciceronianus, in 1528, renewed the irritation; in this he gave a sort of preference to Badius over Budæus, in respect to style alone; observing that the latter had great excellences of another kind. The French scholars made this a national quarrel, pretending that Erasmus was prejudiced against their country. He defends himself in his epistles so prolixly and elaborately, as to confirm the suspicion, not of this absurdly imputed dislike to the French, but of some little desire to pique Budæus. Epigrams in Greek were written at Paris against him by Lascaris and Toussain; and thus Erasmus, by an unlucky inability to restrain his pen from sly sarcasm, multiplied the enemies, whom an opposite part of his character, its spirit of temporising and timidity, was always raising up. Erasm. Epist. mvxi. et alibi.

This rather unpleasing correspondence between two great men, professing friendship, yet covertly jealous of each other, is not ill described by Von der Hardt, in the Historia Litteraria Reformationis. Mirum dictu, qui undique aculei, sub mellitissima oratione, inter blandimenta continua. Genius utriusque argutissimus, qui vellendo et acerbe pungendo nullibi videretur referre sanguinem aut vulnus in'erre. Possint profecto hæ literæ Budæum inter et Erasmum illustre esse et incomparabile exemplar delicatissimæ sed et perquam aculeatæ concertationis, quæ videretur suavissimo absolvi risu et velut familiarissimo palpo. De alterutrius integritate neuter visus dubitare; uterque tamen semper auceps, tot annis commercio frequentissimo. Dissimulandi artificium inexplicabile, quod attenti lectoris admirationem vehat, eumque præ dissertationum dulcedine subamara in stuporem vertat. p. 46.

gantly ; but they were of comparatively superficial erudition, and had neither his keen wit nor his vigour of intellect. As to theological learning, the great Lutheran divines must have been at least his equals in respect of Scriptural knowledge, and some of them possessed an acquaintance with Hebrew, of which Erasmus knew nothing ; but he had probably the advantage in the study of the fathers. It is to be observed, that by far the greater part of his writings are theological. The rest either belong to philology and ancient learning, as the Adages, the Ciceronianus, and the various grammatical treatises, or may be reckoned effusions of his wit, as the Colloquies and the Encomium Moriæ.

39. Erasmus, about 1517, published a very enlarged edition of his Adages, which had already grown with the His Adages severe on kings. growth of his own erudition. It is impossible to distinguish the progressive accessions they received without a comparison of editions ; and some probably belong to a later period than the present. The Adages, as we read them, display a surprising extent of intimacy with Greek and Roman literature.[s] Far the greater portion is illustrative ; but Erasmus not unfrequently sprinkles his explanations of ancient phrase with moral or literary remarks of some poignancy. The most remarkable, in every sense, are those which reflect with excessive bitterness and freedom on kings and priests. Jortin has slightly alluded to some of these ; but they may deserve more particular notice, as displaying the character of the man, and perhaps the secret opinions of his age.

40. Upon the adage, Frons occipitio prior, meaning, that every one should do his own business, Erasmus takes Instances in illustration. the opportunity to observe, that no one requires more attention to this than a prince, if he will act as a real prince, and not as a robber. But at present our kings and bishops are only the hands, eyes, and ears of others, careless of the state, and of everything but their own pleasure.[t] This, how-

---

[s] In one passage, under the proverb Herculei labores, he expatiates on the immense labour with which this work, his Adages, had been compiled ; mentioning, among other difficulties, the prodigious corruption of the text in all Latin and Greek manuscripts, so that it scarce ever happened that a passage could be quoted from them without a certainty or suspicion of some erroneous reading.

[t] Chil. i. cent. ii. 19.

ever, is a trifle. In another proverb he bursts out : ' Let any one turn over the pages of ancient or modern history, scarcely in several generations will you find one or two princes whose folly has not inflicted the greatest misery on mankind.' And after much more of the same kind : ' I know not whether much of this is not to be imputed to ourselves. We trust the rudder of a vessel, where a few sailors and some goods alone are in jeopardy, to none but skilful pilots ; but the state, wherein the safety of so many thousands is concerned, we put into any hands. A charioteer must learn, reflect upon, and practise his art ; a prince need only be born. Yet government, as it is the most honourable, so is it the most difficult of all sciences. And shall we choose the master of a ship, and not choose him who is to have the care of many cities, and so many souls ? But the usage is too long established for us to subvert. Do we not see that noble cities are erected by the people ; that they are destroyed by princes ? that the community grows rich by the industry of its citizens, is plundered by the rapacity of its princes ? that good laws are enacted by popular magistrates, are violated by these princes ? that the people love peace ; that princes excite war ? ' [u]

41. ' It is the aim of the guardians of a prince,' he exclaims in another passage, ' that he may never become a man. The nobility, who fatten on public calamity, endeavour to plunge him into pleasures, that he may never learn what is his duty. Towns are burned, lands are wasted, temples are plundered, innocent citizens are slaughtered, while the prince is playing at dice, or dancing, or amusing himself

---

[u] Quin omnes et veterum et neotericorum annales evolve, nimirum ita comperies, vix sæculis aliquot unum aut alterum extitisse principem, qui non insigni stultitiâ maximam perniciem invexerit rebus humanis. . . Et haud scio, an nonnulla hujus mali pars nobis ipsis sit imputanda. Clavum navis non committimus nisi ejus rei perito, quod quatuor vectorum aut paucarum mercium sit periculum ; et rempublicam, in qua tot hominum millia periclitantur, cuivis committimus. Ut auriga fiat aliquis discit artem, exercet, meditatur ; at ut princeps sit aliquis, satis esse putamus natum esse. Atqui rectè gerere principatum, ut est munus omnium longe pulcherrimum, ita est omnium etiam multo difficillimum. Deligis, cui navem committas, non deligis cui tot urbes, tot hominum capita credas ? Sed istud receptius est, quam ut convelli possit.

An non videmus egregia oppida a populo condi, a principibus subverti ? rempublicam civium industria ditescere, principum rapacitate spoliari ? bonas leges ferri a plebeiis magistratibus, a principibus violari ? populum studere paci, principes excitare bellum ?

with puppets, or hunting, or drinking. O race of the Bruti, long since extinct! O blind and blunted thunderbolts of Jupiter! We know indeed that those corrupters of princes will render account to Heaven, but not easily to us.' He passes soon afterwards to bitter invective against the clergy, especially the regular orders.[x]

42. In explaining the adage, Sileni Alcibiadis, referring to things which, appearing mean and trifling, are really precious, he has many good remarks on persons and things, of which the secret worth is not understood at first sight. But thence passing over to what he calls inversi Sileni, those who seem great to the vulgar, and are really despicable, he expatiates on kings and priests, whom he seems to hate with the fury of a philosopher of the last century. It must be owned he is very prolix and declamatory. He here attacks the temporal power of the church with much plainness; we cannot wonder that his Adages required mutilation at Rome.

43. But by much the most amusing and singular of the Adages is Scarabæus aquilam quærit; the meaning of which, in allusion to a fable that the beetle, in revenge for an injury, destroyed the eggs of the eagle, is explained to be, that the most powerful may be liable to the resentment of the weakest. Erasmus here returns to the attack upon kings still more bitterly and pointed than before. There is nothing in the Contre un of La Boetie, nothing, we may say, in the most seditious libel of our own time, more indignant and cutting against regal government than this long declamation : 'Let any physiognomist, not a blunderer in his trade, consider the look and features of an eagle, those rapacious and wicked eyes, that threatening curve of the beak, those cruel cheeks, that stern front, will he not at once recognise the image of a king, a magnificent and majestic king? Add to these a dark, ill-omened colour, an unpleasing, dreadful, appalling voice, and that threatening scream, at which every kind

---

[x] Miro studio curant tutores, ne unquam vir sit princeps. Adnituntur optimates, ii qui publicis malis saginantur, ut voluptatibus sit quam effœminatissimus, ne quid eorum sciat, quæ maxime decet scire principem. Exuruntur vici, vastantur agri, diripiuntur templa, trucidantur immeriti cives, sacra profanaque miscentur, dum princeps interim otiosus ludit aleam, dum saltitat, dum oblectat se morionibus, dum venatur, dum amat, dum potat. O Brutorum genus jam olim extinctum! o fulmen Jovis aut cæcum aut obtusum! Neque dubium est, quin isti principum corruptores pœnas Deo daturi sint, sed sero nobis.

of animal trembles. Every one will acknowledge this type, who has learned how terrible are the threats of princes, even uttered in jest. At this scream of the eagle the people tremble, the senate shrinks, the nobility cringes, the judges concur, the divines are dumb, the lawyers assent, the laws and constitutions give way; neither right nor religion, neither justice nor humanity avail. And thus while there are so many birds of sweet and melodious song, the unpleasant and unmusical scream of the eagle alone has more power than all the rest.' [y]

44. Erasmus now gives the rein still more to his fancy. He imagines different animals, emblematic no doubt of mankind, in relation to his eagle. 'There is no agreement between the eagle and the fox, not without great disadvantage to the vulpine race; in which however they are perhaps worthy of their fate, for having refused aid to the hares when they sought an alliance against the eagle, as is related in the Annals of Quadrupeds, from which Homer borrowed his Battle of the Frogs and Mice.' [z] I suppose that the foxes mean the nobility, and the hares the people. Some allusions to animals that follow I do not well understand. Another is more pleasing: 'It is not surprising,' he says, 'that the eagle agrees ill with the swans, those poetic birds; we may wonder more, that so warlike an animal is often overcome by them.' He sums up all thus : 'Of all birds the

---

[y] Age si quis mihi physiognomon non omnino malus vultum ipsum et os aquilæ diligentius contempletur, oculos avidos atque improbos, rictum minacem, genas truculentas, frontem torvam, denique illud quod Cyrum Persarum regem tantopere delectavit in principe γρυπὸν, nonne plane regium quoddam simulacrum agnoscet, magnificum et majestatis plenum. Accedit huc et color ipse funestus, teter et inauspicatus, fusco squalore nigricans. Unde etiam quod fuscum est et subnigrum, aquilum vocamus. Tum vox inamœna, terribilis, exanimatrix, ac minax ille querulusque clangor, quem nullum animantium genus non expavescit. Jam hoc symbolum protinus agnoscit, qui modo periculum fecerit, aut viderit certè, quam sint formidandæ principum minæ, vel joco prolatæ. . . Ad hanc, inquam, aquilæ stridorem illico pavitat omne vulgus, contrahit sese senatus, observit nobilitas,

obsecundant judices, silent theologi, assentantur jurisconsulti, cedunt leges, cedunt instituta ; nihil valet fas nec pietas, nec æquitas, nec humanitas. Cumque tam multæ sint aves non ineloquentes, tam multæ canoræ, tamque variæ sint voces ac modulatus qui vel saxa possint flectere, plus tamen omnibus valet insuavis ille et minime musicus unius aquilæ stridor.

[z] Nihil omnino convenit inter aquilam et vulpem. quanquam id sane non mediocri vulpinæ gentis malo ; quo tamen haud scio an dignæ videri debeant, quæ quondam leporibus συμμαχίαν adversus aquilam petentibus auxilium negarint, ut refertur in Annalibus Quadrupedum, a quibus Homerus Βατραχομυομαχίαν mutuatus est. . . Neque vero mirum quod illi parum convenit cum oloribus, ave nimirum poetica ; illud mirum, ab iis sæpenumero vinci tam pugnacem belluam.

eagle alone has seemed to wise men the apt type of royalty; not beautiful, not musical, not fit for food; but carnivorous, greedy, plundering, destroying, combating, solitary, hateful to all, the curse of all, and with its great powers of doing harm, surpassing them in its desire of doing it.' [a]

45. But the eagle is only one of the animals in the proverb. After all this bile against those whom the royal bird represents, he does not forget the beetles. These of course are the monks, whose picture he draws with equal bitterness and more contempt. Here, however, it becomes difficult to follow the analogy, as he runs a little wildly into mythological tales of the Scarabæus, not easily reduced to his purpose. This he discloses at length: 'There is a wretched class of men, of low degree, yet full of malice; not less dingy, nor less filthy, nor less vile than beetles; who nevertheless by a certain obstinate malignity of disposition, though they can never do good to any mortal, become frequently troublesome to the great. They frighten by their ugliness, they molest by their noise, they offend by their stench; they buzz round us, they cling to us, they lie in ambush for us, so that it is often better to be at enmity with powerful men than to attack these beetles, whom it is a disgrace even to overcome, and whom no one can either shake off, or encounter, without some pollution.' [b]

46. It must be admitted, that this was not the language

---

[a] Ex universis avibus una aquila viris tam sapientibus idonea visa est, quæ regis imaginem repræsentet, nec formosa, nec canora, nec esculenta, sed carnivora, rapax, prædatrix, populatrix, bellatrix, solitaria, invisa omnibus, pestis omnium; quæ cum plurimum nocere possit, plus tamen velit quam possit.

[b] Sunt homunculi quidam, infimæ quidem sortis, sed tamen malitiosi, non minus atri quam scarabæi, neque minus putidi, neque minus abjecti; qui tamen pertinaci quadam ingenii malitia, cum nulli omnino mortalium prodesse possint, magnis etiam sæpenumero viris facessunt negotium. Territant nigrore, obstrepunt stridore, obturbant fœtore; circumvolitant, hærent, insidiantur, ut non paulo satius sit cum magnis aliquando viris simultatem suscipere, quam hos lacessere scarabæos, quos pudeat etiam vicisse, quosque nec excutere pos-

sis, neque conflictari cum illis queas, nisi discedas contaminatior. Chil. iii. cent. vii. 1.

In a letter to Budæus, Ep. ccli., Erasmus boasts of his παρρησία in the Adages, naming the most poignant of them; but says, in proverbio ἀετὸν κάνθαρος μαιεύεται, plane lusimus ingenio. This proverb, and that entitled Sileni Alcibiadis, had appeared before 1515; for they were reprinted in that year by Frobenius, separately from the other Adages, as appears by a letter of Beatus Rhenanus in Appendice ad Erasm. Epist. Ep. xxviii. Zasius, a famous jurist, alludes to them in another letter, Ep. xxvii., praising 'fluminosas disserendi undas, amplificationis immensam ubertatem.' And this in truth is the character of Erasmus's style. The Sileni Alcibiadis were also translated into English, and published by John Gough; see

to conciliate; and we might almost commiserate the sufferance of the poor beetles thus trod upon; but Erasmus knew that the regular clergy were not to be conciliated, and resolved to throw away the scabbard. With respect to his invectives against kings, they proceeded undoubtedly, like those, less intemperately expressed, of his friend More in the Utopia, from a just sense of the oppression of Europe in that age by ambitious and selfish rulers. Yet the very freedom of his animadversions seems to plead a little in favour of these tyrants, who, if they had been as thorough birds of prey as he represents them, might easily have torn to pieces the author of this somewhat outrageous declamation, whom on the contrary they honoured and maintained. In one of the passages above quoted, he has introduced, certainly in a later edition, a limitation of his tyrannicidal doctrine, if not a palinodia, in an altered key. ' Princes,' he says, ' must be endured, lest tyranny should give way to anarchy, a still greater evil. This has been demonstrated by the experience of many states; and lately the insurrection of the German boors has taught us, that the cruelty of princes is better to be borne than the universal confusion of anarchy.' I have quoted these political ebullitions rather diffusely, as they are, I believe, very little known, and have given the original in my notes, that I may be proved to have no way over-coloured the translation, and also that a fair specimen may be presented of the eloquence of Erasmus, who has seldom an opportunity of expressing himself with so much elevation, but whose rapid, fertile, and lively, though not very polished style, is hardly more exhibited in these paragraphs than in the general character of his writings.

47. The whole thoughts of Erasmus began now to be occupied with his great undertaking, an edition of the Greek Testament with explanatory annotations and a continued paraphrase. Valla, indeed, had led the inquiry as a commentator; and the Greek text without notes was already printed at Alcalá by direction of Cardinal Ximenes; though this edition, commonly styled the Complutensian,

His Greek Testament.

Dibdin's Typographical Antiquities, article 1433.
  There is not a little severity in the remarks which Erasmus makes on princes and nobles in the Moriæ Encomium. But with them he seems through life to have been a privileged person.

did not appear till 1522. That of Erasmus was published at
Basle in 1516. It is strictly therefore the princeps editio.
He employed the press of Frobenius, with whom he lived
in friendship. Many years of his life were spent at Basle.

48. The public, in a general sense of the word, was
hardly yet recovered enough from its prejudices to Patrons of
give encouragement to letters. But there were not letters in Germany.
wanting noble patrons, who, besides the immediate advantages
of their favour, bestowed a much greater indirect benefit on
literature, by making it honourable in the eyes of mankind.
Learning, which is held pusillanimous by the soldier, unprofitable by the merchant, and pedantic by the courtier,
stands in need of some countenance from those before whom
all three bow down; wherever at least, which is too commonly
the case, a conscious self-respect does not sustain the scholar
against the indifference or scorn of the prosperous vulgar.
Italy was then, and perhaps has been ever since, the soil
where literature, if it has not always most flourished, has
stood highest in general estimation. But in Germany also,
at this time, the emperor Maximilian, whose character is
neither to be estimated by the sarcastic humour of the Italians,
nor by the fond partiality of his countrymen, and especially
his own, in his self-delineation of Der Weiss Kunig, the
White King, but really a brave and generous man of lively
talents; Frederic, justly denominated the Wise, elector of
Saxony; Joachim elector of Brandenburg; Albert archbishop
of Mentz, were prominent among the friends of genuine
learning. The university of Wittenberg, founded by the
second of these princes in 1502, rose in this decad to great
eminence, not only as the birthplace of the Reformation, but
as the chief school of philological and philosophical literature.
That of Frankfort on the Oder was established by the elector
of Brandenburg in 1506.

49. The progress of learning, however, was not to be a
march through a submissive country. Ignorance, Resistance
which had much to lose, and was proud as well to learning.
as rich, ignorance in high places, which is always incurable,
because it never seeks for a cure, set itself sullenly and
stubbornly against the new teachers. The Latin language,
taught most barbarously through books whose very titles,
Floresta, Mammotrectus, Doctrinale puerorum, Gemma

gemmarum, bespeak their style,[c] with the scholastic logic and divinity in wretched compends, had been held sufficient for all education. Those who had learned nothing else could of course teach nothing else, and saw their reputation and emoluments gone all at once by the introduction of philological literature and real science. Through all the palaces of Ignorance went forth a cry of terror at the coming light—'A voice of weeping heard and loud lament.' The aged giant was roused from sleep, and sent his dark hosts of owls and bats to the war. One man above all the rest, Erasmus, cut them to pieces with irony or invective. They stood in the way of his noble zeal for the restoration of letters.[d] He began his attack in his Encomium Moriæ, the

---

[c] Eichhorn, iii. 273, gives a curious list of names of these early grammars; they were driven out of the schools about this time. Mammotrectus, after all, is a learned word; it means μαμμοθρεπτὸς, that is, a boy taught by his grandmother; and a boy taught by his grandmother means one taught gently.

Erasmus gives a lamentable accouut of the state of education when he was a boy, and probably later: Deum immortalem! quale sæculum erat hoc, cum magno apparatu disticha Joannis Garlandini adolescentibus operosis et prolixis commentariis enarrabantur! cum ineptis versiculis dictandis, repetendis et exigendis magna pars temporis, absumeretur; cum disceretur Floresta et Floretus; nam Alexandrum inter tolerabiles numerandum arbitror.

I will take this opportunity of mentioning that Erasmus was certainly born in 1465, not in 1467, as Bayle asserts, whom Le Clerc and Jortin have followed. Burigni perceived this; and it may be proved by many passages in the Epistles of Erasmus. Bayle quotes a letter of Feb. 1516, wherein Erasmus says, as he transcribes it: Ago annum undequinquagesimum. But in the Leyden edition, which is the best, I find Ego jam annum ago primum et quinquagesimum. Epist. cc. Thus he says also, 15th March, 1528: Arbitror me nunc ætatem agere, in quo M. Tullius decessit. Some other places I have not taken down. His epitaph at Basle calls him, jam septuagenarius, and he died in 1536. Bayle's proofs of the birth of Erasmus in 1467 are so unsatisfactory, that I wonder how Le Clerc

should have so easily acquiesced in them. The Biographie universelle, sets down 1467 without remark.

[d] When the first lectures in Greek were given at Oxford about 1519, a party of students arrayed themselves, by the name of Trojans, to withstand the innovators by dint of clamour and violence, till the king interfered to support the learned side. See a letter of More, giving an account of this, in Jortin's Appendix, p. 662. Cambridge, it is to be observed, was very peaceable at this time, and suffered those who liked it to learn something worth knowing. The whole is so shortly expressed by Erasmus, that his words may be quoted. Anglia duas habet Academias. . . . In utraque traduntur Græcæ literæ, sed Cantabrigiæ tranquillè, quod ejus scholæ princeps sit Joannes Fischerus, episcopus Roffensis, non eruditione tantum sed et vitâ theologicâ. Verum Oxoniæ cum juvenis quidam non vulgariter doctus satis feliciter Græcè profiteretur, barbarus quispiam in populari concione magnis et atrocibus conviyiis debacchari cœpit in Græcas literas. At Rex, ut non indoctus ipse, ita bonis literis favens, qui tum forte in propinquo erat, re per Morum et Pacœum cognitâ, denunciavit ut volentes ac lubentes Græcanicam literaturaṁ amplecterentur. Ita rabulis impositum est silentium. Appendix, p. 667. See also Erasm. Epist. ccclxxx.

Antony Wood, with rather an excess of academical prejudice, insinuates that the Trojans, who waged war against Oxonian Greek, were 'Cambridge men,

Praise of Folly. This was addressed to Sir Thomas More,
and published in 1511. Eighteen hundred copies were

as it is reported.' He endeavours to exaggerate the deficiencies of Cambridge in literature at this time, as if 'all things were full of rudeness and barbarousness;' which the above letters of More and Erasmus show not to have been altogether the case. On the contrary, More says that even those who did not learn Greek contributed to pay the lecturer.

It may be worth while to lay before the reader part of two orations by Richard Croke, who had been sent down to Cambridge by Bishop Fisher, chancellor of the university. As Croke seems to have left Leïpsic in 1518, they may be referred to that, or perhaps more probably the following year. It is evident that Greek was now just incipient at Cambridge.

Maittaire says of these two orations of Richard Croke : Editio rarissima, cujusque unum duntaxat exemplar inspexisse mihi contigit. The British Museum has a copy, which belonged to Dr. Farmer ; but he must have seen another copy, for the last page of this being imperfect, he has filled it up with his own hand. The book is printed at Paris by Colinæus in 1520.

The subject of Croke's orations, which seem not very correctly printed, is the praise of Greece and of Greek literature, addressed to those who already knew and valued that of Rome, which he shows to be derived from the other. Quin ipsæ quoque vocnlationes Romanæ Græcis longe insuaviores, minusque concitatæ sunt, cum ultima semper syllaba rigeat in gravem, contraque apud Græcos et inflectatur nonnunquam et acuatur. Croke of course spoke Greek accentually. Greek words, in bad types, frequently occur through this oration.

Croke dwells on the barbarous state of the sciences, in consequence of the ignorance of Greek. Euclid's definition of a line was so ill translated, that it puzzled all the geometers till the Greek was consulted. Medicine was in an equally bad condition ; had it not been for the labours of learned men, Linacre, Cop, Ruel, quorum opera felicissime loquuntur Latinè Hippocrates, Galenus et Dioscorides, cum summa ipsorum invidia, qui, quod canis in præsepi, nec

Græcam linguam discere ipsi voluerunt, nec aliis ut discerent permiserunt. He then urges the necessity of Greek studies for the theologian, and seems to have no respect for the Vulgate above the original.

Turpe sanè erit, cum mercator sermonem Gallicum, Illyricum, Hispanicum, Germanicum, vel solius lucri causa avide ediscat, vos studiosos Græcum in manus vobis traditum rejicere, quo et divitiæ et eloquentia et sapientia comparari possunt. Imo perpendite rogo viri Cantabrigienses, quo nunc in loco vestræ res sitæ sunt. Oxonienses quos ante hæc in omni scientiarum genere vicistis, ad literas Græcas perfugere, vigilant, jejunant, sudant et algent; nihil non faciunt ut eas occupent. Quod si contingat, actum est de fama vestra. Erigent enim de vobis tropæum nunquam succumbuturi. Habent duces præter cardinalem Cantuariensem, Wintoniensem, cæteros omnes Angliæ episcopos, excepto uno Roffensi, summo semper fautore vestro, et Eliensi, &c.

Favet præterea ipsis sancta Grocini et theologo digna severitas, Linacri πολυμάϑεια et acre judicium, Tunstali non legibus magis quam utrique linguæ familiaris facundia, Stopleii triplex lingua, Mori candida et eloquentissima urbanitas, Pacei mores doctrina et ingenium, ab ipso Erasmo, optimo eruditionis censore, commendati ; quem vos olim habuistis Græcarum literarum professorem, utinamque potuissetis retinere. Succedo in Erasmi locum ego, bone Deus, quam infra illum, et doctrinâ et famâ, quamquam me, ne omnino nihili fiam, principes viri, theologici doctores, jurium etiam et medicinæ, artium præterea professores innumeri, et præceptorem agnovere, et quod plus est, a scholis ad ædes, ab ædibus ad scholas honorificentissime comitati perduxere. Dii me perdant, viri Cantabrigienses, si ipsi Oxonienses stipendio multorum nobilium præter victum me non invitavere. Sed ego pro mea in hanc academiam et fide et observantia, &c.

In his second oration Croke exhorts the Cantabrigians not to give up the study of Greek. Si quisquam omnium sit qui vestræ reipublicæ bene consulere debeat, is ego sum, viri Cantabrigienses.

printed, and speedily sold; though the book wanted the attraction that some later editions possess, the curious and amusing engravings from designs of Holbein. It is a poignant satire against all professions of men, and even against princes and peers; but the chief objects are the mendicant orders of monks. 'Though this sort of men,' he says, 'are so detested by every one, that it is reckoned unlucky so much as to meet them by accident, they think nothing equal to themselves, and hold it a proof of their consummate piety, if they are so illiterate as not to be able to read. And when their asinine voices bray out in the churches their psalms, of which they understand the notes, but not the words,[e] then it is they fancy that the ears of the saints above are enraptured with the harmony;' and so forth.

50. In this sentence Erasmus intimates, what is abundantly confirmed by other testimony, that the mendicant orders had lost their ancient hold upon the people. There was a growing sense of the abuses prevailing in the church, and a desire for a more Scriptural and spiritual religion. We have seen already that this was the case seventy years before. And in the intermediate period the exertions of a few eminent men, especially Wessel of

(margin note: Unpopularity of the monks.)

Optime enim vobis esse cupio, et id nisi facerem, essem profecto longe ingratissimus. Ubi enim jacta literarum mearum fundamenta, quibus tantum tum apud nostrates, tum vero apud exteros quoque principes, favoris mihi comparatum est; quibus ea fortuna, ut licet jam olim consanguineorum iniquitate paterna hæreditate sim spoliatus, ita tamen adhuc vivam, ut quibusvis meorum majorum imaginibus videar non indignus. He was probably of the ancient family of Croke. Peter Mosellanus calls him, in a letter among those of Erasmus, juvenus cum imaginibus.

Audio ego plerosque vos a litteris Græcis dehortatos esse. Sed vos diligenter expendite, qui sint, et plane non alios fore comperitis, quam qui igitur linguam oderunt Græcam, quia Romanam non norunt. Cæterum jam deprehendo quid facturi sint, qui nostras literas odio prosequuntur, confugiunt videlicet ad religionem, cui uni dicent omnia postpo-

nenda. Sentio ego cum illis, sed unde quæso orta religio, nisi è Græciâ? quid enim novum testamentum, excepto Matthæo? quid enim vetus? nunquid Deo auspice a septuaginta Græcè redditum? Oxonia est colonia vestra; uti olim non sine summa laude a Cantabrigia deducta, ita non sine summo vestro nunc dedecore, si doctrina ab ipsis vos vinci patiamini. Fuerunt olim illi discipuli vestri, nunc erunt præceptores? Utinam quo animo hæc a me dicta sunt, eo vos dicta interpretemini; crederetisque, quod est verissimum, si quoslibet alios, certe Cantabrigienses minime decere literarum Græcarum esse desertores.

The great scarcity of this tract will serve as an apology for the length of these extracts, illustrating, as they do, the commencement of classical literature in England.

[e] Numeratos illos quidem, sed non intellectos.—[I conceive that I have given the meaning rightly.—1842.]

Groningen, had not been wanting to purify the doctrines
and discipline of the clergy.   More popular writers assailed
them with satire.   Thus everything was prepared for the
blow to be struck by Luther; better indeed than he was
himself; for it is well known that he began his attack on
indulgences with no expectation or desire of the total breach
with the see of Rome which ensued.[f]

51. The Encomium Moriæ was received with applause by
all who loved merriment, and all who hated the The book excites odium.
monks; but grave men, as usual, could not bear to
see ridicule employed against grave folly and hypocrisy.   A
letter of one Dorpius, a man, it is said, of some merit, which
may be read in Jortin's Life of Erasmus,[g] amusingly
complains that while the most eminent divines and lawyers
were admiring Erasmus, his unlucky Moria had spoiled all,
by letting them see that he was mischievously fitting asses'
ears to their heads.   The same Dorpius, who seems, though
not an old man, to have been a sworn vassal of the giant
Ignorance, objects to anything in Erasmus's intended edition
of the Greek Testament which might throw a slur on the
accuracy of the Vulgate.

52. Erasmus was soon in a state of war with the monks;
and in his second edition of the New Testament, Erasmus attacks the
printed in 1518, the notes, it is said, are full of monks.
invectives against them.   It must be confessed that he had
begun the attack, without any motive of provocation, unless
zeal for learning and religion is to count for such, which the
parties assailed could not be expected to admit, and they
could hardly thank him for 'spitting on their gaberdine.'   No
one, however, knew better how to pay his court; and he
wrote to Leo X. in a style rather too adulatory, which in
truth was his custom in addressing the great, and contrasts
with his free language in writing about them.   The custom
of the time affords some excuse for this panegyrical tone
of correspondence, as well as for the opposite extreme of
severity.

---

[f] Seckendorf, Hist. Lutheranismi, p.
226.   Gerdes, Hist. Evang. sæc. xvi.
renovat. vols. i. and iii. Milner's Church
History, vol. iv.   Mosheim, sæc. xv. et
xvi.   Bayle, art. Wessel.   For Wessel's
character as a philosopher, who boldly
opposed the scholastics of his age, see
Brucker, iii. 859.
    [g] ii. 336.

53. The famous contention between Reuchlin and the
German monks, though it began in the preceding
decennial period, belongs chiefly to the present. In
the year 1509, one Pfeffercorn, a converted Jew, induced the
inquisition at Cologne to obtain an order from the Emperor
for burning all Hebrew books except the Bible, upon the
pretext of their being full of blasphemies against the
Christian religion. The Jews made complaints of this injury ; but before it could take place, Reuchlin, who had been
consulted by the Emperor, remonstrated against the destruction of works so curious and important, which, from his
partiality to Cabbalistic theories, he rated above their real
value. The order was accordingly superseded, to the great
indignation of the Cologne inquisitors, and of all that party
throughout Germany which resisted the intellectual and religious progress of mankind. Reuchlin had offended the
monks by satirising them in a comedy, perhaps the Sergius,
which he permitted to be printed in 1506. But the struggle
was soon perceived to be a general one; a struggle between
what had been and what was to be. Meiners has gone so far
as to suppose a real confederacy to have been formed by the
friends of truth and learning through Germany and France,
to support Reuchlin against the mendicant orders, and to
overthrow, by means of this controversy, the embattled
legions of ignorance.[h] But perhaps the passages he adduces
do not prove more than their unanimity and zeal in the
cause. The attention of the world was first called to it
about 1513 ; that is, it assumed about that time the character of a war of opinions, extending, in its principle and
consequences, beyond the immediate dispute.[i] Several books
were published on both sides; and the party in power
employed its usual argument of burning what was written
by its adversaries. One of these writings is still known, the
Epistolæ Obscurorum Virorum ; the production, it is said,
of three authors, the principal of whom was Ulric von Hutten
a turbulent, hot-headed man, of noble birth and quick parts,
and a certain degree of learning, whose early death seems
more likely to have spared the reformers some degree of

*Their con-
tention with
Reuchlin.*

---

[h] Lebensbeschreib. i. 144 et seqq.

[i] Meiners brings many proofs of the interest taken in Reuchlin, as the champion, if not the martyr, of the good cause.

shame, than to have deprived them of a useful supporter.[k] Few books have been more eagerly received than these Epistles at their first appearance in 1516,[m] which surely proceeded rather from their suitableness to the time, than from much intrinsic merit; though it must be presumed that the spirit of many temporary allusions, which delighted or offended that age, is now lost in a mass of vapid nonsense and bad grammar, which the imaginary writers pour out. Erasmus, though not intimately acquainted with Reuchlin, could not but sympathise in a quarrel with their common enemies in a common cause. In the end the controversy was referred to the pope; but the pope was Leo; and it was hoped that a proposal to burn books, or to disgrace an illustrious scholar, would not sound well in his ears. But Reuchlin was disappointed, when he expected acquittal, by a mandate to supersede, or suspend, the process commenced against him by the inquisition of Cologne, which might be taken up at a more favourable time.[n] This dispute has always been reckoned of high importance; the victory in public opinion, though not in judicature, over the adherents to the old system, prostrated them so utterly, that from this time the study of Greek and Hebrew became general among the German youth; and the cause of the Reformation was identified in their minds with that of classical literature.[o]

---

[k] Herder, in his Zerstreute Blätter, v. 329, speaks with unreasonable partiality of Ulric von Hutten; and Meiners has written his life with an enthusiasm which seems to me quite extravagant. Seckendorf, p. 130, more judiciously observes that he was of little use to the Reformation. And Luther wrote about him in June, 1521: Quid Huttenus petat vides. Nollem vi et cæde pro evangelio certari, ita scripsi ad hominem. Melanchthon of course disliked such friends. Epist. Melanchth. p. 45 (1647), and Camerarius, Vita Melanchth. Erasmus could not endure Hutten; and Hutten, when he found this out, wrote virulently against Erasmus. Jortin, as biographer of Erasmus, treats Hutten perhaps with too much contempt; but this is nearer justice than the veneration of the modern Germans. Hutten wrote Latin pretty well, and had a good deal of wit; his satirical libels, consequently, had great circulation and popularity, which, in respect of such writings is apt, in all ages, to produce an exaggeration of their real influence. In the mighty movement of the Reformation, the Epistolæ Obscurorum Virorum had about as much effect as the Mariage de Figaro in the French Revolution. A dialogue severely reflecting on Pope Julius II., called Julius exclusus, of which Jortin suspects Erasmus, in spite of his denial, ii. 595, is given by Meiners to Hutten.

[m] Meiners, in his Life of Hutten, Lebensbesch. iii. 73, inclines to fix the publication of the first part of the Epistles in the beginning of 1517: though he admits an earlier date to be not impossible.

[n] Meiners, i. 197.

[o] Sleidan, Hist. de la Réformat. l. ii. Brucker, iv. 366. Mosheim. Eichhorn, iii. 238, vi. 16. Bayle, art. Hochstrat. None of these authorities are equal in ful-

54. We are now brought, insensibly perhaps, but by neces-
Origin of the sary steps, to the great religious revolution which
Reforma-
tion. has just been named. I approach this subject with
some hesitation, well aware that impartiality is no protection
against unreasonable cavilling; but neither the history of
literature, nor of human opinion upon the most important
subjects, can dispense altogether with so extensive a portion
of its materials. It is not required, however, in a work
of this nature, to do much more than state shortly the
grounds of dispute, and the changes wrought in the public
mind.

55. The proximate cause of the Reformation is well known.
Indulgences, or dispensations granted by the pope from the
heavy penances imposed on penitents after absolution by
the old canons, and also, at least in later ages, from the pains
of purgatory, were sold by the papal retailers with the most
indecent extortion, and eagerly purchased by the superstitious
multitude, for their own sake, or that of their deceased
friends. Luther, in his celebrated theses, propounded at
Wittenberg, in November, 1517, inveighed against the
erroneous views inculcated as to the efficacy of indulgences,
and especially against the notion of the pope's power over
souls in purgatory. He seems to have believed that the
dealers had exceeded their commission, and would be disavowed by the pope. This, however, was very far from being
the case; and the determination of Leo to persevere in
defending all the abusive prerogatives of his see drew
Luther on to levy war against many other prevailing usages
of the church, against several tenets maintained by the most
celebrated doctors, against the divine right of the papal
supremacy, and finally to renounce all communion with a
power which he now deemed an antichristian tyranny. This
absolute separation did not take place till he publicly burned
the pope's bull against him, and the volumes of the canon law,
at Wittenberg, in November, 1520.

---

ness to Meiners, Lebensbeschreibungen, berühmter Männer, i. 98–212; which I did not consult so early as the rest. But there is also a very copious account of the Reuchlinian controversy, including many original documents, in the second part of Von der Hardt's Historia Litteraria Reformationis.

56. In all this dispute Luther was sustained by a prodigious force of popular opinion.   It was perhaps in Popularity the power of his sovereign, Frederic elector of of Luther. Saxony, to have sent him to Rome, in the summer of 1518, according to the pope's direction.   But it would have been an odious step in the people's eyes, and a little later would have been impossible.   Miltitz, an envoy despatched by Leo in 1519 upon a conciliatory errand, told Luther that 25,000 armed men would not suffice to make him a prisoner, so favourable was the impression of his doctrine upon Germany. And Frederic himself, not long afterwards, wrote plainly to Rome, that a change had taken place in his country; the German people were not what they had been; there were many men of great talents and considerable learning among them, and the laity were beginning to be anxious about a knowledge of Scripture; so that unless Luther's doctrine, which had already taken root in the minds of a great many both in Germany and other countries, could be refuted by better arguments than mere ecclesiastical fulminations, the consequence must be so much disturbance in the empire as would by no means redound to the benefit of the Holy See.[p] In fact, the university of Wittenberg was crowded with students and others, who came to hear Luther and Melanchthon. The latter had at the very beginning embraced his new master's opinions with a conviction which he did not in all respects afterwards preserve.   And though no overt attempts to innovate on the established ceremonies had begun in this period, before the end of 1520 several preached against them, and the whole north of Germany was full of expectation.

57. A counterpart to the reformation that Luther was thus effecting in Saxony might be found at the Simultaneous reform same instant in Switzerland, under the guidance of by Zwingle. Zwingle.   It has been disputed between the advocates of these leaders, to which the priority in the race of reform belongs.   Zwingle himself declares, that in 1516, before he

---

[p] Seckendorf. This remarkable letter will be found also in Roscoe's Leo X., Appendix, No. 185. It bears date April, 1520. See also a letter of Petrus Mosel- lanus, in Jortin's Erasmus, ii. 353; and Luther's own letter to Leo, of March, 1519.

had heard of Luther, he began to preach the Gospel at
Zurich, and to warn the people against relying upon human
authority.[q] But that is rather ambiguous, and hardly enough
to substantiate his claim. In 1518, which of course is after
Luther's appearance on the scene, the Swiss reformer was
engaged in combating the venders of indulgences, though
with less attention from the Court of Rome. Like Luther,
he had the support of the temporal magistrate, the council of
Zurich. Upon the whole, they proceeded so nearly with equal
steps, and were so little connected with each other, that it
seems difficult to award either any honour of precedence.[r]

58. The German nation was, in fact, so fully awakened
Reformation to the abuses of the church, the denial of papal
prepared
beforehand. sovereignty in the councils of Constance and Basle

---

[q] Zwingle apud Gerdes, i. 103.

[r] Milner, who is extremely partial in
the whole of this history, labours to extenuate the claims of Zwingle to independence in the preaching of reformation;
and even pretends that he had not separated from the Church of Rome in 1523,
when Adrian VI. sent him a civil letter.
But Gerdes shows at length that the
rupture was complete in 1520. See also
the article Zwingle, in Biogr. universelle.

The prejudice of Milner against Zwingle throughout is striking, and leads him
into much unfairness. Thus he asserts
him, v. 510, to have been consenting to
the capital punishment of some Anabaptists at Zurich. But, not to mention that
their case was not one of mere religious
dissidence, it does not by any means
appear that he approved their punishment, which he merely relates as a fact.
A still more gross misrepresentation occurs in p. 526.—[Capito says, in a letter
to Bullinger (1536): Antequam Lutherus
in lucem emerserit, Zwinglius et ego
inter nos communicavimus de pontifice
dejiciendo, etiam cum ille vitam degeret
in eremitorio. Nam utrique ex Erasmi
consuetudine, et lectione bonorum auctorum, qualecunque judicium tum sobo-
lescebat. Gerdes, p. 117.—1842.]

[A late writer, as impartial as he is
learned and penetrating, thus contrasts
the two founders of the Reformation.
'If we compare him [Zwingle] with
Luther, we find that he had no such
tremendous tempests to withstand as

those which shook the most secret depths
of Luther's soul. As he had never devoted himself with equal ardour to the
Established Church, he had not now to
break loose from it with such violent
and painful struggles. It was not the
profound love of the faith, and of its
connection with redemption, in which
Luther's efforts originated, that made
Zwingle a reformer ; he became so chiefly
because, in the course of his study of
Scripture in search of truth, he found the
church and the received morality at variance with its spirit. Nor was Zwingle
trained at an university, or deeply imbued with the prevalent doctrinal opinions. To found a high school, firmly
attached to all that was worthy of attachment, and dissenting only on certain
most important points, was not his vo-
cation. He regarded it much more as
the business and duty of his life to bring
about the religious and moral reformation of the republic that had adopted
him, and to recall the Swiss Confedera-
tion to the principles upon which it was
originally founded. While Luther's main
object was a reform of doctrine which,
he thought, would be necessarily followed by that of life and morals, Zwingle
aimed directly at the improvement of
life ; he kept mainly in view the practical significancy of Scripture as a whole ;
his original views were .of a moral and
political nature : hence his labours were
tinged with a wholly peculiar colour.'
Ranke's Hist. of Reformation, vol. iii.
p. 7.—1847.]

had been so effectual in its influence on the public mind,
though not on the external policy of church and state, that
if neither Luther nor Zwingle had ever been born, there can
be little question that a great religious schism was near at
hand. These councils were to the Reformation what the
Parliament of Paris was to the French Revolution. Their
leaders never meant to sacrifice one article of received faith;
but the little success they had in redressing what they de-
nounced as abuses, convinced the laity that they must go
much farther for themselves. What effect the invention of
printing, which in Italy was not much felt in this direction,
exerted upon the serious minds of the Teutonic nations, has
been already intimated, and must appear to every reflecting
person. And when this was followed by a more extensive acquaintance with the New Testament in the Greek language,
nothing could be more natural than that inquisitive men
should throw away much of what seemed the novel superstructure of religion, and what in other times such men had
rarely ventured, should be encouraged by the obvious change
in the temper of the multitude to declare themselves. We
find that Pellican and Capito, two of the most learned scholars
in western Germany, had come, as early as 1512, to reject
altogether the doctrine of the real presence. We find also
that Œcolampadius had begun to preach some of the
Protestant doctrines in 1514.[s] And Erasmus, who had so
manifestly prepared the way for the new reformers, continued,
as it is easy to show from the uniform current of his letters,
beyond the year 1520, favourable to their cause. His enemies
were theirs, and he concurred in much that they preached,
especially as to the exterior practices of religion. Some,
however, of Luther's tenets he did not and could not approve; and he was already disgusted by that intemperance
of language and conduct, which, not long afterwards, led him
to recede entirely from the Protestant side.[t]

---

[s] Gerdes, i. 117, 124, et post. In
fact, the precursors of the Reformation
were very numerous, and are collected
by Gerdes in his first and third volumes,
though he has greatly exaggerated the
truth, by reckoning as such Dante and
Petrarch, and all opponents of the temporal power of the papacy. Wessel may,
upon the whole, be fairly reckoned
among the Reformers.

[t] In 1519 and 1520, even in his letters to Albert archbishop of Mentz, and
others by no means partial to Luther, he
speaks of him very handsomely, and with
little or no disapprobation, except on account of his intemperance, though pro-

59. It would not be just, probably, to give Bossuet credit
Dangerous tenets of Luther. in every part of that powerful delineation of Luther's theological tenets with which he begins the History of the Variations of Protestant Churches. Nothing, perhaps, in polemical eloquence is so splendid as this chapter. The eagle of Meaux is there truly seen, lordly of form, fierce of eye, terrible in his beak and claws. But he is too determined a partisan to be trusted by those who seek the truth without regard to persons and denominations. His quotations from Luther are short, and in French; I have failed in several attempts to verify the references. Yet we are not to follow the reformer's indiscriminate admirers in dissembling altogether, like Isaac Milner, or in slightly censuring, as others have done, the enormous paradoxes which deform his writings, especially such as fall within the present period. In maintaining salvation to depend on faith as a single condition, he not only denied the importance, in a religious sense, of a virtuous life, but asserted that every one, who felt within himself a full assurance that his sins were remitted, (which, according to Luther, is the proper meaning of Christian faith,) became incapable of sinning at all, or at least of forfeiting the favour of God, so long, but so long only, as that assurance should continue. Such expressions are sometimes said by Seckendorf and Mosheim to have been thrown out hastily, and without precision; but I fear it will be found on examination that they are very definite and clear, the want of precision and perspicuity being rather in those which are alleged as inconsistent with them, and as more consonant to the general doctrine of the Christian church.[u] It must not be supposed for a moment, that Luther,

---

fessing only a slight acquaintance with his writings. The proofs are too numerous to be cited. He says, in a letter to Zwinglo, as late as 1521, Videor mihi fere omnia docuisse, quæ docet Lutherus, nisi quod non tam atrociter, quodque abstinui a quibusdam ænigmatis et paradoxis. This is quoted by Gerdes, i. 153, from a collection of letters of Erasmus, published by Hottinger, but not contained in the Leyden edition. Jortin seems not to have seen them.

[u] See in proof of this Luther's works, vol. i. passim (edit. 1554). The first

work of Melanchthon, his Loci Communes, published in 1521, when he followed Luther more obsequiously in his opinions than he did in after-life, is equally replete with the strongest Calvinism. This word is a little awkward in this place; but I am compelled to use it, as most intelligible to the reader; and I conceive that these two reformers went much beyond the language of Augustin, which the schoolmen thought themselves bound to recognise as authority though they might elude its spirit. I find the first edition of Melanchthon's

whose soul was penetrated with a fervent piety, and whose integrity as well as purity of life are unquestioned, could mean to give any encouragement to a licentious disregard of moral virtue; which he valued, as in itself lovely before God as well as man, though, in the technical style of his theology, he might deny its proper obligation. But his temper led him to follow up any proposition of Scripture to every consequence that might seem to result from its literal meaning; and he fancied that to represent a future state as the motive of virtuous action, or as any way connected with human conduct, for better or worse, was derogatory to the free grace of God, and the omnipotent agency of the Spirit in converting the soul.[x]

Loci Commentes in Von der Hardt, Historia Litteraria Reformationis, a work which contains a great deal of curious matter. It is called by him, opus rarissimum, not being in the edition of Melanchthon's theological works; which some have ascribed to the art of Peucer, whose tenets were widely different.

[x] I am unwilling to give these pages too theological a cast by proving this statement, as I have the means of doing, by extracts from Luther's own early writings. Milner's very prolix history of this period is rendered less valuable by his disingenuous trick of suppressing all passages in these treatises of Luther which display his Antinomian paradoxes in a strong light. Whoever has read the writings of Luther up to the year 1520 inclusive, must find it impossible to contradict my assertion. In treating of an author so full of unlimited propositions as Luther, no positive proof as to his tenets can be refuted by the production of inconsistent passages.

[It was to be expected that what I have here said, and afterwards, in Ch. VI., concerning Luther, would grate on the ears of many very respectable persons, whose attachment to the Reformation, and admiration of his eminent character, could not without much reluctance admit that degree of censure which I have felt myself compelled to pass upon him. Two Edinburgh reviewers, for both of whom I feel great respect, have at different times remarked what seemed to them an undue severity; and a late writer, Archdeacon Hare, in his notes to a series of Sermons on the Mission of the Comforter, 1846, has animadverted on it at great length, and with a sufficiently uncompromising spirit. I am unwilling to be drawn on this occasion into controversy, or to follow my prolix antagonist through all his observations upon my short paragraphs; both because I have in my disposition a good deal of stulta clementia, which leads me to take pity on paper, or rather on myself; and for a better reason, namely, that notwithstanding what the Archdeacon calls my 'aversion' to Luther,' I really look upon him as a great man, endowed with many virtues, and an instrument of Providence for a signal good. I am also particularly reluctant, at the present time, to do in any manner the drudgery of the Philistines, and while those who are not more in my good graces than the Archdeacon's, and who had hardly sprouted up when my remarks on Luther were first written, are depreciating the Protestant cause with the utmost animosity, to strengthen any prejudice against it. But I must as shortly as possible, and perhaps more shortly than an adequate exposition of my defence would require, produce the passages in Luther's own writings which have compelled me to speak out as strongly as I have done.

I may begin by observing, that in charging Luther, especially in his early writings, with what goes generally by the name of Antinomianism (that is, with representing faith alone as the condition of acceptance with God, not merely for those who for the first time embrace the Gospel, but for all who have been

60. Whatever may be the bias of our minds as to the truth of Luther's doctrines, we should be careful, in con-

baptized and brought up in its profession, and in so great a degree that no sins whatever can exclude a faithful man from salvation), I have maintained no paradox, but what has been repeatedly alleged, not only by Romanist, but Protestant theologians. This, however, is not sufficient to prove its truth; and I am therefore under the necessity of quoting a few out of many passages. But I repeat that I have not the remotest intention of charging Luther with wilful encouragement to an immoral life. The Antinomian scheme of religion, which indeed was not called by that name in Luther's age (the word, as applied to the followers of Agricola, involving only a denial of the obligation of the Mosaic law *as such*, moral as well as ceremonial), is only one mode in which the disinterestedness of virtuous actions has been asserted, and may be held by men of the utmost sanctity, though it must be exceedingly dangerous in its general promulgation. Thus we find it substantially though without intemperance, in some Essays by a highly respected writer, Mr. Thomas Erskine, on the Unconditional Freeness of the Gospel. Nothing is more repugnant to my principles than to pass moral reprobation on persons because I differ, however essentially, from their tenets. Let us leave that to Rome and Oxford; though Luther unfortunately was the last man who could claim this liberty of prophesying for himself on the score of his charity and tolerance for others.

Archdeacon Hare is a man of so much fairness, and so intensely persuaded of being in the right, that he produces himself the leading propositions of Luther, from which others, like myself, have deduced our own very different inferences as to his doctrine.

In the treatise de Captivitate Babylonica, 1520, we find these celebrated words: ' Ita vides quam dives sit homo Christianus et baptisatus, qui etiam volens non potest perdere salutem suam quantiscunque peccatis, nisi nolit credere. Nulla enim peccata eum possunt damnare nisi sola incredulitas Cætera omnia, si redeat vel stet fides in promissionem divinam baptisato factam, in momento absorbentur per eandem fidem, imo veritatem Dei, quia seipsum negare

non potest, si tu eum confessus fueris, et promittenti fideliter adhæseris. It may be pretended, that however paradoxically Luther has expressed himself, he meant to assert the absolute incompatibility of *habitual* sins with a justifying faith. But even if his language would always bear this meaning, it is to be kept in mind, that faith (πιστις) can never be more than inward persuasion or assurance, whereof, *subjectively*, each man must judge for himself; and though to the eyes of others a true faith may be wanting, it is not evident that men of enthusiastic minds may not be fully satisfied that they possess it.

Luther indeed has, in another position, often quoted, taken away from himself this line of defence :—Si in fide posset fieri adulterium, peccatum non esset. Disputat. 1520. Archdeacon Hare observes on this, that 'it is logically true,' p. 794. This appears to me a singular assertion. The hypothesis of Luther is, that a sinful action might be committed in a state of faith ; and the consequent of the proposition is, that in such case it would not be a sin at all. Grant that he held the supposition to be impossible, which no doubt he sometimes does though we should hardly draw that inference from the passage last cited, or from some others, still, in reasoning *ex absurdo*, we are bound to argue rightly upon the assumed hypothesis. But all his notions about sin and merit were so preposterously contradictory to natural morality and religion, that they could not have been permanently received without violating the moral constitution of the human mind. Thus, in the Heidelberg Propositions, 1518, we read: Opera hominum ut semper speciosa sint, bonaque videantur, probabile tamen est ea esse peccata mortalia. . . . Opera Dei ut semper sint deformia malaque videantur, verè tamen sunt merita immortalia . . . Non sic sunt opera hominum mortalia (de bonis, ut apparent, loquimur), ut eadem sint crimina . . . Non sic sunt opera Dei merita (de his quæ per hominem fiunt, loquimur), ut eadem non sint peccata . . . Justorum opera essent mortalia, nisi pio Dei timore ab ipsismet justis ut mortalia timerentur. Such a series of propositions occasions a sort of bewilderment in the understanding, so

sidering the Reformation as a part of the history of mankind, not to be misled by the superficial and ungrounded

unlike are they to the usual tone of moral precept and sentiment.

I am indebted to Archdeacon Hare for another, not at all less singular passage, in a letter of Luther to Melanchthan in 1521, which I have also found in the very able, though very bitter, Vie de Luther, by M. Audin, Paris, 1839. I do not see the necessity of giving the context, or of explaining on what occasion the letter was written; on the ground that, where a sentence is complete in itself, and contains a general assertion of an author's own opinion, it is not to be limited by reference to anything else. Sufficit, Luther says, quod agnovimus per divitias gloriæ Dei Agnum, qui tollit peccata mundi; ab hoc non avellet nos peccatum, etiamsi millies millies uno die fornicamur aut occidamus. Putas tam parvum esse pretium et redemtionem pro peccatis nostris factam in tanto et tali agno? Ora fortiter; es enim fortissimus peccator.

It appears that Mr. Ward has translated 'uno die' by 'every day;' for which the Archdeacon animadverts on him: 'This mistranslation serves his purpose of blasting Luther's fame, inasmuch as it substitutes a hellish horror, —the thought that a continuous life of the most atrocious sin can co-exist with faith and prayer, and Christ and righteousness,—for that which, justly offensive as it may be, is so mainly from its peculiar Lutheran extravagance of expression.' p. 794. No one will pretend that Mr. Ward ought not to have been more accurate. But I confess that the difference does not strike me as immensely great. Luther, I cannot help thinking, would have written 'unoquoque die' as readily as 'uno,' if the word had suggested itself. He wanted to assert the efficacy of Christ's imputed righteousness in the most forcible terms, by weighing it against an impossible accumulation of offences. It is no more than he had said in the passage quoted above from the treatise De Captivitate Babylonica; non potest perdere salutem suam quantiscunque peccatis; expressed still more offensively.

The real question is not what interpretation an astute advocate, by making large allowance for warmth of temper, peculiarities of expression, and the necessity of inculcating some truths more forcibly by being silent on others, may put on the writings of Luther (for very few will impute to him either a defective sense of moral duties in himself, or a disposition to set his disciples at liberty from them), but what was the evident tendency of his language. And this, it should be remembered, need not be judged solely by the plain sense of words, though that is surely sufficient. The danger of these exaggerations, the mildest word that I can use, and one not adequate to what I feel, was soon shown in the practical effect of Lutheran preaching. Munzer and Knipperdolling, with the whole rabble of anabaptist fanatics, were the legitimate brood of Luther's early doctrine. And even if we set these aside, it is certain that we find no testimonies to any reform of manners in the countries that embraced it. The Swiss Reformation, the English, and the Calvinistic churches generally, make a far better show in this respect.

This great practical deficiency in the Lutheran reformation is confessed by their own writers. And it is attested by a remarkable letter of Willibald Pirckheimer, announcing the death of Albert Durer to a correspondent at Vienna in 1528, which may be found in Reliquien von Albrecht Dürer, Nuremberg, 1828, p. 168. In this he takes occasion to inveigh against the bad conduct of the reformed party at Nuremberg, and seems as indignant at the Lutherans as he had ever been against popery, though without losing his hatred for the latter. I do not quote the letter, which is long, and in obsolete German; and perhaps it may display too much irritation, natural to an honest man who has been disappointed in his hopes from a revolution; but the witness he bears to the dishonest and dissolute manners which had accompanied the introduction of Lutheranism is not to be slightly regarded; considering the respectability of Pirckheimer, and his known co-operation with the first reform.

I have been thought to speak too disparagingly of Luther's polemical writings, especially that against the bishops, by the expression 'bellowing in bad Latin.' Perhaps it might be too contemptuous towards a great men; but I

representations which we sometimes find in modern writers. Such is this, that Luther, struck by the absurdity of the prevailing superstitions, was desirous of introducing a more rational system of religion; or, that he contended for freedom of inquiry, and the boundless privileges of individual judgment; or, what others have been pleased to suggest, that his zeal for learning and ancient philosophy led him to attack the ignorance of the monks, and the crafty policy of the church, which withstood all liberal studies.

had been disgusted by the perusal of them. Those who have taken exception (in the Edinburgh Review) are probably little conversant with Luther's writings. But, independently of the moral censure which his virulence demands, we are surely at liberty to say that it is in the worst taste, and very unlikely to convince or conciliate any man of good sense. One other grave objection to the writings of Luther I have not hitherto been called upon to mention; but I will not wholly omit his scandalous grossness, especially as Archdeacon Hare has entered upon an elaborate apology for it. We all know quite as well as he does, that the manners of different ages, different countries, and different conditions of life, are not alike; and that what is universally condemned in some periods has been tolerated in others. Such an excuse may often be made with great fairness; but it cannot be made for Luther. We have writings of his contemporaries, we have writings of grave men in ages less polished than his own. No serious author of the least reputation will be found who defiles his pages, I do not say with such indelicacy, but with such disgusting filthiness as Luther. He resembles Rabelais alone in this respect, and absolutely goes beyond him. Audin, whose aim is to destroy as far as possible the moral reputation of Luther, has collected a great deal more than Bossuet would have deigned to touch; and, considering this object, in the interests of his own religion, I do not know how he can be blamed, though I think that he should have left more passages untranslated. Those taken from the Colloquia Mensalia might perhaps be forgiven, and the blame thrown on the gossiping retailer of his table-talk; but in all his attacks on popes and cardinals, Luther disgraces himself by a nasty and stupid brutality. The great cause, also, of the marriage of priests ceases to be holy and honourable in his advocacy.

And I must express my surprise that Archdeacon Hare should vindicate, against Mr. Ward, the Sermo di Matrimonio, preached at Wittenberg, 1522; for though he says there are four sermons with this title of Luther's works, I have little doubt that Mr. Ward was led to this by Audin, who makes many quotations from it. ' The date of this sermon, 1522, when many of the inmates of the convents were quitting them, and when the errors of the anabaptists were beginning to spread, shows that there was urgent need for the voice of wisdom to set forth the true idea, relations, and obligations of marriage; nor could this be done without an exposition and refutation of the manifold scandalous errors and abuses concerning it, bred and propagated by the papacy.' p. 771. A very rational sentence! but utterly unlike Luther's sermon, which is far more in the tone of the anabaptists than against them. But without dwelling on this, and referring to Audin, vol. ii. p. 34, whose quotations cannot be forgeries, or to the shorter extracts in Bossuet, Hist. des Variations, c. 6, § 11, I shall only observe, that if the voice was that of wisdom, it was not that of Christianity. But here I conclude a note far longer than I wished to make it, the discussion being akin to the general subject of these volumes, and forced upon me by a direct attack of many pages. For Archdeacon Hare himself I have all the respect which his high character, and an acquaintance of long duration, must naturally have created.—1847.]

61. These notions are merely fallacious refinements, as every man of plain understanding, who is ac- Real expla-
nation of quainted with the writings of the early reformers, them. or has considered their history, must acknowledge. The doctrines of Luther, taken altogether, are not more rational, that is, more conformable to what men, à priori, would expect to find in religion, than those of the church of Rome ; nor did he ever pretend that they were so. As to the privilege of free inquiry, it was of course exercised by those who deserted their ancient altars, but certainly not upon any theory of a right in others to judge amiss, that is, differently from themselves. Nor, again, is there any foundation for imagining that Luther was concerned for the interests of literature. None had he himself, save theological ; nor are there, as I apprehend, many allusions to profane studies, or any proof of his regard to them, in all his works. On the contrary, it is probable that both the principles of this great founder of the Reformation, and the natural tendency of so intense an application to theological controversy, checked for a time the progress of philological and philosophical literature on this side of the Alps.[y] Every solution of the conduct of the reformers must be nugatory, except one, that they were men absorbed by the conviction that they were fighting the battle of God. But among the population of Germany or Switzerland, there was undoubtedly another predominant feeling ; the sense of ecclesiastical oppression, and scorn for the worthless swarm of monks and friars. This may be said to have divided the propagators of the Reformation into such as merely pulled down, and such as built upon the ruins. Ulric von Hutten may pass for the type of the one, and Luther himself of the other. And yet it is hardly correct to say of Luther, that he erected his system on the ruins of popery. For it was rather

---

[y] Erasmus, after he had become exasperated with the reformers, repeatedly charges them with ruining literature. Ubicunque regnat Lutheranismus, ibi literarum est interitus. Epist. mvi. (1528). Evangelicos istos, cum multis aliis, tum hoc nomine præcipue odi, quod per eos ubique languent, frigent, jacent, intereunt bonæ literæ, sine quibus quid est hominum vita ? Amant viaticum et uxorem, cætera pili non faciunt. Hos fucos longissime arcendos censeo a vestro contubernio. Ep. dccccxlvi. (eod. ann.) There were, however, at this time, as well as afterwards, more learned men on the side of the Reformation than on that of the church.

the growth and expansion in his mind of one positive dogma, justification by faith, in the sense he took it (which can be easily shown to have preceded the dispute about indulgences[z]), that broke down and crushed successively the various doctrines of the Romish church; not because he had originally much objection to them, but because there was no longer room for them in a consistent system of theology.[a]

62. The laws of synchronism, which we have hitherto *Orlando Furioso.* obeyed, bring strange partners together, and we may pass at once from Luther to Ariosto. The Orlando Furioso was first printed at Ferrara in 1516. This edition contained forty cantos, to which the last six were added in 1532. Many stanzas, chiefly of circumstance, were interpolated by the author from time to time.

63. Ariosto has been, after Homer, the favourite poet of *Its popularity.* Europe. His grace and facility, his clear and rapid stream of language, his variety and beauty of invention, his very transitions of subject, so frequently censured by critics, but artfully devised to spare the tediousness that hangs on a protracted story, left him no rival in general popularity. Above sixty editions of the Orlando Furioso

---

[z] See his disputations at Wittenberg, 1516; and the sermons preached in the same and the subsequent year.

[a] The best authorities for the early history of the Reformation are Seckendorf, Hist. Lutheranismi, and Sleidan, Hist. de la Réformation, in Courayer's French translation; the former being chiefly useful for the ecclesiastical, the latter for political history. But as these confine themselves to Germany, Gerdes (Hist. Evangel. Reformat.) is necessary for the Zuinglian history, as well as for that of the northern kingdoms. The first sections of Father Paul's History of the Council of Trent are also valuable. Schmidt, Histoire des Allemands, vols. vi. and vii., has told the story on the side of Rome speciously and with some fairness ; and Roscoe has vindicated Leo. X. from the imputation of unnecessary violence in his proceeding against Luther. Mosheim is always good, but concise ; Milner far from concise, but highly prejudiced, and in the habit of giving his quotations in English, which is not quite satisfactory to a lover of truth.

The essay on the influence of the Reformation by Villers, which obtained a prize from the French Institute, and has been extolled by a very friendly, but better-informed writer in the Biographie universelle, appears to me the production of a man who had not taken the pains to read any one work contemporaneous with the Reformation, or even any compilation which contains many extracts. No wonder that it does not represent in the slightest degree, the real spirit of the times, or the tenets of the reformers. Thus, e. gr., 'Luther,' he says, 'exposed the abuse of the traffic of indulgences, and the danger of believing that heaven and the rémission of all crimes could be bought with money ; while a sincere repentance and an amended life were the only means of appeasing the divine justice.' (P. 65, Engl. transl.) This at least is not very like Luther's Antinomian contempt for repentance and amendment of life ; it might come near to the notions of Erasmus.

were published in the sixteenth century. 'There was not one,' says Bernardo Tasso, 'of any age, or sex, or rank, who was satisfied after more than a single perusal.' If the change of manners and sentiments have already in some degree impaired this attraction, if we cease to take interest in the prowess of Paladins, and find their combats a little monotonous, this is perhaps the necessary lot of all poetry, which, as it can only reach posterity through the medium of contemporary reputation, must accommodate itself to the fleeting character of its own time. This character is strongly impressed on the Orlando Furioso; it well suited an age of war, and pomp, and gallantry; an age when chivalry was still recent in actual life, and was reflected in concentrated brightness from the mirror of romance.

64. It has been sometimes hinted as an objection to Ariosto, that he is not sufficiently in earnest, and Want of leaves a little suspicion of laughing at his subject. seriousness. I do not perceive that he does this in a greater degree than good sense and taste permit. The poets of knight errantry might in this respect be arranged in a scale, of which Pulci and Spenser would stand at the extreme points; the one mocking the absurdities he coolly invents, the other, by intense strength of conception, full of love and faith in his own creations. Between these Berni, Ariosto, and Boiardo take successively their places; none so deeply serious as Spenser, none so ironical as Pulci. It was not easy in Italy, especially after the Morgante Maggiore had roused the sense of ridicule, to keep up at every moment the solemn tone which Spain endured in the romances of the sixteenth century; nor was this consonant to the gaiety of Ariosto. It is the light carelessness of his manner which constitutes a great part of its charm.

65. Castelvetro has blamed Ariosto for building on the foundations of Boiardo.[b] He seems to have had A continua-tion of originally no other design than to carry onward, a Boiardo. little better than Agostini, that very attractive story; having written, it is said, at first only a few cantos to please his

---

[b] Poetica d'Aristotele (1570). It violates, he says, the rule of Aristotle, ἀρχή ἐστιν ὁ ἐξ ἀνάγκης μὴ μετ' ἀλλό ἐστι. Ca-millo Pellegrini, in his famous controversy with the Academicians of Florence, repeats the same censure.

friends.[c] Certainly it is rather singular that so great and
renowned a poet should have been little more than the
continuator of one who had so lately preceded him; though
Salviati defends him by the example of Homer; and other
critics, with whom we shall perhaps not agree, have thought
this the best apology for writing a romantic instead of an
heroic poem. The story of the Orlando Innamorato must be
known before we can well understand that of the Furioso.
But this is nearly what we find in Homer; for who can
reckon the Iliad anything but a fragment of the tale of Troy?
It was indeed less felt by the compatriots of Homer, already
familiar with that legendary cyclus of heroic song, than it is
by the readers of Ariosto, who are not in general very well
acquainted with the poem of his precursor. Yet experience
has even here shown that the popular voice does not echo
the complaint of the critic. This is chiefly owing to the
want of a predominant unity in the Orlando Furioso, which
we commonly read in detached parcels. The principal unity
that it does possess, distinct from the story of Boiardo, consists in the loves and announced nuptials of Rogero and
Bradamante, the imaginary progenitors of the house of Este;
but Ariosto does not gain by this condescension to the vanity
of a petty sovereign.

66. The inventions of Ariosto are less original than those
In some
points in-
ferior.
of Boiardo, but they are more pleasing and various.
The tales of old mythology and of modern romance
furnished him with those delightful episodes we all admire,
with his Olimpia and Bireno, his Ariodante and Geneura,
his Cloridan and Medoro, his Zerbino and Isabella. He is
more conversant with the Latin poets, or has turned them
to better account, than his predecessor. For the sudden
transitions in the middle of a canto or even a stanza, with
which every reader of Ariosto is familiar, he is indebted to
Boiardo, who had himself imitated in them the metrical
romancers of the preceding age. From them also, that
justice may be rendered to those nameless rhymers, Boiardo
drew the individuality of character, by which their heroes
were distinguished, and which Ariosto has not been so care-

---

[c] Quadrio, Storia d'ogni Poesia, vi. 606.

ful to preserve. His Orlando has less of the honest simplicity, and his Astolfo less of the gay boastfulness, that had
been assigned to them in the cyclus.

67. Corniani observes of the style of Ariosto, what we may
all perceive on attending to it to be true, that he is   Beauties of
sparing in the use of metaphors, contenting himself   its style.
generally with the plainest expression ; by which, if he loses
something in dignity, he gains in perspicuity. It may be
added, that he is not very successful in figurative language,
which is sometimes forced and exaggerated. Doubtless this
transparency of phrase, so eminent in Ariosto, is the cause
that he is read and delighted in by the multitude, as well as
by the few; and it seems also to be the cause that he can
never be satisfactorily rendered into any language less
musical, and consequently less independent upon an ornamental dress in poetry than his own, or one which wants the
peculiar advantages, by which conventional variations in the
form of words, and the liberty of inversion, as well as the
frequent recurrence of the richest and most euphonious
rhymes, elevate the simplest expression in Italian verse
above the level of discourse. Galileo, being asked by what
means he had acquired the remarkable talent of giving perspicuity and grace to his philosophical writings, referred it
to the continual study of Ariosto. His similes are conspicuous for their elaborate beauty; they are familiar to
every reader of this great poet; imitated, as they usually
are, from the ancients, they maintain an equal strife with
their models, and occasionally surpass them. But even the
general strain of Ariosto, natural as it seems, was not un-
premeditated, or left to its own felicity; his manuscript at
Ferrara, part of which is shown to strangers, bears numerous
alterations, the *pentimenti*, if I may borrow a word from a
kindred art, of creative genius.

68. The Italian critics love to expatiate in his praise,
though they are often keenly sensible to his defects.   Accompa-
                                                        nied with
The variety of style and of rhythm in Ariosto, it is   faults.
remarked by Gravina, is suitable to that of his subject. His
rhymes, the same author observes, seem to spring from the
thoughts, and not from the necessities of metre. He describes
minutely, but with much felicity, and gives a clear idea of

every part; like the Farnesian Hercules, which seems
greater by the distinctness of every vein and muscle.[d]
Quadrio praises the correspondence of the sound to the
sense. Yet neither of these critics is blindly partial. It is
acknowledged, indeed, by his warmest advocates, that he
falls sometimes below his subject, and that trifling and
feeble lines intrude too frequently in the Orlando Furioso.
I can hardly regret, however, that in the passages of flattery
towards the house of Este, such as that long genealogy
which he deduces in the third canto, his genius has deserted
him, and he degenerates, as it were wilfully, into prosaic
tediousness. In other allusions to contemporary history, he
is little better. I am hazarding deviation from the judgment
of good critics when I add, that in the opening stanza of
each canto, where the poet appears in his own person, I find
generally a deficiency of vigour and originality, a poverty of
thought and of emotion, which is also very far from unusual
in the speeches of his characters. But these introductions
have been greatly admired.

69. Many faults of language in Ariosto are observed by his
Its place as countrymen. They justly blame also his inobser-
a poem. vance of propriety, his hyperbolical extravagance,
his harsh metaphors, his affected thoughts. These are sufficiently obvious to a reader of reflecting taste; but the
enchantment of his pencil redeems every failing, and his
rapidity, like that of Homer, leaves us little time to censure
before we are hurried forward to admire. The Orlando
Furioso, as a great single poem, has been very rarely surpassed in the living records of poetry. He must yield to
three, and only three, of his predecessors. He has not the
force, simplicity, and truth to nature of Homer, the exquisite style and sustained majesty of Virgil, nor the
originality and boldness of Dante. The most obvious parallel
is Ovid, whose Metamorphoses, however, are far excelled by
the Orlando Furioso, not in fertility of invention, or variety
of images and sentiments, but in purity of taste, in grace of
language, and harmony of versification.

---

[d] Ragi on Poetica, p. 104.

70. No edition of Amadis de Gaul has been proved to exist before that printed at Seville in 1519, which Amadis de yet is suspected of not being the first.[e] This famous Gaul. romance, which in its day was almost as popular as the Orlando Furioso itself, was translated into French by Herberay between 1540 and 1557, and into English by Munday in 1619. The four books by Vasco de Lobeyra grew to twenty by successive additions, which have been held by lovers of romance far inferior to the original. They deserve at least the blame, or praise, of making the entire work unreadable by the most patient or the most idle of mankind. Amadis de Gaul can still perhaps impart pleasure to the susceptible imagination of youth ; but the want of deep or permanent sympathy leaves a naked sense of unprofitableness in the perusal, which must, it should seem, alienate a reader of mature years. Amadis at least obtained the laurel at the hands of Cervantes, speaking through the barber and curate, while so many of Lobeyra's unworthy imitators were condemned to the flames.

71. A curious dramatic performance, if it may deserve such an appellation, was represented at Paris in 1511, and published in 1516. It is entitled Le Gringore. Prince des Sots et la Mère sotte, by one Peter Gringore, who had before produced some other pieces of less note, and bordering more closely on the moralities. In the general idea there was nothing original. A prince of fools had long ruled his many-coloured subjects on the theatre of a joyous company, les Enfans sans souci, who had diverted the citizens of Paris with their buffoonery, under the name, perhaps, of moralities, while their graver brethren represented the mysteries of Scripture and legend. But the chief aim of La Mère sotte was to turn the pope and court of Rome into ridicule during the sharp contest of Louis XII. with Julius II. It consists of four parts, all in verse. The first of these is called The Cry, and serves as a sort of prologue, summoning all fools of both sexes to see the prince of fools play on Shrove Tuesday. The second is the Folly. This is an irregular

---

[e] Brunet, Man. du Libraire.

dramatic piece, full of poignant satire on the clergy, but especially on the pope. A third part is entitled The Morality of the Obstinate Man; a dialogue in allusion to the same dispute. Finally comes an indecent farce, unconnected with the preceding subject. Gringore, who represented the character of La Mère sotte, was generally known by that name, and assumed it in his subsequent publications.[f]

72. Gringore was certainly at a great distance from the Italian stage, which had successfully adapted the plots of Latin comedies to modern stories. But, among the *barbarians*, a dramatic writer, somewhat younger than he, was now beginning to earn a respectable celebrity, though limited to a yet uncultivated language, and to the inferior class of Society. Hans Sachs, a shoemaker of Nuremberg, born in 1494, is said to have produced his first carnival play (Fast-nacht spiel) in 1517. He belonged to the fraternity of poetical artisans, the meister singers of Germany, who, fron the beginning of the fourteenth century, had a succession of mechanical (in every sense of the word) rhymers to boast, for whom their countrymen felt as much reverence as might have sufficed for more genuine bards. In a spirit which might naturally be expected from artisans, they required a punctual observance of certain arbitrary canons, the by-laws of the corporation Muses, to which the poet must conform. These, however, did not diminish the fecundity, if they repressed the excursiveness, of our meister-singers, and least of all that of Hans Sachs himself, who poured forth, in about forty years, fifty-three sacred and seventy-eight profane plays, sixty-four farces, fifty-nine fables, and a large assortment of other poetry. These dramatic works are now scarce, even in Germany; they appear to be ranked in the same class as the early fruits of the French and English theatres. We shall mention Hans Sachs again in another chapter.[g]

Hans Sachs.

---

[f] Beauchamps, Recherches sur le Théâtre français. Goujet, Bibl. française, xi. 212. Niceron, vol. xxxiv. Bouterwek, Gesch. der Französischen Poesie, v. 113. Biogr. univers. The works of Gringore, says the last authority, are rare, and sought by the lovers of our old poetry because they display the state of manners at the beginning of the sixteenth century.

[g] Biogr. univ. Eiehhorn. iii. 948. Bouterwek, ix. 381. Heinsius, iv. 150. Retrospective Review, vol. x.

73. No English poet, since the death of Lydgate, had arisen whom it could be thought worth while to Stephen mention.[h] Many, perhaps, will not admit that Hawes. Stephen Hawes, who now meets us, should be reckoned in that honourable list. His ' Pastime of Pleasure, or the Historie of Graunde Amour and La bel Pucel,' finished in 1506, was printed by Wynkyn de Worde in 1517. From this title we might hardly expect a moral and learned allegory, in which the seven sciences of the trivium and quadrivium, besides a host of abstract virtues and qualities, play their parts, in living personality, through a poem of about six thousand lines. Those who require the ardent words or the harmonious grace of poetical diction will not frequently be content with Hawes. Unlike many of our older versifiers, he would be judged more unfavourably by extracts than by a general view of his long work. He is rude, obscure, full of pedantic Latinisms, and probably has been disfigured in the press; but learned and philosophical, reminding us frequently of the school of James I. The best, though probably an unexpected parallel for Hawes is John Bunyan : their inventions are of the same class, various and novel, though with no remarkable pertinence to the leading subject, or naturally consecutive order ; their characters, though abstract in name, have a personal truth about them, in which Phineas Fletcher, a century after Hawes, fell much below him ; they render the general allegory subservient to inculcating a system, the one of philosophy, the other of religion. I do not mean that the Pastime of Pleasure is equal in merit, as it certainly has not been in success, to the Pilgrim's Progress. Bunyan is powerful and picturesque from his concise simplicity ; Hawes, has the common failings of our old writers, a tedious and languid diffuseness, an expatiating on themes of pedantry in which the reader takes no interest, a weakening of every picture and every reflection by ignorance of the touches that give effect. But if we consider the ' Historie of Graunde Amour ' less as a poem to be read than as a measure of the author's mental power,

---

[h] I have adverted in another place to Alexander Barclay's translation of the Ship of Fools from Sebastian Brandt; and I may here observe, that he has added many original strokes on his own countrymen, especially on the clergy.

we shall not look down upon so long and well-sustained an allegory. In this style of poetry much was required, that no mind ill-stored with reflection, or incapable of novel combination, could supply ; a clear conception of abstract modes, a familiarity with the human mind, and with the effects of its qualities on human life, a power of justly perceiving and vividly representing the analogies of sensible and rational objects. Few that preceded Hawes have possessed more of these gifts than himself.

74. This poem was little known till Mr. Southey reprinted it in 1831 ; the original edition is very rare. Warton had given several extracts, which, as I have observed, are disadvantageous to Hawes, and an analysis of the whole ;[i] but though he praises the author for imagination, and admits that the poem has been unjustly neglected, he has not dwelt enough on the erudition and reflection it displays. Hawes appears to have been educated at Oxford, and to have travelled much on the Continent. He held also an office in the court of Henry VII. We may reckon him therefore among the earliest of our learned and accomplished gentlemen ; and his poem is the first fruits of that gradual ripening of the English mind, which must have been the process of the laboratory of time, in the silence and darkness of the fifteenth century. It augured a generation of grave and stern thinkers, and the omen was not vain.

75. Another poem, the Temple of Glass, which Warton

Change in English language.   had given to Hawes, is now by general consent restored to Lydgate. Independently of external proof, which is decisive,[k] it will appear that the Temple of Glass is not written in the English of Henry VIII.'s reign. I mention this only for the sake of observing, that in following the line of our writers in verse and prose, we find the old obsolete English to have gone out of use about the accession of Edward IV. Lydgate and Bishop Pecock, especially the latter, are not easily understood by a reader not habituated to their languages : he requires a glossary, or must help himself out

---

[i] Hist. of Engl. Poetry, iii. 54.

[k] See note in Price's edition of Warton, ubi supra : to which I add, that the

Temple of Glass is mentioned in the Paston Letters, ii. 90, long before the time of Hawes.

by conjecture.[m] In the Paston Letters, on the contrary, in
Harding the metrical chronicler, or in Sir John Fortescue's
Discourse on the difference between an absolute and limited

[m] [The language of Bishop Pecock is
more obsolete than that of Lydgate, or
any other of his contemporaries ; and
this may also be observed with respect
to Wicliffe's translation of the Bible.
Yet even he has many French and Latin
words, though in a smaller proportion
than Chaucer and Gower, or even Mandeville and Trevisa. In a passage of Mandeville, quoted by Burnet (Specimens of
Early English Writers, vol. i. p. 16), I
counted 41 French and 53 Saxon words,
omitting particles and a few common
pronouns, which, of course, belong to the
latter. But this is not in the usual ratio ;
and in Trevisa I found the Saxon to be as
two to one. The form *ben* for *be* occurs
more often in Trevisa than in Mandeville, which may probably be owing to
ancient or modern transcribers.   Both
these writers seem to have undergone
some repairs as to orthography and an-
tique terminations.   In Wicliffe's translation, made about 1380, the preponderance of Saxon, counting only nouns,
verbs, and adverbs, is considerably
greater, probably nearly three to one ;
those who have included pronouns and
particles (all which are notoriously
Teutonic) have brought forward a much
higher ratio of Saxon even in modern
books; especially if, like Mr. Sharon
Turner and Sir James Mackintosh, they
reckon each word as often as it occurs.
I have never counted a single word, in
any of these experiments, more than
once ; and my results have certainly
given a much greater proportion of
French and Latin than these writers
have admitted. But this is in reference
to later periods of the language than that
with which we have to do.

Pecock, and probably Wicliffe before
him, was apparently studious of a sort
of archaism. He preserves the old terminations which were going into disuse,
perhaps from a tenaciousness of purity
in language, which we often find in
literary men. Hence we have in him,
as in Wicliffe, *schulen* for *shall*, *wolden*
for *would*, *tho* for *them*, and *her* for *their*;
and this almost invariably.   Now we
possess hardly any prose exactly of
Pecock's age, about 1440, with the
exception of the Rolls of Parliament.

These would be of material authority for
the progress of our language, if we could
be sure that they have been faithfully
transcribed ; but I have been informed
that this is not altogether the case. It
is possible, therefore, that modern forms
of language have been occasionally substituted for the more ancient. I should
not conceive that this has very frequently
occurred, as there has evidently been a
general intention to preserve the original
with accuracy : there is no designed mo-
dernisation, even of orthography. But
in the Rolls of Parliament, during the
reign of Henry VI., we rarely find the
termination *en* to the infinitive mood ;
though I have observed it twice about
1459, and probably it occurs oftener.
In the participle it continued longer,
even to the 16th century; as in Fabian,
who never employs this termination in
the infinitive. And in the present tense,
we find *usen* in Fortescue ; *ben* for *be*,
and a few more plurals, in Caxton. Some
inferior writers adopt this plural down
to the reign of Henry VIII.

Caxton republished the translation
of Higden's Polychronicon by Trevisa,
made about a hundred years before, in
the new English of his own age. ' Certainly,' he says, ' our language now used
varyeth far from that which was spoken
when I was born ; for we English men
ben born under the denomination of the
moon, which is never stedfast, but ever
wavering; waxing one season, and waneth
and decreaseth another season.   And
common English that is spoken in one
shire varyeth from another.'   He then
tells a story of one *axing* for eggs in
Kent, when the good wife replied she
could speak no French; at last the word
eyren being used she understood it.
Caxton resolved to employ a mean between the common and the ancient
English, ' not over rude ne curious,
but in such terms as should be understood.'   The difference between the old
copy of Trevisa and Caxton's moderni-
sation is perhaps less than from the
above passage we might expect ; but
possibly we have not the former in its
perfect purity of text.   Trevisa was a
parson in Cornwall, and Caxton tells us
that he himself learned his English in

monarchy, he finds scarce any difficulty; antiquated words and forms of termination frequently occur; but he is hardly sensible that he reads these books much less fluently than those of modern times. These were written about 1470. But in Sir Thomas More's History of Edward V., written about 1509, or in the beautiful ballad of the Nut-brown Maid, which we cannot place very far from the year 1500, but which, if nothing can be brought to contradict the internal evidence, I should incline to refer to this decennium, there is not only a diminution of obsolete phraseology, but a certain modern turn and structure, both in the verse and prose, which denotes the commencement of a new era, and the establishment of new rules of taste in polite literature. Every one will understand that a broad line cannot be traced for the beginning of this change: Hawes, though his English is very different from that of Lydgate, seems to have had a great veneration for him, and has imitated the manner of that school, to which, in a marshalling of our poets, he unquestionably belongs. Skelton, on the contrary, though ready enough to coin words, has comparatively few that are obsolete.

76. The strange writer, whom we have just mentioned, seems to fall well enough within this decad; though his poetical life was long, if it be true that he received the laureate crown at Oxford in 1483, and was also the author of a libel on Sir Thomas More, ascribed to him by Ellis, which, alluding to the Nun of Kent, could hardly be written before 1533.[n] But though this piece is somewhat in Skelton's manner, we find it said that he died in

Skelton.

---

the Weald of Kent, 'where I doubt not is spoken as brode and rude English as is in any place in England.'

Caxton has a fluent and really good style: he is even less obsolete than Fortescue, an older man and a lawyer, who for both reasons might adhere to antiquity. Yet in him we have *eyen* for *eyes*, *syn* for *afterwards*, and a few more marks of antiquity. In Lord Rivers's preface to his 'Dictionary of Philosophers,' 1477, as quoted in the introduction to Todd's edition of Johnson's Dictionary, there is no archaism at all. But the first book that I have read

through without detecting any remnant of obsolete forms (excepting of course the termination of the third person singular in *eth*, which has not been wholly disused for a hundred years, and may indeed be found in Reid's Inquiry into the Human Mind, published in 1764, and later), is Sir Thomas More's History of Edward V.—1847.]

[n] Ellis's Specimens, vol. ii. [Skelton was Laureate at Oxford in 1490: it does not appear how long before. But he had written an Elegy on Edward IV. in 1483.—1853.]

1529, and it is probably the work of an imitator. Skelton is certainly not a poet, unless some degree of comic humour, and a torrent-like volubility of words in doggrel rhyme, can make one; but this uncommon fertility, in a language so little copious as ours was at that time, bespeaks a mind of some original vigour. Few English writers come nearer in this respect to Rabelais, whom Skelton preceded. His attempts in serious poetry are utterly contemptible; but the satirical lines on Cardinal Wolsey were probably not ineffective. It is impossible to determine whether they were written before 1520. Though these are better known than any poem of Skelton's, his dirge on Philip Sparrow is the most comic and imaginative.[o]

77. We must now take a short survey of some other departments of literature during this second decad Oriental of the sixteenth century. The Oriental languages languages. become a little more visible in bibliography than before. An Æthiopic, that is, Abyssinian grammar, with the Psalms in the same language, was published at Rome by Potken in 1513; a short treatise in Arabic at Fano in 1514, being the first time those characters had been used in type; a Psalter in 1516, by Giustiniani at Genoa, in Hebrew, Chaldee, Arabic, and Greek;[p] and a Hebrew Bible, with the Chaldee paraphrase and other aids, by Felice di Prato, at Venice in 1519. The Book of Job in Hebrew appeared at Paris in 1516. Meantime the magnificent polyglott Bible of Alcalá proceeded under the patronage of Cardinal Ximenes, and was published in five volumes folio, between the years 1514 and 1517. It contains in triple columns the Hebrew, the Septuagint Greek, and Latin Vulgate; the Chaldee paraphrase of the Pentateuch by Onkelos being also printed at the foot

---

[o] This last poem is reprinted in Southey's Selections from the older Poets. Extracts from Skelton occur also in Warton, and one in the first volume of the Somers Tracts. Mr. Dyce has published a collective edition of Skelton's works.

[p] It is printed in eight columns, which Gesner, apud Bayle, Justiniani, Note D., thus describes: Quarum prima habet Hebræam editionem, secunda Latinam interpretationem respondentem Hebrææ de verbo in verbum, tertia Latinam communem, quarta Græcam, quinta Arabicam, sexta paraphrasim, sermone quidem Chaldæo, sed literis Hebraicis conscriptam; septima Latinam respondentem Chaldeæ, ultima vero, id est cctava, continet scholia, hoc est, annotationes sparsas et intercisas.

of the page.[q]   Spain, therefore, had found men equal to
superintend this arduous labour. Lebrixa was still living,
though much advanced in years; Stunica and a few other
now obscure names were his coadjutors. But that of Demetrius Cretensis appears among these in the title-page,
to whom the principal care of the Greek was doubtless intrusted; and it is highly probable that all the early Hebrew
and Chaldee publications demanded the assistance of Jewish
rabbis.

78. The school of Padua, renowned already for its medi-
Pompona-   cal science as well as for the cultivation of the Aris-
tius.   totelian philosophy, laboured under a suspicion of
infidelity, which was considerably heightened by the work of
Pomponatius, its most renowned professor, on the immortality of the soul, published in 1516. This book met with
several answerers, and was publicly burned at Venice; but
the patronage of Bembo sustained Pomponatius at the court
of Leo; and he was permitted by the Inquisition to reprint
his treatise with some corrections. He defended himself by
declaring that he merely denied the validity of philosophical
arguments for the soul's immortality, without doubting in
the least the authority of revelation, to which, and to that
of the church, he had expressly submitted. This, however,
is the current language of philosophy in the sixteenth and
seventeenth centuries, which must be judged by other presumptions. Brucker and Ginguéné are clear as to the real
disbelief of Pomponatius in the doctrine, and bring some
proofs from his other writings, which seem more unequivocal
than any that the treatise De Immortalitate affords. It is
certainly possible, and not uncommon, for men to deem the
arguments on that subject inconclusive, so far as derived
from reason, while they assent to those that rest on revelation. It is on the other hand impossible for a man to believe
inconsistent propositions, when he perceives them to be so.
The question therefore can only be, as Buhle seems to have
seen, whether Pomponatius maintained the rational argu-

---

[q] Andrès, xix. 35. An observation in
the preface to the Complutensian edition
has been often animadverted upon, that
they print the Vulgate between the Hebrew and the Greek, like Christ between
two thieves. The expression, however it
may have been introduced, is not to be
wholly defended; but at that time it was
generally believed that the Hebrew text
had been corrupted by the Jews.

ments for a future state to be repugnant to known truths, or merely insufficient for conviction; and this a superficial perusal of his treatise hardly enables me to determine; though there is a presumption on the whole, that he had no more religion than the philosophers of Padua generally kept for a cloak. That university was for more than a century the focus of atheism in Italy.[r]

79. We may enumerate among the philosophical writings of this period, as being first published in 1516, a treatise full two hundred years older, by Raymond Lully, a native of Majorca, one of those innovators in philosophy, who, by much boasting of their original discoveries in the secrets of truth, are taken by many at their word, and gain credit for systems of science, which those who believe in them seldom trouble themselves to examine, or even understand. Lully's principal treatise is his Ars Magna, being, as it professes, a new method of reasoning on all subjects. But this method appears to be only an artificial disposition, readily obvious to the eye, of subjects and predicables, according to certain distinctions; which, if it were meant for anything more than a topical arrangement, such as the ancient orators employed to aid their invention, could only be compared to the similar scheme of using machinery instead of mental labour devised by the philosophers of Laputa. Leibnitz is of opinion that the method might be convenient in extempore speaking; which is the utmost limit that can be assigned to its usefulness. Lord Bacon has truly said of this, and of such idle or fraudulent attempts to substitute trick for science, that they are, 'not a lawful method, but a method of imposture, which is to deliver knowledges in such manner, as men may speedily come to make a show of learning, who have it not;' and that they are 'nothing but a mass of words of all arts, to give men

[marginal notes: Raymond Lully. His method.]

---

[r] Tiraboschi, vol. viii. Corniani. Ginguéné. Brucker. Buhle. Niceron. Biogr. universelle. The two last of these are more favourable than the rest to the intentions of the Paduan philosopher.

Pomponatius, or Peretto, as he was sometimes called, on account of his diminutive stature, which he had in common with his predecessor in philosophy, Marsilius Ficinus, was ignorant of Greek, though he read lectures on Aristotle. In one of Sperone's dialogues (p. 120, edit. 1596) he is made to argue, that if all books were read in translations, the time now consumed in learning languages might be better employed.

countenance, that those which use the terms might be thought to understand them.

80. The writings of Lully are admitted to be very obscure ; and those of his commentators and admirers, among whom the meteors of philosophy, Cornelius Agrippa and Jordano Bruno, were enrolled, are hardly less so. But, as is usual with such empiric medicines, it obtained a great deal of celebrity, and much ungrounded praise, not only for the two centuries which intervened between the author's age and that of its appearance from the press, but for a considerable time afterwards, till the Cartesian philosophy drove that to which the art of Lully was accommodated from the field ; and even Morhof, near the end of the seventeenth century, avows that, though he had been led to reckon it a frivolous method[s] he had very much changed his opinion on fuller examination. The few pages which Brucker has given to Lully do not render his art very intelligible ;[t] but they seem sufficient to show its uselessness for the discovery of truth. It is utterly impossible, as I conceive, for those who have taken much pains to comprehend this method, which is not the case with me, to give a precise notion of it in a few words, even with the help of diagrams, which are indispensably required.[u]

---

[s] Morhof, Polyhistor, l. ii. c. 5. But if I understand the ground on which Morhof rests his favourable opinion of Lully's art, it is merely for its usefulness in suggesting middle terms to a syllogistic disputant.

[t] Brucker, iv. 9–21. Ginguéné, who observes that Brucker's analysis, à sa manière accoutumée, may be understood by those who have learned Lully's method, but must be very confused to others, has made the matter a great deal more unintelligible by his own attempt to explain it. Hist. litt. de l'Italie, vii. 497. I have found a better development of the method in Alstedius, Clavis Artis Lullianæ (Argentor. 1633), a staunch admirer of Lully. But his praise of the art, when examined, is merely as an aid to the memory, and to disputation, de quavis quæstione utramque in partem disputandi. This is rather an evil than a good ; and though mnemonical contrivances are not without utility, it is probable that much better

could be found than that of Lully.

[u] Buhle has observed that the favourable reception of Lully's method is not surprising, since it really is useful in the association of ideas, like all other topical contrivances, and may be applied to any subject, though often not very appropriately, suggesting materials in extemporary speaking, and, notwithstanding its shortness, professing to be a complete system of topics ; but whoever should try it must be convinced of its inefficacy in reasoning. Hence he thinks that such men as Agrippa and Bruno kept only the general principle of Lully's scheme, enlarging it by new contrivances of their own. Hist. de Philos. ii. 612. See also an article on Lully in the Biographie universelle. Tennemann calls the Ars Magna a logical machine to let men reason about everything without study or reflection. Manuel de la Philos. i. 380. But this seems to have been much what Lully reckoned its merit.

81. The only geographical publication which occurs in this period is, an account of the recent discoveries in America, by Peter Martyr of Anghiera, a Milanese, who passed great part of his life in the court of Madrid. The title is, De Rebus Oceanicis decades tres; but it is, in fact, a series of epistles, thirty in number, written, or feigned to be written, at different times as fresh information was received; the first bearing date a few days only after the departure of Columbus in 1493; while the two last decads are addressed to Leo X. An edition is said to have appeared in 1516, which is certainly the date of the author's dedication to Charles V.; yet this edition seems not to have been seen by bibliographers. Though Peter Martyr's own account has been implicitly believed by Robertson and many others, there seems strong internal presumption against the authenticity of these epistles in the character they assume. It appears to me evident that he threw the intelligence he had obtained into that form many years after the time. Whoever will take the trouble of comparing the two first letters in the decads of Peter Martyr with any authentic history, will, I should think, perceive that they are a negligent and palpable imposture, every date being falsified, even that of the year in which Columbus made his great discovery. It is a strange instance of oversight in Robertson that he has uniformly quoted them as written at the time, for the least attention must have shown him the contrary. And it may here be mentioned, that a similar suspicion may be reasonably entertained with respect to another collection of epistles by the same author, rather better known than the present. There is a folio volume with which those who have much attended to the history of the sixteenth century are well acquainted, purporting to be a series of letters from Anghiera to various friends between the years 1488 and 1522. They are full of interesting facts, and would be still more valuable than they are, could we put our trust in their genuineness as strictly contemporary documents. But though Robertson has almost wholly relied upon them in his account of the Castilian insurrection, and even in the Biographie universelle no doubt is raised as to their being truly written at their several dates, yet La Monnoye (if I remember right, certainly

some one) long since charged the author with imposture, on the ground that the letters, into which he wove the history of his times, are so full of anachronisms as to render it evident that they were fabricated afterwards. It is several years since I read these epistles; but I was certainly struck with some palpable errors in chronology, which led me to suspect that several of them were wrongly dated, the solution of their being feigned not occurring to my mind as the book is of considerable reputation.[x] A ground of suspicion hardly less striking is, that the letters of Peter Martyr are too exact for verisimilitude; he announces events with just the importance they ought to have, predicts nothing but what comes to pass, and must in fact be either an impostor (in an innocent sense of the word), or one of the most sagacious men of his time. But if not exactly what they profess to be, both these works of Anghiera are valuable as contemporary history; and the first mentioned in particular, De Rebus Oceanicis, is the earliest account we possess of the settlement of the Spaniards in Darien, and of the whole period between Columbus and Cortes.

82. It would be embarrassing to the reader were we to pursue any longer that rigidly chronological division by short decennial periods, which has hitherto served to display the regular progress of European literature, and especially of classical learning. Many other provinces were now cultivated, and the history of each is to be traced separately from the rest, though frequently with mutual reference,

---

[x] The following are specimens of anachronism, which seem fatal to the genuineness of these epistles, and are only selected from others. In the year 1489 he writes to a friend (Arias Barbosa): In peculiarem te nostræ tempestatis morbum, qui appellatione Hispanâ Bubarum dicitur, ab Italis morbus Gallicus, medicorum Elephantiam alii, alii aliter appellant, incidisse præcipitem, libero ad me scribis pede. Epist. 68. Now if we should even believe that this disease was known some years before the discovery of America and the siege of Naples, is it probable that it could have obtained the name of morbus Gallicus before the latter era? In February, 1511, he communicates the absolution of the Venetians by Julius II., which took place in February, 1510. Epist. 451. In a letter dated at Brussels, Aug. 31, 1520 (Epist. 689), he mentions the burning of the canon law at Wittenberg by Luther, which is well known to have happened in the ensuing November.—[Mr. Prescott, in his excellent History of Ferdinand and Isabella, vol. ii. p. 78, has expressed his dissent from this suspicion that P. Martyr's letters were written after the time, and ascribes the anachronisms to the misplacing of some letters by the original editor. This will probably account for some of them; but my suspicion is not wholly removed.—1842.]

and with regard, as far as possible, to their common unity. In the period immediately before us, that unity was chiefly preserved by the diligent study of the Latin and Greek languages; it was to the writers in those languages that the theologian, the civil lawyer, the physician, the geometer and philosopher, even the poet, for the most part, and dramatist, repaired for the materials of their knowledge, and the nourishment of their minds. We shall begin, therefore, by following the further advances of philological literature; and some readers must here, as in other places, pardon what they will think unnecessary minuteness in so general a work as the present, for the sake of others who set a value on precise information.

CHAPTER V.

HISTORY OF ANCIENT LITERATURE IN EUROPE FROM
1520 TO 1550.

Classical Taste of the Italians—Ciceronians—Erasmus attacks them—
Writings on Roman Antiquity—Learning in France—Commentaries of
Budæus—Progress of Learning in Spain, Germany, England—State of
Cambridge and Oxford—Advance of Learning still slow—Encyclopædic
Works.

1. ITALY, the genial soil where the literature of antiquity
Superiority had been first cultivated, still retained her superi-
of Italy in
taste.   ority in the fine perception of its beauties, and in
the power of retracing them by spirited imitation.   It was
the land of taste and sensibility; never surely more so than
in the age of Raffaelle as well as Ariosto.   Far from the
clownish ignorance so long predominant in the Transalpine
aristocracy, the nobles of Italy, accustomed to a city life,
and to social festivity, more than to war or the chace, were
always conspicuous for their patronage, and, what is more
important than mere patronage, their critical skill in matters of art and elegant learning.   Among the ecclesiastical
order this was naturally still more frequent.   If the successors of Leo X. did not attain so splendid a name, they
were, perhaps, after the short reign of Adrian VI., which,
if we may believe the Italian writers, seemed to threaten
an absolute return of barbarism,[y] not less munificent or

---

[y] Valerianus, in his treatise De In-
felicitate Litteratorum, a melancholy
series of unfortunate authors, in the
manner, though not quite with the spirit
and interest, of Mr. D'Israeli, speaks of
Adrian VI. as of another Paul II. in
hatred of literature. Ecce adest musarum et eloquentiæ, totiusque nitoris
hostis acerrimus, qui literatis omnibus
inimicitias minitatur, quoniam, ut ipse
dictitabat, Terentiani essent, quos cum
odisse atque etiam persequi cœpisset,
voluntarium alii exilium, alias atque
alias alii latebras quærentes, tamdiu la-
tuere, quoad Dei beneficio, altero imperii anno decessit, qui si aliquanto
diutius vixisset, Gotica illa tempora
adversus bonas literas videbatur suscita-
turus. Lib. ii. p. 34. It is but fair to
add, that Erasmus ascribes to Adrian
the protection of letters in the Low
Countries.   Vix nostra phalanx susti-
nuisset hostium conjurationem, ni Adri-
anus tum Cardinalis, postea Romanus
pontifex, hoc edidisset oraculum : Bonas
literas non damno, hæreses et schismata

sedulous in encouraging polite and useful letters. The first part indeed of this period of thirty years was very adverse to the progress of learning; especially in that disastrous hour when the lawless mercenaries of Bourbon's army were led on to the sack of Rome. In this, and in other calamities of the same kind, it happened that universities and literary academies were broken up, that libraries were destroyed or dispersed. That of Sadolet, having been with difficulty saved in the pillage of Rome, was dispersed, in consequence of shipwreck during its transport to France.[z] A better era commenced with the pacification of Italy in 1531. The subsequent wars were either transient, or partial in their effects. The very extinction of all hope for civil freedom, which characterised the new period, turned the intellectual energies of an acute and ardent people towards those tranquil pursuits which their rulers would both permit and encourage.

2. The real excellence of the ancients in literature as well as art gave rise to an enthusiastic and exclusive ad- Admiration miration of antiquity, not unusual indeed in other of antiquity. parts of Europe, but in Italy a sort of national pride which all partook. They went back to the memory of past ages for consolation in their declining fortunes, and conquered their barbarian masters of the north in imagination with Cæsar and Marius. Every thing that reminded them of the slow decay of Rome, sometimes even their religion itself, sounded ill in their fastidious ears. Nothing was so much at heart with the Italian scholars as to write a Latin style, not only free from barbarism, but conformable to the standard of

---

damno. Epist. mclxxvi. There is not indeed much in this: but the Biographie universelle (Suppl., art. Busleiden) informs us that this pope was compelled to interfere in order to remove the impediments to the foundation of Busleiden's Collegium Trilingue ad Louvain. It is well known that Adrian VI. was inclined to reform some abuses in the church, enough to set the Italians against him. See his life, in Bayle, Note D.

[z] Cum enim direptis rebus cæteris, libri soli superstites ab hostium injuria intacti, in navim conjecti, ad Galliæ lit-

tus jam pervecti essent, incidit in vectores, et in ipsos familiares meos pestilentia. Quo metu ii permoti, quorum ad littora navis appulsa fuerat, onera in terram exponi non permisere. Ita asportati sunt in alienas et ignotas terras; exceptisque voluminibus paucis, quæ deportavi mecum huc proficiscens, mei reliqui illi tot labores quos impenderamus, Græcis præsertim codicibus conquirendis undique et colligendis, mei tanti sumptus, meæ curæ, omnes iterum jam ad nihilum reciderunt. Sadolet, Epist. lib. i. p. 23. (Colon. 1554.)

what is sometimes called the Augustan age, that is, of the period from Cicero to Augustus. Several of them affected to be exclusively Ciceronian.

3. Sadolet, one of the apostolic secretaries under Leo X.

Sadolet.

and Clement VII., and raised afterwards to the purple by Paul III., stood in as high a rank as any for purity of language without affectation, though he seems to have been reckoned of the Ciceronian school. Except his Epistles, however, none of Sadolet's works are now read, or even appear to have been very conspicuous in his own age; though Corniani has given an analysis of a treatise on education.[a] A greater name, in point of general lite-

Bembo.

rary reputation, was Peter Bembo, a noble Venetian, secretary with Sadolet to Leo, and raised, like him, to the dignity of a cardinal by Paul III. Bembo was known in Latin and Italian literature; and in each language both as a prose writer and a poet. We shall thus have to regard four claims which he prefers to a niche in the temple of fame, and we shall find none of them ungrounded. In pure Latin style he was not perhaps superior to Sadolet, but would not have yielded to any competitor in Europe. It has been told, in proof of Bembo's scrupulous care to give his compositions the utmost finish, that he kept forty portfolios, into which every sheet entered successively, and was only taken out to undergo his corrections, before it entered into the next limbo of this purgatory. Though this may not be quite true, it

---

[a] Niceron says of Sadolet's Epistles, which form a very thick volume: Il y a plusieurs choses dignes d'être remarquées dans les lettres de Sadolet; mais elles sont quelquefois trop diffuses, et par conséquent ennuyeuses à lire. I concur in this: yet it may be added, that the Epistles of Cicero would sometimes be tedious, if we took as little interest in their subjects as we commonly do in those of Sadolet. His style is uniformly pure and good; but he is less fastidious than Bembo, and does not use circuity to avoid a theological expression. They are much more interesting, at least than the ordinary Latin letters of his contemporaries, such as those of Paulus Manutius. An uniform goodness of heart and love of right prevail in the epistles of Sadolet. His desire of ecclesiastical reformation in respect of morals has caused him to be suspected of a bias towards Protestantism; and a letter in the most flattering terms, which he wrote to Melanchthon, but which that learned man did not answer, has been brought in corroboration of this; yet the general tenor of his letters refutes this surmise; his theology, which was wholly semi-Pelagian, must have led him to look with disgust on the early Lutheran school (Epist. l. iii. p. 121, and l. ix. p. 410); and after Paul III. bestowed on him the purple, he became a staunch friend of the court of Rome, though never losing his wish to see a reform of its abuses. This will be admitted by every one who takes the trouble to run over Sadolet's epistles.

is but an exaggeration of the laborious diligence by which he must often have reduced his sense to feebleness and vacuity. He was one of those exclusive Ciceronians who, keenly feeling the beauties of their master's eloquence, and aware of the corruption which, after the age of Augustus, came rapidly over the purity of style, rejected with scrupulous care not only every word or phrase which could not be justified by the practice of what was called the golden age, but even insisted on that of Cicero himself, as the only model they thought absolutely perfect. Paulus Manutius, one of the most rigorous, though of the most eminent among these, would not employ the words of Cicero's correspondents, though as highly accomplished and polite as himself. This fastidiousness was of course highly inconvenient in a language constantly applicable to the daily occurrences of life in epistles or in narration, and it has driven Bembo, according to one of his severest critics, into strange affectation and circuity in his Venetian history. It produced also, what was very offensive to the more serious reader, and is otherwise frigid and tasteless, an adaptation of heathen phrases to the usages and even the characters of Christianity.[b] It has been remarked also, that in his great solicitude about the choice of words, he was indifferent enough to the value of his meaning; a very common failing of elegant scholars, when they write in a foreign language. But if some praise is due, as surely it is, to the art of reviving that consummate grace and richness which enchants every successive generation in the periods of Cicero, we must place Bembo, had we nothing more than this to say of him, among the ornaments of literature in the sixteenth century.

4. The tone which Bembo and others of that school were

---

[b] This affectation had begun in the preceding century, and was carried by Campano in his Life of Braccio di Montone to as great an extreme as by Bembo or any Ciceronian of his age. Bayle (Bembus, Note B.) gives some odd instances of it in the latter. Notwithstanding his laborious scrupulosity as to language, Bembo is reproached by Lipsius, and others of a more advanced stage of critical knowledge, with many faults of Latin, especially in his letters. Ibid. Sturm says of the letters of Bembo: Ejus epistolæ scriptæ mihi magis quam missæ esse videntur. Indicia sunt hominis otiosi et imitatoris speciem magis rerum quam res ipsas consectantis. Ascham, Epist. cccxci.

[The origin of the Ciceronian controversy will have some light thrown on it by the Epistles of Politian, lib. v. 1-4. —1842.]

studiously giving to ancient literature, provoked one of the
Ciceronianus most celebrated works of Erasmus, the dialogues
of Erasmus. entitled Ciceronianus. The primary aim of these
was to ridicule the fastidious purity of that sort of writers
who would not use a case or tense for which they could not
find authority in the works of Cicero. A whole winter's
night, they thought, was well spent in composing a single
sentence; but even then it was to be revised over and over
again. Hence they wrote little except elaborated epistles.
One of their rules, he tells us, was never to speak Latin, if
they could help it, which must have seemed extraordinary
in an age when it was the common language of scholars from
different countries. It is certain, indeed, that the practice
cannot be favourable to very pure Latinity.

5. Few books of that age give us more insight into its
literary history and the public taste than the Ciceronianus.
In a short retrospect Erasmus characterises all the considerable writers in Latin since the revival of letters, and endeavours to show how far they wanted this Ciceronian elegance for which some were contending. He distinguishes
in a spirit of sound taste between a just imitation which leaves
free scope for genius, and a servile following of a single
writer. 'Let your first and chief care,' he says, 'be to
understand thoroughly what you undertake to write about.
That will give you copiousness of words, and supply you with
true and natural sentiments. Then will it be found how your
language lives and breathes, how it excites and hurries away
the reader, and how it is a just image of your own mind.
Nor will that be less genuine which you add to your own by
imitation.'

6. The Ciceronianus, however, goes in some passages
beyond the limited subject of Latin style. The controversy
had some reference to the division between the men of learning and the men of taste, between the lovers of the solid
and of the brilliant, in some measure also to that between
Christianity and Paganism, a garb which the incredulity of
the Italians affected to put on. All the Ciceronian party,
except Longolius, were on the other side of the Alps.[c] The

---

[c] Though this is generally said, on
the authority of Erasmus himself, Peter
Bunel is asserted by some French scholars of great name, and particularly by

object of the Italian scholars was to write pure Latin, to
glean little morsels of Roman literature, to talk a heathenish
philosophy in private, and leave the world to its own abuses.
That of Erasmus was to make men wiser and better by wit,
sense, and learning.

7. Julius Cæsar Scaliger wrote against the Ciceronianus
with all that unmannerly invective which is the dis- Scaliger's
grace of many scholars, and very much his own. against it.
His vanity blinded him to what was then obvious to Europe,
that with considerable learning, and still better parts, he
was totally unworthy of being named with the first man in
the literary republic. Nor in fact had he much right to take
up the cause of the Ciceronian purists, with whom he had
no pretension to be reckoned, though his reply to Erasmus is
not ill-written. It consists chiefly in a vindication of Cicero's
life and writings against some passages in the Ciceronianus
which seem to affect them, scarcely touching the question
of Latin style. Erasmus made no answer, and thus escaped
the danger of retaliating on Scaliger in his own phrases.

8. The devotedness of the Italians to Cicero was displayed
in a more useful manner than by this close imita- Editions of
tion. Pietro Vettori (better known as Victorius), Cicero.
professor of Greek and Roman literature at Florence, published an entire edition of the great orator's writings in
1534. But this was soon surpassed by a still more illustrious scholar, Paulus Manutius, son of Aldus, and his successor in the printing-house at Venice. His edition of Cicero
appeared in 1540 ; the most important which had hitherto
been published of any ancient author. In fact, the notes of
Manutius, which were subsequently very much augmented,[d]
form at this day in great measure the basis of interpretation
and illustration of Cicero, as what are called the Variorum
editions will show. A further accession to Ciceronian litera-

---

Henry Stephens, to have equalled in
Ciceronian purity the best of the Italians;
and Paulus Manutius owns him as his
master, in one of his epistles : Ego ab
illo maximum habebam beneficium, quod
me cum Politianis et Erasmis nescio quibus miserè errantem, in hanc rectè scribendi viam primus induxerat. In a later
edition, for Politianis et Erasmis, it was

thought more decent to introduce Phi-
lelphis et Campanis. Bayle, art. Bunel,
Nota A. The letters of Bunel, written
with great purity, were published in
1551. It is to be observed, that he had
lived much in Italy. Erasmus does not
mention him in the Ciceronianus.

[d] Renouard, Imprimerie des Aldes.

ture was made by Nizolius in his Observationes in M. Tullium Ciceronem, 1535. This title hardly indicates that it is a dictionary of Ciceronian words, with examples of their proper senses. The later and improved editions bear the title of Thesaurus Ciceronianus. I find no critical work in this period of greater extent and labour than that of Scaliger de Causis Latinæ Linguæ; by 'causis' meaning its principles. It relates much to the foundations of the language, or the rules by which its various peculiarities have been formed. He corrects many alleged errors of earlier writers, and sometimes of Valla himself; enumerating, rather invidiously, 634 of such errors in an index. In this book he shows much acuteness and judgment.

9. The Geniales Dies of Alexander ab Alexandro, a Alexander ab Alexandro. Neapolitan lawyer, published in 1522, are on the model of Aulus Gellius, a repertory of miscellaneous learning, thrown together without arrangement, on every subject of Roman philology and antiquities. The author had lived with the scholars of the fifteenth century, and even remembered Philelphus; but his own reputation seems not to have been extensive, at least through Europe. 'He has known every one,' says Erasmus, in a letter; 'no one knows who he is.'[e] The Geniales Dies has had better success in later ages than most early works of criticism, a good edition having appeared, with Variorum notes, in 1673. It gives, like the Lectiones Antiquæ of Cælius Rhodiginus, an idea of the vast extent to which the investigation of Latin antiquity had been already carried.

10. A very few books of the same class belong to this Works on Roman antiquities. period; and may deserve mention, although long since superseded by the works of those to whom we have just alluded, and who filled up and corrected their outline. Marlianus on the Topography of Rome, 1534, is admitted, though with some hesitation, by Grævius into his

---

[e] Demiror quis sit ille Alexander ab Alexandro. Novit omnes celebres Italiæ viros, Philelphum, Pomponium Lætum, Hermolaum, et quos non? Omnibus usus est familiariter; tamen nemo novit illum. Appendix, ad Erasm. Epist. ccclxxiii. (1533.) Bayle also remarks that Alexander is hardly mentioned by his contemporaries. Tiraqueau, a French lawyer of considerable learning, undertook the task of writing critical notes on the Geniales Dies about the middle of the century, correcting many of the errors which they contained.

Thesaurus Antiquitatum Romanarum, while he absolutely
sets aside the preceding labours of Blondus Flavius and
Pomponius Lætus. The Fasti Consulares were first published by Marlianus in 1549 ; and a work on the same subject in 1550 was the earliest production of the great Sigonius.
Before these the memorable events of Roman history had
not been critically reduced to a chronological series. A
treatise by Raphael of Volterra de Magistratibus et Sacer-
dotibus Romanorum is very inaccurate and superficial.[f]
Mazochius, a Roman bookseller, was the first who, in 1521,
published a collection of inscriptions. This was very imperfect, and full of false monuments. A better appeared in
Germany by the care of Apianus, professor of mathematics
at Ingoldstadt, in 1534.[g]

11. It could not be expected that the elder and more
copious fountain of ancient lore, the Greek language, Greek less
would slake the thirst of Italian scholars as readily studied in Italy.
as the Latin. No local association, no patriotic sentiment,
could attach them to that study. Greece itself no longer
sent out a Lascaris or a Musurus ; subdued, degraded, barbarous in language and learning, alien, above all, by insuperable enmity, from the church, she had ceased to be a
living guide to her own treasures. Hence we may observe,
even already, not a diminution, but a less accelerated increase
of Greek erudition in Italy. Two, however, among the most
considerable editions of Greek authors, in point of labour,
that the century produced, are the Galen by Andrew of Asola
in 1525, and the Eustathius from the press of Bladus at
Rome in 1542.[h] We may add, as first editions of Greek
authors, Epictetus, at Venice, in 1528, and Arrian in 1535 ;
Ælian, at Rome, in 1545. The Etymologicum Magnum of
Phavorinus, whose real name was Guarino, published at
Rome in 1523, was of some importance, while no lexicon
but the very defective one of Craston had been printed. The
Etymologicum of Phavorinus, however, is merely ' a com-
pilation from Hesychius, Suidas, Phrynichus, Harpocration,
Eustathius, the Etymologica, the lexicon of Philemon, some

---

[f] It is published in Sallengre, Novus
Thesaurus Antiquit. vol. iii.
[g] Burmann, præfat. in Gruter, Corpus

Inscriptionum.
[h] Gresswell's Early Parisian Greek
Press, p. 14.

treatises of Trypho, Apollonius, and other grammarians and various scholiasts. It is valuable as furnishing several important corrections of the authors from whom it was collected, and not a few extracts from unpublished grammarians.[i]

12. Of the Italian scholars, Vettori, already mentioned,
Schools of classical learning. seems to have earned the highest reputation for his skill in Greek. But there was no considerable town in Italy, besides the regular universities, where public instruction in the Greek as well as Latin tongue was not furnished, and in many cases by professors of fine taste and recondite learning, whose names were then eminent; such as Bonamico, Nizzoli, Parrhasio, Corrado, and Maffei, commonly called Raphael of Volterra. Yet, according to Tiraboschi, something was still wanting to secure these schools from the too frequent changes of teachers, which the hope of better salaries produced, and to give the students a more vigorous emulation, and a more uniform scheme of discipline.[k] This was to be supplied by the followers of Ignatius Loyola. But their interference with education in Italy did not begin in quite so early a period as the present.

13. If we cross the Alps, and look at the condition of
Budæus; his Commentaries on Greek. learning in countries which we left in 1520 rapidly advancing on the footsteps of Italy, we shall find that, except in purity of Latin style, both France and Germany were now capable of entering the lists of fair competition. France possessed, by general confession, the most profound Greek scholar in Europe, Budæus. If this could before have been in doubt, he raised himself to a pinnacle of philological glory by his Commentarii Linguæ Græcæ, Paris, 1529. The publications of the chief Greek authors by Aldus, which we have already specified, had given a compass of reading to the scholars of this period which those of the fifteenth century could not have possessed. But, with the exception of the Etymologicum of Phavorinus, just mentioned, no attempt had been made by a native of

---

[i] Quarterly Review, vol. xxii. Roscoe's Leo, ch. xi. Stephens is said to have inserted may parts of this lexicon of Guarino in his Thesaurus. Niceron, xxii. 141.

[k] Vol. viii. 114; x. 312. Ginguéné,

vii. 232, has copied Tiraboschi's account of these accomplished teachers with little addition, and probably with no knowledge of the original sources of information.

western Europe to interpret the proper meaning of Greek words; even he had confined himself to compiling from the grammarians. In this large and celebrated treatise, Budæus has established the interpretation of a great part of the language. All later critics write in his praise. There will never be another Budæus in France, says Joseph Scaliger, the most envious and detracting, though the most learned, of the tribe.[m] But, referring to what Baillet and Blount have collected from older writers,[n] we will here insert the character of these Commentaries which an eminent living scholar has given.

14. 'This great work of Budæus has been the text-book and common storehouse of succeeding lexicogra- Its cha- phers. But a great objection to its general use was racter. its want of arrangement. His observations on the Greek language are thrown together in the manner of a commonplace book, an inconvenience which is imperfectly remedied by an alphabetical index at the end. His authorities and illustrations are chiefly drawn from the prose writers of Greece, the historians, orators, and fathers. With the poets he seems to have had a less intimate acquaintance. His interpretations are mostly correct, and always elegantly expressed; displaying an union of Greek and Latin literature which renders his Commentaries equally useful to the students of both languages. The peculiar value of this work consists in the full and exact account which it gives of the Greek legal and forensic terms, both by literal interpretation, and by a comparison with the corresponding terms in Roman jurisprudence. So copious and exact is this department of the work, that no student can read the Greek orators to the best advantage unless he consults the Commentaries of Budæus. It appears from the Greek epistle subjoined to the work that the illustration of the forensic language of Athens and Rome was originally all that his plan embraced; and that when circumstances tempted him to extend the limits of his work, this still continued to be his chief object.'[o]

---

[m] Scaligerana, i. 33.

[n] Baillet, Jugemens des Savans, ii. 328 (Amst. 1725). Blount, in Budæo.

[o] Quarterly Review, vol. xxii., an article ascribed to the Bishop of London. The Commentaries of Budæus are written in a very rambling and desultory manner, passing from one subject to another

15. These Commentaries of Budæus stand not only far
Greek grammars and lexicons. above anything else in Greek literature before the middle of the sixteenth century, but are alone in their class. What comes next, but at a vast interval, is the Greek grammar of Clenardus, printed at Louvain in 1530. It was, however, much beyond Budæus in extent of circulation, and probably, for this reason, in general utility. This grammar was continually reprinted with successive improvements, and, defective as, especially in its original state, it must have been, was far more perspicuous than that of Gaza, though not, perhaps, more judicious in principle. It was for a long time commonly used in France ; and is in fact the principal basis of those lately or still in use among us; such as the Eton Greek grammar. The proof of this is, that they follow Clenardus in most of his innovations, and too frequently for mere accident, in the choice of instances.[p] The account of syntax in this grammar as well as that of Gaza, is very defective. A better treatise, in this respect, is by Varenius of Malines, Syntaxis Linguæ Græcæ, printed at Louvain about 1532. Another Greek grammar by Vergara, a native of Spain, has been extolled by some of the older critics and depreciated by

---

as a casual word may suggest the transition. Sic enim, he says, hos commentarios scribere instituimus, ut quicquid in ordinem seriemque scribendi incurreret, vel ex diverticulo quasi obviam se offerret, ad id digredi. A large portion of what is valuable in this work has been transferred by Stephens in his Thesaurus. The Latin criticisms of Budæus have also doubtless been borrowed.

Budæus and Erasmus are fond of writing Greek in their correspondence. Others had the same fancy; and it is curious that they ventured upon what has wholly gone out of use since the language has been so well understood. But probably this is the reason that later scholars have avoided it. Neither of these great men shine much in elegance or purity. One of Budæus, Aug. 15, 1519 (in Erasm. Epist. cccclv.), seems often incorrect, and in the mere style of a schoolboy.

[p] Clenardus seems first to have separated simple from contracted nouns, thus making ten declensions. Wherever he differs from Gaza, our popular grammars seem in general to have followed

him. He tells us, that he had drawn up his own for the use of his private pupils. Baillet observes, that the grammar of Clenardus, notwithstanding the mediocrity of his learning, has had more success than any other; those who have followed having mostly confined themselves to correcting and enlarging it. Jugemens des Savans, ii. 164. This is certainly true, as far as England is concerned; though the Eton grammar is in some degree an improvement on Clenardus.

[This was stated rather too strongly in my first edition. A learned person at the head of one of our public schools, in a communication with which he has favoured me, does not think, on a comparison of the two works, that the Eton Greek grammar owes very much to that of Clenardus, though there is no doubt much that may have been borrowed from him, and is inclined to believe that it was formed upon one published by the university of Padua, which contains the Eton grammar *totidem verbis*, and a great deal of other matter.

Of this Paduan grammar I am wholly

others.[q]   A Greek lexicon, of which the first edition was printed at Basle in 1537, is said to abound in faults and inaccuracies of every description.   The character given of it by Henry Stephens, even when it had been enlarged, if not improved, does not speak much for the means that the scholars of this age had possessed in labouring for the attainment of Greek learning.[r]

16. The most remarkable editions of Greek authors from the Parisian press were those of Aristophanes in 1528, and of Sophocles in 1529 ; the former printed by Gourmont, the latter by Colinæus; the earliest edition of Dionysius Halicarnassensis in 1546, and of Dio Cassius in 1548; both by Robert Stephens.   The first Greek edition of the Elements of Euclid appeared at Basle, in 1533, of Diogenes Laertius the same year, of five books of Diodorus in 1539, of Josephus in 1544 ; the first of Polybius in 1530, at Haguenau. Besides these editions of classical authors, Basil, and other of the Greek fathers, occupied the press of Frobenius, under the superintendence of Erasmus.   The publications of Latin authors by Badius Ascensius continued till his death in 1535. Colinæus began to print his small editions of the same class at Paris about 1521.   They are in that cursive character

(margin note: Editions of Greek authors.)

---

ignorant : if published before that of Clenardus, it must be of some interest in literary history. But certainly the grammar of Clenardus differs considerably from that of Gaza, by distinguishing contracted from simple nouns, as separate declensions, surely a great error; and by dividing the conjugations of verbs into thirteen, which Gaza makes but four, ending in ω, and one in μι. The choice of words for examples with Clenardus is very often the same as in our modern grammars, though not so constantly as I had at first supposed. It would be easy to point out rules in that grammarian which have been copied verbatim by his successors.—1842.]

   [q] Vergara de omnibus Græcæ linguæ grammaticæ partibus, 1573; rather 1537, for 'deinde Parisiis, 1550,' follows in Antonio, Bibl. Nova.

   [r] H. Stephanus de typographiæ suæ statu. Gesner himself says of this lexicon, which sometimes bore his name :

Circa annum 1537, lexicon Græco-Latinum, quod jam ante a diversis et innominatis nescio quibus miserè satis consarcinatum erat, ex Phavorini Camertis Lexico Græco ita auxi, ut nihil in eo extaret, quod non ut singulari fide, ita labore maximo adjicerem ; sed typographus me inscio, et præter omnem expectationem meam, exiguam duntaxat accessionis meæ partem adjecit, reservans sibi forte auctarium ad sequentes etiam editiones. He proceeds to say that he enlarged several other editions down to 1556, when the last that had been enriched by his additions appeared at Basle. Cæterum hoc anno, quo hæc scribo, 1562, Genevæ prodiisse audio longe copiosissimum emendatissimumque Græcæ linguæ thesaurum a Rob. Constantino incomparabilis doctrinæ viro, ex Joannis Crispini officinâ. Vide Gesneri Biblioth. Universalis, art. Conrad Gesner : this is part of a long account given here by Gesner of his own works.

which Aldus had first employed.[s] The number of such editions, both in France and Germany, became far more considerable than in the preceding age. They are not, however,
in general, much valued for correctness of text; nor had
many considerable critics even in Latin philology yet appeared on this side of the Alps. Robert Stephens
stands almost alone, who, by the publication of his
Thesaurus in 1535, augmented in a subsequent edition of
1543, may be said to have made an epoch in this department
of literature. The preceding dictionaries of Calepio and
other compilers had been limited to an interpretation of single
words, sometimes with reference to passages in the authors
who had employed them. This produced, on the one hand,
perpetual barbarisms and deviations from purity of idiom,
while it gave rise in some to a fastidious hypercriticism, of
which Valla had given an example.[t] Stephens first endeavoured to exhibit the proper use of words, not only in all
the anomalies of idiom, but in every delicate variation of
sense to which the pure taste and subtle discernment of the
best writers had adapted them. Such an analysis is perhaps
only possible with respect to a language wherein the extant
writers, and especially those who have acquired authority,
are very limited in number; and even in Latin, the most extensive dictionary, such as has grown up long since the days of
Robert Stephens, under the hands of Gesner, Forcellini, and
Facciolati, or such as might still improve upon their labour,
could only approach an unattainable perfection. What Stephens himself achieved would now be deemed far too defective for general use; yet it afforded the means of more purity
in style than any could in that age have reached without
unwearied exertion. Accordingly it is to be understood that
while a very few scholars, chiefly in Italy, had acquired a
facility and exactness of language which has seldom been surpassed, the general style retained a great deal of barbarism,
and neither in single words, nor always in mere grammar,
can bear a critical eye. Erasmus is often incorrect, espe-

Marginal note: Latin Thesaurus of R. Stephens.

---

[s] Gresswell's History of the Early Parisian Greek Press.
[t] Vives de causis corrupt. art. (Opera
Lud. Vives, edit. Basle, 1555, i. 358.)

He observes in another work, that there
was no full and complete dictionary of
Latin. Id. p. 475.

cially in his epistles, and says modestly of himself in the
Ciceronianus, that he is hardly to be named among writers
at all, unless blotting a great deal of paper with ink is enough
to make one. He is however among the best of his contemporaries, if a vast command of Latin phrase, and a spirited
employment of it, may compensate for some want of accuracy. Budæus, as has been already said, is hard and unpolished. Vives assumes that he has written his famous and
excellent work on the corruption of the sciences with some
elegance ; but this he says in language which hardly war-
rants the boast.[u] In fact, he is by no means a good writer.
But Melanchthon excelled Erasmus by far in purity of diction, and correctness of classical taste. With him we may
place Calvin in his Institutes, and our countryman Sir John
Cheke, as distinguished from most other Cisalpine writers by
the merit of what is properly called style. The praise, however, of writing pure Latin, or the pleasure of reading it, is
dearly bought when accompanied by such vacuity of sense as
we experience in the elaborate epistles of Paulus Manutius,
and the Ciceronian school in Italy.

17. Francis I. has obtained a glorious title, the Father
of French literature. The national propensity (or Progress of learning in France.
what once was such) to extol kings may have had
something to do with this ; for we never say the same of
Henry VIII. In the early part of his reign he manifested
a design to countenance ancient literature by public endowments. War, and unsuccessful war, sufficiently diverted his
mind from this scheme. But in 1531, a season of peace, he
established the royal college of three languages in the university of Paris, which did not quite deserve its name till
the foundation of a Latin professorship in 1534. Vatable
was the first professor of Hebrew, and Danes of Greek. In
1545 it appears that there were three professors of Hebrew
in the royal college, three of Greek, one of Latin, two of
mathematics, one of medicine, and one of philosophy. But

---

[u] Nitorem præterea sermonis addidi
aliquem, et quod non expediret res pul-
cherrimas sordidè ac spuriè vestiri, et
ut studiosi elegantiarum [orum ?] literarum non perpetuo in vocum et sermonis
cognitione adhærescerent ; quod hactenus
fere accidit, tædio nimirum infrugiferæ
ac horridæ molestiæ, quæ in percipiendis
artibus diutissimè erat devorata. i. 324.

this college had to encounter the jealousy of the university, tenacious of its ancient privileges, which it fancied to be trampled upon, and stimulated by the hatred of the pretended philosophers, the scholastic dialecticians, against philological literature. They tried to get the parliament on their side; but that body, however averse to innovation, of which it gave in this age, and long afterwards, many egregious proofs, was probably restrained by the king's known favour to learning from obstructing the new college as much as the university desired.[x] Danes had a colleague and successor as Greek professor in a favourite pupil of Budæus, and a good scholar, Toussain, who handed down the lamp in 1547 to one far more eminent, Turnebus. Under such a succession of instructors, it may be naturally presumed that the knowledge of Greek would make some progress in France. And no doubt the great scholars of the next generation were chiefly trained under these men. But the opposition of many, and the coldness almost of all, in the ecclesiastical order, among whom that study ought principally to have flourished, impeded in the sixteenth century, as it has perhaps ever since, the diffusion of Grecian literature in all countries of the Romish communion. We do not find much evidence of classical, at least of Greek, learning in any university of France, except that of Paris, to which students repaired from every quarter of the kingdom.[y] But a few once distinguished names of the age of Francis I. deserve to be mentioned. William Cop, physician to the king, and John Ruel, one of the earliest promoters of botanical science, the one translator of Galen, the other of Dioscorides; Lazarus Baif, a poet of some eminence in that

---

[x] The faculty of theology in 1530 condemned these propositions: 1. Scripture cannot be well understood without Greek and Hebrew; 2. A preacher cannot explain the epistle and gospel without these languages. In the same year they summoned Danes and Vatable with two more to appear in parliament, that they might be forbidden to explain Scripture by the Greek and Hebrew without permission of the university; or to say, the Hebrew, or the Greek, is so and so; lest they should injure the credit of the Vulgate. They admitted, however, that the study of Hebrew and Greek was praiseworthy in skilful and orthodox theologians, disposed to maintain the inviolable authority of the Vulgate. Contin. de Fleury, Hist. ecclésiast. xxvii. 233. See also Gaillard, Hist. de François I., vi. 289.

[y] We find, however, that a Greek and Latin school was set up in the diocese of Sadolet (Carpentras), about 1533: he endeavoured to procure a master from Italy, and seems, by a letter of the year 1540, to have succeeded. Sadol. Epist. lib. ix. and xvi.

age, who rendered two Greek tragedies into French verse;
with a few rather more obscure, such as Petit, Pin, Deloin,
De Chatel, who are cursorily mentioned in literary history,
or to whom Erasmus sometimes alludes.   Let us not forget
John Grollier, a gentleman who, having filled with honour
some public employments, became the first perhaps on this
side of the Alps who formed a very extensive library and
collection of medals.   He was the friend and patron of the
learned during a long life; a character little affected in that
age by private persons of wealth on the less sunny side of the
Alps.   Grollier's library was not wholly sold till the latter
part of the seventeenth century.[z]

18. In Spain the same dislike of innovation stood in the
way.   Greek professorships existed, however, in the Learning in
universities; and Nunnes, usually called Pincianus Spain.
(from the Latin name for the city of Valladolid), a disciple
of Lebrixa, whom he surpassed, taught the language at
Alcalá, and afterwards at Salamanca.   He was the most
learned man whom Spain had possessed; and his edition of
Seneca, in 1536, has obtained the praise of Lipsius.[a]   Resende,
the pupil of Arias Barbosa and Lebrixa in Greek, has been
termed the restorer of letters in Portugal.   None of the
writings of Resende, except a Latin grammar, published in
1540, fall within the present period; but he established,
about 1531, a school at Lisbon, and one afterwards at Evora,
where Estaço, a man rather better known, was educated.[b]
School divinity and canon law over-rode all liberal studies
throughout the Peninsula; of which the catalogue of books
at the end of Antonio's Bibliotheca Nova is a sufficient
witness.

19. The first effects of the great religious schism in Germany were not favourable to classical literature.[c] Effects of
An all-absorbing subject left neither relish nor Reformation
                                                  on learning.
leisure for human studies.   Those who have made the
greatest advances in learning were themselves generally
involved in theological controversy; and, in some countries,
had to encounter either personal suffering on account of

---

[z] Biog. univ. Grollier.   [b] Biogr. univ.
[a] Antonio, Bibl. Nova. Biogr. univ.   [c] Erasm. Epist. passim.

their opinions, or, at least, the jealousy of a church that hated the advance of knowledge. The knowledge of Greek and Hebrew was always liable to the suspicion of heterodoxy. In Italy, where classical antiquity was the chief object, this dread of learning could not subsist. But few learned much of Greek in these parts of Europe without some reference to theology,[d] especially to the grammatical interpretation of the Scriptures. In those parts which embraced the Reformation a still more threatening danger arose from the distempered fanaticism of its adherents. Men who interpreted the Scripture by the Spirit could not think human learning of much value in religion ; and they were as little likely to perceive any other advantage it could possess. There seemed, indeed, a considerable peril, that through the authority of Carlostadt, or even of Luther, the lessons of Crocus and Mosellanus would be totally forgotten.[e] And this would very probably have been the case, if one man, Melanchthon, had not perceived the necessity of preserving human learning as a bulwark to theology itself against the wild waves of enthusiasm. It was owing to him that both the study of the Greek and Latin languages, and that of the Aristotelian philosophy, were maintained in Germany.[f] Nor did his activity content itself with animating the universities. The schools of preparatory instruction, which had hitherto furnished merely the elements of grammar, throwing the whole burthen of philological learning on the universities, began before the middle of the century to be improved by Melanchthon, with the assistance of a friend, even superior to him, probably, in that walk of literature, Joachim Camerarius. 'Both these great men,' says Eichhorn, ' laboured upon one plan, upon the same principle, and with equal zeal ; they were, in the strictest sense, the fathers of that pure taste and solid learning by which the next generation was distinguished.' Under the names of Lycæum or Gymnasium, these German schools gave a more complete

---

[d] Erasm. Adag. chil. iv. c. v. § 1. Vives, apud Meiners, Vergl. der Sitten, ii. 737.

[e] Seckendorf, p. 198.

[f] [It is said by Melchior Adam, Vitæ Philosophorum, p. 87, that when Me-

lanchthon first lectured on the Philippics of Demosthenes in 1524, he had but four hearers, and these were obliged to transcribe from their teacher's copy.— 1842.]

knowledge of the two languages, and sometimes the elements
of philosophy.[g]

20. We derive some acquaintance with the state of
education in this age from the writings of John ~Sturm's ac-~
Sturm, than whom scarce any one more contri- ~man schools.~
buted to the cause of letters in Germany. He became in 1538, and continued for above forty years,
rector of a celebrated school at Strasburg. Several treatises on education, especially one, De Literarum Ludis
rectè instituendis, bear witness to his assiduity. If the
scheme of classical instruction which he has here laid down
may be considered as one actually in use, there was a solid
structure of learning erected in the early years of life,
which none of our modern academies would pretend to
emulate. Those who feel any curiosity, about the details
of this course of education, which seems almost too rigorous
for practice, will find the whole in Morhof's Polyhistor.[h]
It is sufficient to say, that it occupies the period of life
between the ages of six and fifteen, when the pupil is presumed to have acquired a very extensive knowledge of the
two languages. Trifling as it may appear to take notice of
this subject, it serves at least as a test of the literary pre-
eminence of Germany. For we could, as I conceive, trace
no such education in France, and certainly not in England.

21. The years of the life of Camerarius correspond to
those of the century. His most remarkable works ~Learning in~
fall partly into the succeeding period; but many ~Germany.~
of the editions and translations of Greek authors, which
occupied his laborious hours, were published before 1550.
He was one of the first who knew enough of both languages, and of the subjects treated, to escape the reproach
which has fallen on the translators of the fifteenth century.
His Thucydides, printed in 1540, was superior to any
preceding edition. The universities of Tubingen and
Leipsic owed much of their prosperity to his superintending
care. Next to Camerarius among the German scholars, we
may place Simon Grynæus, professor of Greek at Heidelberg in 1523, and translator of Plutarch's Lives. Micyllus,

---

[g] Eichhorn, iii. 254 et post.   [h] Lib. ii. c. 10.

his successor in this office, and author of a treatise De re metricâ, of which Melanchthon speaks in high terms of praise, was more celebrated than most of his countrymen for Latin poetry. Yet in this art he fell below Eobanus Hessus, whose merit is attested by the friendship of Erasmus, Melanchthon, and Camerarius, as well as by the best verses that Germany had to boast. It would be very easy to increase the list of scholars in that empire; but we should find it more difficult to exhaust the enumeration. Germany was not only far elevated in literary progress above France, but on a level, as we may fairly say, with Italy herself. The university of Marburg was founded in 1526, that of Copenhagen in 1539, of Konigsberg in 1544, of Jena in 1548.

22. We come now to investigate the gradual movement of learning in England, the state of which about 1520 we have already seen. In 1521 the first Greek characters appear in a book printed at Cambridge, Linacre's Latin translation of Galen de Temperamentis, and in the titlepage, but there only, of a treatise περὶ Διψάδων, by Bullock. They are employed several times for quotations in Linacre de Emendata Structura Orationis, 1524.[1] This treatise is chiefly a series of grammatical remarks, relating to distinctious in the Latin language now generally known. It must have been highly valuable, and produced a considerable effect in England, where nothing of that superior criticism had been attempted. In order to judge of its proper merit, it should be compared with the antecedent works of Valla and Perotti. Every rule is supported by authorities; and Linacre, I observe, is far more cautious than Valla in asserting what is not good Latin, contenting himself, for the most part, with showing what is. It has been remarked that, though Linacre formed his own style on the model of Quintilian, he took most of his authorities from Cicero. This treatise, the firstfruits of English erudition, was well received, and frequently printed on the

In England Linacre.

---

[1] The author begins by bespeaking the reader's indulgence for the Greek printing. Pro tuo candore, optime lector, æquo animo feras, si quæ literæ in exemplis Hellenismi vel tonis, vel spiritibus, vel affectionibus careant. Iis enim non satis erat instructus typographus, videlicet recens ab eo fusis characteribus Græcis, nec parata ea copia quæ ad hoc agendum opus est.

Continent. Melanchthon recommended its use in the schools
of Germany. Linacre's translation of Galen has been praised
by Sir John Cheke, who in some respects bears rather hardly
on his learned precursor.[k]

23. Croke, who became tutor to the duke of Richmond,
son of Henry VIII., did not remain at Cambridge long after
the commencement of this period. But in 1524, Robert
Wakefield, a scholar of some reputation, who had been professor in a German university, opened a public Lectures in
lecture there in Greek, endowed with a salary by the univer-sities.
the king. We know little individually of his hearers; but,
notwithstanding the confident assertions of Antony Wood,
there can be no doubt that Cambridge was, during the whole
of this reign, at least on a level with the sister university,
and indeed, to speak plainly, above it. Wood enumerates
several persons educated at Oxford about this time, sufficiently skilled in Greek to write in that language, or to
translate from it, or to comment upon Greek authors. The
list might be enlarged by the help of Pits; but he is less of
a scholar than Wood. This much, after all, appears, that
the only editions of classical authors published in England
before 1540, except those already mentioned, are five of
Virgil's Bucolics, two of a small treatise of Seneca, with one
of Publius Syrus; all evidently for the mere use of school-
boys. We may add one of Cicero's Philippics, printed for
Pinson in 1521; and the first book of his epistles at Oxford
in 1529. Lectures in Greek and Latin were, however, established in a few colleges at Oxford.

24. If Erasmus, writing in 1528, is to be believed, the
English boys were wont to disport in Greek epi- Greek per-
grams.[m] But this must be understood as only ap- haps taught to boys.
plicable to a very few, upon whom some extraordinary pains
had been bestowed. Thus Sir Thomas Elyot, in his Governor,
first published in 1531, points out a scheme of instruction
which comprehends the elements of the Greek language.
There is no improbability in the supposition, and some

---

[k] Johnson's Life of Linacre.
[m] An tu credidisses unquam fore, ut
apud Britannos aut Batavos pueri Græcè

garrirent, Græcis epigrammatiis non infeliciter luderent? Dial. de Pronuntiatione, p. 48, edit. 1528.

evidence to support it, that the masters of our great schools,
a Lily, a Cox, an Udal, a Nowell, did not leave boys of quick
parts wholly unacquainted with the rudiments of a language
they so much valued.[n] It tends to confirm this supposition,
that in the statutes of the new cathedrals established by
Henry in 1541, it is provided that there shall be a grammar
school for each, with a head master, 'learned in Latin and
Greek.' Such statutes, however, are not conclusive evidences that they were put in force.[o] In the statutes of
Wolsey's intended foundation at Ipswich, some years earlier,
though the course of instruction is amply detailed, we do
not find it extend to the merest elements of Greek.[p] It is
curious to compare this with the course prescribed by Sturm
for the German schools.

25. But English learning was chiefly indebted for its more
Teaching of
Smith at
Cambridge. rapid advance to two distinguished members of the
university of Cambridge ; Smith, afterwards secre-
tary of state to Elizabeth, and Cheke. The former began to
read the Greek lecture in 1533 ; and both of them, soon
afterwards, combined to bring in the true pronunciation
of Greek, upon which Erasmus had already written. The
early students of that language, receiving their instructions
from natives, had acquired the vicious uniformity of sounds
belonging to the corrupted dialect. Reuchlin's school, of
which Melanchthon was one, adhered to this, and were
called Itacists, from the continual recurrence of the sound of
Iota in modern Greek, being thus distinguished from the
Etists of Erasmus's party.[q] Smith and Cheke proved, by

---

[n] Churton, in his Life of Nowell, says
that the latter taught the Greek Testament to the boys at Westminster School,
referring for authority to a passage in
Strype, which I have not been able to
find. There is nothing at all improbable
in the fact. These inquiries will be
deemed too minute by some in this age.
But they are not unimportant in their
bearing on the history of literature ; and
an exaggerated estimate of English learning in the age of the Reformation generally prevails. Sir Thomas Pope, founder
of Trinity College, Oxford, observes, in
a letter to Cardinal Polo in 1556, that
when he was 'a young scholar at Eton,

the Greek tongue was growing apace ;
the study of which is now alate much
decayed.' Warton, iii. 279. I do not
think this implies more than a reference
to the time, which was about 1520 : he
means thnt Greek was beginning to be
studied in England.

[o] Warton, iii. 265.

[p] Strype's Ecclesiastical Memorials,
Appendix, No. 35.

[q] Eichhorn, iii. 217. Melanchthon,
in his Greek grammar, follows Reuchlin ;
Luscinius is on the side of Erasmus.
Ibid. In very recent publications I observe that attempts have been made to
set up again the 'lugubres sonos, et

testimonies of antiquity, that the latter were right; and 'by this revived pronunciation,' says Strype, 'was displayed the flower and plentifulness of that language, the variety of vowels, the grandeur of diphthongs, the majesty of long letters, and the grace of distinct speech.'[r] Certain it is, that about this time some Englishmen began to affect a knowledge of Greek. Sir Ralph Sadler, in his embassy to the king of Scotland, in 1540, had two or three Greek words embroidered on the sleeves of his followers, which led to a ludicrous mistake on the part of the Scotch bishops. Scotland, however, herself was now beginning to receive light; the Greek language was first taught in 1534 at Montrose, which continued for many years to be what some call a flourishing school.[s] But the whole number of books printed in Scotland before the middle of the century has been asserted to be only seven. No classical author, or even a grammar, is among these.[t]

26. Cheke, successor of Smith as lecturer in Greek at Cambridge, was appointed the first royal professor of that language in 1540, with a respectable salary. *Succeeded by Cheke.* He carried on Smith's scheme, if indeed it were not his own, for restoring the true pronunciation, in spite of the strenuous opposition of Bishop Gardiner, chancellor of the university. This prelate, besides a literary controversy in letters between himself and Cheke, published at Basle in 1555, interfered, in

---

illud flebile iota' of the modern Greeks. To adopt their pronunciation, even if right, would be buying truth very dear.

[r] Strype's Life of Smith, p. 17. 'The strain I heard was of a higher mood.' I wonder what author honest John Strype has copied or translated in this sentence; for he never leaves the ground so far in his own style.

[s] M'Crie's Life of Knox, i. 6, and Note C. p. 342.

[t] The list in Herbert's History of Printing, iii. 468, begins with the breviary of the church of Aberdeen; the first part printed at Edinburgh in 1509, the second in 1510. A poem without date, addressed to James V., de suscepto regni regimine, which seems to be in Latin, and must have been written about 1528, comes the nearest to a learned work. Two editions of Lindsay's poems,

two of a translation of Hector Boece's chronicles, two of a temporary pamphlet called Scotland's Complaint, with one of the statutes of the kingdom, printed in pursuance of an act of parliament passed in 1540, and a religious tract by one Balnaves, compose the rest. [But this list appears to be not quite accurate. A collection of pamphlets in the Scottish dialect has been discovered, printed at Edinburgh in 1508, and therefore older than the breviary in the foregoing enumeration. Pinkerton's Scottish Poems, 1792, vol. i. p. 22. On the other hand, it is contended that no edition of Lindsay's poems, printed in Scotland, is older than 1568. Pinkerton's Ancient Scottish Poems (a different publication from the former), 1786, vol. i. p. 104.— 1842.]

a more orthodox way, by prohibiting the new style of speech in a decree which, for its solemnity, might relate to the highest articles of faith. Cheke however in this, as in greater matters, was on the winning side; and the corrupt pronunciation was soon wholly forgotten.

27. Among the learned men who surrounded Cheke at Cambridge, none was more deserving than Ascham;

Ascham's character of Cambridge. whose knowledge of ancient languages was not shown in profuse quotation, or enveloped in Latin phrase, but served to enrich his mind with valuable sense, and taught him to transfer the firmness and precision of ancient writers to our own English, in which he is nearly the first that deserves to be named, or that is now read. He speaks in strong terms of his university. 'At Cambridge also, in St. John's College, in my time, I do know that not so much the good statutes as two gentlemen of worthy memory, Sir John Cheke and Dr. Redman, by their own example of excellency in learning, of godliness in living, of diligence in studying, of counsel in exhorting, by good order in all things, did breed up so many learned men in that one college of St. John's at one time as I believe the whole university of Louvain in many years was never able to afford.'[u] Lectures in humanity, that is, in classical literature, were, in 1535, established by the king's authority in all colleges of the university of Oxford where they did not already exist; and in the royal injunctions at the same time for the reformation of

---

[u] Ascham's Schoolmaster. In the Life of Ascham by Grant, prefixed to the former's epistles, he enumerates the learned of Cambridge about 1530. Ascham was himself under Pember, homini Græcæ linguæ admirabili facultate excultissimo. The others named are Day, Redman, Smith, Cheke, Ridley, Grindal (not the archbishop), Watson, Haddon, Pilkington, Horn, Christopherson, Wilson, Seton, et infiniti alii excellenti doctrinâ præditi. Most of these are men afterwards distinguished in the church on one side or the other. This is a sufficient refutation of Wood's idle assertion of the superiority of Oxford; the fact seems to have been wholly otherwise. Ascham himself, in a letter without date, but evidently written about the time that the controversy of Cheke and Gardiner began, praises thus the learning of Cambridge:—Aristoteles nunc et Plato, quod factum est etiam apud nos hic quinquennium, in sua lingua a pueris leguntur Sophocles et Euripides sunt hic familiariores, quam olim Plautus fuerat, cum tu hic eras. Herodotus, Thucydides, Xenophon, magis in ore et manibus omnium tenentur, quam tum Titus Livius, etc. Ibid. p. 74. What then can be thought of Antony Wood when he says, 'Cambridge was in the said king's reign overspread with barbarism and ignorance, as 'tis often mentioned by several authors?' Hist. and Antiq. of Oxford, A.D. 1545.

academical studies a regard to philological learning is enforced.[x]

28. Antony Wood, though he is by no means always consistent, gives rather a favourable account of the state of philological learning at Oxford in the last years of Henry VIII. There can, indeed, be no doubt that it had been surprisingly increasing in all England through his reign. More grammar schools, it is said by Knight, were founded in thirty years before the Reformation, meaning, I presume, the age of Henry, than in three hundred years preceding. But the suddenness with which the religious establishment was changed on the accession of Edward, and still more the rapacity of the young king's council, who alienated or withheld the revenues designed for the support of learning, began to cloud the prospect before the year 1550.[y] Wood, in reading whom allowance is to be made for a strong, though not quite avowed bias towards the old system of ecclesiastical and academical government, inveighs against the visitors of the university appointed by the crown in 1548, for burning and destroying valuable books. And this seems to be confirmed by other evidence. It is true that these books, though it was a vile act to destroy them, would have been more useful to the English antiquary than to the classical student. Ascham, a contemporary Protestant, denies that the university of Cambridge declined at all before the accession of Mary in 1553.

Wood's account of Oxford.

29. Edward himself received a learned education, and, according to Ascham, read the Ethics of Aristotle in Greek. Of the princess Elizabeth, his favourite pupil, we have a similar testimony.[z] Mary was not by any

Education of Edward and his sisters.

---

[x] Warton, iii. 272.

[y] Strype, ii. 258. Todd's Cranmer, ii. 33.

[z] Of the king he says : Dialecticam didicit, et nunc Græcè discit Aristotelis Ethica. Eo progressus est in Græca lingua, ut in philosophia Ciceronis ex Latinis Græca facillime faciat. Dec. 1550. Ascham, Epist. iv. Elizabeth spoke French and Italian as well as English ; Latin fluently and correctly ; Greek tolerably. She began every day by reading the Greek Testament, and

afterwards the orations of Isocrates, and tragedies of Sophocles. Some years afterwards, in 1555, he writes of her to Sturm : Domina Elizabeth et ego una legimus Græcè orationes Æschinis et Demosthenis περὶ στεφάνου. Illa prælegit mihi, et primo aspectu tam scienter intelligit non solum proprietatem linguæ et oratoris sensum, sed totam causæ contentionem, populi scita, consuetudinem et mores illius urbis, ut summopere admireris. p. 53. In 1560 he asserts that there are not four persons, in court or

means illiterate. It is hardly necessary to mention Jane Grey and the wife of Cecil. Their proficiency was such as to excite the admiration of every one, and is no measure of the age in which they lived. And their names carry us on a little beyond 1550, though Ascham's visit to the former was in that year.

30. The reader must be surprised to find that, notwith-standing these high and just commendations of our scholars, no Greek grammars or lexicons were yet printed in England, and scarcely any works in that or the Latin language. In fact, there was no regular press in either university at this time, though a very few books had been printed in each about 1520 ; nor had they one till near the end of Elizabeth's reign. Reginald Wolfe, a German printer, obtained a patent, dated April 19, 1541, giving him the ex-clusive right to print in Latin, Greek, and Hebrew, and also Greek and Latin grammars, though mixed with English, and charts and maps. But the only productions of his press before the middle of the century are two homilies of Chry-sostom, edited by Cheke in 1543. Elyot's Latin and English Dictionary, 1538, was the first, I believe, beyond the mere vocabularies of school boys; and it is itself but a meagre performance.[a] Latin grammars were of course so frequently published, that it has not been worth while to take notice of them. But the Greek and Latin lexicon of Hadrian Junius, though dedicated to Edward VI., and said to have been com-piled in England (I know not how this could be the case), being the work of a foreigner, and printed at Basle, in 1548, cannot be reckoned as part of our stock.[b]

The progress of learning is still slow.

---

college (in aula, in academia), who know Greek better than the Queen.

Habemus Angliæ reginam, says Eras-mus long before of Catherine, feminam egregiè doctam, cujus filia Maria scribit bene Latinas epistolas. Thomæ Mori domus nihil aliud quam musarum est domicilium. Epist. MXXXIV.

[a] Elyot boasts that this ' contains a thousand more Latin words than were together in any one dictionary published in this realm at the time when I first be-gan to write this commentary.' Though far from being a good, or even, according to modern notions, a tolerable diction-

ary, it must have been of some value at the time. It was afterwards much aug-mented by Cooper.

[b] Wood ascribes to one Tolley or Tol-leius a sort of Greek grammar, Progym-nasmata Linguæ Græcæ, dedicated to Edward VI. And Pits, in noticing also other works of the same kind, says of this : Habentur Monachii in Bavaria in bibliotheca ducali. As no mention is made of such a work by Herbert or Dibdin, I had been inclined to think its existence apocryphal. It is certainly foreign.

[I have since my first edition seen this

31. It must appear, on the whole, that under Edward VI. there was yet rather a commendable desire of learn- Want of books and public libra-ries. ing, and a few vigorous minds at work for their own literary improvement, than any such diffusion of knowledge as can entitle us to claim for that age an equality with the chief continental nations. The means of acquiring true learning were not at hand. Few books, as we have seen, useful to the scholar, had been published in England; those imported were of course expensive. No public libraries of any magnitude had yet been formed in either of the universities; those of private men were exceedingly few. The king had a library, of which honourable mention is made; and Cranmer possessed a good collection of books at Lambeth; but I do not recollect any other person of whom this is recorded.

32. The progress of philological literature in England was connected with that of the Reformation. The Destruction of monas-teries no injury to learning. learned of the earlier generation were not at all Pro-testants, but their disciples were zealously such. They taunted the adherents of the old religion with igno-rance; and though by that might be meant ignorance of the Scriptures, it was by their own acquaintance with languages that they obtained their superiority in this respect. And here I may take notice, that we should be deceived by acquiescing in the strange position of Warton, that the dis-solution of the monasteries in 1536 and the next two years gave a great temporary check to the general state of letters in England.[c] This writer is inconsistent with himself; for no one had a greater contempt for the monastic studies, dia-lectics and theology. But, as a desire to aggravate, in every

---

book in the British Museum. Its title is: Progymnasmata Græcæ grammatices autore David Tavelego medico. Ant-werp, 1547. It is dedicated to Edward VI.; and the dedication is dated at Ox-ford, Kal. Jul. 1546; but the privilege to print is at Bruxelles, Nov. 13, 1546. The author says it had been written eight years, as well as a Latin grammar already printed. Græca vero rudimenta nondum prodiere in publicum. It does not appear that Tavelegus, called Tol-ley and Taulæus by others, was precep-tor to the young prince. The grammar is very short, and seems to be a com-

pendium of Clenardus. It is remark-able that in this copy, which appears to have been presented to Edward, he is called VI. while his father was still living. Κύριε σώσον τὸν Ἐδούαρδον ἕκτον πρωτόγονον τοῦ βασίλεως. This is on an illuminated page adorned with the prince's feather, and the lines sub-scribed:—

Principis Edwardi sunt hæc insignia sexti,
Cujus honos nomenque precor subsistat in
    ævum.

—1842.]

  [c] History of Engl. Poetry, iii. 268.

possible respect, the supposed mischiefs of the dissolution of
monasteries is abundantly manifest in many writers later
than Warton, I shall briefly observe, that men are deceived,
or deceive others, by the equivocal use of the word learning.
If good learning, *bonæ literæ*, which for our present purpose
means a sound knowledge of Greek and Latin, was to be
promoted, there was no more necessary step in doing so
than to put down bad learning, which is worse than ignorance, and which was the learning of the monks, so far as
they had any at all. What would Erasmus have thought
of one who should in his days have gravely intimated, that
the abolition of monastic foundations would retard the progress of literature? In what Protestant country was it accompanied with such a consequence, and from whom, among
the complaints sometimes made, do we hear this cause
assigned? I am ready to admit, that in the violent courses
pursued by Henry VIII. many schools attached to monasteries were broken up, and I do not think it impossible that
the same occurred in other parts of Europe. It is also to be
fully stated and kept in mind, that by the Reformation the
number of ecclesiastics and consequently of those requiring
what was deemed a literary education was greatly reduced.
The English universities, as we are well aware, do not contain
by any means the number of students that frequented them
in the thirteenth century. But are we therefore a less
learned nation than our fathers of the thirteenth century?
Warton seems to lament, that 'most of the youth of the
kingdom betook themselves to mechanical or other illiberal
employments, the profession of letters being now supposed to
be without support or reward.' Doubtless many who would
have learned the Latin accidence, and repeated the breviary,
became useful mechanics. But is this to be called, not
rewarding the profession of letters? and are the deadliest
foes of the Greek and Roman muses to be thus confounded
with their worshippers? The loss of a few schools in the
monasteries was well compensated by the foundation of
others on a more enlightened plan and with much better instructors, and after the lapse of some years the communication of substantial learning came in the place of that tincture
of Latin which the religious orders had supplied. Warton,

it should be remarked, has been able to collect the names of
not more than four or five abbots and other regulars, in the
time of Henry VIII., who either possessed some learning
themselves, or encouraged it in others.

33. We may assist our conception of the general state of
learning in Europe by looking at some of the books   Ravisius
which were then deemed most usefully subsidiary   Textor.
to its acquisition. Besides the lexicons and grammatical
treatises that have been mentioned, we have a work first
published about 1522, but frequently reprinted, and in
much esteem, the Officina of Ravisius Textor. Of this book
Peter Danes, a man highly celebrated in his day for erudition, speaks as if it were an abundant storehouse of knowledge, admirable for the manner of its execution, and comparable to any work of antiquity. In spite of this praise, it is
no more than a common-place book from Latin authors, and
from translations of the Greek, and could deserve no regard
except in a half-informed generation.

34. A far better evidence of learning, was given by Conrad
Gesner, a man of prodigious erudition, in a con-   Conrad
tinuation of his Bibliotheca Universalis (the earliest   Gesner.
general catalogue of books with an estimate of their merits),
to which he gave the rather ambitious title of Pandectæ
Universales, as if it were to hold the same place in general
science that the Digest of Justinian does in civil law. It is
a sort of index to all literature, containing references only,
and therefore less generally useful, though far more learned
and copious in instances, than the Officina of Ravisius. It
comprehends, besides all ancient authors, the schoolmen and
other writers of the middle ages. The references are sometimes very short, and more like hints to one possessed of a
large library than guides to the general student. In connexion with the Bibliotheca Universalis, it forms a literary
history or encyclopædia, of some value to those who are
curious to ascertain the limits of knowledge in the middle of
the sixteenth century.

CHAPTER VI.

HISTORY OF THEOLOGICAL LITERATURE IN EUROPE FROM 1520 TO 1550.

Advance of the Reformation — Differences of Opinion — Erasmus — The Protestant Opinions spread farther — Their Prevalence in Italy — Reaction of Church of Rome — Theological Writings — Luther — Spirit of the Reformation — Translations of Scripture.

1. THE separation of part of Europe from the church of Progress of Rome is the great event that distinguishes these the Reformation. thirty years. But as it is not our object to traverse the wide field of civil or ecclesiastical history, it will suffice to make a few observations rather in reference to the spirit of the times than to the public occurrences that sprung from it. The new doctrine began to be freely preached, and with immense applause of the people, from the commencement of this period, or, more precisely, from the year 1522, in many parts of Germany and Switzerland; the Duke of Deuxponts in that year, or, according to some authorities, in 1523, having led the way in abolishing the ancient ceremonies; and his example having been successively followed in Saxony, Hesse, Brandenburg, Brunswick, many imperial cities, and the kingdoms of Denmark and Sweden, by the disciples of Luther; while those who adhered to Zwingle made similar changes in Zurich and in several other cantons of Switzerland.[a]

2. The magistrates generally proceeded, especially at the Interference outset, with as great caution and equity as were of civil power practicable in so momentous a revolution; though perhaps they did not always respect the laws of the empire. They commonly began by allowing freedom of preaching, and

---

Dr. Seckendorf, Gerdes.

forbad that any one should be troubled about his religion. This, if steadily acted upon, repressed the tumultuous populace, who were eager for demolishing images, the memorials of the old religion, as much as it did the episcopal courts, which, had they been strong enough, might have molested those who so plainly came within their jurisdiction. The Reformation depended chiefly on zealous and eloquent preachers ; the more eminent secular clergy, as well as many regulars, having espoused its principles. They encountered no great difficulty in winning over the multitude ; and when thus a decisive majority was obtained, commonly in three or four years from the first introduction of free preaching, the government found it time to establish, by a general edict, the abolition of the mass, and of such ceremonies as they did not deem it expedient to retain. The conflict between the two parties in Germany seems to have been less arduous than we might expect. It was usually accompanied by an expulsion of the religious of both sexes from their convents—a measure, especially as to women, unjust and harsh ;[b] and sometimes by an alienation of ecclesiastical revenues to the purposes of the state ; but this was not universal in Germany, nor was it countenanced by Luther. I cannot see any just reason to charge the Protestant princes of the empire with having been influenced generally by such a motive. In Sweden, however,

---

[b] Wilibald Pirckheimer wrote to Melanchthon, complaining that a convent of nuns at Nuremberg, among whom were two of his sisters, had been molested and insulted because they would not accept confessors appointed by the senate. Res eo deducta est ut quicunque miserandas illas offendere et incessere audet, obsequium Deo se præstitisse arbitretur. Idque non solum a viris agitur, sed et a mulieribus ; et illis mulieribus, quarum liberis omnem exhibuere caritatem. Non solum enim viris, qui alios docere contendunt, se ipsos vero minime emendant, urbs nostra referta est, sed et mulieribus curiosis, garrulis et otiosis, quæ omnia potius quam domum propriam gubernare satagunt. Pirckheimer Opera, Frankf. 1610, p. 375. He was a moderate man, concurring with the Lutherans in most of their doctrine, but against the violation of monastic vows. Several letters passed between him and Erasmus. The latter, though he could not approve the hard usage of women, hated the monks so much, that he does not greatly disapprove what was done towards them. In Germaniâ multa virginum ac monachorum monasteria crudeliter direpta sunt. Quidam magistratus agunt moderatius. Ejecerunt eos duntaxat, qui illic non essent professi, et vetuerunt novitios recipi ; ademerunt illis curam virginum, et jus alibi concionandi quam in suis monasteriis. Breviter, absque magistratus permissu nihil licet illis agere. Videntur huc spectare, ut ex monasteriis faciant parochias. Existimant enim hos conjuratos phalangas et tot privilegiis armatos diutius ferri non posse. (Basil. Aug. 1525.) Epist. Dcccliv. Multis in locis durè tractati sunt monachi ; verum plerique cum sint intolerabiles, alia tamen ratione corrigi non possunt. Epist. Dcclvii.

the proceedings of Gustavus Vasa, who confiscated all ecclesiastical estates, subject only to what he might deem a sufficient maintenance for the possessors, have very much the
appearance of arbitrary spoliation.[c]

3. But while these great innovations were brought in by
Excitement of revolutionary spirit. the civil power, and sometimes with too despotic a
contempt of legal rights, the mere breaking up of
old settlements had so disturbed the minds of the
people, that they became inclined to further acts of destruction, and more sweeping theories of revolution. It is one of
the fallacious views of the Reformation, to which we have
adverted in a former page, to fancy that it sprang from any
notions of political liberty, in such a sense as we attach to
the word. But, inasmuch as it took away a great deal of
coercive jurisdiction exercised by the bishops, without substituting much in its place, it did unquestionably relax the
bonds of laws not always unnecessary ; and inasmuch as the
multitude were in many parts instrumental in destroying by
force the exterior symbols of the Roman worship, it taught
them a habit of knowing and trying the efficacy of that
popular argument. Hence the insurrection of the German
peasants in 1525 may, in a certain degree, be ascribed to the
influence of the new doctrine; and, in fact, one of their
demands was the establishment of the Gospel. But as the
real cause of that rebellion was the oppressive yoke of their
lords, which, in several instances before the Reformation was
thought of, had led to similar efforts at relief, we should not
lay too much stress on this additional incitement.[d]

4. A more immediate effect of overthrowing the ancient
Growth of fanaticism. system was the growth of fanaticism, to which, in
its worst shape, the Antinomian extravagances of
Luther yielded too great encouragement. But he was the
first to repress the pretences of the Anabaptists ;[e] and when

---

[c] Gerdes, Hist. Evangel. Reform.,
Seckendorf, et alii supra nominati. The
best account I have seen of the Reformation in Denmark and Sweden is in the
third volume of Gerdes, p. 279, &c.

[d] Seckendorf.

[e] Id. Melanchthon was a little stag-
gered by the first Anabaptists, who appeared during the concealment of Luther

in the Castle of Wartburg. Magnis rationibus, he says, adducor certè ut con-
temnere eos nolim, nam esse in iis spiritus quosdam multis argumentis apparet,
sed de quibus judicare præter Martinum
nemo facile possit. As to infant baptism, he seemed to think it a difficult
question. But the Elector observed
that they passed for heretics already,

he saw the danger of general licentiousness which he had
unwarily promoted, he listened to the wiser counsels of
Melanchthon, and permitted his early doctrine upon justification to be so far modified, or mitigated in expression, that
it ceased to give apparent countenance to immorality;
though his differences with the church of Rome, as to the
very question from which he had started, thus became of
less practical importance, and less tangible to ordinary minds
than before.[f] Yet in his own writings we may find to the
last such language as to the impossibility of sin in the
justified man, who was to judge solely by an internal assurance as to the continuance of his own justification, as
would now be universally condemned in all our churches,
and is hardly to be heard from the lips of the merest en-
thusiast.

5. It is well known that Zuinglius, unconnected with
Luther in throwing off his allegiance to Rome, took Differences
in several respects rather different theological views, and Zwingle.
but especially in the article of the real presence, asserted by
the Germans as vigorously as in the church of Rome, though
with a modification sufficient, in the spirit of uncompromising
orthodoxy, to separate them entirely from her communion,
but altogether denied by the Swiss and Belgian reformers.
The attempts made to disguise this division of opinion, and
to produce a nominal unanimity by ambiguous and inco-

---

and it would be unwise to moot a new
point. Luther, when he came back, rejected the pretences of the Anabaptists
at once.

[f] See two remarkable passages in
Seckendorf, part ii. p. 90 and p. 106.
The era of what may be called the palinodia of early Lutheranism was in 1527,
when Melanchthon drew up instructions
for the visitation of the Saxon churches.
Luther came into this; but it produced
that jealousy of Melanchthon among the
rigid disciples, such as Amsdorf and Justus Jonas, which lead to the molestation
of his latter years. In 1537 Melanchthon writes to a correspondent; Scis me
quædam minus horridè dicere, de præ-
destinatione, de assensu voluntatis, de
necessitate obedientiæ nostræ, de peccato mortali. De his omnibus scio re
ipsa Lutherum sentire eadem, sed ineru-
diti quædam ejus φορτικώτερα dicta,
cum non videant quo pertineant, nimium
amant. Epist. p. 115 (edit 1647).

I am not convinced that this apology
for Luther is sufficient. Words are of
course to be explained, when ambiguous,
by the context and scope of the argument. But when single detached aphorisms, or even complete sentences in a
paragraph, bear one obvious sense, I do
not see that we can hold the writer ab-
solved from the imputation of that
meaning because he may somewhere
else have used a language inconsistent
with it. If the Colloquia Mensalia are
to be fully relied upon, Luther continued to talk in the same Antinomian
strain as before, though he grew sometimes more cautious in writing. See
chap. xii. of that work.

herent jargon, belong to ecclesiastical history, of which they form a tedious and not very profitable portion.[g]

6. The Lutheran princes, who the year before had ac-quired the name of Protestants, by their protest against the resolutions of the majority in the diet of Spire, presented in 1530 to that held at Augsburg the celebrated Confession, which embodies their religious creed. It has been said that there are material changes in subsequent editions, but this is denied by the Lutherans. Their denial can only be as to the materiality, for the fact is clear.[h]

Confession of Augsburg.

7. Meantime, it was not all the former opponents of abuses in the church who now served under the banner of either Luther or Zwingle. Some few, like Sir Thomas More, went violently back to the extreme of maintaining the whole fabric of superstition; a greater

Conduct of Erasmus.

---

[g] [The Zuinglian doctrine which denies the real, in the sense of literal and substantial, presence of Christ's body and blood in the symbols of bread and wine, was apparently in opposition to the usual language of the church. It had been, however, remarkably supported in the ninth century by one Bertram, or Ratramm, abbot of Corvey; and there is no reason to think that he was advancing a novel and heterodox opinion, though certainly it was not one to which all were ready to accede. The history of his book is well known: but it seems as if the book itself were not; when some, with Dr. Lingard, pretend that he believed in transubstantiation, and others, with Mr. Alexander Knox, suppose him to have held the unintelligible middle hypothesis, which they prefer. Bertram writes with more candour and clearness than some Protestants of the School of Bucer and Calvin; and states the question tersely thus: Utrum quod in cœna Domini fidelium ore sumitur, corpus et sanguis Christi in mysterio sive figura fiat, an in veritate; determining for the former.

Erasmus would, as he tells us, have assented to the Zuinglian tenets, if he could have believed the church to have remained so long in a portentous error. Nisi me moveret tantus ecclesiæ consensus, possim in Œcolampadii sententiam pedibus discedere; nunc in eo persisto,

quod mihi tradit scripturarum interpres ecclesia. Ep. mliii. And some time before, in a letter to Pirckheimer, he intimates his preference of the doctrine of Œcolampadius above that of Luther, if both were private opinions, but prefers the authority of the church to either. Mihi non displiceret Œcolampadii sententia, nisi obstaret consensus ecclesiæ. Nec enim video quid agat corpus insensibile nec utilitatem allaturum si sentiretur, modo adsit in symbolis gratia spiritualis. Et tamen ab ecclesiæ consensu non possum discedere, nec unquam discessi. Tu sic dissentis ab Œcolampadio, ut cum Luthero sentire malis, quam cum ecclesia. Ep. Dcccxxiii. Sadolet thought, like Erasmus, that the whole church could not have been in so great an error as the corporal presence would be, if false, for so many ages. Sadoleti Epistolæ, p. 161.—1842.]

[h] Bossuet, Variations des Églises protestantes, vol. i. Seckendorf, p. 170. Clement, Bibliothèque curieuse, vol. ii. In the editions of 1531 we read: De cœna Domini docent, quod corpus et sanguis Christi vere adsint, et distribuantur vescentibus in cœna Domini, et improbant secus docentes. In those of 1540 it runs thus: De cœna Domini docent, quod cum pane et vino vere exhibeantur corpus et sanguis Christi vescentibus in cœna Domini.

number, without abandoning their own private sentiments, shrunk, for various reasons, from an avowed separation from the church. Such we may reckon Faber Stapulensis, the most learned Frenchman of that age, after Budæus ; such perhaps was Budæus himself ;[i] and such were Bilibaldus Pirckheimer,[m] Petrus Mosellanus, Beatus Rhenanus, and Wimpfeling, all men of just renown in their time. Such, above all, we may say, was Erasmus, the precursor of bolder prophets than himself, who, in all his la'ter years, stood in a very unenviable state, exposed to the shafts of two parties who forgave no man that moderation which was a reproach to themselves. At the beginning of this period he had certainly an esteem for Melanchthon, Œcolampadius, and other reformers ; and though already shocked by the violence of Luther, which he expected to ruin the cause altogether, had not begun to speak of him with disapprobation.[n] In several points of opinion he professed to coincide with the German reformers ; but his own temper was not decisive ; he was capable of viewing a subject in various lights ; his learning, as well as natural disposition, kept him irresolute ; and it might not be easy to determine accurately the tenets of so voluminous a theologian. One thing was manifest, that he had greatly contributed to the success of the Reformation. It was said, that Erasmus had laid the egg, and Luther had hatched it. Erasmus afterwards, when more alienated from the new party, observed that he had laid a hen's egg, but Luther had hatched a crow's.[o] Whatever was the bird, it

---

[i] Budæus was suspected of Protestantism, and disapproved many things in his own church ; but the passages quoted from him by Gerdes, i. 186, prove that he did not mean to take the leap.

[m] Gerdes, vol. i. § 66–83. We have seen above the moderation of Pirckheimer in some respects. I am not sure, however, that he did not comply with the Reformation after it was established at Nuremberg.

[n] Male metuo misero Luthero ; sic undique fervet conjuratio ; sic undique irritantur in illum principes, ac præcipuè Leo pontifex. Utinam Lutherus meum secutus consilium, ab odiosis illis ac seditiosis abstinuisset. Plus erat fructûs et minus invidiæ. Parum esset unum

hominem perire ; si res hæc illis succedit, nemo feret illorum insolentiam. Non conquiescent donec linguas ac bonas literas omnes subverterint. Epist. Dxxviii. Sept. 1520.

Lutherus, quod negari non potest, optimam fabulam susceperat, et Christi pene aboliti negotium summo cum orbis applausu cœperat agere. Sed utinam rem tantam gravioribus ac sedatioribus egisset consiliis, majoreque cum animi calamique moderatione ; atque utinam in scriptis illius non essent tam multa bona, aut sua bona non vitiâsset malis haud ferendis. Epist. Dcxxxv. 3rd Sept. 1521.

[o] Epist. Dccxix. Dec. 1524.

pecked still at the church.   In 1522 came out the Colloquies
of Erasmus, a book even now much read, and deserving to be
so.   It was professedly designed for the instruction and
amusement of youth; but both are conveyed at the expense
of the prevalent usages in religion.   The monkish party
could not be blind to its effect.   The faculty of theology at
Paris, in 1526, led by one Beda, a most bigoted enemy of
Erasmus, censured the Colloquies for slighting the fasts of
the church, virginity, monkery, pilgrimages, and other
established parts of the religious system.   They incurred of
course the displeasure of Rome, and have several times been
forbidden to be read in schools.   Erasmus pretended that in
his 'Ιχθυοφαγία he only turned into ridicule the abuse of
fasting, and not the ordinances of the church.   It would be
difficult, however, to find out this distinction in the dialogue,
or, indeed, any thing favourable to the ecclesiastical cause in
the whole book of Colloquies.   The clergy are every where
represented as idle and corrupt.   No one who desired to
render established institutions odious could set about it in
a shorter or surer way; and it would be strange if Erasmus
had not done the church more harm by such publications
than he could compensate by a few sneers at the reformers
in his private letters.   In the single year 1527 Colinæus
printed 24,000 copies of the Colloquies, all of which were
sold.

8. But about the time of this very publication we find
Estimate   Erasmus growing by degrees more averse to the
of it.   radical innovations of Luther.   He has been severely blamed for this by most Protestants; and doubtless,
so far as an undue apprehension of giving offence to the
powerful, or losing his pensions from the emperor and king
of England migh influence him, no one can undertake his
defence.   But it is to be remembered, that he did not by any
means espouse all the opinions either of Luther or Zwingle;
that he was disgusted at the virulent language too common among the reformers, and at the outrages committed
by the populace; that he anticipated great evils from the
presumptuousness of ignorant men in judging for themselves
in religion; that he probably was sincere in what he always
maintained as to the necessity of preserving the communion

of the Catholic church, which he thought consistent with
much latitude of private faith; and that, if he had gone
among the reformers, he must either have concealed his real
opinions more than he had hitherto done, or lived, as Melanchthon did afterwards, the victim of calumny and oppression. He had also to allege, that the fruits of the Reformation had by no means shown themselves in a more
virtuous conduct; and that many heated enthusiasts were
depreciating both all profane studies, and all assistance of
learning in theology.[p]

---

[p] The letters of Erasmus, written
under the spur of immediate feelings,
are a perpetual commentary on the mischiefs with which the Reformation, in
his opinion, was accompanied. Civitates
aliquot Germaniæ implentur erroribus,
desertoribus monasteriorum, sacerdoti-
bus conjugatis, plerisque famelicis ac
nudis. Nec aliud quam saltatur, editur,
bibitur ac subatur; nec docent nec dis-
cunt; nulla vitæ sobrietas, nulla sin-
ceritas. Ubicunque sunt, ibi jacent
omnes bonæ disciplinæ cum pietate.
(1527.) Epist. DCCCII. Satis jam diu
audivimus, Evangelium, Evangelium,
Evangelium; mores Evangelicos deside-
ramus. Epist. DCCCCXLVI. Duo tantum
quærunt, censum et uxorem. Cætera
præstat illis Evangelium, hoc est, potes-
tatem vivendi ut volunt. Epist. MVI.
Tales vidi mores (Basileæ) ut etiamsi
minus displicuissent dogmata, non pla-
cuisset tamen cum hujusmodi [sic] fœdus
inire. Epist. MLXVI. Both these last are
addressed to Pirckheimer, who was
rather more a Protestant than Erasmus;
so that there is no fair suspicion of temporising. The reader may also look at
the 788th and 793rd Epistles, on the
wild doctrines of the Anabaptists and
other reformers, and at the 731st, on
the effects of Farel's first preaching at
Basle in 1525. See also Bayle, Farel,
note B.

It is become very much the practice
with our English writers to censure
Erasmus for his conduct at this time.
Milner rarely does justice to any one
who did not servilely follow Luther.
And Dr. Cox, in his life of Melanchthon, p. 35, speaks of a third party,
'at the head of which the learned,
witty, vascillating, avaricious, and artful
Erasmus is unquestionably to be placed.'

I do not deny his claim to this place,
but why the last three epithets? Can
Erasmus be shown to have vacillated in
his tenets? If he had done so, it might
be no great reproach; but his religious
creed was nearly that of the moderate
members of the church of Rome, nor
have I observed any proof of a change
in it. But vacillation, some would reply, may be imputed to his conduct. I
hardly think this word is applicable;
though he acted from particular impulses, which might make him seem a
little inconsistent in spirit, and certainly
wrote letters not always in the same
tone, according to his own temper at
the moment, or that of his correspondent. Nor was he avaricious; at least I
know no proof of it: and as to the epi-
thet artful, it ill applies to a man who
was perpetually involving himself by
an unguarded and imprudent behaviour.
Dr. Cox proceeds to charge Erasmus
with seeking a cardinal's hat. But of
this there is neither proof nor probability; he always declared his reluctance
to accept that honour, and I cannot
think that in any part of his life he
went the right way to obtain it.

Those who arraign Erasmus so severely (and I am not undertaking the
defence of every passage in his voluminous Epistles) must proceed either on
the assumption that no man of his
learning and ability could honestly remain in the communion of the church
of Rome, which is the height of bigotry
and ignorance; or that, according to his
own religious opinions, it was impossible
for him to do so. This is somewhat
more tenable, inasmuch as it can only
be answered by a good deal of attention
to his writings. But from various passages in them, it may be inferred that,

9. In 1524, Erasmus, at the instigation of those who were resolved to dislodge him from a neutral station his timidity rather affected, published his Diatribe de libero arbitrio, selecting a topic upon which Luther, in the opinion of most reasonable men, was very open to attack. Luther answered in a treatice, De servo arbitrio, flinching not, as suited his character, from any tenet because it seemed paradoxical, or revolting to general prejudice. The controversy ended with a reply of Erasmus, entitled Hyperaspistes. It is not to be understood, from the titles of these tracts, that the question of free will was discussed between Luther and Erasmus in a philosophical

His controversy with Luther.

---

though his mind was not made up on several points, and perhaps for that reason, he thought it right to follow, in assent as well as conformity, the catholic tradition of the church, and, above all, not to separate from her communion. The reader may consult, for Erasmus's opinions on some chief points of controversy, his Epistles, DCCCXXIII. DCCCCLXXVII. (which Jortin has a little misunderstood), MXXXV. MLIII. MXCIII. And see Jortin's own fair statement of the case, i. 274.

Melanchthon had doubtless a sweeter temper and a larger measure of human charities than Erasmus, nor would I wish to vindicate one great man at the expense of another. But I cannot refrain from saying, that no passage in the letters of Erasmus is read with so much pain as that in which Melanchthon, after Luther's death, and writing to one not very friendly, says of his connexion with the founder of the Reformation, Tuli servitutem pæne deformem, &c. Epist. Melanchthon, p. 21 (edit. 1647). But the characters of literary men are cruelly tried by their correspondence, especially in an age when more conventional dissimulation was authorised by usage than at present.

[q] Seckendorf took hold of a few words in a letter of Erasmus, to insinuate that he had taken a side against his conscience in writing his treatise De libero arbitrio. Jortin, acute as he was, seems to have understood the passage the same way, and endeavours to explain away the sense, as if he meant only that he had undertaken the task unwillingly. Milner of course repeats the imputation; though it must be owned that, perceiving the absurdity of making Erasmus deny what in all his writings appears to have been his real opinion, he adopts Jortin's solution. I am persuaded that they are all mistaken, and that Erasmus was no more referring to his treatise against Luther than to the Trojan war. The words occur in an answer to a letter of Vives, written from London, wherein he had blamed some passages in the Colloquies on the usual grounds of their freedom as to ecclesiastical practices. Erasmus, rather piqued at this, after replying to the observations, insinuates to Vives that the latter had not written of his own free will, but at the instigation of some superior. Verum, ut ingenuè dicam, perdidimus liberum arbitrium. Illic mihi aliud dictabat animus, aliud scribebat calamus. By a figure of speech far from unusual, he delicately suggests his own suspicion as Vives's apology. And the next letter of Vives leaves no room for doubt: Liberum arbitrium non perdidimus, quod tu asserueris,—words that could have no possible meaning, upon the hypothesis of Seckendorf. There is nothing in the context that can justify it; and it is equally difficult to maintain the interpretation Jortin gives of the phrase, aliud dictabat animus, aliud scribebat calamus, which can mean nothing but that he wrote what he did not think. The letters are DCCCXXIX. DCCCLXXI. DCCCLXXVI. in Erasmus's Epistles; or the reader may turn to Jortin, i. 413.

sense; though Melanchthon in his Loci Communes, like the
modern Calvinists, had combined the theological position of
the spiritual inability of man with the metaphysical tenet
of general necessity.   Luther on most occasions, though not
uniformly, acknowledged the freedom of the will as to indifferent actions, and also as to what they called the works of
the law.   But he maintained that, even when regenerated
and sanctified by faith and the Spirit, man had no spiritual
free will; and as before that time he could do no good, so
after it he had no power to do ill; nor indeed could he, in a
strict sense, do either good or ill, God always working in
him, so that all his acts were properly the acts of God,
though man's will being of course the proximate cause, they
might, in a secondary sense, be ascribed to him.   It was this
that Erasmus denied, in conformity with the doctrine afterwards held by the council of Trent, by the church of England, and, if we may depend on the statements of writers
of authority, by Melanchthon and most of the later Lutherans.   From the time of this controversy Luther seems to
have always spoken of Erasmus with extreme ill-will; and
if the other was a little more measured in his expressions,
he fell not a jot behind in dislike.[r]

10. The Epistles of Erasmus, which occupy two folio
volumes in the best edition of his works, are a Character
of his
vast treasure for the ecclesiastical and literary his- Epistles.
tory of his times.[s]   Morhof advises the student to common-
place them; a task which, even in his age, few would have

---

[r] Many of Luther's strokes at Erasmus occur in the Colloquia Mensalia,
which I quote from the translation.
'Erasmus can do nothing but cavil and
flout; he cannot confute.' 'I charge
you in my will and testament, that you
hate and loathe Erasmus, that viper.'
ch. xliv. 'He called Erasmus an epi-
cure and ungodly creature, for thinking
that if God dealed with men here on
earth as they deserved, it would not go
so ill with the good, or so well with the
wicked.' ch. vii. Lutherus, says the
other, sic respondit (diatribæ de libero
arbitrio) ut antehac in neminem virulentius; et homo suavis post editum
librum per literas dejerat se in me esse

animo candidissimo, ac propemodum
postulat, ut ipsi gratias agam, quod me
tam civiliter tractavit, longe aliter scrip-
turus si cum hoste fuisset res. Ep.
DCCCXXXVI.

[s] [Many of the epistles of Erasmus
were published by Rhenanus from the
press of Frobenius about 1519. He pretended to be angry, and that Frobenius
had done this against his will; which
even Jortin perceives to be untrue.
Epist. DVII. This was a little like Voltaire, to whose physiognomy that of
Erasmus has often been observed to
bear some resemblance; and he has
been suspected of other similar tricks.—
1842.]

spared leisure to perform, and which the good index of the
Leyden edition renders less important. Few men carry on
so long and extensive a correspondence without affording
some vulnerable points to the criticism of posterity. The
failings of Erasmus have been already adverted to; it is
from his own letters that we derive our chief knowledge of
them. An extreme sensibility to blame in his own person,
with little regard to that of others; a genuine warmth of
friendship towards some, but an artificial pretence of it too
frequently assumed; an inconsistency of profession both
as to persons and opinions, partly arising from the different
character of his correspondents, but in a great degree from
the varying impulses of his ardent mind, tend to abate
that respect which the name of Erasmus at first excites,
and which, on a candid estimate of his whole life, and
the tenor even of this correspondence, it ought to retain.
He was the first conspicuous enemy of ignorance and superstition, the first restorer of Christian morality on a Scriptural foundation, and, notwithstanding the ridiculous assertion of some moderns that he wanted theological learning,
the first who possessed it in its proper sense, and applied it
to its proper end.

11. In every succeeding year the letters of Erasmus be-
His alienation tray increasing animosity against the reformers.
from the re He had long been on good terms with Zwingle
formers in-
creases. and Œcolampadius, but became so estranged by
these party differences, that he speaks of their death with a
sort of triumph.[t] He still, however, kept up some inter-

---

[t] Bene habet, quod duo Coryphæi pe-
rierint, Zuinglius in acie, Œcolampadius
paulo post febri et apostemate. Quod si
illis favisset ενναλιος, actum fuisset de
nobis. Epist. MCCV. It is of course to
be regretted that Erasmus allowed this
passage to escape him, even in a letter.
With Œcolampadius he had long carried
on a correspondence. In some book
the latter had said, Magnus Erasmus
noster. This was at a time when much
suspicion was entertained of Erasmus,
who writes rather amusingly, in Feb.
1525, to complain; telling Œcolampadius
that it was best neither to be praised nor
blamed by his party, but if they must

speak of him, he would prefer their
censure to being styled *noster*. Epist.
DCCXXVIII. Milner quotes this, leaving
poor Erasmus to his reader's indignation for what he would insinuate to be a
piece of the greatest baseness. But, in
good truth, what right had Œcolampadius to use the word *noster*, if it could
be interpreted as claiming Erasmus to
his own side? He was not theirs, as
Œcolampadius well knew, in exterior
profession, nor theirs in the course they
had seen fit to pursue.
It is just towards Erasmus to mention, that he never dissembled his affection for Lewis Berquin, the first martyr

course with Melanchthon. The latter years of Erasmus could not have been happy; he lived in a perpetual irritation from the attacks of adversaries on every side; his avowed dislike of the reformers by no means assuaging the virulence of his original foes in the church, or removing the suspicion of lukewarmness in the orthodox cause. Part of this should fairly be ascribed to the real independence of his mind in the formation of his opinions, though not always in their expression, and to their incompatibility with the extreme doctrines of either side. But an habitual indiscretion, the besetting sin of literary men, who seldom restrain their wit, rendered this hostility far more general than it need have been, and, accompanied as it was with a real timidity of character, exposed him to the charge of insincerity, which he could better palliate by the example of others than deny to have some foundation. Erasmus died in 1536, having returned to Basle, which, on pretence of the alterations in religion, he had quitted for Friburg in Brisgau a few years before. No differences of opinion had abated the pride of the citizens of Basle in their illustrious visitor. Erasmus lies interred in their cathedral, the earliest, except Œcolampadius, in the long list of the literary dead which have rendered that cemetery conspicuous in Europe.

12. The most striking effect of the first preaching of the Reformation was that it appealed to the ignorant; and though political liberty, in the sense we use the word, cannot be reckoned the aim of those who introduced it, yet there predominated that revolutionary spirit which loves to witness destruction for its own sake, and that intoxicated self-confidence which renders folly mischievous. Women took an active part in religious dispute; and though in some respects the Roman Catholic religion is very congenial to the female sex, we cannot be surprised that many ladies might be good Protestants against the right of any to judge better than themselves. The translation of the New Testament by Luther in 1522,

Appeal of the reformers to the ignorant.

to Protestantism in France, who was burned in 1528, even in the time of his danger. Epist. dcccclxxvi. Erasmus had no more inveterate enemies than in the university of Paris.

and of the Old a few years later, gave weapons to all dis-
putants; it was common to hold conferences before the
burgomasters of German and Swiss towns, who settled the
points in controversy, one way or other, perhaps as well as
the learned would have done.

13. We cannot give any attention to the story of the
Reformation, without being struck by the extraordinary analogy it bears to that of the last fifty
years. He who would study the spirit of this
mighty age may see it reflected as in a mirror from the
days of Luther and Erasmus. Man, who, speaking of him
collectively, has never reasoned for himself, is the puppet
of impulses and prejudices, be they for good or for evil.
These are, in the usual course of things, traditional notions and sentiments, strengthened by repetition, and running into habitual trains of thought. Nothing is more
difficult, in general, than to make a nation perceive anything as true, or seek its own interest in any manner, but
as its forefathers have opined or acted. Change in these
respects has been, even in Europe, where there is most of
flexibility, very gradual; the work, not of argument or instruction, but of exterior circumstances slowly operating
through a long lapse of time. There have been, however,
some remarkable exceptions to this law of uniformity, or,
if I may use the term, of *secular variation*. The introduction of Christianity seems to have produced a very rapid
subversion of ancient prejudices, a very conspicuous alteration of the whole channel through which moral sentiments
flow, in nations that have at once received it. This has also
not unfrequently happened through the influence of Mo-
hammedism in the East. Next to these great revolutions in
extent and degree, stand the two periods we have begun by
comparing; that of the Reformation in the sixteenth century,
and that of political innovation wherein we have long lived.
In each, the characteristic features are a contempt for
antiquity, a shifting of prejudices, an inward sense of self-
esteem leading to an assertion of private judgment in the
most uninformed, a sanguine confidence in the amelioration
of human affairs, a fixing of the heart on great ends, with
a comparative disregard of all things intermediate. In

Parallel of those times with the present.

each there has been so much of alloy in the motives, and, still more, so much of danger and suffering in the means, that the cautious and moderate have shrunk back, and sometimes retraced their own steps rather than encounter evils, which at a distance they had not seen in their full magnitude.   Hence we may pronounce with certainty what Luther, Hutten, Carlostadt, what again More, Erasmus, Melanchthon, Cassander, would have been in the nineteenth century, and what our own contemporaries would have been in their times.   But we are too apt to judge others, not as the individualities of personal character and the varying aspects of circumstances rendered them, and would have rendered us, but according to our opinion of the consequences, which, even if estimated by us rightly, were such as they could not determinately have foreseen.

14. In 1531 Zwingle lost his life on the field of battle. It was the custom of the Swiss that their pastors should attend the citizens in war to exhort the *Calvin.* combatants and console the dying.   But the reformers soon acquired a new chief in a young man superior in learning and probably in genius, John Calvin, a native of *His Institutes.* Noyon in Picardy.   His Institutions, published in 1536, became the text-book of a powerful body, who deviated in some few points from the Helvetic school of Zwingle.   They are dedicated to Francis I., in language, good, though not perhaps as choice as would have been written in Italy, temperate, judicious, and likely to prevail upon the general reader, if not upon the king.   This treatise was the most systematic and extensive defence and exposition of the Protestant doctrine which had appeared. Without the overstrained phrases and wilful paradoxes of Luther's earlier writings, the Institutes of Calvin seem to contain most of his predecessor's theological doctrine, except as to the corporal presence.   He adopted a middle course as to this, and endeavoured to distinguish himself from the Helvetic divines.   It is well known that he brought forward the predestinarian tenets of Augustin more fully than Luther, who seems, however, to have maintained them with equal confidence.   They appeared to Calvin, as doubtless they are, clearly deducible from their common doctrine as to the

sinfulness of all natural actions, and the arbitrary irresistible conversion of the passive soul by the power of God. The city of Geneva, throwing off subjection to its bishop, and embracing the reformed religion in 1536, invited Calvin to an asylum, where he soon became the guide and legislator, though never the ostensible magistrate, of the new republic.

15. The Helvetian reformers at Zurich and Bern were now more and more separated from the Lutherans ; and in spite of frequent endeavours to reconcile their differences, each party, but especially the latter, became as exclusive and nearly as intolerant as the church which they had quitted. Among the Lutherans themselves, those who rigidly adhered to the spirit of their founder's doctrine grew estranged, not externally, but in language and affection, from the followers of Melanchthon.[u] Luther himself, who never withdrew his friendship from

Increased differences among reformers.

---

[u] Amsdorfius Luthero scripsit, viperam eum in sinu alere, me significans, omitto alia multa. Epist. Melanchthon. p. 450 (edit. 1647). Luther's temper seems to have grown more impracticable as he advanced in life. Melanchthon threatened to leave him. Amsdorf and that class of men flattered his pride. See the following letters. In one, written about 1549, he says: Tuli etiam antea servitutem pæne deformem cum sæpe Lutherus magis suæ naturæ, in qua φιλονεικία erat haud exigua, quam vel personæ suæ, vel utilitati communi serviret. p. 21. This letter is too apologetical and temporising. Nec movi has controversias quæ distraxerunt rempublicam ; sed incidi in motas, quæ cum et multæ essent et inexplicatæ, quodam simplici studio quærendæ veritatis, præsertim cum multi docti et sapientes initio applauderent, considerare eas cœpi. Et quanquam materias quasdam horridiores autor initio miscuerat, tamen alia vera et necessaria non putavi rejicienda esse. Hæc cum excerpta amplecterer, paulatim aliquas absurdas opiniones vel sustuli vel lenii. Melanchthon should have remembered that no one had laid down these opinions with more unreserve, or in a more 'horrid' way of disputation, than himself in the first edition of his Loci Communes. In these a d other passages he endeavours to strike at Luther for faults which were equally his own, though doubtless not so long persisted in.

Melanchthon, in the first edition of the Loci Communes, which will scarcely be found except in Von der Hardt, sums up the free-will question thus :

Si ad prædestinationem referas humanam voluntatem, nec in externis, nec in internis operibus ulla est libertas, sed eveniunt omnia juxta destinationem divinam.

Si ad opera externa referas voluntatem, quædam videtur esse, judicio naturæ, libertas.

Si ad affectus referas voluntatem, nulla plane libertas est, etiam naturæ judicio. This proves what I have said in another place, that Melanchthon held the doctrine of strict philosophical necessity. Luther does the same, in express words, once at least in the treatise De servo arbitrio, vol. ii. fol. 429 (edit. Wittenberg, 1554).

In an epistle often quoted by others, Melanchthon wrote : Nimis horridæ fuerunt apud nostros disputationes de fato, et disciplinæ nocuerunt. But a more thoroughly ingenuous man might have said *nostræ* for apud nostros. Certain it is, however, that he had changed his opinions considerably before 1540, when he published his Moralis Philosophiæ Epitome, which contains evidence

the latter, seems to have been alternately under his influence and that of inferior men. The Anabaptists, in their
well-known occupation of Munster, gave such proof of the
tremendous consequences of fanaticism, generated, in great
measure, by the Lutheran tenet of assurance, that the paramount necessity of maintaining human society tended more
to silence these theological subtilties than any arguments of
the same class. And from this time that sect itself, if it
did not lose all its enthusiasm, learned how to regulate it in
subordination to legal and moral duties.

16. England, which had long contained the remnants of
Wicliffe's followers, could not remain a stranger *Reformed*
to this revolution. Tyndale's New Testament was *tenets spread in*
printed at Antwerp in 1526; the first translation *England.*
that had been made into English. The cause of this delay
has been already explained ; and great pains were taken to
suppress the circulation of Tyndale's version. But England
was then inclined to take its religion from the nod of a capricious tyrant. Persecution would have long repressed the
spirit of free judgment, and the king, for Henry's life at
least, have retained his claim to the papal honour conferred
on him as defender of the faith, if ' Gospel light,' as Gray
has rather affectedly expressed it, had not ' flashed from
Boleyn's eyes.' But we shall not dwell on so trite a subject. It is less familiar to everyone, that in Italy *In Italy.*
the seeds of the Reformation were early and widely
sown. A translation of Melanchthon's Loci Communes,
under the name of Ippofilo da Terra Nigra, was printed at
Venice in 1521, the very year of its appearance at Wittenberg ; the works of Luther, Zwingle, and Bucer were also
circulated under false names.[x] The Italian translations of
Scripture made in the fifteenth century were continually
reprinted; and in 1530 a new version was published at

---

of his holding the synergism, or activity,
and co-operation with divine grace of
the human will. See p. 39.

 The animosity excited in the violent
Lutherans by Melanchthon's moderation
in drawing up the Confession of Augsburg is shown in Camerarius, Vita Me-

lanchthon. p. 124 (edit. 1696). From
this time it continued to harass him till
his death.

 [x] M'Crie's Hist. of Reformation in
Italy. Epigrams were written in favour of Luther as early as 1521. p 32.

Venice by Brucioli, with a preface written in a Protestant
tone.[y] The great intercourse of Italy with the Cisalpine
nations through war and commerce, and the partiality of
Renée of France, Duchess of Ferrara, to the new doctrines,
whose disciples she encouraged at her court, under the pretext of literature, contributed to spread an active spirit of
inquiry. In almost every considerable city, between 1525
and 1540, we find proofs of a small band of Protestants,
not in general abandoning the outward profession of the
church, but coinciding in most respects with Luther or
Zwingle. It has lately been proved that a very early proselyte to the Reformation, and one whom we should least
expect to find in that number, was Berni, before the completion, if not the commencement, of his labour on the Orlando Innamorato; which he attempted to render in some
places the vehicle of his disapprobation of the church. This
may account for the freedom from indecency which distinguishes that poem, and contrasts with the great licentiousness
of Berni's lighter and earlier productions.[z]

---

[y] Id. p. 53, 55.
[z] This curious and unexpected fact
was brought to light by Mr. Panizzi,
who found a short pamphlet of extreme
scarcity, and unnoticed, I believe, by
Zeno or any other bibliographer (except
Niceron, xxxviii. 76), in the library of
Mr. Grenville. It is written by Peter
Paul Vergerio, and printed at Basle in
1554. This contains eighteen stanzas,
intended to have been prefixed by Berni
to the twentieth canto of the Orlando
Innamorato. They are of a decidedly
Protestant character. For these stanzas
others are substituted in the printed
editions, much inferior, and, what is
remarkable, almost the only indecent
passage in the whole poem. Mr. Panizzi
is of opinion that great liberties have
been taken with the Orlando Innamorato, which is a posthumous publication,
the earliest edition being at Venice,
1541, five years after the author's death.
Vergerio, in this tract, the whole of
which has been reprinted by Mr. P. in
iii. 361 of his Boiardo, says of Berni:
Costui quasi agli ultimi suoi anni non
fù altro che carne e mondo; di che ci
fanno ampia fede alcuni suoi capitoli e

poesie, delle quali egli molti fogli im-
brattò. Ma perchè il nome suo era
scritto nel libro della vita, ne era possi-
bile ch' egli potesse fuggire delle mani
del celeste padre, &c. Veggendo egli che
questo gran tiranno non permittea onde
alcuno potesse comporre all' aperta di
quei libri, per li quali altri possa pene-
trare nella cognizione del vero, andando
attorno per le man d' ognuno un certo
libro profano chiamato innamoramento
d' Orlando, che era inetto e mal com-
posto, il Berna [sic] s' immaginò di fare
un bel trattato; e ciò fù ch' egli si pose
a racconciare le rime e le altre parti di
quel libro, di che esso n' era ottimo ar-
tefice, e poi aggiungendovi di suo alcune
stanze, pensò di entrare con questa oc-
casione e con quel mezzo (insin che
d' altro migliore ne avesse potuto avere)
ad insegnare la verità dell' Evangelio,
&c. Whether Vergerio is wholly to be
trusted in all this account, more of
which will be found on reference to
Panizzi's edition of the Orlando Innamorato, I must leave to the competent
reader. The following expressions of
Mr. P., though, I think, rather strong,
will show the opinion of one conversant

17. The Italians are an imaginative, but not essentially a superstitious people, or liable, nationally speak- Italian ing, to the gloomy prejudices that master the heterodoxy. reason. Among the classes whose better education had strengthened and developed the acuteness and intelligence so general in Italy, a silent disbelief of the popular religion was far more usual than in any other country. In the majority, this has always taken the turn of a complete rejection of all positive faith; but at the era of the Reformation especially, the substitution of Protestant for Romish Christianity was an alternative to be embraced by men of more serious temperaments. Certain it is, that we find traces of this aberration from orthodoxy, in one or the other form, through much of the literature of Italy, sometimes displaying itself only in censures of the vices of the clergy; censures from which, though in other ages they had been almost universal, the rigidly Catholic party began now to abstain. We have already mentioned Pontanus and Mantuan. Trissino, in his Italia Liberata, introduces a sharp invective against the church of Rome.[a] The Zodiacus Vitæ of Manzolli, whose assumed Latin name, by which he is better known, was Palingenius Stellatus, teems with invectives against the monks, and certainly springs from a Protestant source.[b] The first edition is of

---

with the literature and history of those times:—'The more we reflect on the state of Italy at that time, the more have we reason to suspect that the reforming tenets were as popular among the higher classes in Italy in those days, as liberal notions in ours.' p. 361.

[a] This passage, which is in the sixteenth canto, will be found in Roscoe's Leo X., Append. No. 164; but the reader would be mistaken in supposing, as Roscoe's language seems to imply, that it is only contained in the first edition of 1548. The fact is that Trissino cancelled these lines in the unsold copies of that edition, so that very few are found to contain them; but they are restored in the edition of the Italia Liberata printed at Verona in 1729.

[b] The Zodiacus Vitæ is a long moral poem, the books of which are named

from the signs of the zodiac. It is not very poetical, but by no means without strong passages of sense and spirit in a lax Horatian metre. The author has said more than enough to incur the suspicion of Lutheranism.

I have observed several proofs of this; the following will suffice:—

Sed tua præsertim non intret limina quisquam
Frater, nec monachus, vel quavis lege sacerdos.
Hos fuge; pestis enim nulla hac immanior; hi sunt
Fæx hominum, fons stultitiæ, sentina malorum,
Agnorum sub pelle lupi, mercede colentes,
Non pietate, Deum; falsa sub imagine vecti
Decipiunt stolidos, ac religionis in umbra
Mille actus vetitos, et mille piacula condunt, &c.
                              Leo (lib. v.)

I could find, probably, more decisive Lutheranism in searching through the poem, but have omitted to make notes in reading it.

1537, at Basle. But no one writer is more indignantly severe than Alamanni.[c]

18. This rapid, though rather secret progress of heresy

Its progress in the literary classes. among the more educated Italians could not fail to alarm their jealous church. They had not won over the populace to their side; for, though censures on the superior clergy were listened to with approbation in every country, there was little probability that the Italians would generally abjure modes of worship so congenial to their national temper, as to have been devised, or retained from heathen times, in compliance with it. Even of those who had associated with the reformers, and have been in consequence reckoned among them, some were far from intending to break off from a church which had been identified with all their prejudices and pursuits. Such was Flaminio, one of the most elegant of poets and best of men; and such was the accomplished and admirable Vittoria Colonna.[d] But those who had drunk deeper of the cup of free thought had no other resource, when their private assemblies had been detected, and their names proscribed, than to fly beyond the Alps. Bernard Ochino, a Capuchin preacher of great eminence, being summoned to Rome, and finding his death resolved upon, fled to Geneva. His apostasy struck his admirers with astonishment, and possibly put the Italians more on their guard against others. Peter Martyr, well known afterwards in England, soon followed him; the academy of Modena, a literary society highly distinguished, but long suspected of heresy, was compelled, in 1542, to subscribe a declaration of faith; and though Lombardy was still full of secret Protestants, they lived in continual terror of persecution during the rest of this period. The small reformed church of Ferrara was broken up in 1550; many were imprisoned, and one put to death.[e]

---

[c] Ahi cieca gente, che l' hai troppo 'n pregio;
Tu credi ben, che questa ria semenza
Habbian più d' altri gratia e privilegio;
Ch' altra trovi hoggi in lei vera scienza,
Che dissimulazion, menzogne e frodi.
Beato 'l mondo, che sarà mai senza, &c.
                                    Satira i.

The twelfth Satire concludes with a similar execration, in the name of Italy, against the church of Rome.

[d] M'Crie discusses at length the opinions of these two, p. 164–177, and seems to leave those of Flaminio in doubt; but his letters, published at Nuremberg in 1571, speak in favour of his orthodoxy.

[e] Besides Dr. M'Crie's History of the Reformation in Italy, which has thrown a collected light upon a subject interest-

19. Meantime the natural tendency of speculative minds to press forward, though checked at this time by the inflexible spirit of the leaders of the Reformation, gave rise to some theological novelties. A Spanish physician, Michael Reves, commonly called Servetus, was the first to open a new scene in religious innovation. The ancient controversies on the Trinity had long subsided; if any remained whose creed was not unlike that of the Arians, we must seek for them among the Waldenses, or other persecuted sects. But even this is obscure; and Erasmus, when accused of Arianism, might reply with apparent truth, that no heresy was more extinct. Servetus, however, though not at all an Arian, framed a scheme, not probably quite novel, which is a difficult matter, but sounding very unlike what was deemed orthodoxy. Being an imprudent and impetuous man, he assailed the fundamental doctrines of reformers as much as of the Catholic church with none of the management necessary in such cases, as the title of his book, printed in 1531, De Trinitatis erroribus, is enough to show. He was so little satisfied with his own performance, that in a second treatise, called Dialogues on the Trinity, he retracts the former as ill-written, though without having changed any of his opinions. These works are very scarce, and obscurely worded, but the tenets seem to be nearly what are called Sabellian.[f]

20. The Socinian writers derive their sect from a small knot of distinguished men, who met privately at Vicenza about 1540; including Lælius Socinus, at that time too young to have had any influence, Ochino, Gentile, Alciati, and some others. This fact has been doubted by Mosheim and M'Crie, and does not rest on much evidence; while some of the above names are rather improbable.[g] It is certain, however, that many of the Italian reformers held anti-Trinitarian opinions, chiefly of the Arian form. M'Crie

Servetus.

Arianism in Italy.

ing and little familiar, I have made use of his predecessor Gerdes, Specimen Italiæ reformatæ; of Tiraboschi, viii. 150; of Giannone, iv. 108, et alibi; and of Galluzzi, Istoria del Gran Ducato, ii. 292, 369.

[f] The original editions of the works of Servetus very rarely occur; but there are reprints of the last century, which themselves are by no means common.

[g] Lubienecius, Hist. Reformat. Polonicæ. M'Crie's Hist. of Reformation in Italy, p. 154.

suggests that these had been derived from Servetus; but it does not appear that they had any acquaintance, or concurred, in general, with him, who was very far from Arianism; and it is much more probable that their tenets originated among themselves. If, indeed, it were necessary to look for an heresiarch, a Spanish gentleman, resident at Naples, by name Valdes, is far more likely than Servetus. It is agreed that Valdes was one of the chief teachers of the Reformation in Italy; and he has also been supposed to have inclined towards Arianism.[h]

21. Even in Spain, the natural soil of tenacious supersti-
Protestants
in Spain
and Low
Countries.
tion, and the birthplace of the Inquisition, a few seeds of Protestantism were early sown. The first writings of Luther were translated into Spanish soon after their appearence; the Holy Office began to take alarm about 1530. Several suspected followers of the new creed were confined in monasteries, and one was burnt at Valladolid in 1541.[i] But in no country where the Reformation was severely restrained by the magistrate did it spread so extensively as in the Netherlands. Two Augustine monks were burned at Brussels in 1523, and their death had the effect, as Erasmus tells us, of increasing prodigiously the number of heretics.[k] From that time a bitter persecution was carried on, both by destroying books, and punishing their readers; but most of the seventeen provinces were full of sectaries.

22. Deeply shaken by all this open schism and lurking disaffection, the church of Rome seemed to have little hope

---

[h] Dr. M'Crie is inclined to deny the Arianism of Valdes, and says it cannot be found in his writings (p. 122); others have been of a different opinion. See Chalmers's Dictionary, art. Valdesso, and Bayle. His Considerations were translated into English in 1638. I can find no evidence as to this point one way or the other in the book itself, which betrays a good deal of fanaticism, and confidence in the private teaching of the Spirit. The tenets are high Lutheranism as to human action, and derived perhaps from the Loci Communes of Melanchthon. Beza condemned the book.

[i] M'Crie's Hist. of Reformation in Spain.

[k] Cœpta est carnificina. Tandem Bruxellæ tres Augustinenses [duo?] publicitus affecti sunt supplicio. Quæris exitum? Ea civitas antea purissima cœpit habere Lutheri discipulos, et quidem non paucos. Sævitum est et in Hollandiâ. Quid multis? Ubicunque fumos excitavit nuncius, ubicunque sævitiam exercuit Carmelita, ibi diceres fuisse factam hæresion sementem. Ep. mclxiii. The history of the Reformation in the Low Countries has been copiously written by Gerard Brandt, to whose second and third books I refer the reader.

but in the superstition of the populace, the precarious support of the civil power, or the quarrels of her adver- Order of
saries.   But she found an unexpected source of Jesuits.
strength in her own bosom; a green shoot from the yet living
trunk of an aged tree. By a bull, dated the 27th of September, 1540, Paul III. established the order of Jesuits, planned
a few years before by Ignatius Loyola.   The leading rules of
this order were, that a general should be chosen for life,
whom every Jesuit was to obey as he did God; and that
besides the three vows of the regulars, poverty, chastity, and
obedience, he should promise to go wherever the pope should
command. They were to wear no other dress than the clergy
usually did; no regular hours of prayer were enjoined; but
they were bound to pass their time usefully for their neighbours, in preaching, in the direction of consciences, and the
education of youth.   Such were the principles of an institution which has, more effectually than any other, exhibited
the moral power of a united association in moving the great
unorganised mass of mankind.

23. The Jesuits established their first school in 1546, at
Gandia in the kingdom of Valencia, under the aus- Their popu-
pices of Francis Borgia, who derived the title of larity.
duke from that city.   It was erected into a university by the
pope and king of Spain.[m]   This was the commencement of
that vast influence they were speedily to acquire by the
control of education.   They began about the same time to
scatter their missionaries over the East.   This had been one
of the great objects of their foundation.   And when news
was brought, that thousands of barbarians had flocked to the
preaching of Francis Xavier, that he had poured the waters
of baptism on their heads, and raised the cross over the pro-
strate idols of the East, they had enough, if not to silence
the envy of competitors, at least to secure the admiration of
the Catholic world.   Men saw in the Jesuits courage and
self-devotion, learning and politeness; qualities the want of
which had been the disgrace of monastic fraternities.   They
were formidable to the enemies of the church; and those who
were her friends cared little for the jealousy of the secular

---

[m] Fleury, Hist. ecclés. xxix. 221.

clergy, or for the technical opposition of lawyers. The mischiefs and dangers that might attend the institution were
too remote for popular alarm.

24. In the external history of Protestant churches, two
Council of   events, not long preceding the middle of the six-
Trent.   teenth century, served to compensate each other,
—the unsuccessful league of the Lutheran princes of Germany, ending in their total defeat, and the establishment
of the reformed religion in England by the council of
Edward VI. It admits, however, of no doubt, that the
principles of the Reformation were still progressive, not
only in those countries where they were countenanced by
the magistrate, but in others, like France and the Low
Countries, where they incurred the risk of martyrdom.
Meantime Paul III. had, with much reluctance, convoked
a general council at Trent. This met on the 13th of December, 1545; and after determining a large proportion of
the disputed problems in theology, especially such as related
to grace and original sin, was removed by the pope, in
March 1547, to his own city of Bologna, where they sat but
a short time before events occurred which compelled them
to suspend their sessions. They did not re-assemble till
1551.

25. The greatest difficulties which embarrassed the
Its chief   council of Trent appear to have arisen from the
difficulties.   clashing doctrines of scholastic divines, especially
the respective followers of Thomas Aquinas and Duns
Scotus, embattled as rival hosts of Dominicans and Franciscans.[n] The fathers endeavoured, as far as possible, to avoid
any decision, which might give too unequivocal a victory to
either; though it has generally been thought, that the
former, having the authority of Augustin, as well as their
own great champion, on their side, have come off, on the
whole, superior in the decisions of the council.[o] But we

---

[n] Fleury, xxix. 154, et alibi. F. Paul,
lib. ii. and iii. passim.

[o] It is usual for Protestant writers to
inveigh against the Tridentine fathers.
I do not assent to their decisions, which
is not to the purpose, nor vindicate the
intrigues of the papal party. But I must

presume to say, that, reading their proceedings in the pages of that very able
and not very lenient historian to whom
we have generally recourse, an adversary
as decided as any that could have come
from the reformed churches, I find
proofs of much ability, considering the

must avoid these subtilties, into which it is difficult not to slide when we touch on such topics.

26. In the history of the Reformation, Luther is incomparably the greatest name. We see him, in the skilful composition of Robertson, the chief figure Character of Luther. of a group of gownsmen, standing in contrast on the canvas with the crowned rivals of France and Austria, and their attendant warriors, but blended in the unity of that historic picture. This amazing influence on the revolutions of his own age, and on the opinions of mankind, seems to have produced, as is not unnatural, an exaggerated notion of his intellectual greatness. It is admitted on all sides, that he wrote his own language with force and purity; and he is reckoned one of its best models. The hymns in use with the Lutheran church, many of which are his own, possess a simple dignity and devoutness, never, probably, excelled in that class of poetry, and alike distinguished from the poverty of Sternhold or Brady, and from the meretricious ornament of later writers. But from the Latin works of Luther few readers, I believe, will rise without disappointment. Their intemperance, their coarseness, their inelegance, their scurrility, their wild paradoxes, that menace the foundations of religious morality, are not compensated, so far at least as my slight acquaintance with them extends, by much strength or acuteness, and still less by any impressive eloquence. Some of his treatises, and we may instance his reply to Henry VIII., or the book 'against the falsely-named order of bishops,' can be described as little else than bellowing in bad Latin. Neither of these books display, as far as I can judge, any striking ability. It is not to be imagined that a man of his vivid parts fails to perceive any advantage which may offer itself in that close grappling, sentence by sentence, with an adversary, which fills most of his controversial writings; and in scornful irony he had no superior.

---

embarrassments with which they had to struggle, and of an honest desire of reformation, among a large body, as to those matters which, in their judgment, ought to be reformed. The notes of Courayer on Sarpi's history, though he is not much less of a Protestant than his original, are more candid, and generally very judicious. Pallavicini I have not read; but what is valuable in him will doubtless be found in the continuation of Fleury, vol. xxix. et alibi.

His epistle to Erasmus, prefixed to the treatise De servo arbitrio, is bitterly insolent in terms as civil as he could use. But the clear and comprehensive line of argument, which enlightens the reader's understanding, and resolves his difficulties, is always wanting. An unbounded dogmatism, resting on an absolute confidence in the infallibility, practically speaking, of his own judgment, pervades his writings; no indulgence is shown, no pause allowed, to the hesitating; whatever stands in the way of his decisions, the fathers of the church, the schoolmen and philosophers, the canons and councils, are swept away in a current of impetuous declamation; and as every thing contained in Scripture, according to Luther, is easy to be understood,[p] and can only be understood in his sense, every deviation from his doctrine incurs the anathema of perdition. Jerome, he says, far from being rightly canonised, must, but for some special grace, have been damned for his interpretation of St. Paul's Epistle to the Romans.[q] That the Zuinglians, as well as the whole church of Rome, and the Anabaptists, were shut out by their tenets from salvation, is more than insinuated in numerous passages of Luther's writings. Yet he had passed himself through several changes of opinion. In 1518 he rejected auricular confession; in 1520 it was both useful and necessary; not long afterwards it was again laid aside. I have found it impossible to reconcile, or to understand, his tenets concerning faith and works; and can only perceive, that, if there be any reservation in favour of the latter, not merely sophistical, of which I am hardly well convinced, it consists in distinctions too subtle for the people to apprehend. These are not the oscillations of the balance in a calm understanding, conscious of the difficulty which so often attends the estimate of opposite presumptions, but alternate gusts of dogmatism, during which, for the time, he was as tenacious of his judgment as if it had been uniform.

27. It is not impossible that some offence will be taken

---

[p] [This, however, is only for those who are illuminated by the Spirit. Spiritus enim requiritur ad totam Scripturam, et ad quamlibet ejus partem intelligendam. Vol. ii. fol. 428, edit.

Wittenberg, 1554.—1842.]
[q] Infernum potius quam cœlum Hieronymus meruit; tantum abest ut ipsum canonizare aut sanctum esse audeam dicere. Id. fol. 478.

at this character of his works by those who have thought
only of the man; extraordinary as he doubtless was in himself, and far more so as the instrument of mighty changes
on earth. Many of late years, especially in Germany,
without holding a single one of Luther's more peculiar
tenets, have thought it necessary to magnify his intellectual
gifts. Frederic Schlegel is among these; but in his panegyric there seems a little wish to insinuate that the reformer's powerful understanding had a taint of insanity.
This has not unnaturally occurred to others, from the
strange tales of diabolical visions Luther very seriously
recounts, and from the inconsistencies as well as the extravagance of some passages. But the total absence of self-
restraint, with the intoxicating effects of presumptuousness,
is sufficient to account for aberrations, which men of regular
minds construe into actual madness. Whether Luther were
perfectly in earnest as to his personal interviews with the
devil, may be doubtful; one of them he seems to represent
as internal.

28. Very little of theological literature, published between
1520 and 1550, except such as bore immediately Theological
on the great controversies of the age, has obtained Erasmus.
sufficient reputation to come within our researches, which,
upon this most extensive portion of ancient libraries, do
not extend to disturb the slumbers of forgotten folios. The
Paraphrase of Erasmus was the most distinguished work
in Scriptural interpretation. Though not satisfactory to
the violent of either party, it obtained the remarkable
honour of being adopted in the infancy of our own Protestantism. Every parish church in England, by an order of
council in 1547, was obliged to have a copy of this paraphrase. It is probable, or rather obviously certain, that
this order was not complied with.[r]

29. The Loci Communes of Melanchthon have already
been mentioned. The writings of Zwingle, collectively published in 1544, did not attain equal reputation: with more

---

[r] Jortin says that, ' taking the Annotations and the Paraphrase of Erasmus
together, we have an interpretation of
the New Testament as judicious and exact as could be made in his time, and to
which very few deserve to be preferred
of those which have since been published.' ii. 91.

of natural ability than erudition, he was left behind in the
general advance of learning. Calvin stands on higher
ground. His Institutes are still in the hands of
that numerous body who are usually denominated
from him. The works of less conspicuous advocates of the
Reformation which may fall within this earlier period of
controversy will not detain us; nor is it worth while to do
more on this occasion than mention the names of a few once
celebrated men in the communion of Rome, Vives, Cajetan,
Melchior, Cano, Soto, and Catharin.[s] The two latter were
prominent in the council of Trent, the first being of the
Dominican party, or that of Thomas Aquinas, which was
virtually that of Augustin; the second a Scotist, and in some
points deviating a little from what passed for the more orthodox tenets either in the Catholic or Protestant churches.[t]

*Melanch-
thon.
Romish
writers.*

30. These elder champions of a long war, especially the
Romish, are, with a very few exceptions, known only
by their names and lives. These are they, and many
more there were down to the middle of the seventeenth century,
at whom, along the shelves of an ancient library, we look
and pass by. They belong no more to man, but to the worm,
the moth, and the spider. Their dark and ribbed backs,
their yellow leaves, their thousand folio pages, do not more
repel us than the unprofitableness of their substance. Their
prolixity, their barbarous style, the perpetual recurrence, in
many, of syllogistic forms, the reliance, by way of proof, on
authorities that have been abjured, the temporary and partial
disputes, which can be neither interesting nor always intelligible at present, must soon put an end to the activity of
the most industrious scholar.[u] Even the coryphæi of the
Reformation are probably more quoted than read, more
praised than appreciated; their works, though not scarce,
are voluminous and expensive; and it may not be invidious to
surmise, that Luther and Melanchthon serve little other
purpose, at least in England, than to give an occasional air
of erudition to a theological paragraph, or to supply its
margin with a reference that few readers will verify. It will

*This lite-
rature nearly
forgotten.*

---

    [s] Eichhorn, v. 210–226.   Andrès,   [t] Sarpi and Fleury, passim.
xviii. 236.   [u] Eichhorn.

be unnecessary to repeat this remark hereafter; but it must
be understood as applicable, with such few exceptions as will
from time to time appear, throughout at least the remainder
of the sixteenth century.

31. No English treatise on a theological subject, published
before the end of 1550, seems to deserve notice in
the general literature of Europe, though some may Sermons.
be reckoned interesting in the history of our Reformation.
The Sermons of Latimer, however, published in 1548, are
read for their honest zeal and lively delineation of manners.
They are probably the best specimens of a style then prevalent in the pulpit, and which is still not lost in Italy, nor
among some of our own sectaries; a style that came at once
home to the vulgar, animated and effective, picturesque and
intelligible, but too unsparing both of ludicrous associations and common-place invective. The French have some
preachers, earlier than Latimer, whose great fame was obtained in this manner, Maillard and Menot. They belong to
the reign of Louis XII. I am but slightly acquainted with
the former, whose sermons, printed if not preached in Latin,
with sometimes a sort of almost macaronic intermixture of
French, appeared to me very much inferior to those of
Latimer. Henry Stephens, in his Apologie pour Hérodote,
has culled many passages from these preachers, in proof of
the depravity of morals in the age before the Reformation.
In the little I have read of Maillard, I did not find many
ridiculous, though some injudicious passages; but those who
refer to the extracts of Niceron, both from him and Menot,
will have as much gratification as consummate impropriety
and bad taste can furnish.[x]

32. The vital spirit of the Reformation, as a great working in the public mind, will be inadequately dis- Spirit of the
cerned in the theological writings of this age. Two Reformation.
controversies overspread their pages, and almost efface more

---

[x] Niceron, vols. xxiii. and xxiv. If
these are the original sermons, it must
have been the practice in France, as it
was in Italy, to preach in Latin; but
Eichhorn tells us that the sermons of
the fifteenth century, published in Germany, were chiefly translated from the
mother-tongue. vi, 113. Tauler certainly
preached in German, yet Eichhorn in
another place, iii. 282, seems to represent Luther and his Protestant associates
as the first who used that language in
the pulpit.

important and more obvious differences between the old and
the new religions. Among the Lutherans, the tenet of justification or salvation by faith alone, called, in the barbarous
jargon of polemics, solifidianism, was always prominent : it
was from that point their founder began ; it was there that,
long afterwards, and when its original crudeness had been
mellowed, Melanchthon himself thought the whole principle
of the contest was grounded.[y] In the disputes again of the
Lutherans with the Helvetic reformers, as well as in those
of the latter school, including the church of England, with
that of Rome, the corporal or real presence (which are generally synonymous with the writers of that century) in the
Lord's supper was the leading topic of debate. But in the
former of these doctrines, after it had been purged from the
Antinomian extravagances of Luther, there was found, if
not absolutely a verbal, yet rather a subtle, and by no means
practical difference between themselves and the church of
Rome ;[z] while, in the Eucharistic controversy, many of the
reformers bewildered themselves, and strove to perplex their
antagonists, with incompatible and unintelligible propositions, to which the mass of the people paid as little regard
as they deserved. It was not for these trials of metaphysical
acuteness that the ancient cathedrals shook in their inmost
shrines; and though it would be very erroneous to deny,
that many not merely of the learned laity, but of the inferior
ranks, were apt to tread in such thorny paths, we must look
to what came closer to the apprehension of plain men for
their zeal in the cause of reformed religion, and for the
success of that zeal. The abolition of saint-worship, the
destruction of images, the sweeping away of ceremonies, of
absolutions, of fasts and penances, the free circulation of the
Scriptures, the communion in prayer by the native tongue,
the introduction, if not of a good, yet of a more energetic
and attractive style of preaching than had existed before ;
and besides this, the eradication of monkery which they
despised, the humiliation of ecclesiastical power which they
hated, the immunity from exactions which they resented,

---

[y] Melanchth. Epist. p. 290, ed. Peucer, 1570.
[z] Burnet on Eleventh Article.

these are what the north of Europe deemed its gain by the
public establishment of the Reformation, and to which the
common name of Protestantism was given. But it is rather
in the history, than in the strictly theological literature of
this period, that we are to seek for the character of that
revolution in religious sentiment, which ought to interest
us from its own importance, and from its analogy to other
changes in human opinion.

33. It is often said, that the essential principle of Protestantism, and that for which the struggle was made, Limits of
was something different from all we have mentioned, private
judgment.
a perpetual freedom from all authority in religious belief, or
what goes by the name of the right of private judgment.
But, to look more nearly at what occurred, this permanent
independence was not much asserted, and still less acted
upon.   The Reformation was a change of masters ; a voluntary one, no doubt, in those who had any choice ; and in this
sense, an exercise, for the time, of their personal judgment.
But no one having gone over to the Confession of Augsburg,
or that of Zurich, was deemed at liberty to modify those
creeds at his pleasure.   He might of course become an Anabaptist or an Arian ; but he was not the less a heretic in
doing so, than if he had continued in the church of Rome.
By what light a Protestant was to steer, might be a problem
which at that time, as ever since, it would perplex a theologian to decide ; but in practice, the law of the land, which
established one exclusive mode of faith, was the only safe,
as, in ordinary circumstances, it was, upon the whole, the
most eligible guide.

34. The adherents to the church of Rome have never
failed to cast two reproaches on those who left Passions
them : one, that the reform was brought about by instrumental
in Reform-
intemperate and calumnious abuse, by outrages of ation.
an excited populace, or by the tyranny of princes ; the
other, that after stimulating the most ignorant to reject the
authority of their church, it instantly withdrew this liberty
of judgment, and devoted all who presumed to swerve from
the line drawn by law, to virulent obloquy, or sometimes to
bonds and death.   These reproaches, it may be a shame for
us to own, ' can be uttered, and cannot be refuted.'   But,

without extenuating what is morally wrong, it is permitted
to observe, that the Protestant religion could, in our human
view of consequences, have been established by no other
means.   Those who act by calm reason are always so few in
number, and often so undeterminate in purpose, that without the aid of passion and folly no great revolution can be
brought about.   A persuasion of some entire falsehood, in
which every circumstance converges to the same effect on the
mind; an exaggerated belief of good or evil disposition in
others; a universal inference peremptorily derived from
some particular case; these are what sway mankind, not the
simple truth with all its limits and explanations, the fair
partition of praise and blame, or the measured assent to probability that excludes not hesitation.   That condition of the
heart and understanding which renders men cautious in their
judgment, and scrupulous in their dealings, unfits them for
revolutionary seasons.   But of this temper there is never
much in the public.   The people love to be told that they
can judge; but they are conscious that they can act.   Whether a saint in sculpture ought to stand in the niches of their
cathedrals, it was equally tedious and difficult to inquire;
that he could be defaced, was certain; and this was achieved.
It is easy to censure this as precipitancy; but it was not a
mere act of the moment; it was, and much more was of the
same kind, the share that fell naturally to the multitude in
a work which they were called to fulfil, and for which they
sometimes encountered no slight danger.

35. But if it were necessary, in the outset of the Reformation, to make use of that democratic spirit of
destruction, by which the populace answered to the
bidding of Carlostadt or of Knox, if the artisans of
Germany and Switzerland were to be made arbiters of controversy, it was not desirable that this reign of religious
anarchy should be more than temporary.   Protestantism,
whatever, from the generality of the word, it may since be
considered, was a positive creed; more distinctly so in the
Lutheran than in the Helvetic churches, but in each, after
no great length of time, assuming a determinate and dogmatic character.   Luther himself, as has been already observed, built up before he pulled down; but the Confession

Establish-
ment of
new dog-
matism.

of Augsburg was the first great step made in giving the
discipline and subordination of regular government to the
rebels against the ancient religion.　In this, however, it was
taken for granted, that their own differences of theological
opinion were neither numerous nor inevitable; a common
symbol of faith, from which no man could dissent without
criminal neglect of the truth or blindness to it, seemed
always possible, though never attained; the pretensions of
catholic infallibility were replaced by a not less uncompromising and intolerant dogmatism, availing itself, like the
other, of the secular power, and arrogating to itself, like the
other, the assistance of the Spirit of God.　The mischiefs
that have flowed from this early abandonment of the right
of free inquiry are as evident as its inconsistency with the
principles upon which the reformers had acted for themselves; yet, without the Confession of Augsburg and similar
creeds, it may be doubtful whether the Protestant churches
would have possessed a sufficient unity to withstand their
steady, veteran adversaries, either in the war of words, or in
those more substantial conflicts to which they were exposed
for the first century after the Reformation.　The schism of
the Lutheran and Helvetic Protestants did injury enough to
their cause; a more multitudinous brood of sectaries would,
in the temper of those times, have been such a disgrace as it
could not have overcome.　It is still very doubtful whether
the close phalanx of Rome can be opposed, in ages of strong
religious zeal, by anything except established or at least
confederate churches.

36. We may conclude this section with mentioning the
principal editions or translations of Scripture, pub-　Editions of
lished between 1520 and 1550.　The Complutensian　Scripture.
edition of the New Testament, suspended since the year
1514, when the printing was finished, became public in 1522.
ThePolyglott of the Old Testament, as has been before mentioned, had appeared in 1517.　An edition of the Greek
Testament was published at Strasburg by Cephalæus in
1524, and of the Septuagint in 1526.　The New Testament
appeared at Haguenau in 1521, and from the press of Colinæus at Paris in 1534; another at Venice in 1538.　But
these, which have become very scarce, were eclipsed in reputa-

tion by the labours of Robert Stephens, who printed three editions in 1546, 1549, and 1550 ; the two former of a small size, the last in folio. In this he consulted more manuscripts than any earlier editor had possessed; and his margin is a register of their various readings. It is therefore, though far from the most perfect, yet the first endeavour to establish the text on critical principles.

37. The translation of the Old and New Testament by Luther is more renowned for the purity of its German idiom than for its adherence to the original text. Simon has charged him with ignorance of Hebrew ; and when we consider how late he came to the study of either that or the Greek language, and the multiplicity of his employments, it may be believed that his knowledge of them was far from extensive.[a] From this translation, however, and from the Latin Vulgate, the English one of Tyndale and Coverdale, published in 1535 or 1536, is avowedly taken.[b] Tyndale had printed his version of the New Testament in 1526. That of 1537, commonly called Matthews's Bible, from the name of the printer, though in substance the same as Tyndale's, was superintended by Rogers, the first martyr in the persecution of Mary, who appears to have had some skill in the original languages. The Bible of 1539, more usually called Cranmer's Bible, was certainly revised by comparison with the original. It is, however, questionable whether there was

Translations of Scripture.

English.

[a] Simon, Hist. critique du V. T. p. 432. Andrès, xix. 169. Eichhorn, however, says that Luther's translation must astonish any impartial judge, who reflects on the lamentable deficiency of subsidiary means in that age. iii. 317. The Lutherans have always highly admired this work on account of its pure Germanism : it has been almost as ill spoken of among Calvinists as by the Catholics themselves. St. Aldegonde says it is farther from the Hebrew than any one he knows ; ex qua manavit nostra, ex vitiosa Germanicâ facta vitiosior Belgico-Teutonica. Gerdes, iii. 60.

[b] Tyndale's translation of the Pentateuch had been published in 1530. It has been much controverted of late years whether he were acquainted or not with Hebrew.

[Tyndale's translation of the Greek Testament, so far as it is made from the Latin at all, is from that of Erasmus, not from the Vulgate. But it is said that he frequently adheres to the original where Erasmus departs from it ; so that he must be reckoned sufficiently acquainted with Greek. See Historical Accounts of English Versions of the Scriptures, prefixed to the English Hexapla, printed in 1841.
Coverdale had other versions to assist him besides that of Luther and the Vulgate. But his own was executed with a rapidity absolutely incompatible with deliberate consideration, even if his learning had been greater than it was.—1847.]

either sufficient leisure, or adequate knowledge of the Hebrew and Greek languages, in the reign of Henry VIII., to consummate so arduous a task as the thorough censure of the Vulgate text.

38. Brucioli of Venice published a translation of the Scriptures into Italian, which he professes to have formed upon the original text.[c] It was retouched by Marmocchini, and printed as his own in 1538. Zaccarias, a Florentine monk, gave another version in 1542, taken chiefly from his two predecessors. The earlier translation of Malerbi passed through twelve editions in this century.[d] The Spanish New Testament by Francis de Enzina was printed at Antwerp in 1543, as the Pentateuch in the same language was by some Jews at Constantinople in 1547.[e] Olaus Petri, the chief ecclesiastical adviser of Gustavus Vasa, translated the Scriptures into Swedish, and Palladius into Danish, before the middle of the century. But in no language were so many editions of Scripture published as in that of Flanders or Holland; the dialects being still more slightly different, I believe, at that time than they are now. The old translation from the Vulgate, first printed at Delft in 1497, appeared several times before the Reformation from the presses of Antwerp and Amsterdam. A Flemish version of the New Testament from that of Luther came out at Antwerp in 1522, the very year of its publication at Wittenberg; and twelves times more in the next five years. It appears from the catalogue of Panzer, that the entire Bible was printed in the Flemish or Dutch language, within the

In Italy and Low Countries.

---

[c] The truth of this assertion is denied by Andrès, xix. 188.

[d] M'Crie's Reformation in Italy, p. 43.

[e] This translation, which could have been of little use, was printed in Hebrew characters, with the original, and with a version in modern Greek, but in the same characters. It was reprinted in 1553 by some Italian Jews, in the ordinary letter. This Spanish translation is of considerable antiquity. appearing by the language to be of the twelfth century; it was made for the use of the Spanish Jews, and preserved privately in their synagogues and schools. This is one out of several translations of Scripture that were made in Spain during the middle ages; one of them, perhaps, by order of Alfonso X. Andrès, xix. 151. But in the sixteenth century, even before the alarm about the progress of heresy began in Spain, a stop was put to their promulgation, partly through the suspicions entertained of the half-converted Jews. Id. 183. The translation of Enzina, a suspected Protestant, was of course not well received, and was nearly suppressed. Id. ibid. M'Crie's Hist. of the Reformation in Spain.

first thirty-six years of the sixteenth century, in fifteen editions, one of which was at Louvain, one at Amsterdam, and the rest at Antwerp. Thirty-four editions of the New Testament alone in that language appeared within the same period ; twenty-four of them at Antwerp.[f] Most of these were taken from Luther, but some from the Vulgate. There can be no sort of comparison between the number of these editions, and consequently the eagerness of the people of the Low Countries for Biblical knowledge, considering the limited extent of their language, and anything that could be found in the Protestant states of the empire.

39. Notwithstanding the authority given to the Vulgate by the church of Rome, it has never been forbidden either to criticise the text of that version, or to publish a new one. Sanctes Pagninus, an oriental scholar of some reputation, published a translation of the Old and New Testament at Lyons in 1528. This has been reckoned too literal, and consequently obscure and full of solecisms. That of Sebastian Munster, a more eminent Hebraist, printed at Basle in 1534, though not free from Oriental idioms, which indeed very few translations have been, or perhaps rightly can be, and influenced, according to some, by the false interpretations of the rabbins, is more intelligible. Two of the most learned and candid Romanists, Huet and Simon, give it a decided preference over the version of Pagninus. Another translation by Leo Juda and Bibliander, at Zurich in 1543, though more elegant than that of Munster, deviates too much from the literal sense. This was reprinted at Paris in 1545 by Robert Stephens, with notes attributed to Vatable.[g]

40. The earliest Protestant translation in French is that by Olivetan at Neufchâtel in 1535. It has been said that Calvin had some share in this edition; which, however, is of little value, except from its scarcity, if it be true that the text of the version from the Vulgate by Faber Stapulensis has been merely retouched. Faber had printed this, in successive portions, some time before ; at first

Latin translations.

French translations.

---

f Panzer, Annales Typographici, Index.

g Simon, Hist. crit. du V. T. Biogr.

univ. Eichhorn, v. 565 et post. Andrès, xix. 165.

in France; but the Parliament of Paris, in 1525, having prohibited his translation, he was compelled to have recourse to the press of Antwerp. This edition of Faber appeared several times during the present period. The French Bible of Louvain, which is that of Faber, revised by the command of Charles V., appeared as a new translation in 1550.[h]

[h] Simon, Hist. crit. du V. T. Biogr. univ. Eichhorn, v. 565 et post. Andrès, xix. 165.

CHAPTER VII.

HISTORY OF SPECULATIVE, MORAL, AND POLITICAL PHILOSOPHY,
AND OF JURISPRUDENCE, IN EUROPE, FROM 1520 TO 1550.

Sect. I.   1520—1550.

Speculative Philosophy.

1. UNDER this head we shall comprehend not only what passes
<small>Logic in-
cluded under
this head.</small> by the loose, yet not unintelligible appellation,
metaphysics, but those theories upon the nature
of things, which, resting chiefly upon assumed dogmas, could
not justly be reduced to the division of physical science.
The distinction may sometimes be open to cavil; but every
man of a reflecting mind will acknowledge the impossibility
of a rigorous classification of books. The science of logic,
not only for the sake of avoiding too many partitions, but on
account of its peculiar connexion, in this period of literature,
with speculative philosophy, will be comprised in the same
department.

2. It might be supposed that the old scholastic philosophy,
<small>Slow defeat
of scholastic
philosophy.</small> the barbarous and unprofitable disputations which
occupied the universities of Europe for some hun-
dred years, would not have endured much longer against
the contempt of a more enlightened generation. Wit and
reason, learning and religion, combined their forces to overthrow the idols of the schools. They had no advocates able
enough to say much in their favour; but established possession, and that inert force which ancient prejudices retain,
even in a revolutionary age, especially when united with
civil and ecclesiastical authority, rendered the victory of
good sense and real philosophy very slow.

3. The defenders of scholastic disputation availed themselves of the common-place plea, that its abuses It is sustain-
furnished no conclusion against its use. The bar- ed by the
universities
barousness of its terminology might be in some and regulars.
measure discarded; the questions which had excited ridicule
might be abandoned to their fate; but it was still contended
that too much of theology was involved in the schemes of
school philosophy erected by the great doctors of the church
to be sacrificed for heathen or heretical innovations. The
universities adhered to their established exercises; and
though these, except in Spain, grew less active, and provoked
less emulation, they at least prevented the introduction of
any more liberal course of study. But the chief supporters
of scholastic philosophy, which became, in reality or in
show, more nearly allied to the genuine authority of Aristotle, than it could have been, while his writings were unknown or ill-translated, were found, after the revival of
letters, among the Dominican or Franciscan orders; to
whom the Jesuits, inferior to none in acuteness, lent, in
process of time, their own very powerful aid.[a] Spain was,
above all countries, and that for a very long time, the asylum
of the schoolmen; and this seems to have been one among
many causes which have excluded, as we may say the
writers of that kingdom, with but few exceptions, from the
catholic communion of European literature.

4. These men, or many of them, at least towards the
middle of the century, were acquainted with the Commentators on
writings of Aristotle. But commenting upon the Aristotle.
Greek text, they divided it into the smallest fragments,
gave each a syllogistic form, and converted every proposition into a complex series of reasonings, till they ended,
says Buhle, in an endless and insupportable verbosity. 'In
my own labours upon Aristotle,' he proceeds, 'I have
sometimes had recourse, in a difficult passage, to these scholastic commentators, but never gained any thing else by my
trouble than an unpleasant confusion of ideas; the little

---

[a] Brucker, iv. 117 et post. Buhle has drawn copiously from his predecessor, ii. 448.

there is of value being scattered and buried in a chaos of endless words.'[b]

5. The scholastic method had the reformers both of re-
Attack of ligion and literature against it.   One of the most
Vives on
scholastics. strenuous of the latter was Ludovicus Vives, in his great work, De corruptis artibus et tradendis disciplinis. Though the main object of this is the restoration of what were called the studies of humanity (humaniores literæ), which were ever found incompatible with the old meta-physics, he does not fail to lash the schoolmen directly in parts of this long treatise, so that no one, according to Brucker, has seen better their weak points, or struck them with more effect.   Vives was a native of Valencia, and at one time preceptor to the princess Mary in England.[c]

6. In the report of the visitation of Oxford, ordered by
Contempt of Henry VIII. in 1535, contempt for the scholastic
them in Eng-
land. philosophy is displayed in the triumphant tone of conquerors.   Henry himself had been an admirer of Thomas Aquinas.   But the recent breach with the see of Rome made it almost necessary to declare against the schoolmen, its steadiest adherents.   And the lovers of ancient learning, as well as the favourers of the Reformation, were gaining ground in the English Government.[d]

7. But while the subtle, though unprofitable, ingenuity
Veneration of the Thomists and Scotists was giving way, the
for Aristotle. ancient philosophy, of which that of the scholastic doctors was a corruption, restored in its genuine lineaments, kept possession of the field with almost redoubled honour. What the doctors of the middle ages had been in theology, that was Aristotle in all physical and speculative science;

---

[b] ii. 417.

[c] Brucker, iv. 86. Meiners (Vergleich. der Sitten, ii. 730–755) has several extracts from Vives as to the scholasti-cism of the beginning of this century. He was placed by some of his contem-poraries in a triumvirate with Erasmus and Budæus. [This treatise of Vives is in seven books. The first is general ; the second treats of the corrupt teach-ing of grammar ; the third of logic ; the fourth of rhetoric ; the fifth of medi-cine and mathematics ; the sixth of

ethics ; the last of the civil law. Thus, on every side except theology, which he certainly did not mean to represent as standing in no need of correction, he wages war against the universities and their system.—1842]

[d] Wood's Hist. of University of Ox-ford.   The passage wherein Antony Wood deplores the 'setting Duns in Bocardo' has been often quoted by those who make merry with the lamentations of ignorance.

and the church admitted him into an alliance of dependency
for her own service.　The Platonic philosophy, to which
the patronage of the Medici and the writings of Ficinus
had given countenance in the last century, was much fallen,
nor had, at this particular time, any known supporters in
Europe.　Those who turned their minds to physical knowledge, while they found little to their purpose in Plato, were
furnished by the rival school with many confident theories
and some useful truth.　Nor was Aristotle without adherents among the conspicuous cultivators of polite literature; who willingly paid that deference to a sage of Greece,
which they blushed to show for a barbarian dialectician of
the thirteenth century.　To them at least he was indebted
for appearing in a purer text, and in more accurate versions;
nor was the criticism of the sixteenth century more employed
on any other writer.　By the help of philology, as her
bounden handmaid, philosophy trimmed afresh her lamp.
The true peripatetic system, according to so competent a
judge as Buhle, was first made known to the rest of Europe
in the sixteenth century; and the new disciples of Aristotle,
endeavouring to possess themselves of the spirit as well as
literal sense of his positions, prepared the way for a more
advanced generation to poise their weight in the scale of
reason.[e]

8. The name of Aristotle was sovereign in the continental
universities; and the union between his philosophy, Melanchthon
or what bore that title, and the church, appeared countenances
him.
so long established, that they must stand or fall together.
Luther accordingly, in the commencement of the Reformation, inveighed against the Aristotelian logic and metaphysics,
or rather against those sciences themselves; nor was Melanchthon at that time much behind him.　But time ripened
in this, as it did in theology, the disciple's excellent understanding; and he even obtained influence enough over the
master to make him retract some of that invective against
philosophy, which at first threatened to bear down all human
reason.　Melanchthon became a strenuous advocate of Aristotle, in opposition to all other ancient philosophy.　He

---

[e] Buhle, ii. 462.

introduced into the university of Wittenberg, to which all
Protestant Germany looked up, a scheme of dialectics and
physics, founded upon the peripatetic school, but improved,
as Buhle tells us, by his own acuteness and knowledge.
Thus in his books logic is taught with a constant reference
to rhetoric; and the physical science of antiquity is enlarged
by all that had been added in astronomy and physiology.
It need hardly be said, that the authority of Scripture was
always resorted to as controlling a philosophy which had
been considered unfavourable to natural religion.[f]

9. I will not contend, after a very cursory inspection of
His own phi-
losophical
treatises.
this latter work of Melanchthon, against the elaborate panegyric of Buhle; but I cannot think the
Initia Doctrinæ Physicæ much calculated to advance the
physical sciences. He insists very fully on the influence of
the stars in producing events which we call fortuitous, and
even in moulding the human character; a prejudice under
which this eminent man is well known to have laboured.
Melanchthon argues sometimes from the dogmas of Aristotle, sometimes from a literal interpretation of Scripture,
so as to arrive at strange conclusions. Another treatise,
entitled De animâ, which I have not seen, is extolled by
Buhle as comprehending not only the psychology but the
physiology also of man, and as having rendered great service in the age for which it was written. This universality
of talents, and we have not yet adverted to the ethics and
dialectics of Melanchthon, enhanced his righ reputation; nor
is it surprising that the influence of so great a name should
have secured the preponderance of the Aristotelian philosophy in the Protestant schools of Germany for more than
a century.

10. The treatise of the most celebrated Aristotelian of
Aristotelians
of Italy.
his age, Pomponatius, on the immortality of the
soul, has been already mentioned. In 1525 he
published two books, one on incantations, the other on fate
and freewill. They are extremely scarce, but, according
to the analysis of Brucker, indicate a scheme of philosophy
by no means friendly to religion.[g] I do not find any other

---

[f] Buhle, ii. 427.   [g] Brucker, iv. 166.

of the Aristotelian school who falls within the present
thirty years, of sufficient celebrity to deserve mention in
this place.   But the Italian Aristotelians were divided into
two classes ; one, to which Pomponatius belonged, following
the interpretation of the ancient Greek scholiasts, especially Alexander of Aphrodisea; the other, that of the
famous Spanish philosopher of the twelfth century, Averroes, who may rather be considered an heresiarch in the
peripatetic church, than a genuine disciple of its founder.
The leading tenet of Averroism was the numerical unity
of the soul of mankind, notwithstanding its partition among
millions of living individuals.[h] This proposition, which it
may seem difficult to comprehend, and which Buhle deems
a misapprehension of a passage in Aristotle, natural enough
to one who read him in a bad Arabic version, is so far
worthy of notice, that it contains the germ of an atheistical
philosophy, which spread far, as we shall hereafter see, in
the latter part of this century, and in the seventeenth.

11. Meantime the most formidable opposition to the
authority of Aristotle sprang up in the very centre
of his dominions ; a conspiracy against the sovereign

University of Paris.

in his court itself.   For, as no university had been equal in
renown for scholastic acuteness to that of Paris, there was
none so tenacious of its ancient discipline.   The very study
of Greek and Hebrew was a dangerous innovation in the
eyes of its rulers, which they sought to restrain by the intervention of the civil magistrate.   Yet here, in their own
schools, the ancient routine of dialectics was suddenly disturbed by an audacious hand.

12. Peter Ramus (Ramée), a man of great natural acuteness, an intrepid, though too arrogant a spirit, and
a sincere lover of truth, having acquired a con-

New logic of Ramus.

siderable knowledge of languages as well as philosophy in
the university, where he originally filled, it is said, a menial
office in one of the colleges, began publicly to attack the
Aristotelian method of logic, by endeavouring to substitute
a new system of his own.   He had been led to ask himself,

---

[h] See Bayle, Averroes, note E, to which I omitted to refer on a former mention
of the subject, p. 197.

he tells us, after three years passed in the study of logic, whether it had rendered him more conversant with facts, more fluent in speech, more quick in poetry, wiser, in short, any way than it had found him; and being compelled to answer all this in the negative, he was put on considering, whether the fault were in himself, or in his course of study. Before he could be quite satisfied as to this question, he fell accidentally upon reading some dialogues of Plato; in which, to his infinite satisfaction, he found a species of logic very unlike the Aristotelian, and far more apt, as it appeared, to the confirmation of truth. From the writings of Plato, and from his own ingenious mind, Ramus framed a scheme of dialectics, which immediately shook the citadel of the Stagirite; and, though in itself it did not replace the old philosophy, contributed very powerfully to its ultimate decline. The Institutiones Dialecticæ of Ramus were published in 1543.

13. In the first instance, however, he met with the strenuous opposition which awaits such innovators. The university laid their complaint before the parliament of Paris; the king took it out of the hands of the parliament; and a singular trial was awarded as to the merits of the rival systems of logic, two judges being nominated by Goveanus, the prominent accuser of Ramus, two by himself, and a fifth by the king. Francis, it seems, though favourable to the classical scholars, whose wishes might generally go against the established dialectics, yet, perhaps from connecting this innovation with those in religion, took the side of the university; and after a regular hearing, though, as is alleged, a very partial one, the majority of the judges pronouncing an unfavourable decision, Ramus was prohibited from teaching, and his book was suppressed. This prohibition, however, was taken off a few years afterwards, and his popularity as a lecturer in rhetoric gave umbrage to the university. It was not till some time afterwards that his system spread over part of the Continent.[1]

It meets with unfair treatment.

---

[1] Launoy de variâ Aristot. fortuna in Acad. Paris. The sixth stage of Aristotle's fortune Launoy reckons to be the Ramean controversy, and the victory of the Greek philosopher. He quotes a passage from Omer Talon, which shows that the trial was conducted with much unfairness and violence, p. 112. See

14. Ramus has been once mentioned by Lord Bacon, certainly no bigot to Aristotle, with much contempt, Its merits and charac-
and another time with limited praise.[k] It is, how- ter.
ever, generally admitted by critical historians of philosophy,
that he conferred material obligations on science by decrying
the barbarous logic of the schoolmen.   What are the merits
of his own method, is a different question.   It seems evidently to have been more popular and convenient than that
in use.   He treated logic as merely the art of arguing to
others, *ars disserendi*; and, not unnaturally from this definition, comprehended in it much that the ancients had placed
in the province of rhetoric, the invention and disposition of
proofs in discourse.

15. ' If we compare,' says Buhle, ' the logic of Ramus with
that which was previously in use, it is impossible Buhle's ac-
not to recognise its superiority.   If we judge of it count of it.
by comparison with the extent of the science itself and the
degree of perfection it has attained in the hands of modern
writers, we shall find but an imperfect and faulty attempt.'
Ramus neglected, he proceeds to say, the relation of the
reason to other faculties of the mind, the sources of error,
and the best means of obviating them, the precautions
necessary in forming and examining our judgments.   His
rules display the pedantry of system as much as those of the
Aristotelians.[m]

16. As the logic of Ramus appears to be of no more direct
utility than that of Aristotle in assisting us to determine the
absolute truth of propositions, and consequently could not
satisfy Lord Bacon, so perhaps it does not interfere with the
proper use of syllogisms, which indeed, on a less extended

---

also Brucker, v. 548-583, for a copious
account of Ramus ; and Buhle, ii. 579-
602 ; also Bayle.

[k] Hooker also says with severe irony ;
' In the poverty of that other new-
devised aid, two things there are notwithstanding singular. Of marvellous
quick despatch it is, and doth show
them that have it as much almost in
three days as if it had dwelt threescore
years with them,' &c.   Again : ' Because the curiosity of man's wit doth
many times with peril wade farther in

the search of things than were convenient, the same is thereby restrained
into such generalities, as every where
offering themselves, are apparent unto
men of the weakest conceit that need
be : so as following the rules and precepts thereof, we may find it to be an
art, which teacheth the way of speedy
discourse, and restraineth the mind of
man, that it may not wax over-wise.'
Eccles. Pol. i. § 6.
[m] Buhle, ii. 593, 595.

scale than in Aristotle, form part of the Ramean dialectics.
Like all those who assailed the authority of Aristotle, he kept
no bounds in depreciating his works ; aware, no doubt, that
the public, and especially younger students, will pass more
readily from admiration to contempt, than to a qualified
estimation, of any famous man.

17. While Ramus was assaulting the stronghold of Aristotelian despotism, the syllogistic method of ar-
gumentation, another province of that extensive
empire, its physical theory, was invaded by a still more
audacious, and, we must add, a much more unworthy innovator, Theophrastus Paracelsus. Though few of this extraordinary person's writings were published before the middle
of the century, yet as he died in 1541, and his disciples
began very early to promulgate his theories, we may introduce his name more appropriately in this than in any later
period. The system, if so it may be called, of Paracelsus had
a primary regard to medicine, which he practised with the
boldness of a wandering empiric. It was not unusual in
Germany to carry on this profession; and Paracelsus employed his youth in casting nativities, practising chiromancy,
and exhibiting chemical tricks. He knew very little Latin,
and his writings are as unintelligible from their style as
their substance. Yet he was not without acuteness in his
own profession; and his knowledge of pharmaceutic chemistry was far beyond that of his age. Upon this real
advantage he founded those extravagant theories which
attracted many ardent minds in the sixteenth century, and
were afterwards woven into new schemes of fanciful philosophy. His own models were the oriental reveries of the
Cabbala, and the theosophy of the mystics. He seized hold
of a notion which easily seduces the imagination of those
who do not ask for rational proof, that there is a constant
analogy between the macrocosm, as they called it, of external nature, and the microcosm of man. This harmony and
parallelism of all things, he maintains, can only be made
known to us by divine revelation; and hence all heathen
philosophy has been erroneous. The key to the knowledge
of nature is in the Scriptures only, studied by means of the
Spirit of God communicating an interior light to the contem-

Paracelsus.

plative soul. So great an obscurity reigns over the writings
of Paracelsus, which, in Latin at least, are not originally his
own, for he had but a scanty acquaintance with that language, that it is difficult to pronounce upon his opinions,
especially as he affects to use words in senses imposed by
himself : the development of his physical system consisted in
an accumulation of chemical theorems, none of which are
conformable to sound philosophy.[n]

18. A mixture of fanaticism and imposture is very palpable in Paracelsus, as in what he calls his Ga- His impos-
balistic art, which produces by imagination and tures.
natural faith, ' per fidem naturalem ingenitam,' all magical
operations, and counterfeits by these means whatever we see
in the external world. Man has a sidereal as well as material body, an astral element, which all do not partake in
equal degrees; and therefore the power of magic, which is
in fact the power of astral properties, or of producing those
effects which the stars naturally produce, is not equally
attainable by all. This astral element of the body survives
for a time after death, and explains the apparition of dead
persons; but in this state it is subject to those who possess
the art of magic, which is then called necromancy.

19. Paracelsus maintained the animation of every thing;
all minerals both feed and render their food. And And extra-
besides this life of every part of nature, it is peopled vagancies.
with spiritual beings, inhabitants of the four elements, subject to disease and death like man. These are the silvains
(sylphs,) undines, or nymphs, gnomes, and salamanders. It
is thus observable that he first gave these names, which rendered afterwards the Rosicrucian fables so celebrated. These
live with man, and sometimes, except the salamanders, bear
children to him; they know future events, and reveal them
to us; they are also guardians of hidden treasures, which
may be obtained by their means.[o] I may perhaps have said
too much about paradoxes so absurd and mendacious; but

---

[n] Brucker, iv. 646–684, has copiously
descanted on the theosophy of Paracelsus ; and a still more enlarged account
of it will be found in the third volume
of Sprengel's Geschichte der Arzney-
kunste, which I use in the French
translation. Buhle is very brief in this
instance, though he has a general partiality to mystical rhapsodies.

[o] Sprengel, iii. 305.

literature is a garden of weeds as well as flowers; and Paracelsus forms a link in the history of opinion, which should
be not overlooked.

20. The sixteenth century was fertile in men, like Para-

Cornelius
Agrippa.

celsus, full of arrogant pretensions, and eager to
substitute their own dogmatism for that they endeavoured to overthrow. They are, compared with Aristotle,
like the ephemeral demagogues who start up to a power they
abuse as well as usurp on the overthrow of some ancient
tyranny. One of these was Cornelius Agrippa, chiefly remembered by the legends of his magical skill. Agrippa had
drunk deep at the turbid streams of cabbalistic philosophy,
which had already intoxicated two men of far greater merit,
and born for greater purposes, Picus of Mirandola and
Reuchlin. The treatise of Agrippa on occult philosophy is a
rhapsody of wild theory and juggling falsehood. It links,
however, the theosophy of Paracelsus and the later sect of
Behmenists with an Oriental lore, venerable in some measure
for its antiquity, and full of those aspirations of the soul to
break her limits, and withdraw herself from the dominion of
sense, which soothed, in old time, the reflecting hours of
many a solitary sage on the Ganges and the Oxus. The
Jewish doctors had borrowed much from this eastern source,
and especially the leading principle of their Cabbala, the
emanation of all finite being from the infinite. But this
philosophy was in all its successive stages mingled with
arbitrary, if not absurd, notions as to angelic and demoniacal
intelligences, till it reached a climax in the sixteenth
century.

21. Agrippa, evidently the precursor of Paracelsus, builds

His pre-
tended phi-
losophy.

his pretended philosophy on the four elements, by
whose varying forces the phænomena of the world
are chiefly produced; yet not altogether, since there are
occult forces of greater efficacy than the elementary, and
which are derived from the soul of the world, and from the
influence of the stars. The mundane spirit actuates every
being, but in different degrees, and gives life and form to
each; form being derived from the ideas which the Deity has
empowered his intelligent ministers, as it were by the use
of his seal, to impress. A scale of being, that fundamental

theorem of the emanative philosophy, connects the higher
and lower orders of things; and hence arises the power of
magic; for all things have, by their concatenation, a sympathy with those above and below them, as sound is propagated along a string. But besides these natural relations,
which the occult philosophy brings to light, it teaches us
also how to propitiate and influence the intelligences, mundane, angelic, or demoniacal, which people the universe.
This is best done by fumigations with ingredients corresponding to their respective properties. They may even thus
be subdued, and rendered subject to man. The demons are
clothed with a material body, and attached to the different
elements; they always speak Hebrew, as the oldest tongue.[p]
It would be trifling to give one moment's consideration to
this gibberish, were it not evidently connected with superstitious absurdities, that enchained the mind of Europe for
some generations. We see the credence in witchcraft and
spectral appearances, in astrology and magical charms, in
demoniacal possessions, those fruitful springs of infatuation,
wretchedness, and crime, sustained by an impudent parade
of metaphysical philosophy. The system of Agrippa is the
mere creed of magical imposture, on which Paracelsus, and
still more Jacob Behmen, grafted a sort of religious mysticism. But in their general influence these theories were
still more pernicious than the technical pedantry of the
schools. A Venetian monk, Francis Georgius, published a
scheme of blended Cabbalistic and Platonic, or Neo-Platonic,
philosophy in 1525; but having no collateral pretensions to
fame, like some other worshippers of the same phantom, he
can only be found in the historians of obsolete paradoxes.[q]

22. Agrippa has left, among other forgotten productions,
a treatise on the uncertainty of the sciences, which *His sceptical*
served in some measure to promote a sceptical *treatise.*
school of philosophy; no very unnatural result of such theories as he had proposed. It is directed against the imperfections sufficiently obvious in most departments of science,
but contains nothing which has not been said more ably

---

[p] Brucker, iv. 410. Sprengel, iii. [q] Brucker. iv. 374–386. Buhle, ii. 367.
226. Buhle, ii. 368.

since that time.   It is remarkable that he contradicts much
that he had advanced in favour of the occult philosophy, and
of the art of Raymond Lully.[r]

23. A man far superior to both Agrippa and Paracelsus
was Jerome Cardan: his genius was quick, versatile,
fertile, and almost profound ; yet no man can read
the strange book on his own life, wherein he describes, or
pretends to describe, his extraordinary character, without suspecting a portion of insanity ; a suspicion which the hypothesis of wilful falsehood would, considering what the book
contains, rather augment than diminish.   Cardan's writings
are extremely voluminous ; the chief that relate to general
philosophy are those entitled De subtilitate et varietate
rerum.   Brucker praises these for their vast erudition, supported by innumerable experiments and observations on
nature, which furnish no trifling collection of facts to readers
of judgment; while his incoherence of ideas, his extravagance of fancy, and confused method, have rendered him of
little service to philosophy.   Cardan professed himself a
staunch enemy of Aristotle.[s]

Cardan. (margin note)

SECT. II.   1520—1550.

On Moral and Political Philosophy.

24 BY moral philosophy, we are to understand not only systems of ethics, and exhortations to virtue, but that
survey of the nature or customs of mankind which
men of reflecting minds are apt to take, and by which they
become qualified to guide and advise their fellows.   The influence of such men, through the popularity of their writings,
is not the same in all periods of society ; it has sensibly

Influence of moral writers. (margin note)

---

[r] Brucker. Buhle.
[s] Brucker, v. 85.   Cardan had much
of the same kind of superstition as Paracelsus and Agrippa.   He admits, as the
basis of his physical philosophy, a sympathy between the heavenly bodies and
our own ; not only general, but distribu-
tive ; the sun being in harmony with the
heart, the moon with the animal juices.

All organised bodies he held to be animated, so that there is no principle
which may not be called nature.   All is
ruled by the properties of numbers.
Heat and moisture are the only real
qualities in nature ; the first being the
formal. the second the material cause of
all things.   Sprengel, iii. 278.

abated in modern times, and is chiefly exercised through
fiction, or at least a more amusing style than was found
sufficient for our forefathers ; and from this change of
fashion, as well as from the advance of real knowledge, and
the greater precision of language, many books once famous
have scarcely retained a place in our libraries, and never lie
on our tables.

25. In this class of literature, good writing, such at least
as at the time appears to be good, has always been Cortegiano of
the condition of public esteem.   They form a large Castiglione.
portion of the classical prose in every language.   And it is
chiefly in this point of view that several of the most distinguished can deserve any mention at present.   None was more
renowned in Italy than the Cortegiano of Castiglione, the
first edition of which is in 1528.   We here find both the
gracefulness of the language in this, perhaps its best age, and
the rules of polished life in an Italian court.   These, indeed,
are rather favourably represented, if we compare them with
all we know of the state of manners from other sources; but
it can be no reproach to the author that he raised the
standard of honourable character above the level of practice.
The precepts, however, are somewhat trivial, and the expression diffuse; faults not a little characteristic of his contemporaries.   A book of this kind that is serious without depth
of thought or warmth of feeling cannot be read through with
pleasure.

26. At some distance below Castiglione, in merit, and
equally in reputation, we may place the dialogues of Sperone
Speroni, a writer whose long life embraced two ages of
Italian literature.   These dialogues belong to the first, and
were published in 1544.   Such of them as relate to moral
subjects, which he treats more theoretically than Castiglione,
are solemn and dry ; they contain good sense in good language ; but the one has no originality, and the other no
spirit.

27. A Spanish prelate in the court of Charles obtained an
extraordinary reputation in Europe by a treatise so Marco Au-
utterly forgotten at present, that Bouterwek has relio of
Guevara.
even omitted his name.   This was Guevara, author of Marco
Aurelio, or the Golden Book.   It contains several feigned

letters of the emperor Marcus Aurelius, which probably in a credulous age passed for genuine, and gave vogue to the book. It was continually reprinted in different languages for more than a century; scarce any book except the Bible, says Casaubon, has been so much translated, or so frequently printed.[t] It must be owned that Guevara is dull; but he wrote in the infancy of Spanish literature.[u] It is fair to ob-

---

[t] [This was afterwards greatly enlarged by the author, and the title, Relox de principes, the watch or dial of princes, added to the former. The counterfeited letters are in this second work interspersed amidst a farrago of trite moral and religious reflections.— 1842.]

Bayle speaks of Guevara's Marco Aurelio with great contempt; its reputation had doubtless much declined before that time.

[u] [The account of Guevara in the former edition, though conformable to the bibliographers, stood in need of some correction, which the learned Dr. W. West of Dublin has enabled me to give. ' There are some circumstances connected with the Relox not generally known, which satisfactorily account for various erroneous statements that have been made on the subject by writers of high authority. The fact is, that Guevara, about the year 1518, commenced a life and letters of M. Aurelius, which purported to be a translation of a Greek work he found at Florence. Having some time afterwards lent this in MS. to the emperor, it was surreptitiously copied, and printed, as he informs us himself, first in Seville, and afterwards in Portugal. This was the famous Libro aureo, or Golden Book, which for more than a century afterwards was so very popular, and which was so often translated. Guevara himself subsequently published it (1529), with considerable additions under the title mentioned by you, but still, as I have already stated, forming but one treatise. An Italian translation of this was published in Venice in 1606, and there is also a Latin translation; but it was never so popular, nor so often reprinted, as the Golden Book, its original form. I have a copy of this letter in the original Spanish, printed at Antwerp in 1529, and have seen another, printed at Toledo in 1554, so that even after the

author published it in an enlarged and altered form, it was apparently preferred. The English Translation of the "Golden Boke of Marcus Aurelius, Emperour and eloquent Oratour," was made from the French in 1532, by Lord Berners, the translator of Froissart. According to Lowndes it was first printed by Berthelet in 1534, in octavo. My edition, by the same printer, is in quarto, 1539. I cannot discover from what French translation the English was made, the earliest mentioned by Brunet being 1535. It must, however, have been very accurate, as the English, though taken from the Spanish only at second hand, through the French, follows it so closely as to have the appearance of a literal translation made directly from it. I have likewise the Aldine edition of the Italian version with additions (Venice, 1546). Antonio, Watts, and Lowndes, all seem to have been unaware of the literary history of the two works.'

In a subsequent letter Dr. West observes, that the evidence of his statement is easily given from the language of Guevara himself, towards the conclusion of the prologue to the Relox de principes.

The following passage at the beginning of an edition of this work in the British Museum without a title-page, but referred by a pencil note in the flyleaf to the date of Seville, 1540, will confirm Dr. West's assertion :—

Comienca el primero libro del famosissimo emperador Marco Aurelio con el Relox de principes nuevamente añadido, compuesto por el muy reverendo y magnifico señor Don Antonio de Guevara, obispo de Guadix, predicador y coronista del emperador y rey Don Carlos quinto deste nombre; á cuya imperial celsitad se dirige la presente obra. En la qual son añadidas ciertas cartas del emperador Marco Aurelio, que si quitaron en otras impressiones que se hizieron antes desta, y tractase en este primero libro quanta

serve, that Guevara seems uniformly a friend to good and just government, and that he probably employs Roman stories as a screen to his satire on the abuses of his time. Antonio and Bayle censure this as a literary forgery more severely than is quite reasonable. Andrés extols the style very highly.[x]

28. Guevara wrote better, or more pleasingly, in some other moral essays. One of them, Menosprecio di corte y alabanza d'aldea, indifferently translated into English by Thomas Tymme in 1575, contains some eloquent passages; and being dictated apparently by his own feelings, instead of the spirit of book-making, is far superior to the more renowned Marco Aurelio. Antonio blames Guevara for affectation of antithesis, and too studious a desire to say everything well. But this sententious and antithetical style of the Spanish writers is worthy of our attention; for it was imitated by their English admirers, and formed a style much in vogue in the reigns of Elizabeth and James. Thus, to take a very short specimen from Tymme's translation: ' In the court,' says Guevara, ' it profits little to be wise, forasmuch as good service is soon forgotten, friends soon fail, and enemies augment, the nobility doth forget itself, science is forgotten, humility despised, truth cloaked and hid, and good counsel refused.'

His Menosprecio di corte.

---

excelencia es en el principe ser buen christiano, y quantos males se sigue de ser tyrano.

The second book is announced as follows:—Comienca el segundo libro llamado Relox de principes, en el qual va encorporado otró muy famoso libro llamado Marco Aurelio; trata el autor en el presente libro della manera que los principes y grandes señores se han de aver con sus mujeres, y de como han de criar á sus hijos.

I have not searched for the numerous editions of the Golden Book, but one in Spanish (Antwerp, 1529), which I have seen, contains only the original fiction of Marcus Aurelius, without the Dial of Princes. Dr. West is probably right in supposing that the former was the celebrated work which was so often printed throughout Europe; but there are several editions of the second in different languages. One in Italian, Venice, 1584, contains a fourth book, purporting to be the genuine work of Guevara, and translated from the Spanish in 1562. But whether this appears in any Spanish edition I do not know.

The account given of Guevara in the Biographic universelle is plainly written in ignorance of the facts for which I am indebted to my learned correspondent. —1842.]

[x] vii. 148. In 1541 Sir Thomas Elyot published ' The image of government compiled of the acts and sentences of Alexander Severus," as the work of Encolpius, an imaginary secretary to that emperor. Some have thought this genuine, or at least no forgery of Elyot's; but I see little reason to doubt that he imitated Guevara. Fabric. Bibl. Lat. and Herbert.

This elaborately condensed antithetical manner cannot have been borrowed from the Italians, of whom it is by no means a distinguishing feature.

29. Bouterwek has taken notice of a moral writer contem-
Perez d'Oliva. porary with Guevara, though not so successful in his own age, Perez d'Oliva. Of him, Andrès says, that the slight specimen he has left in his dialogue on the dignity of man displays the elegance, politeness, and vigour of his style. 'It is written,' says Bouterwek, 'in a natural and easy manner; the ideas are for the most part clearly and accurately developed, and the oratorical language, particularly where it is appropriately introduced, is powerful and picturesque.'ʸ

30. The writings of Erasmus are very much dedicated to
Ethical writings of Erasmus and Melanchthon. the inculcation of Christian ethics. The Enchiridion Militis Christiani, the Lingua, and, above all, the Colloquies, which have this primary object in view, may be distinguished from the rest. The Colloquies are, from their nature, the most sportive and amusing of his works; the language of Erasmus has no prudery, nor his moral code, though strict, any austerity; it is needless to add, that his piety has no superstition. The dialogue is short and pointed, the characters display themselves naturally, the ridicule falls, in general, with skill and delicacy; the moral is not forced, yet always in view; the manners of the age, in some of the colloquies, as in the German Inn, are humorously and agreeably represented. Erasmus, perhaps, in later times, would have been successful as a comic writer. The works of Vives breathe an equally pure spirit of morality. But it is unnecessary to specify works of this class, which, valuable as they are in their tendency, form too much the staple literature of every generation to be enumerated in its history. The treatise of Melanchthon, Moralis Philosophiæ Epitome, stands on different grounds. It is a compendious system of ethics, built in great measure on that of Aristotle, but with such variation as the principles of Christianity, or his own judgment, led him to introduce. Hence, though he exhorts young students, as the result of his own

---

ʸ Bouterwek, p. 309. Andrès, vii. 149.

long reflection on the subject, to embrace the Peripatetic theory of morals, in preference to those of the Stoic or Epicurean school,[z] and contends for the utility of moral philosophy, as part of the law of God, and the exposition of that of nature, he admits that the reason is too weak to discern the necessity of perfect obedience, or the sinfulness of natural appetite.[a]   In this epitome, which is far from servilely following the Aristotelian dogmas, he declares wholly against usury, less wise in this than Calvin, and asserts the magistrate's right to punish heretics.

31. Sir Thomas Elyot's Governor, published in 1531, though it might also find a place in the history of political philosophy, or of classical literature, seems best to fall under this head ; education of youth being certainly no insignificant province of moral science.   The author was a gentleman of good family, and had been employed by the king in several embassies.   The Biographia Britannica pronounces him 'an excellent grammarian, poet, rhetorician, philosopher, physician, cosmographer, and historian.'   For some part of this sweeping eulogy we have no evidence ; but it is a high praise to have been one of our earliest English writers of worth ; and though much inferior in genius to Sir Thomas More, equal perhaps in learning and sagacity to any scholar of the age of Henry VIII.   The plan of Sir Thomas Elyot in his Governor, as laid down in his dedication to the

Sir T. Elyot's Governor.

---

[z] Ego vero qui has sectarum controversias diu multumque agitavi, ἄνω καὶ κάτω στρέφων, ut Plato facere praecipit, valde adhortor adolescentulos, ut repudiatis Stoicis et Epicureis, amplectantur Peripatetica. Praefat. ad Mor. Philos. Epist. (1549.)

[a] Id. p. 4.   The following passage, taken nearly at random, may serve as a fair specimen of Melanchthon's style :—

Primum cum necesse sit legem Dei, item magistratuum leges nosse, ut disciplinam teneamus ad coercendas cupiditates, facile intelligi potest, hanc philosophiam etiam prodesse, quae est quaedam domestica disciplina, quae cum demonstrat fontes et causas virtutum, accendit animos ad earum amorem ; abeunt enim studia in mores, atque hoc magis invitantur animi, quia quo propius aspicimus res bonas, eo magis ipsas et admi-

ramur et amamus. Hic autem perfecta notitia virtutis quaeritur. Neque vero dubium est, quin, ut Plato ait, sapientia, si quod ejus simulacrum manifestum in oculos incurreret, acerrimos amores excitaret. Nulla autem fingi effigies potest, quae propius exprimat virtutem et clarius ob oculos ponat spectantibus, quam haec doctrina. Quare ejus tractatio magnam vim habet ad excitandos animos ad amorem rerum honestarum, praesertim in bonis ac mediocribus ingeniis. p. 6.

He tacitly retracts in this treatise all he had said against freewill in the first edition of the Loci Communes ; in hac quaestione moderatio adhibenda est, ne quas amplectamur opiniones immoderatas in utramque partem, quae aut moribus officiant, aut beneficia Christi obscurent. p. 34.

king, is bold enough, It is 'to describe in our vulgar
tongue the form of a just public weal, which matter I have
gathered as well of the sayings of most noble authors Greek
and Latin, as by mine own experience, I being continually
pained in some daily affairs of the public weal of this most
noble realm almost from my childhood.'   But it is far from
answering to this promise.   After a few pages on the superiority of regal over every other government, he passes to the
subject of education, not of a prince only, but any gentleman's son, with which he fills up the rest of his first book.

32. This contains several things worthy of observation.
Severity of   He advises that children be used to speak Latin
education.   from their infancy, and either learn Latin and Greek
together, or begin with Greek.   Elyot deprecates ' cruel and
yrous schoolmasters, by whom the wits of children be dulled,
whereof we need no better author to witness than daily
experience.'[b]   All testimonies concur to this savage ill-
treatment of boys in the schools of this period.   The fierce-
ness of the Tudor government, the religious intolerance, the
polemical brutality, the rigorous justice, when justice it was,
of our laws, seem to have engendered a hardness of character, which displayed itself in severity of discipline, when it
did not even reach the point of arbitrary or malignant
cruelty.   Every one knows the behaviour of Lady Jane
Grey's parents towards their accomplished and admirable
child ; the slave of their temper in her brief life ; the victim
of their ambition in death.   The story told by Erasmus of
Colet is also a little too trite for repetition.   The general
fact is indubitable ; and I think we may ascribe much of the
hypocrisy and disingenuousness, which were so unfortunately
too much displayed in this and the first part of the next
century, to the rigid scheme of domestic discipline so
frequently adopted ; though I will not say but that we owe
some part of the firmness and power of self-command, which
were equally manifest in the English character, to the same
cause.

33. Elyot dwells much and justly on the importance of
elegant arts, such as music, drawing, and carving, by which

---

[b] Chap. x.

he means sculpture, and of manly exercises, in liberal education ; and objects with reason to the usual prac- He seems to
tice of turning mere boys at fifteen to the study of avoid politics.
the laws.[c] In the second book he seems to come back to his
original subject, by proposing to consider what qualities a
governor ought to possess.   But this soon turns to long
common-place ethics, copiously illustrated out of ancient
history, but perhaps, in general, little more applicable to
kings than to private men, at least those of superior station.
It is plain that Elyot did not venture to handle the political
part of his subject as he wished to do.   He seems worthy,
upon the whole, on account of the solidity of his reflections,
to hold a higher place than Ascham, to whom, in some
respects, he bears a good deal of resemblance.

34. Political philosophy was not yet a common theme with
the writers of Europe, unless so far as the moral Nicolas
duties of princes may have been vaguely touched Machiavel.
by Guevara or Elyot, or their faults strongly, but incidentally adverted to by Erasmus and More.   One great luminary,
however, appeared at this time, though, as he has been
usually deemed, rather a sinister meteor, than a benignant
star.   It is easy to anticipate the name of Nicolas Machiavel.
His writings are posthumous, and were first published at
Rome early in 1532, with an approbation of the pope.   It is
certain, however, that the treatise called The Prince was
written in 1513, and the Discourses on Livy about the same
time.[d] Few are ignorant that Machiavel filled for nearly
fifteen years the post of secretary to that government of
Florence which was established between the expulsion of the
Medici in 1494 and their return in 1512.   This was in fact
the remnant of the ancient oligarchy, which had yielded to
the ability and popular influence of Cosmo and Lorenzo de'
Medici.   Machiavel, having served this party, over which
the gonfalonier Pietro Soderini latterly presided, with great
talents and activity, was naturally involved in their ruin ;
and having undergone imprisonment and torture on a charge

---

[c] Chap. xiv.
[d] There are mutual references in each
of these books to the other, from which

Ginguéné has reasonably inferred that
they were in progress at the same time.
Hist. litt. de l'Italie, viii. 46.

of conspiracy against the new government, was living in retired poverty, when he set himself down to the composition of his two political treatises. The strange theories that have been brought forward to account for the Prince of Machiavel could never be revived after the publication of Ginguéné's history of Italian literature, and the article on Machiavel in the Biographie universelle, if men had not sometimes a perverse pleasure in seeking refinements after the simple truth has been laid before them.[e] His own language may assure us of what certainly is not very improbable, that his object was to be employed in the service of Julian de' Medici, who was at the head of the state in Florence, almost in the situation of a prince, though without the title; and that he wrote this treatise to recommend himself in his eyes. He had been faithful to the late powers; but these powers were dissolved; and in a republic, a dissolved government, itself the recent creature of force and accident, being destitute of the prejudice in favour of legitimacy, could have had little chance of reviving again. It is probable, from the general tenor of Machiavel's writings, that he would rather have lived under a republic than under a prince; but the choice was not left; and it was better, in his judgment, to serve a master usefully for the state, than to waste his life in poverty and insignificance.

35. We may also in candour give Machiavel credit for sincerity in that animated exhortation to Julian which concludes the last chapter of The Prince, where he calls him forth to the noble enterprise of rescuing Italy from the barbarians. Twenty years that beautiful land had been the victim of foreign armies, before whom in succession every native state had been humiliated or overthrown. His acute mind easily perceived that no republican institutions would possess stability or concert enough to cast off this yoke. He formed, therefore, the idea of a prince; one raised newly to power, for Italy furnished no hereditary line; one sustained by a native army, for he deprecates the employment of mercenaries; one loved, but feared also, by

His motives in writing The Prince.

---

[e] Ginguéné has taken great pains with his account of Machiavel, and I do not know that there is a better. The Biographie universelle has a good anonymous article. Tiraboschi had treated the subject in a most slovenly manner.

the many; one to whom, in so magnanimous an undertaking
as the liberation of Italy, all her cities would render a willing
obedience.   It might be, in part, a strain of flattery in which
he points out to Julian of Medici a prospect so disproportionate, as we know historically, to his opportunities and his
character ; yet it was one also perhaps of sanguine fancy and
unfeigned hope.

36. None of the explanations assigned for the motives of
Machiavel in the Prince is more groundless than Some of his
one very early suggested, that by putting the house rules not
immoral.
of Medici on schemes of tyranny he was artfully luring them
to their ruin.   Whether this could be reckoned an excuse,
may be left to the reader; but we may confidently affirm
that it contradicts the whole tenor of that treatise.   And,
without palliating the worst passages, it may be said that
few books have been more misrepresented.   It is very far
from true, that he advises a tyrannical administration of
government, or one likely to excite general resistance, even
to those whom he thought, or rather knew from experience,
to be placed in the most difficult position for retaining
power, by having recently been exalted to it.   The Prince,
he repeatedly says, must avoid all that will render him
despicable or odious, especially injury to the property of
citizens, or to their honour.[f] This will leave him nothing to
guard against but the ambition of a few.   Conspiracies, which
are of little importance while the people are well affected,
become unspeakably dangerous as soon as they are hostile.[g]
Their love, therefore, or at least the absence of their hatred,
is the basis of the governor's security, and far better than any
fortresses.[h]   A wise prince will honour the nobility, at the
same time that he gives content to the people.[i] If the
observance of these maxims is likely to subvert a ruler's
power, he may be presumed to have designed the ruin of the
Medici.   The first duke in the new dynasty of that house,
Cosmo I., lived forty years in the practice of all that
Machiavel would have advised, for evil as well as good ; and
his reign was not insecure.

---

[f] c. xvii. and xix.   [g] c. xix.   è non essere odiato de' popoli
[h] c. xx. : la miglior fortezza che sia   [i] c. xix.

37. But much of a darker taint is found in The Prince.
But many Good faith, justice, clemency, religion, should be
dangerous. ever in the mouth of the ideal ruler; but he must
learn not to fear the discredit of any actions which he finds
necessary to preserve his power.[k]   In a new government it is
impossible to avoid the charge of cruelty ; for new states are
always exposed to dangers.   Such cruelties perpetrated at
the outset and from necessity, ' if we may be permitted to
speak well of what is evil,' may be useful; though when
they become habitual and unnecessary, they are incompatible
with the continuance of this species of power.[m]   It is best to
be both loved and feared ; but if a choice must be made, it
should be of the latter.   For men are naturally ungrateful,
fickle, dissembling, cowardly, and will promise much to a
benefactor, but desert him in his need, and will break the
bonds of love much sooner than those of fear.   But fear does
not imply hatred ; nor need a prince apprehend that, while
he abstains from the properties and the lives of his subjects.
Occasions to take the property of others never cease, while
those of shedding blood are rare ; and besides, a man will
sooner forgive the death of his father than the loss of his
inheritance.[n]

38. The eighteenth chapter, on the manner in which
Its only pal- princes should observe faith, might pass for a satire
liation. on their usual violations of it, if the author did not
too seriously manifest his approbation of them.   The best
palliation of this, and of what else has been justly censured
in Machiavel, is to be derived from his life and times.
These led him to consider every petty government as in a
continual state of self-defence against treachery and violence,
from its ill-affected citizens, as well as from its ambitious
neighbours.   It is very difficult to draw the straight line of
natural right in such circumstances ; and neither perhaps
the cool reader of a remote age, nor the secure subject of a
well-organised community, is altogether a fair arbiter of what
has been done or counselled in days of peril and necessity ;
relatively, I mean, to the persons, not to the objective
character of actions.   There is certainly a steadiness of

---

[k] c. xvi. xviii.   [m] c. viii.   [n] c. xvii.

moral principle and Christian endurance which tells us that
it is better not to exist at all than to exist at the price of
virtue ; but few indeed of the countrymen and contemporaries
of Machiavel had any claim to the practice, whatever they
might have to the profession, of such integrity. His crime
in the eyes of the world, and it was truly a crime, was to
have cast away the veil of hypocrisy, the profession of a
religious adherence to maxims which at the same moment
were violated.[o]

39. The Discourses of Machiavel upon the first books of
Livy, though not more celebrated than The Prince, His Dis-
have been better esteemed. Far from being exempt Livy. courses on
from the same bias in favour of unscrupulous politics, they
abound with similar maxims, especially in the third book ;
but they contain more sound and deep thinking on the spirit
of small republics than could be found in any preceding
writer that has descended to us ; more, probably, in a practical sense, than the Politics of Aristotle, though they are
not so comprehensive. In reasoning upon the Roman government, he is naturally sometimes misled by confidence in
Livy ; but his own acquaintance with modern Italy was in
some measure the corrective that secured him from the errors
of ordinary antiquaries.

40. These discourses are divided into three books, and contain 143 chapters with no great regard to arrange- Their lead-
ment ; written probably as reflections occasionally ples. ing princi-
presented themselves to the author's mind. They are built
upon one predominant idea ; that the political and military
annals of early Rome having had their counterparts in a
great variety of parallel instances which the recent history of
Italy furnished, it is safe to draw experimental principles
from them, and to expect the recurrence of similar consequences in the same circumstances. Though this reasoning
may easily mislead us, from an imperfect estimate of the

---

[o] Morhof has observed that all the
arts of tyranny which we read in Machiavel had been unfolded by Aristotle;
and Ginguéné has shown this in some
measure from the eleventh chapter of the
fifth book of the latter's Politics. He
might also have quoted the Œconomics;
the second book, however, of which, full
of the stratagems and frauds of Dionysius, though nearly of the age of Aristotle, is not genuine. Mitford, with his
usual partiality to tyrants (chap. xxxi.
sect. 8), seems to think them all laud-
able.

conditions, and does not give a high probability to our anticipations, it is such as those entrusted with the safety
of commonwealths ought not to neglect. But Machiavel
sprinkles these discourses with thoughts of a more general
cast, and often applies a comprehensive knowledge of history,
and a long experience of mankind.

41. Permanence, according to Machiavel, is the great aim
of government.[p] In this very common sentiment among
writers accustomed to republican forms, although experience
of the mischiefs generally attending upon change might lead
to it, there is, no doubt, a little of Machiavel's original taint,
the reference of political ends to the benefit of the rulers
rather than that of the community. But the polity which
he seems for the most part to prefer, though he does not
speak explicitly, nor always perhaps consistently, is one
wherein the people should at least have great weight.   In
one passage he recommends, like Cicero and Tacitus, the
triple form, which endeavours to conciliate the power of a
prince with that of a nobility and a popular assembly ; as
the best means of preventing that cycle of revolutions through
which, as he supposes, the simpler institutions would naturally, if not necessarily, pass ; from monarchy to aristocracy,
from that to democracy, and finally to monarchy again ;
though, as he observes, it rarely happens that there is time
given to complete this cycle, which requires a long course of
ages, the community itself, as an independent state, being
generally destroyed before the close of the period.[q] But,
with his predilection for a republican polity, he yet saw its
essential weakness in difficult circumstances ; and hence observes that there is no surer way to ruin a democracy than to
set it on bold undertakings, which it is sure to misconduct.[r]
He has made also the profound and important remark, that
states are rarely either formed or reformed except by one
man.[s]

42. Few political treatises can even now be read with more

---

[p] l. i. c. ii.
[q] c. ii. and vi.
[r] c. liii.
[s] c. 9. Corniani, iv. 70, has attempted
to reduce into system the Discourses of
Machiavel, which have no regnlar arrangement, so that nearly the same
thoughts recur in different chapters.

advantage than the Discourses of Machiavel; and in pro-
portion as the course of civil society tends farther Their use and influence.
towards democracy, and especially if it should lead to
what seems the inevitable consequence of democracy, a considerable subdivision of independent states, they may acquire
an additional value. The absence of all passion, the continual reference of every public measure to a distinct end, the
disregard of vulgar associations with names or persons, render him, though too cold of heart for a very generous reader,
a sagacious and useful monitor for any one who can employ
the necessary methods of correcting his theorems. He
formed a school of subtle reasoners upon political history,
which, both in Italy and France, was in vogue for two centuries; and, whatever might be its errors, has hardly been
superseded for the better by the loose declamation that some
dignify with the name of philosophical politics, and in which
we continually find a more flagitious and undisguised abandonment of moral rules for the sake of some idol of a general
principle than can be imputed to the Prince of Machiavel.

43. Besides these two works, the History of Florence
is enough to immortalise the name of Nicolas Ma- His History of Florence.
chiavel. Seldom has a more giant stride been made
in any department of literature than by this judicious, clear,
and elegant history: for the preceding historical works,
whether in Italy or out of it, had no claims to the praise of
classical composition, while this has ranked among the
greatest of that order. Machiavel was the first who gave at
once a general and a luminous development of great events
in their causes and connexions, such as we find in the first
book of his History of Florence. That view of the formation
of European societies, both civil and ecclesiastical, on the
ruins of the Roman empire, though it may seem now to contain only what is familiar, had never been attempted before,
and is still, for its conciseness and truth, as good as any that
can be read.

44. The little treatises of Giannotti and Contarini on the
republic of Venice, being chiefly descriptive of actual Treatises on Venetian Government.
institutions, though the former, a Florentine by
birth, sometimes reasons upon and even censures them,

would not deserve notice, except as they display an attention to the workings of a most complicated, and at the same time a most successful machine. The wonderful permanency, tranquillity, and prosperity of Venice became the admiration of Europe, and especially, as was most natural, of Italy; where she stood alone, without internal usurpation or foreign interference, strong in wisdom more than in arms, the survivor of many lines of petty princes, and many revolutions of turbulent democracy, which had, on either side of the Apennine, run their race of guilt and sorrow for several preceding centuries.[t]

45. Calvin alone, of the reformers in this period, has touched upon political government as a theme of rational discussion; though he admits that it is needless to dispute which is the best form of polity, since private men have not the right of altering that under which they live. The change from monarchy to despotism, he says, is easy; nor is that from aristocracy to the dominion of a few much more difficult; but nothing is so apt to follow as sedition from a popular regimen. But upon the whole he considers an aristocratic form to be far better than the other two, on account of the vices and infirmity of human nature.[u]

Calvin's political principles.

Sect. III.   1501—1510.

Jurisprudence.

46. Under the name jurisprudence, we are not yet to seek for writings on that high department of moral philosophy, which treats of the rules of universal justice, by which positive legislation and courts of judicature ought to be directed. Whatever of this kind may appear in works of this period arises incidentally out of their subject, and does not constitute their essence. According to the primary and established sense of the word, especially

Jurisprudence confined to Roman law.

---

[t] These are both published in Grævius, Thesaur. Antiq. Italiæ. See, too, Ginguéné, viii. 186.
[u] Calv. Inst. l. iv. c. 20, § 8.

the Continent, jurisprudence is the science of the Roman
law, and is seldom applied to any other positive system, but
least of all to the law of nature. Yet the application of this
study has been too extensive in Europe, and the renown of
its chief writers too high, to admit of our passing wholly
over this department of literature, as we do some technical
and professional subjects.

47. The civil or Roman law is comprehended in four
leading divisions (besides some later than the time The laws not well arranged.
of Justinian), very unequal in length, but altogether
forming that multifarious collection usually styled the Corpus Juris Civilis. As this has sometimes been published
in a single, though a vast and closely printed volume, it may
seem extraordinary that by means of arranged indexes, marginal references, and similar resources, it was not, soon after
it came into use as a standard authority, or, at least, soon
after the invention of printing, reduced into a less disorderly
state than its present disposition exhibits. But the labours
of the older jurists, in accumulating glosses or short marginal
interpretations, were more calculated to multiply than to
disentangle the intricacies of the Pandects.

48. It is at first sight more wonderful, that many nations
of Europe, instead of selecting the most valuable Adoption of the entire system.
portion of the civil law, as directory to their own
tribunals, should have bestowed decisive authority on that
entire unwieldy body which bore the name of Justinian ;
laws which they could not understand, and which, in great
measure, must, if understood, have been perceived to clash
with the new order of human society. But the homage paid
to the Roman name, the previous reception of the Theodosian
code in the same countries, the vague notion of the Italians,
artfully encouraged by one party, that the Conrads and
Frederics were really successors of the Theodosii and Justi-
nians, the frequent clearness, acuteness, and reasonableness
of the decisions of the old lawyers which fill the Pandects, the
immense difficulty of separating the less useful portion, and
of obtaining public authority for a new system, the deference,
above all, to great names, which cramped every effort of the
human mind in the middle ages, will sufficiently account for

the adoption of a jurisprudence so complicated, uncertain, unintelligible and ill fitted to the times.

49 The portentous ignorance of the earlier jurists in every thing that could aid their textual explana- tions has been noticed in the first chapter of this volume. This could not hold out long after the revival of learning. Budæus, in his Observations on the Pandects, was the first to furnish better verbal interpreta- tions; but his philological erudition was not sustained by that knowledge of the laws themselves which nothing but long labour could impart.[x] Such a knowledge of the Latin language as even after the revival of letters was given in the schools, or, we may add, as is now obtained by those who are counted learned among us, is by no means sufficient for the understanding those Roman lawyers, whose short decisions, or, as we should call them, opinions, occupy the fifty books of the Pandects. They had not only a technical terminology, as is perhaps necessary in professional usage, but many words and phrases not merely technical occur, as to the names and notions of things, which the classical authors, especially such as are commonly read, do not contain. Yet these writers of antiquity, when diligently pursued, throw much light upon jurisprudence; they assist conjecture, if they do not afford proof, as to the meaning of words; they explain allusions, they connect the laws with their temporary causes or general principles; and if they seem a little to lead us astray from the great object of jurisprudence, the adjudication of right, it was still highly important, in the conditions that Europe had imposed upon herself, to ascertain what it was that she had chosen to obey.

50. Ulric Zasius, a professor at Friburg, and Garcia d'Erzilla, whose Commentaries were printed in 1515, should have the credit, according to Andrès, of leading the way to a more elegant jurisprudence.[y] The former of these is known, in some measure, as a scholar and

Side notes: Utility of general learning to lawyers. — Alciati; his reform of law.

---

[x] Gravina, Origines Jur. Civ. p. 211.

[y] Andrès, xvi. 143. Savigny agrees with Andrès as to the merits of Zasius, and observes that the revival of the study of the laws in their original sources, instead of the commentators, had been announced by several signs be- fore the sixteenth century. Ambrogio Traversari had recommended this, and Lebrixa wrote against the errors of Ac- cursius, though in a superficial manner. Gesch. des Römischen Rechts, vi. 364.

a correspondent of Erasmus ; for the latter I have to depend
on the testimony of his countryman.   But the general voice
of Europe has always named Andrew Alciati of Milan as the
restorer of the Roman law.   He taught, from the year 1518
to his death in 1550, in the universities of Avignon, Milan,
Bourges, Paris, and Bologna.   Literature became with him
the handmaid of law ; the historians of Rome, her antiquaries, her orators and poets, were called upon to elucidate
the obsolete words and obscure allusions of the Pandects ;
to which, the earlier as well as the more valuable and
extensive portion of the civil law, this method of classical
interpretation is chiefly applicable.   Alciati had another
advantage, denied to his predecessors of the middle ages, in
the possession of the Byzantine jurists; with whom, says
Gravina, the learning of Roman law had been preserved in
a more perfect state amidst other vestiges of the empire, and
while almost extinguished in Italy by the barbarians, had
been in daily usage at Constantinople down to its capture.
Alciati was the first who taught the lawyers to write with
purity and elegance.   Erasmus has applied to him the eulogy
of Cicero on Scævola, that he was the most jurisprudent of
orators, and the most eloquent of lawyers.   But he deserved
also the higher praise of sweeping away the rubbish of con-
flicting glosses, which had so confounded the students by
their contrary subtilties, that it had become a practice to
count, instead of weighing, their authorities.   It has been
regretted that he made little use of philosophy in the exposition of law ; but this could not have been attempted in the
sixteenth century without the utmost danger of misleading
the interpreter.[z]

51. The practical lawyers, whose prejudices were nourished by their interests, conspired with the pro-   Opposition
fessors of the old school to clamour against the   to him.
introduction of literature into jurisprudence.   Alciati was
driven sometimes from one university to another by their
opposition ; but more frequently his restless disposition and
his notorious desire of gain were the causes of his migra-
tions.   They were the means of diffusing a more liberal

---

[z] Bayle, art. Alciati.   Gravina, p. 206.   Tiraboschi, ix. 115.   Corniani, v. 57.

course of studies in France as well as Italy, and especially
in the great legal university of Bourges. He stood not,
however, alone in scattering the flowers of polite literature
over the thorny brakes of jurisprudence. An
eminent Spaniard, Antonio Agustino, might perhaps be placed almost on a level with him. The first work
of Agustino, Emendationes Juris Civilis, was published in
1544. Andrès, seldom deficient in praising his compatriots,
pronounces such an eulogy on the writings of Agustino, as
to find no one but Cujacius worthy of being accounted his
equal, if indeed he does not give the preference in genius
and learning to the older writer.[a] Gravina is less diffusely
panegyrical; and in fact it is certain that Agustino, though
a lawyer of great erudition and intelligence, has been eclipsed
by those for whom he prepared the way.

Agustino.

* Vol. xvi. p. 148.

CHAPTER VIII.

HISTORY OF THE LITERATURE OF TASTE IN EUROPE FROM
1520 TO 1550.

SECT. I.   1520—1550.

Poetry in Italy—In Spain and Portugal—In France and Germany—In
England—Wyatt and Surrey—Latin Poetry.

1. THE singular grace of Ariosto's poem had not less distinguished it than his fertility of invention and bril-   Poetry of
liancy of language.   For the Italian poetry, since   Bembo.
the days of Petrarch, with the exception of Lorenzo and
Politian, the boasts of Florence, had been very deficient in
elegance; the sonnets and odes of the fifteenth century, even
those written near its close, by Tibaldeo, Serafino d'Aquila,
Benivieni, and other now obscure names, though the list of
poets in Crescimbeni will be found very long, are hardly
mentioned by the generality of critics but for the purpose of
censure; while Boiardo, who deserved most praise for bold
and happy inventions, lost much of it through an unpolished
and inharmonious style.   In the succeeding period, the faults
of the Italian school were entirely opposite; in Bembo, and
those who, by their studious and servile imitation of one
great master, were called Petrarchists, there was an elaborate
sweetness, a fastidious delicacy, a harmony of sound, which
frequently served as an excuse for coldness of imagination
and poverty of thought.   'As the too careful imitation of
Cicero,' says Tiraboschi, 'caused Bembo to fall into an
affected elegance in his Latin style, so in his Italian poetry,
while he labours to restore the manner of Petrarch, he displays more of art than of natural genius.   Yet by banishing

the rudeness of former poetry, and pointing out the right path, he was of no small advantage to those who knew how to imitate his excellences and avoid his faults.' [a]

2. The chief care of Bembo was to avoid the unpolished lines which deformed the poetry of the fifteenth century in the eyes of one so exquisitely sensible to the charms of diction. It is from him that the historians of Italian literature date the revival of the Petrarcan elegance; of which a foreigner, unless conversant with the language in all its varieties, can hardly judge, though he may perceive the want of original conception, and the monotony of conventional phrases, which is too frequently characteristic of the Italian sonnet. Yet the sonnets of Bembo on the death of his Morosina, the mother of his children, display a real tenderness not unworthy of his master; and the canzone on that of his brother has obtained not less renown; though Tassoni, a very fastidious critic, has ridiculed its centonism, or studious incorporation of lines from Petrarch; a practice which the habit of writing Latin poetry, wherein it should be sparingly employed, but not wholly avoided, would naturally encourage.[b]

Its beauties and defects.

3. The number of versifiers whom Italy produced in the sixteenth century was immensely great. Crescimbeni gives a list of eighty earlier than 1550, whom he selects from many hundred ever-forgotten names. By far the larger proportion of these confined themselves to the sonnet and the canzone or ode; and the theme is generally love, though they sometimes change it to religion. A conventional phraseology, an interminable repetition of the beauties and coldness of perhaps an ideal, certainly to us an unknown mistress, run through these productions; which so much resemble each other as sometimes to suggest to any one who reads the Sceltas which bring together many extracts from these poets, no other parallel than that of the hooting of owls in concert; a sound melancholy and not unpleasing to all ears in its way, but monotonous, unintellectual, and manifesting as little real sorrow or sentiment in the bird as these compositions do in the poet.[c]

Character of Italian poetry.

---

[a] Vol. x. p. 3.
[b] Tiraboschi, ibid. Corniani, iv. 102.

[c] Muratori himself observes the tantalising habit in which sonnetteers in-

4. A few exceptions may certainly be made. Alamanni, though the sonnet is not his peculiar line of strength, and though he often follows the track of ^{Alamanni.} Petrarch with almost servile imitation, could not, with his powerful genius, but raise himself above the common level. His Lygura Pianta, a Genoese lady, the heroine of many sonnets, is the shadow of Laura ; but when he turns to the calamities of Italy and his own, that stern sound is heard again, that almost reminds us of Dante and Alfieri.   The Italian critics, to whom we must of course implicitly defer as to the grace and taste of their own writers, speak well of Molza, and some other of the smaller poets ; though they are seldom exempt from the general defects above mentioned. But none does Crescimbeni so much extol as a Vittoria poetess, in every respect the most eminent of her Colonna. sex in Italy, the widow of the Marquis of Pescara, Vittoria Colonna, surnamed, he says, by the public voice, the divine. The rare virtues and consummate talents of this lady were the theme of all Italy, in that brilliant age of her literature ; and her name is familiar to the ordinary reader at this day. The canzone dedicated to the memory of her illustrious husband is worthy of both.[d]

5. The satires of Ariosto, seven in number, and composed in the Horatian manner, were published after his Satires of death in 1534.   Tiraboschi places them at the head Alamanni. of that class of poetry.   The reader will find an analysis of these satires, with some extracts, in Ginguéné.[e]   The twelve satires of Alamanni, one of the Florentine, exiles, of which the first edition is dated in 1532, though of earlier publi- cation than those of Ariosto, indicate an acquaintance with them.   They are to one another as Horace and Juvenal, and

---

dulge themselves, of threatening to die for love, which never comes to any thing ; quella volgare smania che mostrano gl' amanti di voler morire, e che tante volte s' ode in bocca loro, ma non mai viene ad effetto.

[d] Crescimbeni della volgar Poesia, vols. ii. and iii.   For the character of Vittoria Colonna, see ii. 360.   Roscoe (Leo X. iii. 314) thinks her canzone on her husband in no respect inferior to

that of Bembo on his brother.   It is rather by a stretch of chronology that this writer reckons Vittoria, Berni, and several more, among the poets of Leo's age.

[e] ix. 100–129.   Corniani, iv. 55.   In one passage of the second satire Ariosto assumes a tone of higher dignity than Horace ever ventured, and inveighs against the Italian courts in the spirit of his rival Alamanni.

as their fortunes might lead us to expect; one gay, easy, full
of the best form of Epicurean philosophy, cheerfulness, and
content in the simpler enjoyments of life ; the other ardent,
scornful, unsparing, declamatory, a hater of vice, and no great
lover of mankind, pouring forth his moral wrath in no feeble
strain. We have seen in another place his animadversions
on the court of Rome; nor does anything in Italy escape his
resentment.[f] The other poems of Alamanni are of a very
miscellaneous description; eclogues, little else than close imitations of Theocritus and Virgil, elegies, odes, hymns, psalms,
fables, tragedies, and what were called *selve*, a name for all
unclassed poetry.

6. Alamanni's epic, or rather romantic poem, the Avarchide,
is admitted by all critics to be a work of old age,
little worthy of his name. But his poem on agriculture, La Coltivazione, has been highly extolled. A certain
degree of languor seems generally to hang on Italian blank
verse; and in didactic poetry it is not likely to be overcome.
The Bees of Rucellai is a poem written with exquisite sweetness of style; but the critics have
sometimes forgotten to mention, that it is little else than a
free translation from the fourth Georgic.[g] No one has ever
pretended to rescue from the charge of dulness and
insipidity the epic poem of the father of blank verse,
Trissino, on the liberation of Italy from the Goths by Beli-
sarius. It is, of all long poems that are remembered at all,
the most unfortunate in its reputation.

7. A very different name is that of Berni, partly known
by his ludicrous poetry, which has given that style
the appellation of Poesia Bernesca, rather on account
of his excellence than originality, for nothing is so congenial
to the Italians,[h] but far more by his *ri-faccimento*, or re-

Marginal notes: Alamanni. Rucellai. Trissino. Berni.

---

[f] The following lines, which conclude
the twelfth and last satire, may serve as
a specimen of Alamanni's declamatory
tone of invective, and his bitter attacks
on Rome, whom he is addressing :—

O chi vedesse il ver, vedrebbe come
Più disnor tu, che 'l tuo Luther Martino
Porti a te stessa, e più gravose some ;
Non la Germania, nò ; ma l' ocio, il vino,
Avarizia, ambition, lussuria e gola,
Ti mena al fin, che già veggiam vicino.
Non pur questo dico io, non Francia sola,

Non pur la Spagna, tutta Italia ancora
Che ti tien d' heresia, di vizi scuola.
E che nol crede, ne dimandi ogn', ora
Urbin, Ferrara, l' Orso, e la Colonna,
La Marca, il Romagnuol, ma più che plora
Per te servendo, che fù d' altri donna.

[g] Roscoe's Leo, iii. 351. Tiraboschi,
x. 85. Algarotti, and Corniani (v. 116),
who quotes him, do not esteem the
poem of Rucellai highly.

[h] Corniani, iv. 252. Roscoe, iii. 323.

moulding of the poem of Boiardo. The Orlando Innamorato, an ill-written poem, especially to Tuscan ears, had been encumbered by the heavy continuation of Agostini. Yet if its own intrinsic beauties of invention would not have secured it from oblivion, the vast success of the Orlando Furioso, itself only a continuation, and borrowing most of its characters from Boiardo's poem, must have made it impossible for Italians of any curiosity to neglect the primary source of so much delight. Berni, therefore, undertook the singular office of writing over again the Orlando Innamorato, preserving the sense of almost every stanza, though every stanza was more or less altered, and inserting nothing but a few introductory passages, in the manner of Ariosto, to each canto.[i] The genius of Berni, playful, satirical, flexible, was admirably fitted to perform this labour; the rude Lombardisms of the lower Po gave way to the racy idiom of Florence; and the Orlando Innamorato has descended to posterity as the work of two minds, remarkably combined in this instance; the sole praise of invention, circumstance, description, and very frequently that of poetical figure and sentiment, belonging to Boiardo; that of style, in the peculiar and limited use of the word, to Berni. The character of the poem, as thus adorned, has sometimes been misconceived. Though Berni is almost always sprightly, he is not, in this romance, a burlesque or buffoon poet.[k] I once heard Foscolo prefer him to Ariosto. A foreigner, not so familiar with the peculiari-

---

[i] The first edition of the Rifaccimento is in 1541, and the second in 1542. In that of 1545 the first eighty-two stanzas are very different from those that correspond in former editions; some that follow are suspected not to be genuine. It seems that we have no edition on which we can wholly depend. No edition of Berni appeared from 1545 to 1725, though Domenichi was printed several times. This reformer of Boiardo did not alter the text nearly so much as Berni. Panizzi, vol. ii.

[k] Tiraboschi, vii. 195, censures Berni for 'motti e racconti troppo liberi ed empi, che vi ha inseriti.' Ginguéné exclaims, as well he may against this imputation. Berni has inserted no stories; and unless it were the few stanzas against monastic hypocrisy that remain at the

head of the twentieth canto, it is hard to say what Tiraboschi meant by impieties. But though Tiraboschi must have read Berni, he has here chosen to copy Zeno, who talks of 'il poema di Boiardo, rifatto dal Berni, e di serio trasformato in ridicolo, e di onesto in iscandaloso, e però giustamente dannato dalla chiesa.' (Fontanini, p. 273.) Zeno, even more surely than Tiraboschi, was perfectly acquainted with Berni's poem : how could he give so false a character of it ? Did he copy some older writer ? and why ? It seems hard not to think that some suspicion of Berni's bias towards Protestantism had engendered a prejudice against his poem, which remained when the cause had been forgotttn, as it certainly was in the days of Zeno and Tiraboschi.

ties of language, would probably think his style less brilliant and less pellucid ; and it is in execution alone that he claims to be considered as an original poet. The Orlando Innamorato was also remoulded by Domenichi in 1545 ; but the excellence of Berni has caused this feeble production to be nearly passed over by the Italian critics.[m]

8. Spain now began to experience one of those revolu-

Spanish poets.

tions in fashionable taste which await the political changes of nations. Her native poetry, whether Castilian or Valencian, had characteristics of its own, that placed it in a different region from the Italian. The short heroic, amatory, or devotional songs, which the Peninsular dialects were accustomed to exhibit, were too ardent, too hyperbolical for a taste which, if not correctly classical, was at least studious of a grace not easily compatible with extravagance. But the continual intercourse of the Spaniards with Italy, partly subject to their sovereign, and the scene of his wars, accustomed their nobles to relish the charms of a sister language, less energetic, but more polished than their

Boscan. Garcilasso.

own. Two poets, Boscan and Garcilasso de la Vega, brought from Italy the softer beauties of amorous poetry, embodied in the regular sonnet, which had hitherto been little employed in the Peninsula. These poems seem

---

[m] 'The ingenuity,' says Mr. Panizzi, 'with which Berni finds a resemblance between distant objects, and the rapidity with which he suddenly connects the most remote ideas; the solemn manner in which he either alludes to ludicrous events or utters an absurdity ; the air of innocence and naïveté with which he presents remarks full of shrewdness and knowledge of the world; that peculiar *bonhomie* with which he seems to look kindly and at the same time unwillingly on human errors or wickedness ; the keen irony which he uses with so much appearance of simplicity and aversion to bitterness : the seeming singleness of heart with which he appears anxious to excuse men and actions, at the very moment that he is most inveterate in exposing them ; these are the chief elements of Berni's poetry. Add to this the style, the loftiness of the verse contrasting with the frivolity of the argument, the gravest conception expressed in the most homely manner ; the seasonable use of strange metaphors and of similes sometimes sublime, and for this very reason the more laughable, when considered with relation to the subject which they are intended to illustrate, form the most remarkable features of his style." p. 120.

'Any candid Italian scholar who will peruse the Rifaccimento of Berni with attention will be compelled to admit that, although many parts of the poem of Boiardo have been improved in that work, such has not always been the case; and will, moreover, be convinced that some parts of the Rifaccimento, besides those suspected in former times, are evidently either not written by Berni, or have not received from him, if they be his, such corrections as to be worthy of their author.' p. 141. Mr. P. shows in several passages his grounds for this suspicion.

not to have been printed till 1543, when both Boscan and
Garcilasso were dead, and their new school had already met
with both support and opposition at the court of Valladolid.
The national character is not entirely lost in these poets;
love still speaks with more impetuous ardour, with more
plaintive sorrow than in the contemporary Italians; but the
restraints of taste and reason are perceived to control his
voice. An eclogue of Garcilasso, called Salicio and Nemoroso,
is pronounced by the Spanish critics to be one of the finest
works in their language. It is sadder than the lament of
saddest nightingales. We judge of all such poetry differently
in the progressive stages of life.

9. Diego Mendoza, one of the most remarkable men for
variety of talents whom Spain has produced, ranks
with Boscan and Garcilasso as a reformer of Cas- Mendoza.
tilian poetry. His character as a soldier, as the severe
governor of Siena, as the haughty minister of Charles at
the court of Rome and the council of Trent is notorious in
history.[n] His epistles, in an Horatian style, full of a masculine and elevated philosophy, though deficient in harmony
and polish, are preferred to his sonnets; a species of composition where these faults are more perceptible; and for which,
at least in the style then popular, the stern understanding
of Mendoza seems to have been ill adapted. 'Though he
composed,' says Bouterwek, 'in the Italian manner with less
facility than Boscan and Garcilasso, he felt more correctly
than they or any other of his countrymen the difference
between the Spanish and Italian languages, with respect to
their capabilities for versification. The Spanish admits of
none of those pleasing elisions, which, particularly when
terminating vowels are omitted, render the mechanism of
Italian versification so easy, and enable the poet to augment
or diminish the number of syllables according to his pleasure; and this difference in the two languages renders the
composition of a Spanish sonnet a difficult task. Still more
does the Spanish language seem hostile to the soft termination of a succession of feminine rhymes; for the Spanish

---

[n] Sadolet, in one of his epistles dated
1532 (lib. vi. p. 309, edit. 1554), gives
an interesting character of Mendoza, then
young, who had visited him at Carpentras on his way to Rome; a journey undertaken solely for the sake of learning.

poet, who adopts this rule of the Italian sonnet, is compelled
to banish from his rhymes all infinitives of verbs, together with
a whole host of sonorous substantives and adjectives.   Mendoza therefore availed himself of the use of masculine rhymes
in his sonnets; but this metrical licence was strongly censured
by all partisans of the Italian style.   Nevertheless, had he
given to his sonnets more of the tenderness of Petrarch, it is
probable that they would have found imitators.   Some of
them, indeed, may be considered as successful productions,
and throughout all the language is correct and noble.' °

10. The lyric poems of Mendoza, written in the old national
Saa di   style, tacitly improved and polished, are preferred
Miranda.   by the Spaniards to his other works.   Many of them
are printed in the Romancero General.   Saa di Miranda,
though a Portuguese, has written much in Castilian, as well
as in his own language.   Endowed by nature with the
melancholy temperament akin to poetic sensibility, he fell
readily into the pastoral strain, for which his own language
is said to be peculiarly formed.   The greater and better part
of his eclogues, however, are in Castilian.   He is said to
have chosen the latter language for imagery, and his own for
reflection.ᴾ   Of this poet, as well as of his Castilian contemporaries, the reader will find a sufficient account in Bouterwek
and Sismondi.

11. Portugal, however, produced one who did not abandon
her own soft and voluptuous dialect, Ribeyro; the
Ribeyro.   first distinguished poet she could boast.   His strains
are chiefly pastoral, the favourite style of his country, and
breathe that monotonous and excessive melancholy, with
which it requires some congenial emotion of our own to
sympathise.   A romance of Ribeyro, Menina e Moça, is one
of the earliest among the few specimens of noble prose which
we find in that language.   It is said to be full of obscure
allusions to real events in the author's life, and cannot be
read with much interest; but some have thought that it is
the prototype of the Diana of Montemayor, and the whole
school of pastoral romance, which was afterwards admired in
Europe for an entire century.   We have, however, seen that
the Arcadia of Sannazzaro has the priority; and I am not

• P. 198.   ᴾ Bouterwek, p. 240.   Sismondi.

aware that there is any specific distinction between that
romance and this of Ribeyro. It may be here observed, that
Ribeyro should in strictness have been mentioned before ; his
eclogues seem to have been written, and possibly published,
before the death of Emanuel in 1521. The romance however
was a later production.[q]

12. The French versifiers of the age of Francis I. are not
few. It does not appear that they rise above the   French
level of the three preceding reigns, Louis XI.,   poetry.
Charles VIII., and Louis XII. ; some of them mistaking
insipid allegory for the creations of fancy, some tamely describing the events of their age, others, with rather more
spirit, satirising the vices of mankind, and especially of the
clergy ; while many, in little songs, expressed their ideal
love with more perhaps of conventional gallantry than
passion or tenderness,[r] yet with some of those light and
graceful touches which distinguish this style of French
poetry. Clement Marot ranks far higher. The
psalms of Marot, though famous in their day, are   Marot.
among his worst performances. His distinguishing excellence is a naïveté, or pretended simplicity, of which it is the
highest praise to say, that it was the model of La Fontaine.
This style of humour, than which nothing is more sprightly
or diverting, seems much less indigenous among ourselves,
if we may judge by our older literature, than either among
the French or Italians.

13. In the days of Marot, French poetry had not put on
all its chains. He does not observe the regular   Their metri-
alternation of masculine and feminine rhymes, nor   cal structure.
scruple to use the open vowel, the suppression of a mute *e*
before a consonant in scanning the verse, the carrying on
the sense, without a pause, to the middle of the next line.
These blemishes, as later usage accounts them, are common
to Marot with all his contemporaries. In return, they dealt
much in artificial schemes of recurring words or lines, as
the chant royal, where every stanza was to be in the same
rhyme, and to conclude with the same verse ; or the ron-

---

[q] Bouterwek, Hist. of Portuguese   vols. x. and xi. passim. Auguis, Recueil
Liter. p. 24. Sismondi, iv. 280.   des Anciens Poètes français, vols. ii. and
  [r] Goujet, Bibliothèque française,   iii.

deau, a very popular species of metre long afterwards, wherein two or three initial words were repeated at the refrain or close of every stanza.[s]

14. The poetical and imaginative spirit of Germany, subdued as it had long been, was never so weak as in this century. Though we cannot say that this poverty of genius was owing to the Reformation, it is certain that the Reformation aggravated very much in this sense the national debasement. The controversies were so scholastic in their terms, so sectarian in their character, so incapable of alliance with any warmth of soul, that, so far as their influence extended, and that was to a large part of the educated classes, they must have repressed every poet, had such appeared, by rendering the public insensible to his superiority. The Meister-Singers were sufficiently prosaic in their original constitution; they neither produced, nor perhaps would have suffered to exhibit itself, any real excellence in poetry. But they became in the sixteenth century still more rigorous in their requisitions of a mechanical conformity to rule ; while at the same time they prescribed a new code of law to the versifier, that of theological orthodoxy. Yet one man, of more brilliant fancy and powerful feeling than the rest, Hans Sachs, the shoemaker of Nuremberg, stands out from the crowd of these artisans. Most conspicuous as a dramatic writer, his copious muse was silent in no line of verse. Heinsius accounts the bright period of Hans Sachs's literary labours to have been from 1530 to 1538 ; though he wrote much both sooner and after that time. His poems of all kinds are said to have exceeded six thousand; but not more than one-fourth of them are in print. In this facility of composition he is second only to Lope de Vega; and it must be presumed that uneducated, unread, accustomed to find his public in his own class, so wonderful a fluency was accompanied by no polish, and only occasionally by gleams of vigour and feeling. The German critics are divided concerning the genius of Hans Sachs: Wieland and Goethe gave him lustre at one time by their eulogies ; but these having been as ex-

German poetry.

Hans Sachs.

---

[s] Goujet, Bibl. française, xi. 36. Pasquier, Recherches de la France, l. vii. Gaillard, Vie de François I, vii. 20. c. 5. Auguis, vol. iii.

aggerated as the contempt of a former generation, the place
of the honest and praiseworthy shoemaker seems not likely
to be fixed very high ; and there has not been demand enough
for his works, some of which are very scarce, to encourage
their republication.[t]

15. The Germans, constitutionally a devout people, were
never so much so as in this first age of Protes- German
tantism.   And this, in combination with their hymns.
musical temperament, displayed itself in the peculiar line of
hymns.   No other nation has so much of this poetry.   At
the beginning of the eighteenth century, the number of
religious songs was reckoned at 33,000, and that of their
authors at 500.   Those of Luther have been more known
than the rest; they are hard and rude, but impressive and
deep.   But this poetry, essentially restrained in its flight,
could not develop the creative powers of genius.[u]

16. Among the few poems of this age none has been so
celebrated as the Theuerdanks of Melchior Pfint- Theuerdanks
zing, secretary to the emperor Maximilian ; a of Pfintzing.
poem at one time attributed to the master, whose praises it
records, instead of the servant.   This singular work, published originally in 1517, with more ornament of printing
and delineation than was usual, is an allegory, with scarce
any spirit of invention or language ; wherein the knight
Theuerdanks, and his adventures in seeking the marriage
of the princess Ehrreich, represent the memorable union of
Maximilian with the heiress of Burgundy.   A small number of German poets are commemorated by Bouterwek and
Heinsius, superior no doubt in ability to Pfintzing, but so
obscure in our eyes, and so little extolled by their countrymen, that we need only refer to their pages.

17. In the earlier part of this period of thirty years,
we can find very little English poetry.   Sir David English
Lyndsay, an accomplished gentleman and scholar Lyndsay.
of Scotland, excels his contemporary Skelton in such qualities, if not in fertility of genius.   Though inferior to Dunbar in vividness of imagination and in elegance of language, he shows a more reflecting and philosophical mind ;

---

[t] Heinsius, iv. 150.   Bouterwek, ix. 381.   Retrospective Review, vol. x.
[u] Bouterwek. Heinsius.

and certainly his satire upon James V. and his court is more poignant than the other's panegyric upon the Thistle. But in the ordinary style of his versification he seems not to rise much above the prosaic and tedious rhymers of the fifteenth century. His descriptions are as circumstantial without selection as theirs; and his language, partaking of a ruder dialect, is still more removed from our own. The poems of Lyndsay are said by Herbert to have been printed in 1540, and would be among the first fruits of the Scottish press; but one of these, the Complaint of the Papingo, had appeared in London two years before.[x] Lyndsay's poetry is said to have contributed to the Reformation in Scotland; in which, however, he is but like many poets of his own and preceding times. The clergy were an inexhaustible theme of bitter reproof.

18. ' In the latter end of King Henry VIII.'s reign,' says Puttenham in his Art of Poesie, ' sprung up a new company of courtly makers, of whom Sir Thomas Wyatt the elder and Henry Earl of Surrey were the two chieftains, who having travelled into Italy, and there tasted the sweet and stately measures and style of the Italian poesie, as novices newly crept out of the schools of Dante, Ariosto, and Petrarch, they greatly polished our rude and homely manner of vulgar poesie, from that it had bene before, and for that cause may justly be sayd the first reformers of our English meeter and stile. In the same time or not long after was the Lord Nicolas Vaux, a man of much facilitie in vulgar makings.'[y] The poems of Sir Thomas Wyatt, who died in 1544, and of the Earl of Surrey, executed in 1547, were first published in 1557, with a few by other hands, in a scarce little book called Tottel's Miscellanies. They were, however, in all probability, known before; and it seems necessary to mention them in this period, as they mark an important epoch in English literature.

Wyatt and Surrey.

19. Wyatt and Surrey, for we may best name them in the order of time, rather than of civil or poetical rank, have had recently the good fortune to be recommended by an editor of extensive acquaintance with literature, and of still

---

[x] [Pinkerton, however, denies that there is any genuine Scots edition before 1568.—1842.]   [y] Puttenham, book i. ch. 31.

superior taste. It will be a gratification to read the following comparison of the two poets, which I extract the more
willingly that it is found in a publication somewhat bulky
and expensive for the mass of readers.

20. 'They were men whose minds may be said to have
been cast in the same mould; for they differ only Dr. Nott's
in those minuter shades of character which always character of them.
must exist in human nature; shades of difference so infinitely varied, that there never were and never will be two
persons in all respects alike.   In their love of virtue and
their instinctive hatred and contempt of vice, in their freedom from personal jealousy, in their thirst after knowledge
and intellectual improvement, in nice observation of nature,
promptitude to action, intrepidity and fondness for romantic
enterprise, in magnificence and liberality, in generous support of others and high-spirited neglect of themselves, in con-
stancy in friendship, and tender susceptibility of affections
of a still warmer nature, and in every thing connected with
sentiment and principle, they were one and the same; but
when those qualities branch out into particulars, they will be
found in some respects to differ.

21. 'Wyatt had a deeper and more accurate penetration
into the characters of men than Surrey had; hence arises
the difference in their satires.   Surrey, in his satire against
the citizens of London, deals only in reproach; Wyatt, in
his, abounds with irony, and those nice touches of ridicule
which make us ashamed of our faults, and therefore often
silently effect amendment.[z]   Surrey's observation of nature
was minute; but he directed it towards the works of nature
in general, and the movements of the passions, rather than
to the foibles and characters of men: hence it is that he

---

[z] Wyatt's best poem in this style, the
Epistle to John Poins, is a very close
imitation of the tenth satire of Alamanni; it is abridged, but every thought
and every verse in the English is taken
from the Italian.   Dr. Nott has been
aware of this; but it certainly detracts a
leaf from the laurel of Wyatt, though he
has translated well.

The lighter poems of Wyatt are more
unequal than those of Surrey; but his
Ode to his Lute does not seem inferior
to any production of his noble compe-

titor. The sonnet in which he intimates
his secret passion for Anne Boleyn,
whom he describes under the allegory of
a doe, bearing on her collar—

Noli me tangere : I Cæsar's am,

is remarkable for more than the poetry,
though that is pleasing.   It may be
doubtful whether Anne were yet queen;
but in one of Wyatt's latest poems, he
seems to allude penitentially to his passion for her.

excels in the description of rural objects, and is always tender
and pathetic.   In Wyatt's Complaint we hear a strain of
manly grief which commands attention, and we listen to it
with respect for the sake of him that suffers.   Surrey's dis-
tress is painted in such natural terms, that we make it our
own, and recognise in his sorrows emotions which we are
conscious of having felt ourselves.

22. ' In point of taste and perception of propriety in composition, Surrey is more accurate and just than Wyatt; he
therefore seldom either offends with conceits, or wearies with
repetition, and when he imitates other poets, he is original
as well as pleasing.   In his numerous translations from Petrarch, he is seldom inferior to his master; and he seldom
improves upon him.   Wyatt is almost always below the
Italian, and frequently degrades a good thought by expressing
it so that it is hardly recognisable.   Had Wyatt attempted a
translation of Virgil, as Surrey did, he would have exposed
himself to unavoidable failure.' [a]

23. To remarks so delicate in taste and so founded in
knowledge, I should not venture to add much of my
own.   Something however may generally be admitted to modify the ardent panegyrics of an editor.   Those
who, after reading this brilliant passage, should turn for the
first time to the poems either of Wyatt or of Surrey, might
think the praise too unbounded, and, in some respects,
perhaps, not appropriate.   It seems to be now ascertained,
after sweeping away a host of foolish legends and tradition-
ary prejudices, that the Geraldine of Surrey, Lady Elizabeth
Fitzgerald, was a child of thirteen, for whom his passion,
if such it is to be called, began several years after his own
marriage.[b]   But in fact there is more of the conventional tone
of amorous song, than of real emotion, in Surrey's poetry.
The

> Easy sighs, such as men draw in love,

are not like the deep sorrows of Petrarch, or the fiery trans-
ports of the Castilians.

24. The taste of this accomplished man is more striking

Perhaps rather exaggerated.

---

[a] Nott's edition of Wyatt and Surrey,
ii. 156.
[b] Surrey was born about 1518, married Lady Frances Vere in 1535, fell in
love, if so it was, in 1541, with Geraldine, who was born in 1528.

than his poetical genius.   He did much for his own country
and his native language.   The versification of Surrey Surrey im-
differs very considerably from that of his predeces- versification.
sors.   He introduced, as Dr. Nott says, a sort of involution
into his style, which gives an air of dignity and remoteness
from common life.   It was, in fact, borrowed from the licence
of Italian poetry, which our own idiom has rejected.   He
avoids pedantic words, forcibly obtruded from the Latin, of
which our earlier poets, both English and Scots, had been
ridiculously fond.   The absurd epithets of Hoccleve, Lydgate,
Dunbar, and Douglas are applied equally to the most different
things, so as to show that they annexed no meaning to them.
Surrey rarely lays an unnatural stress on final syllables,
merely as such, which they would not receive in ordinary
pronunciation; another usual trick of the school of Chaucer.
His words are well chosen and well arranged.

25. Surrey is the first who introduced blank verse into our
English poetry.   It has been doubted whether it Introduces
had been previously employed in Italian, save in blank verse.
tragedy; for the poems of Alamanni and Rucellai were not
published before many of our noble poet's compositions had
been written.   Dr. Nott, however, admits that Boscan and
other Spanish poets had used it.   The translation by Surrey
of the second book of the Æneid, in blank verse, is among
the chief of his productions.   No one had, before his time,
known how to translate or imitate with appropriate expression.   But the structure of his verse is not very harmonious,
and the sense is rarely carried beyond the line.

26. If we could rely on a theory, advanced and ably supported by his editor, Surrey deserves the still more Dr. Nott's
conspicuous praise of having brought about a great hypothesis
as to his
revolution in our poetical numbers.   It had been metre.
supposed to be proved by Tyrwhitt, that Chaucer's lines are
to be read metrically, in ten or eleven syllables, like the
Italian, and, as I apprehend, the French of his time.   For
this purpose, it is necessary to presume that many terminations, now mute, were syllabically pronounced; and where
verses prove refractory after all our endeavours, Tyrwhitt has
no scruple in declaring them corrupt.   It may be added, that
Gray, before the appearance of Tyrwhitt's essay on the ver-

sification of Chaucer, had adopted without hesitation the
same hypothesis.[c]   But, according to Dr. Nott, the verses of
Chaucer, and of all his successors down to Surrey, are merely
rhythmical, to be read by cadence, and admitting of considerable variety in the number of syllables, though ten may
be the more frequent.   In the manuscripts of Chaucer, the
line is always broken by a cæsura in the middle, which is
pointed out by a virgule; and this is preserved in the early
editions down to that of 1532.   They come near, therefore,
to the short Saxon line, differing chiefly by the alternate
rhyme, which converts two verses into one.   He maintains
that a great many lines of Chaucer cannot be read metrically,
though harmonious as verses of cadence.   This rhythmical
measure he proceeds to show in Hoccleve, Lydgate, Hawes,
Barclay, Skelton, and even Wyatt; and thus concludes that
it was first abandoned by Surrey, in whom it very rarely
occurs.[d]

27. This hypothesis, it should be observed, derives some
additional plausibility from a passage in Gascoyne's ' Notes
of instruction concerning the making of verse or rhyme in
English,' printed in 1575.   ' Whosoever do peruse and well
consider his (Chaucer's) works, he shall find that, although
his lines are not always of one self-same number of syllables,
yet being read by one that hath understanding, the longest
verse, and that which hath most syllables in it, will fall (to
the ear) correspondent unto that which hath fewest syllables ;
and likewise that which hath fewest syllables shall be found
yet to consist of words that have such natural sound, as may
seem equal in length to a verse which hath many more syllables of lighter accents.'

28. A theory so ingeniously maintained, and with so much
But seems induction of examples, has naturally gained a good
too exten-
sive. deal of credit.   I cannot, however, by any means
concur in the extension given to it.   Pages may be read in
Chaucer, and still more in Dunbar, where every line is regularly and harmoniously decasyllabic ; and though the cæsura
may perhaps fall rather more uniformly than it does in
modern verse, it would be very easy to find exceptions, which

---

[c] Gray's Works (edit. Mathias), ii. 1.
[d] Nott's Dissertation, subjoined to the second volume of his Wyatt and Surrey.

could not acquire a rhythmical cadence by any artifice of the reader.[g]   The deviations from the normal type, or deca-syllable line, were they more numerous than, after allowance for the licence of pronunciation, as well as the probable corruption of the text, they appear to be, would not, I conceive, justify us in concluding that it was disregarded.   For these aberrant lines are much more common in the dramatic blank verse of the seventeenth century.   They are, doubtless, vestiges of the old rhythmical forms ; and we may readily allow that English versification had not, in the fifteenth or even sixteenth centuries, the numerical regularity of classical or Italian metre.   In the ancient ballads, Scots and English, the substitution of the anapæst for the iambic foot is of perpetual recurrence, and gives them a remarkable elasticity and animation ; but we never fail to recognise a uniformity of measure, which the use of nearly equipollent feet cannot, on the strictest metrical principles, be thought to impair.

29. If we compare the poetry of Wyatt and Surrey with that of Barclay or Skelton, about thirty or forty years before, the difference must appear wonderful. Politeness of Wyatt and Surrey. But we should not, with Dr. Nott, attribute this wholly to superiority of genius.   It is to be remembered that the later poets wrote in a court, and in one which, besides the aristocratic manners of chivalry, had not only inbibed a great deal of refinement from France and Italy, but a considerable tinge of ancient literature.   Their predecessors were less educated men, and they addressed a more vulgar class of readers.   Nor was this polish of language peculiar to Surrey and his friend.   In the short poems of Lord Vaux, and of others about the same time, even in those of Nicholas Grimoald, a lecturer at Oxford, who was no courtier, but had

---

* Such as these among multitudes more :—

A lover, and a lusty bachelor.
Chaucer.

But reason, with the shield of gold so shene.
Dunbar.

The rock, again the river resplendent.—Id.

Lydgate apologises for his own lines,—

Because I know the verse therein is wrong,
As being some too short, and some too long,—

in Gray, ii. 4.   This seems at once to exclude the rhythmical system, and to account for the imperfection of the metrical.   Lydgate has, perhaps, on the whole, more aberrations from the deca-syllable standard than Chaucer.

Puttenham, in his Art of Poesie (1586), book ii. ch. 3, 4, though he admits the licentiousness of Chaucer, Lydgate, and other poets, in occasionally disregarding the cæsura, does not seem to doubt that they wrote by metrical rules ; which indeed is implied in this censure.   Dr. Nott's theory does not admit a disregard of cæsura.

acquired a classical taste, we find a rejection of obsolete and trivial phrases, and the beginnings of what we now call the style of our older poetry.

30. No period since the revival of letters has been so conspicuous for Latin poetry as the present. Three names of great reputation adorn it, Sannazarius, Vida, Fracastorius. The first of these, Sannazarius, or San Nazaro, or Actius Sincerus, was a Neapolitan, attached to the fortunes of the Aragonese line of kings; and following the last of their number, Frederic, after his unjust spoliation, into France, remained there till his master's death. Much of his poetry was written under this reign, before 1503; but his principal work, De Partu Virginis, did not appear till 1522. This has incurred not unfair blame for the intermixture of classical mythology, at least in language, with the Gospel story; nor is the latter very skilfully managed. But it would be difficult to find its equal for purity, elegance, and harmony of versification. The unauthorised word, the doubtful idiom, the modern turn of thought, so common in Latin verse, scarce ever appear in Sannazarius; a pure taste enabled him to diffuse a Virgilian hue over his language; and a just ear united with facility in command of words, rendered his versification melodious and varied beyond any competitor. The Piscatory Eclogues of Sannazarius, which are perhaps better known, deserve at least equal praise; they seem to breathe the beauty and sweetness of that fair bay they describe. His elegies are such as may contend with Tibullus. If Sannazarius does not affect sublimity, he never sinks below his aim; the sense is sometimes inferior to the style, as he is not wholly free from conceits; [f] but it would perhaps be more difficult to find cold and posaic passages in his works than in those of any other Latin poet in modern times.

Latin poetry,

Sannazarius.

31. Vida of Cremona is not by any means less celebrated than Sannazarius; his poem on the Art of Poetry, and that on the Game of Chess, were printed in 1527; the Christiad, an epic poem, as perhaps it deserves to

Vida.

---

[f] The following lines, on the constellation Taurus, are more puerile than any I have seen in this elegant poet:—

Torva bovi facies; sed qua non altera cœlo
Dignior, imbriferum quæ cornibus inchoet
    annum,
Nec *quæ tam claris mugitibus astra lacessat.*

be called, in 1535; and that on Silk Worms in 1537. Vida's precepts are clear and judicious, and we admire in his Game of Chess especially, and the poem on Silk Worms, the skill with which the dry rules of art, and descriptions the most appa-rently irreducible to poetical conditions, fall into his elegant and classical language. It has been observed, that he is the first who laid down rules for imitative harmony, illustrating them by his own example. The Christiad shows not so much, I think, of Vida's great talents, at least in poetical language; but the subject is better managed than by Sanna-zarius. Yet notwithstanding some brilliant passages, among which the conclusion of the second book De Arte Poetica is prominent, Vida appears to me far inferior to the Neapolitan poet. His versification is often hard and spondaic, the elisions too frequent, and the cæsura too much neglected. The language, even where the subject best admits of it, is not always so elevated as we should desire.

32. Fracastorius has obtained his reputation by the Syphilis, published in 1530; and certainly, as he thought fit to make choice of the subject, there is *Fracastorius.* no reader but must admire the beauty and variety of his digressions, the vigour and nobleness of his style. Once only has it been the praise of genius to have delivered the rules of practical art in all the graces of the most delicious poetry, without inflation, without obscurity, without affectation, and generally perhaps with the precision of truth. Fracastorius, not emulous in this of the author of the Georgics, seems to have made Manilius, rather, I think, than Lucretius, his model in the didactic portion of his poem.

33. Upon a fair comparison we should not err much, in my opinion, by deciding that Fracastorius is the greater *Latin verse* poet, and Sannazarius the better author of Latin *not to be disdained.* verses. In the present age it is easy to anticipate the super-cilious disdain of those who believe it ridiculous to write Latin poetry at all, because it cannot, as they imagine, be written well. I must be content to answer, that those who do not know when such poetry is good, should be as slow to contra-dict those who do, as the ignorant in music to set themselves against competent judges. No one pretends that Sannazarius was equal to Ariosto. But it may be truly said, that his

poetry, and a great deal more that has been written in Latin, beyond comparison excels most of the contemporary Italian; we may add, that its reputation has been more extended and European.

34. After this famous triumvirate, we might reckon several Other Latin in different degrees of merit. Bembo comes forward poets in Italy. again in these lists.   His Latin poems are not numerous; that upon the lake Benacus is the best known. He shone more, however, in elegiac than hexameter verse. This is a common case in modern Latin, and might be naturally expected of Bembo, who had more of elegance than of vigour.   Castiglione has left a few poems, among which the best is in the archaic lapidary style, on the statue of Cleopatra in the Vatican.   Molza wrote much in Latin; he is the author of the epistle to Henry VIII., in the name of Catherine, which has been ascribed to Joannes Secundus. It is very spirited and Ovidian.   These poets were, perhaps, surpassed by Naugerius and Flaminius; both, but especially the latter, for sweetness and purity of style, to be placed in the first rank of lyric and elegiac poets in the Latin language. In their best passages, they fall not by any means short of Tibullus or Catullus.   Aonius Palearius, though his poem on the Immortality of the Soul is equalled by Sadolet himself to those of Vida and Sannazarius, seems not entitled to anything like such an eulogy.   He became afterwards suspected of Lutheranism, and lost his life on the scaffold at Rome. We have in another place mentioned the Zodiacus Vitæ of Palingenius Stellatus, whose true name was Manzolli.   The Deliciæ Poetarum Italorum present a crowd of inferior imitations of classical models; but I must repeat that the volumes published by Pope, and entitled Poemata Italorum, are the best evidences of the beauties of these poets.

35. The Cisalpine nations, though at a vast distance from In Germany. Italy, cannot be reckoned destitute, in this age, of respectable Latin poets.   Of these the best known, and perhaps upon the whole the best, is Joannes Secundus, who found the doves of Venus in the dab-chicks of Dutch marshes.   The Basia, however, are far from being superior to his elegies, many of which, though not correct, and often sinning by false quantity, a fault pretty general with these

early Latin poets, especially on this side of the Alps, are
generally harmonious, spirited, and elegant. Among the Germans, Eobanus Hessus, Micyllus, professor at Heidelberg, and
Melanchthon, have obtained considerable praise.

Sect. II.   1520—1550.

State of Dramatic Representation in Italy—Spain and Portugal—France—
Germany—England.

36. WE have already seen the beginnings of the Italian
comedy, founded in its style, and frequently in its $_{\text{Italian}}$
subjects, upon Plautus.   Two of Ariosto's comedies $^{\text{comedy.}}$
have been mentioned, and two more belong to this period.
Some difference of opinion has existed with respect to their
dramatic merit.   But few have hesitated to place above
them the Mandragola and Clitia of a great contemporary
genius, Machiavel.   The Mandragola was pro- $_{\text{Machiavel.}}$
bably written before 1520, but certainly in the
fallen fortunes of its author, as he intimates in the prologue.
Ginguéné, therefore, forgot his chronology, when he supposes Leo X. to have been present, as cardinal, at its representation.[g]   It seems, however, to have been acted before
this pope at Rome.   The story of the Mandragola, which
hardly bears to be told, though Ginguéné has done it, is said
to be founded on a real and recent event at Florence, one
of its striking resemblances to the Athenian comedy.   It
is admirable for its comic delineations of character, the
management of the plot, and the liveliness of its
idiomatic dialogue.   Peter Aretin, with little of $^{\text{Aretin.}}$
the former qualities, and inferior in all respects to Machiavel,
has enough of humorous extravagance to amuse the reader.
The licentiousness of the Italian stage in its contempt of
morality, and even, in the comedies of Peter Aretin, its
bold satire on the great, remind us rather of Athens than
of Rome; it is more the effrontery of Aristophanes than the
pleasant freedom of Plautus.   But the depravity which

---

[g] Ginguéné, vi. 222.

had long been increasing in Italy gained in this first part of the sixteenth century a zenith which it could not surpass, and from which it has very gradually receded. These comedies are often very satirical on the clergy ; the bold strokes of Machiavel surprise us at present ; but the Italian stage had something like the licence of a masquerade ; it was a tacit agreement that men should laugh at things sacred within those walls, but resume their veneration for them at the door.[h]

37. Those who attempted the serious tone of tragedy were less happy in their model; Seneca generally represented to them the ancient buskin. The Canace of Sperone Speroni, the Tullia of Martelli, and the Orbecche of Giraldi Cinthio, esteemed the best of nine tragedies he has written, are within the present period. They are all works of genius. But Ginguéné observes how little advantage the first of these plays afforded for dramatic effect, most of the action passing in narration. It is true that he could hardly have avoided this without aggravating the censures of those who, as Crescimbeni tells us, thought the subject itself unfit for tragedy.[i] The story of the Orbecche is taken by Cinthio from a novel of his own invention, and is remarkable for its sanguinary and disgusting circumstances. This became the characteristic of tragedy in the sixteenth century; not by any means peculiarly in England, as some half-informed critics of the French school used to pretend. The Orbecche, notwithstanding its passages in the manner of Titus Andronicus, is in many parts an impassioned and poetical tragedy. Riccoboni, though he censures the general poverty of style, prefers one scene in the third act to anything on the stage : ' If one scene were sufficient to decide the question, the Orbecche would be the finest play in the world '[k] Walker observes that this is the first tragedy wherein the prologue is separated from the play, of which, as is very well known,

Tragedy.

Sperone.
Cinthio.

---

[h] Besides the plays themselves, see Ginguéné, vol. vi., who gives more than a hundred pages to the Calandra, and to the comedies of Ariosto, Machiavel, and Aretin. Many of the old comedies are reprinted in the great Milan collection of Classici Italiani. Those of Machiavel and Ariosto are found in most editions of their works.

[i] Della volgar Poesia, ii. 391. Alfieri went still farther than Sperone in his Mirra. Objections of a somewhat similar kind were made to the Tullia of Martelli.

[k] Hist. du Théâtre italien, vol. i.

it made a part on the ancient theatre. But in Cinthio, and in other tragic writers long afterwards, the prologue continued to explain and announce the story.[m]

38. Meantime, a people very celebrated in dramatic literature was forming its national theatre. A few attempts were made in Spain to copy the classical model. But these seem not to have gone beyond translation, and had little effect on the public taste. Others in imitation of the Celestina, which passed for a moral example, produced tedious scenes, by way of mirrors of vice and virtue, without reaching the fame of their original. But a third class was far more popular, and ultimately put an end to competition. The founders of this were Torres Naharro, in the first years of Charles, and Lope de Rueda, a little later. 'There is very little doubt,' says Bouterwek, 'that Torres Naharro was the real inventor of the Spanish comedy. He not only wrote his eight comedies in redondillas in the romance style, but he also endeavoured to establish the dramatic interest solely on an ingenious combination of intrigues, without attaching much importance to the development of character, or the moral tendency of the story. It is besides probable, that he was the first who divided plays into three acts, which, being regarded as three days' labour in the dramatic field, were called jornadas. It must therefore be unreservedly admitted that these dramas, considered both with respect to their spirit and their form, deserve to be ranked as the first in the history of the Spanish national drama; for in the same path which Torres Naharro first trod the dramatic genius of Spain advanced to the point attained by Calderon, and the nation tolerated no dramas except those which belonged to the style which had thus been created.'[o]

Spanish drama.

Torres Naharro.

39. Lope de Rueda, who is rather better known than his predecessor, was at the head of a company of players, and was limited in his inventions by the capacity of his troop and of the stage upon which they were to appear. Cervantes calls him the great Lope de Rueda,

Lope de Rueda.

[m] Walker, Essay on Italian Tragedy. Ginguéné, vi. 61, 69.
[o] p. 285. Andrès thinks Naharro low, insipid, and unworthy of the praise of Cervantes, v. 136.

even when a greater Lope was before the world. ‘He was
not,’ to quote again from Bouterwek, ‘inattentive to general
character, as is proved by his delineation of old men, clowns,
&c., in which he was particularly successful. But his principal aim was to interweave in his dramas a succession of
intrigues; and as he seems to have been a stranger to the
art of producing stage effect by striking situations, he made
complication the great object of his plots. Thus mistakes,
arising from personal resemblances, exchanges of children,
and such-like common-place subjects of intrigue, form the
ground-work of his stories, none of which are remarkable
for ingenuity of invention. There is usually a multitude of
characters in his dramas, and jests and witticisms are freely
introduced, but these in general consist of burlesque disputes
in which some clown is engaged.’ P

40. The Portuguese Gil Vicente may perhaps contend with
Torres Naharro for the honour of leading the dra-
matists of the Peninsula. His Autos indeed, as
has been observed, do not, so far as we can perceive, differ
from the Mysteries, the religious dramas of France and
England. Bouterwek, strangely forgetful of these, seems to
have assigned a character of originality, and given a precedence, to the Spanish and Portuguese Autos which they
do not deserve. The specimen of one of these by Gil
Vicente, given in the history of Portuguese Literature, is
far more extravagant and less theatrical than our John
Parfre’s contemporary mystery of Candlemas Day. But a
few comedies, or, as they are more justly styled, farces, remain; one of which, mentioned by the same author, is
superior in choice and management of the fable to most of
the rude productions of that time. Its date is unknown:
Gil Vicente’s dramatic compositions of various kinds were
collectively published in 1562; he had died in 1557, at a
very advanced age.

41. ‘These works,’ says Bouterwek of the dramatic productions of Gil Vicente in general, ‘display a true poetic
spirit, which however accommodated itself entirely to the
age of the poet, and which disdained cultivation. The dramatic genius of Gil Vicente is equally manirest from his

_____

P p. 282.

power of invention, and from the natural turn and facility
of his imitative talent.   Even the rudest of these dramas is
tinged with a certain degree of poetic feeling.'[q]   The want
of complex intrigue, such as we find afterwards in the Castilian drama, ought not to surprise us in these early compositions.

42. We have no record of any original dramatic composition belonging to this age in France, with the ex- Mysteries
ception of mysteries and moralities, which are very and morali-
abundant.   These were considered, and perhaps France.
justly, as types of the regular drama.   ' The French morality,'
says an author of that age, ' represents, in some degree, the
tragedy of the Greeks and Romans ; particularly because it
treats of serious and important subjects ; and if it were contrived in French that the conclusion of the morality should
be always unfortunate, it would become a tragedy.   In the
morality we treat of noble and virtuous actions, either true,
or at least probable ; and choose what makes for our instruction in life.'[r]   It is evident from this passage and the whole
context, that neither tragedy nor comedy were yet known.
The circumstance is rather remarkable, when we consider the
genius of the nation, and the politeness of the court.   But
from about the year 1540 we find translations from Latin and
Italian comedies into French.   These probably were not represented.   Les Amours d'Érostrate, by Jacques Bourgeois,
published in 1545, is taken from the Suppositi of Ariosto.
Sibilet translated the Iphigenia of Euripides in 1549, Bou-
chetel the Hecuba in 1550, and Lazarus Baif two other plays
about the same time.   But a great dramatic revolution was
now prepared by the strong arm of the state.   The first
theatre had been established at Paris about 1400 by the
Confrairie de la Passion de N. S., for the representation of
Scriptural mysteries.   This was suppressed by the parlia-

---

[q] Hist. of Portuguese Lit. p. 83–111.
It would be vain to look elsewhere for
so copious an account of Gil Vicente,
and very difficult probably to find his
works.   See, too, Sismondi, Hist. de la
Litt. du Midi, iv. 448.
    [A much fuller account of Gil Vi-
cente has since been given in the Qua-
terly Review for January 1847.]
    [r] Sibilet, Art poétique (1548), apud

Beauchamps, Recherches sur le Théâtre
français, i. 82.
    In the Jardin de Plaisance, an anony-
mous undated poem, printed at Lyons
probably before the end of the fifteenth
century, we have rules given for composing moralities.   Beauchamps (p. 86)
extracts some of these ; but they seem
not worth copying.

ment in 1547, on account of the scandal which this devout
buffoonery had begun to give. The company of actors purchased next year the Hôtel de la Bourgogne, and were
authorised by the parliament to represent profane subjects,
'lawful and decent' (licites et honnêtes), but enjoined to
abstain from 'all mysteries of the passion or other sacred
mysteries.' [s]

43. In Germany, meantime, the pride of the meister-singers,
German the-
atre. Hans
Sachs. Hans Sachs, was alone sufficient to pour forth a plen-
teous stream for the stage. His works, collectively
printed at Nuremberg in five folio volumes, 1578, and reprinted in five quartos at Kempten, 1606, contain 197 dramas
among the rest. Many of his comedies in one act, called
Schwanken, are coarse satires on the times. Invention,
expression, and enthusiasm, if we may trust his admirers, are
all united in Hans Sachs. [t]

44. The mysteries founded upon Scriptural or legendary
Moralities
and similar
plays in Eng-
land. histories, as well as the moralities, or allegorical
dramas, which, though there might be an intermix-
ture of human character with abstract personification,
did not aim at that illusion which a possible fable affords,
continued to amuse the English public. Nor were they confined, as perhaps they were before, to churches and monasteries. We find a company of players in the establishment
of Richard III. while Duke of Gloucester; and in the
subsequent reigns, especially under Henry VIII., this seems
to have been one of the luxuries of the great. The frugal
Henry VII. maintained two distinct sets of players; and his
son was prodigally sumptuous in every sort of court exhibition, bearing the general name of revels, and superintended
by a high priest of jollity, styled the Abbot of Misrule. The
dramatic allegories, or moral plays, found a place among
them. It may be presumed that from their occasionality, or
want of merit, far the greater part have perished. [u] Three

---

[s] Beauchamps, i. 91.
[t] Hans Sachs has met with a very
laudatory critic in the Retrospective Review, x. 113, who even ventures to assert that Goethe has imitated the old
shoemaker in Faust.
The Germans had many plays in this
age. Gesner says, in his Pandectæ Uni-

versales: Germanicæ fabulæ multæ extant. Fabula decem ætatum et Fusio
stultorum Colmariæ actæ sunt. Fusio
edita est 1537, chartis quatuor. Qui
volet hoc loco plures ascribat in vulga-
ribus linguis, nos ad alia festinamus.

[u] Collier's Annals of the Stage, i. 34,
&c.

or four, which we may place before 1550, are published in
Hawkins's Ancient Drama and Dodsley's Old Plays; one is
extant, written by Skelton, the earliest that can be referred
to a known author.[x] A late writer, whose diligence seems to
have almost exhausted our early dramatic history, has retrieved the titles of a few more. The most ancient of these
moral plays he traces to the reign of Henry VI. They became
gradually more complicated, and approached nearer to a
regular form. It may be observed that a line is not easily
defined between the Scriptural mysteries and the legitimate
drama; the choice of the story, the succession of incidents,
are those of tragedy; even the intermixture of buffoonery
belongs to all our ancient stage; and it is only by the mean-
ness of the sentiments and diction that we exclude the Candlemas Day, which is one of the most perfect of the mysteries,
or even those of the fifteenth century, from our tragic series.[y]
Nor were the moralities, such as we find them in the reign
of Henry VIII., at a prodigious distance from the regular
stage: deviations from the original structure of these, as Mr.
Collier has well observed, ' by the relinquishment of abstract
for individual character, paved the way, by a natural and
easy gradation, for tragedy and comedy, the representations
of real life and manners.'[z]

45. The moralities were, in this age, distinguished by the
constant introduction of a witty, mischievous, and They are
turned to re-
profligate character, denominated the Vice. This ligious satire.
seems originally to have been an allegorical representation of
what the word denotes; but the Vice gradually acquired a
human individuality, in which he came very near to our
well-known Punch. The devil was generally introduced in
company with the Vice, and had to endure many blows
from him. But the moralities had another striking characteristic in this period. They had always been religious, but
they now became theological. In the crisis of that great
revolution then in progress, the stage was found a ready and

---

[x] Warton, iii. 188.
[y] Candlemas Day, a mystery, on the
murder of the Innocents, is published in
Hawkins's Early English Drama. It is
by John Parfre, and may be referred to
the first years of Henry VIII.

[z] Hist. of English Dramatic Poetry,
ii. 260. This I quote by its proper title;
but it is in fact the same work as the
Annals of the Stage, so far as being incorporated, and sold together, renders it
the same.

impartial instrument for the old or the new faith. Luther
and his wife were satirised in a Latin morality represented
at Gray's Inn, in 1529. It was easy to turn the tables on the
clergy. Sir David Lyndsay's satire of the Three Estatis, a
direct attack upon them, was played before James V. and his
queen at Linlithgow, in 1539 ;[a] and in 1543 an English statute was made, prohibiting all plays and interludes which
meddle with the interpretation of Scripture. In 1549 the
council of Edward VI. put a stop by proclamation to all kinds
of stage-plays.[b]

46. Great indulgence, or a strong antiquarian prejudice is
Latin play. required to discover much genius in these moralities
and mysteries. There was, however, a class of dramatic productions that appealed to a more instructed audience.
The custom of acting Latin plays prevailed in our universities
at this time, as it did long afterwards. Whether it were
older than the fifteenth century seems not to be proved ; and
the presumption is certainly against it. 'In an original
draught,' says Wharton, ' of the statutes of Trinity College at
Cambridge, founded in 1546, one of the chapters is entitled,
' De Præfecto ludorum qui imperator dicitur,' under whose
direction and authority Latin comedies and tragedies are to
be exhibited in the hall at Christmas.'[c] It is probable that
Christopherson's tragedy of Jephthah, and another by Grimoald on John the Baptist, both older than the middle of the
century, were written for academical representation. - Nor
was this confined to the universities. Nicolas Udal, head
master of Eton, wrote several plays in Latin to be acted in
the long nights of winter by his boys.[d] And if we had to
stop here, it might seem an unnecessary minuteness to take
notice of the diversions of school-boys, especially as the same

---

[a] Warton, iv. 23.
[b] Collier, i. 144.
[c] Hist. of Engl. Poetry, iii. 205.
[d] Udal was not the first, if we could
trust Harwood's Alumni Etonenses, who
established an Eton theatre. Of Rightwise, who succeeded Lily as master of
St. Paul's, it is said by him, that he was
' a most eminent grammarian, and wrote
the tragedy of Dido from Virgil, which
was acted before Cardinal Wolsey with
great applause by himself and other scho-

lars of Eton.' But as Rightwise left
Eton for King's College in 1508, this
cannot be true, at least so far as Wolsey
is concerned. It is said afterwards in the
same book of one Hallewell, who went to
Cambridge in 1532, that he wrote 'the
tragedy of Dido.' Which should we believe, or were there two Didos ? But
Harwood's book is not reckoned of much
authority beyond the mere records
which he copied.

is recorded of other teachers besides Udal. But there is
something more in this. Udal has lately become First English
known in a new and more brilliant light, as the comedy.
father of English comedy. It was mentioned by Warton, but
without any comment, that Nicolas Udal wrote some English
plays to be represented by his scholars ; a passage from one
of which is quoted by Wilson in his Art of Logic, dedicated
to Edward VI.[e] It might have been conjectured, by the help
of this quotation, that these plays were neither of the class
of moralities or mysteries, nor mere translations from Plautus
and Terence, as it would not have been unnatural at first to
suppose. Within a few years, however, the comedy from
which Wilson took his extract has been discovered. It was
printed in 1565, but probably written not later than 1540.
The title of this comedy is Ralph Roister Doister, a name
uncouth enough, and from which we should expect a very
barbarous farce. But Udal, an eminent scholar, knew how
to preserve comic spirit and humour without degenerating
into licentious buffoonery. Ralph Roister Doister, in spite
of its title. is a play of some merit, though the wit may seem
designed for the purpose of natural merriment rather than
critical glory. We find in it, what is of no slight value, the
earliest lively picture of London manners among the gallants
and citizens, who furnished so much for the stage down to
the civil wars. And perhaps there is no striking difference in
this respect between the dramatic manners under Henry VIII.
and James I. This comedy, for there seems no kind of reason why it should be refused that honourable name, is much
superior to Gammar Gurton's Needle, written twenty years
afterwards, from which it has wrested a long established precedence in our dramatic annals.[f]

---

[e] Hist. of Engl. Poetry, iii. 213.

[f] See an analysis with extracts of
Ralph Roister Doister, in Collier's Hist.
of Dram. Poetry, ii. 445–460.

['The plot,' Mr. C. observes, ' of
Ralph Roister Doister is amusing and
well conducted, with an agreeable intermixture of serious and comic dialogue,
and a variety of character to which no
other piece of a similar date can make
any pretension. When we recollect that
it was perhaps written in the reign of

Henry VIII., we ought to look upon it
as a masterly production. Had it followed Gammar Gurton's Needle by as
many years as it preceded it, it would
have been entitled to our admiration on
its own separate merits, independent of
any comparison with other pieces. The
character of Matthew Merrygreeke here
and there savours a little of the vice of
the moralities ; but his humour never
depends upon the accidents of dress and
accoutrements.'—1842.]

Romances and Novels—Rabelais.

47. The popularity of Amadis de Gaul gave rise to a class
Romances of   of romances, the delight of the multitude in the
chivalry.   sixteenth century, though since chiefly remembered
by the ridicule and ignominy that has attached itself to their
name—those of knight errantry.   Most of these belong to
Spanish or Portuguese literature.   Palmerin of Oliva, one of
the earliest, was published in 1525.   Palmerin, less fortunate
than his namesake of England, did not escape the penal flame
to which the barber and curate consigned many also of his
younger brethren.   It has been observed by Bouterwek, that
every respectable Spanish writer, as well as Cervantes, resisted the contagion of bad taste which kept the prolix mediocrity of these romances in fashion.[g]

48. A far better style was that of the short novel, which
the Italian writers, especially Boccaccio, had ren-
Novels.   dered popular in Europe.   But, though many of
these were probably written within this period of thirty years,
none of much distinction come within it, as the date of
their earliest publication, except the celebrated Belphegor of
Machiavel.[h]   The amusing story of Lazarillo de Tormes was
certainly written by Mendoza in his youth.   But it did not
appear in print within our present period.[i]   This is the first

---

[g] Hist. of Spanish Literature, p. 304.
Dunlop's Hist. of Fiction, vol. ii.
  [h] I cannot make another exception
for Il Pellegrino by Caviceo of Parma,
the first known edition of which, published at Venice in 1526, evidently
alludes to one earlier: diligentemente
in lingua tosca corretto, e novamente
stampato et historiato.   The editor
speaks of the book as obsolete in orthography and style.   It is probably, however, not older than the last years of
the fifteenth century, being dedicated
to Lucrezia Borgia.   It is a very prolix
and tedious romance, in three books
and two hundred and nineteen chapters,
written in a semi-poetical, diffuse style,
and much in the usual manner of love

stories.   Ginguéné and Tiraboschi do
not mention it ; the Biographie universelle does.
  Mr. Dunlop has given a short account
of a French novel, entitled, Les Aven-
tures de Lycidas et de Cléorithe, which
he considers as the earliest and best
specimen of what he calls the spiritual
romance, unmixed with chivalry or
allegory.   Hist. of Fiction, iii. 51.   It
was written in 1529, by Basire, archdeacon of Sens.   I should suspect that
there had been some of this class already
in Germany ; they certainly became
common in that country afterwards.
  [i] [Nicolas Antonio tells us, that the
first edition of Lazarillo de Tormes was
in 1586.   But Brunet mentions one

known specimen in Spain of the picaresque, or rogue style, in which the adventures of the low and rather dishonest part of the community are made to furnish amusement for the great. The Italian novelists are by no means without earlier instances; but it became the favourite, and almost peculiar class of novel with the Spanish writers about the end of the century.

49. But the most celebrated, and certainly the most brilliant performance in the path of fiction, that belongs to this age, is that of Rabelais. Few books are less _{Rabelais.} likely to obtain the praise of a rigorous critic; but few have more the stamp of originality, or show a more redundant fertility, always of language, and sometimes of imagination. He bears a slight resemblance to Lucian, and a considerable one to Aristophanes. His reading is large, but always rendered subservient to ridicule; he is never serious in a single page, and seems to have had little other aim, in his first two volumes, than to pour out the exuberance of his animal gaiety. In the latter part of Pantagruel's history, that is, the fourth and fifth books, one published in 1552, the other, after the author's death, in 1561, a dislike to the church of Rome, which had been slightly perceived in the first volumes, is not at all disguised; but the vein of merriment becomes gradually less fertile, and weariness steals on before the close of a work which had long amused while it disgusted us. Allusions to particular characters are frequent, and, in general, transparent enough, with the aid of a little information about contemporaneous history, in several parts of Rabelais; but much of what has been taken for political and religious satire cannot, as far as I perceive, be satisfactorily traced beyond the capricious imagination of the author. Those who have found Montluc, the famous bishop of Valence, in Panurge, or Antony of Bourbon, father of Henry IV., in Pantagruel, keep no measures with chronology. Panurge is so admirably conceived, that we may fairly

---

printed at Burgos in 1554, and three at Antwery in 1553 and 1555. Supplément au Manuel du Libraire, art. Hurtado. The following early edition also is in the British Museum, of which I transcribe the titlepage :—La Vida de Lazarillo de Tormes y de sus fortunas y adversidades, nuevamente impressa, corregida, y de nuevo añadida en esta segunda impression. Vendense en Alcalá de Henares, en casa de Salzedo, librero, año de N. D. 1554. A colophon recites the same date and place of impression, —1842.]

reckon him original; but the germ of the character is in the gracioso, or clown, of the extemporaneous stage; the roguish, selfish, cowardly, cunning attendant, who became Panurge in the plastic hands of Rabelais, and Sancho in those of Cervantes. The French critics have not in general done justice to Rabelais, whose manner was not that of the age of Louis XIV. The Tale of a Tub appears to me by far the closest imitation of it, and to be conceived altogether in a kindred spirit; but in general those who have had reading enough to rival the copiousness of Rabelais have wanted his invention and humour, or the riotousness of his animal spirits.

Sect. IV.   1520—1550.

Struggle between Latin and Italian Languages—Italian and Spanish polite
Writers—Criticism in Italy—In France and England.

50. Among the polished writers of Italy, we meet on every side the name of Bembo; great in Italian as well as in Latin literature, in prose as in verse. It is now the fourth time that it occurs to us; and in no instance has he merited more of his country. Since the fourteenth century, to repeat what has been said before, so absorbing had become the love of ancient learning, that the natural language, beautiful and copious as it really was, and polished as it had been under the hands of Boccaccio, seemed to a very false-judging pedantry scarce worthy of the higher kinds of composition. Those, too, who with enthusiastic diligence had acquired the power of writing Latin well, did not brook so much as the equality of their native language. In an oration delivered at Bologna in 1529 before the emperor and pope, by Romolo Amaseo, one of the good writers of the sixteenth century. he not only pronounced a panegyric upon the Latin tongue, but contended that the Italian should be reserved for shops and markets, and the conversation of the vulgar;[k] nor was this doctrine, probably in rather a less degree, uncommon during that age. A dialogue of Sperone

Contest of Latin and Italian languages.

---

[k] Tiraboschi, x. 389.

relates to this debated question, whether the Latin or Italian
language should be preferred ; one of the interlocutors (probably Lazaro Buonamici, an eminent scholar) disdaining the
latter as a mere corruption.   It is a very ingenious performance, well conducted on both sides, and may be read with
pleasure.   The Italians of that age are as clever in criticism
as they are wearisome on the common-places of ethics.   It
purports to have been written the year after the oration of
Romolo Amaseo, to which it alludes.

51. It is an evidence of the more liberal spirit that generally accompanies the greatest abilities, that Bembo,   Influence of
superior even to Amaseo in fame as a Latin writer,   Bembo in this.
should have been among the first to retrieve the honour of
his native language by infusing into it that elegance and
selection of phrase which his taste had taught him in Latin,
and for which the Italian is scarcely less adapted.   In the
dialogue of Sperone quoted above, it is said that ' it was
the general opinion no one would write Italian who could
write Latin; a prejudice in some measure lightened by the
poem of Politian on the tournament of Julian de' Medici,
but not taken away till Bembo, a Venetian gentleman, as
learned in the ancient languages as Politian, showed that
he did not disdain his maternal tongue.' [m]

52. It is common in the present age to show as indiscri-
minating a disdain of those who wrote in Latin as   Apology for
they seem to have felt towards their own literature.   Latinists.
But the taste and imagination of Bembo are not given to
every one ; and we must remember, in justice to such men as
Amaseo, who, though they imitate well, are yet but imitators
in style, that there was really scarce a book in Italian prose
written with any elegance, except the Decamerone of Boccaccio ; the manner of which, as Tiraboschi justly observes,
however suitable to those sportive fictions, was not very well
adapted to serious eloquence.[n]   Nor has the Italian language,

---

[m] p. 430 (edit. 1596).
[n] x. 402.   [Bettinelli speaks not very
favourably of the style of the Decameron.   Certo è, che il costumare, il
dipingere, l' arte del dialogo, la grazia
de' motti, la verità e varietà di caratteri nel Decamerone fanno un' opera
molto eloquente.   Ma certo è non meno,

che affettata è la sua rotondità di pe-
riodo, faticosa la costruzione, dure e
spiacevoli le trasposizioni, etc.   L' altre
opere sue di fatto non sono autorevoli
fuorchè in Crusca.   Risorgimento d' Italia dopo il Millesimo, vol. i. p. 192.—
1842.]

we may add, in its very best models, attained so much energy
and condensation as will satisfy the ear or the understanding
of a good Latin scholar; and there can be neither pedantry
nor absurdity in saying, that it is an inferior organ of human
thought. The most valid objection to the employment of
Latin in public discourses or in moral treatises is its exclusion of those whose advantage we are supposed to seek, and
whose sympathy we ought to excite. But this objection,
though not much less powerful in reality than at present,
struck men less sensibly in that age, when long use of the
ancient language, in which even the sermons of the clergy
were frequently delivered, had taken away the sense of its
impropriety.[o]

53. This controversy points out some degree of change in
Character of public opinion, and the first stage of that struggle
the contro-
versy. against the aristocracy of erudition, which lasted
more or less for nearly two centuries, till, like other struggles
of still more importance, it ended in the victory of the many.
In the days of Poggio and Politian, the native Italian no
more claimed an equality, than the plebeians of Rome
demanded the consulship in the first years of the republic.
These are the revolutions of human opinion, bearing some
analogy and parallelism to those of civil society, which it is
the business of an historian of literature to indicate.

54. The life of Bembo was spent, after the loss of his
Life of great patron Leo X., in literary elegance at Padua.
Bembo. Here he formed an extensive library and collection
of medals; and here he enjoyed the society of the learned,
whom that university supplied, or who visited him from other
parts of Italy and Europe. Far below Sadolet in the solid
virtues of his character, and not probably his superior in
learning, he has certainly left a greater name, and contributed
more to the literary progress of his native country. He died

---

[o] Sadolet himself had rather discouraged Bembo from writing Italian, as
appears from one of his epistles, thanking his friend for the present of a book,
perhaps Le Prose. Sed tu fortasse con-
jicis ex eo, illa mihi non placere, quod
te avocare solebam ab illis literis. Fa-
ciebam ego id quidem, sed consilio, ut
videbar, bono. Cum enim in Latinis
major multo inesset dignitas, tuque in
ea facultate princeps mihi longe viderere,
non tam abstrahebam te illinc, quam huc
vocabam. Nec studium reprehendebam
in illis tuum, sed te majora quædam
spectare debere arbitrabar. Epist. lib.
ii. p. 55.

at an advanced age in 1547; having a few years before obtained a cardinal's hat on the recommendation of Sadolet.[p]

55. The style of some other Italian and Spanish writers, Castiglione, Sperone, Machiavel, Guevara, Oliva, has been already adverted to when the subject of their writings was before us; and it would be tedious to dwell upon them again in this point of view. The Italians have been accustomed to associate almost every kind of excellence with the word cinquecento. They extol the elegant style and fine taste of those writers. But Andrès has remarked, with no injustice, that if we find purity, correctness, and elegance of expression in the chief prose writers of this century, we cannot but also acknowledge an empty prolixity of periods, a harsh involution of words and clauses, a jejune and wearisome circuity of sentences, with a striking deficiency of thought. ' Let us admit the graces of mere language in the famous authors of this period; but we must own them to be far from models of eloquence, so tedious and languid as they are.'[q]   The Spanish writers of the same century, he says afterwards, nourished as well as the Italian with the milk of antiquity, transfused the spirit and vigour of these ancients into their own compositions, not with the servile imitation of the others, nor seeking to arrange their phrases and round their periods, the source of languor and emptiness, so that the best Spanish prose is more flowing and harmonious than the contemporary Italian.[r]

Character of Italian and Spanish style.

56. The French do not claim, I believe, to have produced at the middle of the sixteenth century any prose writer of a polished or vigorous style, Calvin excepted, the dedication of whose Institutes in French to Francis I. is a model of purity and elegance for the age.[s]   Sir Thomas More's Life of Edward V., written about 1509, appears to me the first example of good English language; pure and perspicuous, well-chosen, without vulgarisms or pedantary.[t]   His polemical tracts are inferior,

English writers.

More.

---

[p] Tiraboschi, ix. 296. Corniani, iv. 99. Sadolet. Epist. lib. xii. p. 555.
[q] Andrès, vii. 68.
[r] Id. 72.
[s] Neufchâteau, Essai sur les meilleurs ouvrages dans la langue française, p. 135.

[t] This has been reprinted entire in Holingshed's Chronicle ; and the reader may find a long extract in the preface to Todd's edition of Johnson's Dictionary. I should name the account of Jane Shore as a model of elegant narration.

but not ill-written. We have seen that Sir Thomas Elyot
had some vigour of style. Ascham, whose Toxophilus, or
Dialogue on Archery, came out in 1544, does not
Ascham.
excel him. But his works have been reprinted in
modern times, and are consequently better known than those
of Elyot. The early English writers are seldom select enough
in their phrases to bear such a critical judgment as the
academicians of Italy were wont to exercise.

57. Next to the models of style, we may place those writings which are designed to form them. In all sorts
Italian
criticism. of criticism, whether it confines itself to the idioms
of a single language, or rises to something like a general
principle of taste, the Italian writers had a decided priority
in order of time as well as of merit. We have already mentioned the earliest work, that of Fortunio, on Italian grammar. Liburnio, at Venice, in 1521, followed with his Volgari
Eleganzie. But this was speedily eclipsed by a work of
Bembo, published in 1525, with the rather singular title, Le
Prose. These observations on the native language, commenced more than twenty years before, are written in dialogue, supposed to originate in the great controversy of that
age, whether it were worthy of a man of letters to employ his
mother-tongue instead of Latin. Bembo well defended the
national cause; and by judicious criticism on the
Bembo.
language itself and the best writers in it, put an end
to the most specious argument under which the advocates of
Latin sheltered themselves,—that the Italian, being a mere
assemblage of independent dialects, varying not only in pronunciation and orthography, but in their words and idioms,
and having been written with unbounded irregularity and
constant adoption of vulgar phrases, could afford no certain
test of grammatical purity or graceful ornament. It was
thought necessary by Bembo to meet this objection by the
choice of a single dialect; and though a Venetian, he had no
hesitation to recognise the superiority of that spoken in
Florence. The Tuscan writers of that century proudly make
use of his testimony in aid of their pretensions to dictate
the laws of Italian idiom. Varchi says, 'The Italians cannot
be sufficiently thankful to Bembo, for having not only purified their language from the rust of past ages, but given it

such regularity and clearness, that it has become what we now see.' This early work, however, as might be expected, has not wholly escaped the censure of a school of subtle and fastidious critics, in whom Italy became fertile.[u]

58. Several other treatises on the Italian language appeared even before the middle of the century; though few comparatively with the more celebrated and elaborate labours of criticism in its latter portion. None seem to deserve mention, unless it be the Observations of Lodovico Dolce, (Venice, 1550,) which were much improved in subsequent editions. Of the higher kind of criticism, which endeavours to excite and guide our perceptions of literary excellence, we find few or no specimens, even in Italy, within this period, except so far as the dialogues of Bembo furnish instances.

59. France was not destitute of a few obscure treatises at this time, enough to lay the foundations of her critical literature. The complex rules of French metre were to be laid down; and the language was irregular in pronunciation, accent, and othography. These meaner, but necessary, elements of correctness occupied three or four writers, of whom Goujet has made brief mention: Sylvius,' or Du Bois, who seems to have been the earliest writer on grammar;[x] Stephen Dolet, better known by his unfortunate fate, than by his eassy on French punctuation;[y] and though Goujet does not name him, we may add an Englishman, Palsgrave, who published a French grammar in English as early as 1530.[z] An earlier production than any of these is the Art de plaine rhétorique, by Peter Fabry, 1521; in which, with the help of some knowledge of Cicero, he attempted, but with little correctness, and often in absurd expressions, to establish the principles of oratory. If his work is no better than Goujet represents it to be, its popularity must denote a low condition of literature in France.[a] The first who aspired to lay down any thing like laws of taste in poetry was Thomas Sibilet, whose Art poétique appeared in 1548. This is in two books; the former relating to the

Grammarians and Critics in France.

---

[u] Ginguéné, vii. 390. Corniani, iv. 111.

[x] [The Sylvius here mentioned was, as I have been informed, James Du Bois, the physician, brother of Francis, who is recorded, p. 278.—1842.]

[y] Goujet, Bibliothèque française, i. 42, 81.

[z] Biogr. univ.: Palsgrave.

[a] Goujet, i. 361.

metrical rules of French verse, the latter giving precepts, short and judicious, for different kinds of composition. It is not, however, a work of much importance.[b]

60. A more remarkable grammarian of this time was Louis Meigret, who endeavoured to reform orthography by adapting it to pronunciation. In a language where these had come to differ so prodigiously as they did in French, something of this kind would be silently effected by the printers; but the bold scheme of Meigret went beyond their ideas of reformation; and he complains that he could not prevail to have his words given to the public in the form he preferred. They were ultimately less rigid; and the new orthography appears in some grammatical treatises of Meigret, published about 1550. It was not, as we know, very successful; but he has credit given him for some improvements which have been retained in French printing. Meigret's French grammer, it has been said, is the first that contains any rational or proper principles of the language. It has been observed, I know not how correctly, that he was the first who denied the name of case to those modifications of sense in nouns which are not marked by inflexion; but the writer to whom I am indebted for this adds, what all will not alike admit, that this limited meaning of the word case, which the modern grammars generally adopt, is rather an arbitrary deviation from their predecessors.[c]

Orthography of Meigret.

61. It would have been strange, if we could exhibit a list of English writers on the subject of our language in the reign of Henry VIII., when it has, at all times, been the most neglected department of our literature. The English have ever been as indocile in acknowledging the rules of criticism, even those which determine the most ordinary questions of grammar, as the Italians and French have been voluntarily obedient. Nor had they as yet drunk deep enough of classical learning to discriminate, by any steady principle, the general beauties of composition. Yet among the scanty rivulets that the English press furnished, we find 'The Art or Craft of Rhetoryke,' dedicated by Leonard Cox to Hugh Faringdon, abbot of Reading. This book, which though now very scarce, was translated into Latin, and twice

Cox's Art of Rhetoric.

---

[b] Goujet, iii. 92.   [c] Biogr. univ. : Meigret ; a good article. Goujet, i. 83.

printed at Cracow, in the year 1526,[d] is the work of a schoolmaster and man of reputed learning. The English edition
has no date, but was probably published about 1524. Cox
says : ' I have partly translated out of a work of rhetoric
written in the Latin tongue, and partly compiled of my own,
and so made a little treatise in manner of an introduction
into this aforesaid science, and that in the English tongue,
remembering that every good thing, after the saying of the
philosopher, the more common the better it is.' His art of
rhetoric follows the usual distribution of the ancients, both
as to the kinds of oration and their parts; with examples,
chiefly from Roman history, to direct the choice of arguments.
It is hard to say how much may be considered as his own.
The book is in duodecimo, and contains but eighty-five pages ;
it would of course be unworthy of notice in a later period.

---

[d] Panzer

CHAPTER IX.

ON THE SCIENTIFIC AND MISCELLANEOUS LITERATURE OF
EUROPE, FROM 1520 TO 1550.

Sect. I.

On Mathematical and Physical Science.

1. The first translation of Euclid from the Greek text was
Geometrical made by Zamberti of Venice, and appeared in 1505.
treatises. It was republished at Basle in 1537. The Spherics
of Theodosius and the Conics of Apollonius were translated
by men, it is said, more conversant with Greek than with
geometry. A higher praise is due to Werner of Nuremberg,
the first who aspired to restore the geometrical analysis of
the ancients. The treatise of Regiomontanus on triangles
was first published in 1533. It may be presumed that its
more important contents were already known to geometers.
Montucla hints that the editor Schæner may have introduced
some algebraic solutions which appear in this work; but
there seems no reason to doubt, that Regiomontanus was
sufficiently acquainted with that science. The treatise of
Vitello on optics, which belongs to the thirteenth century,
was first printed in 1533.[a]

2. Oronce Finée, with some reputation in his own times,
has, according to Montucla, no pretension to the
Fernel. name of a geometer; and another Frenchman, Fernel,
better known as a physician, who published a Cosmotheoria
in 1527, though he first gave the length of a degree of the
meridian, and came not far from the truth, arrived at it by
so unscientific a method, being in fact no other than counting
the revolutions of a wheel along the main road, that he

---

[a] Montucla, Kästner.

cannot be reckoned much higher.[b]   These are obscure names in comparison with Joachim, surnamed Rhœticus from his native country.   After the publication of Rhœticus. the work of Regiomontanus on trigonometry, he conceived the project of carrying those labours still farther; and calculated the sines, tangents, and secants, the last of which he first reduced to tables, for every minute of the quadrant, to a radius of unity followed by fifteen ciphers; one of the most remarkable monuments, says Montucla, of human patience, or rather of a devotion to science, the more meritorious that it could not be attended with much glory.   But this work was not published till 1594, and then not so complete as Rhœticus had left it.[c]

3. Jerome Cardan is, as it were, the founder of the higher algebra: for, whatever he may have borrowed from others, we derive the science from his Ars Magna, Cardan and Tartaglia. published in 1545.   It contains many valuable discoveries; but that which has been most celebrated is the rule for the solution of cubic equations, generally known by Cardan's name, though he had obtained it from a Cubic equa- tions. man of equal genius in algebraic science, Nicolas Tartaglia. The original inventor appears to have been Scipio Ferreo, who, about 1505, by some unknown process, discovered the solution of a single case; that of $x^3 + p\, x = q$.   Ferreo imparted the secret to one Fiore, or Floridus, who challenged Tartaglia to a public trial of skill, not unusual in that age. Before he heard of this, Tartaglia, as he assures us himself, had found out the solution of two other forms of cubic equation; $x^3 + p\, x^2 = q$; and $x^3 - p\, x^2 = q$.   When the day of trial arrived, Tartaglia was able not only to solve the problems offered by Fiore, but to baffle him entirely by others which resulted in the forms of equation, the solution of which had been discovered by himself.   This was in 1535; and four years afterwards Cardan obtained the secret from Tartaglia under an oath of secresy.   In his Ars Magna, he did not

---

[b] Montucla, ii. 316. Kästner, ii. 329. [It has lately been shown by Professor de Morgan (Philosophical Magazine for December, 1841), that Montucla, Delambre, and others have made an egregious error about Fernel's measurement, which they have reduced to French toises, in direct opposition to what he has said himself. He estimates the degree of latitude at 68·096 Italian miles (equal to 63 or 64 English), and consequently falls very short of the truth.—1842.]

[c] Montucla, i. 582. Biogr. univ.: art. Joachim. Kästner, i. 561.

hesitate to violate this engagement; and, though he gave
Tartaglia the credit of the discovery, revealed the process to
the world.[d] He has said himself, that by the help of Ferrari,
a very good mathematician, he extended his rule to some
cases not comprehended in that of Tartaglia; but the best
historian of early algebra seems not to allow this claim.[e]

4. This writer, Cossali, has ingeniously attempted to trace
Beauty of the discovery. the process by which Tartaglia arrived at this discovery;[f] one which, when compared with the other
leading rules of algebra, where the invention, however useful,
has generally lain much nearer the surface, seems an astonishing effort of sagacity. Even Harriott's beautiful
generalisation of the composition of equations was prepared
by what Cardan and Vieta had done before, or might have
been suggested by observation in the less complex cases.[g]

---

[d] Playfair, in his second dissertation in the Encyclopædia Britannica, though he cannot but condemn Cardan, seems to think Tartaglia rightly treated for having concealed his discovery; and others have echoed this strain. Tartaglia himself says, in a passage I have read in Cossali, that he meant to have divulged it ultimately; but in that age money as well as credit was to be got by keeping the secret; and those who censure him wholly forget, that the solution of cubic equations was, in the actual state of algebra, perfectly devoid of any utility to the world.

[e] Cossali, Storia Critica d' Algebra (1797), ii. 96, &c. Hutton's Mathematical Dictionary. Montucla, i. 591. Kästner, i. 152.

[f] Ibid. p. 145. Tartaglia boasts of having discovered, by a geometrical construction, that the cube of $p+q=p^3+p^2 q+p q^2+q^3$. I give the modern formula, but literal algebra was unknown to him.

[g] Cardan strongly expresses his sense of this recondite discovery. And as the passage in which he retraces the early progress of algebra is short, and is quoted from Cardan's works, which are scarce in England, by Kästner, who is himself not very commonly known here, I shall transcribe the whole passage as a curiosity for our philomaths. Hæc ars olim a Mahomete Mosis Arabis filio initium sumpsit. Etenim hujus rei locuples testis Leonardus Pisanus. Reliquit autem

capitula quatuor, cum suis demonstrationibus quas nos locis suis ascribemus. Post multa vero temporum intervalla tria capitula derivativa addita illis sunt, incerto autore, quæ tamen cum principalibus a Luca Paciolo posita sunt. Demum etiam ex primis, alia tria derivativa, a quodam ignoto viro inventa legi, hæc tamen minimè in lucem prodierant, cum essent aliis longe utiliora, nam cubi et numeri et cubi quadrati æstimationem docebant. Verum temporibus nostris Scipio Ferreus Bononiensis, capitulum cubi et rerum numero æqualium [$x^3+p x=q$] invenit, rem sane pulchram et admirabilem: *cum omnem humanam subtilitatem, omnis ingenii mortalis claritatem ars hæc superet, donum profecto cœleste, experimentum autem virtutis animorum, atque adeo illustre, ut qui hæc attigerit nihil non intelligere posse se credat.* Hujus æmulatione Nicolaus Tartalea Brixellensis, amicus noster, cum in certamen cum illius discipulo Antonio Maria Florido venisset, capitulum idem ne vinceretur invenit, qui mihi ipsum multis precibus exoratus tradidit. Deceptus enim ego verbis Lucæ Pacioli, qui ultra sua capitula generale ullum aliud esse posse negat (quanquam tot jam antea rebus a me inventis sub manibus esset), desperabam tamen invenire quod quærere non audebam.[1] Inde autem illo habito demonstrationem venatus, in-

[1] [This was very erroneously printed in the first edition; in consequence, as I believe, of a mistake I had made in transcription.—1842.]

5. Cardan, though not entitled to the honour of this discovery, nor even equal, perhaps, in mathematical   Cardan's
genius to Tartaglia, made a great epoch in the   veries.
science of algebra; and, according to Cossali and Hutton,
has a claim to much that Montucla has unfairly or carelessly
attributed to his favourite Vieta. ' It appears,' says Dr.
Hutton, ' from this short chapter (lib. x. cap. 1 of the Ars
Magna), that he had discovered most of the principal properties of the roots of equations, and could point out the
number and nature of the roots, partly from the signs of the
terms, and partly from the magnitude and relations of the
co-efficients.' Cossali has given the larger part of a quarto
volume to the algebra of Cardan ; his object being to establish
the priority of the Italian's claim to most of the discoveries
ascribed by Montucla to others, and especially to Vieta.
Cardan knew how to transform a complete cubic equation
into one wanting the second term ; one of the flowers which
Montucla has placed on the head of Vieta ; and this he explains so fully that Cossali charges the French historian of
mathematics with having never read the Ars Magna.[h]
Leonard of Pisa had been aware that quadratic equations
might have two positive roots ; but Cardan first perceived, or
at least first noticed, the negative roots, which he calls ' fictæ
radices.'[i] In this perhaps there is nothing extraordinary ;
the algebraic language must early have been perceived by
such acute men as exercised themselves in problems to give
a double solution of every quadratic equation ; but, in fact,
the conditions of these problems, being always numerical,
were such as to render a negative result practically false, and
impertinent to the question. It is therefore, perhaps, without much cause that Cossali triumphs in the ignorance shown
of negative values by Vieta, Bachet, and even Harriott,
though Cardan had pointed them out ;[k] since we may better

tellexi complura alia posse haberi. Ac
eo studio, auctaque jam confidentia, per
me partim, ac etiam aliqua per Ludo-
vicum Ferrarium, olim alumnum nostrum, inveni. Porro quæ ab his inventa
sunt, illorum nominibus decorabuntur,
cætera quæ nomine carent nostra sunt.
At etiam demonstrationes, præter tres
Mahometis, et duas Ludovici, omnes
nostræ sunt, singulæque capitibus suis

præponentur, inde regula addita, sub-
jicietur experimentum. Kästner, p. 152.
The passage in italics is also quoted by
Cossali, p. 159.
    [h] p. 164.
    [i] Montucla gives Cardan the credit
due for this ; at least in his second edition (1799), p. 595.
    [k] i. 23.

say, that they did not trouble themselves with what, in the
actual application of algebra, could be of no utility.   Cardan
also is said to have discovered that every cubic equation has
one or three real roots ; and (what seems hardly probable in
the state of science at that time) that there are as many
positive or true roots as changes of sign in the equation ; that
the co-efficient of the second term is equal to the sum of the
roots, so that where it is wanting, the positive and negative
values must compensate each other ; [m] and that the known
term is the product of all the roots.   Nor was he ignorant
of a method of extracting roots by approximation ; but in
this again the definiteness of solution, which numerical problems admit and require, would prevent any great progress
from being made.[n]   The rules are not perhaps all laid down
by him very clearly ; and it is to be observed, that he confined
himself chiefly to equations not above the third power ;
though he first published the method of solving biquadratics,
invented by his coadjutor Ferrari.   Cossali has also shown
that the application of algebra to geometry, and even to the
geometrical construction of problems, was known in some
cases by Tartaglia and Cardan ; thus plucking another feather
from the wing of Vieta, or of Descartes.   It is a little amusing
to see that, after Montucla had laboured with so much success
to despoil Harriott of the glory which Wallis had, perhaps
with too national a feeling, bestowed upon him for a long list
of discoveries contained in the writings of Vieta, a claimant
by an older title started up in Jerome Cardan, who, if we
may trust his accomplished advocate, seems to have established
his right at the expense of both.

6. These anticipations of Cardan are the more truly wonderful, when we consider that the symbolical language of
algebra, that powerful instrument not only in expediting the
processes of thought, but in suggesting general truths to

---

[m] It must, apparently, have been
through his knowledge of this property
of the co-efficient of the second term,
that Cardan recognised the existence of
equal roots, even when affected by the
same sign (Cossali, ii. 362) ; which, considered in relation to the numerical problems then in use, would seem a kind of
absurdity.

[n] Kästner, p. 161.   In one place Cos-

sali shows that Cardan had transported
all the quantities of an equation to one
side, making the whole equal to zero ;
which Wallis has ascribed to Harriott,
as his leading discovery, p. 324.   Yet in
another passage we find Cossali saying :
Una somma di quantità uguale al zero
avea un' aria mostruosa, e non sapeasi di
equazion si fatta concepire idea. p.
159.

the mind, was nearly unknown in his age. Diophantus, Fra Luca, and Cardan make use occasionally of letters to express indefinite quantities besides the *res* or *cosa*, sometimes written shortly, for the assumed unknown number of an equation. But letters were not yet substituted for known quantities. Michael Stifel, in his Arithmetica Integra, Nuremberg, 1544, is said to have first used the signs + and −, and numeral exponents of powers.[o] It is very singular that discoveries of the greatest convenience, and apparently not above the ingenuity of a parish schoolmaster, should have been overlooked by men of extraordinary acuteness, like Tartaglia, Cardan, and Ferrari, and hardly less so, that by dint of this acuteness, they dispensed with the aid of these contrivances, in which we suppose that so much of the utility of algebraic expression consists.

Imperfections of algebraic language.

7. But the great boast of science during this period is the treatise of Copernicus on the revolutions of the heavenly bodies, in six books, published at Nuremberg, in 1543.[p] This founder of modern astronomy was born at Thorn, of a good family, in 1473; and after receiving the best education his country furnished, spent some years in Italy, rendering himself master of all the mathematical and astronomical science at that time attainable. He became possessed afterwards of an ecclesiastical benefice in his own country. It appears to have been about 1507, that, after meditating on various schemes besides the Ptolemaic, he began to adopt and confirm in writing that of Pythagoras, as alone capable of explaining the planetary motions with that simplicity which gives a presumption of truth in the works of nature.[q] Many years of exact obervations confirmed his

Copernicus.

---

[o] Hutton, Kästner.

[p] The titlepage and advertisement of so famous a work, and which so few of my readers will have seen, are worth copying from Kästner, ii. 595. Nicolai Copernici Torinensis, de revolutionibus orbium cœlestium libri vi.

Habes in hoc opere jam recens nato et edito, studiose lector, motus stellarum tam fixarum quam erraticarum, cum ex veteribus tum etiam ex recentibus observationibus restitutos; et novis insuper ac admirabilibus hypothesibus ornatos. Habes etiam tabulas expeditissimas, ex quibus eosdem ad quodvis tempus quam facillime calculare poteris. Igitur eme, lege, fruere. Αγεωμετρητος ουδεις εισιτω. Noribergæ, apud Joh. Petreium, anno MDxliii.

[q] This is the proper statement of the Copernican argument, as it then stood; it rested on what we may call a metaphysical probability, founded upon its beauty and simplicity; for it is to be remembered that the Ptolemaic hypothesis explained all the phænomena then known. Those which are only to be solved by the supposition of the earth's

mind in the persuasion that he had solved the grandest problem which can occupy the astronomer. He seems to have completed his treatise about 1530 ; but perhaps dreaded the bigoted prejudices which afterwards oppressed Galileo. Hence he is careful to propound his theory as an hypothesis; though it is sufficiently manifest that he did not doubt of its truth. It was first publicly announced by his disciple Joachim Rhœticus, already mentioned for his trigonometry, in the Narratio de Revolutionibus Copernici, printed at Dantzic in 1540. The treatise of Copernicus himself, three years afterwards, is dedicated to tne pope, Paul III., as if to shield himself under that sacred mantle. But he was better protected by the common safeguard against oppression. The book reached him on the day of his death; and he just touched with his hands the great legacy he was to bequeath to mankind. But many years were to elapse before they availed themselves of the wisdom of Copernicus. The progress of his system, even among astronomers, as we shall hereafter see, was exceeding slow.[r] We may just mention here, that no kind of progress was made in mechanical or optical science during the first part of the sixteenth century.

Sect. II.

On Medicine and Anatomy.

8. The revival of classical literature had an extensive influence where we might not immediately anticipate it, on the science of medicine. Jurisprudence itself though nomi-

---

motion were discovered long afterwards. This excuses the slow reception of the new system, interfering as it did with so many prejudices, and incapable of that kind of proof which mankind generally demand.

[r] Gassendi, Vita Copernici. Biogr. univ. Montucla. Kästner. Playfair. Gassendi, p. 14–22, gives a short analysis of the great work of Copernicus de orbium cœlestium revolutionibus, p. 22. The hypothesis is generally laid down in the first of the six books. One of the most remarkable passages in Copernicus is his conjecture that gravitation was not a central tendency, as had been supposed, but an attraction common to matter, and probably extending to the heavenly bodies, though it does not appear that he surmised their mutual influences in virtue of it : gravitatem esse affectionem non terræ totius, sed partium ejus propriam, qualem soli etiam et lunæ cæterisque astris convenire credibile est. These are the words of Copernicus himself, quoted by Gassendi, p. 19.

nally and exclusively connected with the laws of Rome was
hardly more indebted to the restorers of ancient Revival of
learning than the art of healing, which seems to cine.
own no mistress but nature, no code of laws but those which
regulate the human system. But the Greeks, among their
other vast superiorities above the Arabians, who borrowed so
much, and so much perverted what they borrowed, were not
only the real founders, but the best teachers of medicine; a
science which in their hands seems, more than any other, to
have anticipated the Baconian philosophy ; being founded on
an induction proceeding by select experience, always observant, always cautious, and ascending slowly to the generalities
of theory. But instead of Hippocrates and Galen, the Arabians brought in physicians of their own, men, doubtless,
of considerable, though inferior merit, and substituted arbitrary or empirical precepts for the enlarged philosophy of the
Greeks. The scholastic subtilty also obtruded itself even into
medicine ; and the writings of the middle ages on these subjects are alike barbarous in style and useless in substance.
Pharmacy owes much to this oriental school, but it has retained no reputation in physiological or pathological science.

9. Nicolas Leonicenus, who became professor at Ferrara
before 1470, was the first restorer of the Hippocratic Linacre and
method of practice. He lived to a very advanced sicians.
age, and was the first translator of Galen from the Greek.[s]
Our excellent countryman, Linacre, did almost as much for
medicine. The College of Physicians, founded by Henry
VIII. in 1518, venerates him as its original president. His
primary object was to secure a learned profession, to rescue
the art of healing from mischievous ignorance, and to guide
the industrious student in the path of real knowledge, which
at that time lay far more through the regions of ancient
learning than at present. It was important, not for the
mere dignity of the profession, but for its proper ends, to
encourage the cultivation of the Greek language, or to
supply its want by accurate versions of the chief medical
writers.[t] Linacre himself, and several eminent physicians
on the Continent, Cop, Ruel, Gonthier, Fuchs, by such

---

[s] Biogr. univ. Sprengel, Hist. de la　　[t] Johnson's Life of Linacre, p. 207,
Médecine (traduite par Jourdan), vol. ii.　279. Biogr. Britann.

labours in translation, restored the school of Hippocrates. That of the Arabians rapidly lost ground, though it preserved through the sixteenth century an ascendancy in Spain; and some traces of its influence, especially the precarious empiricism of judging diseases by the renal secretion, without sight of the patient, which was very general in that age, continued long afterwards in several parts of Europe.[u]

10. The study of Hippocrates taught the medical writers of this century to observe and describe like him.
Medical innovators. Their works, chiefly indeed after the period with which we are immediately concerned, are very numerous, and some of them deserve much praise, though neither the theory of the science, nor the power of judiciously observing and describing, was yet in a very advanced state. The besetting sin of all who should have laboured for truth, an undue respect for authority, made Hippocrates and Galen, especially the former, as much the idols of the medical world, as Augustin and Aristotle were of theology and metaphysics. This led to a pedantic erudition, and contempt of opposite experience, which rendered the professors of medicine an inexhaustible theme of popular ridicule. Some, however, even at an early time, broke away from the trammels of implicit obedience to the Greek masters. Fernel, one of the first physicians in France, rejecting what he could not approve in their writings, gave an example of free inquiry. Argentier of Turin tended to shake the influence of Galen by founding a school which combated many of his leading theories.[x] But the most successful opponent of the
Paracelsus. orthodox creed was Paracelsus. Of his speculative philosophy, or rather the wild chimæras which he borrowed or devised, enough has been said in former pages. His reputation was originally founded on a supposed skill in medicine; and it is probable that, independently of his real merit in the application of chemistry to medicine, and in the employment of very powerful agents, such as antimony, the fanaticism of his pretended philosophy would exercise that potency

---

[u] Sprengel, vol. iii. passim.

[x] Id. 204. 'Argentier,' he says, 'was the first to lay down a novel and true principle, that the different faculties of the soul are not inherent in certain distinct parts of the brain.'

over the bodily frame, to which disease has, in recent experience, so often yielded.[y]

11. The first important advances in anatomical knowledge since the time of Mundinus were made by Berenger Anatomy. of Carpi, in his commentary upon that author, Berenger. printed at Bologna in 1521, which it was thought worth while to translate into English as late as 1664, and in his Isagogæ breves in anatomiam, Bologna, 1522. He followed the steps of Mundinus in human dissection, and thus gained an advantage over Galen. Hence we owe to him the knowledge of several specific differences between the human structure and that of quadrupeds. Berenger is asserted to have discovered two of the small bones of the ear, though this is contested on behalf of Achillini. Portal observes, that though some have regarded Berenger as the restorer of the science of anatomy, it is hard to strip one so much superior to him as Vesalius of that honour.[z]

12. Every early anatomist was left far behind when Vesalius, a native of Brussels, who acquired in early youth an extraordinary reputation on this side of the Vesalius. Alps, and in 1540 became professor of the science at Pavia, published at Basle, in 1543, his great work, de Corporis humani Fabrica. If Vesalius was not quite to anatomy what Copernicus was to astronomy, he has yet been said, a little hyperbolically, to have discovered a new world. A superstitious prejudice against human dissection had confined the ancient anatomists in general to pigs and apes, though Galen, according to Portal, had some experience in the former. Mundinus and Berenger, by occasionally dissecting the human body, had thrown much additional light on its structure; and the superficial muscles, those immediately under the integuments, had been studied by Da Vinci and others for the purposes of painting and sculpture. Vesalius first gave a complete description of the human body, with designs, which, at the time, were ascribed to Titian. We have here, therefore, a great step made in science; the precise estimation of Vesalius's discoveries must be sought, of course, in anatomical history.[a]

---

[y] Sprengel, vol. iii.   [z] Hist. de l'Anatomie, i. 277.
[a] Portal, i. 394–433.

13. ' Vesalius,' says Portal, in the rapturous strain of one
Portal's account of him. devoted to his own science, ' appears to me one of
the greatest men who ever existed.   Let the astro-
nomers vaunt their Copernicus, the natural philosophers
their Galileo and Torricelli, the mathematicians their Pascal,
the geographers their Columbus, I shall always place Vesalius above all their heroes.   The first study for man is man.
Vesalius has had this noble object in view, and has admirably
attained it; he has made on himself and his fellows such discoveries as Columbus could only make by travelling to the
extremity of the world.   The discoveries of Vesalius are of
direct importance to man : by acquiring fresh knowledge of
his own structure, man seems to enlarge his existence; while
discoveries in geography or astronomy affect him but in a
very indirect manner.'   He proceeds to compare him with
Winslow, more than a century later, in order to show how
little had been done in the intermediate time.   Vesalius
seems not to have known the osteology of the ear.   His
account of the teeth is not complete ; but he first clearly
described the bones of the feet.   He has given a full account
of the muscles, but with some mistakes, and was ignorant of
a very few.   In his account of the sanguineous and nervous
systems, the errors seem more numerous.   He describes the
intestines better than his predecessors, and the heart very
well; the organs of generation not better than they, and
sometimes omits their discoveries; the brain admirably, little
having since been added.

14. The zeal of Vesalius and his fellow-students for ana-
His human dissections. tomical science led them to strange scenes of ad-
venture.   Those services, which have since been
thrown on the refuse of mankind, they voluntarily undertook.

Entire affection scorneth nicer hands.

They prowled by night in charnel-houses, they dug up the
dead from the grave, they climbed the gibbet, in fear and
silence, to steal the mouldering carcass of the murderer; the
risk of ignominious punishment, and the secret stings of
superstitious remorse, exalting no doubt the delight of these
useful, but not very enviable, pursuits.[b]

---

b Portal, p. 395.

15. It may be mentioned here, that Vesalius, after living for some years in the court of Charles and Philip as Fate of Vesalius. their physician, met with a strange reverse, characteristic enough of such a place. Being absurdly accused of having dissected a Spanish gentleman before he was dead, Vesalius only escaped capital punishment, at the instance of the Inquisition, by undertaking a pilgrimage to Jerusalem, during which he was shipwrecked, and died of famine in one of the Greek island.[c]

16. The best anatomists were found in Italy. But Francis I. invited one of these, Vidus Vidius, to his Other anatomists. royal college at Paris; and from that time France had several of respectable name. Such were Charles Etienne, one of the great typographical family, Sylvius and Gonthier.[d] A French writer about 1540, Levasseur, has been thought to have known, at least, the circulation of the blood through the lungs, as well as the valves of the arteries and veins, and their direction, and its purpose; treading closely on an anticipation of Harvey.[e] But this seems to be too hastily inferred. Portal has erroneously supposed the celebrated passage of Servetus on the circulation of the blood to be contained in his book de Trinitatis erroribus, published in 1531,[f] whereas it is really found in the Chrstianismi Restitutio, which did not appear till 1553.

17. The practice of trusting to animal dissection, from which it was difficult for anatomists to extricate Imperfection of the science. themselves, led some men of real merit into errors. They seem also not to have profited sufficiently by the writings of their predecessors. Massa of Venice, one of the greatest of this age, is ignorant of some things known to Berenger. Many proofs occur in Portal how imperfectly the elder anatomists could yet demonstrate the more delicate parts of the human body.

---

[c] Portal. Tiraboschi, ix. 34. Biogr. univ. [Sprengel, Hist. de la Médecine, vol. iv. p. 6, treats the cause of the pilgrimage of Vesalius, assigned by these writers, as a fable.—1842.]

[d] Portal, i. 330 et post.

[e] Portal, p. 373, quotes the passage, which at first seems to warrant this inference, but is rather obscurely worded. We shall return to this subject when we arrive at Harvey.

[f] P. 300.

Sect. III.

On Natural History.

18. The progress of natural history, in all its departments,
was very slow, and should of course be estimated by
the additions made to the valuable materials collected by Aristotle, Theophrastus, Dioscorides, and Pliny.
The few botanical treatises that had appeared before this
time were too meagre and imperfect to require mention.
Otto Brunfels of Strasburg was the first who published, in
1530, a superior work, Herbarum vivæ Eicones, in three
volumes folio, with 238 wooden cuts of plants.[g] Euricius
Cordus of Marburg, in his Botanilogicon, or dialogues on
plants, displays, according to the Biographie universelle, but
little knowledge of Greek, and still less observation of nature.
Cordus has deserved more praise (though this seems
better due to Lorenzo de' Medici), as the first who
established a botanical garden. This was at Marburg, in
1530.[h] But the fortunes of private physicians were hardly
equal to the cost of an useful collection. The university of
Pisa led the way by establishing a public garden in 1545,
according to the date which Tiraboschi has determined.
That of Padua had founded a professorship of botany in
1533.[i]

Botany.

Botanical gardens.

19. Ruel, a physician of Soissons, an excellent Greek
scholar, had become known by a translation of
Dioscorides in 1516, upon which Huet has bestowed high praise. His more celebrated treatise, De Natura Stirpium, appeared at Paris in 1536, and is one of the
handsomest offsprings of that press. It is a compilation from
the Greek and Latin authors on botany, made with taste and

Ruel.

---

[g] Biogr. univ.

[h] Id. Andrès, xiii. 80. Eichhorn,
iii. 304. See, too, Roscoe's Leo X.,
iv. 125, for some pleasing notices of
the early studies in natural history.
Pontanus was fond of it; and his poem
on the cultivation of the lemon, orange,
and citron (De hortis Hesperidum)
shows an acquaintance with some of the
operations of horticulture. The garden
of Bembo was also celebrated. Theophrastus and Dioscorides were published
in Latin before 1500. But it was not
till about the middle of the sixteenth
century that botany, through the commentaries of Matthioli on Dioscorides,
began to assume a distinct form, and to
be studied as a separate branch.

[i] ix. 10.

judgment. His knowledge, however, derived from experience was not considerable, though he has sometimes given the French names of species described by the Greeks, so far as his limited means of observation and the difference of climate enabled him. Many later writers have borrowed from Ruel their general definitions and descriptions of plants, which he himself took from Theophrastus.[k]

20. Ruel, however, seems to have been left far behind by Leonard Fuchs, professor of medicine in more than one German university, who has secured a verdant immortality in the well-known Fuchsia. Besides many works on his own art, esteemed in their time, he published at Basle in 1542, his Commentaries on the History of Plants, containing above 500 figures, a botanical treatise frequently reprinted, and translated into most European languages. ' Considered as a naturalist, and especially as a botanist, Fuchs holds a distinguished place, and he has thrown a strong light on that science. His chief object is to describe exactly the plants used in medicine; and his prints, though mere outlines, are generally faithful. He shows that the plants and vegetable products mentioned by Theophrastus, Dioscorides, Hippocrates, and Galen had hitherto been ill known.' [m]

21. Matthioli, an Italian physician, in a peaceful retreat near Trent, accomplished a laborious repertory of medical botany in his Commentaries on Dioscorides, published originally, 1544, in Italian, but translated by himself into Latin, and frequently reprinted throughout Europe. Notwithstanding a bad arrangement, and the author's proneness to credulity, it was of great service at a time when no good work on that subject was in existence in Italy; and its reputation seems to have been not only general, but of long duration.[n]

22. It was not singular that much should have been published, imperfect as it might be, on the natural history of plants, while that of animal nature, as a matter of science, lay almost neglected. The importance of

Fuchs.

Matthioli.

Low state of zoology.

---

[k] Biogr. univ. (by M. du Petit Thouars).
[m] Id.

[n] Tiraboschi, ix. 2. Andrès, xiii. 85. Corniani, vi. 5.

vegetable products in medicine was far more extensive and
various ; while the ancient treatises, which formed substantially the chief knowledge of nature possessed in the sixteenth century, are more copious and minute on the botanical
than the animated kingdom. Hence we find an absolute
dearth of books relating to zoology. That of P. Jovius de
piscibus Romanis is rather one of a philologer and a lover of
good cheer than a naturalist, and treats only of the fish eaten
at the Roman tables.[o] Gillius de vi et natura animalium is
little else than a compilation from Ælian and other ancient
authors, though Niceron says that the author has interspersed some observations of his own.[p] No work of the least
importance, even for that time, can perhaps be traced in
Europe on any part of zoology, before the Avium præcipu-
arum historia of our countryman Turner, published at Cologne in 1548, though this is confined to species described
by the ancients. Gesner, in his Pandects, which bear date
in the same year, several times refers to it with commendation.[q]

23. Agricola, a native of Saxony, acquired a perfect knowledge of the processes of metallurgy from the miners
of Chemnitz, and perceived the immense resources
that might be drawn from the abysses of the earth. ' He is
the first mineralogist,' says Cuvier, ' who appeared after the
revival of science in Europe. He was to mineralogy what
Gesner was to zoology ; the chemical part of metallurgy, and
especially what relates to assaying, is treated with great care,
and has been little improved down to the end of the eighteenth
century. It is plain that he was acquainted with the classics,
the Greek alchemists, and many manuscripts. Yet he believed in the goblins to whom miners ascribe the effects of
mephitic exhalations.'[r]

Agricola.

---

[o] Andrès, xiii. 143. Roscoe's Leo X.,
ubi supra.
[p] Vol. xxiii. Biogr. univ. Andrès,
xiii. 144.
[q] Pandect. Univers. lib. 14. Gesner may be said to make great use of
Turner ; a high compliment from so
illustrious a naturalist. He quotes also
a book on quadrupeds lately printed in
German by Michael Herr. Turner,
whom we shall find again as a naturalist,
became afterwards dean of Wells, and
was one of the early Puritans. See
Chalmers's Dictionary.
[r] Biogr. univ.

Sect. IV.

On Oriental Literature.

24. The study of Hebrew was naturally one of those which flourished best under the influence of Protestantism. It was exclusively connected with Scriptural inter- Hebrew. pretation; and could neither suit the polished irreligion of the Italians, nor the bigotry of those who owned no other standard than the Vulgate translation. Sperone observes in one of his dialogues, that as much as Latin is prized in Italy, so much do the Germans value the Hebrew language.[s] We have anticipated in another place the translations of the Old Testament by Luther, Pagninus, and other Hebraists of this age. Sebastian Munster published the first grammar and lexicon of the Chaldee dialect in 1527. His Hebrew Grammar had preceded in 1525. The Hebrew Lexicon of Pagninus appeared in 1529; and that of Munster himself in 1543. Elias Levita, the learned Jew who has been already mentioned, deserves to stand in Elias Levita. this his natural department above even Munster. Among several works that fall within this period we may notice the Masorah (Venice, 1538, and Basle, 1539), wherein he excited the attention of the world by denying the authority and antiquity of vowel points, and a Lexicon of the Chaldee and Rabbinical dialects, in 1541. ‘Those,’ says Simon, ‘who would thoroughly understand Hebrew should read the Treatises of Elias Levita, which are full of important observations necessary for the explanation of the sacred text.’[t] Pellican, one of the first who embraced the principles Pellican. of the Zuinglian reform, has merited a warm eulogy from Simon for his Commentarii Bibliorum (Zurich, 1531–1536, five volumes in folio), especially for avoiding that display of rabbinical learning which the German Hebraists used to affect.[u]

25. Few endeavours were made in this period towards the cultivation of the other Oriental languages. Pagnino printed

---

[s] P. 102 (edit. 1596).　　[t] Biogr. univ.　　[u] Id.

an edition of the Koran at Venice in 1530 ; but it was imme-
Arabic and Oriental Literature. diately suppressed ; a precaution hardly required
while there was no one able to read it. But it may
have been supposed, that the leaves of some books, like that
recorded in the Arabian Nights, contain an active poison that
·does not wait for the slow process of understanding their
contents. Two crude attempts at introducing the Eastern
tongues were made soon afterwards. One of these was by
William Postel, a man of some parts and more reading, but
chiefly known, while he was remembered at all, for mad
reveries of fanaticism, and an idolatrous veneration for a
saint of his own manufacture, La Mère Jeanne, the Joanna
Southcote of the sixteenth century. We are only concerned
at present with his collection of alphabets, twelve in number,
published at Paris in 1538. The greater part of these are
Oriental. An Arabic Grammar followed the same year ;
but the types are so very imperfect, that it would be difficult
to read them. A polyglot alphabet on a much larger scale
appeared at Pavia the next year, through the care of Tesco
Ambrogio, containing those of forty languages. Ambrogio
gave also an introduction to the Chaldee, Syriac, and Arme-
nian ; but very defective, at least, as to the two latter. Such
rude and incorrect publications hardly deserve the name of
beginnings. According to Andrès, Arabic was publicly
taught at Paris by Giustiniani, and at Salamanca by
Clenardus. The Æthiopic version of the New Testament
was printed at Rome in 1548.

Sect. V.

On Geography and History.

26. The curiosity natural to mankind had been gratified
Geography of Grynæus. by various publications since the invention of printing, containing either the relations of ancient tra-
vellers, such as Marco Polo, or of those under the Spanish or
Portuguese flags, who had laid open two new worlds to the
European reader. These were for the first time collected,
to the number of seventeen, by Simon Grynæus, a learned

professor at Basle, in Novus orbis regionum et insularum veteribus incognitarum, printed at Paris in 1532. We find in this collection, besides an introduction to cosmography by Sebastian Munster, a map of the world bearing the date 1531. The Cosmography of Apianus, professor at Ingoldstadt, published in 1524, contains also a map of the four quarters of the world. In this of Grynæus's collection, a rude notion of the eastern regions of Asia appears. Sumatra is called Taprobane, and placed in the 150th meridian. A vague delineation of China and the adjacent sea is given; but Catay is marked farther north. The island of Gilolo, which seems to be Japan, is about 240° east longitude. South America is noted as Terra Australis recenter inventa, sed nondum plane cognita; and there is as much of North America as Sebastian Cabot had discovered, a little enlarged by lucky conjecture. Magellan, by circumnavigating the world, had solved a famous problem. We find accordingly in this map an attempt to divide the globe by the 360 meridians of longitude. The best account of his voyage, that by Pigafetta, was not published till 1556; but the first, Maximilianus de insulis Moluccis, appeared in 1523.

27. The Cosmography of Apianus, above mentioned, was reprinted with additions by Gemma Frisius in 1533 and 1550. It is, however, as a work of mere geo- *Apianus.* graphy, very brief and superficial; though it may exhibit as much of the astronomical part of the science as the times permitted. That of Sebastian Munster, published in 1546, notwithstanding its title, extends only to *Munster.* the German empire.[x] The Isolario of Bordone (Venice, 1528) contains a description of all the islands of the world, with maps.[y]

---

[x] Eichhorn, iii. 294.

[y] Tiraboschi, ix. 179. [The best map, probably, of this period is one in the British Museum, executed in France before 1536, as is inferred from the form of the French king's crown, which was altered in that year. This map is generally superior to some which were engraved at a later time, and represents the figure of the African continent. It has excited some attention in consequence of an apparent delineation of Australia, under the name of Java grande. But this, which seems to come immediately from some Italian work, may be traced to Marco Polo, the great father of geographical conjecture in the middle ages. He gives an account, such as he picked up in China, of two islands, Java major and Java minor. The continent delineated in this French map is only the island of Java, vastly enlarged. —1842.]

28. A few voyages were printed before the middle of the
century, which have, for the most part, found their
Voyages.   way into the collection of Ramusio. The most
considerable is the History of the Indies, that is, of the
Spanish dominions in America, by Gonzalo Her-
Oviedo.   nandez, sometimes called Oviedo, by which name
he is recorded in the Biographie universelle. The author
had resided for some years in St. Domingo. He published a
summary of the general and natural history of the Indies in
1526; and twenty books of this entire work in 1535. The
remaining thirty did not appear till 1783. In the long list
of geographical treatises given by Ortelius, a small number
belong to this earlier period of the century. But it may be
generally said, that the acquaintance of Europe with the
rest of the world could as yet be only obtained orally from
Spanish and Portuguese sailors or adventurers, and was such
as their falsehood and blundering would impart.

29. It is not my design to comprehend historical litera-
Historical   ture, except as to the chief publications, in these
works.   volumes; and it is hitherto but a barren field; for
though Guicciardini died in 1540, his great history did not
appear till 1564. Some other valuable histories, those of
Nardi, Segni, Varchi, were also kept back through political
or other causes, till a comparatively late period. That of
Paulus Jovius, which is not in very high estimation, appeared in 1550, and may be reckoned, perhaps, after that of
Machiavel, the best of this age. Upon this side of the Alps,
several works of this class, to which the historical student
has recourse, might easily be enumerated; but none of a
philosophical character, or remarkable for beauty of style.
I should, however, wish to make an exception for the
Memoirs of the Chevalier Bayard, written by his secretary,
and known by the title of Le Loyal Serviteur; they are full
of warmth and simplicity. A chronicle bearing the name of
Carion, but really written by Melanchthon, and published in
the German language, 1532, was afterwards translated into
Latin, and became the popular manual of universal history.[z]
But ancient and mediæval history was as yet very imperfectly
made known to those who had no access to its original

---

[z] Bayle, art. Carion. Eichhorn, iii. 285.

sources. Even in Italy little had yet been done with critical or even extensive erudition.

30. Italy in the sixteenth century was remarkable for the number of her literary academies; institutions which, though by no means peculiar to her, have in no other country been so general or so conspicuous. We have already taken notice of that established by Aldus Manutius at Venice early in this century, and of those of older date, which had enjoyed the patronage of princes at Florence and Naples, as well as of that which Pomponius Lætus and his associates, with worse auspices, had endeavoured to form at Rome The Roman academy, after a long season of persecution or neglect, revived in the genial reign of Leo X. 'Those were happy days,' says Sadolet in 1529, writing to Angelo Colocci, a Latin poet of some reputation, 'when in your suburban gardens, or mine on the Quirinal, or in the circus, or by the banks of the Tiber, we held those meetings of learned men, all recommended by their own virtues and by public reputation. Then it was that after a repast, which the wit of the guests rendered exquisite, we heard poems or orations recited to our great delight, productions of the ingenious Casanuova, the sublime Vida, the elegant and correct Beroaldo, and many others still living or now no more.'[a] Corycius, a wealthy German, encouraged the good-humoured emulation of these Roman luminaries.[b] But the miserable reverse, that not long after the death of Leo befel Rome, put an end to this academy, which was afterwards replaced by others of less fame.

Italian academies.

31. The first academies of Italy had chiefly directed their attention to classical literature; they compared manuscripts, they suggested new readings, or new interpretations, they deciphered inscriptions and coins, they sat in judgment on a Latin ode, or debated the propriety of a phrase. Their own poetry had, perhaps, never been neglected; but it was not till the writings of Bembo founded a new code of criticism in the Italian language, that they

They pay regard to the language.

---

[a] Sadolet, Epist. p. 225 (edit. 1554).   Roscoe has quoted this interesting letter.
[b] Roscoe, iii. 480.

began to study it minutely, and judge of compositions with that fastidious scrupulousness which they had been used to exercise upon modern Latinity. Several academies were established with a view to this purpose, and became the self-appointed censors of their native literature. The reader will remember what has been already mentioned, that there was a peculiar source of verbal criticism in Italy, from the want of a recognised standard of idiom. The very name of the language was long in dispute. Bembo maintained that Florentine was the proper appellation. Varchi and other natives of the city have adhered to this very restrictive monopoly. Several, with more plausibility, contended for the name Tuscan; and this, in fact, was so long adopted, that it is hardly yet, perhaps, altogether out of use. The majority, however, were not Tuscans; and while it is generally agreed that the highest purity of their language is to be found in Tuscany, the word Italian has naturally prevailed as its denomination.

32. The academy of Florence was instituted in 1540 to illustrate and perfect the *Tuscan* language, especially by a close attention to the poetry of Petrarch. Their admiration of Petrarch became an exclusive idolatry; the critics of this age would acknowledge no defect in him, nor excellence in any different style. Dissertations and commentaries on Petrarch, in all the diffuseness characteristic of the age and the nation, crowd the Italian libraries. We are, however, anticipating a little in mentioning them; for few belong to so early a period as the present. But by dint of this superstitious accuracy in style, the language rapidly acquired a purity and beauty which has given the writers of the sixteenth century a value in the eyes of their countrymen not always so easily admitted by those who, being less able to perceive the delicacy of expression, are at leisure to yawn over their frequent tediousness and inanity.

Their fondness for Petrarch.

33. The Italian academies which arose in the first half of the century, and we shall meet with others hereafter, are too numerous to be reckoned in these pages. The most famous were the Intronati of Siena, founded in 1525, and devoted, like that at Florence, to the improvement of their language; the Infiammati of Padua, founded by

They become numerous.

some men of high attainments in 1534; and that of Modena, which, after a short career of brilliancy, fell under such suspicions of heresy, and was subjected to such inquisitorial jealousy about 1542, that it never again made any figure in literary history.[c]

34. Those academies have usually been distinguished by little peculiarities, which border sometimes on the ridiculous, but serve probably, at least in the beginning, to keep up the spirit of such societies. They took names humorously quaint; they adopted devices and distinctions, which made them conspicuous, and inspired a vain pleasure in belonging to them. The Italian nobility, living a good deal in cities, and restrained from political business, fell willingly into these literary associations. They have, perhaps, as a body, been better educated, or at least, better acquainted with their own literature and with classical antiquity, than men of equal rank in other countries. This was more the case in the sixteenth century than at present. Genius and erudition have been always honoured in Italy; and the more probably that they have not to stand the competition of overpowering wealth, or of political influence. *Their distinctions.*

35. Academies of the Italian kind do not greatly favour the vigorous advances in science, and much less the original bursts of genius, for which men of powerful minds are designed by nature. They form an oligarchy pretending to guide the public taste, as they are guided themselves, by arbitrary maxims and close adherence to precedents. The spirit of criticism which they foster is a salutary barrier against bad taste and folly, but is too minute and scrupulous in repressing the individualities that characterise real talents, and ends by producing an unblemished mediocrity, without the powers of delight or excitement, for which alone the literature of the imagination is desired. *Evils connected with them.*

36. In the beginning of this century several societies were set on foot in Germany, for the promotion of ancient learning, besides that already mentioned, of the Rhine, established by Camerarius of Dalberg and Conrad Celtes in the preceding age. Wimpfeling presided over one *They succeed less in Germany.*

---

[c] Tiraboschi, viii. ch. 4, is my chief authority about the Italian academies of this period.

at Strasburg in 1514, and we find another at Augsburg in 1518. It is probable that the religious animosities which followed stood in the way of similar institutions; or they may have existed without obtaining much celebrity.[d]

37. Italy was rich, far beyond any other country, in public and private libraries. The Vatican, first in dignity, in antiquity, and in number of books, increased under almost every successive pope, except Julius II., the least favourable to learning of them all. The Laurentian library, purchased by Leo X., before his accession to the papacy, from a monastery at Florence, which had acquired the collection after the fall of the Medici in 1494, was restored to that city by Clement VII., and placed in the newly-erected building which still contains it. The public libraries of Venice and Ferrara were conspicuous; and even a private citizen of the former, the Cardinal Grimani, is said to have left one of 8000 volumes; at that time, it appears, a remarkable number.[e] Those of Heidelberg and Vienna, commenced in the fifteenth century, were still the most distinguished in Germany; and Cardinal Ximenes founded one at Alcalá.[f] It is unlikely that many private libraries of great extent existed in the empire; but the trade of bookselling, though not yet, in general, separated from that of printing, had become of considerable importance.

Libraries.

---

[d] Jugler, in his Hist. Litteraria, mentions none between that of the Rhine, and one established at Weimar in 1617. p. 1994.

[e] Tiraboschi, viii. 197–219.

[f] Jugler, Hist. Litteraria, p. 206 et alibi.

PART II.

ON THE LITERATURE OF THE LATTER HALF OF THE
SIXTEENTH CENTURY.

CHAPTER I.

HISTORY OF ANCIENT LITERATURE IN EUROPE, FROM
1550 TO 1600.

SECT. I.

*Progress of Classical Learning—Principal Critical Scholars—Editions of
ancient Authors—Lexicons and Grammars—Best Writers of Latin—
Muretus—Manutius—Decline of Taste—Scaliger—Casaubon—Classical Learning in England under Elizabeth.*

1. IN the first part of the sixteenth century we have seen
that the foundations of a solid structure of classical
learning had been laid in many parts of Europe; Progress of
philology.
the superiority of Italy had generally become far less conspicuous, or might perhaps be wholly denied; in all the German
empire, in France, and even in England, the study of ancient
literature had been almost uniformly progressive. But it
was the subsequent period of fifty years, which we now approach, that more eminently deserved the title of an age of
scholars, and filled our public libraries with immense fruits
of literary labour. In all matters of criticism and philology,
what was written before the year 1550 is little in comparison
with what the next age produced.

2. It may be useful in this place to lay before the reader
at one view the dates of the first editions of Greek First editions
and Latin authors, omitting some of inconsiderable of classics.
reputation or length. In this list I follow the authority of
Dr. Dibdin, to which no exception will probably be taken:—

Ælian	1545.	*Rome.*
Æschylus	1518.	*Venice, Aldus.*
Æsop	1480 ?	*Milan.*
Ammianus	1474.	*Rome.*
Anacreon	1554.	*Paris.*

Antoninus	1558.	*Zurich.*
Apollonius Rhodius	1496.	*Florence.*
Appianus	1551.	*Paris.*
Apuleius	1469.	*Rome.*
Aristophanes	1498.	*Venice.*
Aristoteles	1495–8.	*Venice.*
Arrian	1535.	*Venice.*
Athenæus	1514.	*Venice.*
Aulus Gellius	1469.	*Rome.*
Ausonius	1472.	*Venice.*
Boethius	Absque anno.	circ. 1470.
Cæsar	1469.	*Rome.*
Callimachus	Absque anno.	*Florence.*
Catullus	1472.	*Venice.*
Ciceronis Opera	1498.	*Milan.*
Cicero de Officiis	1465.	*Mentz.*
—— Epistolæ Famil.	1467.	} *Rome.*
—— Epistolæ ad Attic.	1469.	
—— de Oratore	1465.	*Mentz and Subiac .*
—— Rhetorica	1490.	*Venice.*
—— Orationes	1471.	*Rome.*
—— Opera Philosoph.	{ 1469. 1471.	} *Rome.*
Claudian	Absque anno.	*Brescia.*
Demosthenes	1504.	*Venice.*
Diodorus, v. lib.	1539.	*Basle.*
—— xv. lib.	1559.	*Paris.*
Diogenes Laertius	1533.	*Basle.*
Dio Cassius	1548.	*Paris.*
Dionysius Halicarn.	1546.	*Paris.*
Epictetus	1528.	*Venice.*
Euripides	1513.	*Venice.*
Euclid	1533.	*Basle.*
Florus	1470.	*Paris.*
Herodian	1513.	*Venice.*
Herodotus	1502.	*Venice.*
Hesiod. Op. et Dies	1493.	*Milan.*
—— Op. omnia	1495.	*Venice.*
Homer	1488.	*Florence.*
Horatius	Absque anno.	
Isocrates	1493.	*Milan.*
Josephus	1544.	*Basle.*
Justin	1470.	*Venice.*
Juvenal	Absque anno.	*Rome.*
Livius	1469.	*Rome.*
Longinus	1584.	*Basle.*
Lucan	1469.	*Rome.*
Lucian	1496.	*Florence.*
Lucretius	1473	*Brescia.*
Lysias	1513.	*Venice.*
Macrobius	1472.	*Venice.*
Manilius	Ante 1474.	*Nuremberg.*
Martialis	1471.	*Ferrara.*
Oppian	1515.	*Florence.*
Orpheus	1500.	*Florence.*
Ovid	1471.	*Bologna.*
Pausanias	1516.	*Venice.*

Petronius	1476 ?	
Phædrus	1596.	*Troyes.*
Photius	1601.	*Augsburg.*
Pindar	1513.	*Venice.*
Plato	1513.	*Venice.*
Plautus	1472.	*Venice.*
Plinii Nat. Hist.	1469.	*Venice.*
—— Epist.	1471.	
Plutarch Op. Moral.	1509.	*Venice.*
—— Vitæ	1517.	*Venice.*
Polybius	1530.	*Haguenow.*
Quintilian	1470.	*Rome.*
Quintus Curtius	Absque anno.	*Rome.*
Sallust	1470.	*Paris.*
Seneca	1475.	*Naples.*
Senecæ Tragediæ	1484.	*Ferrara.*
Silius Italicus	1471.	*Rome.*
Sophocles	1512.	*Venice.*
Statius	1472 ?	
Strabo	1516.	*Venice.*
Suetonius	1470.	*Rome.*
Tacitus	1468 ?	*Venice.*
Terence	Ante 1470 ?	*Strasburg.*
Theocritus	1493.	*Milan.*
Thucydides	1502.	*Venice.*
Valerius Flaccus	1474.	*Rome.*
Valerius Maximus	Ante 1470 ?	*Strasburg.*
Velleius Paterculus	1520.	*Basle.*
Virgil	1469.	*Rome.*
Xenophon	1516.	*Florence.*

3. It will be perceived that even in the middle of this century, some far from uncommon writers had not yet been given to the press. But most of the rest had Change in character of learning. gone through several editions, which it would be tedious to enumerate; and the means of acquiring an extensive, though not in all respects very exact, erudition might perhaps be nearly as copious as at present. In consequence, probably, among other reasons, of these augmented stores of classical literature, its character underwent a change. It became less polished and elegant, but more laborious and profound. The German or Cisalpine type, if I may use the word, prevailed over the Italian, the school of Budæus over that of Bembo; nor was Italy herself exempt from its ascendancy. This advance of erudition at the expense of taste was perhaps already perceptible in 1550, for we cannot accommodate our arbitrary divisions to the real changes of things; yet it was not hitherto so evident in Italy, as it became in the latter part of the century. The writers of this age, between 1550 and

1600, distinguish themselves from their predecessors, not
only by a disregard for the graces of language, but by a more
prodigal accumulation of quotations, and more elaborate
efforts to discriminate and to prove their positions. Aware
of the censors whom they may encounter in an increasing
body of scholars, they seek to secure themselves in the event
of controversy, or to sustain their own differences from those
who have gone already over the same ground. Thus books
of critical as well as antiquarian learning often contain little
of original disquisition, which is not interrupted at every
sentence by quotation, and in some instances are hardly
more than the adversaria, or common-place books, in which
the learned were accustomed to register their daily observations in study. A late German historian remarks the contrast between the Commentary of Paulus Cortesius on the
scholastic philosophy, published in 1503, and the Mythologia
of Natalis Comes, in 1551. The first, in spite of its subject,
is classical in style, full of animation and good sense; the
second is a tedious mass of quotations, the materials of a
book rather than a book, without a notion of representing
any thing in its spirit and general result.[a] This is, in great
measure, a characteristic of the age, and grew worse towards
the end of the century. Such a book as the Annals of Baronius, the same writer says, so shapeless, so destitute of
every trace of eloquence, could not have appeared in the age
of Leo. But it may be added, that, with all the defects of
Baronius, no one, in the age of Leo, could have put the
reader in the possession of so much knowledge.

4. We may reckon among the chief causes of this diminution of elegance in style, the increased culture
of the Greek language; not certainly that the
great writers in Greek are inferior models to those in
Latin, but because the practice of composition was confined
to the latter. Nor was the Greek really understood, in
its proper structure and syntax, till a much later period.
It was however a sufficiently laborious task, with the defective aids then in existence, to learn even the single words
of that most copious tongue; and in this some were eminently successful. Greek was not very much studied in

Cultivation of Greek.

---

[a] Ranke, Die Päpste des 16ten und 17ten Jahrhunderts, i. 484.

Italy; we may perhaps say, on the contrary, that no one native of that country, after the middle of the century, except Angelus Caninius and Æmilius Portus, both of whom lived wholly on this side of the Alps, acquired any remarkable reputation in it; for Petrus Victorius had been distinguished in the earlier period. It is to France and Germany that we should look for those who made Grecian literature the domain of scholars. It is impossible to mention every name, but we must select the more eminent; not, however, distinguishing the labourers in the two vineyards of ancient learning, since they frequently lent their service alternately to each.

5. The university of Paris, thanks to the encouragement given by Francis I., stood in the first rank for phi- Principal lological learning; and as no other in France could Turnebus. pretend to vie with her, she attracted students from every part. Toussain, Danes, and Dorat were conspicuous professors of Greek. The last was also one of the celebrated pleiad of French poets, but far more distinguished in the dead tongues than in his own. But her chief boast was Turnebus, so called by the gods, but by men Tournebœuf, and, as some have said, of a Scots family, who must have been denominated Turnbull.[b] Turnebus was one of those industrious scholars who did not scorn the useful labour of translating Greek authors into Latin, and is among the best of that class. But his reputation is chiefly founded on the Adversaria, the first part of which appeared in 1564, the second in 1565, the third, posthumously, in 1580. It is wholly miscellaneous, divided into chapters, merely as resting-places to the reader; for the contents of each are mostly a collection of unconnected notes. Such books, truly adversaria or common-places, were not unusual; but can of course only be read in a desultory manner, or consulted upon occasion. The Adversaria of Turnebus contains several thousand explanations of Latin passages. They are eminent for conciseness, few remarks exceeding half a page, and the greater

---

[b] Biogr. univ. The penultimate of Turnebus is made both short and long by the Latin poets of the age, but more commonly the latter, which seems contrary to what we should think right. Even Greek will not help us, for we find him called both τουρνεϐος and τουρυνηϐος. Maittaire, Vitæ Stephanor. vol. iii.

part being much shorter. He passes without notice from one subject to another the most remote, and has been so much too rapid for his editor, that the titles of each chapter, multifarious as they are, afford frequently but imperfect notions of its contents. The phrases explained are generally difficult; so that this miscellany gives a high notion of the erudition of Turnebus, and it has furnished abundant materials to later commentators. The best critics of that and the succeeding age, Gesner, Scaliger, Lipsius, Barthius, are loud in his praises; nor has he been blamed, except for his excess of brevity and rather too great proneness to amend the text of authors, wherein he is not remarkably successful.[c] Montaigne has taken notice of another merit in Turnebus, that with more learning than any who had gone before for a thousand years, he was wholly exempt from the pedantry characteristic of scholars, and could converse upon topics remote from his own profession, as if he had lived continually in the world.

6. A work very similar in its nature to the Adversaria of Turnebus was the Variæ Lectiones of Petrus Vic-

Petrus Victorius.

torius (Vettori), professor of Greek and Latin rhetoric at Florence during the greater part of a long life, which ended in 1585. Thuanus has said, with some hyperbole, that Victorius saw the revival and almost the extinction of learning in Italy.[d] No one, perhaps, deserved more praise in the restoration of the text of Cicero; no one, according to Huet, translated better from Greek; no one was more accurate in observing the readings of manuscripts, or more cautious in his own corrections. But his Variæ Lectiones, in 38 books, of which the first edition appeared in 1583, though generally extolled, has not escaped the severity

---

[c] Blount, Baillet. The latter begins his collection of these testimonies by saying that Turnebus has had as many admirers as readers, and is almost the only critic whom envy has not presumed to attack. Baillet, however, speaks of his correction of *Greek* and Latin passages. I have not observed any of the former in the Adversaria: the book, if I am not mistaken, relates wholly to Latin criticism. Muretus calls Turnebus, ' Homo immensa quadam doc-

trinæ copia instructus, sed interdum nimis propere, et nimis cupidè amplexari solitus est ea quæ in mentem venerant.' Variæ Lectiones, l. x. c. 18. Muretus as usual with critics, *vineta cædit sua:* the same charge might be brought against himself.

[d] Petrus Victorius longæva ætate id consecutus est, ut literas in Italia renascentes et pæne extinctas viderit. Thuanus ad ann. 1585, apud Blount.

of Scaliger, who says that there is less of valuable matter in
the whole work than in one book of the Adversaria of Turnebus.[e] Scaliger, however, had previously spoken in high
terms of Victorius: there had been afterwards, as he admits,
some ill-will between them; and the tongue or pen of this
great scholar was never guided by candour towards an opponent. I am not acquainted with the Variæ Lectiones of Victorius except through my authorities.

7. The same title was given to a similar miscellany by
Marc Antony Muretus, a native of Limoges. The
first part of this, containing eight books, was pub-   Muretus.
lished in 1559, seven more books in 1586, the last four in
1600. This great classical scholar of the sixteenth century
found in the eighteenth one well worthy to be his editor,
Ruhnkenius of Leyden, who has called the Variæ Lectiones
of Muretus 'a work worthy of Phidias;' an expression
rather amusingly characteristic of the value which verbal
critics set upon their labours. This book of Muretus contains only miscellaneous illustrations of passages which
might seem obscure, in the manner of those we have already
mentioned. Sometimes he mingles conjectural criticisms;
and in many chapters only points out parallel passages, or
relates incidentally some classical story. His emendations
are frequently good and certain, though at other times we may
justly think him too bold.[f] Muretus is read with far more
pleasure than Turnebus; his illustrations relate more to the
attractive parts of Latin criticism, and may be compared to
the miscellaneous remarks of Jortin.[g] But in depth of eru-

---

[e] Scaligerana Secunda.

[f] The following will serve as an instance. In the speech of Galgacus
(Taciti vita Agricolæ), instead of 'libertatem non in præsentia laturi,' which
indeed is unintelligible enough, he would
read, 'in libertatem, non in populi Romani servitium nati.' Such a conjecture
would not be endured in the present state
of criticism. Muretus, however, settles
it in the current style; vulgus quid probet, quid non probet, nunquam laboravi.

[g] The following titles of chapters, from
the eighth book of the Variæ Lectiones,
will show the agreeable diversity of
Muretus's illustrations:—

1. Comparison of poets to bees, by
Pindar, Horace, Lucretius. Line of
Horace—

Necte meo Lamiæ coronam;

illustrated by Euripides.

2. A passage in Aristotle's Rhetoric, lib. ii., explained differently
from P. Victorius.

3. Comparison of a passage in the
Phædrus of Plato, with Cicero's translation.

4. Passage in the Apologia Socratis,
corrected and explained.

5. Line in Virgil, shown to be imitated from Homer.

dition he is probably much below the Parisian professor. Muretus seems to take pleasure in censuring Victorius.

8. Turnebus, Victorius, Muretus, with two who have been Gruter's mentioned in the first part of this volume, Cœlius Thesaurus Criticus. Rhodiginus and Alexander ab Alexandro, may be reckoned the chief contributors to this general work of literary criticism in the sixteenth century. But there were many more, and some of considerable merit, whom we must pass over. At the beginning of the next century, Gruter collected the labours of preceding critics in six very thick and closely printed volumes, to which Paræus, in 1623, added a seventh, entitled 'Lampas, sive Fax Liberalium Artium,' but more commonly called Thesaurus Criticus. A small portion of these belong to the fifteenth century, but none extend beyond the following. Most of the numerous treatises in this ample collection belong to the class of Adversaria, or miscellaneous remarks. Though not so studiously concise as those of Turnebus, each of these is generally contained in a page or two, and their multitude is consequently immense. Those who now by glancing at a note obtain the result of the patient diligence of these men, should feel some respect for their names, and some admiration for their acuteness and strength of memory. They had to collate the

---

6. Slips of memory in P. Victorius, noticed.

7. Passage in Aristotle's Rhetoric explained from his Metaphysics.

8. Another passage in the same book explained.

9. Passage in Cicero pro Rabirio, corrected.

10. Imitation of Æschines in two passages of Cicero's 3rd Catilinarian oration.

11. Imitation of Æschines and Demosthenes in two passages of Cicero's Declamation against Sallust. [Not genuine.]

12. Inficetus is the right word, not infacetus.

13. Passage in 5th book of Aristotle's Ethics, corrected.

14. The word διαψευδεσθαι, in the 2nd book of Aristotle's Rhetoric, not rightly explained by Victorius.

15. The word Asinus, in Catullus (Carm. 95), does not signify an ass,

but a mill-stone.

16. Lines of Euripides, ill-translated by Cicero.

17. Passage in Cicero's Epistles misunderstood by Politian and Victorius.

18. Passage in the Phædrus explained.

19. Difference between accusation and invective, illustrated from Demosthenes and Cicero.

20. Imitation of Æschines by Cicero. Two passages of Livy amended.

21. Mulieres eruditas plerumque libidinosas esse, from Juvenal and Euripides.

22. Nobleness of character displayed by Iphicrates,

23. That Hercules was a physician, who cured Alcestis when given over.

24. Cruelty of king Dejotarus, related from Plutarch.

25. Humane law of the Persians.

whole of antiquity, they plunged into depths which the indolence of modern philology, screening itself under the garb
of fastidiousness, affects to deem unworthy to be explored,
and thought themselves bound to become lawyers, physicians,
historians, artists, agriculturists, to elucidate the difficulties
which ancient writers present. It may be doubted also,
whether our more recent editions of the classics have preserved all the important materials which the indefatigable
exertions of the men of the sixteenth century accumulated.
In the present state of philology, there is incomparably more
knowledge of grammatical niceties, at least in the Greek
language, than they possessed, and more critical acuteness
perhaps in correction, though in this they were not always
deficient; but for the exegetical part of criticism—the interpretation and illustration of passages, not corrupt, but
obscure—we may not be wrong in suspecting that more has
been lost than added in the eighteenth and present centuries
to the *savans in us,* as the French affect to call them, whom
we find in the bulky and forgotten volumes of Gruter.

9. Another and more numerous class of those who devoted
themselves to the same labour, were the editors of   Editions
Greek and Roman authors. And here again it is   of Greek
and Latin
impossible to do more than mention a few, who   authors.
seem, in the judgment of the best scholars, to stand above
their contemporaries. The early translations of Greek,
made in the fifteenth century, and generally very defective
through the slight knowledge of the language that even the
best scholars then possessed, were replaced by others more
exact: the versions of Xenophon by Leunclavius, of Plutarch
by Xylander, of Demosthenes by Wolf, of Euripides and Aristides by Canter, are greatly esteemed. Of the first, Huet says,
that he omits or perverts nothing, his Latin often answering
to the Greek, word for word, and preserving the construction
and arrangement, so that we find the original author complete, yet with a purity of idiom, and a free and natural air,
not often met with.[h]   Stephens, however, according to
Scaliger, did not highly esteem the learning of Leunclavius.[i] France, Germany, and the Low Countries, beside Basle

---

[h] Baillet. Blount. Niceron, vol. xxvi.   [i] Scaligerana Secunda.

and Geneva, were the prolific parents of new editions, in
many cases very copiously illustrated by erudite commentaries.

10. The Tacitus of Lipsius is his best work, in the opinion
of Scaliger and in his own. So great a master was
he of this favourite author, that he offered to repeat
any passage with a dagger at his breast, to be used against
him on a failure of memory.[k] Lipsius, after residing several
years at Leyden, in the profession of the reformed religion,
went to Louvain, and discredited himself by writing in
favour of the legendary miracles of that country, losing
sight of all his critical sagacity. The Protestants treated
his desertion and these later writings with a contempt which
has perhaps sometimes been extended to his productions of a
superior character. The article on Lipsius, in Bayle, betrays
some of this spirit; and it appears in other Protestants,
especially Dutch critics. Hence they undervalue his Greek
learning, as if he had not been able to read the language,
and impute plagiarism, when there seems to be little ground
for the charge. Casaubon admits that Lipsius has translated
Polybius better than his predecessors, though he does not
rate his Greek knowledge very high.[m]

11. Acidalius, whose premature death robbed philological
literature of one from whom much had been expected,[n] Paulus
Manutius, and Petrus Victorius, are to be named with honour
for the criticism of Latin authors, and the Lucretius of
Giffen or Giphanius, published at Antwerp, 1566, is still esteemed.[o] But we may select the Horace of Lambinus
as a conspicuous testimony to the classical learning
of this age. It appeared in 1561. In this he claims to have
amended the text, by the help of ten manuscripts, most of
them found by him in Italy, whither he had gone in the
suite of Cardinal Tournon. He had previously made large
collections for the illustration of Horace, from the Greek

Side notes: Tacitus of Lipsius. Horace of Lambinus.

[k] Niceron, xxiv. 119.

[m] Casaub. Epist. xxi. A long and
elaborate critique on Lipsius will be
found in Baillet, vol. ii. (4to. edit.), art.
437. See also Blount, Bayle, and
Niceron.

[n] The notes of Acidalius (who died
at the age of 28, in 1595) on Tacitus,
Plautus, and other Latin authors, are
much esteemed. He is a bold corrector
of the text. The Biographie universelle has a better article than that in the
34th volume of Niceron.

[o] Biogr. univ.

philosophers and poets, from Athenæus, Stobæus, and Pausanias, and other sources with which the early interpreters had been less familiar. Those commentators, however, among whom Hermannus Figulus, Badius Ascensius, and Antonius Mancinellus, as well as some who had confined themselves to the Ars Poetica, namely, Grisolius, Achilles Statius (in his real name Estaço, one of the few good scholars of Portugal), and Luisinius, are the most considerable, had not left unreaped a very abundant harvest of mere explanation. But Lambinus contributed much to a more elegant criticism, by pointing out parallel passages, and by displaying the true spirit and feeling of his author. The text acquired a new aspect, we may almost say, in the hands of Lambinus, at least when we compare it with the edition of Landino in 1482; but some of the gross errors in this had been corrected by intermediate editors. It may be observed, that he had far less assistance from prior commentators in the Satires and Epistles than in the Odes. Lambinus, who became professor of Greek at Paris in 1561, is known also by his editions of Demosthenes, of Lucretius, and of Cicero.[p] That of Plautus is in less esteem. He has been reproached with a prolixity and tediousness, which has naturalised the verb *lambiner* in the French language. But this imputation is not, in my opinion, applicable to his commentary upon Horace, which I should rather characterise as concise. It is always pertinent and full of matter. Another charge against Lambinus is for rashness in conjectural[q]

---

[p] This edition by Lambinus is said to mark the beginning of one of the seven ages in which those of the great Roman orator have been arranged. The first comprehends the early editions of separate works. The second begins with the earliest entire edition, that of Milan, in 1498. The third is dated from the first edition which contains copious notes, that of Venice, by Petrus Victorius, in 1534. The fourth, from the more extensive annotations given not long afterwards by Paulus Manutius. The fifth, as has just been said, from this edition by Lambinus, in 1566, which has been thought too rash in correction of the text. A sixth epoch was made by Gruter, in 1618; and this period is reckoned to comprehend most editions of that and the succeeding century; for the seventh and last age dates, it seems, only from the edition of Ernesti, in 1774. Biogr. univ. art. Cicero. See Blount, for discrepant opinions expressed by the critics about the general merits of Lambinus.

[q] Henry Stephens says that no one had been so audacious in altering the text by conjecture as Lambinus. In Manutio non tantam quantam in Lambino audaciam, sed valde tamen periculosam et citam. Maittaire, Vitæ Stephanorum, p. 401. It will be seen that Scaliger finds exactly the same fault with Stephens himself.

emendation, no unusual failing of ingenious and spirited editors.

12. Cruquius (de Crusques) of Ypres, having the advantage of several new manuscripts of Horace, which he dis-
Of Cruquius. covered in a convent at Ghent, published an edition with many notes of his own, besides an abundant commentary, collected from the glosses he found in his manuscripts, usually styled the Scholiast of Cruquius. The Odes appeared at Bruges, 1565; the Epodes at Antwerp, 1569; the Satires in 1575: the whole together was first published in 1578. But the Scholiast is found in no edition of Cruquius's Horace before 1595.[r] Cruquius appears to me inferior as a critic to Lambinus; and borrowing much from him as well as Turnebus, seldom names him except for censure. An edition of Horace at Basle, in 1580, sometimes called that of the forty commentators, including a very few before the extinction of letters, is interesting in philological history, by the light it throws on the state of criticism in the earlier part of the century, for it is remarkable that Lambinus is not included in the number, and it will, I think, confirm what has been said above in favour of those older critics.

13. Henry Stephens, thus better known among us than by
Henry Ste- his real surname Etienne, the most illustrious (if in-
phens. deed he surpassed his father) of a family of great printers, began his labours at Paris in 1554, with the princeps editio of Anacreon.[s] He had been educated in that city under Danes, Toussain, and Turnebus;[t] and, though equally learned in both languages, devoted himself to Greek, as being more neglected than Latin.[u] The press of Stephens

***

[r] Biogr. univ.

[s] Almeloveen, Vitæ Stephanorum, p. 60. Maittaire, p. 200. An excellent life of Henry Stephens, as well as others of the rest of his family, was written by Maittaire, but which does not supersede those formerly published by Almeloveen. These together are among the best illustrations of the philological history of the 16th century that we possess. They have been abridged, with some new matter, by Mr. Gresswell, in his Early History of the Parisian Greek Press.

[t] Almeloveen, p. 70. His father

made him learn Greek before he had acquired Latin. Maittaire, p. 198.

[u] The life of Stephens in the 36th volume of Niceron is long and useful. That in the Biographie universelle is not bad, but enumerates few editions published by this most laborious scholar, and thus reduces the number of his works to twenty-six. Huet says (whom I quote from Blount) that Stephens may be called 'The Translator par excellence;' such is his diligence and accuracy, so happy his skill in giving the character of his author, so great his perspicuity and elegance.

might be called the central point of illumination to Europe. In the year 1557 alone, he published, as Maittaire observes, more editions of ancient authors than would have been sufficient to make the reputation of another scholar. His publications, as enumerated by Niceron (I have not counted them in Maittaire), amount to 103, of which by far the greater part are classical editions, more valuable than his original works. Baillet says of Henry Stephens, that he was second only to Budæus in Greek learning, though he seems to put Turnebus and Camerarius nearly on the same level. But perhaps the majority of scholars would think him superior, on the whole, to all the three ; and certainly Turnebus, whose Adversaria are confined to Latin interpretation, whatever renown he might deserve by his oral lectures, has left nothing that could warrant our assigning him an equal place.[x] Scaliger, however, accuses Henry Stephens of spoiling all the authors he edited by wrong alterations of the text.[y] This charge is by no means unfrequently brought against the critics of this age.

14. The year 1572 is an epoch in Greek literature, by the publication of Stephens's Thesaurus. A lexicon had been published at Basle in 1562, by Robert Constantin, who, though he made use of that famous press, lived at Caen, of which he was a native. Scaliger speaks in a disparaging tone both of Constantin and his lexicon. But its general reputation has been much higher. A modern critic observes, that ' a very great proportion of the explanations

Lexicon of Constantin.

---

[x] [The works of Turnebus, 3 vols. folio, bound in one, contain, 1. his commentaries on Latin authors; 2. his translations from Greek; 3. his miscellaneous writings, including the Adversaria. Turnebus did comparatively little for Greek, except in the way of translation. —1842.]

[y] Omnes quotquot edidit, editve libros, etiam meos, suo arbitrio jam corrupit et deinceps corrumpet. Scalig. Prima, p. 96. Against this sharp, and perhaps rash, judgment, we may set that of Maittaire, a competent scholar, though not like Scaliger, and without his arrogance and scorn of the world. Henrici editiones ideo miror, quod eas, quam

posset accuratissime aut ipse aut per alios, quos complures noverat, viros eruditos, ad omnium tum manuscriptorum tum impressorum codicum fidem, non sine maximo delectu et suo (quo maximè in Græcis præsertim pollebat) aliorumque judicio elaboravit. Vitæ Stephanorum, t. ii. p. 284. No man perhaps ever published so many editions as Stephens; nor was any other printer of so much use to letters; for he knew much more than the Aldi or the Juntas. Yet he had planned many more publications, as Maittaire has collected from what he has dropped in various places. p. 469.

and authorities in Stephens's Thesaurus are borrowed from
it.'ᶻ   We must presume that this applies to the first edition ;
for the second, enlarged by Æmilius Portus, which is more
common, did not appear till 1591.ᵃ 'The principal defects
of Constantin,' it is added, ' are first, the confused and ill-
digested arrangement of the interpretation of words, and,
secondly, the absence of all distinction between primatives
and derivatives.' It appears by a Greek letter of Constantin,
prefixed to the first edition, that he had been assisted in his
labours by Gesner, Henry Stephens, Turnebus, Camerarius,
and other learned contemporaries. He gives his authorities,
if not so much as we should desire, very far more than the
editors of the former Basle lexicon. This lexicon, as was
mentioned in another place, is extremely defective and full
of errors, though a letter of Grynæus, prefixed to the edition
of 1539, is nothing but a strain of unqualified eulogy, little
warranted by the suffrage of later scholars. I found, however, on a loose calculation, the number of words in this
edition to be not much less than 50,000.ᵇ

ᶻ Quarterly Review, vol. xxvii.

ᵃ The first edition of this Lexicon
sometimes bears the name of Crespin,
the printer at Basle ; and both Baillet
and Bayle have fallen into the mistake
of believing that there were two different works. See Niceron, vol. xxvii.

ᵇ Henry Stephens in an epistle, De
suæ Typographiæ statu ad quosdam
amicos, gives an account of his own
labours on the Thesaurus. The following passage on the earlier lexicons may
be worth reading :—Iis quæ circumfe-
runtur lexicis Græco-Latinis primam
imposuit manum monachus quidam,
frater Johannes Crastonus, Placentinus,
Carmelitanus ; sed cum is jejunis expo-
sitionibus, in quibus vernaculo etiam
sermone interdum, id est Italico, utitur,
contentus fuisset, perfunctoriè item con-
structiones verborum indicasset, nullos
autorum locos proferens ex quibus illæ
pariter et significationes cognosci pos-
sent ; multi postea certatim multa hinc
inde sine ullo delectu ac judicio excerpta
inseruerunt. Donec tandem indoctis
typographis de augenda lexicorum mole
inter se certantibus, et præmia iis qui id
præstarent proponentibus, quæ jejunæ,
et, si ita loqui licet, macilentæ antea

erant expositiones, adeo pingues et
crassæ redditæ sunt, ut in illis passim
nihil aliud quam Bœoticam suem agnos-
camus. Nam pauca ex Budæo, aliisque
idoneis autoribus, et ea quidem parum
fideliter descripta, utpote parum intel-
lecta, multa contra ex Lapo Florentino,
Leonardo Aretino, aliisque ejusdem
farinæ interpretibus, ut s¹miles habent
labra lactucas, in opus illud transtule-
runt. Ex iis quidem certe locis in
quorum interpretatione felix fuit Laurentius Valla, paucissimos protulerunt ;
sed pro perverso suo judicio, perversis-
simas quasque ejus interpretationes,
quales prope innumeras a me annotatas
in Latinis Herodoti et Thucydidis edi-
tionibus videbis, delegerunt egregii illi
lexicorum seu consarcinatores seu inter-
polatores, quibus, tamquam gemmis,
illa insignirent. Quod si non quam
multa, sed duntaxat quam multorum
generum errata ibi sint, commemorare
velim, merito certe exclamabo, τί πρῶ-
τον, τί δ᾿ ἔπειτα, τι δ᾿ ὑστάτιον καταλέξω ;
vix enim ullum vitii genus posse a nobis
cogitari aut fingi existimo, cujus ibi
aliquod exemplum non extat. p. 156.
He produces afterwards some gross instances of error.

15. Henry Stephens had devoted twelve years of his laborious life to his own immense work, large materials Thesaurus for which had been collected by his father. In com- phens; prehensive and copious interpretation of words it not only left far behind every earlier dictionary, but is still the single Greek lexicon; one which some have ventured to abridge or enlarge, but none have presumed to supersede. Its arrangement, as is perhaps scarce necessary to say, is not according to an alphabetical, but a radical order; that is, the supposed roots following each other alphabetically, every derivative or compound, of whatever initial letter, is placed after the primary word. This method is certainly not very convenient to the uninformed reader; and perhaps, even with a view to the scientific knowledge of the language, it should have been deferred for a more advanced stage of etymological learning. The Thesaurus embodies the critical writings of Budæus and Camerarius, with whatever else had been contributed by the Greek exiles of the preceding age and by their learned disciples. Much, no doubt, has since been added to what we find in the Thesaurus of Stephens, as to the nicety of idiom and syntax, or to the principles of formation of words, but not, perhaps, in copiousness of explanation, which is the proper object of a dictionary. 'The leading defects conspicuous in Stephens,' it is said by the critic already quoted, 'are inaccurate or falsified quotations, the deficiency of several thousand words, and a wrong classification both of primitives and derivatives. At the same time, we ought rather to be surprised that, under existing disadvantages, he accomplished so much even in this last department, than that he left so much undone.'

16. It has been questioned among bibliographers, whether there are two editions of the Thesarus; the first in abridged by 1572, the second without a date, and probably after Scapula. 1580. The affirmative seems to be sufficiently proved.[c] The sale, however, of so voluminous and expensive a work did not

---

[c] Niceron (vol. xxvi.) contends that the supposed second edition differs only by a change in the titlepage, wherein we find rather an unhappy attempt at wit, in the following distich aimed at Scapula:—

Quidam επιτεμνων me capulo tenus abdidit ensem:
Æger eram a scapulis; sanus at huc redeo.

But it seems that Stephens, in his Palæstra de Justi Lipsii Latinitate, mentions this second edition, which is said

indemnify its author; and it has often been complained of, that Scapula, who had been employed under Stephens, injured his superior by the publication of his well-known abridgment in 1579. The fact, however, that Scapula had possessed this advantage rests on little evidence, and his preface, if it were true, would be the highest degree of effrontery :[d] it was natural that some one would abridge so voluminous a lexicon. Literature, at least, owes an obligation to Scapula.[e] The temper of Henry Stephens, restless and uncertain, was not likely to retain riches : he passed several years in wandering over Europe, and having wasted a considerable fortune amassed by his father, died in a public hospital at Lyons, in 1598,[f] 'opibus,' says his biographer, 'atque etiam ingenio destitutus in nosocomio.'

---

by those who have examined it to have fewer typographical errors than the other, though it is admitted that the leaves might be intermixed without inconvenience, so close is the resemblance. Vid. Maittaire, p. 356–360. Brunet, Man. du Libr. Gresswell, vol. ii. p. 289.

[d] [Incidi forte in Thesaurum ab Henrico Stephano conscriptum. Gresswell's Greek Press, ii. 284.—1842.]

[e] Maittaire says that Scapula's lexicon is as perfidious to the reader as its author was to his master, and that Dr. Busby would not suffer his boys to use it. p. 358. But this has hardly been the general opinion. See Quarterly Review, *ubi suprà*.

[f] Casaubon writes frequently to Scaliger about the strange behaviour of his father-in-law, and complains that he had not even leave to look at the books in the latter's library, which he himself scarce ever visited. Nôsti hominem, nôsti mores, nôsti quid apud eum possim, hoc est, quam nihil possim, qui videtur in suam perniciem conspirâsse. Epist. 21. And, still more severely, Epist. 41. Nam noster, etsi vivens valensque, pridem numero hominum, certe doctorum, eximi meruit; ea est illius inhumanitas, et quod invitus dico, delirium; qui libros quoslibet veteres, ut Indici gryphi aurum, aliis invidet, sibi perire sinit, sed quid ille habeat aut non, juxta scio ego cum ignavissimo. After Stephens's death, he wrote in kinder terms than he had done before; but regretting some publications, by which the

editor of Casaubon's letters thinks he might mean the Apologie pour Hérodote, and the Palæstra de Justi Lipsii Latinitate; the former of which, a very well-known book, contains a spirited attack on the Romish priesthood, but with less regard either for truth or decorum in the selection of his stories than became the character of Stephens; and the latter is of little pertinence to its avowed subject. Henry Stephens had long been subject to a disorder natural enough to laborious men, quædam actionum consuetarum satietas et fastidium, Maittaire, p. 248.

Robert Stephens had carried with him to Geneva, in 1550, the punches of his types, made at the expense of Francis I., supposing that they were a gift of the king. On the death, however, of Henry Stephens, they were claimed by Henry IV., and the senate of Geneva restored them. They had been pledged for 400 crowns, and Casaubon complains as of a great injury, that the estate of Stephens was made answerable to the creditor when the pledge was given up to the king of France. See Le Clerk's remarks on this in Bibliothèque choisie, vol. xix. p. 219. Also a vindication of Stephens by Maittaire from the charge of having stolen them (Vitæ Stephanorum, i. 34); and again in Gresswell's Parisian Press, i. 399. He seems above the suspicion of theft; but whether he had just cause to think the punches were his own, it is now impossible to decide.

17. The Hellenismus of Angelus Caninius, a native of the Milanese, is merely a grammar. Tanaquil Faber Hellenismus prefers it not only to that of Clenardus, but to all of Caninius. which existed even in his own time. It was published at Paris in 1555. Those who do not express themselves so strongly, place him above his predecessors. Caninius is much fuller than Clenardus; the edition by Crenius (Leyden, 1700) containing 380 pages. The syntax is very scanty; but Caninius was well conversant with the mutations of words, and is diligent in noting the differences of dialects, in which he has been thought to excel. He was acquainted with the digamma, and with its Latin form. I will take this opportunity of observing that the Greek grammar of Vergara's Vergara, mentioned in the first part of this work grammar. (p. 339), and of which I now possess the Paris edition of 1557, printed by William Morel (ad Complutensem editionem excusum et restitutum), appears superior to those of Clenarnus or Varenius. This book is doubtless very scarce; it is plain that Tanaquil Faber, Baillet, Morhof, and, I should add, Nicolas Antonio, had never seen it,[g] nor is it mentioned by Brunet or Watts.[h] There is, however, a copy in the British Museum. Scaliger says that it is very good, and that Caninius has borrowed from it the best parts.[i] Vergara had, of course, profited by the commentaries of Budæus, the great source of Greek philology in western Europe; but he displays, as far as I can judge by recollection more than comparison, an ampler knowledge of the rules of Greek than any of his other contemporaries. This grammar contains 438 pages, more than 100 of which are given to the syntax. A small grammar by Nunnez, or Pincianus, published at Valencia in 1555, seems chiefly borrowed from Clenardus or Vergara.

---

[g] Blount, Baillet.

[h] Antonio says it was printed at Alcalá, 1573; deinde Parisiis, 1550. The first is of course a false print; if the second is not so likewise, he had never seen the book.

[i] Scaligerana Secunda. F. Vergara, Espagnol, a composé une bonne grammaire grecque, mais Caninius a pris tout le meilleur de tous, et a mis du sien aussi quelque chose dans son Hellenismus. This, as Bayle truly observes, reduces the eulogies Scaliger has elsewhere given Caninius to very little. Scaliger's loose expressions are not of much value. Yet he who had seen Vergara's grammar might better know what was original in others than Tanaquil Faber, who had never seen it.

18. Peter Ramus, in 1557, gave a fresh proof of his
Grammars of acuteness and originality, by publishing a Greek
Ramus and
Sylburgius. grammar, with many important variances from his
precursors. Scaliger speaks of it with little respect; but he
is habitually contemptuous towards all but his immediate
friends.[k] Lancelot, author of the Port Royal grammar,
praises highly that of Ramus, though he reckons it too
intricate. This grammar I have not seen in its original
state, but Sylburgius published one in 1582, which he professes to have taken from the last edition of the Ramean
grammar. It has been said that Laurence Rhodomann was
the first who substituted the partition of the declensions of
Greek nouns into three for that of Clenardus, who introduced or retained the prolix and unphilosophical division
into ten.[m] But Ramus is clearly entitled to this credit. It
would be doubted whether he is equally to be praised, as he
certainly has not been equally followed, in making no distinction of conjugations, nor separating the verbs in μι
from those in ω, on the ground that their general flexion is
the same. Much has been added to this grammar by Sylburgius himself, a man in the first rank of Greek scholars;

---

[k] Scaligerana. Casaubon, it must be owned, who had more candour than Scaliger, speaks equally ill of the grammar of Ramus. Epist. 878.

[m] Morhof, l. iv. c. 6. Preface to translation of Matthiæ's Greek Grammar. The learned author of this preface has not alluded to Ramus, and though he praises Sylburgius for his improvements in the mode of treating grammar, seems unacquainted with that work which I mention in the text. Two editions of it are in the British Museum, 1582 and 1600; but, upon comparison, I believe that there is no difference between them.

The best of these grammars of the 16th century bear no sort of comparison with those which have been latterly published in Germany. And it seems strange at first sight, that the old scholars, such as Budæus, Erasmus, Camerarius, and many more, should have written Greek, which they were fond of doing, much better than from their great ignorance of many fundamental rules of syntax we could have anticipated. But reading continually and thinking in Greek, they found comparative accuracy by a secret tact, and by continual imitation of what they read. Language is always a mosaic work, made up of associated fragments, not of separate molecules; we repeat, not the simplest words, but the phrases and even the sentences we have caught from others. Budæus wrote Greek without knowing its grammar, that is, without a distinct notion of moods or tenses, as men speak their own language tolerably well without having ever attended to a grammatical rule. Still many faults must be found in such writing on a close inspection. The case was partly the same in Latin during the middle ages, except that Latin was at that time better understood than Greek was in the sixteenth century; not that so many words were known, but those who wrote it best had more correct notions of the grammar.

'especially,' as he tells us, in 'the latter books, so that it may be called rather a supplement than an abridgment of the grammar of Ramus.' The syntax in this grammar is much better than in Clenardus, from whom some have erroneously supposed Sylburgius to have borrowed; but I have not compared him with Vergara.[n] The Greek grammar of Sanctius is praised by Lancelot; yet from what he tells us of it, we may infer that Sanctius, though a great master of Latin, being comparatively unlearned in Greek, displayed such temerity in his hypotheses as to fall into very great errors. The first edition was printed at Antwerp in 1581.

19. A few more books of a grammatical nature, falling within the present period, may be found in Morhof, Baillet, and the bibliographical collections; but neither in number nor importance do they deserve much notice.[o] In a more miscellaneous philology, the Commentaries of Camerarius, 1551, are superior to any publication of the kind since that of Budæus in 1529. The Novæ Lectiones of William Canter, though the work of a very young man, deserve to be mentioned as almost the first effort of an art which has done much for ancient literature—that of restoring a corrupt text, through conjecture, not loose and empirical, but guided by a skilful sagacity, and upon principles which we may without impropriety not only call scientific, but approximating sometimes to the logic of the Novum Organum. The earlier critics, not always possessed of many manuscripts, had recourse, more indeed in Latin than in Greek, to conjectural emendation; the prejudice against which, often carried too far by those who are not sufficiently aware of the enormous ignorance and carelessness which ordinary manuscripts display, has also been heightened by the random and sometimes very improbable guesses of editors. Canter, be-

(margin note: Camerarius, Canter, Robortellus.)

---

[n] Vossius says of the grammarians in general, ex quibus doctrinæ et industriæ laudem maxime mihi meruisse videntur Angelus Caninius et Fridericus Sylburgius. Aristarchus, p. 6. It is said that, in his own grammar, which is on the basis of Clenardus, Vossius added little to what he had taken from the two former. Baillet, in Caninio.

[o] In the British Museum is a book by one Guillon, of whom I find no account in biography, called Gnomon, on the quantity of Greek syllables. This seems to be the earliest work of the kind; and he professes himself to write against those who think 'quidvis licere in quantitate syllabarum.' It is printed at Paris, 1556; and it appears by Watts that there are other editions.

sides the practice he showed in his Novæ Lectiones, laid
down the principles of his theory in a 'Syntagma de Ratione
emendandi Græcos Auctores,' reprinted in the second volume
of Jebb's edition of Aristides.　He here shows what letters are
apt to be changed into others by error of transcription, or
through a source not perhaps quite so obvious—the uniform
manner of pronouncing several vowels and diphthongs among
the later Greeks, which they were thus led to confound,
especially when a copyist wrote from dictation.　But besides
these corruptions, it appears by the instances Canter gives,
that almost any letters are liable to be changed into almost
any others.　The abbreviations of copyists are also great
causes of corruption, and require to be known by those who
would restore the text.　Canter, however, was not altogether
the founder of this school of criticism.　Robortellus, whose
vanity and rude contempt of one so much superior to himself
as Sigonius, has perhaps caused his own real learning to be
undervalued, had already written a treatise entitled 'De Arte
sive Ratione corrigendi Antiquorum Libros Disputatio;' in
which he claims to be the first who devised this art, 'nunc
primum à me excogitata.'　It is not a bad work, though
probably rather superficial according to our present views.
He points out the general characters of manuscripts, and the
different styles of handwriting; after which he proceeds to
the rules of conjecture, making good remarks on the causes
of corruption and consequent means of restoration.　It is
published in the second volume of Gruter's Thesaurus Criticus.　Robortellus, however, does not advert to Greek manuscripts, a field upon which Canter first entered.　The Novæ
Lectiones of William Canter are not to be confounded with
the Variæ Lectiones of his brother Theodore, a respectable
but less eminent scholar.　Canter, it may be added, was the
first, according to Boissonade, who in his edition of Euripides, restored some sort of order and measure to the
choruses.[p]

---

[p] Biogr. univ. The Life of Canter
in Melchior Adam is one of the best his
collection contains; it seems to be copied
from one by Miræus.　Canter was a man
of great moral as well as literary excellence; the account of his studies and
mode of life in this biography is very
interesting.　The author of it dwells
justly on Canter's skill in exploring the
text of manuscripts, and in observing
the variations of orthography.　See also
Blount, Baillet, Niceron, vol. xxix., and
Chalmers.

20. Sylburgius, whose grammar has been already praised, was of great use to Stephens in compiling the Thesaurus; it has even been said, but perhaps with Editions by Sylburgius. German partiality, that the greater part of its value is due to him.[q] The editions of Sylburgius, especially those of Aristotle and Dionysius of Halicarnassus, are among the best of that age; none, indeed, containing the entire works of the Stagirite, is equally esteemed.[r] He had never risen above the station of a schoolmaster in small German towns, till he relinquished the employment for that of superintendent of classical editions in the press of Wechel, and afterwards in that of Commelin. But the death of this humble and laborious man, in 1596, was deplored by Casaubon as one of the heaviest blows that learning could have sustained.

21. Michael Neander, a disciple of Melanchthon and Camerarius, who became rector of a flourishing school at Isfeld in Thuringia soon after 1550, and Neander. remained there till his death in 1595, was certainly much inferior to Sylburgius; yet to him Germany was chiefly indebted for keeping alive, in the general course of study, some little taste for Grecian literature, which towards the end of the century was rapidly declining. The 'Erotemata Græcæ Linguæ' of Neander, according to Eichhorn, drove the earlier grammars out of use in the schools.[s] But the publications of Neander appear to be little more than such

---

[q] Melchior Adam, p. 193. In the article of the Quarterly Review, several times already quoted, it is said that the Thesaurus 'bears much plainer marks of the sagacity and erudition of Sylburgius than of the desultory and hasty studies of his master, than whom he was more clear-sighted;' a compliment at the expense of Stephens, not perhaps easily reconcilable with the eulogy a little before passed by the reviewer on the latter, as the greatest of Greek scholars except Casaubon. Stephens says of himself, quem habuit (Sylburgius), novo quodam more dominum simul ac præceptorem, quod ille beneficium pro sua ingenuitate agnoscit (apud Maittaire, p. 421). But it has been remarked that Stephens was not equally ingenuous, and never acknowledges any obligation to Sylburgius, p. 583. Scaliger says, Stephanus non solus fecit Thesaurum; plusieurs y ont mis la main; and in another place, Sylburgius a travaillé au Trésor de H. Etienne. But it is impossible for us to apportion the disciple's share in this great work; which might be more than Stephens owned, and less than the Germans have claimed. Niceron, which is remarkable, has no life of Sylburgius.

[r] The Aristotle of Sylburgius is properly a series of editions of that philosopher's separate works, published from 1584 to 1596. It is in great request when found complete, which is rarely the case. It has no Latin translation.

[s] Geschichte der Cultur, iii. 277.

extracts from the Greek writers as he thought would be useful in education.[t] Several of them are gnomologies, or collections of moral sentences from the poets; a species of compilation not uncommon in the sixteenth and seventeenth centuries, but neither exhibiting much learning nor favourable to the acquisition of a true feeling for ancient poetry. The Thesaurus of Basilius Faber, another work of the same class, published in 1571, is reckoned by Eichhorn among the most valuable school-books of this period, and continued to be used and reprinted for two hundred years.[u]

22. Conrad Gesner belongs almost equally to the earlier and later periods of the sixteenth century. En-
Gesner. dowed with unwearied diligence, and with a mind capacious of omnifarious erudition, he was probably the most comprehensive scholar of the age. Some of his writings have been mentioned in another place. His ' Mithridates, sive de Differentiis Linguarum,' is the earliest effort on a great scale to arrange the various languages of mankind by their origin and analogies. He was deeply versed in Greek literature, and especially in the medical and physical writers; but he did not confine himself to that province. It may be noticed here, that in his Stobæus, published in 1543, Gesner first printed Greek and Latin in double columns.[x] He was followed by Turnebus, in an edition of Aristotle's Ethics (Paris, 1555), and the practice became gradually general, though some sturdy scholars, such as Stephens and Sylburgius, did not comply with it. Gesner seems to have had no expectation that the Greek text would be much read, and only recommends it as useful in conjunction with the Latin.[y] Scaliger, however, deprecates so indolent a mode of study, and ascribes the decline of Greek learning to these unlucky double columns.[z]

23. In the beginning of the century, as has been shown

---

[t] Niceron, vol. xxx.

[u] Eichhorn, 274.

[x] This I give only on the authority of Chevillier, Origines de l'Imprimerie de Paris.

[y] Id. p. 240.

[z] Scalig. Secunda. Accents on Latin words, it is observed by Scaliger (in the Scaligerana Prima), were introduced within his memory; and, as he says, which would be more important, the points called comma and semicolon, of which Paulus Manutius was the inventor. But in this there must be some mistake; for the comma is frequent in books much older than any edited by Manutius.

in the first part of this volume, the prospects of classical literature in Germany seemed most auspicious. Decline of Schools and universities, the encouragement of taste in Germany. liberal princes, the instruction of distinguished professors, the formation of public libraries, had given an impulse, the progressive effects of which were manifest in every Protestant state of the empire. Nor was any diminution of this zeal and taste discernible for a few years. But after the death of Melanchthon in 1560, and of Camerarius in 1574, a literary decline commenced, slow but uniform and permanent, during which Germany had to lament a strange eclipse of that lustre which had distinguished the preceding age. This was first shown in an inferiority of style, and in a neglect of the best standards of good writing. The admiration of Melanchthon himself led in some measure to this; and to copy his manner (genus dicendi Philippicum, as it was called) was more the fashion than to have recourse to his masters, Cicero and Quintilian.[a] But this, which would have kept up a very tolerable style, gave way, not long afterwards, to a tasteless and barbarous turn of phrase, in which all feeling of propriety and elegance was lost. This has been called Apuleianismus, as if that indifferent writer of the third century had been set up for imitation, though probably it was the mere sympathy of bad taste and incorrect expression. The scholastic philosophy came back about the same time into the German universities, with all its technical jargon, and triumphed over the manes of Erasmus and Melanchthon. The disciples of Paracelsus spread their mystical rhapsodies far and wide, as much at the expense of classical taste as of sound reason. And when we add to these untoward circumstances the dogmatic and polemical theology, studious of a phraseology certainly not belonging to the Augustan age, and the necessity of writing on many other subjects almost equally incapable of being treated in good language, we cannot be much astonished that a barbarous and slovenly Latinity should become characteristic of Germany, which, even in later ages, very few of its learned men have been able to discard.[b]

---

[a] Eichhorn, iii. 268. The Germans usually said Philippus for Melanchthon.

[b] Melchior Adam, after highly praising Wolf's translation of Demosthenes,

24. In philological erudition we have seen that Germany
German long maintained her rank, if not quite equal to
learning. France, in this period, yet nearer to her than to any
third nation. We have mentioned several of the most
Greek verses distinguished; and to these we might add many
of Rhodo-
mann. names from Melchior Adam, the laborious biographer of his learned countrymen; such as Oporinus, George
Fabricius, Frischlin, and Crusius, who first taught the Romaic
Greek in Germany. One, rather more known than these,
was Laurence Rhodomann. He was the editor of several
authors; but his chief claim to a niche in the temple seems
to rest upon his Greek verses, which have generally been
esteemed superior to any of his generation. The praise does
not imply much positive excellence; for in Greek composition, and especially in verse, the best scholars of the sixteenth
century make but an indifferent figure. Rhodomann's Life
of Luther is written in Greek hexameters. It is also a
curious specimen of the bigotry of his church. He boasts
that Luther predicted the deaths of Zuingle, Carlostadt, and
Œcolampadius as the punishment of their sacramentarian
hypothesis. The lines will be found in a note,[c] and may
serve as a fair specimen of as good Greek as could perhaps
be written in that age of celebrated erudition. But some
other poems of Rhodomann, which I have not seen, are more
praised by the critics.

25. But, at the expiration of the century, few were left

---

proceeds to boast of the Greek learning
of Germany, which, rather singularly, he
seems to ascribe to this translation:
Effecit ut ante ignotus plerisque Demosthenes nunc familiariter nobiscum ver-
setur in scholis et academiis. Est sanè
quod gratulemur Germaniæ nostræ,
quod per Wolfium tantorum fluminum
eloquentiæ particeps facta est. Faten-
tur ipsi Græci, qui reliqui sunt hodie
Constantinopoli, præ cæteris eruditi, et
Christianæ religionis amantes, totum
musarum chorum, relicto Helicone, in
Germaniam transmigrâsse. (Vitæ Philosophorum.) Melchior Adam lived in
the early part of the seventeenth century, when this high character was
hardly applicable to Germany; but his
panegyric must be taken as designed for

the preceding age, in which the greater
part of his eminent men flourished.
Besides this, he is so much a compiler
that this passage may not be his own.

[c] Και τα μεν ως τετελεστο μετα χρονον, ως
μεμορητο.
ως γαρ δωδεκαμηνος ελιξ τριτος ετρεχε Φοιβου,
δη τοτε μοιρα, θεου κρυφι·ην πρησσουσα με-
νοινην,
μαντοσυναις επεθηκε θεοφραδεεσσι τελευτην
ανδρος, ος ουτιν' απρηκτον απο κραδιης βαλε
μυθον.
αμφω γαρ στυγερου πλαγξηνορε δογματος
αρχω
Οικιολαμπαδιον και Κιγκλιον εφθασεν ατη
ποτμου δακρυοεντος· ινα φριξειε και αλλος
ατρεκιης προς κεντρον αναιδεα ταρσον ιαψαι.
ουδε μεν οξυμορους Καρολοσταδιος φυγε ποι-
νας,
τον δε γαρ αντιβολων κρυερω μετα φασματι
δαιμων
εξαπινης εταραξε, και ηρπασεν ου χρεος ηεν.

besides Rhodomann of the celebrated philologers of Germany;
nor had a new race arisen to supply their place. Learning
Æmilius Portus, who taught with reputation at declines;
Heidelberg, was a native of Ferrara, whose father, a Greek
by origin, emigrated to Genoa on account of religion. The
state of literature, in a general sense, had become sensibly de-
teriorated in the empire. This was most perceptible, or perhaps only perceptible, in its most learned provinces, those
which had embraced the Reformation. In the opposite
quarter there had been little to lose, and something was
gained. In the first period of the Reformation, the Catholic
universities, governed by men whose prejudices were insuperable even by appealing to their selfishness, except in
Catholic
had kept still in the same track, educating their Germany.
students in the barbarous logic and literature of the middle
ages, careless that every method was employed in Protestant
education to develop and direct the talents of youth; and
this had given the manifest intellectual superiority, which
taught the disciples and contemporaries of the first reformers
a scorn for the stupidity and ignorance of the popish party,
somewhat exaggerated, of course, as such sentiments generally are, but dangerous above measure to its influence. It
was therefore one of the first great services which the Jesuits
performed to get possession of the universities, or to found
other seminaries for education. In these they discarded the
barbarous school-books then in use, put the rudimentary
study of the languages on a better footing, devoted themselves, for the sake of religion, to those accomplishments
which religion had hitherto disdained; and by giving a taste
for elegant literature, with as much solid and scientific
philosophy as the knowledge of the times and the prejudices
of the church would allow, both wiped away the reproach of
ignorance, and drew forth the native talents of their novices
and scholars. They taught gratuitously, which threw, however unreasonably, a sort of discredit upon salaried professors;[d] it was found that boys learned more from them in

---

[d] Mox, ubi paululum firmitatis acces-
sit, pueros sine mercede docendos et
erudiendos susceperunt; quo artificio non
vulgarem vulgi favorem emeruere, cri-
minandis præsertim aliis doctoribus,
quorum doctrina venalis esset, et scholæ
nulli sine mercede paterent, et interdum
etiam doctrina peregrina personarent.

six months than in two years under other masters; and, probably for both these reasons, even Protestants sometimes withdrew their children from the ordinary gymnasia and placed them in Jesuit colleges. No one will deny that, in their classical knowledge, particularly of the Latin language, and in the elegance with which they wrote it, the order of Jesuits might stand in competition with any scholars of Europe. In this period of the sixteenth century, though not perhaps in Germany itself, they produced several of the best writers whom it could boast.[e]

26. It is seldom that an age of critical erudition is one Philological works of Stephens. also of fine writing; the two have not perhaps a natural incompatibility with each other, but the bond-woman too often usurps the place of the free-woman, and the auxiliary science of philology controls, instead of adorning and ministering to the taste and genius of original minds. As the study of the Latin language advanced, as better editions were published, as dictionaries and books of criticism were more carefully drawn up, we naturally expect to find it written with more correctness, but not with more force and truth. The Expostulation of Henry Stephens de Latinitate Falso Suspecta, 1576, is a collection of classical authorities for words and idioms, which seem so like French, that the reader would not hesitate to condemn them. Some among these, however, are so familiar to us as good Latin, that we can hardly suspect the dictionaries not to have contained them. I have not examined any earlier edition than that of Calepin's dictionary, as enlarged by Paulus Manutius, of the date of 1579, rather after this publication by Henry Stephens; and certainly it does not appear to want these words, or to fail in sufficient authority for them.

27. In another short production by Stephens, De Latini- Style of Lipsius. tate Lipsii Palæstra, he turns into ridicule the affected style of that author, who ransacked all his stores of learning to perplex the reader. A much later writer, Scioppius, in his Judicium de Stylo Historico, points

---

Incredibile dictu est, quantum hæc cri-
minatio valuerit. Hospinian, Hist. Jesuitarum, l. ii. c. 1. fol. 84. See also
l. i. fol. 59.

[e] Ranke, ii. 32. Eichhorn, iii. 266.
The latter scarcely does justice to the
Jesuits as promoters of learning in their
way.

out several of the affected and erroneous expressions of
Lipsius. But he was the founder of a school of bad writers,
which lasted for some time, especially in Germany. Seneca
and Tacitus were the authors of antiquity whom Lipsius
strove to emulate. ' Lipsius,' says Scaliger, ' is the cause
that men have now little respect for Cicero, whose style he
esteems about as much as I do his own. He once wrote
well, but his third century of epistles is good for nothing.'[f]
But a style of point and affected conciseness will always have
its admirers, till the excess of vicious imitation disgusts the
world.[g]

28. Morhof, and several authorities quoted by Baillet,
extol the Latin Grammar of a Spaniard, Emanuel Minerva of
Alvarez, as the first in which the fancies of the Sanctius.
ancient grammarians had been laid aside. Of this work I
know nothing farther. But the Minerva of another native of
Spain, Sanchez, commonly called Sanctius, the first edition
of which appeared at Salamanca in 1587, far excelled any
grammatical treatise that had preceded it, especially as to
the rules of syntax, which he had reduced to their natural
principles, by explaining apparent anomalies. He is called
the prince of grammarians, a divine man, the Mercury
and Apollo of Spain, the father of the Latin language, the
common teacher of the learned, in the panegyrical style of
the Lipsii or Scioppii.[h] The Minerva, enlarged and corrected at different times by the most eminent scholars,
Scioppius, Perizonius, and others more recent, still retains a
leading place in philology. ' No one among those,' says

[f] Scaligerana Secunda.

[g] Miræus, quoted in Melchior Adam's
Life of Lipsius, praises his eloquence,
with contempt of those who thought
their own feeble and empty writing
like Cicero's. See also Eichhorn, iii.
299 ; Baillet, who has a long article on
the style of Lipsius and the school it
formed (Jugemens des Savans, vol. ii.
p. 192, 4to edition) ; and Blount ; also
the note M in Bayle's article on Lipsius. The following passage of Scioppius I transcribe from Blount :—'In
Justi Lipsii stylo, scriptoris ætate nostra
clarissimi, istæ apparent dotes ; acumen,

venustas, delectus, ornatus vel nimius,
cum vix quicquam proprie dictum ei
placeat, tum schemata nullo numero,
tandem verborum copia ; desunt autem
perspicuitas, puritas, æquabilitas, collo-
catio, junctura et numerus oratorius.
Itaque oratio ejus est obscura, non paucis barbarismis et solœcismis, pluribus
vero archaismis et idiotismis, innumeris
etiam neoterismis inquinata, compre-
hensio obscura, compositio fracta et in
particulas concisa, vocum similium aut
ambiguarum puerilis captatio.'

[h] Baillet.

its last editor, Bauer, 'who have written well upon grammar, has attained such reputation and even authority as the
famous Spaniard whose work we now give to the press.'
But Sanctius has been charged with too great proneness to
censure his predecessors, especially Valla, and with an excess
of novelty in his theoretical speculations.

29. The writers who in this second moiety of the sixteenth
Orations of Muretus. century appear to have been most conspicuous for
purity of style, were Muretus, Paulus Manutius,
Perpinianus, Osorius, Maphæus, to whom we may add our
own Buchanan, and perhaps Haddon. Muretus is celebrated
for his Orations, published by Aldus Manutius in 1576.
Many of these were delivered a good deal earlier. Ruhn-
Panegyric of Ruhnkenius. kenius, editor of the works of Muretus, says that
he at once eclipsed Bembo, Sadolet, and the whole
host of Ciceronians; expressing himself so perfectly in that
author's style that we should fancy ourselves to be reading him,
did not the subject betray a modern hand. 'In learning,' he
says, 'and in knowledge of the Latin language, Manutius
was not inferior to Muretus; we may even say that his zeal
in imitating Cicero was still stronger, inasmuch as he seemed
to have no other aim all his life than to bear a perfect resemblance to that model. Yet he rather followed than overtook
his master, and in this line of imitation cannot be compared
with Muretus. The reason of this was, that nature had
bestowed on Muretus the same kind of genius that she had
given to Cicero, while that of Manutius was very different.
It was from this similarity of temperament that Muretus
acquired such felicity of expression, such grace in narration,
such wit in raillery, such perception of what would gratify
the ear in the structure and cadence of his sentences. The
resemblance of natural disposition made it a spontaneous act
of Muretus to fall into the footsteps of Cicero; while, with
all the efforts of Manutius, his dissimilar genius led him
constantly away; so that we should not wonder when the
writings of one so delight us that we cannot lay them down,
while we are soon wearied with those of the other, correct
and polished as they are, on account of the painful desire of
imitation which they betray. No one, since the revival of
letters,' Ruhnkenius proceeds, 'has written Latin more cor-

rectly than Muretus; yet even in him a few inadvertencies may be discovered.[i]

30. Notwithstanding the panegyric of so excellent a scholar, I cannot feel this very close approximation of Muretus to the Ciceronian standard; and it even seems to me that I have not rarely met with modern Latin of a more thoroughly classical character. His style is too redundant and florid, his topics very trivial. Witness the whole oration on the battle of Lepanto, where the greatness of his subject does not raise them above the level of a school-boy's exercise. The celebrated eulogy on the St. Bartholomew massacre, delivered before the Pope, will serve as a very fair specimen to exemplify the Latinity of Muretus.[k] Scaliger, invidious for the most part in his characters of contemporary scholars, declares that no one since Cicero had written so well as Muretus, but that he adopted the Italian diffuseness, and says little in many words. This observation seems perfectly just.

Defects of his style.

31. The epistles of Paulus Manutius are written in what we may call a gentleman-like tone, without the virulence or querulousness that disgusts too often in the compositions of literary men. Of Panvinius, Robortellus, Sigonius, his own peculiar rivals, he writes in a friendly spirit, and tone of eulogy. His letters are chiefly addressed to the great classical scholars of his age. But

Epistles of Manutius.

---

[i] Mureti opera, cura Ruhnkenii, Lugd. 1789.

[k] O noctem illam memorabilem et in fastis eximiæ alicujus notæ adjectione signandam, quæ paucorum seditiosorum interitu regem a præsenti cædis periculo, regnum a perpetua bellorum civilium formidine liberavit! Qua quidem nocte stellas equidem ipsas luxisse solito nitidius arbitror, et flumen Sequanam majores undas volvisse, quo citius illa impurorum hominum cadavera evolveret et exoneraret in mare. O felicissimam mulierem Catharinam, regis matrem, quæ cum tot annos admirabili prudentia parique solicitudine regnum filio, filium regno conservasset, tum demum secura regnantem filium adspexit! O regis fratres ipsos quoque beatos! quorum alter cum, qua ætate cæteri vix adhuc arma tractare incipiunt, eâ ipse quater

commisso prælio fraternos hostes fregis-set ac fugasset hujus quoque pulcherri-mi facti præcipuam gloriam ad se potissi-mum voluit pertinere; alter, quamquam ætate nondum ad rem militarem idonea erat, tanta tamen est ad virtutem indole, ut neminem nisi fratrem in his rebus gerendis æquo animo sibi passurus fuerit anteponi. O diem denique illum ple-num lætitiæ et hilaritatis, quo tu, beatis-sime pater, hoc ad te nuncio allato, Deo immortali, et Divo Ludovico regi, cujus hæc in ipso pervigilio evenerant, gratias acturus, indictas a te supplicationes pe-des obiisti! Quis optabilior ad te nun-cius adferri poterat? aut nos ipsi quod felicius optare poteramus principium pontificatus tui, quam ut primis illis mensibus tetram illam caliginem, quasi exorto sole, discussam cerneremus? vol. i. p. 177, edit. Ruhnken.

on the other hand, though exclusively on literary subjects, they deal chiefly in generalities; and the affectation of copying Cicero in every phrase gives a coldness and almost an air of insincerity to the sentiments. They have but one note, the praise of learning; yet it is rarely that they impart to us much information about its history and progress. Hence they might serve for any age, and seem like pattern forms for the epistles of a literary man. In point of mere style there can be no comparison between the letters of a Sadolet or Manutius on the one hand, and those of a Scaliger, Lipsius, or Casaubon on the other. But while the first pall on the reader by their monotonous elegance, the others are full of animation and pregnant with knowledge. Even in what he most valued, correct Latin, Manutius, as Scioppius has observed, is not without errors. But the want of perfect dictionaries made it difficult to avoid illegitimate expressions which modern usage suggested to the writer.[m]

32. Manutius, as the passage above quoted has shown, is not reckoned by Ruhnkenius quite equal to Muretus, at least in natural genius. Scioppius thinks him consummate in delicacy and grace. He tells us that Manutius could hardly speak three words of Latin, so that the Germans who came to visit him looked down on his deficiency. But this, Scioppius remarks, as Erasmus had done a hundred years before, was one of the rules observed by the Italian scholars to preserve the correctness of their style. They perceived that the daily use of Latin in speech must bring in a torrent of barbarous phrases, which, ' claiming afterwards the privileges of acquaintance' (quodam familiaritatis jure), would obtrude their company during compositiou, and render it difficult for the most accurate writer to avoid them.[n]

Care of the Italian Latinists.

33. Perpinianus, a Valencian Jesuit, wrote some orations, hardly remembered at present, but Ruhnkenius has placed him along with Muretus, as the two Cisalpines (if that word may be so used for brevity) who have

Perpinianus, Osorius, Maphæus.

---

[m] Scioppius, Judicium de Stylo Historico.

[n] Id. p. 65. This was so little understood in England, that, in some of our colleges, and even schools, it was the regulation for the students to speak Latin when within hearing of their superiors. Even Locke was misled into recommending this preposterous barbarism.

excelled the Italians in Latinity. A writer of more celebrity was Osorius, a Portuguese bishop, whose treatise on Glory, and, what is better known, his History of the Reign of Emanuel, have placed him in a high rank among the imitators of the Augustan language. Some extracts from Osorius de Gloria will be found in the first volume of the Retrospective Review. This has been sometimes fancied to be the famous work of Cicero with that title, which Petrarch possessed and lost, and which Petrus Alcyonius has been said to have transferred to his own book De Exilio. But for this latter conjecture there is, I believe, neither evidence nor presumption; and certainly Osorius, if we may judge from the passages quoted, was no Cicero. Lord Bacon has said of him, that 'his vein was weak and waterish,' which these extracts confirm. They have not elegance enough to compensate for their verbosity and emptiness. Dupin, however, calls him the Cicero of Portugal.[o] Nor is less honour due to the Jesuit Maffei (Maphæus), whose chief work is the History of India, published in 1586. Maffei, according to Scioppius, was so careful of his style, that he used to recite the breviary in Greek, lest he should become too much accustomed to bad Latin.[p] This may perhaps be said in ridicule of such purists. Like Manutius, he was tediously elaborate in correction; some have observed that his History of India has scarce any value except for its style.[q]

34. The writings of Buchanan, and especially his Scottish history, are written with strength, perspicuity, and neatness.[r] Many of our own critics have extolled the Latinity of Walter Haddon. His Orations were published in 1567. They belong to the first years of this period. But they seem hardly to deserve any high praise. Haddon had certainly laboured at an imitation of Cicero, but without catching his manner, or getting rid of the florid, semi-poetical tone of the fourth century. A specimen, taken much at ran-

Buchanan, Haddon.

---

[o] Niceron, vol. ii.
[p] De Stylo Hist. p. 71.
[q] Tiraboschi. Niceron, vol. v. Biogr. univ.
[r] Le Clerc, in an article of the Bibliothèque choisie, vol. viii., pronounces

a high eulogy on Buchanan, as having written better than any one else in verse and prose; that is, as I understand him, having written prose better than any one who has written verse so well, and the converse.

dom, but rather favourable than otherwise, from his oration
on the death of the young brothers of the house of Suffolk,
at Cambridge, in 1550, is given in a note.[s] Another work of
a different kind, wherein Haddon is said to have been concerned jointly with Sir John Cheke, is the Reformatio Legum
Ecclesiasticarum, the proposed code of the Anglican Church,
drawn up under Edward VI. It is, considering the subject,
in very good language.

35. These are the chief writers of this part of the sixteenth
Sigonius, century who have attained reputation for the polish
De Conso- and purity of their Latin style. Sigonius ought,
latione.
perhaps, to be mentioned in the same class, since his writings exhibit not only perspicuity and precision, but as much
elegance as their subjects would permit. He is also the acknowledged author of the treatise De Consolatione, which
long passed with many for a work of Cicero. Even Tiraboschi was only undeceived of this opinion by meeting with
some unpublished letters of Sigonius, wherein he confesses
the forgery.[t] It seems, however, that he had inserted some
authentic fragments. Lipsius speaks of this counterfeit with
the utmost contempt, but after all his invective can scarcely
detect any bad Latinity.[u] The Consolatio is, in fact, like
many other imitations of the philosophical writings of Cicero,

---

[s] O laboriosam et si non miseram,
certe mirabiliter exercitam, tot cumula-
tam funeribus Cantabrigiam! Gravi nos
vulnere percussit hyems, æstas saucios
ad terram afflixit. Calendæ Martiæ stan-
tem adhuc Academiam nostram et erec-
tam vehementer impulerunt, et de priori
statu suo depresserunt. Idus Juliæ nu-
tantem jam et inclinatam oppresserunt.
Cum magnus ille fidei magister et excellens noster in vera religione doctor,
Martinus Bucerus, frigoribus hybernis
conglaciavisset, tantam in ejus occasu
plagam accepisse videbamur, ut majorem
non solum ullam expectaremus, sed ne
posse quidem expectari crederemus. Verum postquam inundantes, et in Cantabrigiam effervescentes æstivi sudores,
illud præstans et aureolum par Suffol-
ciensium fratrum, tum quidem peregri-
natum a nobis, sed tamen plane nostrum
obruerunt, sic ingemuimus, ut infinitus
dolor vix ullam tanti mali levationem
invenire possit. Perfectus omni scientia

pater, et certe senex incomparabilis,
Martinus Bucerus, licet nec reipublicæ
nec nostro, tamen suo tempore mortuus
est, nimirum ætate, et annis et morbo
affectus. Suffolcienses autem, quos ille
florescentes ad omnem laudem, tanquam
alumnos disciplinæ reliquit suæ, tam
repente sudorum fluminibus absorpti
sunt, ut prius mortem illorum audire-
mus, quam morbum animadverteremus.
[t] Biogr. univ. art. Sigonio.
[u] Lipsii Opera Critica. His style is
abusive, as usual in this age. Quis autem ille suaviludius qui latere se posse
censuit sub illâ personâ? Male meher-
cule de seculo nostro judicavit. Quid
enim tam dissimile ab illo auro, quam
hoc plumbum? ne simia quidem Ciceronis esse potest, nedum ut ille. . . .
Habes judicium meum, in quo si aliqua
asperitas, ne mirere. Fatua enim hæc
superbia tanto nomini se inserendi dig-
nissima insectatione fuit.

resembling their original in his faults of verbosity and want
of depth, but flowing and graceful in language. Lipsius,
who affected the other extreme, was not likely to value that
which deceived the Italians into a belief that Tully himself
was before them. It was, at least, not everyone who could
have done this like Sigonius.

36. Several other names, especially from the Jesuit col-
leges, might, I doubt not, be added to the list of good Latin writers by any competent scholar, who should prosecute the research through public libra- *Decline of taste and learning in Italy.*
ries by the aid of the biographical dictionaries. But more
than enough may have been said for the general reader.
The decline of classical literature in this sense, to which we
have already alluded, was the theme of complaint towards
the close of the century, and above all in Italy. Paulus
Manutius had begun to lament it long before. But Latinus
Latinius himself, one of the most learned scholars of that
country, states positively, in 1584, that the Italian universities were forced to send for their professors from Spain
and France.[x] And this abandonment by Italy of her former
literary glory was far more striking in the next age, an age
of science, but not of polite literature. Ranke supposes that
the attention of Italy being more turned towards mathematics and natural history, the study of the ancient writers,
which do not contribute greatly to these sciences, fell into
decay. But this seems hardly an adequate cause, nor had
the exact sciences made any striking progress in the period
immediately under review. The rigorous orthodoxy of the
church, which in some measure revived an old jealousy of
heathen learning, must have contributed far more to the
effect. Sixtus V. notoriously disliked all profane studies,
and was even kept with difficulty from destroying the antiquities of Rome, several of which were actually demolished
by his bigoted and barbarous zeal.[y] No other pope, I believe, has been guilty of what the Romans always deemed
sacrilege. In such discouraging circumstances we could
hardly wonder at what is reported, that Aldus Manutius,
having been made professor of rhetoric at Rome, about 1589,

---

[x] Tiraboschi, x. 387.   [y] Ranke, i. 476.

could only get one or two hearers. But this, perhaps, does not rest on very good authority.[z] It is agreed that the Greek language was almost wholly neglected at the end of the century, and there was no one in Italy distinguished for a knowledge of it. Baronius must be reckoned a man of laborious erudition; yet he wrote his annals of the ecclesiastical history of twelve centuries, without any acquaintance with that tongue.

37. The two greatest scholars of the sixteenth century, being rather later than most of the rest, are yet unnamed; Joseph Scaliger and Isaac Casaubon.

Joseph Scaliger.

The former, son of Julius Cæsar Scaliger, and, in the estimation at least of some, his inferior in natural genius, though much above him in learning and judgment, was perhaps the most extraordinary master of general erudition that has ever lived. His industry was unremitting through a length of life; his memory, though he naturally complains of its failure in latter years, had been prodigious; he was, in fact, conversant with all ancient, and very extensively with modern literature. The notes of his conversations, taken down by some of his friends, and well known by the name of Scaligerana, though full of vanity and contempt of others, and though not always perhaps faithful registers of what he said, bear witness to his acuteness, vivacity, and learning.[a] But

---

[z] Ranke, 482. Renouard, Imprimerie des Aldes, iii. 197, doubts the truth of this story, which is said to come on the authority alone of Rossi, a writer who took the name of Erythræus, and has communicated a good deal of literary miscellaneous information, but not always such as deserves confidence.

[a] The Scaligerana Prima, as they are called, were collected by Francis Vertunien, a physician of Poitiers; the Secunda, which are much the longest, by two brothers, named De Vassan, who were admitted to the intimacy of Scaliger at Leyden. They seem to have registered all his table-talk in common-place books alphabetically arranged. Hence, when he spoke at different times of the same person or subject, the whole was published in an undigested, incoherent, and sometimes self-contradictory paragraph. He was not strict about consist-

ency, as men of his temper seldom are in their conversation, and one would be slow in relying on what he has said; but the Scaligerana, with its many faults, deserves perhaps the first place among those amusing miscellanies known by the name of Ana.

It was little to the honour of the Scaligers, father and son, that they lay under the strongest suspicions of extreme credulity, to say nothing worse, in setting up a descent from the Scala princes of Verona, though the world could never be convinced that their proper name was not Burden, of a plebeian family, and known as such in that city. Joseph Scaliger, took as his device, Fuimus Troes; and his letters, as well as the Scaligerana, bear witness to the stress he laid on this pseudo-genealogy. Lipsius observes on this, with the true spirit which a man of letters ought to feel,

his own numerous and laborious publications are the best testimonials to these qualities. His name will occur to us more than once again. In the department of philology, he was conspicuous as an excellent critic, both of the Latin and Greek languages ; though Bayle, in his own paradoxical, but acute and truly judicious spirit, has suggested, that Scaliger's talents and learning were too great for a good commentator ; the one making him discover in authors more hidden sense than they possessed, the other leading him to perceive a thousand allusions which had never been designed. He frequently altered the text in order to bring these more forward ; and in his conjectures is bold, ingenious, and profound, but not always very satisfactory.[b] His critical writings are chiefly on the Latin poets ; but his knowledge of Greek was eminent ; and, perhaps, it may not be too minute to notice as a proof of it, that his verses in that language, if not good according to our present standard, are at least much better than those of Casaubon. The latter, in an epistle to Scaliger, extols his correspondent as far above Gaza or any modern Greek in poetry, and worthy to have lived in Athens with Aristophanes and Euripides. This cannot be said of his own attempts, in which their gross faultiness is as manifest as their general want of spirit.

38. This eminent person, a native of Geneva[c]—that little

that it would have been a great honour for the Scalas to have descended from the Scaligers, who had more real nobility than the whole city of Verona. (Thuana, p. 14.) But unfortunately the vain, foolish, and vulgar part of mankind cannot be brought to see things in that light, and both the Scaligers knew that such princes as Henry II. and even Henry IV. would esteem them more for their ancestry than for their learning and genius.

The epitaph of Daniel Heinsius on Joseph Scaliger, pardonably perhaps on such an occasion, mingles the real and fabulous glories of his friend.

Regius a Brenni deductus sanguine sanguis
Qui dominos rerum tot numerabat avos,
Cui nihil indulsit sors, nil natura negavit,
Et jure imperii conditor ipse sui,
Invidiæ scopulus, sed cœlo proximus, illa,
Illa Juliades conditur, hospes, humo.
Centum illic proavos et centum pone triumphos,
Sceptraque Veronæ sceptrigerosque Deos ;

Mastinosque, Canesque, et totam ab origine gentem,
Et quæ præterea non bene nota latent.
Illic stent aquilæ priscique insignia regni,
Et ter Cæsareo munere fulta domus.
Plus tamen invenies quicquid sibi contulit ipse,
Et minimum tantæ nobilitatis eget.
Aspice tot linguas, totumque in pectore mundum ;
Innumeras gentes continet iste locus.
Crede illic Arabas, desertaque nomina Pœnos,
Et crede Armenios Æthiopasque tegi.
Terrarum instar habes ; et quam natura negavit
Laudem uni populo, contigit illa viro.

[b] Niceron, vol. xxiii. Blount, Biogr. univ.

[c] The father of Casaubon was from the neighbourhood of Bordeaux. He fled to Geneva during a temporary persecution of the Huguenots, but returned home afterwards. Casaubon went back to Geneva in his nineteenth year for the sake of education. See his life by his son Meric, prefixed to Almeloveen's edition of his epistles.

city, so great in the annals of letters—and the son-in-law
Isaac Casau-
bon. of Henry Stephens, rose above the horizon in 1583,
when his earliest work, the Annotations on Diogenes
Laertius, was published; a performance of which he was
afterwards ashamed, as being unworthy of his riper studies.
Those on Strabo, an author much neglected before, followed
in 1587. For more than twenty years Casaubon employed
himself upon editions of Greek writers, many of which, as
that of Theophrastus, in 1593, and that of Athenæus, in
1600, deserve particular mention. The latter, especially,
which he calls, 'molestissimum, difficillimum et tædii ple-
nissimum opus,' has always been deemed a noble monument
of critical sagacity and extensive erudition. In conjectural
emendation of the text, no one hitherto had been equal to
Casaubon. He may probably be deemed a greater scholar
than his father-in-law Stephens, or even, in a critical sense,
than his friend Joseph Scaliger. These two lights of the
literary world, though it is said that they had never seen
each other,[d] continued till the death of the latter in regular
correspondence and unbroken friendship. Casaubon, queru-
lous but not envious, paid freely the homage which Scaliger
was prepared to exact, and wrote as to one superior in age,
in general celebrity, and in impetuosity of spirit. Their
letters to each other, as well as to their various other correspondents, are highly valuable for the literary history of the
period they embrace; that is, the last years of the present,
and the first of the ensuing century.

39. Budæus, Camerarius, Stephens, Scaliger, Casaubon,
General
result. appear to stand out as the great restorers of ancient
learning, and especially of the Greek language. I
do not pretend to appreciate them by deep skill in the subject, or by a diligent comparison of their works with those
of others, but from what I collect to have been the more
usual suffrage of competent judges. Canter, perhaps, or
Sylburgius, might be rated above Camerarius; but the last
seems, if we may judge by the eulogies bestowed upon him,
to have stood higher in the estimation of his contemporaries.
Their labours restored the integrity of the text in the far

---

[d] Morhof, l. i. c. xv. s. 57.

greater part of the Greek authors—though they did not yet possess as much metrical knowledge as was required for that of the poets—explained most dubious passages, and nearly exhausted the copiousness of the language. For another century mankind was content, in respect of Greek philology, to live on the accumulations of the sixteenth; and it was not till after so long a period had elapsed, that new scholars arose, more exact, more philosophical, more acute in 'knitting up the ravelled sleeve' of speech, but not, to say the least, more abundantly stored with erudition than those who had cleared the way, and upon whose foundations they built.

40. We come, in the last place, to the condition of ancient learning in this island; a subject which it may be interesting to trace with some minuteness, though we can offer no splendid banquet, even from the reign of the Virgin Queen. Her accession was indeed a happy epoch in our literary as well as civil annals. She found a great and miserable change in the state of the universities since the days of her father. Plunder and persecution, the destroying spirits of the last two reigns, were enemies against which our infant muses could not struggle.[e] Ascham, however, denies that there was much decline of learning at Cambridge before the time of Mary. The influence of her reign was not indirectly alone, but by deliberate purpose, injurious to all useful knowledge.[f] It was in

Learning in England, under Edward and Mary.

---

[e] The last editor of Wood's Athenæ Oxonienses bears witness to having seen chronicles and other books mutilated, as he conceives, by the Protestant visitors of the university under Edward. 'What is most,' he says, 'to the discredit of Cox (afterwards bishop of Ely), was his unwearied diligence in destroying the ancient manuscripts and other books in the public and private libraries at Oxford. The savage barbarity with which he executed this hateful office can never be forgotten,' &c. p. 468. One book only of the famous library of Humphrey, duke of Gloucester, bequeathed to Oxford, escaped mutilation. This is a Valerius Maximus. But as Cox was really a man of considerable learning, we may ask whether there is evidence to lay these Vandal proceedings on him rather than on his colleagues?

[f] 'And what was the fruit of this seed? Verily, judgment in doctrine was wholly altered; order in discipline very much changed; the love of good learning began suddenly to wax cold; the knowledge of the tongues, in spite of some that therein had flourished, was manifestly contemned, and so the way of right study manifestly perverted; the choice good authors of malice confounded; old sophistry. I say not well, not old, but that new rotten sophistry, began to beard and shoulder logic in their own tongue; yea, I know that heads were cast together, and counsel devised, that Duns, with all the rabble of barbarous questionists, should have dispossessed, of their places and room, Aristotle, Plato, Tully, and Demosthenes; whom good Mr. Redman, and those two worthy stars of the university, Mr. Cheke and Mr. Smith, with their

contemplation, he tells us (and surely it was congenial enough to the spirit of that government), that the ancient writers should give place in order to restore Duns Scotus and the scholastic barbarians.

41. It is indeed impossible to restrain the desire of noble Revival minds for truth and wisdom. Scared from the under Eliza-beth. banks of Isis and Cam, neglected or discountenanced by power, learning found an asylum in the closets of private men, who laid up in silence stores for future use. And some of course remained out of those who had listened to Smith and Cheke, or the contemporary teachers of Oxford. But the mischief was effected, in a general sense, by breaking up the course of education in the universities. At the beginning of the new queen's reign, but few of the clergy, to whichever mode of faith they might conform, had the least tincture of Greek learning, and the majority did not understand Latin.[g] The Protestant exiles, being far the most learned men of the kingdom, brought back a more healthy tone of literary diligence. The universities began to revive. An address was delivered in Greek verses to Elizabeth at Cambridge in 1564, to which she returned thanks in the same language.[h] Oxford would not be outdone. Lawrence, regius professor of Greek, as we are told by Wood, made an oration at Carfax, a spot often chosen for public exhibition, on her visit to the city in 1566; when her majesty, thanking the university in the same tongue, observed, 'it was the best Greek speech she had ever heard.'[i] Several slight proofs of classical learning appear from this time in the 'History and Antiquities of Oxford;' marks of a progress, at first slow and silent, which I only mention because nothing more important has been recorded.

42. In 1575, the queen having been now near twenty Greek Lec-tures atCam-bridge. years on the throne, we find, on positive evidence, that lectures on Greek were given in St. John's College, Cambridge; which, indeed, few would be disposed

---

scholars, had brought to flourish as notably in Cambridge, as ever they did in Greece and in Italy; and for the doctrine of those four, the four pillars of learning, Cambridge then giving no place to no university, neither in France,

Spain, Germany, nor Italy.'—p. 317.
    [g] Hallam's Constit. Hist. of Eng. i. 249.
    [h] Peck's Desiderata Curiosa, p. 270.
    [i] Wood, Hist. and Antiq. of Oxford.

to doubt, reflecting on the general character of the age and the length of opportunity that had been afforded. It is said in the life of Mr. Bois, or Boyse, one of the revisers of the translation of the Bible under James, that 'his father was a great scholar, being learned in the Hebrew and Greek excellently well, which, considering the manners, that I say not, the looseness of the times of his education, was almost a miracle.' The son was admitted at St. John's in 1575. 'His father had well educated him in the Greek tongue before his coming; which caused him to be taken notice or in the college. For besides himself there was but one there who could write Greek. Three lectures in that language were read in the college. In the first, grammar was taught, as is commonly now done in schools. In the second, an easy author was explained in the grammatical way. In the third was read somewhat which might seem fit for their capacities who had passed over the other two. A year was usually spent in the first, and two in the second.'[k] It will be perceived that the course of instruction was still elementary; but it is well known that many, or rather most students, entered the universities at an earlier age than is usual at present.[m]

43. We come very slowly to books, even subsidiary to education, in the Greek language. And since this cannot be conveniently carried on to any great extent without books, though I am aware that some contri- Few Greek editions in England.

---

[k] Peck's Desiderata Curiosa, p. 327. Chalmers.

[m] It is probable that Cambridge was at this time better furnished with learning than Oxford. Even Wood does not give us a favourable notion of the condition of that university in the first part of the queen's reign. Oxford was for a long time filled with popish students, that is, with conforming partisans of the former religion; many of whom, from time to time, went off to Douay. Leicester, as chancellor of the university, charged it, in 1582, and in subsequent years, with great neglect of learning; the disputations had become mere forms, and the queen's lecturers in Greek and Hebrew seldom read. It was as bad in all the other sciences. Wood's Antiquities and Athenæ, *passim*. The col-

leges of Corpus Christi and Merton were distinguished beyond the rest in the reign of Elizabeth; especially the former, where Jewel read the lecture in rhetoric, (at an earlier time, of course,) Hooker in logic, and Raynolds in Greek. Leicester succeeded in *puritanizing*, as Wood thought, the university, by driving off the old party, and thus rendering it a more effective school of learning.

Harrison, about 1586, does not speak much better of the universities: 'the quadrivials, I mean arithmetic, music, geometry, and astronomy, are now small regarded in either of them.' Description of Britain, p. 252. Few learned preachers were sent out from them, which he ascribes, in part, to the poor endowments of most livings.

vances were employed as substitutes for them, and since it
was as easy to publish either grammars or editions of ancient
authors in England as on the Continent, we can, as it seems,
draw no other inference from the want of them than the
absence of any considerable demand. I shall therefore enumerate all the books instrumental to the study of Greek
which appeared in England before the close of the century.

44. It has been mentioned in another place that two alone
had been printed before 1550. In 1553 a Greek version
of the second Æneid, by George Etherege, was published.
Two editions of the Anglican liturgy in Latin and Greek, by
Whitaker, one of our most learned theologians, appeared in
School books 1569 ;[n] a short catechism in both languages, 1573
enumerated. and 1578. We find also in 1578 a little book
entitled χριστιανισμου στοιχειωσις εις την παιδων ωφελειαν
ἑλληνιστι και λατινιστι εκτεθεισα. This is a translation, made
also by Whitaker, from Nowell's Christianæ Pietatis Prima
Institutio, ad Usum Scholarum Latine Scripta. The Biographia Britannica puts the first edition of this Greek version in
1575; and informs us also that Nowell's lesser Catechism
was published in Latin and Greek, 1575; but I do not find
any confirmation of this in Herbert or Watts. In 1575,
Grant, master of Westminster School, published Græcæ
Linguæ Spicilegium, intended evidently for the use of his
scholars ; and in 1581 the same Grant superintended an
edition of Constantin's Lexicon, probably in the abridgment
under the name of the Basle printer Crespin, enriching it
with four or five thousand new words, which he most likely
took from Stephens's Thesaurus. A Greek, Latin, French,
and English lexicon, by John Barret or Baret, in 1580,[o] and
another by John Morel (without the French), in 1583,
are recorded in bibliographical works; but I do not know
whether any copies have survived.

45. It appears, therefore, that before even the middle of
Greek taught the queen's reign the rudiments of the Greek lan-
in schools. guage were imparted to boys at Westminster School,
and no doubt also at those of Eton, Winchester, and St.

---

[n] Scaliger says of Whitaker, O qu'il   of this dictionary in 1573, but without
étoit bien docte ! Scalig. Secunda.   the Greek.
[o] Chalmers mentions an earlier edition

Paul's.[p] But probably it did not yet extend to many others. In Ascham's Schoolmaster, a posthumous treatise, published in 1570, but evidently written some years after the accession of Elizabeth, while very detailed, and, in general, valuable rules are given for the instruc ion of boys in the Latin language, no intimation is found that Greek was designed to be taught. In the statutes of Witton School in Cheshire, framed in 1558, the founder says:—' I will there were always taught good literature, both Latin and Greek.'[q] But this seems to be only an aspiration after an hopeless excellence ; for he proceeds to enumerate the Latin books intended to be used, without any mention of Greek. In the statutes of Merchant Taylors' School, 1561, the high master is required to be ' learned in good and clean Latin literature, and also in Greek, if such may be gotten.'[r] These words are copied from those of Colet, in the foundation of St. Paul's School. But in the regulations of Hawkshead School in Lancashire, 1588, the master is directed ' to teach grammar and the principles of the Greek tongue.'[s] The little tracts, indeed, above mentioned, do not lead us to believe that the instruction, even at Westminster, was of more than the slightest kind. They are but verbal translations of known religious treatises, wherein the learner would be assisted by his recollection at almost every word. But in the rules laid down by Mr. Lyon, founder of Harrow School, in 1590, the books designed to be taught are enumerated, and comprise some Greek orators and historians, as well as the poems of Hesiod.[t]

---

[p] Harrison mentions, about the year 1586, that at the great collegiate schools of Eton, Winchester, and Westminster, boys ' are well entered in the knowledge of the Latin and Greek tongues and rules of versifying.' Description of England, prefixed to Hollingshed's Chronicles, p. 254 (4to. edition). He has just before taken notice of 'the great number of grammar-schools throughout the realm, and those very liberally endowed for the relief of poor scholars, so that there are not many corporate towns now under the queen's dominion that have not one grammar-school at the least, with a sufficient living for a master

and usher appointed for the same.'
[q] Carlisle's Endowed Schools, vol. i. p. 129.
[r] Id. vol. ii. p. 49.
[s] Id. vol. i. p. 656.
[t] Id. vol. ii. p. 136. I have not discovered any other proofs of Greek education in Mr. Carlisle's work. In the statutes or regulations of Bristol School, founded in the sixteenth century, it is provided that the head master should be ' well learned in the Latin, Greek, and Hebrew.' But these must be modern, as appears, *inter alia*, by the words, ' well affected to the Constitution in Church and State.'

46. We have now, however, descended very low in the
Greek better century. The twilight of classical learning in Eng-
known after
1580. land had yielded to its morning. It is easy to trace
many symptoms of enlarged erudition after 1580. Scot, in
his Discovery of Witchcraft 1584, and doubtless many other
writers, employ Greek quotations rather freely; and the use
of Greek words, or adaptation of English forms to them, is
affected by Webb and Puttenham in their treatises on poetry.
Greek titles are not infrequently given to books; it was a
pedantry that many affected. Besides the lexicons above
mentioned, it was easy to procure, at no great price, those of
Constantin and Scapula. We may refer to the ten years
after 1580 the commencement of that rapid advance which
gave the English nation, in the reign of James, so respectable
a place in the republic of letters. In the last decennium of
the century, the Ecclesiastical Polity of Hooker is a monument of real learning, in profane as well as theological antiquity. But certainly the reading of our scholars in this
period was far more generally among the Greek fathers than
the classics. Even this, however, required a competent acquaintance with the language.

47. The two universities had abandoned the art of printing
Editions of since the year 1521. No press is known to have
Greek. existed afterwards at Cambridge till 1584, or at
Oxford till 1586, when six homilies of Chrysostom in Greek
were published at a press erected by Lord Leicester at his
own expense. The first book of Herodotus came out at the
same place in 1591; the treatise of Barlaam on the Papacy
in 1592; Lycophron in the same year; the Knights of Aristophanes in 1593; fifteen orations of Demosthenes in 1593
and 1597; Agatharcides in the latter year. One oration of
Lysias was printed at Cambridge in 1593. The Greek Testament appeared from the London press in 1581, in 1587,
and again in 1592; a treatise of Plutarch, and three orations
of Isocrates, in 1587; the Iliad in 1591. These, if I have
overlooked none, or if none have been omitted by Herbert,
are all the Greek publications (except grammars, of which
there are several, one by Camden, for the use of Westminster

---

u Herbert.

School, in 1597,[x] and one in 1600, by Knolles, author of
the History of the Turks) that fall within the sixteenth
century; and all apparently, are intended for classes in the
schools and universities.[y]

48. It must be expected that the best Latin writers were
more honoured than those of Greece. Besides gram- and of Latin
mars and dictionaries, which are too numerous to classics.
mention, we find not a few editions, though principally for
the purposes of education: Cicero de Officiis (in Latin and
English), 1553; Virgil, 1570; Sallust, 1570 and 1571;
Justin, 1572; Cicero de Oratore, 1573; Horace and Juvenal,
1574. It is needless to proceed lower, when they become
more frequent. The most important classical publication
was a complete edition of Cicero, which was, of course, more
than a school book. This appeared at London in 1585, from
the press of Ninian Newton. It is said to be a reprint from
the edition of Lambinus.

49. It is obvious that foreign books must have been
largely imported, or we should place the learning of the Eliza-

---

[x] This grammar by Camden was probably founded on that of Grant, above
mentioned; cujus rudimenta, says Smith,
the author of Camden's life, cum multa
ex parte laborarent deficerentque, non
tam reformanda, quam de novo institu-
enda censens, observationibus quas ex
Græcis omne genus scriptoribus acri judicio et longo usu collegerat, sub seve-
rum examen revocatis, grammaticam
novam non soli scholæ cui præerat, sed
universis per Angliam scholis deinceps
inservituram, eodem anno edidit.—p.
19, edit. 1691.

[I have since been informed by the
learned correspondent to whom I have
alluded in p. 338, that, 'after some
search and inquiry, I feel no doubt the
author of the Eton grammar was Camden, and that it was originally compiled
by him when he was head master of
Westminster School, for the use of that
school, in 1595. Thence it was very
likely to have been adopted at Eton by
his friend Sir Henry Savile, who was
made provost the year after Camden's
grammar appeared. I have an edition
before me, bearing date 1595, in usum
Regiæ Scholæ Westmonasteriensis. It
is what is now called the Eton Grammar, totidem verbis. But Camden's gram-

mar was superseded by Busby's at Westminster about 1650, having gone through
more than thirty editions.'—1842.]

The excessive scarcity of early school-
books makes it allowable to mention the
Progymnasma Scholasticum of John
Stockwood, an edition of which, with
the date of 1597, is in the Inner Temple
Library. It is merely a selection of
epigrams from the Anthologia of H.
Stephens, and shows but a moderate expectation of proficiency from the studious youth for whom it was designed;
the Greek being written in interlinear
Latin characters over the original, ad
faciliorem eorundem lectionem. A literal translation into Latin follows, and
several others in metre. Stockwood had
been master of Tunbridge School:
Scholæ Tunbridgiensis olim ludima-
gister; so that there may possibly have
been earlier editions of this little book,

[y] The arrangement of editions recorded in Herbert, following the names
of the printers, does not afford facilities
for any search. I may, therefore, have
omitted one or two trifles, and it is
likely that I have; but the conclusion will
be the same. Angli, says Scaliger, nunquam excuderunt bonos libros veteres,
tantum vulgares.

bethan period as much too low as it has ordinarily been
Learning lower than in Spain. exaggerated. But we may feel some surprise that so
little was contributed by our native scholars. Certain
it is that, in most departments of literature, they did not yet
occupy a distinguished place. The catalogue, by Herbert, of
books published down to the end of the century, presents no
favourable picture of the queen's reign. Without instituting
a comparison with Germany or France, we may easily make
one with the classed catalogue of books printed in Spain,
which we find at the close of the Bibliotheca Nova of Nicolas
Antonio. Greek appears to have been little studied in Spain,
though we have already mentioned a few grammatical works;
but the editions of Latin authors, and the commentators
upon them, are numerous ; and upon the whole it is undeniable that in most branches of erudition, so far as we can
draw a conclusion from publications, Spain, under Philip II.
held a higher station than England under Elizabeth. The
poverty of the English church, the want of public libraries,
and the absorbing influence of polemical theology, will account for much of this ; and I am not by any means inclined
to rate our English gentlemen of Elizabeth's age for useful
and even classical knowledge below the hidalgos of Castile.
But this class were not the chief contributors to literature.
It is, however, in consequence of the reputation for learning
acquired by some men distinguished in civil life, such as
Smith, Sadler, Raleigh, and even by ladies, among whom the
queen herself, and the accomplished daughters of Sir Antony
Cooke, Lady Cecil, and Lady Russell, are particularly to be
mentioned, that the general character of her reign has been,
in this point of view, considerably overrated. No Englishman ought, I conceive, to suppress this avowal, or to feel any
mortification in making it : with the prodigious development
of wisdom and genius that illustrated the last years of
Elizabeth, we may well spare the philologers and antiquaries
of the Continent.

50. There had arisen, however, towards the conclusion of
Improve- ment at the end of the century. the century, a very few men of such extensive learning as entitled them to an European reputation. Sir
Henry Savile stood at the head of these : we may
justly deem him the most learned Englishman, in profane
literature, of the reign of Elizabeth. He published, in 1581,

a translation of part of Tacitus, with annotations not very copious or profound, but pertinent, and deemed worthy to be rendered into Latin in the next century by the younger Gruter, and reprinted on the Continent.[z] Scaliger speaks of him with personal ill-will, but with a respect he seldom showed to those for whom he entertained such sentiments. Next to Savile we may rank Camden, whom all foreigners name with praise for the Britannia. Hooker has already been mentioned; but I am not sure that he could be said to have much reputation beyond our own shores. I will not assert that no other was extensively known even for profane learning; in our own biographical records several may be found, at least esteemed at home. But our most studious countrymen long turned their attention almost exclusively to theological controversy, and toiled over the prolix volumes of the fathers; a labour not to be defrauded of its praise, but to which we are not directing our eyes on this occasion.[a]

51. Scotland had hardly as yet partaken of the light of letters; the very slight attempts at introducing an enlarged scheme of education, which had been made thirty years before, having wholly failed in consequence of the jealous spirit that actuated the chiefs of the old religion, and the devastating rapacity that disgraced the partisans of the new. But in 1575, Andrew Melville was appointed principal of the university of Glasgow, which he found almost broken up and abandoned. He established so solid and extensive a system of instruction, wherein the best Greek authors were included, that Scotland, in some years' time, instead of sending her own natives to foreign universities, found students from other parts of Europe repairing to her own.[b] Yet Ames has observed that no Greek characters appear in any book printed in Scotland before 1599. This assertion has been questioned by Herbert. In the treatise of Buchanan, De Jure Regni (Edinburgh, 1580), I have remarked that the Greek quotations are inserted with a pen. It is at least

Marginal note: Learning in Scotland.

---

[z] They are contained in a small volume, 1649, with Savile's other treatise on the Roman Militia.

[a] It is remarkable that in Jewel's Defence of the Apology, by far the most learned work in theological erudition which the age produced, he quotes the Greek fathers in Latin; and there is a scanty sprinkling of Greek characters throughout this large volume.

[b] M'Crie's Life of Melville, vol. i. p. 72.

certain that no book in that language was printed north of
the Tweed within this century, nor any Latin classic, nor
dictionary, nor any thing of a philological nature except two
or three grammars. A few Latin treatises by modern authors
on various subjects appeared. It seems questionable whether
any printing-press existed in Ireland : the evidence to be collected from Herbert is precarious; but I know not whether
any thing more satisfactory has since been discovered.

52. The Latin language was by no means so generally
Latin little employed in England as on the Continent. Our
used in
writing.   authors have from the beginning been apt to prefer
their mother-tongue, even upon subjects which, by the usage
of the learned, were treated in Latin; though works relating
to history, and especially to ecclesiastical antiquity, such as
those of Parker and Godwin, were sometimes written in that
language. It may be alleged that very few books of a philosophical class appeared at all in the far-famed reign of
Elizabeth. But probably such as Scot's Discovery of Witchcraft, Rogers's Anatomy of the Mind, and Hooker's Ecclesiastical Polity, would have been thought to require a learned
dress in any other country. And we may think the same of
the great volumes of controversial theology; as Jewel's Defence of the Apology, Cartwright's Platform, and Whitgift's
Reply to it. The free spirit, not so much of our government,
as of the public mind itself, and the determination of a large
portion of the community to choose their religion for themselves, rendered this descent from the lofty grounds of learning indispensable. By such a deviation from the general
laws of the republic of letters, which, as it is needless to say,
was by no means less practised in the ensuing age, our
writers missed some part of that general renown they might
have challenged from Europe; but they enriched the minds
of a more numerous public at home; they gave their own
thoughts with more precision, energy, and glow; they in-
vigorated and amplified their native language, which became
in their hands more accommodated to abstract and philosophical disquisition, though, for the same reason, more formal
and pedantic, than any other in Europe. This observation
is as much intended for the reigns of James and Charles as
for that of Elizabeth.

Sect. II.

Principal Writers on Antiquities—Manutius, Sigonius, Lipsius—
Numismatics—Mythology—Chronology of Scaliger.

53. THE attention of the learned had been frequently directed, since the revival of letters, to elucidate the antiquities of
Rome, her customs, rites, and jurisprudence. It was more
laborious than difficult to common-place all extant Early works
Latin authors ; and by this process of comparison, ties.
most expressions, perhaps, in which there was no corruption
of the text, might be cleared up. This seems to have produced the works already mentioned, of Cælius Rhodiginus
and Alexander ab Alexandro, which afford explanations of
many hundred passages that might perplex a student.
Others had devoted their time to particular subjects, as
Pomponius Lætus, and Raphael of Volterra, to the distinctions of magistrates ; Marlianus, to the topography of
ancient Rome ; and Robortellus, to family names. It must
be confessed that most of these early pioneers were rather
praiseworthy for their diligence and good-will, than capable
of clearing away the more essential difficulties that stood in
the way : few treatises, written before the middle of the
sixteenth century, have been admitted into the collections of
Grævius and Sallengre. But soon afterwards an abundant
light was thrown upon the most interesting part of Roman
antiquity, the state of government and public law, by four
more eminent scholars than had hitherto explored that field,
Manutius, Panvinius, and Sigonius in Italy, Gruchius (or
Grouchy) in France.

54. The first of these published in 1558 his treatise De
Legibus Romanorum; and though that De Civitate P. Manutius
did not appear till 1585. Grævius believes it to have Laws.
been written about the same time as the former. Manutius
has given a good account of the principal laws made at
Rome during the republic; not many of the empire. Augus-
tinus, however, archbishop of Tarragona, had preceded him
with considerable success ; and several particular laws were
better illustrated afterwards by Brisson, Balduin, and Gotho-

fred. It will be obvious to any one, very slightly familiar with the Roman law, that this subject, as far as it relates to the republican period, belongs much more to classical antiquity than to jurisprudence.

55. The second Treatise of Manutius, De Civitate, dis-
Manutius, cusses the polity of the Roman republic. Though
De Civitate. among the very first scholars of his time, he will not always bear the test of modern acuteness. Even Grævius, who himself preceded the most critical age, frequently corrects his errors. Yet there are marks of great sagacity in Manutius; and Niebuhr, who has judged the antiquaries of the sixteenth century as they generally deserve, might have found the germ of his own celebrated hypothesis, though imperfectly developed, in what this old writer has suggested; that the populus Romanus originally meant the inhabitants of Rome intra pomœria, as distinguished from the cives Romani, who dwelt beyond that precinct in the territory.[c]

56. Onuphrius Panvinius, a man of vast learning and
Panvinius industry, but of less discriminating judgment, and
Sigonius. who did not live to its full maturity, fell short, in his treatise De Civitate Romana, of what Manutius (from whom, however, he could have taken nothing) has achieved on the same subject, and his writings, according to Grævius, would yield a copious harvest to criticism.[d] But neither of

[c] The first paragraph of the preface to Niebuhr's History deserves to be quoted. 'The History of Rome was treated, during the first two centuries after the revival of letters, with the same prostration of the understanding and judgment to the written letter that had been handed down, and with the same fearfulness of going beyond it, which prevailed in all the other branches of knowledge. If any one had asserted a right of examining the credibility of the ancient writers, and the value of their testimony, an outcry would have been raised against his atrocious presumption. The object aimed at was, in spite of all internal evidence, to combine what was related by them; at the utmost, one authority was in some one particular instance postponed to another as gently as possible, and without inducing any further results. Here and there, indeed, a free-born mind, such

as Glareanus, broke through these bonds; but infallibly a sentence of condemnation was forthwith pronounced against him: besides, such men were not the most learned, and their bold attempts were only partial, and were wanting in consistency. In this department, as in others, men of splendid talents and the most copious learning conformed to the narrow spirit of their age; their labours extracted from a multitude of insulated details what the remains of ancient literature did not afford united in any single work, a systematic account of Roman antiquities. What they did in this respect is wonderful; and this is sufficient to earn for them an imperishable fame.'

[d] In Onuphrio Panvinio fuerunt multæ literæ, multa industria, sed tanta ingenii vis non erat, quanta in Sigonio et Manutio, quorum scripta longe sunt limatiora.

Paulus Manutius calls Panvinius, ille

the two was comparable to Sigonius of Modena,[e] whose works
on the Roman government not only form an epoch in this
department of ancient literature, but have left, in general,
but little for his successors. Mistakes have of course been
discovered, where it is impossible to reconcile, or to rely
upon, every ancient testimony; and Sigonius, like the other
scholars, of his age, might confide too implicitly in his
authorities. But his treatises, De Jure Civium Romanorum,
1560, and De Jure Italiæ, 1562, are still the best that can be
read in illustration of the Roman historians and the orations
of Cicero. Whoever, says Grævius, sits down to the study of
these orations without being acquainted with Sigonius, will
but lose his time. In another treatise, published in 1574,
De Judiciis Romanorum, he goes through the whole course of
judicial proceedings, more copiously than Heineccius, the
most celebrated of his successors, and with more exclusive
regard to writers of the republican period. The Roman
Antiquities of Grævius contain several other excellent pieces
by Sigonius, which have gained him the indisputable character of the first antiquary, both for learning and judgment,
whom the sixteenth century produced. He was engaged in
several controversies ; one with Robortellus,[f] another with a
more considerable antagonist, Gruchius, a native of
Rouen, and professor of Greek at Bordeaux, who in   Gruchius.
his treatise De Comitiis Romanorum, 1555, was the first that
attempted to deal with a difficult and important subject.
Sigonius and he interchanged some thrusts, with more urba-
nity and mutual respect than was usual in that age. An

antiquitatis helluo, spectatæ juvenis industriæ . . . sæpe litigat obscuris de rebus cum Sigonio nostro, sed utriusque
bonitas, mutuus amor, excellens ad cog-
noscendam veritatem judicium facit ut
inter eos facile conveniat. Epist. lib. ii.
p. 81.

[e] It appears from some of the Lettere
Volgari of Manuzio, that the proper
name of Sigonius was not Sigonio, but
Sigone. Corniani (vol. vi. p. 151) has
made the same observation on the authority of Sigone's original unpublished
letters. But the biographers, as well
as Tiraboschi, though himself an inhabitant of the same city, do not advert
to it.

[f] The treatises of Robortellus, republished in the second volume of Gruter's
Lampas, are full of vain-glory and affected scorn of Sigonius. Half the chapters are headed, Error Sigonii. One of
their controversies concerned female
prænomina, which Robortellus denied
to be ancient, except in the formula of
Roman marriage, Ubi tu Cajus, ego
Caja ; though he admits that some appear in late inscriptions. Sigonius
proved the contrary by instances from
republican times. It is evident that
they were unusual, but several have
been found in inscriptions. See Grævius,
vol. ii. in præfatione.

account of this controversy, which chiefly related to a passage in Cicero's oration, De Lege Agraria, as to the confirmation of popular elections by the comitia curiata, will be found in the preface to the second volume of Grævius, wherein the treatises themselves are published. Another contemporary writer, Latino Latini, seems to have solved the problem much better than either Grouchy or Sigone. But both parties were misled by the common source of error in the most learned men in the sixteenth century, an excess of confidence in the truth of ancient testimony. The words of Cicero, who often spoke for an immediate purpose, those of Livy and Dionysius, who knew but imperfectly the primitive history of Rome, those even of Gellius or Pomponius, to whom all the republican institutions had become hardly intelligible, were deemed a sort of infallible text, which a modern might explain as best he could, but must not be presumptuous enough to reject.

57. Besides the works of these celebrated scholars, one by Sigonius on Athenian polity. Zamoscius, a young Pole, De Senatu Romano (1563), was so highly esteemed, that some have supposed him to have been assisted by Sigonius. The latter, among his other pursuits, turned his mind to the antiquities of Greece, which had hitherto, for obvious reasons, attracted far less attention than those of ancient Italy. He treated the constitution of the Athenian republic so fully, that, according to Gronovius, he left little for Meursius and others who trod in his path.[g] He has, however, neglected to quote the very words of his authorities, which alone can be satisfactory to a diligent reader, translating every passage, so that hardly any Greek words occur in a treatise expressly on the Athenian polity. This may be deemed a corroboration of what has been said above, as to the decline of Greek learning in Italy.

58. Francis Patrizzi was the first who unfolded the military system of Rome. He wrote in Italian a treatise Della Milizia Romana, 1583, of which a translation will be found in the tenth volume of Grævius.[h]

---

[g] Nonnulla quidem variis locis attigit Meursius et alii, sed teretiore prorsus et rotundo magis ore per omnia Sigonius.

Thesaur. Antiq. Græc. vol. v.
[h] Primus Romanæ rei militaris præstantiam Polybium secutus detexit, cui

It is divided into fifteen parts, which seem to comprehend the whole subject: each of these again is divided into sections; and each section explains a text from the sixth book of Polybius, or from Livy. But he comes down no lower in history than those writers extend, and is consequently not aware of, or but slightly alludes to, the great military changes that ensued in later times. On Polybius he comments sentence by sentence. He had been preceded by Robortellus, and by Francis duke of Urbino, in endeavouring to explain the Roman castrametation from Polybius. Their plans differ a little from his own.[i] Lipsius, who some years afterwards wrote on the same subject, resembles Patrizzi in his method of a running commentary on Polybius. Scaliger, who disliked Lipsius very much, imputes to him plagiarism from the Italian antiquary.[k] But I do not perceive, on a comparison of the two treatises, much pretence for this insinuation. The text of Polybius was surely common ground, and I think it possible that the work of Patrizzi, which was written in Italian, might not be known to Lipsius. But whether this were so or not, he is much more full and satisfactory than his predecessor, who, I would venture to hint, may have been a little over-praised. Lipsius, however, seems to have fallen into the same error of supposing that the whole history of the Roman militia could be explained from Polybius.

59. The works of Lipsius are full of accessions to our

quantum debeant qui post illum in hoc argumento elaborarunt, non nesciunt viri docti qui Josephi Scaligeri epistolas, aut Nicii Erythræi Pinacothecam legerunt. Nonnulli quidem rectius et explicatius sunt tradita de hac doctrina post Patricium a Justo Lipsio et aliis, qui in hoc stadio cucurrerunt; ut non difficulter inventis aliquid additur aut in iis emendatur, sed præclare tamen fractæ glaciei laus Patricio est tribuenda. Grævius in præfat. ad decimum volumen. This book has been confounded by Blount and Ginguéné with a later work of Patrizzi, entitled Paralleli Militari, Rome, 1594, in which he compared the military art of the ancients with that of the moderns, exposing, according to Tiraboschi (viii. 494), his own ignorance of the subject.

[i] All these writers err, in common, I believe, with every other before General Roy, in his Military Antiquities of the Romans in Britain (1793), in placing the prætorium, or tent of the general, near the front gate of the camp, called Porta Prætoria, instead of the opposite, Porta Decumana. Lipsius is so perplexed by the assumption of this hypothesis, that he struggles to alter the text of Polybius.

[k] Scalig. Secunda. In one of Casaubon's epistles to Scaliger, he says:— Franciscus Patritius solus mihi videtur digitum ad fontes intendisse, quem ad verbum alii, qui hoc studium tractarunt, cum sequuntur tamen ejus nomen ne semel quidem memorarunt. Quod equidem magis miratus sum in illis de quorum candore dubitare piaculum esse putassem.

knowledge of Roman antiquity, and he may be said to have
Lipsius and   stood as conspicuous on this side of the Alps as Si-
other anti-
quaries.   gonius in Italy. His treatise on the amphitheatre,
1584, completed what Panvinius, De Ludis Circensibus, had
begun. A later work, by Peter Fabre, president in the parliament of Toulouse, entitled ' Agonisticon, sive de Re Athle-
tica,' 1592, relates to the games of Greece as well as Rome,
and has been highly praised by Gronovius. It will be found
in the eighth volume of the Thesaurus Antiquitatum Græcarum. Several antiquaries traced the history of Roman
families and names; such as Fulvius Ursinus, Sigonius, Panvinius, Pighius, Castalio, Golzius.[m] A Spaniard of immense
erudition, Petrus Ciaconius (Chacon), besides many illustrations of ancient monuments, especially the rostral column of
Duilius, has left a valuable treatise, De Triclinio Romano,
1588.[n] He is not to be confounded with Alfonsus Ciaconius,
a native also of Spain, but not of the same family, who wrote
an account of the column of Trajan. Pancirollus, in his
Notitia Dignitatum, or rather his commentary on a public
document of the age of Constantine so entitled, threw light
on that later period of imperial Rome.

60. The first contribution that England made to ancient
Savile on Ro-   literature in this line was the ' View of Certain
man militia.   Military Matters, or Commentaries concerning Roman Warfare,' by Sir Henry Savile, in 1598. This was
translated into Latin, and printed at Heidelberg, as early as
1601. It contains much information in small compass, extending only to about 130 duodecimo pages. Nor is it borrowed, as far as I could perceive, from Patrizzi or Lipsius,
but displays an independent and extensive erudition.

61. It would encumber the reader's memory were these
pages to become a register of books. Both in this and the
succeeding periods we can only select such as appear, by the
permanence, or, at least, the immediate lustre of their reputation, to have deserved of the great republic of letters better
than the rest. And in such a selection it is to be expected
that the grounds of preference or of exclusion will occasionally not be obvious to all readers, and possibly would not

[m] Grævius, vol. vii.   [n] Blount, Niceron, vol. xxxvi.

be deemed, on re-consideration, conclusive to the author. In names of the second or third class there is often but a shadow of distinction.

62. The foundations were laid, soon after the middle of the century, of an extensive and interesting science —that of ancient medals. Collections of these had Numisma-
tics. been made from the time of Cosmo de' Medici, and perhaps still earlier; but the rules of arranging, comparing, and explaining them were as yet unknown, and could be derived only from close observation, directed by a profound erudition. Eneas Vico of Venice, in 1555, published 'Discorsi sopra le Medaglie degl' Antichi;' 'in which he justly boasts,' says Tiraboschi, 'that he was the first to write in Italian on such a subject; but he might have added that no one had yet written upon it in any language.' [o] The learning of Vico was the more remarkable in that he was by profession an engraver. He afterwards published a series of imperial medals, and another of the empresses; adding to each a life of the person and explanation of the reverse. But in the latter he was excelled by Sebastian Erizzo; a noble Venetian, who four years after Vico published a work with nearly the same title. This is more fully comprehensive than that of Vico; medallic science was reduced in it to fixed principles, and it is particularly esteemed for the erudition shown by the author in explaining the reverses.[p] Both Vico and Erizzo have been sometimes mistaken; but what science is perfect in its commencement? It has been observed that the latter, living at the same time, in the same city, and engaged in the same pursuit, makes no mention of his precursor; a consequence, no doubt, of the jealous humour so apt to prevail with the professors of science, especially when they do not agree in their opinions. This was the case here; Vico having thought ancient coins and medals identical, while Erizzo made a distinction between them, in which modern critics in numismatic learning have generally thought him in the wrong. The medallic collections, published by Hubert Golzius, a Flemish engraver, who had examined most of the private cabinets in Europe, from 1557 to 1579, acquired great

---

[o] Tiraboschi, ix. 226. Ginguéné, vii. 292. Biogr. univ.   [p] Idem.

reputation, and were long reckoned the principal repertory of that science. But it seems that suspicions entertained by many of the learned have been confirmed, and that Golzius has published a great number of spurious and even of imaginary medals; his own good faith being also much implicated in these forgeries.[q]

63. The ancient mythology is too closely connected with all classical literature to have been neglected so long as numismatic antiquity. The compilations of Rhodiginus and Alexander ab Alexandro, besides several other works, and indeed all annotations on Greek and Latin authors, had illustrated it. But this was not done systematically; and no subject more demands a comparison of authorities, which will not always be found consistent or intelligible. Boccaccio had long before led the way, in his Genealogiæ Deorum; but the erudition of the fourteenth century could clear away but little of the cloud that still in some measure hangs over the religion of the ancient world. In the first decad of the present period we find a work of considerable merit for the times, by Lilio Gregorio Giraldi, one of the most eminent scholars of that age, entitled Historia de Diis Gentium. It had been preceded by one of inferior reputation, the Mythologia of Natalis Comes. 'Giraldi,' says the Biographie universelle, 'is the first who has treated properly this subject, so difficult on account of its extent and complexity. He made use not only of all Greek and Latin authors, but of ancient inscriptions, which he has explained with much sagacity. Sometimes the multiplicity of his quotations renders him obscure, and sometimes he fails in accuracy, through want of knowing what has since been brought to light. But the Historia de Diis Gentium is still consulted.'

64. We can place in no other chapter but the present a work, to which none published within this century is superior, and perhaps none is equal, in originality, depth of erudition, and vigorous encountering of difficulty—that of Joseph Scaliger, De Emendatione Temporum. The first edition of this appeared in 1583; the second, which is

Mythology. [marginal note]

Scaliger's Chronology. [marginal note]

---

q Biogr. univ.

much enlarged and amended, in 1598; and a third, still better, in 1609. Chronology, as a science, was hitherto very much unknown; all ancient history, indeed, had been written in a servile and uncritical spirit, copying dates, as it did everything else, from the authorities immediately under the compiler's eye, with little or no endeavour to reconcile discrepancies, or to point out any principles of computation. Scaliger perceived that it would be necessary to investigate the astronomical schemes of ancient calendars, not always very clearly explained by the Greek and Roman writers, and requiring much attention and acuteness, besides a multifarious erudition, oriental as well as classical, of which he alone in Europe could be reckoned master. This work, De Emendatione Temporum, is in the first edition divided into eight books. The first relates to the lesser equal year, as he denominates it, or that of 360 days, adopted by some eastern nations, and founded, as he supposes, on the natural lunar year, before the exact period of a lunation was fully understood; the second book is on the true lunar year, and some other divisions connected with it; the third on the greater equal year, so called, or that of 365 days; the fourth on the more accurate schemes of the solar period. In the fifth and sixth books he comes to particular epochs, determining in both many important dates in profane and sacred history. The seventh and eighth discuss the modes of computation, and the terminal epochs used in different nations, with miscellaneous remarks and critical emendations of his own. In later editions these two books are thrown into one. The great intricacy of many of these questions, which cannot be solved by testimonies often imperfect and inconsistent, without much felicity of conjecture, serves to display the surprising vigour of Scaliger's mind, who grapples like a giant with every difficulty. Le Clerc has censured him for introducing so many conjectures, and drawing so many inferences from them, that great part of his chronology is rendered highly suspicious.[r] But, whatever may be his merit in the determination of particular dates, he is certainly the first who laid the foundations of the science. He justly calls it

----

[r] Parrhasiana, ii. 363.

' Materia intacta et a nobis nunc primum tentata.' Scaliger
in all this work is very clear, concise, and pertinent, and
seems to manifest much knowledge of physical astronomy,
though he was not a good mathematician, and did little
credit to his impartiality by absolutely rejecting the Gregorian
calendar.

65. The chronology of Scaliger has become more celebrated
Julian   through his invention of the Julian period; a name
period.   given, in honour of his father,[s] to a cycle of 7980
years, beginning 4713 before Christ, and consequently before
the usual date of the creation of the world. He was very
proud of this device: ' it is impossible to describe,' he says,
' its utility; chronologers and astronomers cannot extol it too
much.' And what is more remarkable, it was adopted for
many years afterwards, even by the opponents of Scaliger's
chronology, and is almost as much in favour with Petavius
as with the inventor.[t] This Julian period is formed by
multiplying together the years of three cycles once much in
use—the solar of twenty-eight, according to the old calendar,
the lunar or Metonic of nineteen, and the indiction, an
arbitrary and political division, introduced about the time of
Constantine, and common both in the church and empire,
consisting of fifteen years. Yet I confess myself unable to
perceive the great advantage of this scheme. It affords, of
course, a fixed terminus from which all dates may be reckoned
in progressive numbers, better than the era of the creation,
on account of the uncertainty attending that epoch; but the
present method of reckoning them in a retrograde series
from the birth of Christ, which seems never to have occurred
to Scaliger or Petavius, is not found to have much practical
inconvenience. In other respects, the only real use that the
Julian period appears to possess is, that dividing any year in
it by the numbers 28, 19, or 15, the remainder above the
quotient will give us the place such year holds in the

---

[s] [This, though commonly said, appears to be an erroneous supposition. Scaliger himself gives a different reason, and one much more natural: Periodum Julianum vocavimus, quia ad annum Julianum accommodata est. For this I am indebted to the Études historiques of Daunou, vol. iii. p. 366.—1847.]   [t] Usus illius opinione major est in chronicis, quæ ab orbe condito vel alio quovis initio ante æram Christianam inchoantur. Petav. Rationarium Temporum, part ii. lib. i. c. 14.

cycle, by the proper number of which it has been divided. Thus, if we desire to know what place in the Metonic cycle the year of the Julian period 6402, answering to the year of our Lord 1689, held, or in other words, what was the Golden Number, as it is called, of that year, we must divide 6402 by 19, and we shall find in the quotient a remainder 18; whence we perceive that it was the eighteenth year of a lunar or Metonic cycle. The adoption of the Gregorian calendar, which has greatly protracted the solar cycle by the suppression of one bissextile year in a century, as well as the general abandonment of the indiction, and even of the solar and lunar cycles, as divisions of time, have diminished whatever utility this invention may have originally possessed.

CHAPTER II.

HISTORY OF THEOLOGICAL LITERATURE IN EUROPE FROM 1550 TO 1600.

Progress of Protestantism—Re-action of the Catholic Church—The Jesuits —Causes of the Recovery of Catholicism—Bigotry of Lutherans— Controversy on Free-will — Trinitarian Controversy —Writings on Toleration—Theology in England—Bellarmin— Controversy on Papal Authority—Theological Writers—Ecclesiastical Histories—Translations of Scripture.

1. In the arduous struggle between prescriptive allegiance to the Church of Rome and rebellion against its authority, the balance continued for some time after the commencement of this period to be strongly swayed in favour of the reformers. A decree of the diet of Augsburg in 1555, confirming an agreement made by the emperor three years before, called the Pacification of Passau, gave the followers of the Lutheran confession for the first time an established condition, and their rights became part of the public law of Germany. No one, by this decree, could be molested for following either the old or the new form of religion; but those who dissented from that established by their ruler were only to have the liberty of quitting his territories, with time for the disposal of their effects. No toleration was extended to the Helvetic or Calvinistic, generally called the Reformed party; and by the Ecclesiastical Reservation, a part of the decree to which the Lutheran princes seem not to have assented, every Catholic prelate of the empire quitting his religion was declared to forfeit his dignity.

Diet of Augsburg in 1555.

2. This treaty, though incapable of warding off the calamities of a future generation, might justly pass not only for a basis of religious concord, but for a signal triumph of the Protestant cause; such as, a few years before, it would have required all their steadfast faith in the arm of Providence to anticipate. Immediately after its enactment, the principles of the Confession of Augsburg,

Progress of Protestantism.

which had been restrained by fear of the imperial laws
against heresy, spread rapidly to the shores of the Danube,
the Drave, and the Vistula. Those half-barbarous nations,
who might be expected, by a more general analogy, to
remain longest in their ancient prejudices, came more
readily into the new religion than the civilised people of
the south. In Germany itself the progress of the Reformation was still more rapid: most of the Franconian and
Bavarian nobility, and the citizens of every considerable
town, though subjects of Catholic princes, became Protestant; while in Austria it has been said that not more than
one-thirtieth part of the people continued firm in their
original faith. This may probably be exaggerated; but a
Venetian ambassador in 1558 (and the reports of the
envoys of that republic are remarkable for their judicious-
ness and accuracy) estimated the Catholics of the German
empire at only one-tenth of the population.[a] The universities produced no defenders of the ancient religion. For
twenty years no student of the university of Vienna had
become a priest. Even at Ingolstadt it was necessary to
fill with laymen offices hitherto reserved for the clergy.
The prospect was not much more encouraging in France.
The Venetian ambassador in that country (Micheli, whom
we know by his reports of England under Mary) declares
that in 1561 the common people still frequented the
churches, but all others, especially the nobility, had fallen
off; and this defection was greatest among the younger
part.

3. This second burst of a revolutionary spirit in religion
was as rapid, and perhaps more appalling to its
opponents than that under Luther and Zwingle Its causes.
about 1520. It was certainly prepared by long working in
the minds of a part of the people; but most of its opera-
tion was due to that generous sympathy which carries mankind along with any pretext of common interest in the
redress of wrong. A very few years were sufficient to

---

[a] Ranke, vol. ii. p. 125, takes a general survey of the religious state of the
empire about 1563.

make millions desert their altars, abjure their faith, loathe, spurn, and insult their gods: words hardly too strong, when we remember how the saints and the Virgin had been honoured in their images, and how they and those were now despised. It is to be observed, that the Protestant doctrines had made no sensible progress in the south of Germany before the Pacification of Passau in 1552, nor much in France before the death of Henry II. in 1559. The spirit of reformation, suppressed under his severe administration, burst forth when his weak and youthful son ascended the throne, with an impetuosity that threatened for a time the subversion of that profligate despotism by which the house of Valois had replaced the feudal aristocracy. It is not for us here to discriminate the influences of ambition and oligarchical factiousness from those of high-minded and strenuous exertion in the cause of conscience.

4. It is not surprising that some Catholic governments Wavering of wavered for a time, and thought of yielding to a Catholic princes. storm which might involve them in ruin. Even as early as 1556, the duke of Bavaria was compelled to make concessions which would have led to a full introduction of the Reformation. The emperor Ferdinand I. was tolerant in disposition, and anxious for some compromise that might extinguish the schism; his successor, Maximilian II., displayed the same temper so much more strongly, that he incurred the suspicion of a secret leaning towards the reformed tenets. Sigismund Augustus, king of Poland, was probably at one time wavering which course to adopt; and though he did not quit the church of Rome, his court and the Polish nobility became extensively Protestant; so that, according to some, there was a very considerable majority at his death who professed that creed. Among the Austrian and Hungarian nobility, as well as the burghers in the chief cities, it was held by so preponderating a body that they obtained a full toleration and equality of privileges. England, after two or three violent convulsions, became firmly Protestant; the religion of the court being soon followed with sincere good-will by the people. Scotland, more unanimously and impetuously, threw off the yoke of Rome.

The Low Countries very early caught the flame, and sustained the full brunt of persecution at the hands of Charles and Philip.

5. Meantime the infant Protestantism of Italy had given some signs of increasing strength, and began more and more to number men of reputation; but, unsupported by popular affection, or the policy of princes, it was soon wholly crushed by the arm of power. The reformed church of Locarno was compelled in 1554 to emigrate in the midst of winter, and took refuge at Zurich. That of Lucca was finally dispersed about the same time. A fresh storm of persecution arose at Modena in 1556; many lost their lives for religion in the Venetian States before 1560; others were put to death at Rome. The Protestant countries were filled with Italian exiles, many of them highly gifted men, who, by their own eminence, and by the distinction which has in some instances awaited their posterity, may be compared with those whom the revocation of the Edict of Nantes long afterwards dispersed over Europe. The tendency towards Protestantism in Spain was of the same kind, but less extensive, and certainly still less popular than in Italy. The Inquisition took it up, and applied its usual remedies with success. But this would lead us still farther from literary history than we have already wandered.

Extinguished in Italy, and Spain.

6. This prodigious increase of the Protestant party in Europe after the middle of the century did not continue more than a few years. It was checked and fell back, not quite so rapidly or so completely as it came on, but so as to leave the antagonist church in perfect security. Though we must not tread closely on the ground of political history, nor discuss too minutely any revolutions of opinion which do not distinctly manifest themselves in literature, it seems not quite foreign from the general purpose of these volumes, or at least a pardonable digression, to dwell a little on the leading causes of this retrograde movement of Protestantism; a fact as deserving of explanation as the previous excitement of the Reformation itself, though, from its more negative nature, it has not drawn so much of the attention of mankind. Those who behold the outbreaking of great revolutions in civil society or in religion, will not easily believe

Re-action of Catholicity;

that the rush of waters can be stayed in its course, that a pause of indifference may come on, perhaps very suddenly, or a re-action bring back nearly the same prejudices and passions as those which men had renounced. Yet this has occurred not very rarely in the annals of mankind, and never on a larger scale than in the history of the Reformation.

7. The church of Rome, and the prince whom it most especially in strongly influenced, Philip II., acted on an unre-Germany. mitting, uncompromising policy of subduing, instead of making terms with its enemies. In Spain and Italy the Inquisition soon extirpated the remains of heresy. The fluctuating policy of the French court, destitute of any strong religious zeal, and therefore prone to expedients, though always desirous of one end, is well known. It was, in fact, impossible to conquer a party so prompt to resort to arms and so skilful in their use as the Huguenots. But in Bavaria Albert V., with whom, about 1564, the re-action began, in the Austrian dominions Rodolph II., in Poland Sigismund III., by shutting up churches, and by discountenancing in all respects their Protestant subjects, contrived to change a party once exceedingly powerful into an oppressed sect. The decrees of the council of Trent were received by the spiritual princes of the empire in 1566 ; ' and from this moment,' says the excellent historian who has thrown most light on this subject, ' began a new life for the Catholic church in Germany.' [b] The profession of faith was signed by all orders of men ; no one could be admitted to a degree in the universities nor keep a school without it. Protestants were in some places excluded from the court ; a penalty which tended much to bring about the reconversion of a poor and proud nobility.

8. That could not, however, have been effected by any Discipline of efforts of the princes against so preponderating a the clergy. majority as the Protestant churches had obtained, if the principles that originally actuated them had retained their animating influence, or had not been opposed by more efficacious resistance. Every method was adopted to revive an attachment to the ancient religion, insuperable by the love of novelty or the force of argument. A stricter disci-

---

[b] Ranke, ii. 46. [I quote the German, but this valuable work has now been translated.—1842.]

pline and subordination was introduced among the clergy; they were early trained in seminaries, apart from the sentiments and habits, the vices and virtues of the world. The monastic orders resumed their rigid observances. The Capucins, not introduced into France before 1570, spread over the realm within a few years, and were most active in getting up processions and all that we call foolery, but which is not the less stimulating to the multitude for its folly. It is observed by Davila, that these became more frequent after the accession of Henry III. in 1574.

9. But, far above all the rest, the Jesuits were the instruments of regaining France and Germany to the church they served. And we are the more closely concerned with them here, that they are in this age among the links between religious opinion and literature. We have seen in the last chapter with what spirit they took the lead in polite letters and classical style, with what dexterity they made the brightest talents of the rising generation, which the church had once dreaded and checked, her most willing and effective instruments. The whole course of liberal studies, however deeply grounded in erudition or embellished by eloquence, took one direction, one perpetual aim—the propagation of the Catholic faith. They availed themselves for this purpose of every resource which either human nature or prevalent opinion supplied. Did they find Latin versification highly prized? their pupils wrote sacred poems. Did they observe the natural taste of mankind for dramatic representations, and the repute which that species of literature had obtained? their walls resounded with sacred tragedies. Did they perceive an unjust prejudice against stipendiary instruction? they gave it gratuitously. Their endowments left them in the decent poverty which their vows required, without the offensive mendicancy of the friars.

10. In 1551 Ferdinand established a college of Jesuits at Vienna; in 1556 they obtained one, through the favour of the duke of Bavaria, at Ingolstadt, and in 1559 at Munich. They spread rapidly into other Catholic states of the empire, and some time later into Poland. In France their success was far more equivocal; the Sorbonne declared against them as early as 1554, and they had always

to encounter the opposition of the parliament of Paris. But
they established themselves at Lyons in 1569, and afterwards
at Bordeaux, Toulouse, and other cities. Their three duties
were preaching, confession, and education ; the most powerful levers that religion could employ. Indefatigable and
unscrupulous, as well as polite and learned, accustomed to
consider veracity and candour, when they weakened an argument, in the light of treason against the cause (language
which might seem harsh, were it not almost equally applicable to so many other partisans), they knew how to clear
their reasonings from scholastic pedantry, and tedious quotation, for the simple and sincere understandings whom they
addressed ; yet, in the proper field of controversial theology,
they wanted nothing of sophistical expertness or of erudition. The weak points of Protestantism they attacked with
embarrassing ingenuity ; and the reformed churches did not
cease to give them abundant advantage by inconsistency,
extravagance, and passion.[c]

11. At the death of Ignatius Loyola in 1556, the order
Their col-   that he had founded was divided into thirteen pro-
leges.   vinces, besides the Roman ; most of which were in
the Spanish peninsula or its colonies. Ten colleges belonged
to Castile, eight to Aragon, five to Andalusia. Spain was
for some time the fruitful mother of the disciples, as she had
been of the master. The Jesuits who came to Germany were
called ' Spanish priests.' They took possession of the universities : ' they conquered us,' says Ranke, ' on our own
ground, in our own homes, and stripped us of a part of our
country.' This, the acute historian proceeds to say, sprang
certainly from the want of understanding among the Protestant theologians, and of sufficient enlargement of mind to
tolerate unessential differences. The violent opposition among
each other left the way open to these cunning strangers, who
taught a doctrine not open to dispute.

12. But though Spain for a time supplied the most active

---

[c] Hospinian. Hist. Jesuitarum.
Ranke, vol. ii. p. 32 et post. Tiraboschi, viii. 116. The first of these works
is entirely on one side, and gives no
credit to the Jesuits for their services
to literature. The second is of a very
different class, philosophical and profound, and yet with much more learning,
that is, with a more extensive range of
knowledge, than any writer of Hospinian's age could possess.

spirits in the order, its central point was always at Rome. It was there that the general to whom they had sworn resided; and from thence issued to the remotest lands the voice, which, whatever secret counsels might guide it, appeared that of a single, irresponsible, irresistible will. The Jesuits had three colleges at Rome; one for their own novices, another for German, and a third for English students. Possevin has given us an account of the course of study in Jesuit seminaries, taking that of Rome as a model. It contained nearly 2000 scholars, of various descriptions. ' No one,' he says, ' is admitted without a foundation of grammatical knowledge. The abilities, the dispositions, the intentions for future life, are scrupulously investigated in each candidate; nor do we open our doors to any who do not come up in these respects to what so eminent a school of all virtue requires. They attend divine service daily; they confess every month. The professors are numerous; some teaching the exposition of Scripture, some scholastic theology, some the science of controversy with heretics, some casuistry; many instruct in logic and philosophy, in mathematics, or rhetoric, polite literature, and poetry; the Hebrew and Greek, as well as Latin, tongues are taught. Three years are given to the course of philosophy, four to that of theology. But if any are found not so fit for deep studies, yet likely to be useful in the Lord's vineyard, they merely go through two years of practical, that is, casuistical theology. These seminaries are for youths advanced beyond the inferior classes or schools; but in the latter also religious and grammatical learning go hand in hand.' [d]

13. The popes were not neglectful of such faithful servants. Under Gregory XIII., whose pontificate began in 1572, the Jesuit college at Rome had twenty lecture rooms and 360 chambers for students; a German college was restored after a temporary suspension; and an English one founded by his care; perhaps there was not a Jesuit seminary in the world which was not indebted to his liberality. Gregory also established a Greek college (not of Jesuits) for the education of youths, who there learned to propagate the

Jesuit seminary at Rome.

Patronage of Gregory XIII.

d Possevin, Bibliotheca Selecta, lib. i. c. 39.

Catholic faith in their country.[e] No earlier pope had been more alert and strenuous in vindicating his claims to universal allegiance; nor, as we may judge from the well-known pictures of Vasari in the vestibule of the Sistine chapel, representing the Massacre of St. Bartholomew, more ready to sanction any crime that might be serviceable to the church.

14. The resistance made to this aggressive warfare was for Conversions some time considerable. Protestantism, so late as in Germany and France. 1578, might be deemed preponderant in all the Austrian dominions except the Tyrol.[f] In the Polish diets the dissidents, as they were called, met their opponents with vigour and success. The ecclesiastical principalities were full of Protestants; and even in the chapters some of them might be found. But the contention was unequal, from the different character of the parties: religious zeal and devotion, which fifty years before had overthrown the ancient rites in northern Germany, were now more invigorating sentiments in those who rescued them from further innovation. In religious struggles, where there is anything like an equality of forces, the question soon comes to be which party will make the greatest sacrifice for its own faith. And while the Catholic self-devotion had grown far stronger, there was much more of secular cupidity, lukewarmness, and formality in the Lutheran church. In a very few years the effects of this were distinctly visible. The Protestants of the Catholic principalities went back into the bosom of Rome. In the bishopric of Wurtzburg alone 62,000 converts are said to have been received in the year 1586.[g] The emperor Rodolph and his brother archdukes, by a long series of persecutions and banishment, finally, though not within this century, almost outrooted Protestantism from the hereditary provinces of Austria. It is true that these violent measures were the proximate cause of so many conversions; but if the reformed had been ardent and united, they were much too strong to have been thus subdued. In Bohemia, accordingly, and Hungary, where there was a more steady spirit, they kept their ground. The re-action was not less conspicuous in other countries. It is asserted that the Huguenots had

---

    [e] Ranke, i. 419 et post. Ginguéné, vii. 12. Tiraboschi, viii. 34.
    [f] Ranke, ii. 78.   [g] Id. p. 147.

already lost more than two-thirds of their number in 1580 ;[h] comparatively, I presume, with twenty years before; and the change in their relative position is manifest from all the histories of this period.   In the Netherlands, though the seven United Provinces were slowly winning their civil and religious liberties at the sword's point, yet West Flanders, once in great measure Protestant, became Catholic before the end of the century; while the Walloon provinces were kept from swerving by some bishops of great eloquence and excellent lives, as well as by the influence of the Jesuits planted at St. Omer and Douay.   At the close of this period of fifty years the mischief done to the old church in its first decennium was very nearly repaired; the proportions of the two religions in Germany coincided with those which had existed at the Pacification of Passau.   The Jesuits, however, had begun to encroach a little on the proper domain of the Lutheran church; besides private conversions, which, on account of the rigour of the laws, not certainly less intolerant than in their own communion, could not be very prominent, they had sometimes hopes of the Protestant princes, and had once, in 1578, obtained the promise of John king of Sweden to embrace openly the Romish faith, as he had already done in secret to Possevin, an emissary despatched by the pope on this important errand.   But the symptoms of an opposition, very formidable in a country which has never allowed its kings to trifle with it, made this wavering monarch retrace his steps.   His successor, Sigismund, went farther, and fell a victim to his zeal, by being expelled from the kingdom.

15. This great revival of the papal religion after the shock it had sustained in the first part of the sixteenth century ought for ever to restrain that temerity of prediction so frequent in our ears.   As women sometimes believe the fashion of last year in dress to be wholly ridiculous, and incapable of being ever again adopted by any one solicitous about her beauty, so those who affect to pronounce on future events are equally confident against the possibility of a resurrection of opinions which the majority have for the time ceased to maintain.   In the year 1560, every Protestant

Causes of this revival.

---

[h] Ranke, 121.   The number seems rather startling.

in Europe doubtless anticipated the overthrow of Popery;
the Catholics could have found little else to warrant hope
than their trust in Heaven. The late rush of many nations
towards democratical opinions has not been so rapid and so
general as the change of religion about that period. It is
important and interesting to inquire what stemmed this
current. We readily acknowledge the prudence, firmness,
and unity of purpose, that for the most part distinguished
the court of Rome, the obedience of its hierarchy, the severity
of intolerant laws, and the searching rigour of the Inquisition, the resolute adherence of great princes to the Catholic
faith, the influence of the Jesuits over education; but these
either existed before, or would at least not have been sufficient
to withstand an overwhelming force of opinion. It must be
acknowledged that there was a principle of vitality in that
religion, independent of its external strength. By the side
of its secular pomp, its relaxation of morality, there had
always been an intense flame of zeal and devotion. Superstition it might be in the many, fanaticism in a few; but both
of these imply the qualities which, while they subsist, render
a religion indestructible. That revival of an ardent zeal,
through which the Franciscans had, in the thirteenth century, with some good and much more evil effect, spread a
popular enthusiasm over Europe, was once more displayed
in counteraction of those new doctrines, that themselves
had drawn their life from a similar development of moral
emotion.

16. Even in the court of Leo X., soon after the bursting
A rigid
party in the
church.
forth of the Reformation in Saxony, a small body
was formed by men of rigid piety, and strenuous for
a different species of reform. Sadolet, Caraffa (afterwards
Paul IV.), Cajetan, and Contareni, both the latter eminent
in the annals of the church, were at the head of this party.[1]
Without dwelling on what belongs strictly to ecclesiastical
history, it is sufficient to say that they acquired much weight;
and, while adhering generally to the doctrine of the church
(though Contareni held the Lutheran tenets on justification),
aimed steadily at a restoration of moral discipline, and the

---

[1] Ranke, i. 133.

abolition of every notorious abuse. Several of the regular
orders were reformed, while others were instituted, more
active in sacerdotal duties than the rest. The Jesuits must
be considered as the most perfect type of the rigid party.
Whatever may be objected, perhaps not quite so early, to
their system of casuistry, whatever want of scrupulousness
may have been shown in their conduct, they were men who
never swerved from the path of labour, and, it might be,
suffering, in the cause which they deemed that of God. All
self-sacrifice in such circumstances, especially of the highly-
gifted and accomplished, though the bigot steels his heart
and closes his eyes against it, excites the admiration of the
unsophisticated part of mankind.

17. The council of Trent, especially in its later sessions,
displayed the antagonist parties in the Roman
church, one struggling for lucrative abuses, one
anxious to overthrow them. They may be called the Italian
and Spanish parties; the first headed by the pope's legates,
dreading above all things both the reforming spirit of
Constance and Basle, and the independence either of princes
or of national churches; the other actuated by much of the
spirit of those councils, and tending to confirm that independence. The French and German prelates usually sided
with the Spanish; and they were together strong enough to
establish as a rule, that in every session a decree for reformation should accompany the declaration of doctrine. The
council interrupted in 1547 by the measure that Paul III.
found it necessary for his own defence against these reformers
to adopt, the translation of its sittings to Bologna, with
which the Imperial prelates refused to comply, was opened
again by Julius III. in 1552; and having been once more
suspended in the same year, resumed its labour for the last
time under Pius IV. in 1562. It terminated in 1564, when
the court of Rome, which, with the Italian prelates, had
struggled hard to obstruct the redress of every grievance,
compelled the more upright members of the council to let it
close, after having effected such a reformation of discipline
as they could obtain. That court was certainly successful in
the contest, so far as it might be called one, of prerogative
against liberty; and partially successful in the preservation

Its efforts at Trent.

of its lesser interests and means of influence. Yet it seems impossible to deny that the effects of the council of Trent were on the whole highly favourable to the church for whose benefit it was summoned. The Reformation would never have roused the whole north of Europe, had the people seen nothing in it but the technical problems of theology. It was against ambition and cupidity, sluggish ignorance and haughty pomp, that they took up arms. Hence the abolition of many long-established abuses by the honest zeal of the Spanish and Cisalpine fathers in that council took away much of the ground on which the prevalent disaffection rested.

18. We should be inclined to infer from the language of No compromise in doctrine. some contemporaries that the council might have proceeded farther with more advantage than danger to their church, by complying with the earnest and repeated solicitations of the emperor, the duke of Bavaria, and even the court of France, that the sacramental cup should be restored to the laity, and that the clergy should not be restrained from marriage. Upon this, however, it is not here for us to dilate. The policy of both concessions, but especially of the latter, was always questionable, and has not been demonstrated by the event. In its determinations of doctrine, the council was generally cautious to avoid extremes, and left, in many momentous questions of the controversy, such as the invocation of saints, no small latitude for private opinion. It has been thought by some that they lost sight of this prudence in defining transubstantiation so rigidly as they did in 1551, and thus opposed an obstacle to the conversion of those who would have acquiesced in a more equivocal form of words. But, in truth, no alternative was left upon this point. Transubstantiation had been asserted by a prior council, the Fourth Lateran in 1215, so positively, that to recede would have surrendered the main principle of the Catholic church. And it is also to be remembered, when we judge of what might have been done, as we fancy, with more prudence, that, if there was a good deal of policy in the decisions of the council of Trent, there was no want also of conscientious sincerity ; and that, whatever we may think of this doctrine, it was one which seemed of funda-

mental importance to the serious and obedient sons of the church.[r]

19. There is some difficulty in proving for the council of Trent that universality to which its adherents attach an infallible authority. And this was not held to be a matter of course by the great European powers. Even in France the Tridentine decrees, in matters of faith, have not been formally received, though the Gallican church has never called any of them in question; those relating to matters of discipline are distinctly held not obligatory. The emperor Ferdinand seems to have hesitated about acknowledging the decisions of a council which had at least failed in the object for which it was professedly summoned—the conciliation of all parties to the church. For we find that, even after its

Consultation of Cassander.

---

[r] A strange notion has been started of late years in England, that the council of Trent made important innovations in the previously established doctrines of the Western church; an hypothesis so paradoxical in respect to public opinion, and, it must be added, so prodigiously at variance with the known facts of ecclesiastical history, that we cannot but admire the facility with which it has been taken up. It will appear, by reading the accounts of the sessions of the council, either in Father Paul, or in any more favourable historian, that, even in certain points, such as justification, which had not been clearly laid down before, the Tridentine decrees were mostly conformable with the sense of the majority of those doctors who had obtained the highest reputation; and that upon what are more usually reckoned the distinctive characteristics of the church of Rome, namely, transubstantiation, purgatory, and invocation of the saints and the Virgin, they assert nothing but what had been so ingrafted into the faith of this part of Europe, as to have been rejected by no one without suspicion or imputation of heresy. Perhaps Erasmus would not have acquiesced with good will in *all* the decrees of the council; but was Erasmus deemed orthodox? It is not impossible that the great hurry with which some controversies of considerable importance were despatched in the last sessions, may have had as much to do with the short and vague phrases employed in respect to them, as the prudence I have attributed to the fathers; but the facts will remain the same on either supposition. [1839. The persons alluded to in this note have since changed their ground, and discovered that the council of Trent has not been quite so great an innovator as they had imagined.—1842.]

No general council ever contained so many persons of eminent learning and ability as that of Trent; nor is there ground for believing that any other ever investigated the questions before it with so much patience, acuteness, temper, and desire of truth. The early councils, unless they are greatly belied, would not bear comparison in these characteristics. Impartiality and freedom from prejudice no Protestant will attribute to the fathers of Trent; but where will he produce these qualities in an ecclesiastical synod? But it may be said that they had only one leading prejudice, that of determining theological faith according to the tradition of the Catholic church, as handed down to their own age. This one point of authority conceded, I am not aware that they can be proved to have decided wrong, or at least against all reasonable evidence. Let those who have imbibed a different opinion ask themselves whether they have read Sarpi through with any attention, especially as to those sessions of the Tridentine council which preceded its suspension in 1547.

close, he referred the chief points in controversy to George
Cassander, a German theologian of very moderate sentiments
and temper.   Cassander wrote, at the emperor's request, his
famous Consultation, wherein he passes in review every
article in the Confession of Augsburg, so as to give, if possible, an interpretation consonant to that of the Catholic
church.   Certain it is, that between Melanchthon's desire
of concord in drawing up the Confession, and that of
Cassander in judging of it, no great number of points seem
to be left for dispute.   In another treatise of Cassander, De
Officio Pii Viri in hoc Dissidio Religionis (1561), he holds the
same course that Erasmus had done before, blaming those
who, on account of the stains in the church, would wholly
subvert it, as well as those who erect the pope into a sort of
deity, by setting up his authority as an infallible rule of
faith.   The rule of controversy laid down by Cassander is,
Scripture explained by the tradition of the ancient church;
which is best to be learned from the writings of those who
lived from the age of Constantine to that of Gregory I.,
because, during that period, the principal articles of faith
were most discussed.   Dupin observes that the zeal of
Cassander for the reunion and peace of the church made him
yield too much to the Protestants, and advance some propositions that were too bold. But they were by no means satisfied
with his concessions.   This treatise was virulently attacked
by Calvin, to whom Cassander replied.   No one should hesitate to prefer the spirit of Cassander to that of Calvin ; but
it must be owned that the practical consequence of his
advice would have been to check the profession of the
reformed religion, leaving amendment to those who had little
disposition to amend any thing.   Nor is it by any means
unlikely that this conciliatory scheme, by extenuating dis-
agreements, had a considérable influence in that cessation of
the advance of Protestantism, or rather that recovery of lost
ground by the opposite party, to which we have lately adverted, and of which more proofs were afterwards given.

20. We ought to reckon also among the principal causes
Bigotry of of this change those perpetual disputes, those irre-
Protestant
churches. concilable animosities, that bigotry, above all, and
persecuting spirit, which were exhibited in the Lutheran

and Calvinistic churches. Each began with a common principle — the necessity of an orthodox faith. But this orthodoxy meant evidently nothing more than their own belief as opposed to that of their adversaries; a belief acknowledged to be fallible, yet maintained as certain, rejecting authority in one breath, and appealing to it in the next, and claiming to rest on sure proofs of reason and Scripture, which their opponents were ready with just as much confidence to invalidate.

21. The principle of several controversies which agitated the two great divisions of the Protestant name was still that of the real presence. The Calvinists, as far as their meaning could be divined through a dense mist of nonsense which they purposely collected,[s] were little, if at all, less removed from the Romish and Lutheran parties than the disciples of Zwingle himself, who spoke out more perspicuously. Nor did the orthodox Lutherans fail to perceive this essential discrepancy. Melanchthon, incontestably the most eminent man of their church after the death of Luther, had obtained a great influence over the younger students of theology. But his opinions, half-concealed as they were, and perhaps unsettled, had long been tending to a very different line from those of Luther. The deference exacted by the latter, and never withheld, kept them from any open dissension. But some, whose admiration for the founder of their church was not checked by any scruples at his doctrine, soon began to inveigh against the sacrifice of his favourite tenets which Melanchthon seemed ready to make through timidity, as they believed, or false judgment. To the Romanists he was willing to concede the primacy of the pope and the jurisdiction of bishops; to the Helvetians he was suspected of leaning on the great controversy of the real presence; while, on the still more important questions of faith and works, he not only rejected the Antinomian exaggerations of the high Lutherans, but introduced a doctrine said to be nearly similar to that called Semi-Pelagian; according to which the grace communicated to adult persons so as to draw them to God

Marginal note: Tenets of Melanchthon.

---

[s] See some of this in Bossuet, Variations des Églises protestantes, 1. ix. I do not much trust to Bossuet; but it would be too easy to find similar evidence from our own writers.

required a correspondent action of their own free-will in
order to become effectual. Those who held this tenet were
called Synergists.[t] It appears to be the same, or nearly so,
as that adopted by the Arminians in the next century, but
was not perhaps maintained by any of the schoolmen; nor
does it seem consonant to the decisions of the council of
Trent, nor probably to the intention of those who compiled
the articles of the English Church. It is easy, however, to
be mistaken as to these theological subtilties, which those
who write of them with most confidence do not really discriminate by any consistent or intelligible language.

22. There seems good reason to suspect that the bitterness
A party hostile to him. manifested by the rigid Lutherans against the new
school was aggravated by some political events of
this period; the university of Wittenberg, in which Melanchthon long resided, being subject to the elector Maurice, whose
desertion of the Protestant confederacy and unjust acquisition of the electorate at the expense of the best friends of the
Reformation, though partly expiated by his subsequent conduct, could never be forgiven by the adherents and subjects
of the Ernestine line. Those first protectors of the reformed
faith, now become the victims of his ambition, were reduced
to the duchies of Weimar and Gotha, within the former of
which the university of Jena, founded in 1559, was soon filled
with the sternest zealots of Luther's school. Flacius Illyricus,
most advantageously known as the chief compiler of the
Centuriæ Magdeburgenses, was at the head of this university,
and distinguished by his animosity against Melanchthon,
whose gentle spirit was released by death from the contentions he abhorred in 1560. Bossuet exaggerates the indecision
of Melanchthon on many disputable questions, which, as far
as it existed, is rather perhaps a matter of praise; but his
want of firmness makes it not always easy to determine his
real sentiments, especially in his letters, and somewhat impaired the dignity and sincerity of his mind.

23. After the death of Melanchthon, a controversy, begun
Form of Concord, 1576. by one Brentius, relating to the ubiquity, as it was
called, of Christ's body, proceeded with much heat.
It is sufficient to mention that it led to what is denominated

---

[t] Mosheim.   Bayle, art. Synergistes.

the Formula Concordiæ, a declaration of faith on several matters of controversy, drawn up at Torgau in 1576, and subscribed by the Saxon and most other Lutheran churches of Germany, though not by those of Brunswick, or of the northern kingdoms. It was justly considered as a complete victory of the rigid over the moderate party. The strict enforcement of subscription to this creed gave rise to a good deal of persecution against those who were called Crypto-Calvinists, or suspected of a secret bias towards the proscribed doctrine. Peucer, son-in-law of Melanchthon and editor of his works, was kept for eleven years in prison. And a very narrow spirit of orthodoxy prevailed for a century and a half afterwards in Lutheran theology. But in consequence of this spirit, that theology has been almost entirely neglected and contemned in the rest of Europe, and not many of its books during that period are remembered by name.[u]

24. Though it may be reckoned doubtful whether the council of Trent did not repel some wavering Pro- *Controversy raised by* testants by its unqualified re-enactment of the doc- *Baius.* trine of transubstantiation, it prevented, at least, those controversies on the real presence which agitated the Protestant communions. But in another more extensive and important province of theology, the decisions of the council, though cautiously drawn up, were far from precluding such differences of opinion as ultimately gave rise to a schism in the Church of Rome, and have had no small share in the decline of its power. It is said that some of the Dominican order, who could not but find in their most revered authority, Thomas Aquinas, a strong assertion of Augustin's scheme of divinity, were hardly content with some of the decrees at Trent, as leaving a door open to Semi-Pelagianism.[x] The controversy, however, was first raised by Baius, professor of divinity at Louvain, now chiefly remarkable as the precursor of Jansenius. Many propositions attributed to Baius were censured

---

[u] Hospinian, Concordia Discors, is my chief authority. He was a Swiss Calvinist, and of course very hostile to the Lutheran party. But Mosheim does not vindicate very strongly his own church. See also several articles in Bayle; and Eichhorn, vi. part i. 234.

[x] Du Chesne, Histoire du Baianisme,

vol. i. p. 8. This opinion is ascribed to Peter Soto, confessor to Charles V., who took a part in the re-conversion of England under Mary. He is not to be confounded with the more celebrated Dominic Soto. Both these divines were distinguished ornaments of the council of Trent.

by the Sorbonne in 1560, and by a bull of Pius V. in 1567. He submitted to the latter; but his tenets, which are hardly distinguishable from those of Calvin, struck root, especially in the Low Countries, and seem to have passed from the disciples of Baius to the famous bishop of Ypres in the next century. The bull of Pius apparently goes much farther from the Calvinistic hypothesis than the council of Trent had done. The Jansenist party, in later times, maintained that it was not binding upon the church.[y]

25. These disputes, after a few years, were revived and Treatise of inflamed by the treatise of Molina, a Spanish Jesuit, Molina on in 1588, on free-will. In this he was charged with Free-will. swerving as much from the right line on one side as Baius had been supposed to do on the other. His tenets, indeed, as usually represented, do not appear to differ from those maintained afterwards by the Arminians in Holland and England. But it has not been deemed orthodox in the church of Rome to deviate ostensibly from the doctrine of Augustin in this controversy; and Thomas Aquinas, though not quite of equal authority in the church at large, was held almost infallible by the Dominicans, a powerful order, well stored with learning and logic, and already jealous of the rising influence of the Jesuits. Some of the latter did not adhere to the Semi-Pelagian theories of Molina; but the spirit of the order was roused, and they all exerted themselves successfully to screen his book from the condemnation which Clement VIII. was much inclined to pronounce upon it. They had before this time been accused of Pelagianism by the Thomists, and especially by the partisans of Baius, who procured from the universities of Louvain and Douay a censure of the tenets that some Jesuits had promulgated.[z]

---

[y] Some of the tenets asserted in the articles of the church of England are condemned in this bull, especially the 13th. Du Chesne, p. 78 et post. See Biogr. univ. art. Baius and Bayle. Du Chesne is reckoned an unfair historian by those who favour Baius.

[z] Du Chesne. Biogr. univ. art. Molina. The controversy had begun before the publication of Molina's treatise; and the faculty of Louvain censured thirty-one propositions of the Jesuits in 1587.

Paris, however, refused to confirm the censure. Bellarmin, in 1588, drew up an abstract of the dispute by command of Sixtus V. In this he does not decide in favour of either side, but the pope declared the Jesuit propositions to be sanæ doctrinæ articuli, p. 258. The appearance of Molina's book, which was thought to go much farther towards Pelagianism, renewed the flame. Clement VIII. was very desirous to condemn Molina; but Henry IV., who now

26. The Protestant theologians did not fail to entangle themselves in this intricate wilderness. Melanchthon <small>Protestant</small> drew a large portion of the Lutherans into what was <small>tenets.</small> afterwards called Arminianism; but the reformed churches, including the Helvetian, which, after the middle of the century, gave up many at least of those points of difference which had distinguished them from that of Geneva, held the doctrine of Augustin on absolute predestination, on total depravity, and arbitrary irresistible grace.

27. A third source of intestine disunion lay deep in recesses beyond the soundings of human reason. The <small>Trinitarian</small> doctrine of the Trinity, which theologians agree to <small>Controversy.</small> call inscrutable, but which they do not fail to define and analyse with the most confident dogmatism, had already, as we have seen in a former passage, been investigated by some bold spirits with little regard to the established faith. They had soon, however, a terrible proof of the danger that still was to wait on such momentous aberrations from the prescribed line. Servetus, having, in 1553, published, at Vienne in Dauphiné, a new treatise, called Christianismi Restitutio, and escaping from thence, as he vainly hoped, to the Protestant city of Geneva, became a victim to the bigotry of the magistrates, instigated by Calvin, who had acquired an immense ascendancy over that republic.[a] He did not leave,

---

favoured the Jesuits, interfered for their honour. Cardinal Perron took the same side, and told the pope that a Protestant might subscribe the Dominican doctrine. Ranke, ii. 295 et post. Paul V. was also rather inclined against the Jesuits; but it would have been hard to mortify such good friends, and in 1607 he issued a declaration postponing the decision *sine die*. The Jesuits deemed themselves victorious, as in fact they were. Id. p. 353.

[a] This book is among the scarcest in the world, ipsa raritate rarior, as it is called by Schelhorn. Il est reconnu, says De Bure, pour le plus rare de tous les livres. It was long supposed that no copy existed except that belonging to Dr. Mead, afterwards to the Duke de la Valière, and now in the royal library at Paris. But a second is said to be in the Imperial library at Vienna; and Brunet observes, on connoît à peine

trois exemplaires, which seems to hint that there may be a third. Allwoerden, in his Life of Servetus, published in 1727, did not know where any printed copy could be found, several libraries having been named by mistake, But there were at that time several manuscript copies, one of which he used himself. It had belonged to Samuel Crellius, and afterwards to La Croze, from whom he had borrowed it, and was transcribed from a printed copy, belonging to an Unitarian minister in Transylvania, who had obtained it in England between 1660 and 1670. This celebrated book is a collection of several treatises, with the general title, Christianismi Restitutio. But that of the first and most remarkable part has been differently given. According to a letter from the Abbé Rive, librarian to the Duke de la Valière, to Dutens, which the latter has published

as far as we know, any peculiar disciples.   Many, however,
among the German Anabaptists, held tenets not unlike those

in the second edition of his Origines des
Découvertes attribuées aux Modernes,
vol. ii. p. 359, all former writers on the
subject have been incorrect.   The difference, however, is but in one word.
In Sandius, Niceron, Allwoerden, and
I suppose, others, the title runs : De
Trinitate Divina, quod in ea non sit *indivisibilium* trium rerum illusio, sed vera
substantiæ Dei manifestatio in verbo,
et communicatio in spiritu, libri vii.
The Abbé Rive gives the word *invisi-
bilium*, and this I find also in the additions of Simler to the Bibliotheca
Universalis of Gesner, to which M. Rive
did not advert.   In Allwoerden, however, a distinct heading is given to the
6th and 7th dialogues, wherein the same
title is repeated, with the word *invisibi-
lium* instead of *indivisibilium*.   It is remarked in a note, by Rive or Dutens,
that it was a gross error to put *indivisibilium*, as it makes Servetus say the
contrary of what his system requires.
I am not entirely of this opinion ; and
if I understand the system of Servetus
at all, the word *indivisibilium* is very
intelligible.   De Bure, who seems to
write from personal inspection of the
same copy, which he supposed to be
unique, gives the title with *indivisibilium*.
The Christianismi Restitutio was reprinted at Nuremberg, about 1790, in
the same form as the original edition ;
but I am not aware which word is used
in the title-page; nor would the evidence
of a modern reprint, possibly not taken
immediately from a printed copy, be
conclusive.
The Life of Servetus by Allwoerden,
Helmstadt, 1727, is partly founded on
materials collected by Mosheim, who
put them into the author's hands.   Bar-
bier is much mistaken in placing it
among pseudonymous works, as if Allwoerden had been a fictitious denomination of Mosheim.   Dictionnaire des Ano-
nymes (1824), iii. 555.   The book contains, even in the title-page, all possible
vouchers for its authenticity.   Mosheim
himself says, in a letter to Allwoerden,
non dubitavi negotium hoc tibi committere, atque Historiam Serveti concin-
nandam et apte construendam tradere.
But it appears that Allwoerden added
much from other sources, so that it

cannot reasonably be called the work of
any one else.   The Biographie universelle ascribes to Mosheim a Latin History of Servetus, Helmstadt, 1737; but,
as I believe, by confusion with the former.   They also mention a German
work by Mosheim on the same subject
in 1748.   See Biogr. univ. arts. Mosheim and Servetus.
The analysis of the Christianismi Restitutio, given by Allwoerden, is very
meagre, but he promises a fuller account,
which never appeared.   It is a far more
extensive scheme of theology than had
been promulgated by Servetus in his first
treatises ; the most interesting of his
opinions being, of course, those which
brought him to the stake.   He distinctly
held the divinity of Christ.   Dialogus
secundus modum generationis Christi
docet, quod ipse non sit creatus nec
finitæ potentiæ, sed vere adorandus ve-
rusque Deus.   Allwoerden, p. 214.   He
probably ascribed this divinity to the
presence of the Logos, as a manifestation of God by that name, but denied
its distinct personality in the sense of
an intelligent being differing from the
Father.   Many others may have said something of the same kind, but in more
cautious language, and respecting more
the conventional phraseology of theologians.   Ille crucem, hic diadema.   Servetus, in fact, was burned, not so much
for his heresies, as for some personal
offence he had several years before given
to Calvin.   The latter wrote to Bolsec
in 1546, Servetus cupit huc venire, sed
a me accersitus.   Ego autem nunquam
committam, ut fidem meam eatenus ob-
strictam habeat.   Jam enim constitutum
habeo, si veniat, nunquam pati ut salvus
exeat.   Allwoerden, p. 43.   A similar
letter to Farel differs in some phrases,
and especially by the word *vivus* for
salvus.   The latter was published by
Wytenbogart, in an ecclesiastical history
written in Dutch.   Servetus had, in
some printed letters, charged Calvin
with many errors, which seems to have
exasperated the great reformer's temper,
so as to make him resolve on what he
afterwards executed.
The death of Servetus has perhaps as
many circumstances of aggravation as
any execution for heresy that ever took

of the ancient Arians. Several persons, chiefly foreigners, were burned for such heresies in England under Edward VI., Elizabeth, and James. These Anabaptists were not very learned or conspicuous advocates of their opinions; but some of the Italian confessors of Protestantism were of more importance. Several of these were reputed to be Arians. None, however, became so celebrated as Lælius Socinus, a young man of considerable ability, who is reckoned the proper founder of that sect which takes its name from his family. Prudently shunning the fate of Servetus, he neither published any thing, nor permitted his tenets to be openly known. He was, however, in Poland not long after the commencement of this period; and there seems reason to believe that he left writings, which, coming into the hands of some persons in that country who had already adopted the Arian hypothesis, induced them to diverge still farther from the orthodox line. The Anti-Trinitarians became numerous among the Polish Protestants; and in 1565, having separated from the rest, they began to appear as a distinct society. Faustus, nephew of Lælius Socinus, joined them about 1578; and acquiring a great ascendancy by his talents, gave a name to the sect, though their creed was already conformable to his own. An university, or rather academy, for it never obtained a legal foundation, established at Racow, a small town belonging to a Polish nobleman of their persuasion, about 1570, sent forth men of considerable eminence

place. One of these, and among the most striking, is, that he was not the subject of Geneva, nor domiciled in the city, nor had the Christianismi Restitutio been published there, but at Vienne. According to our laws, and those, I believe, of most civilised nations, he was not amenable to the tribunals of the republic.

The tenets of Servetus are not easily ascertained in all respects, nor very interesting to the reader. Some of them were considered infidel and even pantheistical; but there can be little ground for such imputations, when we consider the tenor of his writings, and the fate which he might have escaped by a retractation. It should be said in justice to Calvin, that he declares himself to have endeavoured to obtain a commu-

tation of the sentence for a milder kind of death. Genus mortis conati sumus mutare, sed frustra. Allwoerden, p. 106. But he has never recovered, in the eyes of posterity, the blow this gave to his moral reputation, which the Arminians, as well as Socinians, were always anxious to depreciate. De Serveto, says Grotius, ideo certi aliquid pronuntiare ausus non sum, quia causam ejus non bene didici; neque Calvino ejus hosti capitali credere audeo, cum sciam quam inique et virulente idem ille Calvinus tractaverit viros multo se meliores Cassandrum, Balduinum, Castellionem. Grot. Op. Theolog. iv. 639. Of Servetus and his opinions he says, in another place, very fairly, Est in illo negotio difficillimo facilis error, p. 655.

and great zeal in the propagation of their tenets. These, indeed, chiefly belong to the ensuing century; but, before the termination of the present, they had begun to circulate books in Holland.[b]

28. As this is a literary, rather than an ecclesiastical history, we shall neither advert to the less learned sectaries, nor speak of controversies which had chiefly a local importance, such as those of the English Puritans with the established church. Hooker's Ecclesiastical Polity will claim attention in a subsequent chapter.

29. Thus, in the second period of the Reformation, those *Religious intolerance.* ominous symptoms which had appeared in its earlier stage, disunion, virulence, bigotry, intolerance, far from yielding to any benignant influence, grew more inveterate and incurable. Yet some there were, even in this century, who laid the foundations of a more charitable and rational indulgence to diversities of judgment, which the principle of the Reformation itself had in some measure sanctioned. It may be said that this tolerant spirit rose out of the ashes of Servetus. The right of civil magistrates to punish heresy with death had been already impugned by some Protestant theologians, as well as by Erasmus. Luther had declared against it; and though Zwingle, who had maintained the same principle as Luther, has been charged with having afterwards approved the drowning of some Anabaptists in the lake of Zurich, it does not appear that his language requires such an interpretation. The early Anabaptists, indeed, having been seditious and unmanageable to the greatest degree, it is not easy to show that they were put to death simply on account of their religion. But the execution of Servetus, with circumstances of so much cruelty, and with no possible pretext but the error of his opinions, brought home to the minds of serious men the importance of considering whether a mere persuasion of the truth of our own doctrines can justify the infliction of capital punishment on those who dissent from them; and how far we can consistently reprobate the persecutions of the church of Rome, while acting so closely after

---

[b] Lubienecius, Hist. Reformat. Polo- nicæ. Rees, History of Racovian Cate- chism. Dupin. Bayle, art. Socinus. Eichhorn. Mosheim.

her example. But it was dangerous to withstand openly
the rancour of the ecclesiastics domineering in the Protestant
churches, or the usual bigotry of the multitude. Melanchthon
himself, tolerant by nature, and knowing enough of the
spirit of persecution which disturbed his peace, was yet unfortunately led by timidity to express, in a letter to Beza,
his approbation of the death of Servetus, though he admits
that some saw it in a different light. Calvin, early in
1554, published a dissertation to vindicate the magistrates
of Geneva in their dealings with this heretic. But
Sebastian Castalio, under the name of Martin ^{Castalio,}
Bellius, ventured to reply in a little tract, entitled ' De
Hæreticis quomodo cum iis agendum sit variorum Sen-
tentiæ.' This is a collation of different passages from the
fathers and modern authors in favour of toleration, to which
he prefixed a letter of his own to the Duke of Wirtemberg,
more valuable than the rest of the work, and, though
written in the cautious style required by the times, containing the pith of those arguments which have ultimately
triumphed in almost every part of Europe. The impossibility of forcing belief, the obscurity and insignificance of
many disputed questions, the sympathy which the fortitude
of heretics produced, and other leading topics, are well
touched in this very short tract, for the preface does not
exceed twenty eight pages in 16mo.[c]

30. Beza answered Castalio, whom he perfectly knew under
the mask of Bellius, in a much longer treatise, answered
' De Hæreticis a Civili Magistratu Puniendis.' It by Beza.
is unnecessary to say that his tone is that of a man who
is sure of having the civil power on his side. As to capital punishments for heresy, he acknowledges that he has
to contend, not only with such sceptics as Castalio, but
with some pious and learned men.[d] He justifies their infliction, however, by the magnitude of the crime, and by

---

[c] This little book has been attributed
by some to Lælius Socinus; I think Castalio more probable. Castalio entertained
very different sentiments from those of
Beza on some theological points, as appears by his dialogues on predestination
and free-will, which are opposed to the
Augustinian system then generally pre-

valent. He seems also to have approxi-
mated to the Sabellian theories of Servetus on the Trinity. See p. 144, edit. 1613.
  [d] Non modo cum nostris academicis,
sed etiam cum piis alioqui et eruditis
hominibus mihi negotium fore prospicio,
p. 208. Bayle has an excellent remark
(Beza, note F.) on this controversy.

the Mosaic law, as well as by precedents in Jewish and
Christian history. Calvin, he positively asserts, used his
influence that the death of Servetus might not be by fire,
for the truth of which he appeals to the Senate ; but though
most lenient in general, they had deemed no less expiation
sufficient for such impiety.[e]

31. A treatise written in a similar spirit to that of
Aconcio. Castalio, by Aconcio, one of the numerous exiles
from Italy, 'De Stratagematibus Satanæ, Basle,
1565,' deserves some notice in the history of opinions,
because it is, perhaps, the first wherein the limitation of
fundamental articles of Christianity to a small number is
laid down at considerable length.   He instances, among
doctrines which he does not reckon fundamental, those of
the real presence and of the Trinity ; and, in general, such
as are not either expressed in Scripture, or deducible from
it by unequivocal reasoning.[f] Aconcio inveighs against capital punishments for heresy ; but his argument, like that
of Castalio, is good against every minor penalty.   'If the
clergy,' he says, ' once get the upper hand, and carry
this point, that, as soon as one opens his mouth, the exe-
cutioner shall be called in to cut all knots with his knife,
what will become of the study of Scripture ? They will
think it very little worth while to trouble their heads with
it; and, if I may presume to say so, will set up every
fancy of their own for truth. O unhappy times !   O
wretched posterity ! If we abandon the arms by which
alone we can subdue our adversary.'   Aconcio was not
improbably an Arian; this may be surmised, not only because he was an Italian Protestant, and because he seems
to intimate it in some passages of his treatise, but on the
authority of Strype, who mentions him as reputed to be
such, while belonging to a small congregation of refugees
in London.[g] This book attracted a good deal of notice :
it was translated both into French and English; and in

---

[e] Sed tanta erat ejus hominis rabies,
tam execranda tamque horrenda impie-
tas, ut Senatus alioqui clementissimus
solis flammis expiari posse existimarit
p. 91.

[f] The account given of this book in

the Biographie universelle is not accurate ; a better will be found in Bayle.

[g] Strype's Life of Grindal, p. 42 ;
see also Bayle. Elizabeth gave him a
pension for a book on fortification.

one language or another, went through several editions. In the next century it became of much authority with the Arminians of Holland.

32. Mino Celso, of Siena, and another of the same class of refugees, in a long and elaborate argument against persecution, De Hæreticis Capitali Suppli- cio non Afficiendis, quotes several authorities from writers of the sixteenth century in his favour.[h] We should add to these advocates of toleration the name of Theodore Koornhert, who courageously stood up in Holland against one of the most encroaching and bigoted hierarchies of that age. Koornhert, averse in other points to the authority of Calvin and Beza, seems to have been a precursor of Arminius; but he is chiefly known by a treatise against capital punishment for heresy, published in Latin after his death. It is extremely scarce, and I have met with no author, except Bayle and Brandt, who speaks of it from direct knowledge.[i] Thus, at the end of the sixteenth century, the simple proposition, that men for holding or declaring heterodox opinions in religion ought not to be burned alive, or otherwise put to death, was itself little else than a sort of heterodoxy; and, though many privately must have been persuaded of its truth, the Protestant churches were as far from acknowledging it as that of Rome. No one had yet pretended to assert the general right of religious worship, which, in fact, was rarely or never conceded to the Romanists in a Protestant country, though the Huguenots shed oceans of blood to secure the same privilege for themselves.

33. In the concluding part of the century, the Protestant

Marginal note: Minus Celsus, Koornhert.

---

[h] Celso was formerly supposed to be a fictitious person, but the contrary has been established. The book was published in 1584, but without name of place. He quotes Aconcio frequently. The following passage seems to refer to Servetus:—Superioribus annis, ad hæretici cujusdam in flammis constantiam, ut ex fide dignis accepi, plures ex astantibus sanæ doctrinæ viri, non posse id sine Dei spiritu fieri persuasum habentes, ac propterea hæreticum martyrem esse plane credentes, ejus hæresin pro veritate complexi, in fide naufragium fecerunt, fol. 109.

[i] Bayle, Biogr. univ. Brandt, Hist. de la Réformation des Provinces unies, i. 435. Lipsius had, in his Politica, inveighed against the toleration of more religions than one in a commonwealth. Ure, seca, ut membrum potius aliquod, quam totum corpus intereat. Koornhert answered this, dedicating his answer to the magistrates of Leyden, who, however, thought fit to publish that they did not accept the dedication, and requested that those who read Koornhert would read also the reply of Lipsius, ibid. This was in 1590, and Koornhert died the same year.

cause, though not politically unprosperous, but rather mani-
Decline of Protestant-ism. festing some additional strength through the great
energies put forth by England and Holland, was less
and less victorious in the conflict of opinion. It might, perhaps, seem to a spectator that it gained more in France by
the dissolution of the League, and the establishment of a
perfect toleration, sustained by extraordinary securities in
the edict of Nantes, than it lost by the conformity of Henry
IV. to the Catholic religion. But, if this is considered more
deeply, the advantage will appear far greater on the other
side ; for this precedent, in the case of a man so conspicuous,
would easily serve all who might fancy they had any public
interest to excuse them, from which the transition would not
be long to the care of their own. After this time, accordingly, we find more numerous conversions of the Huguenots,
especially the nobler classes, than before. They were furnished with a pretext by an unlucky circumstance. In a
public conference, held at Fontainebleau, in 1600, before
Henry IV., from which great expectation had been raised,
Du Plessis Mornay, a man of the noblest character, but
though very learned as a gentleman, more fitted to maintain
his religion in the field than in the schools, was signally
worsted, having been supplied with forged or impertinent
quotations from the fathers, which his antagonist, Perron,
easily exposed. Casaubon, who was present, speaks with
shame, but without reserve, of his defeat ; and it was an
additional mortification that the king pretended ever afterwards to have been more thoroughly persuaded by this conference that he had embraced the truth, as well as gained a
crown. by abandoning the Protestant side.[k]

34. The men of letters had another example, about the
Desertion of Lipsius. same time, in one of the most distinguished of their
fraternity, Justus Lipsius. He left Leyden on some
pretence in 1591 for the Spanish Low Countries, and soon

[k] Scaliger, it must be observed, praises very highly the book of Du Plessis Mornay on the mass, and says that no one after Calvin and Beza had written so well; though he owns that he would have done better not to dispute about religion before the king. Scaligerana Secunda, p. 461. Du Plessis himself, in a publication after the conference of Fontainebleau, retaliated the charge of falsified quotations on Perron. I shall quote hereafter what Casaubon has said on the subject. See the article Mornay, in the Biographie universelle, in which, though the signature seems to indicate a descendant or relation, the inaccuracy of the quotations is acknowledged.

afterwards embraced the Romish faith. Lest his conversion
should be suspected, Lipsius disgraced a name, great at least
in literature, by writing in favour of the local superstitions
of those bigoted provinces. It is true, however, that some,
though the lesser, portion of his critical works were published after his change of religion.

35. The controversial divinity poured forth during this
period is now little remembered. In England it may Jewell's
be thought necessary to mention Jewell's celebrated Apology.
Apology. This short book is written with spirit; the style
is terse, the arguments pointed, the authorities much to the
purpose; so that its effects are not surprising. This treatise
is written in Latin; his Defence of the Apology, a much more
diffuse work, in English. Upon the merits of the controversy of Jewell with the Jesuit Harding, which this defence embraces, I am not competent to give any opinion; in
length and learning it far surpasses our earlier polemical
literature.

36. Notwithstanding the high reputation which Jewell
obtained by his surprising memory and indefatigable English
reading, it cannot be said that many English theolo- theologians.
gians of the reign of Elizabeth were eminent for that learning which was required for ecclesiastical controversy. Their
writings are neither numerous nor profound. Some exceptions ought to be made. Hooker was sufficiently versed in
the fathers, and he possessed also a far more extensive
knowledge of the philosophical writers of antiquity than any
others could pretend. The science of morals, according to
Mosheim, or rather of casuistry, which Calvin had left in
a rude and imperfect state, is confessed to have been first
reduced into some kind of form, and explained with some
accuracy and precision, by Perkins, whose works. however,
were not published before the next century.[m] Hugh Brough-
ton was deep in Jewish erudition. Whitaker and Nowell
ought also to be mentioned. It would not be difficult to
extract a few more names from biographical collections, but
names so obscure that we could not easily bring their merit
as scholars to any sufficient test. Sandys's sermons may be
called perhaps good, but certainly not very distinguished.

---

[m] Mosheim, Chalmers.

The most eminently learned man of the queen's reign seems
to have been Dr. John Rainolds ; and a foreign author of the
last century, Colomies, places him among the first six in
copiousness of erudition whom the Protestant churches had
produced.[n] Yet his works are, I presume, read by nobody,
nor am I aware that they are ever quoted ; and Rainolds
himself is chiefly known by the anecdote, that, having been
educated in the church of Rome, as his brother was in the
Protestant communion, they mutually converted each other in
the course of disputation. Rainolds was on the Puritan side,
and took a part in the Hampton Court conference.

37. As the century drew near its close, the church of Rome
brought forward her most renowned and formidable

Bellarmin. champion, Bellarmin, a Jesuit, and afterwards a
cardinal. No one had entered the field on that side with
more acuteness, no one had displayed more skill in marshalling the various arguments of controversial theology, so as to
support each other and serve the grand purpose of church
authority. 'He does not often,' says Dupin, ' employ reasoning, but relies on the textual authority of Scripture, of the
councils, the fathers, and the consent of the theologians ;
seldom quitting his subject, or omitting any passage useful
to his argument ; giving the objections fairly, and answering
them in few words. His style is not so elegant as that of
writers who have made it their object, but clear, neat, and
brief, without dryness or barbarism. He knew well the tenets
of Protestants, and states them faithfully, avoiding the invective so common with controversial writers.' It is nevertheless alleged by his opponents, and will not seem incredible to
those who know what polemical theology has always been,
that he attempts to deceive the reader, and argues only in
the interests of his cause.[o]

---

[n] Colomesiana. The other five are
Usher, Gataker, Blondel, Petit, and
Bochart. See also Blount, Baillet, and
Chalmers, for testimonies to Rainolds,
who died in 1607. Scaliger regrets his
death, as a loss to all Protestant churches,
as well as that of England. Wood admits that Rainolds was ' a man of infinite reading, and of a vast memory:'
but laments that, after he was chosen
divinity lecturer at Oxford in 1586, the

face of the university was much changed
towards Puritanism. Hist. and Antiq.
In the Athenæ, ii. 14, he gives a very
high character of Rainolds, on the authority of Bishop Hall and others, and
a long list of his works. But as he
wanted a biographer, he has become obscure in comparison with Jewell, who
probably was not at all his superior,

[o] [Casaubon, in one of his epistles,
which I quote from Blount, not having

38. Bellarmin, if we may believe Du Perron, was not unlearned in Greek ;[p] but it is positively, asserted, on the other side, that he could hardly read it, and that he quotes the writers in that language only from translations. Nor has his critical judgment been much esteemed. But his abilities are best testified by Protestant theologians, not only in their terms of eulogy, but indirectly in the peculiar zeal with which they chose him as their worthiest adversary. More than half a dozen books in the next fifty years bear the title of Anti-Bellarminus ; it seemed as if the victory must remain with those who should bear away the *spolia opima* of this hostile general. The Catholic writers, on the other hand, borrow every thing, it has been said, from Bellarmin, as the poets do from Homer.[q]

39. In the hands of Bellarmin, and other strenuous advocates of the church, no point of controversy was neglected. But in a general view we may justly say that the heat of battle was not in the same part of the field as before. Luther and his immediate disciples held nothing so vital as the tenet of justification by faith alone ; while the arguments of Eckius and Cajetan were chiefly designed to maintain the modification of doctrine on that subject which had been handed down to them by the fathers and schoolmen. The differences of the two parties, as to the mode of corporeal presence in the eucharist, though quite sufficient to keep them asunder, could hardly bear much controversy ; inasmuch as the primitive writers, to whom it was usual to appeal, have not, as is universally agreed, drawn these metaphysical distinctions with much preciseness. But when the Helvetic churches, and those bearing the general name of Reformed, became, after the middle of the century, as prominent, to say the least, in theological literature as the Lutheran, this controversy acquired much greater importance ; the persecutions in England and the Netherlands were principally directed against this single heresy of deny-

Topics of controversy changed.

---

observed the passage, says with great acrimony : Est tamen Baronius Bellarmino melior, homine ad strophas, sophismata, mendacia apto, nulli alii rei idoneo. Norma illius viri non est sacra scriptura, sed libido papæ quem ut deum in terris consistat, quam sceleste, quam sæpe mentitur!—1842.]

[p] Perroniana.

[q] Dupin. Bayle. Blount. Eichhorn, vi. part ii. p. 30. Andrès, xviii. 243. Niceron, vol. xxxi.

ing the real presence, and the disputes of the press turned so
generally upon no other topic.

40. In the last part of the century, through the influence
It turns on of some political circumstances, we find a new theme
papal
power. of polemical discussion, more peculiarly characteristic
of the age. Before the appearance of the early reformers,
a republican or aristocratic spirit in ecclesiastical polity,
strengthened by the decrees of the councils of Constance and
Basle, by the co-operation, in some instances, of the national
church with the state in redressing or demanding the redress
of abuses, and certainly also both by the vices of the court of
Rome, and its diversion to local politics, had fully counter-
balanced, or even in a great measure silenced, the bold
pretensions of the school of Hildebrand. In such a lax
notion of papal authority, prevalent in Cisalpine Europe, the
Protestant Reformation had found one source of its success.
But for this cause the theory itself lost ground in the Catholic
church. At the council of Trent the aristocratic or episcopal
party, though it seemed to display itself in great strength,
comprising the representatives of the Spanish and Gallican
churches, was for the most part foiled in questions that
touched the limitations of papal supremacy. From this
time the latter power became lord of the ascendant. ' No
Catholic,' says Schmidt, ' dared after the Reformation to say
one-hundredth part of what Gerson, Peter d'Ailly, and many
others, had openly preached.' The same instinct, of which
we may observe the workings in the present day, then also
taught the subjects of the church that it was no time to
betray jealousy of their own government, when the public
enemy was at their gates.

41. In this resuscitation of the court of Rome, that is,
This upheld of the papal authority, in contradistinction to the
by the
Jesuits. general doctrine and discipline of the Catholic church,
much, or rather most, was due to the Jesuits. Obedience,
not to that abstraction of theologians, the Catholic church,
a shadow eluding the touch and vanishing into emptiness
before the inquiring eye, but to its living acting centre, the
one man, was their vow, their duty, their function. They
maintained, therefore, if not quite for the first time, yet with
little countenance from the great authorities of the schools,

his personal infallibility in matters of faith. They asserted his superiority to general councils, his prerogative of dispensing with all the canons of the church, on grounds of spiritual expediency, whereof he alone could judge. As they grew bolder, some went on to pronounce even the divine laws subject to this control; but it cannot be said that a principle, which seemed so paradoxical, though perhaps only a consequence from their assumptions, was generally received.

42. But the most striking consequence of this novel position of the papacy was the renewal of its claims to temporal power, or, in stricter language, to pronounce the forfeiture of it by lawful sovereigns for offences against religion. This pretension of the Holy See, though certainly not abandoned, had in a considerable degree lain dormant in that period of comparative weakness which followed the great schism of the fourteenth century. Paul III. deprived Henry VIII. of his dominions, as far as a bull could have that effect: but the deposing power was not generally asserted with much spirit against the first princes who embraced the Reformation. In this second part of the century, however, the see of Rome was filled by men of stern zeal and intrepid ambition, aided by the Jesuits and other regulars with an energy unknown before, and favoured also by the political interests of the greatest monarch in Christendom. Two circumstances of the utmost importance gave them occasion to scour the rust away from their ancient weapons— the final prostration of the Romish faith in England by Elizabeth, and the devolution of the French crown on a Protestant heir. Incensed by the former event, Pius V., the representative of the most rigid party in the church, issued in 1570 his famous bull, releasing English Catholics from their allegiance to the queen, and depriving her of all right and title to the throne. Elizabeth and her parliament retaliated by augmented severities of law against these unfortunate subjects, who had little reason to thank the Jesuits for announcing maxims of rebellion which it was not easy to carry into effect. Allen and Persons, secure at St. Omer and Douay, proclaimed the sacred duty of resisting a prince who should break his faith with God and the

people; especially when the supreme governor of the church, whose function it is to watch over its welfare, and separate the leprous from the clean, has adjudged the cause.

43. In the war of the League men became still more familiar with this tenet. Those who fought under that banner did not all acknowledge, or at least would not in other circumstances have admitted, the pope's deposing power; but no faction will reject a false principle that adds strength to its side. Philip II., though ready enough to treat the see of Rome as sharply and rudely as the Italians do their saints when refractory, found it his interest to encourage a doctrine so dangerous to monarchy, when it was directed against Elizabeth and Henry. For this reason we may read with less surprise in Balthazar Ayala, a layman, a lawyer, and judge-advocate in the armies of Spain, the most unambiguous and unlimited assertion of the deposing theory :—'Kings abusing their power may be variously compelled,' he says, 'by the sovereign pontiff to act justly; for he is the earthly vicegerent of God, from whom he has received both swords, temporal as well as spiritual, for the peace and preservation of the Christian commonwealth. Nor can he only control, if it is for the good of this commonwealth, but even depose kings, as God, whose delegate he is, deprived Saul of his kingdom, and as pope Zachary released the Franks from their allegiance to Childeric.'r

and Henry IV.

Deposing power owned in Spain;

44. Bellarmin, the brilliant advocate of whom we have already spoken, amidst the other disputes of the Protestant quarrel, did not hesitate to sustain the papal authority in its amplest extension. His treatise 'De Summo Pontifice, Capite Totius Militantis Ecclesiæ,' forms a portion, and by no means the least important, of those entitled 'The Controversies of Bellarmin,' and first appeared separately in 1586. The pope, he asserts, has no direct temporal authority in the dominions of Christian princes; he cannot interfere with their merely civil affairs, unless they are his feudal vassals; but indirectly, that is, for the sake of some spiritual advantage, all things are submitted to his disposal. He cannot depose these princes, even for a

asserted by Bellarmin.

r Ayala, De Jure et Officiis Bellicis (Antwerp, 1597), p. 32.

just cause, as their immediate superior, unless they are
feudally his vassals; but he can take away and give to others
their kingdoms, if the salvation of souls require it.[s] We
shall observe hereafter how artfully this papal scheme was
combined with the more captivating tenets of popular sovereignty; each designed for the special case, that of Henry IV ,
whose legitimate rights, established by the constitution of
France, it was expected by this joint effort to overthrow.

45. Two methods of delivering theological doctrine had
prevailed in the Catholic church for many ages. Methods of
theological
The one called positive was dogmatic rather than ar- doctrine.
gumentative, deducing its tenets from immediate authorities
of Scripture or of the fathers, which it interpreted and explained for its own purpose. It was a received principle,
conveniently for this system of interpretation, that most
parts of Scripture had a plurality of meaning; and that the
allegorical or analogical senses were as much to be sought
as the primary and literal. The scholastic theology, on the
other hand, which acquired its name, because it was frequently heard in the schools of divinity and employed the
weapons of dialectics, was a scheme of inferences drawn,
with all the subtilty of reasoning, from the same fundamental principles of authority, the Scriptures, the fathers,
the councils of the church. It must be evident upon
reflection, that where many thousand propositions, or sentences easily convertible into them, had acquired the rank of
indisputable truths, it was not difficult to raise a specious
structure of connected syllogisms; and hence the theology
of the schools was a series of inferences from the acknowledged standards of orthodoxy, as their physics were from
Aristotle, and their metaphysics from a mixture of the two.

46. The scholastic method, affecting a complete and
scientific form, led to the compilation of theolo- Loci Com-
gical systems, generally called Loci Communes. munes.
These were very common in the sixteenth and seventeenth
centuries, both in the church of Rome, and, after some
time, in the two Protestant communions. But Luther,
though at first he bestowed immense praise upon the Loci

---

[s] Ranke, ii. 182.

Communes of Melanchthon, grew unfavourable to all systematic theology. His own writings belong to that class we call positive. They deal with the interpretation of Scripture, and the expansion of its literal meaning. Luther rejected, except in a very sparing application, the search after allegorical senses. Melanchthon also, and in general the divines of the Augsburg confession, adhered chiefly to the principle of single interpretation.[t]

47. The Institutes of Calvin, which belong to the preceding part of the century, though not entitled Loci In the Protestant Communes, may be reckoned a full system of deductive theology. Wolfgang Musculus published a treatise with the usual title. It should be observed that, in the Lutheran church, the ancient method of scholastic theology revived after the middle of this century, especially in the divines of Melanchthon's party, one of whose characteristics was a greater deference to ecclesiastical usage and opinion than the more rigid Lutherans would endure to pay. The Loci Theologici of Chemnitz and those of Strigelius were, in their age, of great reputation; the former, by one of the compilers of the Formula Concordiæ, might be read without risk of finding those heterodoxies of Melanchthon which the latter was supposed to exhibit.[u]

48. In the church of Rome the scholastic theology retained an undisputed respect; it was for the here- and Catholic Church. tical Protestants to dread a method of keen logic, by which their sophistry was cut through. The most remarkable book of this kind, which falls within the sixteenth century, is the Loci Theologici of Melchior Canus, published at Salamanca in 1563, three years after the death of the author, a Dominican, and professor in that university. It is of course the theology of the reign and country of Philip II., but Canus was a man acquainted with history, philosophy, and ancient literature. Eichhorn, after giving several pages to an abstract of this volume, pronounces it worthy to be still read. It may be seen by his analysis how Canus, after the manner of the schoolmen, incorporated philosophical with theological science. Dupin,

---

[t] Eichhorn, Gesch. der Cultur. vi. part   part ii.
i. p. 175.   Mosheim, cent. 16, sect. 3,   [u] Eichhorn, 236.   Mosheim.

whose abstract is rather different in substance, calls this an
excellent work, and written with all the elegance we could
desire.[x]

49. Catharin, one of the theologians most prominent in
the council of Trent, though he seems not to have
incurred the charge of heresy, went farther from   Catharin.
the doctrine of Augustin and Aquinas than was deemed
strictly orthodox in the Catholic church. He framed a
theory to reconcile predestination with the universality of
grace, which has since been known in this country by the
name of Baxterianism, and is, I believe, adopted by many
divines at this day. Dupin, however, calls it a new invention,
unknown to the ancient fathers, and never received in the
schools. It has been followed, he adds, by nobody.

50. In the critical and expository department of theological literature, much was written during this Critical and
period, forming no small proportion of the great expository
                                                   writings.
collection called Critici Sacri. In the Romish church, we
may distinguish the Jesuit Maldonat, whose commentaries
on the evangelists have been highly praised by theologians
of the Protestant side; and among these we may name
Calvin and Beza, who occupy the highest place,[y] while below
them are ranked Bullinger, Zanchius, Musculus, Chemnitz,
and several more. But I believe that, even in the reviving
appetite for obsolete theology, few of these writers have yet
attracted much attention. A polemical spirit, it is observed
by Eichhorn, penetrated all theological science, not only in
dogmatical writings, but in those of mere interpretation ; in
catechisms, in sermons, in ecclesiastical history, we find the
author armed for combat, and always standing in imagination
before an enemy.

---

[x] Eichhorn, p. 216-227. Dupin, cent.
16, book 5.

[y] Literas sacras, says Scaliger of Calvin, tractavit ut tractandæ sunt, vere
inquam et pure ac simpliciter sine ullis
argutationibus scholasticis, et divino vir
præditus ingenio multa divinavit quæ
non nisi a linguæ Hebraicæ peritissimis
(cujusmodi tamen ipse non erat), divi-
nari possunt. Scaligerana Prima. A
more detailed and apparently a not un-
candid statement of Calvin's character

as a commentator on Scripture will be
found in Simon, Hist. critique du Vieux
Testament. He sets him, in this respect, much above Luther. See also
Blount, art. Calvin. Scaliger does not
esteem much the learning of Beza, and
blames him for affecting to despise
Erasmus as a commentator. I have
named Beza in the text as superior to
Zanchius and others, in deference to
common reputation, for I am wholly
ignorant of the writings of all.

51. A regular and copious history of the church, from the
Ecclesias- primitive ages to the Reformation itself, was first
tical his-
torians. given by the Lutherans under the title, Centuriæ
Magdeburgenses, from the name of the city where it was
compiled. The principal among several authors concerned,
usually called Centuriatores, was Flacius Illyricus, a most
inveterate enemy of Melanchthon. This work has been more
than once reprinted, and is still, in point of truth and original
research, the most considerable ecclesiastical history on the
Protestant side. Mosheim, or his translator, calls this an
immortal work ;[z] and Eichhorn speaks of it in strong terms
of admiration for the boldness of the enterprise, the labori-
ousness of the execution, the spirit with which it cleared away
a mass of fable, and placed ecclesiastical history on an authentic basis. The faults, both those springing from the
imperfect knowledge and from the prejudices of the compilers, are equally conspicuous.[a] Nearly forty years afterwards, between the years 1588 and 1609, the celebrated
Annals of Cardinal Baronius, in twelve volumes, appeared.
These were brought down by him only to the end of the
twelfth century ; their continuation by Rainaldus, published
between 1646 and 1663, goes down to 1566. It was the
object of Protestant learning in the seventeenth century to
repel the authority and impugn the allegations of Baronius.
Those of his own communion, in a more advanced stage of
criticism, have confessed his mistakes ; many of them arising
from a want of acquaintance with the Greek language, indispensable, as we should now justly think, for one who undertook a general history of the church, but not sufficiently
universal in Italy, at the end of the sixteenth century, to
deprive those who did not possess it of a high character for
erudition. Eichhorn speaks far less favourably of Baronius
than of the Centuriators.[b] But of these two voluminous histories, written with equal prejudice on opposite sides, an impartial and judicious scholar has thus given his opinion :—
52. ' An ecclesiastical historian,' Le Clerc satirically ob-

---

[z] Cent. 16, sect. 3, part ii. c. 9. This
expression is probably in the original ;
but it is difficult to quote Maclaine's
translation with confidence, on account

of the liberties which he took with the
text.
[a] Vol. vi. part ii. p. 149.
[b] Id. p. 180.

serves, ' ought to adhere inviolably to this maxim, that whatever can be favourable to heretics is false, and whatever can be said against them is true; while, on the other hand, all that does honour to the orthodox is unquestionable, and everything that can do them discredit is surely a lie. He must suppress, too, with care, or at least extenuate, as far as possible, the errors and vices of those whom the orthodox are accustomed to respect, whether they know anything about them or no: and must exaggerate, on the contrary, the mistakes and faults of the heterodox to the utmost of his power. He must remember that any orthodox writer is a competent witness against a heretic, and is to be trusted implicitly on his word; while a heretic is never to be believed against the orthodox, and has honour enough done him, in allowing him to speak against his own side, or in favour of our own. It is thus that the Centuriators of Magdeburg, and thus that Cardinal Baronius have written; each of their works having by this means acquired an immortal glory with its own party. But it must be owned that they are not the earliest, and that they have only imitated most of their predecessors in this plan of writing. For many ages men had only sought in ecclesiastical antiquity, not what was really to be found there, but what they conceived ought to be there for the good of their own party.'[c]

Le Clerc's character of them.

53. But in the midst of so many dissentients from each other, some resting on the tranquil bosom of the church, some fighting the long battle of argument, some catching at gleams of supernatural light, the very truths of natural and revealed religion were called in question by a different party. The proofs of this before the middle of the sixteenth century are chiefly to be derived from Italy. Pomponatius has already been mentioned, and some other Aristotelian philosophers might be added. But these, whose scepticism extended to natural theology, belong to the class of metaphysical writers, whose place is in the next chapter. If we limit ourselves to those who directed their attacks against Christianity, it must be presumed that, in an age when the tribunals of justice visited, even with the

Deistical writers.

---

[c] Parrhasiana, vol. i. p. 168.

punishment of death, the denial of any fundamental doctrine, few books of an openly irreligious tendency could appear.[d] A short pamphlet by one Vallée cost him his life in 1584. Some others were clandestinely circulated in France before the end of the century; and the list of men suspected of infidelity, if we could trust all private anecdotes of the time, would be by no means short. Bodin, Montaigne, Charron, have been reckoned among the rejecters of Christianity. The first I conceive to have acknowledged no revelation but the Jewish; the second is free, in my opinion, from all reasonable suspicion of infidelity; the principal work of the third was not published till 1601. His former treatise, ' Des Trois Vérités,' is an elaborate vindication of the Christian and Catholic religion. [e]

54. I hardly know how to insert, in any other chapter than the present, the books that relate to sorcery and demoniacal possessions, though they can only in a very lax sense be ranked with theological literature. The greater part are contemptible in any other light than as evidences of the state of human opinion. Those designed to rescue the innocent from sanguinary prejudices, and chase the real demon of superstition from the mind of man, deserve to be commemorated. Two such works belong to this period. Wierus, a physician of the Netherlands, in a treatise, ' De Præstigiis,' Basle, 1564, combats the horrible prejudice by which those accused of witchcraft were thrown into the flames. He shows a good deal of credulity as to diabolical illusions, but takes these unfortunate persons for the devil's victims rather than his accomplices. Upon the whole, Wierus destroys more superstition than he seriously intended to leave behind.

Wierus. De Præstigiis.

---

[d] The famous Cymbalum Mundi, by Bonaventure des Periers, published in 1538, which, while it continued extremely scarce, had the character of an irreligious work, has proved, since it was reprinted, in 1711, perfectly innocuous, though there are a few malicious glances at priests and nuns. It has always been the habit of the literary world, as much as at present, to speak of books by hearsay. The Cymbalum Mundi is written in dialogue, somewhat in the manner of Lucian, and is rather more lively than books of that age generally are.

[e] Des Trois Vérités contre les Athées, Idolâtres, Juifs, Mahumétans, Hérétiques, et Schismatiques. Bourdeaux, 1593. Charron has not put his name to this book; and it does not appear that he has taken anything from himself in his subsequent work, De la Sagesse.

55. A far superior writer is our countryman Reginald Scot, whose object is the same, but whose views Scot on are incomparably more extensive and enlightened. Witchcraft. He denies altogether to the devil any power of controlling the course of nature. It may be easily supposed that this solid and learned person, for such he was beyond almost all the English of that age, did not escape in his own time, or long afterwards, the censure of those who adhered to superstition. Scot's Discovery of Witchcraft was published in 1584.[f] Bodin, on the other hand, endeavoured to sustain the vulgar notions of Witchcraft in his Démonomanie des Sorciers. It is not easy to conceive a more wretched production; besides his superstitious absurdities, he is guilty of exciting the magistrate against Wierus, by representing him as a real confederate of Satan.

56. We may conclude this chapter by mentioning the principal versions and editions of Scripture. No Authenti- edition of the Greek Testament, worthy to be speci- city of Vulgate. fied, appeared after that of Robert Stephens, whose text was invariably followed. The council of Trent declared the Vulgate translation of Scripture to be authentic, condemning all that should deny its authority. It has been a commonplace with Protestants to inveigh against this decree, even while they have virtually maintained the principle upon which it is founded—one by no means peculiar to the church of Rome—being no other than that it is dangerous to unsettle the minds of the ignorant, or partially learned in religion; a proposition not easily disputable by any man of sense, but, when acted upon, as incompatible as any two contraries can be with the free and general investigation of truth.

57. Notwithstanding this decision in favour of the Vulgate, there was room left for partial uncertainty. The Latin ver- council of Trent, declaring the translation itself to sions and editions by be authentic, pronounced nothing in favour of any Catholics. manuscript or edition; and as it would be easier to put down learning altogether than absolutely to restrain the searching spirit of criticism, it was soon held that the

---

[f] It appears by Scot's book that not only the common, but the more difficult tricks of conjurors were practised in his time; he shows how to perform some of them.

council's decree went but to the general fidelity of the version, without warranting every passage. Many Catholic writers, accordingly, have put a very liberal interpretation on this decree, suggesting such emendations of particular texts as the original seemed to demand. They have even given new translations: one by Arias Montanus is chiefly founded on that of Pagninus, and an edition of the Vulgate, by Isidore Clarius, is said to resemble a new translation, by his numerous corrections of the text from the Hebrew.[g] Sixtus V. determined to put a stop to a licence which rendered the Tridentine provisions almost nugatory. He fulfilled the intentions of the council by causing to be published in 1590 the Sistine Bible; an authoritative edition to be used in all churches. This was, however, superseded by another, set forth only two years afterwards by Clement VIII., which is said to differ more than any other from that which his predecessor had published as authentic; a circumstance not forgotten by Protestant polemics. The Sistine edition is now very scarce. The same pope had published a standard edition of the Septuagint in 1587.[h]

58. The Latin translations made by Protestants in this period were that by Sebastian Castalio, which, in By Protest- search of more elegance of style, deviates from the ants. simplicity, as well as sense, of the original, and fails therefore of obtaining that praise at the hands of men of taste for which more essential requisites have been sacrificed;[i] and that by Tremellius and Junius, published at Frankfort in 1575 and subsequent years. It was retouched some time afterwards by Junius, after the death of his coadjutor. This translation was better esteemed in Protestant countries, especially at first, than by the Catholic critics. Simon speaks of it with little respect. It professedly adheres closely to the Hebrew idiom. Beza gave a Latin version of the New Testament. It is doubtful whether any of these translations have much improved upon the Vulgate.

---

[g] Andrès, xix. 40. Simon, 358.
[h] Andrès, xix. 44. Schelhorn, Amœnit. Literar. vol. ii. 359, and vol. iv. 439.
[i] Andrès, xix. 166. Castalio, according to Simon (Hist. critique du V. T. p. 363), affects politeness to an inconceivable degree of bad taste, especially in such phrases as these in his translation of the Canticles :—Mea columbula, ostende mihi tuum vulticulum ; fac ut audiam tuam voculam, &c. He was, however, Simon says, tolerably acquainted with Hebrew, and spoke modestly of his own translation.

59. The new translations of the Scriptures into modern languages were naturally not so numerous as at an earlier period. Two in English are well known; the *Versions into modern languages.* Geneva Bible of 1560, published in that city by Coverdale, Whittingham, and other refugees, and the Bishop's Bible of 1568. Both of these, or at least the latter, were professedly founded upon the prior versions, but certainly not without a close comparison with the original text. The English Catholics published a translation of the New Testament from the Vulgate at Rheims in 1582. The Polish translation, commonly ascribed to the Socinians, was printed under the patronage of Prince Radzivil in 1563, before that sect could be said to exist, though Lismanin and Blandrata, both of heterodox tenets, were concerned in it.[k] This edition is of the greatest rarity. The Spanish Bible of Ferrara, 1553, and the Sclavonian of 1581, are also very scarce. The curious in bibliography are conversant with other versions and editions of the 16th century, chiefly of rare occurrence.[m]

---

[k] Bayle, art. Radzivil.   [m] Brunet, &c.

END OF THE FIRST VOLUME.